MILLER'S

collectables

collectables

MADELEINE MARSH *GENERAL EDITOR*

2005
VOLUME XVII

MILLER'S COLLECTABLES PRICE GUIDE 2005

Created and designed by
Miller's
The Cellars, High Street
Tenterden, Kent, TN30 6BN
Tel: +44 (0)1580 766411
Fax: +44 (0)1580 766100

First published in Great Britain in 2005
by Miller's, a division of Mitchell Beazley,
imprints of Octopus Publishing Group Ltd,
2–4 Heron Quays, London E14 4JP
Miller's is a registered trademark of
Octopus Publishing Group Ltd

ISBN 1845330358

A CIP record for this book is
available from the British Library

Set in Frutiger

Colour origination by One Thirteen Ltd, Whitstable, Kent, England
Printed and bound by Rotolito Lombarda, Italy

General Editor: Madeleine Marsh
Managing Editor: Valerie Lewis
Production Co-ordinators: Philip Hannath, Kari Moody
Editorial Co-ordinator: Deborah Wanstall
Editorial Assistants: Melissa Hall, Joanna Hill
Production Assistants: Clare Gillingham, Charlotte Smith,
Mel Smith, Ethne Tragett
Senior Advertising Executive: Jill Jackson
Advertising Co-ordinator & Administrator: Melinda Williams
Advertising Executive: Emma Gillingham
Designer: Nick Harris
Advertisement Designer: Simon Cook
Indexer: Hilary Bird
Jacket Design: Alexa Brommer
Production Controller: Jane Rogers
Additional Photography: Emma Gillingham, Dennis O'Reilly, Robin Saker
North American Consultants: Marilynn and Sheila Brass

Front Cover Illustrations:
A hand-painted fan, c1950, 9in (23cm) wide. **£15–20 / €22–30 / $28–38 ⊞ DE**
A Gibson SG Special electric guitar, 1968. **£1,400–1,600 / €2,100–2,400 / $2,600–3,000 ⊞ VRG**
A Pelham Jumpette puppet, 1970s, 9in (23cm) high. **£25–30 / €40–45 / $50–55 ⊞ LAS**
Title page Illustrations:
An amethyst glass scent bottle, 1920s, 5in (12.5cm) high. **£40–45 / €60–70 / $75–85 ⊞ TASV**
A paste brooch, c1960, 4in (10cm) long. **£40–45 / €60–70 / $75–85 ⊞ JBB**
A National Panasonic plastic Toot-A-Loop radio, 1970s, 9in (23cm) high. **£50–60 / €75–90 / $95–110 ⊞ HSR**

Contents

Acknowledgments

We would like to acknowledge the great assistance given by our consultants who are listed below. We would also like to extend our thanks to all the auction houses, their press offices, dealers and collectors who have assisted us in the production of this book.

CHRIS ALBURY
Dominic Winter Book Auctions
The Old School
Maxwell Street, Swindon
Wiltshire SN1 5DR
(Books)

BEVERLEY/BETH
30 Church Street
Alfie's Antique Market
Marylebone,
London NW8 8EP
(Ceramics)

ALAN BLAKEMAN
BBR Elsecar Heritage Centre
Wath Road,
Elsecar, Barnsley
Yorks S74 8AF
(Advertising, Packaging, Bottles, Breweriana)

GLEN BUTLER
Wallis & Wallis
West Street Auction Galleries
Lewes,
East Sussex BN7 2NJ
(Toys)

MIKE DELANEY
www.vintagehornby.co.uk
Tel: 01993 840064
(Trains)

LUCY HOBBS & ANDREW HILTON
Special Auction Services
The Coach House,
Midgham Park
Reading, Berks RG7 5UG
(Commemorative Ware)

LORNA KAUFMANN
Vectis Auctions Ltd
Fleck Way, Thornaby
Stockton-on-Tees TS17 9JZ
(Toys)

SPARKLE MOORE
Alfies Antique Centre
Church Street, London NW8 8DT
(Costume)

MALCOLM PHILLIPS
Comic Book Postal Auctions
40–42 Osnaburgh Street
London NW1 3ND
(Comics)

STEPHEN PHILLIPS
Rellik Antiques
248 Camden High Street
London NW1 8QS
(Punk)

JOHN PYM
Hope & Glory
131a Kensington Church Street
London W8 7LP
(Royal Commemorative)

T. VENNETT-SMITH
11 Nottingham Road
Gotham, Nottinghamshire NG11 0HE
(Autographs)

LESLIE VERRINDER
Tin Tin Collectables
G38–42 Alfie's Antique Market
13–15 Church Street
London NW8 8DT
(Textiles & Fashion)

How To Use This Book

It is our aim to make this guide easy to use. In order to find a particular item, turn to the contents list on page 7 to find the main heading, for example, Books. Having located your area of interest, you will see that larger sections may be sub-divided by subject or maker.
If you are looking for a particular factory, maker or object, consult the index which starts on page 453.

Caption
provides a brief description of the item including the maker's name, medium, date, measurements and in some instances condition.

Information Box
covers relevant collecting information on factories, makers, care, restoration, fakes and alterations.

Further Reading
directs the reader towards additional sources of information.

Price Guide
these are based on actual prices realized at auction or offered for sale by a dealer, shown in £sterling, Euros and $US. Remember that Miller's is a PRICE GUIDE not a PRICE LIST and prices are affected by many variables such as location, condition, desirability and so on. Don't forget that if you are selling, it is quite likely you will be offered less than the price range. Price ranges for items sold at auction tend to include the buyer's premium and VAT if applicable. The exchange rate used in this edition is 1.87 for $ and 1.5 for €.

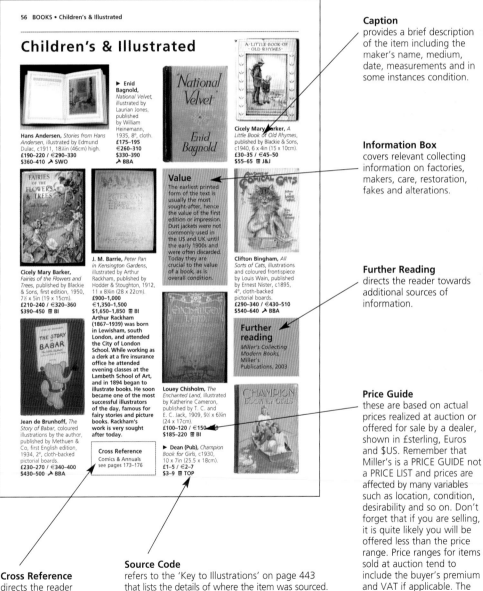

56 BOOKS • Children's & Illustrated

Children's & Illustrated

Hans Andersen, *Stories from Hans Andersen*, illustrated by Edmund Dulac, c1911, 18¼in (46cm) high.
£190–220 / €290–330
$360–410 ➶ SWO

▶ **Enid Bagnold,** *National Velvet,* illustrated by Laurian Jones, published by William Heinemann, 1935, 8°, cloth.
£175–195
€260–310
$330–390
➶ BBA

Cicely Mary Barker, *A Little Book of Old Rhymes,* published by Blackie & Sons, c1940, 6 x 4in (15 x 10cm).
£30–35 / €45–50
$55–65 ⊞ J&J

Cicely Mary Barker, *Fairies of the Flowers and Trees,* published by Blackie & Sons, first edition, 1950, 7½ x 5in (19 x 15cm).
£210–240 / €320–360
$390–450 ⊞ BI

J. M. Barrie, *Peter Pan in Kensington Gardens,* illustrated by Arthur Rackham, published by Hodder & Stoughton, 1912, 11 x 8½in (28 x 22cm).
£900–1,000
€1,350–1,500
$1,650–1,850 ⊞ BI

Value
The earliest printed form of the text is usually the most sought-after, hence the value of the first edition or impression. Dust jackets were not commonly used in the US and UK until the early 1900s and were often discarded. Today they are crucial to the value of a book, as is overall condition.

Clifton Bingham, *All Sorts of Cats,* illustrations and coloured frontispiece by Louis Wain, published by Ernest Nister, c1895, 4°, cloth-backed pictorial boards.
£290–340 / €430–510
$540–640 ➶ BBA

Jean de Brunhoff, *The Story of Babar,* coloured illustrations by the author, published by Methuen & Co, first English edition, 1934, 2°, cloth-backed pictorial boards.
£230–270 / €340–400
$430–500 ➶ BBA

Arthur Rackham (1867–1939) was born in Lewisham, south London, and attended the City of London School. While working as a clerk at a fire insurance office he attended evening classes at the Lambeth School of Art, and in 1894 began to illustrate books. He soon became one of the most successful illustrators of the day, famous for fairy stories and picture books. Rackham's work is very sought after today.

Cross Reference
Comics & Annuals
see pages 173–176

Louey Chisholm, *The Enchanted Land,* illustrated by Katherine Cameron, published by T. C. and E. C. Jack, 1909, 9½ x 6½in (24 x 17cm).
£100–120 / €150–180
$185–220 ⊞ BI

▶ **Dean (Pub),** *Champion Book for Girls,* c1930, 10 x 7in (25.5 x 18cm).
£1–5 / €2–7
$3–9 ⊞ TOP

Further reading
Miller's Collecting Modern Books, Miller's Publications, 2003

Cross Reference
directs the reader to where other related items may be found.

Source Code
refers to the 'Key to Illustrations' on page 443 that lists the details of where the item was sourced. The ➶ icon indicates the item was sold at auction. The ⊞ icon indicates the item originated from a dealer.

Introduction

As the continuing success of *Miller's Collectables Price Guide* demonstrates, the collectables market has expanded rapidly in the past few years. From the 1980s onwards the development of car boot fairs and yard sales has introduced many to the pleasures of collecting at an affordable level, and also helped transform many amateur enthusiasts into part or even full-time dealers. The popularity of antiques programmes on television has been another significant factor in revealing the history and values of objects and demystifying the business of buying and selling at auction. More recently, the internet has played a major part in the development of the collectors market, allowing buyers to look, buy and sell across the world, without even stepping outside the front door.

Some things, however, never change. The only way to learn about objects is to get out there and handle them, and *Miller's Collectables Price Guide* is there to help you every step of the way. This long-established guide is now in its 17th edition, and covers every aspect of the market from Advertising and Packaging to Writing collectables, all arranged in alphabetical order by subject matter.

The 6,000 colour photographs are taken new every year from dealers, auction houses and private collectors. Each entry is given a price range that reflects the current state of the market and these values stretch from rare objects worth three-and four-figure sums to collectables at pocket money prices.

Within every section the objects shown come from a range of different vendors, reflecting the variety of this market place. These sources also provide a matchless list of contacts for every field, no matter how esoteric: fishing equipment, old bottles, vintage money boxes or costume jewellery… whatever your specific interest. Our Key to Illustrations provides the information to put you directly in touch with specialist dealers and salerooms, while the Directory of Collectors Clubs will help you find others who share your particular passion. And passion is what collecting is all about. Everyone wants to know what their antiques and collectables are worth, but prices do not just reflect the intrinsic merit of the object – above all they reflect the desire of the person who wants to own them. Just look at the items

on our Record Breakers page: an old comic, a redundant train nameplate, a Matchbox toy with the wrong type of wheels, an empty whisky jar and a dust jacket without its book. None of these random pieces qualify as fine art, they are not made from precious materials and they have no practical use, yet each one fetched a record-breaking four- or five-figure sum when sold at auction over the past year, thanks to their individual rarity and the passionate enthusiasm of the bibliophiles, the railwayana lovers, the diecast toy enthusiasts and the other collectors who fought for them in the saleroom.

As we at Miller's know there is a collector for everything and each year we come across different subjects and objects. In our Shipping section we mark the 200th anniversary of the battle of Trafalgar and the death of Admiral Lord Nelson, probably the most collectable naval hero of all time. Other new sections in the guide this year range from Mining memorabilia to Theatrical ephemera, where we celebrate the 100th birthday of Peter Pan. There is perhaps a little part in all of us that doesn't want to grow up. Collectors are often inspired by nostalgia, hence the large sections in this book devoted to games, dolls and toys. Rock and pop enthusiasts often return to the favourite bands of their youth and this year we devote a special section to punk. Punks deliberately made themselves look frightening, now it's the prices of original punk clothing that can be scary and, if you kept your Vivienne Westwood bondage trousers, you could be sitting on a fortune. Vintage fashion is an area that has continued to expand, attracting more and more enthusiasts, and objects covered in this guide range from the finest vintage dresses and handbags to a pair of 1970s nylon pants, also quite horrific in their own way. In Ceramics we look at the history of the teapot and in Textiles the story of the tea cosy.

Miller's Collectables Price Guide aims to reflect every taste and every collecting passion and if you have any subjects you would like to see included in this guide, let us know. Thank you for your support and interest and thanks to all the contributors who shared their objects with us. Though the pieces illustrated could not be more different, what unites us all is a love of collecting.

Madeleine Marsh

Advertising & Packaging

In many ways, the subject of advertising and packaging provides the perfect definition of a collectable. Antiques often started life as expensive works of fine art and craftsmanship aimed at people of wealth. Collectables, on the other hand, is a term applied to everyday objects that were often mass-produced. Most of the following items were never meant to be enduring or valuable treasures. Many were designed as promotional freebies or simply as containers for household products. By their very nature, advertising and packaging are ephemeral. Once the package was emptied, the shop refitted or the advertising campaign finished, many of these objects were simply thrown away, hence the rarity of good surviving examples. Value is also affected by condition, the attraction of the image and the nostalgic appeal of the product itself.

Singer sewing machines, OXO, Bovril, Horlicks and many famous names began life in the late 19th and early 20th centuries and are still with us today. Some collectors focus on a specific brand, such as Robertson's gollies (page 50), Guinness (page 75) and Coca Cola. Such is the appeal of these brands that they have spawned their own range of modern collectables created specifically (and often expensively) for the collectors' market. Other enthusiasts focus on one type of object, such as tins.

One of the great attractions of this field is that, thanks to the imagination and the commercial hunger of advertisers and manufacturers, a huge range of material is available, providing objects of every variety and price at every level, and guaranteed to stimulate nostalgic memories of your favourite products.

An F. Dunn, Bootmaker ceramic plate, c1860, 7½in (19cm) diam.
£120–140 / €180–210
$220–260 ⚒ SAS

A Dairy Supply Company ceramic shop counter display, c1880, 15in (38cm) high.
£1,300–1,500 / €1,950–2,250
$2,450–2,800 ⊞ SMI

A box of Link-Boy candles, c1880, 6in (15cm) high.
£40–45 / €60–70
$75–85 ⊞ BS

A Hudson's Soap cast-iron water trough, c1889, 16in (40.5cm) wide.
£320–360 / €480–540
$600–670 ⊞ BS

A butcher's shop papier-mâché display model, with glass eyes, early 20thC, 25in (63.5cm) high.
£630–700 / €950–1,050
$1,200–1,300 ⊞ ARK

A set of Dewhurst's thread drawers, with painted decoration, signs of wear, c1900, 20in (51cm) wide.
£110–125 / €165–190
$210–230 ⊞ Cot

◄ **A C. J. Hardy & Co, Outfitters hat brush,** c1900, 10in (25.5cm) long.
£12–16 / €18–24
$22–30 ⊞ Cot

A Keen's Mustard celluloid tape measure, 1905, 1¾in (4.5cm) diam.
£55–65 / €85–100
$100–120 ⊞ HUX

A Wright's Coal Tar Soap dish, by Royal Doulton, moulded with a dragonfly, c1920, 6in (15cm) diam.
£70–80 / €105–120
$130–150 ↗ G(L)
Royal Doulton produced advertising ceramics for a number of different soap and cosmetic companies, including Wright's Coal Tar Soap, Vinolia soaps and creams and Yardley. Doulton designer Leslie Harradine adapted the famous Yardley London Cries Lavender group figurine in 1924.

A Chairman Cigars ceramic ashtray, c1910, 11in (28cm) high.
£400–450 / €600–680
$750–840 ⊞ JUN

A butcher's ceramic plate, inscribed 'A-La-Mode Beef', c1920, 13in (33cm) diam.
£310–350 / €470–530
$580–650 ⊞ SMI

A Bovril pewter pepper pot, in the form of a castle tower, c1915, 2¾in (7cm) high.
£80–90 / €120–135
$150–170 ⊞ BS

A Calder's 'Bee' Yeast ceramic plate, c1920, 12in (30.5cm) square.
£180–200 / €270–300
$340–370 ⊞ SMI

▶ **A pair of glass florist's signs,** c1920, 20in (51cm) wide.
£100–120
€150–180
$185–220
⊞ HOP

An OXO nickel spoon, 1920s, 8in (20.5cm) long.
£50–60 / €75–90
$95–110 ⊞ BS

▶ **A Hudson Scott & Sons Sempridur Finish notepad,** depicting Diana the Huntress, 1925, 8in (20.5cm) high.
£65–75
€100–115
$120–140
⊞ HUX

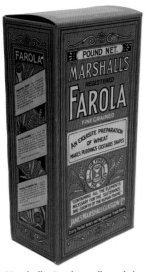

A Spratt's enamel dog bowl,
1920s–30s, 10½in (26.5cm) diam.
£60–70 / €90–105
$110–130 ⊞ B&R

A Nelson's Patent Opaque
Gelatine packet, 1920s–30s,
4½in (11.5cm) wide.
£1–5 / €2–7
$3–9 ⊞ RTT

A Marshall's Farola cardboard shop
display, 1920s, 15in (38cm) high.
£180–200 / €270–300
$340–370 ⊞ AAA

A Victor's Confectionery wooden
delivery box, with metal bands,
c1930, 19in (48.5cm) wide.
£130–150 / €200–230
$250–280 ⊞ B&R

A butcher's rubberoid shop
display figure, modelled as a lamb,
c1930, 16in (40.5cm) high.
£360–400 / €540–600
$670–750 ⊞ SMI

A Wills's Pirate Shag Tobacco
plaster advertising figure, c1930,
15in (38cm) high.
£310–350 / €470–530
$580–650 ⊞ JUN

A J. Scotcher, Baker &
Confectioner delivery handcart,
with original painted decoration,
c1930, 34in (86.5cm) wide.
£900–1,000 / €1,350–1,500
$1,650–1,850 ⊞ B&R

A Kiwi Shoe Polish painted tin
stand, c1930, 17in (43cm) wide.
£115–130 / €175–195
$220–250 ⊞ B&R

▶ A Horlicks glass mixer, c1930,
6in (15cm) high.
£10–15 / €15–22
$19–28 ⊞ AL

▶ **Three Bryant & May match-box covers,** decorated with flowers, 1930s, 3in (7.5cm) high.
£10–15 / €15–22
$19–28 ⊞ HUX

A *Radio Times* **shop calendar,** dated 1930, 14¾ x 10in (37.5 x 25.5cm).
£75–85 / €115–130
$140–160 ⊞ LFi

A Wills's Soccer Roll & Pigtail **wooden cribbage board,** 1930s, 12in (30.5cm) long.
£15–20 / €22–30
$28–38 ⊞ HUX

A pack of Royal Ediswan **playing cards,** 1930s, 4in (10cm) high.
£40–45 / €60–70
$75–85 ⊞ BS

A **Middlemass Chocolate Wembley shop display,** 1930s, 1¼ x 4in (3 x 10cm).
£10–15 / €15–22
$19–28 ⊞ HUX

An OshKosh **advertising clock,** c1938, 19in (48.5cm) diam.
£160–190 / €240–290
$300–360 ↗ JAA
OshKosh B'Gosh, the famous US clothing company, was founded in Oshkosh, Wisconsin in 1895 and made hickory-striped denim bib overalls for railroad workers and farmers. In 1910, the company began producing child-sized overalls as novelty items using the slogan 'Work Clothes for Dad, Play Clothes for Sonny'. However, on a trip to the theatre, the firm's manager heard the line 'Oshkosh B'Gosh' in a vaudeville skit. In 1911 the phrase was adopted as a garment brand name and by 1937 it had become the company's official title. During WWII, OshKosh produced over-alls and 'jungle suits' for US soldiers. After the war, as American casual clothing became fashionable across the world, OshKosh developed as an international brand and is now famous for its children's wear.

A Jacob's Biscuits **shop display dispenser,** 1930s, 42in (106.5cm) wide.
£270–300 / €400–450
$500–560 ⊞ DaM

A **Californian Poppy box,** bottle missing, 1940s, 4in (10cm) high.
£6–10 / €9–15
$12–19 ⊞ LBe

A Bovril ceramic mug, 1940s,
3in (7.5cm) high.
£6–10 / €9–15
$12–19 ⊞ JWK

A Henry Heath cardboard hat box, with a ribbon handle, 1950s,
11in (28cm) diam.
£6–10 / €9–15
$12–19 ⊞ HSt

A Schiaparelli shop display top hat, lined in silk, French, 1950s,
9in (23cm) high.
£130–150 / €195–230
$240–280 ⊞ LBe

A pack of *Financial Times* playing cards, designed by Abram Games,
boxed, 1950s, 4 x 5in (10 x 12.5cm).
£50–55 / €75–85
$95–105 ⊞ RTT
Many celebrated authors began
their careers writing advertising
slogans and many famous
designers have also contributed
to the world of packaging. Born
in Whitechapel, the son of Polish
and Latvian Jewish émigrés,
Abram Games (1914–96) was
one of the most talented graphic
designers of his generation. He
became famous for his WWII
propaganda posters and, after
the war, won the competition
for designing the 1951 Festival
of Britain logo, perhaps his
best-known work. From the
1950s onwards, Games designed
for a wide range of private
companies, including the
Financial Times. Games' work
is sought after by graphic
design enthusiasts.

A Wisdom shop display
wooden toothbrush, c1960,
38in (96.5cm) long.
£130–150 / €195–230
$240–280 ⊞ JUN

Items in the Advertising &
Packaging section have been
arranged in date order.

A Sharp's Toffee glass ashtray,
1960s, 4¾ x 3¼in (12 x 8.5cm).
£7–11 / €11–17
$13–20 ⊞ RTT

**A Robertson's cut-out paper
Albatros aeroplane,** with a Golly
pilot, c1970, 8in (20.5cm) wide.
£10–15 / €15–22
$19–28 ⊞ MRW

**A Bird's Blancmange Powder
box,** with contents, 1970s,
5in (12.5cm) wide.
£4–8 / €6–12
$8–15 ⊞ DaM

A K-tel International Brush-o-Matic brush, boxed, 1970s,
10¼in (26cm) long.
£1–5 / €2–7
$3–9 ⊞ TWI

Advertisement Cards & Showcards

A Wills's Star Cigarettes cardboard shop display, c1900, 5in (12.5cm) wide.
£360–400 / €540–600
$670–750 ⊞ MRW

A Meckumfat Sussex Ground Oats showcard, c1910, 10 x 12in (25.5 x 30.5cm).
£105–120 / €160–180
$195–220 ⊞ MURR

A Hudson's Soap showcard, 1910–20, framed, 24 x 17in (61 x 43cm).
£70–80 / €105–120
$130–150 ⊞ RTT

A Jacob & Co Butter Puffs showcard, c1925, framed, 22in (56cm) high.
£450–500 / €680–750
$840–940 ⊞ HUX

A Mullard Valves cardboard advertising showcard, 1928, 20¼ x 8in (51.5 x 20.5cm).
£180–200 / €270–300
$340–370 ⊞ LFi

A Mansion Polish hanging showcard, illustrated by Harry Rountree, 1920s, framed and glazed, 10 x 7½in (25.5 x 19cm).
£150–175 / €230–260
$280–330 ⊞ AAA

An Ogden's Juggler Tobacco showcard, illustrated by John Hassall, 1920–30, framed and glazed, 21 x 15in (53.5 x 38cm).
£450–500 / €680–750
$840–940 ⊞ AAA

John Hassall

Though many showcards are unsigned and anonymous, others can be attributed to well-known artists which may increase their value. John Hassall (1896–1948) was a respected British poster designer and book illustrator. He studied at the Academie Julien in Paris and, in a career that lasted over 50 years, he produced some much-loved designs, including the famous 'Skegness is So Bracing' poster. Harry Rountree (1878–1950), an illustrator and designer who was taught by John Hassall, produced posters, magazines and children's books and was particularly well-known for his depictions of animals.

◀ **A Vesta Paint showcard,** 1930s, framed and glazed, 24 x 18in (61 x 45.5cm).
£130–145 / €195–220
$240–270 ⊞ JUN

A Hooker's Malted Milk show-card, 1920s, 13¾in (35cm) high.
£30–35 / €45–50
$55–65 ⊞ RTT

▶ **A Lucky Lite flashlite and key chain shop display,** American, 1950s, 11 x 8in (28 x 20.5cm).
£40–45
€60–70
$75–85 ⊞ TWI

A Burrow's Malvern Table Waters showcard, 1930s, 19 x 12in (48.5 x 30.5cm).
£90–100 / €135–150
$170–190 ⊞ Do

A Votrix Vermouth showcard, 1950s, 14½ x 9in (37 x 23cm).
£20–25 / €30–35
$35–45 ⊞ RTT

A Middlemass Forfar Scotch Shortbread shop sign, illustrated by Mabel Lucie Attwell, illuminated, 1950s, 12in (30.5cm) high.
£180–200 / €270–300
$340–370 ⊞ HUX

A SKOL active le bronzage cardboard showcard, 1965, 21in (53.5cm) high.
£25–30 / €40–45
$50–55 ⊞ HUX

Enamel & Tin Signs

A Singer Sewing Machines enamel sign, c1890, framed, 35 x 23½in (89 x 59.5cm).
£360–400 / €540–600
$670–750 ⊞ AAA
Many versions of this sign are known as it has been updated over many years for *The Lady* and *Machine* publications.

Items in the Advertising & Packaging section have been arranged in date order.

A Monsters double-sided enamel sign, c1900, 24in (61cm) wide.
£310–350 / €470–530
$580–650 ⊞ JUN

An Evans' Antiseptic Throat Pastilles enamel sign, 1910–18, 12 x 24in (30.5 x 61cm).
£250–280 / €380–420
$470–520 ⊞ MURR

▶ A Fry's Cocoa enamel sign, c1915, framed, 23 x 18in (58.5 x 45.5cm).
£800–900 / €1,200–1,350
$1,500–1,700 ⊞ AAA

A Cambridge Sausage tin sign, c1910, 8in (20.5cm) wide.
£135–150 / €200–230
$250–280 ⊞ SMI

The Passing Show enamel sign, depicting Lloyd George and the Cabinet, c1913, framed, 27½ x 19½in (70 x 49.5cm).
£900–1,000 / €1,350–1,500
$1,700–1,900 ⊞ AAA
The famous British politicians featured in this advertisement for *The Passing Show* magazine make this rare enamel sign particularly desirable.

◀ A Sharp's Super-Kreem Toffee enamel sign, c1920, framed, 36 x 12in (91.5 x 30.5cm).
£900–1,000
€1,350–1,500
$1,700–1,900 ⊞ AAA
As advertising historian Robert Opie notes in *Miller's Advertising Tins: A Collector's Guide*, Edward Sharp ran a grocery business in the 1870s and began manufacturing toffee in the 1880s. Kreemy Toffee was launched in 1911 and was soon followed by Super-Kreem Toffee. The macaw trademark was used from c1915 together with the slogan 'Sharp's Toffee speaks for itself'. Sir Kreemy Knut was introduced around 1920, and clever advertising helped make Sharp's the best selling toffee manufacturer in the world.

An Avon Brilliant Polish tin finger plate, c1920, 10in (25.5cm) high.
£50–55
€75–85
$95–105 ⊞ BS

A Rowntree's Cocoa enamel sign, 1920s, framed, 12 x 18½in (30.5 x 47cm).
£430–480 / €650–720 $800–900 ⊞ AAA

A Melox Dog Foods double-sided enamel sign, 1920s, 18 x 12in (45.5 x 30.5cm).
£400–450 / €600–680 $750–840 ⊞ AAA

▶ **A Globe Metal Polish enamel sign,** 1920s–30s, 7 x 5in (18 x 12.5cm).
£200–230 / €300–350 $370–430 ⊞ BS

A Tip Top Tea double-sided cut-out enamel sign, 1920s, 19 x 12in (48.5 x 30.5cm).
£340–380 / €510–570 $640–710 ⊞ AAA

◀ **A Sunlight Soap enamel sign,** 1920s–30s, 26 x 36in (66 x 91.5cm).
£270–300 €400–450 $500–560 ⊞ AAA

◀ **A Jena Glass enamel finger plate,** c1930, 8in (20.5cm) high.
£150–175 / €230–260 $280–330 ⊞ JUN

A Cap Corned Beef metal sign, 1940s–50s, 10 x 8in (25.5 x 20.5cm).
£15–20 / €22–30 $28–38 ⊞ RTT

Tins

An F. Perroux le Furet corset tin, French, c1890, 16in (40.5cm) wide.
£300–330 / €450–500
$560–620 ⊞ HUX

A Dunn's Chocolate tin, 1890–1900, 8 x 6in (20.5 x 15cm).
£270–300 / €400–450
$500–560 ⊞ MURR

A chocolate tin, commemorating the Boer War, inscribed 'South Africa', 1900, 6¼in (16cm) wide.
£55–65 / €85–100
$100–120 ⊞ HUX
A number of tins were produced to commemorate the Boer War (1899–1902). In 1900, Queen Victoria sent a tin of chocolate to each soldier fighting in South Africa. The tins were designed by J. S. Fry and included an embossed medallion portrait of the Queen together with a printed inscription and signature in the Royal hand, reading 'I wish you a Happy New Year'. J. S. Fry sent 40,000 of these tins to South Africa. Rival companies, Cadbury and Rowntree, also made their own tins.

A Huntley & Palmer's Floral biscuit tin, with two hinged lids, c1900, 8¼in (21cm) wide.
£80–90 / €120–135
$150–170 ⊞ HUX
This Floral biscuit tin is the second in a series of three tins produced by Huntley & Palmer with two hinged lids. Ivory appeared in 1899 and Mosaic in 1901. In total, 40,000 copies of Floral tins were made.

A biscuit tin, in the form of a ship, 1900, 26½in (67.5cm) long.
£1,000–1,200 / €1,500–1,800
$1,850–2,250 ⊞ HUX
Biscuit tins in the form of transport toys tend to fetch the highest prices and were often produced for the lucrative Christmas market. However, comparatively few of these toy tins were made and, having been played with by children, fewer still survive in good condition.

A J. S. Fry & Sons Chocolate tin money box, by Barringer, Wallis & Manners, Canadian, c1905, 5in (12.5cm) high.
£105–120 / €160–180
$195–220 ⊞ HUX

◄ **A Wellington Knife Polish tin,** c1900, 4½in (11.5cm) high.
£55–65 / €85–100
$100–120 ⊞ BS

A Lefevre-Utile biscuit tin,
in the form of a monogrammed
travelling trunk, French, 1905,
8½in (21.5cm) wide.
**£270–300 / €400–450
$500–560 ⊞ HUX**

A biscuit tin, in the form of a
railway carriage, Spanish, 1905,
6½in (16.5cm) wide.
**£760–850 / €1,150–1,300
$1,400–1,600 ⊞ HUX**

A Huntley & Palmer's tin, in
the form of a pigskin handbag,
c1909, 8in (20.5cm) wide.
**£50–60 / €75–90
$95–110 ⟋ L**
Huntley & Palmer's was founded
in 1822 as a small bakery in
Reading, Berkshire. The business
flourished and in 1844 they
opened a large factory. By the
early 1900s Huntley & Palmer's
was the largest biscuit
manufacturer in the world,
producing over 400 varieties of
biscuit. In the 1830s, the firm
began hand-making large tin
storage boxes for displaying
and transporting their products.
From 1868, they began to
produce small, decorative gift
tins with transfer-printed
decoration, aimed at the individual
purchaser. By the turn of the
century they were manufacturing
shaped biscuit tins in a
wide range of inventive designs. This
Gladstone bag tin first appeared
in 1904 when 65,000 examples
were made. It was reissued
in 1909 and a further 20,000
were produced.

**A sewing machine accessories
tin,** c1910, 5¾in (14.5cm) wide.
**£40–45 / €60–70
$75–85 ⊞ HUX**

A Hospodar Cigarettes tin, c1910,
5½in (14cm) wide.
**£110–130 / €175–195
$220–240 ⊞ HUX**

A Gibson Girl Cigarettes tin,
by Manoli, German, Berlin, 1910,
4½in (11.5cm) wide.
**£50–55 / €75–85
$95–105 ⊞ HUX**

An advertising tin string box,
c1910, 7in (18cm) high.
**£135–150 / €200–230
$250–280 ⊞ SMI**
Edwardian grocers wrapped
goods in paper and then tied
them with string. These
promotional tins, covered with
advertisements, were designed
for the shop counter. The string
would have been kept inside and
then cut to size using the blade
on the top.

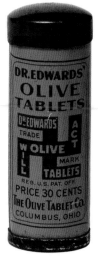

► **A Dr Edwards Olive Tablets tin,**
American, 1914–18, 2½in (6.5cm) high.
**£15–20 / €22–30
$28–38 ⊞ HUX**

A Lipton's Tea tin, 1915,
9in (23cm) high.
**£135–150 / €200–230
$250–280 ⊞ HUX**

A Player's Navy Cut Cigarettes tin, 1915, 4in (10cm) wide.
£25–30 / €40–45
$50–55 ⊞ HUX

A Don Confectionery sweet tin, in the form of a roulette wheel, c1920, 10in (25.5cm) diam.
£90–100 / €135–150
$170–190 ⊞ HUX

A tin, commemorating Napoleon, Dutch, 1920, 11in (28cm) wide.
£115–130 / €175–195
$220–250 ⊞ HUX

A Crawford's biscuit tin, in the form of a tractor, 1925, 7in (18cm) long.
£1,350–1,500 / €2,050–2,250
$2,500–2,800 ⊞ HUX
This is a rare item, hence its value.

A Becos Tobacco tin, German, 1925, 3½in (9cm) wide.
£160–180 / €240–270
$300–340 ⊞ HUX

A Jacob's biscuit tin, in the form of a spinning top, 1925, 8in (20.5cm) high.
£270–300 / €400–450
$500–560 ⊞ HUX

A Dimitrino & Co Egyptian Cigarettes tin, 1920s, 4¼in (11cm) wide.
£80–90 / €120–135
$150–170 ⊞ HUX

A Hall's 'State' Toffee tin, 1920s, 6in (15cm) wide.
£50–60 / €75–90
$95–110 ⊞ MURR

A biscuit tin, with an inkwell in the cover, 1920s, 8½in (21.5cm) wide.
£70–80 / €105–120
$130–150 ⊞ HUX

A Maynards Old London Toffee tin, depicting the Royal Exchange, London, 1920s, 4 x 6½in (10 x 16.5cm).
£20–25 / €30–35
$35–45 ⊞ RTT

A Sharp's Super-Kreem Toffee tin, c1930, 8in (20.5cm) wide.
£6–10 / €9–15
$12–19 ⊞ AL

A Keiller's Toffee tin, depicting Peter Pan, 1930, 12in (30.5cm) wide.
£30–35 / €45–50
$55–65 ⊞ HUX

A blackcurrant drops tin, depicting a member of the Royal Canadian Mounted Police, Canadian, 1930s, 3in (7.5cm) diam.
£25–30 / €40–45
$50–55 ⊞ MRW

A tin, depicting Mickey Mouse, French, c1935, 6¾in (17cm) diam.
£135–150 / €200–230
$250–280 ⊞ HUX

A Brown Beauty Shoe Polish tin, 1930s, 3in (7.5cm) diam.
£2–6 / €3–9
$4–11 ⊞ Do

A Cerebos Table Salt tin, c1950, 10in (25.5cm) high.
£15–20 / €22–30
$28–38 ⊞ AL

A tin, depicting Cinderella, c1950, 3in (7.5cm) diam.
£25–30 / €40–45
$50–55 ⊞ MRW

A Carr's biscuit tin, in the form of a bus, 1950, 10in (25.5cm) wide.
£360–400 / €540–600
$670–750 ⊞ HUX

A Jacob's biscuit tin, depicting a child with a dog, 1950s, 5in (12.5cm) square.
£4–8 / €6–12
$8–15 ⊞ DaM

A Bisto Gravy tin, c1950, 7½in (19cm) high.
£15–20 / €22–30
$28–38 ⊞ AL

A Huntley & Palmer's sweet tin, depicting Noddy cleaning his car, c1956, 5in (12.5cm) diam.
£20–25 / €30–35
$35–45 ⊞ BBe
This is one of a series of 20 tin designs featuring Enid Blyton's famous creation Noddy.

▶ **An A. S. Wilkin Cremona & Red Boy Toffees tin,** decorated with scenes of nursery rhymes, 1950s–60s, 3¾in (9.5cm) diam.
£15–20 / €22–30
$28–38 ⊞ RTT

Aeronautica

A sweet tin, decorated with an airship, c1910, 2½in (6.5cm) wide.
£90–100 / € 135–150
$170–190 ⊞ HUX

A silver-plated Saint Raphael aviation badge, with relief decoration to both sides, 1910, 5in (12.5cm) diam.
£580–650 / € 870–980
$1,050–1,200 ⊞ AU
This badge is the aviation equivalent to a St Christopher plaque for cars. The inscription reads 'St Raphael has taken me and brought me back safe and sound'.

A bronze plaque, commemorating a zeppelin journey around the world, German, 1929, 3¼ x 3in (8.5 x 7.5cm).
£310–350 / € 470–530
$580–650 ⊞ AU

◄ Christopher Beck, *The Crimson Aeroplane*, published by Arthur Pearson Ltd, c1910, 8in (20.5cm) high.
£6–10 / € 9–15
$12–19 ⊞ JUN

A Sonorophone gramophone needle tin, decorated with a Bleriot aeroplane, c1920, 2in (5cm) wide.
£65–75 / € 100–115
$120–140 ⊞ AAA

◄ A poster, advertising model glider flying, c1935, 23¾ x 15¼in (60.5 x 38.5cm).
£70–80 / € 105–120
$130–150 ⋏ NSal

A silver hip flask, in the form of a car radiator, inscribed from the Sopwith family to Amy Johnson, believed to have been a 28th birthday present, 1928, 5in (12.5cm) wide.
£2,800–3,200 / € 4,200–4,800
$5,200–6,000 ⊞ AU
Amy Johnson was born in Hull in 1903 and gained a degree from Sheffield University, which was unusual for women of her day. She then moved to London where she began learning to fly in 1928. Her most famous journey was in 1930 when, in a single-engine Gypsy Moth, she became the first woman to fly alone to Australia. Amy Johnson set several flight records in the 1930s and became an international celebrity. After the outbreak of WWII she joined the Air Transport Auxiliary where her duties included ferrying aircraft from factory airstrips to RAF bases. On one of these missions, on 5 January 1941, she crashed into the Thames Estuary, thus ending the life of Britain's most famous female pilot. Many artefacts associated with Amy Johnson are in British museums and it is rare to find such a piece on the open market.

A Shelley pin dish, decorated with an RAF aircraft, 1937–39, 5in (12.5cm) diam.
£45–50 / € 70–80
$95–105 ⊞ MURR

A postcard, depicting a Hindenburg zeppelin, 1938, 5½in (14cm) wide.
£20–25 / € 30–35
$35–45 ⊞ COB

F. V. Monk and H. T. Winter,
Advance in the Air, published by Blackie & Son, 1930s, 8in (20.5cm) high.
£6–10 / € 9–15
$12–19 ⊞ RTT

▶ **A Steelcraft aeroplane pedal toy,** American, 1930s, 46in (117cm) long.
£340–380 / € 510–570
$640–710 ⊞ BAJ

A model of a Super Marine Spitfire, made from the aluminium of a Spitfire engine, 1939–44, 5in (12.5cm) wide.
£55–65 / € 85–100
$100–120 ⊞ GBM

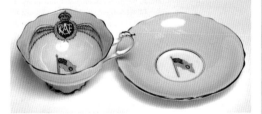

A wooden propeller, c1940, 86in (218.5cm) wide.
£450–500 / € 680–750
$840–940 ⊞ JUN

A Paragon Patriotic Series RAF cup and saucer, c1940, cup 4in (10cm) high.
£130–145 / € 195–220
$240–270 ⊞ BtoB
This item was made for the export market.

◀ **An Elgin aircraft clock,** with 8-day movement, c1941, 2½in (6.5cm) square.
£85–95
€ 130–145
$160–180 ⊞ TIC

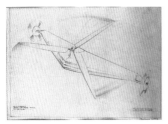

▶ **A Battle of Britain Week window poster,** 1948, 12in (30.5cm) wide.
£15–20
€22–30
$28–38 ⊞ COB

A pencil sketch on paper, by Raymond Fernand Loewy, depicting a Flying Wing helicopter, signed and dated 15 November 1943, 15½ x 21½in (39.5 x 54.5cm).
£1,100–1,300 / €1,650–1,950
$2,050–2,450 ✱ S(P)

A BOAC Strato Cruiser brochure, with poster, labels and information, 1949, 11 x 7in (28 x 18cm).
£20–25 / €30–35
$35–45 ⊞ J&S

A bronze Spitfire table lighter, 1940s, 6in (15cm) high.
£50–60 / €75–90
$95–110 ⊞ COB

An RAF sweetheart emblem on a plastic badge, 1940s, 1¼in (3cm) diam.
£10–15 / €15–22
$19–28 ⊞ HUX

***The Aeroplane* magazine,** November 1956, 12 x 9in (30.5 x 23cm).
£1–5 / €2–7
$3–9 ⊞ JUN

A brass plaque, depicting a Spitfire, 1940s, 12in (30.5cm) wide.
£45–50 / €70–80
$85–95 ⊞ COB

A Coronation Review of the RAF programme, 1953, 11 x 8in (28 x 20.5cm).
£10–15 / €15–22
$19–28 ⊞ J&S

An aluminium aeroplane lamp, with plastic nose cone light, c1950, 12¼in (31cm) high.
£480–580 / €720–870
$900–1,050 ✱ S(P)

▶ **Two Pan Am glasses,** commemorating the Pacific inaugural flight, 1959, 5½in (14cm) high.
£10–15 / €15–22
$19–28 ⊞ RTT

A brass and enamel powder compact, commemorating D-Day, 1950s, 3½in (9cm) diam.
£155–175 / €230–260
$290–330 ⊞ SUW

A FROG plastic model kit, 'The Trail Blazers', 1960s, 4 x 7in (10 x 18cm).
£6–10 / €9–15
$12–19 ⊞ COB

A plastic model of a DC10 aeroplane, by Cesara, Italian, 1978, 29in (73.5cm) wide.
£85–95 / €130–145
$160–180 ⊞ GTM

A BA Concorde postcard, commemorating the first flight from Boeing Field over the Pacific Ocean and back, limited edition of 100, stamped, signed by the pilots, 1984, 7in (18cm) wide.
£12–16 / €18–24
$22–30 ⊞ IQ

A steel airline tiepin, c1960, 3in (7.5cm) wide.
£1–5 / €2–7
$3–9 ⊞ RTT

Seven airline key rings, 1960s, largest 2in (5cm) long.
£1–5 / €2–7
$3–9 each ⊞ COB

A plastic space shuttle radio, model 228, c1981, 10in (25.5cm) wide, boxed.
£6–10 / €9–15
$12–19 ⊞ IQ

Three packs of four Marlboro cigarettes, advertising MEA and Air France, 1960s, 3½in (9cm) high.
£8–12 / €12–18
$15–22 ⊞ HUX

A pack of British Airways playing cards, 1960s, 4 x 2½in (10 x 6.5cm).
£6–10 / €9–15
$12–19 ⊞ RTT

A bronze aviation medal, for the European Motor Glider Championships at Zell-am-See, 1986, 4in (10cm) diam, in original case.
£80–90 / €120–135
$150–170 ⋏ DW

◄ **An Aynsley bone china Concorde Celebration vase,** commemorating 25 years of Concorde supersonic flight, hand-painted and gilded to each side with views of Concorde, limited edition of 100, 2003, 10in (25.5cm) high.
£630–700 / €950–1,050
$1,150–1,300 ⊞ PeJ

Amusement & Slot Machines

Inspired by the traditional game of bagatelle, coin-operated pinball machines took off in the USA in the 1930s. Early machines included the Bingo, Baffle Ball and the Ballyhoo. As the craze for this low-cost type of game swept the penny arcades of depression-torn America, features became more sophisticated. Ball traps improved, electricity was introduced in 1933, bringing flashing lights and scoreboards, and 1937 saw the addition of the bumper. In order to prevent players from cheating by lifting and shaking the machine, manufacturers also came up with the tilt mechanism.

Production ceased during WWII but boomed once again in 1947 when David Gottlieb & Co

introduced the first machine with flippers called the Humpty Dumpty.

For many collectors the 1940s and '50s were the golden age of the pinball machine. Frames and legs were made of wood (metal was introduced later in the 1950s) and individual scores, complete with flashing light bulbs, were incorporated into the back glass. The 1960s saw the introduction of digital scoring and in the 1970s electronic pinball machines, complete with new electronic soundtracks, gradually replaced electro-mechanical models. Vintage pinball machines attract many enthusiasts, particularly in the USA, and are collected for both their aesthetic appeal and their playability.

◀ **An Electra slot machine,** by the Electra Manufacturing Co, with electric shock, c1910, 30in (76cm) high.
£900–1,000 / €1,350–1,500 $1,650–1,850 ⊞ HAK

▶ **A Handani Multiball slot machine,** c1915, 30in (76cm) high.
£1,350–1,500 / €2,000–2,250 $2,500–2,800 ⊞ HAK

An Allwins flick ball machine, c1930, 27in (68.5cm) high.
£520–580 / €780–870 $970–1,100 ⊞ JUN

A Mills cast-iron one-armed bandit, c1930, 30in (76cm) high.
£400–450 / €600–680 $750–840 ⊞ JUN

▶ **A peepshow machine,** 'What did the Diver See?', worn, 1930s, 24in (61cm) wide.
£160–180 / €240–270 $300–340 ⋟ E

A Wonders shooting gallery slot machine, in an oak-mounted case, 1930s, 30¼in (77cm) high.
£400–480 / €600–720 $750–900 ↗ SWO

A L'il Abner gumball machine, depicting characters from *Al Capp* comic strip including Daisy Mae, Mammy and Pappy Yokums, American, c1940, 23½in (59.5cm) high.
£710–850 / €1,100–1,300 $1,350–1,600 ↗ S(P)

A Gottlieb Universe pinball machine, with animated back screen, some paint losses, c1955, 66in (167.5cm) high.
£980–1,200 €1,500–1,800 $1,850–2,200 ↗ JAA

◀ **A Chicago Speedway arcade game,** with pedal accelerator and steering wheel, c1965, 69in (175.5cm) high.
£185–220 / €280–330 $350–410 ↗ JAA

▶ **A Ford gumball machine,** on a chrome stand, American, c1970, 38in (96.5cm) high.
£270–300 / €400–450 $500–560 ⊞ AME

◀ A Data East *Lethal Weapon 3* pinball machine, c1993, 52in (132cm) long.
£1,000–1,200
€ 1,500–1,800
$1,800–2,200 ⊞ AME

A Fireball II pinball machine, 1982, 71in (180.5cm) high.
£1,000–1,200
€ 1,500–1,800
$1,800–2,200 ⊞ MSh

▶ A Bell Fruit *Dr Who* fruit machine, 1983, 74in (188cm) high.
£580–650 / € 870–980
$1,100–1,200 ⊞ AME
It is unusual to find this machine in red.

A Bally Attack from Mars pinball machine, with 1950s theme, American, 1995, 75in (190.5cm) high.
£2,250–2,500
€ 3,400–3,750
$4,200–4,700 ⊞ WAm

A Pachinko Rocky Twin Towers slot machine, Japanese, 2000, 74in (188cm) high.
£1,350–1,500
€ 2,050–2,200
$2,500–2,800 ⊞ AME
This slot machine is hard to find today. The glass panel shows the Twin Towers with a star about to crash into them – for obvious reasons it was withdrawn from the market and is now regarded as a rare collector's item.

Architectural Salvage

A wrought-iron and brass door lock, c1840, 11in (28cm) wide.
£175–195 / €260–290
$330–370 ⊞ OLA

An engraved brass lock, with keep and key, 19thC, 9in (23cm) wide.
£760–850 / €1,150–1,300
$1,400–1,600 ⊞ BS

A Victorian brass door-stop, in the form of a swan, 15½in (39.5cm) high.
£290–350 / €440–530
$540–650 ⋟ NSal

A cast-iron door porter, depicting the Crane and Ewer from *Aesop's Fables*, 19thC, 10½in (26.5cm) high.
£180–200 / €270–300
$330–370 ⊞ MFB

A Victorian stained glass fanlight, the central roundel depicting swallows in a landscape, on a scrolling foliate ground, 42in (106.5cm) wide.
£420–500 / €630–750
$790–940 ⋟ AH

A pair of Aesthetic Movement cast-iron fire dogs, c1880, 9in (23cm) high.
£210–240 / €320–360
$400–450 ⊞ BS

◄ **A wrought-iron range stand,** c1860, 8in (20.5cm) wide.
£18–22 / €27–33
$34–41 ⊞ Cot

A pair of cast-iron pineapple post finials, 19thC, 9in (23cm) high.
£220–250 / €350–390
$410–470 ⋟ WW

Pineapples

Christopher Columbus was the first European to encounter a pineapple and brought accounts of it back in 1493. The name pineapple derived from the fruit's resemblance to the pine cone. In the West Indies pineapples were known as 'nanas' (hence the French word ananas). In the Caribbean, the fruit was the symbol of hospitality and a pineapple left at the entrance to a doorway meant guests were welcome. This custom spread to Europe and North America where pineapple finials were placed on buildings and gateposts.

Another reason for the decorative use of pineapples is that this rare and exotic fruit was a symbol of wealth. Pineapples were first seen in Britain in the 17th century. Charles II was famously painted receiving a pineapple and in the 18th and 19th centuries gentlemen competed to cultivate pineapples in their hot houses. Due to the difficulties of transporting the fruit, fresh pineapple remained an expensive delicacy in Europe until the 20th century.

A copper coal scuttle, c1880, 14in (35.5cm) high.
£100–110 / €150–165
$185–210 ⊞ WAC

A pair of brass beehive door handles, c1880, 3in (7.5cm) high.
£60–70 / €90–105
$110–130 ⊞ OLA

A set of three brass coat hooks, on a wooden board, c1880, hooks 7in (18cm) high.
£90–100 / €135–150
$170–190 ⊞ AL

A pair of nickel-plated bath taps, c1880, 5in (12.5cm) high.
£200–220 / €300–330
$370–410 ⊞ OLA

A pair of brass globe taps, c1890, 5in (12.5cm) high.
£250–280 / €380–420
$470–520 ⊞ OLA

A Bullfinch cast-iron radiator, c1890, 11in (28cm) high.
£50–60 / €75–90
$95–110 ⊞ DaM

An iron weather cock, c1890, 21in (53.5cm) high.
£155–175 / €230–260
$290–330 ⊞ JUN

A Kenrick cast-iron door knocker, c1890, 7in (18cm) high.
£160–180 / €240–270
$300–340 ⊞ OLA
Archibald Kenrick established an iron foundry in West Bromwich in 1791. The firm was known for manufacturing high quality domestic metalware.

◄ **A Regency-style brass curtain rail,** c1900, 72in (183cm) long.
£310–350
€470–530
$580–650
⊞ OLA

A brass electric bell push, 1894, 3½in (9cm) diam.
£150–170 / €230–260
$280–320 ⊞ BS

A wrought-iron brazier, c1900,
19in (48.5cm) diam.
£85–95 / €130–145
$160–180 ⊞ HOP

A cast-iron heating stove, French,
c1900, 19in (48.5cm) wide.
£220–250 / €330–390
$410–470 ⊞ B&R

◄ **A pair of Dennis Ruabon
terracotta pillar caps,** c1900,
18in (45.5cm) high.
£270–300 / €400–450
$500–560 ⊞ HOP

► **A terracotta brick,** with
rose decoration, c1900,
10in (25.5cm) square.
£20–25 / €30–35
$35–45 ⊞ HOP

A Kenrick cast-iron vent cover,
c1900, 9in (23cm) diam.
£110–125 / €165–190
$200–230 ⊞ OLA

**A Doulton 'The
Combination Patent
Lavatory Pan',** c1900,
16in (40.5cm) high.
£500–600 / €750–900
$930–1,100 ➶ E

**A brass electric
light switch,** c1910,
4in (10cm) diam.
£40–45 / €60–70
$75–85 ⊞ JUN

A pine door, Welsh,
c1900, 30in (76cm) wide.
£360–400 / €540–600
$670–750 ⊞ OLA

A copper Pither's Radiant Stove,
early 20thC, 30in (76cm) high.
£360–400 / €540–600
$670–750 ♪ PFK

An enamelled cast-iron sink, with
base, c1930, 27in (68.5cm) wide.
£1,000–1,200 / €1,500–1,800
$1,800–2,200 ⊞ OLA

A brass dolphin door knocker,
c1930, 11in (28cm) long.
£310–350 / €470–530
$580–650 ⊞ OLA

A cast-iron door stop, in the
form of a chicken, French, 1930s,
8½in (21.5cm) wide.
£55–65 / €85–100
$100–120 ⊞ BET

An Art Deco brass letter plate
and knocker, 8in (20.5cm) wide.
£175–195 / €260–290
$330–370 ⊞ SAT

A brass single lever door handle,
1920s, 5in (12.5cm) wide.
£20–25 / €30–35
$35–45 ⊞ BS

A brass and wood 'Ladies' sign,
c1930, 21in (53.5cm) wide.
£70–80 / €105–120
$130–150 ⊞ Cot

An oak log/coal box, with original
liner, c1930, 14in (35.5cm) wide.
£75–85 / €115–130
$140–160 ⊞ SAT

A mahogany lavatory seat,
c1920, 23in (58.5cm) wide.
£250–280 / €380–420
$470–520 ⊞ OLA

A set of three pairs of Art Deco-
style chrome door handles,
c1930, 6in (15cm) high.
£340–380 / €510–570
$640–710 ⊞ OLA

An Art Deco chrome companion
set, c1930, 15in (38cm) high.
£155–175 / €230–260
$290–330 ⊞ SAT

◀ A brass door pull, c1930,
4in (10cm) diam.
£85–95 / €130–145
$160–180 ⊞ OLA

Art Deco

A Gothic Watch Co 14ct white rolled-gold wristwatch, 1920.
£155–175 / €230–260
$290–330 ⊞ **WAC**

A Grimwades jug, decorated with Delhi pattern, 1920–30, 8in (20.5cm) high.
£230–260 / €350–390
$430–490 ⊞ **SCH**

A picture frame, with a bronze model of a deer, on a marble base, c1930, 11in (28cm) high.
£175–195 / €260–290
$330–360 ⊞ **SAT**

A Lalique opalescent glass Coquilles plate, engraved 'R. Lalique', French, c1930, 7½in (19cm) diam.
£200–230 / €290–350
$360–430 ⚲ **G(L)**

A walnut clock, with a quarter-cut face, c1920, 18in (45.5cm) wide.
£350–390 / €530–590
$650–730 ⊞ **SAT**

A set of six silver-gilt and enamel coffee spoons, with ebony coffee bean finials, Birmingham, 1928–29, 3in (7.5cm) long, boxed.
£65–75 / €100–115
$120–140 ⚲ **G(L)**

A mirrored picture frame, on a marble base, c1930, 10in (25.5cm) high.
£130–145 / €195–220
$240–270 ⊞ **SAT**

A porcelain and textile half-doll pincushion, 1920–30, 4½in (11.5cm) high.
£220–250 / €330–380
$410–470 ⊞ **SUW**

A pair of bookends, with bronze models of swifts on marble bases, c1930, 6in (15cm) high.
£150–165 / €220–250
$280–310 ⊞ **SAT**

A Lalique frosted and enamelled glass Dahlia box and cover, the cover moulded with a flowerhead, stencil mark 'R. Lalique', French, c1930, 4½in (11.5cm) diam.
£440–530 / €660–795
$820–990 ⚲ **CDC**

◄ **A suede evening bag,** with gilt mounts and clasp, c1930, 8¼in (21cm) long.
£40–50 / €60–75
$75–85 ⚲ **NSal**

A marble mantel clock, surmounted by a Chiparus-style female figure, c1930, 23¼in (59cm) wide.
£340–410 / €510–610
$640–770 ⚒ L&E
Slender, decorative and often athletic females were a favourite Art Deco subject, particularly in the form of figurines. Romanian artist Demêtre Chiparus specialized in producing bronze and ivory statuettes of exotic women, often inspired by Ballet Russes dancers and Parisian showgirls.

A paste lapel clip, 1930, 3in (7.5cm) wide.
£55–65 / €85–100
$100–120 ⊞ LBe
Patented by Louis Cartier in 1927, the double clip has a favourite piece of Art Deco jewellery that could be clipped onto everything from lapels to shoes.

A mirrored zodiac wall clock, within a stamped copper frame, 1930s, 28¼in (72cm) diam.
£650–780 / €980–1,150
$1,200–1,450 ⚒ L&T

A mahogany jewellery box, c1930, 9in (23cm) wide.
£50–55 / €75–85
$95–105 ⊞ SAT

A pair of Georg Jensen silver Pyramid butter dishes, designed by Harald Nielsen, import mark for 1933, 4¾in (12cm) diam.
£290–350 / €440–530
$540–650 ⚒ G(L)

A Wedgwood model of a deer, by Keith Murray, transfer-printed factory mark, 1930–40, 8in (20.5cm) high.
£90–105 / €135–150
$170–200 ⚒ PF

An oak aneroid barometer, c1930, 24in (61cm) high.
£165–185 / €250–280
$310–350 ⊞ SAT

A hardwood and chrome cake stand, 1930s, 17in (43cm) high.
£85–95 / €130–145
$160–180 ⊞ SAT

◄ **An oak display cabinet,** with sunburst astragal-glazed doors enclosing glass shelves, 1930s, 46¾in (119cm) wide.
£260–310 / €390–470
$490–580 ⚒ Bri

A chrome novelty rabbit cruet set, 1930s, 2in (5cm) wide.
£60–70 / €90–105
$110–130 ↗ DA

A pair of Royal Winton vases, 1930s, 7in (18cm) high.
£200–220
€300–330
$370–410 ⊞ SCH

A bronze figure of a young woman, by Lorenzl, with silver and gold patination, on an onyx stand, some wear to base, marked, 1930s, 9½in (24cm) high.
£280–330 / €350–500
$520–620 ↗ FHF

A Gray's Pottery platter, with hand-painted decoration, 1930s, 14in (35.5cm) wide.
£170–190 / €260–290
$320–360 ⊞ JFME

▶ **A bronze figure of a naked female dancer,** by Strobl, on a marble base, some losses to base, signed, 1930s, 10½in (26.5cm) high.
£180–210
€270–310
$340–400
↗ G(L)

A chrome and glass brooch, 1930s, 3½in (9cm) wide.
£80–90 / €120–135
$150–170 ⊞ LaF

▶ **An Agalin carved Bakelite mirror,** 1930s, 13in (33cm) long.
£180–200
€270–300
$330–370
⊞ SUW

A pair of enamel cufflinks, 1930s, 2in (5cm) wide.
£60–70 / €90–105
$110–130 ⊞ LaF

A pair of Electrolaire chrome and glass two-branch lamps, 1930s, 17in (43cm) high.
£540–600 / €810–900
$1,000–1,100 ⊞ SCH

A set of three resin buttons and a clasp, 1930s, clasp 3¼in (8.5cm) wide.
£50–55 / €75–85
$95–105 ⊞ EV

▶ **A Lucerne rolled-gold and paste wristwatch,** set with *faux* diamonds and rubies, 1940.
£165–185 / €250–280
$310–350 ⊞ WAC

Art Nouveau

An Art Nouveau Orivit pewter and mahogany tray, German, 16in (40.5cm) wide.
£270–300 / €400–450
$500–560 ⊞ WAC

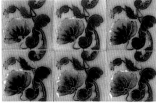

A set of six tiles, decorated with poppies, 1880–1920, 6in (15cm) square.
£95–110 / €140–165
$180–210 ⋏ VSP

▶ **A bronzed lamp,** the marbled glass shade within a cast-bronze frame, the base and handles modelled as two confronting herons, c1900.
£400–480 / €600–720
$750–900 ⋏ LAY

An Art Nouveau Stourbridge glass vase, decorated with trailed green glass, 5in (12.5cm) high.
£190–210 / €290–320
$360–390 ⊞ WAC

An Art Nouveau majolica jardinière stand, with stylized moulded leaf decoration, 38¼in (97cm) high.
£270–320 / €400–480
$500–600 ⋏ JAd

A Porzellanfabrik amphora vase, impressed marks, Austrian, c1900, 20in (51cm) high.
£220–260 / €330–390
$410–490 ⋏ HYD

A Tiffany Favrile glass dish, c1900, 5in (12.5cm) diam.
£115–135 / €175–210
$220–260 ⋏ DuM

A Palme-König glass stick vase, decorated with glass threading, Bohemian, c1900, 8¾in (22cm) high.
£75–90 / €115–135
$140–165 ⋏ JAA

A Palme-König iridescent glass stick vase, decorated with glass threading, Bohemian, c1900, 9in (23cm) high.
£140–165 / €210–250
$260–310 ↗ **JAA**

A wooden photograph frame, carved with a maiden's head, c1900, 9in (23cm) high.
£310–350 / €470–530
$580–650 ⊞ **HaH**

An embossed copper coal box, c1900, 16in (40.5cm) wide.
£170–200 / €260–300
$320–370 ↗ **DA**

A tourmaline and pearl pendant, c1900.
£160–190 / €240–290
$300–360 ↗ **TEN**

A silver and enamel pendant, with an enamel drop, c1900.
£200–240 / €300–360
$370–440 ↗ **TEN**

A WMF silvered cake stand, by Christian Neuwirth, the top inset with a Berlin glazed earthenware panel, impressed and stamped marks, German, c1900, 13¾in (35cm) diam.
£280–330 / €420–500
$520–620 ↗ **L&T**

A Liberty Tudric pewter tea set, by Archibald Knox, comprising three pieces, with whiplash curved decoration, the teapot with a wicker insulated handle, early 20thC, teapot 3¾in (9.5cm) high.
£270–325 / €410–500
$500–620 ↗ **Bri**

A silver-mounted oak photograph frame, decorated with stylized floral motifs, Birmingham 1904, 6¼in (16cm) high.
£210–250 / €320–380
$390–470 ↗ **G(L)**

An oak mantel clock, inlaid with a stylized flower, some damage, c1905, 11½in (29cm) high.
£80–95 / €120–145
$150–180 ↗ **L&E**

▶ **A brass and enamel clasp,** c1920, 3in (7.5cm) wide.
£40–45 / €60–70
$75–85 ⊞ **JBB**

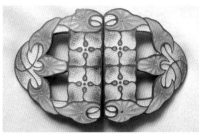

Arts & Crafts

A pair of Linthorpe pottery side plates, moulded with flowers, one restored, signed 'E.P.', c1884, 6½in (16.5cm) diam.
£165–185 / €250–280
$310–350 ⊞ HUN

A pair of Bretby pottery candle-sticks, modelled as Doric columns, c1890, 7¼in (18.5cm) high.
£155–175 / €230–260
$290–330 ⊞ HUN

A Linthorpe two-handled vase, 1890s, 4in (10cm) high.
£175–195 / €260–290
$330–370 ⊞ JFME

▶ **A copper casket,** decorated with two plaques entitled 'Oliver Twist' and 'Bumble', c1900, 9in (23cm) wide.
£200–220
€300–330
$370–420
⊞ WAC

A Murrle Bennett silver and enamel pendant, c1900.
£200–240 / €300–360
$380–450 ➤ G(L)

A footed vase, attributed to Ault, with a crinkle top, c1895, 11in (28cm) high.
£145–165 / €220–250
$270–310 ⊞ HUN

An oak cigar box, with oxidized panels and cabochons, c1900, 11in (28cm) wide.
£200–240 / €300–360
$370–450 ➤ HOLL

LOCATE THE SOURCE

The source of each illustration in Miller's can be found by checking the code letters below each caption with the Key to Illustrations, pages 794–800.

▶ **A Ruskin pottery vase,** 1900s, 13in (33cm) high.
£240–270 / €360–410
$450–500 ⊞ JFME

▶ **A pair of Ault pottery miniature vases,** c1900, 2½in (6.5cm) diam.
£110–125
€165–190
$200–230
⊞ HUN

Autographs

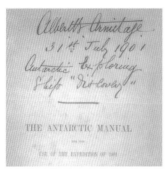

Albert Armitage, a signed and inscribed book *The Antarctic Manual,* edited by George Murray, some damage, 1901, 8°.
£1,900–2,250 / €2,850–3,400
$3,550–4,200 ✗ BBA
Albert Armitage (1864–1943) was the navigator of the *Discovery* and second-in-command to Captain Scott on the National Antarctic Expedition 1901–04. A collection of Armitage material (including this volume) was offered for sale by Bloomsbury Auctions and Armitage's handwritten diary, recording the events of the voyage and his deteriorating relationship with Captain Scott, fetched £36,000 / €54,000 / $67,000.

Winston S. Churchill, a signed and inscribed book *Painting as a Pastime,* with a typed letter from his personal private secretary, 1949, 8°.
£1,350–1,600 / €2,050–2,400
$2,500–3,000 ✗ WilP

▶ **Shirley Eaton,** a signed publicity photograph from *Goldfinger,* 1960s, 10 x 8in (25.5 x 20.5cm).
£35–40 / €50–60
$65–75 ⊞ RaA

Robert Beltrane, a signed photograph from *Star Trek Voyager,* 1990s, 10 x 8in (25.5 x 20.5cm).
£30–35 / €45–50
$55–65 ⊞ CoC

Warwick Davis, a signed photograph of Flitwick from *Harry Potter,* 2002, 10 x 8in (25.5 x 20.5cm).
£35–40 / €50–60
$65–75 ⊞ RaA

Isambard Kingdom Brunel, a signed cheque, 1835, 7in (18cm) wide.
£250–280 / €380–420
$470–520 ⊞ IQ

Bonnie Prince Charlie, a letter signed by Prince Charles Edward Stuart, 1748, 6in (15cm) square.
£2,550–2,850 / €3,850–4,300
$4,750–5,300 ⊞ IQ

Items in the Autographs section have been arranged in alphabetical order.

Marlene Dietrich and James Stewart, a signed photograph from *Destry Rides Again,* c1939, 8 x 10in (20.5 x 25.5cm).
£310–370 / €470–560
$580–690 ✗ VS

General Dwight D. Eisenhower, a signed letter with envelope, 1945, 8 x 5¾in (20.5 x 14.5cm).
£125–150 / €190–230
$230–280 ✗ JAA

Queen Elizabeth II, a signed photograph, 1962, framed, 14 x 10in (35.5 x 25.5cm).
£560–670 / €840–1,000 $1,050–1,250 ⚘ VS

W. C. Fields, a signed and inscribed photograph, c1940, 10 x 8in (25.5 x 20.5cm).
£150–180 / €230–270 $280–330 ⚘ LAY

Judy Garland, a signed cheque with a photograph from *The Wizard of Oz*, 1964, 7in (18cm) wide, framed and glazed.
£300–330 / €450–500 $560–620 ⊞ IQ

Sir Alec Guinness, a signed and inscribed photograph, 1959, 9¾ x 7½in (25 x 19cm).
£80–95 / €120–145 $150–180 ⚘ DW

Paris Jefferson, a signed premium card of Athena from *Xena Warrior Princess*, 2001, 3½ x 2½in (9 x 6.5cm).
£35–40 / €50–60 $65–75 ⊞ NOS

Evel Knievel, a signed promotional card, 1977, 6 x 2in (15 x 5cm).
£55–65 / €85–100 $100–120 ⊞ IQ

L. S. Lowry, a signed letter, with a black and white photograph, 1953, letter 7 x 5in (18 x 12.5cm), framed.
£440–490 / €660–740 $820–920 ⊞ IQ

▶ **J. C. MacKenzie,** an autographed premium card from *Dark Angel*, 2001, 3½ x 2½in (9 x 6.5cm).
£35–40 / €50–60 $65–75 ⊞ NOS

Alexander Alan Milne, an autographed letter, with photograph, early 20thC, letter 6 x 4in (15 x 10cm).
£500–550 / €750–830 $940–1,050 ⊞ IQ

ART GALLERY OF ONTARIO TORONTO

Henry Moore, a signed
Art Gallery of Ontario
exhibition poster, 1980s,
35 x 16in (89 x 40.5cm).
£220–250 / €330–370
$410–470 ⊞ IQ

J. R. R. Tolkien, a signed
and inscribed book
Thucydides Book VI,
signed in two different
coloured inks, dated 1911,
11 x 7½in (28 x 19cm).
£2,000–2,400
€3,000–3,600
$3,750–4,500 ⚑ BBA

► **John Wayne,**
a signed book
*Starring John
Wayne,* by
Gene Fernett,
1969, 10 x 8in
(25.5 x 20.5cm).
£165–195
€250–300
$310–370 ⚑ DW

► **Ayrton Senna,** a signed photograph,
c1994, 10 x 7in (25.5 x 18cm).
£400–450 / €600–680
$750–840 ⊞ CFSD

Christopher Walken, a
signed photograph from
Sleepy Hollow, late 20thC,
8 x 10in (20.5 x 25.5cm).
£40–45 / €60–70
$75–85 ⊞ PICC

Andy Warhol, signed
cover of *Interview* magazine,
1983, 16in (40.5cm) high.
£270–300 / €400–450
$500–560 ⊞ IQ

◄ **Eva Peron,**
a signed menu
card from the
wedding of
Carmen Franco
Polo, daughter of
General Franco
of Spain, also
signed by Juan
Duarte and two
others, 1947.
£940–1,100
€1,400–1,650
$1,750–2,050
⚑ VS

Harry Truman, a signed card, also signed by Bess
Truman, slight damage, 1956, 2 x 4in (5 x 10cm).
£105–125 / €160–190
$195–230 ⚑ VS

Automobilia

As motoring took off in the early 20th century, drivers increasingly sought to personalize their cars with badges and mascots. The first car badge was produced by the AA (Automobile Association), which had been established in 1905 primarily to warn drivers about police speed traps. The society issued their first member's badge in 1906, priced at 5s (25p) for a plain brass badge, and 7s (35p) if it was nickel plated. As the example shown below demonstrates, early AA badges carried the signature of the club's first secretary, Stenson Cooke. The RAC (Royal Automobile Club), established in 1897, brought out their first member's badge in 1907, the year that Edward VII became patron of the club.

Badges were one form of decoration, mascots were another. Car mascots fall into two major categories: factory mascots, commissioned or at least approved by the motor manufacturer and designed for a specific make of vehicle, and accessory mascots – individual designs chosen by drivers themselves and reflecting their tastes and fancies. All manner of figures, animals and other subjects have been portrayed in mascot

form. They could be made from bronze, although zinc, pewter and polished aluminium provided a more affordable alternative.

One of the earliest manufacturers of hood ornaments in the USA was Louis V. Aronson of the Art Metal Company. As well as producing mascots, the company also made lighters and eventually focused on smoking related items, changing its name to the Ronson Corporation. Perhaps the most famous mascot of all time is the Spirit of Ecstasy created by sculptor Charles Sykes for Rolls-Royce in 1910.

Shown below is a bronze of C. S. Rolls (1877–1910). Together with Henry Royce, Rolls founded Rolls-Royce in 1904 and by 1907 their Silver Ghost was already being hailed by the motoring press as 'the best car in the world'. As well as being a leading figure in the field of automobiles, Rolls was a pioneering aviator, beginning with balloons then moving to powered flight. In June 1910, he made the first two-way crossing of the English Channel by aeroplane, and was hailed as a national hero. Tragically, barely a month later he died in an aviation incident at the age of 33.

An Oldfield tyre, from a Studebaker, c1900, 35in (89cm) diam.
£220–250 / €330–380
$410–470 ⊞ OLA

A pottery wall plate, inscribed 'Pirelli', impressed marks, Morocco, early 20thC, 11¾in (30cm) diam.
£70–80 / €105–120
$130–150 ⚘ SWO

A gilded bronze figure of C. S. Rolls, by C. Lorenzini, one of a limited production, signed, 1908–10, 7in (18cm) high.
£1,650–1,850 / €2,500–2,800
$3,100–3,450 ⊞ AU

A brass AA car badge, with impressed Stenson Cooke signature, No. 23142, early 20thC, 5¼in (13.5cm) wide.
£50–60 / €75–90
$95–110 ⚘ G(L)

A coloured lithograph, by Gamy, entitled 'Voitures Crespelle dans le Tour de France 1912', slight damage, French, Paris, 1913, 17¾ x 35½in (45 x 90cm).
£200–240 / €300–360
$380–450 ⚘ NSal

A wooden travelling vanity case, enclosing silver-topped fittings, London 1914, 12in (30.5cm) wide.
£580–650 / €870–980
$1,050–1,200 ⊞ BrL

An aluminium Leyland lorry nameplate, c1920, 12in (30.5cm) wide.
£35–40 / €50–60
$65–75 ⊞ JUN

A Pratts Perfection Spirit matchbox cover, 1916–19, 2½in (6.5cm) wide.
£45–50 / €70–80
$85–95 ⊞ MURR

A nickel-plated pincushion, in the form of a car, 1920s, 4in (10cm) wide.
£25–30 / €40–45
$50–55 ⊞ JUN

A nickel-plated brass car mascot, by the Pierce-Arrow Motor Co, in the form of an archer, American, 1927–28, 5½in (14cm) high.
£450–500 / €680–750
$840–940 ⊞ AU

▶ A Wakefeld Castrol XXL tin sign, 1928, 20in (51cm) high.
£220–250 / €330–380
$410–470 ⊞ MURR

◀ A bronze car mascot, by Generes Co, in the form of a Pekinese, French, Paris, 1925–30, 3in (7.5cm) high.
£180–200
€270–300
$340–370 ⊞ AU

Items in the Automobilia section have been arranged in date order.

A Brooklands official race card, with coloured advertisement, slight damage, 1933, 8 x 5in (20.5 x 12.5cm).
£65–75 / €100–115
$120–140 ⋏ VS

A brass and copper Leyland wall plaque, depicting a tiger, 1920s, 12in (30.5cm) diam.
£270–300 / €400–450
$500–560 ⊞ MURR

A silver-plated bronze plaque, by Drago, inscribed 'Rallye Soleil Cannes', c1938, 2 x 3½in (5 x 9cm).
£270–300 / €400–450
$500–560 ⊞ AU

An album of Hooper & Co leather upholstery samples, early 1930s, 7½ x 11in (19 x 28cm).
£390–470 / €590–710
$730–880 ✣ DW

A Pratts High Test double-sided enamel sign, 1930s, 18in (45.5cm) square.
£30–35 / €45–50
$55–65 ⊞ MURR

A Chenard et Walcker eagle mascot, French, late 1930s, 7in (18cm) wide.
£105–120 / €160–180
$195–220 ⊞ AU

A plaster model of a four-door sedan car, c1950, 29in (74cm) wide.
£560–670 / €840–1,000
$1,050–1,250 ✣ S(P)

Three tin oil pourers, advertising various manufacturers, 1950s, 10in (25.5cm) high.
£25–30 / €40–45
$50–55 each ⊞ JUN

▶ **A pair of Climax glass, chrome and leather goggles,** c1950, 7in (18cm) wide.
£30–35 / €45–50
$55–65 ⊞ JUN

▶ **Seven key rings,** 1950s–60s, largest 2in (5cm) long.
£4–8 / €6–12
$8–15 each ⊞ RTT

A Triumph Trident 'Slippery Sam' plastic plaque, 1970s, 11in (28cm) wide.
£6–10 / €9–15
$12–19 ⊞ COB

▶ **A Morris Minor bone china plaque,** by James Sadler, 2002–03, 8¼in (21cm) diam.
£15–20 / €22–30
$28–38 ⊞ KWCC

Badges

A brass and enamel Sandown Park Racecourse badge, 1897, 1in (2.5cm) wide.
£35–40 / €50–60
$65–75 ⊞ MRW

A brass and enamel Sandown Park Racecourse badge, 1933, 2in (5cm) wide.
£35–40 / €50–60
$65–75 ⊞ MRW

A silver ARP warden's badge, 1939–45, 1in (2.5cm) wide.
£3–7 / €4–10
$6–13 ⊞ MRW

A brass and enamel Newbury Racecourse badge, 1915, 1in (2.5cm) wide.
£50–60 / €75–90
$95–110 ⊞ MRW

A brass Crawford's Biscuits badge, 1930s, 1½in (4cm) high.
£15–20 / €22–30
$28–38 ⊞ HUX

A brass Salvation Army badge, c1940, 2in (5cm) high.
£1–5 / €2–7
$3–9 ⊞ MRW

▶ **A chrome BBC badge,** 1940s, 1in (2.5cm) wide.
£6–10 / €9–15
$12–19 ⊞ HUX

◀ **A white metal RAF sweetheart badge,** c1950, 2in (5cm) wide.
£8–12 / €12–18
$15–22 ⊞ MRW

Two brass and enamel union badges, for Electrical Trades Union and National Union of Sheet Metal Workers and Braziers, 1930–40, 1in (2.5cm) diam.
£10–15 / €15–22
$19–28 each ⊞ MRW

An enamelled Tommy Prattkins badge, 1930s, 1½in (4cm) high.
£180–200 / €270–300
$330–370 ⊞ MURR
Tommy Prattkins was an advertising figure used by Pratts Oil Company in the 1920s and '30s to encourage motorists to use petrol pumps rather than filling up from portable cans. The motoring connection makes this badge desirable to collectors of automobilia.

Two bronze, silver and enamel blood donor badges, 1950, 1in (2.5cm) diam.
£10–15 / €15–22
$19–28 ⊞ MRW

A Coronation button badge, depicting Queen Elizabeth II, 1953, 1½in (4cm) diam.
£1–5 / €2–7
$3–9 ⊞ MRW

A plastic and tin badge, inscribed 'It is time to seek the Lord', 1950s, 1in (2.5cm) diam.
£1–5 / €2–7
$3–9 ⊞ RTT

An enamelled BEA badge, c1960, ½in (1cm) wide.
£4–8 / €6–12
$8–15 ⊞ MRW

An enamelled Robertson's Silver Shred badge, c1960, 1in (2.5cm) wide.
£3–7 / €4–10
$6–13 ⊞ MRW
As well as producing their famous Golly badges, Robertson's also made a series of fruit badges.

An enamelled Royal Lancaster Infirmary nurse's badge, 1964, 1½in (4cm) wide.
£25–30 / €40–45
$50–55 ⊞ MRW

An enamelled Royal Masonic Benevolent Institution steward's badge, 1965, 2in (5cm) high.
£4–8 / €6–12
$8–15 ⊞ MRW

A plastic Pan Am Junior Flyer badge, 1960s, 2½in (6.5cm) wide.
£1–5 / €2–7
$3–9 ⊞ RTT

A British Airways Skyflyers badge, c1970, 3in (7.5cm) wide.
£1–5 / €2–7
$3–9 ⊞ MRW

◀ A silver and enamel Hellingly Hospital Nurses Training School badge, 1975, 1½in (4cm) wide.
£15–20 / €22–30
$28–38 ⊞ MRW

▶ An enamel scouting badge, for Queen Elizabeth II's Silver Jubilee, 1977, 1in (2.5cm) wide.
£1–5 / €2–7
$3–9 ⊞ MRW

A silver and enamel Sussex
Downs School of Nursing badge,
1977, 1½in (4cm) wide.
£25–30 / €40–45
$50–55 ⊞ MRW

An enamelled Wakefield and
District Canine Training Club
badge, c1980, 1in (2.5cm) diam.
£1–5 / €2–7
$3–9 ⊞ MRW

An enamelled Royal College of
Nursing of the United Kingdom
union badge, 1990, 2in (5cm) high.
£2–6 / €3–9
$4–11 ⊞ MRW

Butlin's

Sir William Heygate Edmund Colborne 'Billy'
Butlin (1900–80), opened the first Butlin's
holiday camp at Skegness in 1936, and a British
tradition was born. Due to licensing laws, all
'happy campers' had to wear a badge to prove
they were Butlin's members. Initially badges
cost one shilling (5p) but soon they were made
free of charge. A new design was issued every
season, with different designs for every camp,
and Billy Butlin himself chose the final image.

Badges were so popular with holiday makers
that they would wear them in rows on their
jackets, showing off the number of camps they
had visited and providing free advertising for
Butlin's. Badges were also issued for special clubs
and events such as dance competitions and the
Beaver Clubs for children, and staff had their own
badges. Butlin's stopped issuing badges in 1967
because of cost and also because campers objected
to having pin holes in their holiday clothes.

Three Butlin's Clacton enamelled badges, 1963–67,
largest 1½in (4cm) wide.
£2–6 / €3–9
$4–11 each ⊞ TASV

A Butlin's Filey
enamelled badge, 1962,
1in (2.5cm) wide.
£1–5 / €2–7
$3–9 ⊞ MRW

A Butlin's Filey
enamelled badge, 1948,
1in (2.5cm) wide.
£8–12 / €12–18
$15–22 ⊞ MRW

▶ A Butlin's Minehead
enamelled badge, 1967,
1½in (4cm) diam.
£2–6 / €3–9
$4–11 ⊞ TASV

A Butlin's Beaver Club
enamelled badge, late
1960s, 1in (2.5cm) diam.
£2–6 / €3–9
$4–11 ⊞ MRW

A Butlin's Skegness
enamelled badge, 1967,
1in (2.5cm) wide.
£1–5 / €2–7
$3–9 ⊞ MRW

Gollies

The first golly appeared in a series of American children's books written and illustrated by Florence and Bertha K. Upton from 1895. Featured in the stories with two wooden Dutch dolls, and based on a minstrel figure that the sisters had played with as children, the golly soon became a popular nursery character, inspiring toys and other products including Robertson's famous golly badges.

James Robertson & Sons began producing marmalade in Paisley, Scotland in 1864. Shortly before WWI, John Robertson visited America and returned with a fashionable golly toy. The firm adopted the golly as its trademark in 1914. Golly paper labels were added to jars from 1928 and enamel badges were introduced by the end of the decade. Among earlier subjects were sporting figures such as golfers, cricketers, footballers etc, and sport was to remain a perennially popular theme. Golly badges that were produced before WWII are particularly sought after and distinguishing features include centrally placed 'pop' eyes.

Since badges were made by different manufacturers, the same subject could appear with a range of different variations, thus offering wide scope for the collector. After the war, white (as opposed to yellow) waistcoats were introduced, as well as the first standard golly – a simple standing figure that was sent to people who requested a golly without specifying a particular design. In addition to 'pop' eyes, 1950s' examples had eyes that looked downwards. The 1970s saw the return of yellow waistcoats, the introduction of sideways-looking eyes and a crinkly head as opposed to the round, smooth head. In the 1980s even more activities were represented, and the paint used on the badges changed from enamel to acrylic. Robertson's introduced a collectors' club, which reproduced vintage badges and manufactured special and limited edition models that appeared periodically throughout the 1980s and '90s, and are now popular with enthusiasts. To celebrate the millennium the company issued a limited edition silver badge priced at £25 / €38 / $47.

Although Robertson's tried to keep up with the times by introducing new figures such as the Organic Farmer golly, the image was no longer relevant to the modern age. In response to changing tastes and political correctness the golly, which over the decades had inspired an estimated 20 million badges, was retired in 2002.

A brass and enamel Robertson's Golden Shred golly badge,
Guitar Player, 1950,
1½in (4cm) high.
**£25–30 / €40–45
$50–55 ⊞ TASV**

Items in the Badges section have been arranged in date order.

A brass and enamel Robertson's Golden Shred golly badge,
Cricketer, 1950s–60s,
1½in (4cm) high.
**£25–30 / €40–45
$50–55 ⊞ TASV**

A brass and enamel Robertson's Golden Shred golly badge,
Skater, c1960,
1in (2.5cm) high.
**£15–20 / €22–30
$28–38 ⊞ MRW**

A brass and enamel Robertson's Golden Shred golly badge,
Boy Scouts, c1960,
1in (2.5cm) high.
**£15–20 / €22–30
$28–38 ⊞ MRW
This badge has the 'pop' eyes that also appeared on pre-WWII gollies.**

A brass and enamel Robertson's golly badge, Cricketer, c1980, 1in (2.5cm) high.
£50–60 / €75–90
$95–110 ⊞ MRW
Different versions of this cricketer were produced and the small size of the ball makes this example particularly collectable.

A brass and enamel Robertson's golly badge, Guitar Player, c1970, 1in (2.5cm) high.
£10–15 / €15–22
$19–28 ⊞ MRW

A brass and enamel Robertson's golly badge, Lollipop Man, c1970, 1in (2.5cm) high.
£10–15 / €15–22
$19–28 ⊞ MRW

A brass and enamel Robertson's Golden Shred golly badge, Hockey Player, 1960s, 1in (2.5cm) high.
£10–15 / €15–22
$19–28 ⊞ MRW

► **A brass and enamel Robertson's golly badge,** Darts Player, c1980, 1in (2.5cm) high.
£15–20 / €22–30
$28–38 ⊞ MRW

A brass and enamel Robertson's golly badge, Postman, c1980, 1in (2.5cm) high, in original bag.
£4–8 / €6–12
$8–15 ⊞ MRW

A brass and enamel Robertson's golly badge, Policeman, 1980s, 1in (2.5cm) high.
£30–35 / €45–50
$55–65 ⊞ MRW
This is a rare version of the golly policeman with a bobble on his helmet.

A brass and enamel Robertson's golly badge, Jogger, c1980, 1in (2.5cm) high.
£4–8 / €6–12
$8–15 ⊞ MRW

◄ **A brass and enamel Robertson's golly badge,** Raspberry Fruit, c1980, 1in (2.5cm) high, in original bag.
£50–60 / €75–90
$95–110 ⊞ MRW

A brass and enamel Robertson's golly badge, Footballer, c1980, 1in (2.5cm) high.
£4–8 / €6–12
$8–15 ⊞ MRW

► **A brass and enamel Robertson's golly badge,** Pirate, limited edition, one of five in set, c1990, 1in (2.5cm) high.
£35–40 / €50–60
$65–75 ⊞ MRW

Bicycles

◄ *The Cyclist,*
Xmas No. and
Year Book, three
vols, 1885–88,
large 8°.
£380–450
€ 570–680
$710–840
⚒ **DW**

► **A Ross & Co**
Doctor's Stout
stoneware
bottle, transfer-
printed with a
cyclist, c1880,
8in (20.5cm) high.
£25–30
€ 40–45
$50–55 ⊞ **JUN**

An ashtray, advertising Enfield
cycles, 1900–05, 4½in (11.5cm) diam.
£220–250 / € 330–380
$410–470 ⊞ **MURR**

An Auto Cycle Union Hotel enamel
sign, 1920, 18in (45.5cm) square.
£270–300 / € 400–450
$500–560 ⊞ **MURR**

A can of cycle oil, 1910,
9½in (24cm) high.
£30–35 / € 45–50
$55–65 ⊞ **MURR**

A cast-iron street nameplate, for Cycle Road,
Nottingham, c1910, 26in (66cm) wide.
£115–130 / € 175–195
$220–250 ⊞ **JUN**

LOCATE THE SOURCE

The source of each illustration
in Miller's can be found by
checking the code letters
below each caption with the
Key to Illustrations, pages
794–800.

A Raleigh enamel two-sided sign,
c1930, 14in (35.5cm) wide.
£220–250 / € 330–380
$410–470 ⊞ **JUN**

► **A Halford's catalogue of**
cycle and motor lamps, 1933,
7in (18cm) high.
£10–15 / € 15–22
$19–28 ⊞ **COB**

A pair of Allez drinking bottles,
from a racing bicycle, 1950,
8in (20.5cm) high.
£25–30 / € 40–45
$50–55 ⊞ **AVT**

A Simplex Competition chain wheel gear, c1950, boxed, 7in (18cm) wide.
£45–50 / €70–80
$85–95 ⊞ AVT

A T. D. Cross bicycle freewheel, with 120 teeth, c1950, 3½in (9cm) diam, boxed.
£15–20 / €22–30
$28–38 ⊞ AVT

A Hetchins Magnum Opus touring cycle, with original finish, 1950.
£540–600 / €810–900
$1,000–1,100 ⊞ AVT

▶ A Hopper Cycles advertising poster, 1950s, 31 x 21in (78.5 x 53.5cm).
£270–300 / €400–450
$500–560 ⊞ Do

◀ A Raleigh enamel advertising sign, early 1950s, 30in (76cm) wide.
£1,050–1,200
€1,600–1,800
$1,950–2,250
⊞ MURR

A Frejus racing cycle, original finish, Italian, 1955.
£540–600 / €810–900
$1,000–1,100 ⊞ AVT

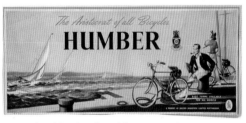

A Humber bicycle advertising poster, late 1950s, 30in (76cm) wide.
£90–100 / €135–150
$170–190 ⊞ IQ

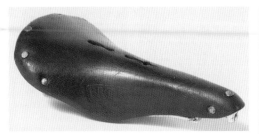

A Brooks B17 leather competition standard racing saddle, 1961, 11in (28cm) wide.
£20–25 / €30–35
$35–45 ⊞ AVT

An EMPI dragster bicycle, 1970s, 72in (183cm) long.
£270–300 / €400–450
$500–560 ⊞ TWI

Books

The book section is divided into different categories including Children's, Modern First Editions (20th-century novels), Gardening & Natural History, and Travel & Topography. In each category books are organized alphabetically, predominantly by author or, where this is not possible, by editor, publisher or illustrator.

Children's books continue to be a flourishing area of the market place. The huge success of contemporary writers such as Philip Pullman and J. K. Rowling has stimulated demand among adult collectors for first editions of their novels, while longer established classics such as Kenneth Grahame's *The Wind in the Willows*, A. A. Milne's Winnie the Pooh stories and C. S. Lewis's Narnia series continue to attract collectors and can make some high prices.

Cinema can also help increase the value of an author's works. Following the *Lord of the Rings* films, demand for Tolkien boomed and a signed first edition of *The Hobbit*, published in 1937 and precursor to the *Lord of the Rings* trilogy, recently fetched an auction record of just over £43,000 / €65,000 / $80,000. Television can be another important factor both in children's and adults' books. When a fictional detective is successfully translated onto the small screen, for example Colin Dexter's Morse or R. D. Wingfield's Frost, interest in the original novels increases. Although in real life most people would deplore crime, the appetite for both reading and collecting crime and suspense novels is seemingly endless, ranging from Agatha Christie mysteries to modern murder stories. Much of the detective fiction illustrated is comparatively recent, written during the last 20 years. The section devoted to modern first editions shows that a work does not have to be old to become collectable and if you buy a new book it may not only be a great read, but also a good investment.

William de Belleroche, *Brangwyn Talks*, published by Chapman & Hall, 1949, 9 x 6in (23 x 15cm), and a letter from Brangwyn.
£180–200 / €270–300
$330–370 ⊞ ADD

▶ **Sir E. A. Wallis Budge,** *The Rosetta Stone and the Decipherment of Egyptian Hieroglyphs,* published by the Religious Tract Society, first edition, London, 1929, 9in (23cm) high.
£35–40 / €50–60
$65–75 ⊞ HTE

Richard Carrickford, *This is Television*, 1960s, 10 x 7¾in (25.5 x 19.5cm).
£5–9 / €8–13
$10–16 ⊞ RTT

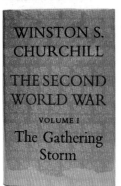

Winston S. Churchill, *The Second World War*, published by Cassell & Co, first edition, 6 vols, 1948, 9 x 6in (23 x 115cm).
£310–350 / €470–530
$580–650 ⊞ BIB

Beniamino Gigli, *The Gigli Memoirs*, published by Cassell & Co, first edition, 1957, 9 x 6in (23 x 15cm), signed by the author.
£40–45 / €60–70
$75–85 ⊞ SDP

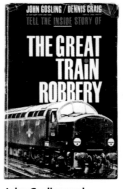

John Gosling and Dennis Craig, *The Great Train Robbery*, published by W. H. Allen & Co, 1964, 9 x 6in (23 x 15cm).
£45–50 / €70–80
$85–95 ⊞ IQ

Mary and Elizabeth Kirby, *Aunt Martha's Corner Cupboard*, 1889, 7¼ x 5¼in (18.5 x 13.5cm).
£8–12 / €12–18
$20–25 ⊞ MSB

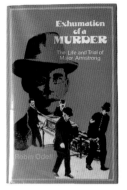

Robin Odell, *Exhumation of a Murder, The Life and Trial of Major Armstrong,* published by George Harrap, signed presentation copy, 1975, 9 x 6in (23 x 15cm).
£110–125 / €165–185 $210–240 ⊞ ADD

Anna Piaggi, *Karl Lagerfeld: A Fashion Journal,* published by Thames & Hudson, 1986, 12 x 9in (30.5 x 23cm).
£20–25 / €30–35 $35–45 ⊞ BIB

► **Gertrude Stein,** *Wars I have Seen,* published by Random House, New York, first edition, 1945, 8in (20.5cm) high.
£30–35 / €45–50 $55–65 ⊞ HTE

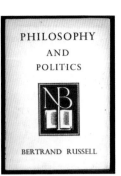

Mrs Alfred Praga, *Easy French Sweets for English Cooks,* published by George Newnes, 1901, 7 x 5in (18 x 12.5cm).
£15–20 / €22–30 $25–35 ⊞ MSB

► **Margaret Thatcher,** *The Path to Power,* published by Harper Collins, 1995, 10 x 6in (25.5 x 15cm).
£20–25 / €30–35 $35–45 ⊞ POL

Bertrand Russell, *Philosophy and Politics,* published by Cambridge Press, 1947, 7½ x 5½in (19 x 14cm).
£10–15 / €15–22 $19–28 ⊞ BIB

Children's & Illustrated

Hans Andersen, *Stories from Hans Andersen*, illustrated by Edmund Dulac, c1911, 18¼in (46cm) high.
£190–220 / €290–330
$360–410 ➹ **SWO**

▶ **Enid Bagnold,** *National Velvet,* illustrated by Laurian Jones, published by William Heinemann, 1935, 8°, cloth.
£175–195
€260–310
$330–390
➹ **BBA**

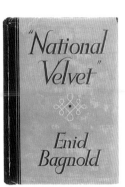

Cicely Mary Barker, *A Little Book of Old Rhymes*, published by Blackie & Sons, c1940, 6 x 4in (15 x 10cm).
£30–35 / €45–50
$55–65 ⊞ **J&J**

Cicely Mary Barker, *Fairies of the Flowers and Trees*, published by Blackie & Sons, first edition, 1950, 7½ x 5in (19 x 15cm).
£210–240 / €320–360
$390–450 ⊞ **BI**

J. M. Barrie, *Peter Pan in Kensington Gardens*, illustrated by Arthur Rackham, published by Hodder & Stoughton, 1912, 11 x 8¾in (28 x 22cm).
€1,350–1,500
$1,650–1,850 ⊞ **BI**

Arthur Rackham (1867–1939) was born in Lewisham, south London, and attended the City of London School. While working as a clerk at a fire insurance office he attended evening classes at the Lambeth School of Art, and in 1894 began to illustrate books. He soon became one of the most successful illustrators of the day, famous for fairy stories and picture books. Rackham's work is very sought after today.

J. J. Bell, *Jack of all Trades*, illustrated by Charles Robinson, published by John Lane, 1900, 4°, pictorial cloth.
£200–240 / €300–360
$370–440 ➹ **BBA**

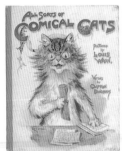

Clifton Bingham, *All Sorts of Cats*, illustrations and coloured frontispiece by Louis Wain, published by Ernest Nister, c1895, 4°, cloth-backed pictorial boards.
£290–340 / €430–510
$540–640 ➹ **BBA**

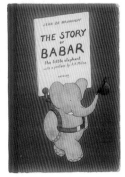

Jean de Brunhoff, *The Story of Babar*, coloured illustrations by the author, published by Methuen & Co, first English edition, 1934, 2°, cloth-backed pictorial boards.
£230–270 / €340–400
$430–500 ➹ **BBA**

▶ **Castell Brothers,** a pig story book, c1900, 4in (10cm) high.
£10–15 / €15–22
$19–28 ⊞ **JUN**

◀ **Louey Chisholm,** *The Enchanted Land*, illustrated by Katherine Cameron, published by T. C. and E. C. Jack, 1909, 9½ x 6¾in (24 x 17cm).
£100–120 / €150–180
$185–220 ⊞ **BI**

Dean (Pub), *Magic Roundabout Fun Pop-Up Book*, 1974, 8in (20.5cm) wide.
£8–12 / €12–18
$15–22 ⊞ **IQ**

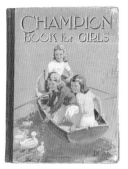

Dean (Pub), *Champion Book for Girls*, c1930, 10 x 7in (25.5 x 18cm).
£1–5 / €2–7
$3–9 ⊞ TOP

Walt Disney, *The Story of Casey Junior*, published by Collins Clear Type Press, c1940, 9 x 7in (23 x 18cm).
£45–50 / €70–80
$85–95 ⊞ J&J

Graham Greene, *The Little Steamroller*, illustrated by Dorothy Craigie, published by Max Parrish, 1966, 8 x 9in (20.5 x 23cm).
£20–25 / €30–35
$35–45 ⊞ J&J

G. A. Henty, *By Pike and Dyke*, published by Blackie, first edition, 1890, 7½ x 5½in (19 x 14cm).
£105–120 / €160–180
$200–220 ⊞ BI

Henrik Ibsen, *Peer Gynt*, illustrated by Arthur Rackham, published by George Harrap, first edition, 1936, 10¼ x 8in (26 x 20.5cm).
£450–500 / €680–750
$840–940 ⊞ BI

Cross Reference
Comics & Annuals
see pages 173–176

Walter Jerrold (ed), *The Big Book of Nursery Rhymes*, coloured plates by Charles Robinson, published by Blackie & Sons, c1910, 4° pictorial cloth, spine gilt.
£250–300 / €380–450
$470–560 ➚ BBA

Walter Jerrold (ed), *The Big Book of Fables*, published by Blackie & Sons, 1912, 9¾ x 8in (25 x 20.5cm)
£135–150 / €200–220
$250–280 ⊞ BI

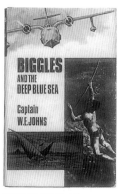

Captain W. E. Johns, *Biggles and the Deep Blue Sea*, published by Brockhampton Press, first edition, 1968, 8°.
£370–440 / €560–660
$690–820 ➚ BBA

Captain W. E. Johns, *Biggles in the Underworld*, published by Brockhampton Press, first edition, 1968, 8°.
£140–165 / €210–250
$260–310 ➚ BBA

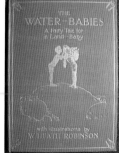

Charles Kingsley, *The Water Babies*, illustrated by W. Heath Robinson, published by Constable, 1915, 8¾ x 7in (22 x 18cm).
£180–200 / €270–300
$330–370 ⊞ BI

Andrew Lang (ed), *The Arabian Nights Entertainments*, frontispiece and illustrations by Henry J. Ford, published by Longman's, Green & Co, 1898, 8°, gilt cloth.
£400–480 / €600–720
$750–900 ➚ BBA

Bertha Lawrence, *Fun and Frolic Stories*, illustrated by Frank Jennens, published by Bruce Publishing Co, c1930, 11 x 8in (28 x 20.5cm).
£5–9 / €8–13
$10–16 ⊞ HeA

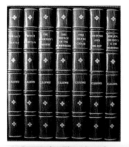

C. S. Lewis, *The Lion the Witch and the Wardrobe*, *The Horse and His Boy*, *The Silver Chair*, *The Voyage of the Dawn Treader*, *The Magician's Nephew*, *Prince Caspian*, *The Last Battle*, 7 vols, two published by Geoffrey Bles, remainder by The Bodley Head, first editions, 1950–56, rebound in morocco, gilt, slip case.
£8,100–9,000
€ 12,200–13,600
$15,100–16,700 ⊞ BI
C. S. Lewis (1898–1963), Christian essayist and science fiction writer, is best known for his novels for children, most famously the Narnia stories.

Michael Molloy, *Time Witches*, published by Chicken House Publishing, first edition, 2002, 8¾ x 5¾in (22 x 14.5cm).
£10–15 / € 15–22
$19–28 ⊞ BIB

Further reading
Miller's Collecting Modern Books, Miller's Publications, 2003

Ada M. Marzials, *The Cobbler and Other Stories*, illustrated by Moira Fry, 1940, 7 x 5in (18 x 12.5cm).
£8–12 / € 12–18
$15–22 ⊞ J&J

Clare Turlay Newberry, *Babette*, published by Hamish Hamilton, 1948, 10 x 8in (25.5 x 20.5cm).
£10–15 / € 15–22
$19–28 ⊞ J&J

▶ **B. Parker,** *Cinderella at the Zoo*, illustrated by Nancy Parker, published by W. & R. Chambers, 2°, pictorial boards.
£420–500 / € 630–750
$780–940 ↗ BBA

David Pelham, *Sam's Pizza Pop-Up Book*, 1996, 7in (8cm) square.
£15–20 / € 22–30
$28–38 ⊞ LAS

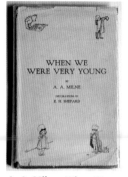

A. A. Milne, *When We Were Very Young*, illustrated by E. H. Shepard, published by Methuen & Co, first edition, 1924, 7½ x 5in (19 x 12.5cm).
£2,250–2,500
€ 3,400–3,800
$4,200–4,700 ⊞ ADD

▶ **B. Parker,** *The Browns:- A Book of Bears*, illustrated by Nancy Parker, published by W. & R. Chambers, 1910, 2°, pictorial boards.
£140–165
€ 210–250
$260–310 ↗ BBA

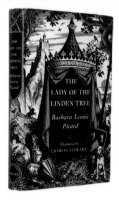

Barbara Leonie Picard, *The Lady of the Linden Tree*, illustrated and signed by Charles Stewart, published by Oxford University Press, 1954, 8 x 6in (20.5 x 15cm).
£15–20 / € 22–30
$28–38 ⊞ ADD

A. A. Milne, *Winnie the Pooh*, illustrated by E. H. Shepard, published by Methuen & Co, 1926, 7½ x 5in (19 x 12.5cm).
£1,500–1,700
€ 2,250–2,550
$2,800–3,200 ⊞ BI

Gladys Peto, *Gladys Peto's Told in the Gloaming*, published by J. F. Shaw & Co, 1920s, 11 x 8in (28 x 20.5cm).
£35–40 / € 50–60
$65–75 ⊞ J&J

◀ **Barbara Leonie Picard,** *The Lady of the Linden Tree*, illustrated and signed by Charles Stewart, published by Oxford University Press, 1954, 8 x 6in (20.5 x 15cm).
£15–20 / € 22–30
$28–38 ⊞ ADD

J. K. Rowling, *Harry Potter and Leopard Walk up to Dragon, Harry Potter and Pearl of Protection from Water, Harry Potter and Golden Armour,* 3 vols, Chinese, Beijing, first editions, 2002, 8°.
£290–350 / €440–530
$540–650 ✦ **BBA**
These three volumes bear the name of J. K. Rowling and have her portrait on the lower flap of each cover, but are piracies, written by a Chinese author. The first title is supposedly the fifth Harry Potter title, published before the genuine fifth was finished, and is the first of a series of fakes that appeared in China and elsewhere. Although printed in large quantities, the books were confiscated after legal action against the Chinese publishers.

Flora Annie Steel, *Tales of the Punjab*, frontispiece and illustrations by J. Lockwood Kipling, published by Macmillan, first edition, 1894, 8°, pictorial gilt cloth.
£370–440 / €560–660
$690–820 ✦ **BBA**

J. R. R. Tolkien, *The Lord of the Rings, The Two Towers, The Return of the King*, 3 vols, published by George Allen & Unwin, first editions, 1954, 1954, 1955, 8¾ x 7½in (22 x 14cm), rebound in gilt green morocco, with a tooled slip case.
£12,600–14,000
€19,000–21,100
$23,500–26,200 ⊞ **BI**

◀ **J. R. R. Tolkien,** *The Lord of the Rings*, 3 vols in 1, published by George Allen & Unwin, 1969, 8°, first deluxe edition on India paper, three folding maps, black buckram decorated in gold and silver, slip case.
£580–690 / €870–1,050
$1,050–1,250 ✦ **BBA**

Theophile Steinlen, *Des Chats, Images sans Paroles*, colour lithograph cover designs by Steinlen, published by Ernest Flammarion, Paris, 1898, large 2°.
£490–580 / €740–870
$910–1,050 ✦ **BBA**

Walter Thornbury, *Historical and Legendary Ballads*, engravings by Dalziel Bros after Whistler, Sandys and Pinwell, published by Chatto & Windus, 1876, 10in (25.5cm) high.
£155–175 / €230–260
$290–330 ⊞ **TDG**

Mary Tourtel (illus), *Old King Cole and other Nursery Rhymes*, a Stump Book, published by Anthony Treheren & Co, 1904, 1½ x 6in (4 x 15cm), buckram with bone toggle.
£50–60 / €75–90
$95–110 ✦ **LAY**

Gardening & Natural History

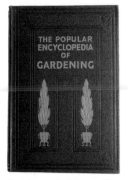

Amalgamated Press, *The Popular Encyclopedia of Gardening*, 3 vols, c1930, 11¼ x 9in (28.5 x 23cm).
**£20–25 / €30–35
$35–45 ⊞ BIB**

Carter's Seeds, *The Blue Book of Gardening*, Catalogue, 1938, 10in (25.5cm) high.
**£30–35 / €45–50
$55–65 ⊞ HOP**

E. T. Cook, *The Century Book of Gardening*, published by Country Life, first edition, 1952, 11 x 9in (28 x 23cm).
**£50–60 / €75–90
$95–110 ⊞ BIB**

F. H. Farthing, *Saturday in My Garden*, published by MacDonald & Co, 1947, 9 x 6in (23 x 15cm).
**£10–15 / €15–22
$19–38 ⊞ BIB**

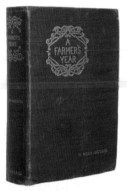

► **Gertrude Jekyll,** *Wall and Water Gardens*, published by George Newnes, c1925, 9 x 6in (23 x 15cm).
**£35–40
€50–60
$65–75 ⊞ BAY**

H. Rider Haggard, *A Farmer's Year*, published by Longman's, Green & Co, first edition, 1899, 8 x 6in (20.5 x 15cm).
**£45–50 / €70–80
$85–95 ⊞ BAY**

Shirley Hibberd, *The Fern Garden*, published by Groombridge & Sons, 1880s, 8in (20.5cm) high.
**£45–50 / €70–80
$85–95 ⊞ HOP**

Robert Tyas, *Favourite Field Flowers*, engravings by Andrews, Houlston and Stoneman, 1850, 7 x 5in (18 x 12.5cm).
**£110–125 / €165–185
$200–230 ⊞ BAY**

Edward Step, *Wild Flowers*, Vol 1, published by Frederick Warne & Co, 1905, 8½ x 6in (21.5 x 15cm).
**£15–20 / €22–30
$28–38 ⊞ BIB**

◄ **M. M. Vilmorin-Andrieux,** *The Vegetable Garden*, edited by William Robinson, published by John Murray, first English edition, 1885, 9in (23cm) high.
**£45–50 / €70–80
$85–95 ⊞ HTE**

Modern First Editions

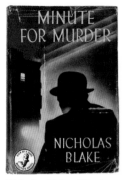

Nicholas Blake, *Minute for Murder*, published by the Crime Club, first edition, 1947, 7¾ x 5¼in (18.5 x 13.5cm).
£35–40 / €50–60
$65–75 ⊞ BIB

Alice Campbell, *Ringed with Fire*, published by Collins Crime Club, first edition, 1943, 8 x 5in (20.5 x 12.5cm).
£155–175 / €230–260
$290–330 ⊞ NW

Agatha Christie, *Why Didn't They Ask Evans?*, published by the Crime Club, first edition, 1932, 8°.
£1,600–1,900
€2,400–2,850
$3,000–3,550 ⋨ BBA

Lindsey Davis, *The Silver Pigs*, published by Sidgwick & Jackson, first edition, 1989, 9½ x 6½in (24 x 16.5cm).
£310–350 / €470–530
$580–650 ⊞ BIB

Colin Dexter, *The Secret of Annexe 3*, published by Macmillan, first edition, 1986, 8¼ x 5¼in (21 x 13.5cm).
£370–420 / €560–630
$690–780 ⊞ BIB

P. C. Doherty, *The Angel of Death*, published by Robert Hale, first edition, 1989, 8 x 5¼in (20.5 x 13.5cm).
£610–680 / €920–1,050
$1,100–1,250 ⊞ BIB

◄ **Charles Frazier,** *Cold Mountain*, published by Sceptre, 1997, 9 x 5½in (23 x 14cm).
£35–40 / €50–60
$65–75 ⊞ BIB

► **Cornelia Funke,** *The Thief Lord*, published by Egmont, first edition, signed by the author, 2000, 8 x 5¼in (20.5 x 13.5cm).
£90–100 / €135–150
$170–190 ⊞ BIB

James Ellroy, *L. A. Confidential*, published by Random Century, first edition, 1990, 9 x 5½in (23 x 14cm).
£100–110 / €150–165
$185–210 ⊞ BIB

Ian Fleming, *You Only Live Twice*, published by Jonathan Cape, first edition, 1964, 8 x 5in (20.5 x 12.5cm).
£6,100–6,800
€9,200–10,300
$11,400–12,700 ⊞ NW

Value

The earliest printed form of the text is usually the most sought-after, hence the value of the first edition or impression. Dust jackets were not commonly used in the US and UK until the early 1900s and were often discarded. Today they are crucial to the value of a book, as is overall condition.

Allen Ginsberg, *Iron Horse,*
published by Coach House Press,
Toronto, first edition, signed and
inscribed by the author, 1973, 8°.
£165–195 / € 250–300
$310–370 ➢ BBA

▶ **George
S. Hellman,**
Peacock's Feather,
published by
Bobbs Merill Co,
Indianapolis, first
edition, signed
and inscribed by
the author, 1932,
9in (23cm) high,
limited edition
of 249 copies
with hand-
printed boards.
£40–45
€ 60–70
$75–85 ⊞ HTE

Patricia Highsmith,
Strangers on a Train,
published by Cresset
Press, first edition, 1950,
7½ x 5¼in (19 x 13.5cm).
£340–380 / € 510–570
$630–710 ⊞ BIB

Dan Kavanagh, *Duffy,*
published by Jonathan
Cape, first edition, 1980,
8¼ x 5½in (21 x 14cm).
£70–80 / € 105–120
$130–150 ⊞ BIB

Items in the Books
section have been
arranged in
alphabetical order.

Donna Leon, *Death
at La Fenice,* published
by Chapmans, first
edition, 1992, 10 x 6¼in
(25.5 x 16cm).
£135–150 / € 200–220
$250–280 ⊞ BIB

Robert Ludlum, *The
Scarlatti Inheritance,*
published by Rupert Hart-
Davis, first edition, 1971,
7¾ x 5¾in (19.5 x 14.5cm).
£45–50 / € 70–80
$85–95 ⊞ BIB

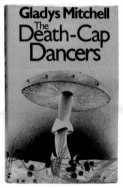

Gladys Mitchell, *The
Death-Cap Dancers,*
published by Michael
Joseph, first edition,
signed by the author,
1981, 8 x 5¼in
(20.5 x 13.5cm).
£135–150 / € 200–220
$250–280 ⊞ BIB

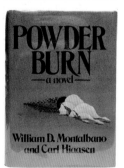

**William D. Montalbano
and Carl Hiaasen,**
Powder Burn, published
by Atheneum, New York,
first edition, 1981,
8½ x 6in (21.5 x 15cm).
£110–125 / € 165–190
$200–230 ⊞ BIB

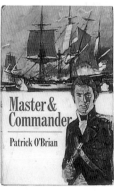

Patrick O'Brian, *Master
& Commander,* published
by Collins, first edition,
1970, 8°.
£400–480 / € 600–720
$750–900 ➢ BBA

Philip Pullman, *Galatea,*
published by Gollancz,
first edition, 1978, 8°.
£280–330 / € 420–500
$520–620 ➢ BBA

▶ **Ruth Rendell,** *Some Lie and Some Die,* published by
Hutchinson, first edition, 1973, 8 x 5in (20.5 x 12.5cm).
£270–300 / € 400–450
$500–560 ⊞ NW

Travel & Topography

Roald Amundsen, *Sydpolen*, 2 vols, published by Kristiania, Norway, first edition, 1912, 8°, plates and illustrations, gilt pictorial cloth.
£260–310 / € 390–470
$490–580 ⚲ BBA

▶ **Henry Lansdell,** *Through Central Asia*, published by Sampson, Low, signed and inscribed by the author, 1887, 8°, folding map, gilt pictorial cloth.
£220–260 / € 330–390
$410–490 ⚲ DW

▶ **Gerald S. Doorly,** *The Voyages of the 'Morning'*, published by Smith, Elder & Co, 1916, 8°, inscribed, plates, 3pp music and folding map.
£3,050–3,650
€ 4,600–5,500
$5,700–6,800 ⚲ BBA
The *Morning* was a relief ship for the 1901–04 National Antarctic Expedition.

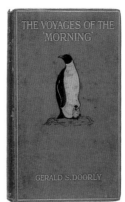

▶ **Captain Willoughby Verner,** *Sketches in the Soudan*, published by R. H. Porter, first edition, 1885, oblong 2°.
£200–240
€ 300–360
$370–440 ⚲ DW

M. Edith Durham, *High Albania*, first edition, 1909, 8°, pictorial cloth.
£170–200 / € 250–300
$320–370 ⚲ DW

Bottles

Nineteenth- and early 20th-century rubbish dumps can still be a treasure trove for bottle diggers. After perhaps more than a century buried under-ground, a quick wash in warm, soapy water can often restore an undamaged bottle to its original sparkle. While many vintage bottles will be worth relatively little, this section also includes some prize discoveries that have achieved high prices at auction. Rarity is all-important when it comes to the value of bottles. Until the 19th century for example, glass wine bottles were scarce and expensive and surviving examples from the 17th and 18th centuries can sell for considerable sums.

The 19th century saw the advent of mass-production and growing demand for ginger beer, mineral waters, medicines and poisons, which, according to a law passed by the British parliament in 1863, had to be contained in distinctively shaped bottles so that even in the dark a potentially dangerous product could be distinguished by touch. With Victorian and Edwardian bottles, collectors look for unusual variations in design, size, colour and, where appropriate (as with stoneware bottles), printed decoration. Stone-ware ginger beer bottles remained popular from early Victorian times until 1928, when Mary Donohoe sued a ginger beer company after finding a snail shell in her opaque bottle, thereby encouraging manufacturers to turn to glass.

With all these bottles, values vary from relatively small amounts for the more common-place examples, to three- or four-figure sums and more for unusual pieces such as mineral water bottles in a rare colour variant or unusually shaped patented poison bottles, many of which were only produced for a limited period. Given that most of these objects were thrown away, buried and then rescued with spades, condition is another factor that affects the price.

◀ **A glass wine bottle,** with 'T. Shepherd' seal, dated 1761, 10in (25.5cm) high.
£620–740 / €930–1,100
$1,200–1,400 ⚘ **LAY**

A ceramic baby feeder, decorated with Oriental scenes, slight damage, 19thC, 6¼in (16cm) wide.
£260–310 / €390–460
$490–580 ⚘ **BBR**

◀ **A set of four ceramic spirit flasks,** inscribed 'Port', 'Brandy', 'Bitters' and 'Gin', with original box-wood stoppers, 19thC, in a wicker basket, 9in (23cm) square.
£330–370
€500–560
$620–690 ⊞ **BS**

A glass Hamilton bottle, embossed 'Hamilton's Patent Aerated Waters sold by R. Johnson, 15 Greek Street, London', with pontil base, 1820–40, 8¼in (21cm) high.
£850–1,000 / €1,300–1,500
$1,600–1,850 ⚘ **BBR**
In the early 1800s Sir William Hamilton developed a torpedo-shaped bottle for mineral waters. As the bottle was stored on its side, the cork was kept wet and swollen, thus keeping the contents fizzy. Early pontil-marked, embossed Hamiltons are among the most desirable mineral water bottles.

◀ **A stoneware slab seal flask,** with 'W. Turner Driffield' seal, c1840, 9in (23cm) high.
£620–740 / €930–1,100
$1,200–1,400 ⚘ **BBR**
Slab seal flasks that are impressed with the proprietor's name are very sought after by collectors. Without its pie-crust-edged seal, this stoneware bottle would be worth considerably less.

◀ **A mallet-shaped ceramic whisky bottle,** inscribed 'The Cream of Highland Whiskies' and 'Thom & Cameron Limited Glasgow', decorated with a portrait of Queen Victoria, 1890s, 7¾in (19.5cm) high.
**£320–380 / €480–570
$600–710** ⚒ BBR

A glass codd bottle, embossed 'Morrells Trustees Oxford Lion Brewery' and 'The Niagra Bottle Barnett & Foster Makers London', c1890, 9in (23cm) high.
**£110–130 / €165–195
$200–240** ⚒ BBR

A glass bullet stopper bottle, embossed 'S. Smart, Chippenham', c1900, 9in (23cm) high.
**£8–12 / €12–18
$15–22** ⊞ OIA

A glass Hamilton bottle and stand, c1900, bottle 9½in (24cm) high.
**£50–55 / €75–85
$95–105** ⊞ JAM

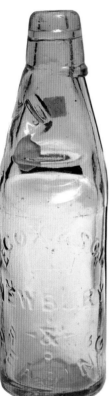

A glass codd bottle, embossed 'Cox & Son, Newbury, Reading', c1900, 9in (23cm) high.
**£1–5 / €2–7
$3–9** ⊞ OIA

Items in the Bottles section have been arranged in date order.

▶ **A stoneware brewery jar,** transfer-printed 'Crown Botanic Brewery, Cardiff', dated 1934, 11in (28cm) high.
**£20–25 / €30–35
$35–45** ⊞ TOP

Ginger Beer Bottles

◄ **A ceramic ginger beer bottle,** by A. W. Buchan, transfer-printed 'Geo Jeff & Co', and with a pixie on a toadstool, minor damage, c1890–1900, 8in (20.5cm) high.
£900–1,050 / €1,350–1,600
$1,700–2,000 ➶ BBR
This is one of the UK's finest and rarest ginger beer bottles.

A stoneware ginger beer bottle, transfer-printed 'Walker & Knight Wine & Spirit Merchants, Chester', c1920, 7in (18cm) high.
£8–12 / €12–18
$15–22 ⊞ JAM

► **A stoneware ginger beer bottle,** transfer-printed 'H. Chandler, Swindon', c1910, 7in (18cm) high.
£15–20 / €22–30
$28–38 ⊞ OIA

◄ **A stoneware ginger beer bottle,** transfer-printed 'Mayo & Rugg, Coventry', c1920, 7in (18cm) high.
£6–10 / €9–15
$12–19 ⊞ JAM

Hot Water Bottles

◄ **A Lambeth Pottery stoneware foot warmer,** transfer-printed 'Doulton's Improved Foot Warmer', 1892, 11in (28cm) wide.
£80–90 / €120–135
$150–170 ⊞ BS

A ceramic foot warmer, transfer-printed 'Keogh Bros, Swindon', 1920s, 10in (25.5cm) wide.
£40–45 / €60–70
$75–85 ⊞ BS

► **A stoneware foot warmer,** transfer-printed 'Olde Fulham Pottery, Estd. 1671', 1920s, 9in (23cm) high.
£50–55 / €75–85
$95–105 ⊞ BS

An A. W. Buchan stoneware two-pint hot water bottle, transfer-printed 'Buchan's Blue Bottle', 1910–20, 12in (30.5cm) high.
£50–55 / €75–85
$95–105 ⊞ MURR

◄ **A stoneware foot warmer,** transfer-printed 'The Peacock Foot Warmer', 1920s–30s, 8in (20.5cm) high.
£60–70 / €90–105
$110–130 ⊞ BS

Medicine & Poison Bottles

A glass medicine bottle, embossed 'Dicey & Co, No. 10 Bow Church Yard, London', 'See that the Words Dicey & Co are Printed in the Stamp' and 'Daffy's Elixir', the neck with an applied lip, 1820–40, 4½in (11.5cm) high.
£700–840 / €1,050–1,250 $1,300–1,550 ⚘ BBR
Early coloured bottles of this successful patent medicine are very collectable. This small sized example is very rare.

A glass medicine bottle, embossed 'Dr Rooke's Solar Elixir', c1890, 5in (12.5cm) high.
£5–9 / €8–13
$10–16 ⊞ OIA

A glass two-pint medicine bottle, embossed 'Warners Safe Cure London', 1890–1900, 11in (28cm) high.
£620–740 / €930–1,100 $1,200–1,400 ⚘ BBR
This bottle is in a rare colour, which contributes to its value.

A stoneware poison bottle, transfer-printed 'Plynine Coy, Edinburgh, Household Ammonia', c1900, 12in (30.5cm) high.
£25–30 / €40–45
$50–55 ⊞ YT

Soda Syphons

◀ **A British Soda Syphon Co mesh-covered glass syphon,** c1900, 20in (51cm) high.
£330–370 / €500–550 $620–690 ⊞ TOP

Further reading
Miller's Bottles & Pot Lids: A Collector's Guide, Miller's Publications, 2002

▶ **An etched glass syphon,** c1930, 11in (28cm) high.
£25–30 / €40–45
$50–55 ⊞ AL

An etched glass syphon, with a copper holder, c1930, syphon holder 14in (35.5cm) high.
£100–115 / €150–180
$190–220 ⊞ JAM

Boxes

A fruitwood seal case, elaborately carved with the arms of Charles II, 1675, 4½in (11.5cm) wide.
£500–600 / €750–900
$930–1,100 ✗ WAL

A mahogany tea box, with satinwood banding and inlaid pinwheel, slight damage, 18thC, 6in (15cm) high.
£200–240 / €300–360
$370–440 ✗ COBB

A Masonic pressed burrwood snuff box, French, c1800, 3in (7.5cm) wide.
£400–450 / €600–680
$750–840 ⊞ NEW

A burr-yew wood tea caddy, with kingwood banding and line inlay, the domed cover enclosing two zinc-lined compartments, damaged and repaired, early 19thC, 7in (18cm) wide.
£170–200 / €260–300
$320–370 ✗ DN

A copper tobacco box, in the form of a peaked cap, 19thC, 4in (10cm) wide.
£200–230 / €200–350
$370–430 ⊞ BS

A brass casket, decorated with religious scenes, lattice work and griffins, Continental, 19thC, 9in (23cm) wide.
£130–155 / €195–230
$250–290 ✗ DA

A George III mahogany tea caddy, with Van Dyke and lattice-inlaid borders, interior part-lined with zinc, 6½in (16.5cm) wide.
£400–480 / €600–720
$750–900 ✗ DN

A filigree and enamel needle-case, c1825, 2¼in (5.5cm) wide.
£150–180 / €230–270
$280–330 ✗ WW

▶ A George III mahogany knife box, with satinwood stringing and inlaid floral medallion, interior missing, 9in (23cm) high.
£100–120 / €150–180
$185–220 ✗ G(L)

A late Victorian Tunbridge ware handkerchief box, 9in (23cm) wide.
£520–580 / €780–870
$980–1,100 ⊞ PGO

An arbutus wood Kilarney box, c1860, 10in (25.5cm) wide.
£310–350 / €470–530
$580–650 ⊞ STA

A Molassine Animal Feed brass tobacco box, c1900, 3½in (9cm) wide.
£130–145 / €195–220
$240–270 ⊞ BS

A Limoges porcelain *pâte-sur-pâte* box and cover, by A. Barriere, early 20thC, 4¾in (12cm) diam.
£110–130 / €165–195
$210–250 ⚲ CAG

A late Victorian velvet sewing box, by Hunt & Roskell, with scrolling brass mounts and a monogram, fitted interior, 9¼in (23.5cm) wide.
£500–600 / €750–900
$930–1,100 ⚲ CHTR

A painted porcelain box, crossed swords mark, French, c1900, 3¾in (9.5cm) wide.
£170–200 / €260–300
$320–370 ⚲ WW

A brass tobacco box, inscribed 'William Neal, Swindon', dated 1914, 3in (7.5cm) wide.
£120–135 / €180–200
$220–250 ⊞ BS

▶ **A Bakelite box of Singer sewing needles,** 1940s–50s, 2in (5cm) high.
£5–9 / €8–13
$10–16 ⊞ RTT

A Tunbridge ware glove box, by Edmund Nye, decorated with a swan, c1855, 9½in (24cm) wide.
£630–700 / €950–1,050
$1,150–1,300 ⊞ AMH

A lacquered papier-mâché box, decorated with panels of Oriental figures, late 19thC, 14in (35.5cm) wide.
£170–200 / €260–300
$320–370 ⚲ G(L)

An Edwardian inlaid cutlery tray, with hinged covers and a silver handle, 16in (40.5cm) wide.
£115–130 / €175–195
$220–250 ⊞ CoHA

Breweriana

The British love of the pub has stimulated a wealth of collectables, many of which are sought after not just in the UK but across the world. Whisky-related items tend to be the most collected, particularly objects commemorating older and smaller breweries. Guinness material is another favourite. Inspired by a visit to Bertram Mills Circus (when it occurred to him that a sea lion could probably balance a pint of Guinness on its nose), artist John Gilroy (1898–1985), created a long-running series of animal figures to advertise Guinness in the 1930s. Often accompanied by a zookeeper (a caricature of Gilroy himself and the only human featured in the series), many animals were represented. The toucan, introduced in 1936, became Guinness' most famous symbol.

Breweriana encompasses many different items; back bar, wall-hung and counter-top objects were designed to promote drinks manufacturers in every conceivable form and medium. Pub jugs are one of the most collected areas, and many famous potteries owed a considerable portion of their revenue to the drinks industry. From its foundation, the Doulton factory produced wares for inns and taverns, and over the decades the names of well over 100 breweries, whisky companies and drinks manufacturers have been found on Doulton products.

Drinking and smoking tend to go together, and another prolific area of breweriana-related ceramics is ashtrays and match strikers, which can be surprisingly decorative and appealing.

A basalt punch pot, with fruiting vine decoration, the finial moulded as a bunch of grapes, 19thC, 6in (15cm) high.
**£150–180 / €230–270
$280–330 ✗ HOLL**

An Uam-Var whisky advertising picture, c1900, 20 x 24in (51 x 61cm), framed.
**£180–200 / €270–300
$330–370 ⊞ JUN**

A Victorian oak spirit stand, with silver-plated mounts, modelled as three barrels on a stand, each with a tap and bucket, with labels for Whiskey, Gin and Brandy, 15in (38cm) high.
**£1,300–1,550 / €2,000–2,350
$2,450–2,900 ✗ BWL**

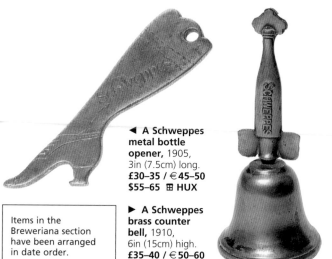

◀ **A Schweppes metal bottle opener,** 1905, 3in (7.5cm) long.
**£30–35 / €45–50
$55–65 ⊞ HUX**

▶ **A Schweppes brass counter bell,** 1910, 6in (15cm) high.
**£35–40 / €50–60
$65–75 ⊞ HUX**

Items in the Breweriana section have been arranged in date order.

A Holt Brewery advertising picture, c1920, 32in (81.5cm) wide, framed.
**£250–280 / €380–420
$470–520 ⊞ JUN**

A Black & White Scotch Whisky metal menu holder, 1925–35, 3½in (9cm) square.
£65–75 / €100–115
$120–140 ⊞ HUX

► A wooden bottle stopper, carved as a kissing couple, c1930, 5in (12.5cm) high.
£35–40 / €50–60
$65–75 ⊞ CAL

An Adnams Nut Brown Ale showcard, c1930s, 9¼ x 14½in (23.5 x 37cm).
£30–35 / €45–50
$55–65 ⊞ RTT

► A Bulmer's Cider cardboard weather house, c1950, 9in (23cm) wide.
£25–30 / €40–45
$50–55 ⊞ IQ

A Zywiec Beer bottle opener, Polish, 1940s–50s, 3½in (9cm) high.
£6–10 / €9–15
$12–19 ⊞ RTT

A musical decanter, modelled as Groucho Marx, Japanese, 1950, 13in (33cm) high.
£80–90 / €120–135
$150–170 ⊞ MF

◄ A Schweppes advertising pin-up, 1950s, 12 x 13½in (30.5 x 34.5cm).
£25–30 / €40–45
$50–55 ⊞ RTT

◄ A Babycham metal lorry mascot, 1950s, 4½in (11.5cm) wide.
£220–250 / €330–380
$410–470 ⊞ MURR

► A Double Diamond advertising figure, by Beswick, hat stopper missing, c1955, 8¼in (21cm) high.
£135–150 / €200–220
$250–280 ⊞ HUX

A set of four Ind Coope lager bottles, brewed to celebrate the marriage of the Prince of Wales and Lady Diana Spencer, 1981, 9in (23cm) high.
£8–12 / €12–18
$15–22 ⊞ IQ

A Bell's Whisky commemorative decanter, inscribed 'To Commemorate the Birth of Prince William of Wales 21st June 1982', 1982, 8in (20.5cm) high, with original presentation box.
£20–25 / €30–35
$35–45 ⚲ BBR

Further reading

Miller's Cool Collectibles, Miller's Publications, 2004

A Bell's Whisky commemorative decanter, inscribed 'The Marriage of Prince Andrew with Miss Sarah Ferguson, 23rd July 1986, Westminster Abbey,' 1986, 7¾in (19.5cm) high, with original contents and presentation box.
£20–25 / €30–35
$35–45 ⚲ BBR

▶ **A Beck's Beer spot-painted glass,** designed by Damien Hurst, c2000, 7in (18cm) high.
£20–25 / €30–35
$35–45 ⊞ PLB

◀ **A Schlitz neon flashing sign,** c1960, 35in (89cm) wide.
£110–130
€165–195
$210–250
⚲ JAA

▶ **A Remy Martin plastic advertising figure,** modelled as a centaur, 1965, 10in (25.5cm) high.
£75–85
€115–130
$140–160 ⊞ HUX

▶ **A Bell's Whisky ceramic commemorative decanter,** by Wade, inscribed 'To Commemorate the Birth of Prince Henry of Wales 15th September 1984', 1984, 8in (20.5cm) high, with original contents and presentation box.
£80–90 / €120–135
$150–170 ⚲ BBR

Ashtrays & Match Strikers

A Pormakwassie Cigars ceramic match striker, with transfer printing, late 19thC, 5½in (14cm) square.
£220–260 / €330–390
$410–490 ✗ BBR

An Ind Coope & Co ashtray/match striker, late 19thC, 6in (15cm) diam.
£180–210 / €270–320
$340–390 ✗ BBR

A Dunville's Whisky ceramic ashtray, by Shelley, depicting an Edwardian lady, repair to rim, c1900, 4¾in (12cm) wide.
£50–60 / €80–90
$95–110 ✗ BBR

A Duniva Scotch match striker, c1900, 4in (10cm) diam.
£35–40 / €50–60
$65–75 ⊞ YT

A Johnnie Walker copper ashtray, 1920s, 5in (12.5cm) diam.
£70–80 / €105–120
$130–150 ⊞ BS

▶ **A Gilbey's Spey Royal Scotch Whisky brass ashtray,** 1920s, 4½in (11.5cm) square.
£60–70 / €90–105
$110–130 ⊞ BS

A Bass ceramic ashtray, 1930s, 4in (10cm) square.
£40–45 / €60–70
$75–85 ⊞ MURR

A Bass Pale Ale ceramic ashtray and match holder, by Cerabel, French, 1930s, 5½in (14cm) wide.
£35–40 / €50–60
$65–75 ⊞ HUX

A Gonzales Sherry ceramic ashtray, 1950, 3½in (9cm) diam.
£8–12 / €12–18
$15–22 ⊞ HUX

A Cantrell & Cochrane ceramic ashtray, 1960, 6in (15cm) diam.
£3–7 / €4–10
$6–13 ⊞ HUX

Guinness

◀ **A Guinness ceramic table lamp,** by Carlton, inscribed 'How grand to be a Toucan Just think what Toucan do', printed mark, 1950s, 10½in (26.5cm) high, with original box.
£300–360 / €450–540
$560–670 ⚒ **G(L)**

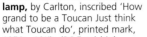

A Guinness celluloid sign, 1950s, 10 x 12in (25.5 x 30.5cm).
£160–180 / €240–270
$300–340 ⊞ **MURR**

A pack of Guinness playing cards, 1950s, 3½ x 2½in (9 x 6.5cm), with original box.
£15–20 / €22–30
$28–38 ⊞ **BOB**

▶ **A Guinness advertising card,** 1950s, 8 x 6in (20.5 x 15cm).
£3–7 / €4–10
$6–13 ⊞ **Do**

◀ **A Guinness candle,** 1960s, 9in (23cm) high.
£8–12
€12–18
$15–22 ⊞ **RTT**

◀ **A Guinness advertising figure,** by Carlton, modelled as a kangaroo with a bottle in her pouch, 1960s, 4in (10cm) wide.
£90–100 / €135–150
$170–190 ⚒ **G(L)**

Jugs

A Greer's O.V.H. Scotch Whisky ceramic water jug, by Doulton, 1910–20, 10in (25.5cm) high.
£105–120 / €160–180
$195–220 ⊞ **MURR**

▶ **A Seagers Gin ceramic water jug,** by Royal Staffordshire Pottery, 1930, 3¾in (9.5cm) high.
£40–45 / €60–70
$75–85 ⊞ **HUX**

◀ **A Robertson's Scotch Whisky enamelled metal jug,** 1920s, 10in (25.5cm) wide.
£85–95 / €130–145
$160–180 ⊞ **MURR**

A Worthington Mayor ceramic water jug, by Beswick, c1950, 9in (23cm) high.
£110–125
€165–190
$200–230
⊞ **JUN**

Buttons

A brass button-cleaning guard,
1843, 7in (18cm) wide.
£15–20 / €22–30
$28–38 ⊞ MRW

**A glass, paper and copper
button,** painted with a depiction of
the Montgolfier brothers' first
successful balloon ascent on 4 June
1783, 1783–85, 1½in (4cm) diam.
£1,150–1,300 / €1,750–1,950
$2,150–2,450 ⊞ TB
In the 18th century buttons were
used principally for decoration.
Gentlemen dandies sported
on their waistcoats rows of large
and elegant buttons which could
be decorated with anything
from paintings to cameos to
precious gemstones. Today,
these handcrafted miniature
works of art are among the most
desirable and costly buttons.

**A copper, glass and parchment
button,** decorated with a
watercolour of a couple fishing,
late 18thC, 1½in (4cm) diam.
£1,150–1,300 / €1,750–1,950
$2,150–2,450 ⊞ TB

**A stamped brass double-face
button,** depicting the head of
Janus, 1850–1900, 1¼in (3cm) diam.
£50–55 / €75–85
$95–105 ⊞ TB

An enamel and brass button,
depicting a windmill and a stream,
French, 1880–90, 1¼in (3cm) diam.
£130–145 / €195–220
$240–270 ⊞ TB

**A set of six silver and paste
buttons,** c1880, 1¼in (3cm) diam.
£18–22 / €27–33
$34–41 ⊞ JBB

An enamel and brass button,
painted with 'The Nut Tree Boy',
within a champlevé border,
late 19thC, 1¼in (3cm) diam.
£120–135 / €180–200
$220–250 ⊞ TB

◀ **A set of five white metal
livery buttons,** each depicting a
stag's head, c1880, ½in (1cm) wide.
£25–30 / €40–45
$50–55 ⊞ MRW

An Art Nouveau silver button,
import marks for Chester 1889,
French, 1in (2.5cm) diam.
£50–55 / €75–85
$95–105 ⊞ TB

A brass livery button, c1900,
1in (2.5cm) diam.
£8–12 / €12–18
$15–22 ⊞ MRW

A set of six buttons, depicting
butterflies, French, c1900,
1in (2.5cm) diam.
£105–120 / €160–180
$195–220 ⊞ JBB

**A stamped silvered- and gilded-
brass button,** depicting Sarah
Bernhardt as L'Aiglon, c1900,
1½in (4cm) diam.
£30–35 / €45–50
$55–65 ⊞ TB
L'Aiglon was one of Sarah
Bernhardt's greatest roles. The
play, written by Edmund
Rostand (1868–1918), was first
performed in 1900.

A set of six gilded-brass buttons,
each with a coloured photograph,
c1910, ½in (1cm) diam,
in a case.
£110–125 / €165–190
$200–230 ⊞ JBB

► **A set of three pearl cartwheel
buttons,** c1910, 2¼in (5.5cm) diam.
£20–25 / €30–35
$35–45 ⊞ EV

◄ **A set of three
silver-coated
moulded-glass
buttons,** c1920,
½in (1cm) diam.
£1–5 / €2–7
$3–9 ⊞ FMN

A stamped brass button,
entitled 'After the Bath', 1918–20,
1in (2.5cm) diam.
£35–40 / €55–60
$65–75 ⊞ TB

**A set of four celluloid plaid
buttons,** 1930s, 2in (5cm) diam.
£15–20 / €22–30
$28–38 ⊞ EV

Six glass fumblies, 1950s, largest
1¼in (3cm) diam.
£1–5 / €2–7
$3–9 ⊞ EV
These large glass buttons are
known as fumblies on account
of their tactile, irregular shapes.

**Seven Kellogg's Rice Krispies
enamelled buttons,** 1960s,
1in (2.5cm) diam.
£1–5 / €2–7
$3–9 each ⊞ JBB

Cameras

A candle slide projector, with a set of slides, German, 19thC, 10in (25.5cm) wide, with original case.
£80–90 / € 120–135
$150–170 ⊞ OIA

An Eastman Kodak No. 2 folding pocket camera, 1899, 7in (18cm) wide.
£70–80 / € 105–120
$130–150 ⊞ APC

An Eastman Kodak folding Brownie camera, 1905, 9in (23cm) wide.
£40–45 / € 60–70
$75–85 ⊞ APC

A mahogany and brass magic lantern, c1910, 28in (71cm) wide.
£360–400 / € 540–600
$670–750 ⊞ JUN

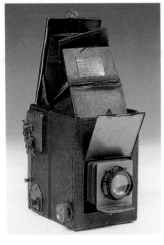

A Graflex Series B reflex camera, for 2¼ x 3¼in film, with Kodak f4.5/ 5½in lens, c1910, with carrying case.
£35–40 / € 45–50
$60–70 ⚹ JAA

An Ernemann Tropen-Klapp teak and brass camera, 1926, 6in (15cm) wide.
£900–1,000 / € 1,350–1,500
$1,700–1,900 ⊞ ARP

A Houghton Ensign Cupid camera, c1922, 4in (10cm) wide.
£60–70 / € 90–105
$110–130 ⊞ APC

A Kodak Eight Model 60 8mm cine camera, with extra lens, c1930, 7in (18cm), wide, with case.
£35–40 / € 50–60
$65–75 ⊞ ARP

A Leitz camera case, with five filters and two film cartridges, 1920–30.
£25–30 / € 40–45
$50–60 ⚹ JAA

◄ **A Purma Special camera,** with portrait lens and filter, c1930, 6in (15cm) wide.
£20–25 / € 30–35
$35–45 ⊞ OIA

An Eastman Kodak Beau Brownie box camera, 1930, 4in (10cm) wide.
£50–60 / €75–90
$95–110 ⊞ APC

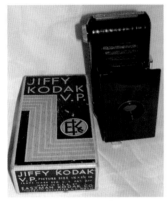

An Eastman Kodak Jiffy Kodak V.P. camera, 1935, 3in (7.5cm) wide, with box.
£30–35 / €45–50
$55–65 ⊞ APC

A Kodak Six Bull's Eye camera, 1938–41.
£4–8 / €6–12
$8–15 ⊞ OIA

▶ A Herbert George Co Donald Duck camera, American, 1946, 5in (12.5cm) wide.
£40–45 / €60–70
$75–85 ⊞ APC

A Kodak Bakelite Hawkette No. 2 camera, 1930s, 6in (15cm) wide.
£55–65 / €85–100
$100–120 ⊞ OIA

A Johnson Star Capacitor Flashgun, 1930s–40s, boxed, 6¼in (16cm) wide.
£7–11 / €11–17
$13–20 ⊞ RTT

A Speed Graphoc camera, with a Kodak Ektar f4.5/101mm lens and Kalart rangefinder, c1940.
£120–140 / €180–210
$220–260 ⊞ JAA

An Eastman Kodak Bakelite Baby Brownie box camera, 1935, 3in (7.5cm) square.
£15–20 / €22–30
$28–38 ⊞ APC

'The dollar camera is at last a fact,' boasted the Eastman Kodak Co in 1900 as it launched the Brownie, which was to become arguably the most famous and popular camera of the 20th century. George Eastman recognized the huge profit to be had from maximizing film sales and this simple and affordable camera was initially targeted at children. It was created by chief designer Frank Brownell, but was in fact named after the Brownies – helpful sprites who featured in the stories of Canadian writer Pat Cox. The Brownie was a huge success and inspired many imitators. It was produced in a range of styles and sizes up until the 1960s when this cheap and practical favourite was supplanted by the Kodak Instamatic.

A Jules Richard Le Glyphoscope, French, c1940, 6in (15cm) high.
£85–95 / €130–145
$160–180 ⊞ ARP

An Ihagee Exakta Varex 35mm SLR camera, with a 180mm Sonnar lens, c1950, 6in (15cm) wide.
£220–250 / €330–280
$410–470 ⊞ ARP

A Van Neck press plate camera, c1950, 8in (20.5cm) wide.
£145–165 / €220–250
$270–310 ⊞ ARP

A Tynar sub-miniature camera, 1950, 3in (7.5cm) wide, in a display box.
£50–60 / €75–90
$95–110 ⊞ APC

A Paillard Bolex 16mm Model 4 camera, with a 25mm Switar lens and a 16mm and a 75mm Schneider lens, with a Hollywood tripod, c1950.
£70–80 / €105–120
$130–150 ➤ JAA

► A Leica 111C camera, with a 90mm Elmar lens, 35mm Summaron lens, and a 135mm Hektor lens, c1950.
£230–260
€340–390
$440–490
➤ JAA

◄ A Paillard Bolex B8 standard 8mm cine camera, with variable shutter, Yvar f1.9/13mm lens, c1953, 5in (12.5cm) high.
£20–25 / €30–35
$35–45 ⊞ CaH

A Soho Myna SK 12 camera, 1950s, 6in (15cm) high.
£15–20 / €22–30
$28–38 ⊞ OIA

A Bell & Howell 16mm 613H cine projector, with a TTH Supertal f1.6/2in lens, c1956, 19in (48.5cm) high.
£115–130 / €175–195
$210–240 ⊞ CaH

◄ A Bell & Howell 16mm movie camera, c1956, 8in (20.5cm) high.
£60–70 / €90–105
$110–130 ⊞ ARP

An Olympus Auto-Eye camera,
1960–63, 5in (12.5cm) wide.
£25–30 / €40–45
$50–55 ⊞ OIA

A Kodak 35mm Retinette IB camera, with Reomar Ctd 45/f2.8 lens and Prontor-500 LK shutter, 1963–66, 5in (12.5cm) wide, with case.
£25–30 / €40–45
$50–55 ⊞ CaH

A Yashica Atoron sub-miniature camera, with fitted case, 1965, 4¼in (11cm) wide.
£50–60 / €75–90
$90–110 ⊞ APC

▶ **A Koda-chrome 16mm magazine film,** in original box, 1970, 6in (15cm) high.
£1–5 / €2–7
$3–9 ⊞ ARP

◀ **A Minolta Minoltina 8mm cine camera,** c1966, 8in (20.5cm) long.
£40–45
€60–70
$75–85 ⊞ ARP

A standard 8mm Quartz 5 Meteor cine camera, with f2.4/9–36mm zoom lens, Russian, c1966, 6in (15cm) high, with lever, pistol grip and case.
£30–35 / €45–50
$55–65 ⊞ CaH

▶ **A Canon Super 8 310 XL cine camera,** with Macro Ctd f1/8.5–25.5mm zoom and manual lens, c1980, 7in (18cm) long, with a cap, wrist strap and case.
£90–100 / €135–150
$170–190 ⊞ CaH

◀ **A Nikon FM2 camera,** with a Micro Nikkor f2.8/55mm lens, c1980, with camera bag.
£140–165
€210–250
$260–310
↗ JAA

▶ **A Canon FTb 35mm camera,** with a Canon f1.8/50mm and 80–200mm auto zoom lens, c1980, with carrying case.
£75–90
€115–135
$140–165 ↗ JAA

Ceramics
Animals

A tin-glazed jug, in the form of a cat, with sponged decoration, script mark, Continental, 19thC, 11½in (29cm) high.
£130–155 / €195–230
$240–290 ✗ WW

A Royal Doulton model of a fox, HN100, slight damage, painted and printed marks, 1913–42, 6in (15cm) high.
£500–600 / €750–900
$940–1,100 ✗ CDC

A Staffordshire stirrup cup, in the form of a dog's head, 19thC, 4½in (11.5cm) long.
£160–190 / €240–290
$300–360 ✗ G(B)

A Gray's Pottery model of a toucan, by Nancy Catford, 1926, 8in (20.5cm) high.
£600–670
€900–1,000
$1,100–1,250
⊞ MMc

◄ **A porcelain Bonzo bath salts container,** 1920s–30s, 5in (12.5cm) high.
£110–125
€165–190
$200–230 ⊞ HYP

A Weiner Werkstätte-style earthenware model of a terrier, impressed mark, Austrian, early 20thC, 12in (30.5cm) high.
£120–140 / €180–210
$220–260 ✗ G(L)

A ceramic Bonzo spill pot, 1920s–30s, 5in (12.5cm) high.
£55–65 / €85–100
$100–120 ⊞ HYP

Bonzo

In 1918, George Studdy began producing a weekly illustration for *The Sketch* entitled 'The Studdy Dog'. After going through several permutations the dog gradually evolved into a stylized boxer/bull terrier. *The Sketch* editor decided he needed a name, and in November 1822 the Studdy Dog was relaunched as Bonzo, and a legend was born. The cartoon canine became a star of stage and screen and was translated into over 100 postcard designs. There were cuddly Bonzos, Bonzo games and puzzles, and memorabilia in the form of everything from ceramics to car mascots. Bonzo reached his height of popularity in the interwar years and original material is highly sought after by collectors today. Bonzo also became one of the most popular names for dogs.

An Art Deco ceramic napkin ring, in the form of a dog, 3in (7.5cm) long.
£25–30 / €40–45
$50–55 ⊞ HeA

A Wemyss pig, by Jan Plitcha, c1930, 4½in (11cm) wide.
£80–90 / €120–135
$150–170 ⊞ CCs

A pair of ceramic book ends, in the form of dogs playing cricket, 1940s, 4in (10cm) high.
£40–45 / €60–70
$75–85 ⊞ RTT

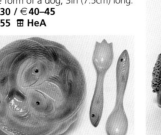

A Shorter & Sons ceramic salad bowl, moulded with fish, with spoons, late 1940s, 10in (25.5cm) diam.
£55–65 / €85–100
$100–120 ⊞ BET

A ceramic model of a poodle, American, 1950s, 4in (10cm) high.
£10–15 / €15–22
$19–28 ⊞ DRE

A Royal Doulton model of an elephant, by Charles Noke, HN2640, 1952–92, 12in (30.5cm) high.
£190–220 / €290–330
$360–410 ⊞ DA

A Wade Disney Blow Up model of Am, 1961, 5¼in (13.5cm) high.
£90–100 / €135–150
$170–190 ⊁ BBR

A Royal Albert model of Beatrix Potter's Appley Dapply, by Albert Hallam, 1971–75, 3½in (9cm) high.
£25–30 / €40–45
$50–55 ⊁ BBR

◄ **A Winstanley pottery cat,** 1990s, 12in (30.5cm) wide.
£40–45
€60–70
$75–85 ⊞ HEI

Belleek

Belleek porcelain was produced in County Fermanagh, Northern Ireland, from 1863. This date saw the introduction of a transfer-printed mark of a round tower with an Irish harp and an Irish Wolfhound above the name Belleek in a ribbon with shamrock leaves at each end. After 1891 the words 'Co Fermanagh Ireland' were added to the mark, and from around 1900 the marks changed again. Belleek production tends to be divided into periods: First Period 1863–90, Second Period 1891–26, Third Period 1926–46, Fourth Period 1946–55, Fifth Period 1955–65 and Sixth Period 1965–80. The post-war periods are also referred to as First Green Period 1946–55, Second Green Period 1955–65 and Third Green Period 1965–80.

▶ **A Belleek tumbler,** with gilt decoration, Irish, First Period, 1863–90, 4in (10cm) high.
£270–300
€400–450
$500–560
⊞ WAA

A Belleek creamer, Irish, Second Period, 1891–1926, 4in (10cm) wide.
£45–50 / €70–80
$85–95 ⋏ JAd

▶ **A Belleek part tea service,** decorated with Echinus pattern, transfer-printed mark, Irish, First Period, 1863–90, teapot 3¾in (9.5cm) high.
£950–1,100 / €1,400–1,650
$1,750–2,050 ⋏ TEN

A Belleek tray, moulded as a shell, printed mark, Irish, Second Period, 1891–1926, 17¼in (44cm) wide.
£180–210 / €270–320
$340–390 ⋏ SWO

Willets Belleek

William Bromley, creator of Irish Belleek, travelled to America in the 1880s to supervise the manufacture of the Belleek formula by American potteries including the Willets Manufacturing Co in Trenton, New Jersey. Willets Belleek, also called Art Porcelaine, was first made in 1887, and as well as producing delicate white ware inspired by Irish prototypes, the company also made a range of porcelain decorated with ormolu and gilding. The printed mark on Belleek was a twisted serpent with the word 'Willets'.

A Willets Belleek vase, decorated with roses, American, early 20thC, 15½in (39.5cm) high.
£490–590 / €740–890
$920–1,100 ⋏ JAA

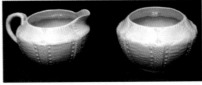

A Belleek biscuit barrel, decorated with Shamrock pattern, Irish, Third Period, 1926–46, 7in (18cm) diam.
£300–350 / €450–530
$560–650 ⊞ MLa

◀ **A Belleek sugar bowl and cream jug,** Irish, Third Period, 1926–46, 3in (7.5cm) high.
£70–80 / €105–120
$130–150 ⊞ MLa

Beswick

A Beswick vase, with drip-glazed decoration, c1930, 11in (28cm) high.
£75–85 / €115–130
$140–160 ⊞ HeA

A Beswick wall plaque, depicting a lady, No. 436, 1930s, 12in (30.5cm) high.
£200–240 / €300–360
$380–450 ➢ DA

A Beswick jug, decorated with flowers, No. 265–2, impressed marks, 1935–40.
£10–15 / €15–22
$19–28 ⊞ ES

A set of Beswick wall plaques, by Arthur Gredington, in the form of swallows, 1939–73, largest 7in (18cm) wide.
£75–85 / €115–130
$140–160 ➢ BBR

A set of Beswick models of ducks, by Mr Watkin, 1941–71, largest 3¼in (8.5cm) high.
£40–45 / €60–70
$75–85 ➢ BBR

A Beswick model of a Sealyham terrier, by Arthur Gredington, entitled 'Forrester Foxglove', 1942–67, 4½in (11.5cm) high.
£60–70 / €90–105
$110–130 ➢ PFK

A Beswick model of a shire horse, by Arthur Gredington, No. 1050, 1946–70, 5½in (14cm) high.
£45–50 / €70–80
$85–95 ➢ BBR

▶ **A Beswick model of Beatrix Potter's Little Pig Robinson,** by Arthur Gredington, 1948–74, 4in (10cm) high.
£120–140 / €180–210
$220–260 ➢ PFK

A Beswick model of a trout, by Arthur Gredington, No. 1390, 1955–75, 3¾in (9.5cm) high.
£45–50 / €70–80
$85–95 ➢ BBR

A Beswick vase, by Colin Melbourne, No. 1399, 1957–63, 6in (15cm) high.
£30–35 / €45–50
$55–65 ✵ BBR

A Beswick model of a cockatoo, No. MN1180, slight damage, 1950s–60s, 8in (20.5cm) high.
£60–70 / €90–105
$110–130 ✵ PSA

▶ **A Beswick wall plaque,** by Albert Hallam and James Hayward, in the form of a huntsman, No. 1505, 1958–62, 9in (23cm) long.
£120–140
€180–210
$220–260 ✵ BBR

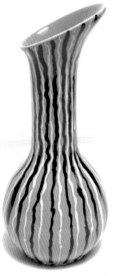

A Beswick vase, No. 1351, c1960, 10in (25.5cm) high.
£45–50 / €70–80
$85–95 ⊞ LUNA

A Beswick model of Beatrix Potter's Ginger, No. BP3B, 1976–82, 4in (10cm) high.
£400–450 / €600–680
$750–840 ⊞ BAC

A Beswick model of Beatrix Potter's Duchess, No. BP6, 1976–82, 4in (10cm) high.
£270–300 / €400–450
$500–560 ⊞ BAC

Cross Reference
Ceramics – Animals
pages 82–83

A Beswick model of Beatrix Potter's Pickles, 1980, 4½in (11.5cm) high.
£150–180 / €230–270
$280–330 ✵ NSal

▶ **A Beswick model of a pig and a piglet,** by Graham Tongue, entitled 'Piggy Back', 1983–94, 6½in (16.5cm) long.
£20–25 / €30–35
$35–45 ✵ BBR

◀ **A Beswick model of Beatrix Potter's Mr Alderman Ptolemy,** No. BP3B, 1980, 3½in (9cm) high.
£45–50 / €70–80
$85–95 ✵ NSal

◀ **A Beswick model of Beatrix Potter's Jemima Puddleduck,** by David Lyttleton, 1983–97, 2¼in (5.5cm) high.
£25–30 / €40–45
$50–55 ✵ BBR

Biscuit Barrels

A Myott biscuit barrel, with hand-painted decoration, c1930, 8in (20.5cm) high.
£120–135 / € 180–200
$220–250 ⊞ BEV

A Parrot & Co biscuit barrel, in the form of a caravan, 1930s, 8in (20.5cm) high.
£125–140 / € 190–210
$230–260 ⊞ LAS

A Hanley biscuit barrel, decorated with a gypsy scene, c1930, 5in (12.5cm) wide.
£80–90 / € 120–135
$135–170 ⊞ BET

Blue & White

A meat dish, transfer-printed with a country house, early 19thC, 20in (51cm) wide.
£290–340 / € 430–510
$540–640 ⚒ DA

A Davenport pearlware spittoon, transfer-printed with a mountain and river, c1820, 4¾in (12cm) diam.
£220–260 / € 330–390
$410–490 ⚒ SWO

A wash bowl, transfer-printed with Eastern Port pattern, slight damage, c1830, 11¼in (28.5cm) diam.
£80–90 / € 120–135
$150–170 ⚒ PFK

A Davenport pap boat, transfer-printed with birds, 19thC, 4¼in (11cm) long.
£160–190 / € 240–290
$300–360 ⚒ BBR
Pap was a semi-liquid food made from bread or meal which was then moistened with milk or water and fed to infants from a pap boat. Nursery wares were often made in blue and white pottery.

A pearlware drainer, printed with an Oriental landscape, 1800–50, 15¼in (38.5cm) wide.
£180–210 / € 270–320
$330–390 ⚒ Bea

A set of five Davies, Cookson & Wilson pearlware plates, decorated with Country Church pattern, c1830, 9in (23cm) diam.
£220–260 / € 330–390
$410–490 ⚒ Bea

A late Georgian ashet, transfer-printed with Bridge pattern, haircracks, 15in (38cm) wide.
£160–190 / €240–290
$300–360 ➤ PFK

A loving cup, with sponged decoration, inscribed with a verse, 19thC, 4in (10cm) high.
£140–165 / €210–250
$260–310 ➤ DA

A feeding bottle, transfer-printed with a chinoiserie pattern, 1850, 6in (15cm) wide.
£330–370 / €500–560
$620–690 ⊞ CuS

Chinoiserie designs were a favourite theme on blue and white ceramics. Perhaps the most famous design of all time is the Willow pattern. Introduced by Spode around 1780, the story is based on a Chinese legend. The daughter of a wealthy mandarin falls in love with a lowly employee. They elope, running away over the bridge, but her father catches them. The young man is killed and the daughter sets fire to her house and dies in the flames. The lovers are reunited in death as a pair of love birds. This pattern (sometimes with slight variations) was produced by many factories.

A platter, possibly Spode, transfer-printed with a basket of flowers, 19thC, 18½in (47cm) wide.
£140–165 / €210–250
$260–310 ➤ GAK

A Swansea meat dish, transfer-printed with Ladies of Llangollen pattern, impressed marks, 19thC, 13½in (34.5cm) wide.
£60–70 / €90–105
$110–130 ➤ SJH

A pair of Victorian plates, transfer-printed with a scene of travellers on a road and distant buildings, one cracked, 10in (25.5cm) diam.
£30–35 / €45–50
$55–65 ➤ G(L)

An Adams vase, c1910, 12in (30.5cm) high.
£105–120 / €160–180
$195–220 ⊞ BET

A Copeland Spode plate, decorated with Italian pattern, 1930s, 9in (23cm) diam.
£15–20 / €22–30
$38–38 ⊞ FOX

The Italian pattern, introduced by Spode c1818 and still in production today, was reputedly inspired by a sketch of the Coliseum in Rome, although its exact origins are uncertain. This hugely popular design appeared on every conceivable shape from tea cups to umbrella stands. Italian themes such as Roman ruins, ancient churches and classical antiquities were a favourite on blue and white pottery and reflected the popularity of the Grand Tour.

Prices

The price ranges quoted in this book reflect the average price a purchaser might expect to pay for a similar item. The price will vary according to the condition, rarity, size, popularity, provenance, colour and restoration of the item, and this must be taken into account when assessing values. Don't forget that if you are selling it is quite likely that you will be offered less than the price range.

Brannam

A C. H. Brannam jug, for Liberty & Co, decorated with a Celtic knot and a verse, c1905, 6in (15cm) high.
£350–390 / €530–590
$650–740 ⊞ MMc

A C. H. Brannam two-handled vase, decorated with fish, signed, c1900, 13¼in (33.5cm) high.
£500–600 / €750–900
$940–1,100 ↗ CHTR

◀ A C. H. Brannam match striker, early 1900s, 5in (12.5cm) high.
£200–230 / €300–350
$370–430 ⊞ MMc

A C. H. Brannam three-handled vase, decorated with incised and relief aquatic motifs, signed, c1900, 37in (94cm) high.
£550–660 / €830–990
$1,050–1,250 ↗ PF

▶ A C. H. Brannam model of a dragon boat, by Reginald Pierce, 1913, 13in (33cm) wide.
£600–670 / €900–1,000
$1,100–1,250 ⊞ MMc

Bretby

◀ A Bretby jardinière and stand, c1900, 46in (117cm) high.
£750–850 / €1,150–1,300
$1,400–1,600 ⊞ MMc

A Bretby vase, with hand-painted decoration, late 19thC, 5in (12.5cm) high.
£15–20 / €22–30
$28–38 ⊞ HEI

Cross Reference
Arts & Crafts
see page 40

A pair of Bretby vases, decorated with fish, 1940s, 10in (25.5cm) high.
£340–380 / €500–570
$620–700 ⊞ SCH

A Bretby figure of Mr Pickwick, No. 3078, mid-20thC, 8in (20.5cm) high.
£15–20 / €22–30
$28–38 ⊞ HeA

Burleigh Ware

Burleigh Ware was a trade name used by the Staffordshire firm of Burgess & Leigh (established 1851). Among the most collectable Burleigh Ware pieces are novelty Art Deco jugs with handles in the shape of birds, animals and figures. Birds (including parrots and kingfishers) were a favourite theme, and since all jugs were hand-painted, quality of decoration varies and will determine the value of a piece. The same design could be produced in different sizes, and since handles could be prone to damage, condition is also an important factor. Burleigh Ware jugs are marked on the base with a factory backstamp and often include the decorator's hand-painted mark.

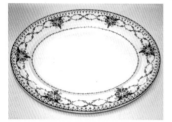

◀ **A pair of Burleigh Ware meat plates,** c1915, 17½in (44.5cm) wide.
£30–35
€45–50
$55–65 ⊞ HEI

A Burleigh Ware jug, moulded with a kingfisher, c1930, 7in (18cm) high.
£130–145 / €195–220
$240–270 ⊞ BEV

A Burleigh Ware jam pot, decorated with Daffodil pattern, c1930, 5in (12.5cm) high.
£65–75 / €100–115
$120–140 ⊞ BEV

A Burleigh Ware jug, moulded with the Pied Piper and his rats, c1930, 8in (20.5cm) high.
£270–300 / €400–450
$490–550 ⊞ BEV

A Burleigh Ware tube-lined vase, decorated by Charlotte Rhead, printed marks, c1930, 8¾in (22cm) high.
£170–200 / €250–300
$310–370 ↗ SWO

A Burleigh Ware jug, moulded with a squirrel, c1930, 7in (18cm) high.
£100–115 / €150–170
$185–210 ⊞ BEV

A Burleigh Ware jug, moulded with a rabbit in a cornfield with poppies, c1930, 7in (18cm) high.
£100–115 / €150–170
$185–210 ⊞ BEV

A Burleigh Ware vase, with moulded decoration of a deer and trees, 1930s, 9in (23cm) high.
£40–45 / €60–70
$75–85 ⊞ BAC

A Burleigh Ware jug, decorated with a flamingo, 1930s, 9½in (24cm) high.
£350–390 / €530–590
$640–710 ⊞ JFME

A Burleigh Ware jug, moulded with a dragon, c1930, 8in (20.5cm) high.
£130–145 / €195–220
$240–270 ⊞ BEV

A Burleigh Ware jug, moulded with a parrot, 1930s, 7½in (19cm) high.
£360–400 / €540–600
$660–730 ⊞ JFME

Candle Extinguishers

◄ **Two Staffordshire candle extinguishers,** modelled as Pierre Marle and Sister Hanrahan, c1870, 3in (7.5cm) high.
£130–145 / €195–220
$240–270 each ⊞ TH

◄ **A Royal Worcester candle extinguisher,** modelled as a young woman tying her bonnet ribbons, printed marks, 1880, 5in (12.5cm) high.
£240–280 / €360–420
$440–510 ⚒ PF

◄ **A Royal Worcester candle extinguisher,** entitled 'Hush', 1920, 3¼in (8.5cm) high.
£1,450–1,650 / €2,200–2,500
$2,650–3,000 ⊞ TH
'Hush', first made in 1929, was the last candle extinguisher of a new design to be produced by the Worcester factory. Decoration on these early models varied tremendously and both clothes and hair can be found in a range of different colours. The figure was reissued by the company in 1976, although the left arm was placed in front rather than behind the body. This pre-WWII example is one of the most sought-after candle extinguishers produced by Worcester, particularly in this colour combination.

A Grainger's Worcester candle extinguisher, modelled as a Tyrolean hat, 1898, 3½in (9cm) high.
£155–175 / €230–260
$280–320 ⊞ GGD

A Volkstedt porcelain candle extinguisher, German, c1900, 2¾in (7cm) high.
£360–400
€540–600
$660–730 ⊞ TH

Carlton Ware

Carlton Ware was manufactured by the Staffordshire-based firm of Wiltshaw & Robinson (1890–1989). Production in the 1920s and '30s ranged from richly enamelled and gilded lustre wares, often inspired by Oriental prototypes, to decorative tea and salad wares, moulded with fruit, vegetables and flowers, which were to prove a best-selling line. Post-war the company reflected contemporary taste with asymmetric designs, two-tone colour schemes and new patterns such as Orbit, which captured the fashion for space-influenced designs. In the 1970s and '80s Carlton Ware became well known for its novelty ceramics, ranging from the highly successful Walking Ware (designed by Roger Mitchell and Danka Napiorkowska) to a range of satirical pieces, modelled as politicians and royalty inspired by the British television series *Spitting Image*.

A Carlton Ware figure of a sailor holding a submarine, decorated with a lucky black cat, c1917, 3in (7.5cm) high.
£140–160 / €220–250
$270–300 ⊞ BtoB

▶ **A Carlton Ware Handcraft jug,** decorated with Flowering Papyrus pattern, 1930s, 8in (20.5cm) high.
£145–165 / €220–250
$270–300 ⊞ JFME

A Carlton Ware Handcraft two-handled dish, c1930, 12in (30.5cm) wide.
£270–300 / €400–450
$500–560 ⊞ BEV

A pair of Carlton Ware vases, decorated with hollyhocks, c1930, 9in (23cm) high.
£320–380 / €480–570
$600–710 ⋏ CHTR

A Carlton Ware Rita coffee service, comprising six coffee cups and saucers, decorated with Sketching Bird pattern, with six silver spoons, Sheffield 1937, in a fitted case.
£600–720 / €900–1,050
$1,150–1,350 ⋏ G(L)

A Carlton Ware jug/two-handled mug, decorated with a face, cover missing, 1930s, 3in (7.5cm) high.
£80–90 / €120–135
$150–170 ⊞ SCH
This jug/mug would be worth double this amount if it still had its cover.

A Carlton Ware two-handled lustre vase, gilded and enamelled with a cockerel beside flowers, impressed and printed marks, 1930s, 5¼in (13cm) high.
£100–120 / €150–180
$185–220 ⋏ PFK

A Carlton Ware Rouge Royale vase, decorated with flowers, 1930s, 5½in (14cm) high.
£145–165 / €220–250
$270–300 ⊞ JFME

A Carlton Ware vase, decorated with Apple Blossom pattern, late 1930s, 4in (10cm) high.
£95–105 / €145–135
$150–170 ⊞ StC

A Carlton Ware Walking Ware egg cup, 1970s, 2½in (6.5cm) high.
£20–25 / €30–35
$35–45 ⊞ BAC

A Carlton Ware Circus napkin ring, 1930s, 3in (7.5cm) wide.
£105–120 / €160–180
$195–220 ⊞ SCH

A pair of Carlton Ware salt and pepper shakers, with hand-painted decoration, 1950s, 3½in (9cm) high.
£20–25 / €30–35
$35–45 ⊞ GRo

A Carlton Ware teapot, decorated with Orbit pattern, c1960, 6in (15cm) high.
£50–55 / €75–85
$95–105 ⊞ BET

A Carlton Ware Walking Ware Brown & Polson gravy boat, 1980s, 6in (15cm) high.
£25–30 / €40–45
$50–55 ⊞ BAC

Two Carlton Ware serving dishes, decorated with dog roses, 1930s, larger 8in (20.5cm) wide.
£60–70 / €90–105
$110–130 each ⊞ CoCo

A Carlton Ware figural toast rack, c1960, 5in (12.5cm) wide.
£50–60 / €75–90
$95–110 ⊞ BEV

A Carlton Ware Walking Ware cup, 1970s, 3½in (9cm) high.
£15–20 / €22–30
$28–38 ⊞ BAC

◄ **A Carlton Ware Walking Ware Brown & Polson gravy boat,** 1980s, 6in (15cm) high.
£25–30 / €40–45
$50–55 ⊞ BAC

Chintz Ware

Chintz ware – tableware printed with an all-over floral pattern inspired by chintz textiles – became particularly popular in the 1920s and '30s. One of the best-known manufacturers was Royal Winton, the trade name used by Grimwades Ltd (established 1885). From the 1920s onwards, the company produced over 60 different chintz patterns and exported their wares across the world, particularly to the USA. Other major chintz ware manufacturers include James Kent, Crown Ducal, Shelley and Midwinter. Some patterns are more desirable than others, and the condition of the transfer-printed design is crucial to value. Collectors want patterns that are clean, crisp and clear, without scratches or fading.

A Crown Ducal cake stand, c1920, 9in (23cm) wide.
£100–115 / € 150–175
$185–210 ⊞ BEV

A Royal Winton teapot, c1930, 5in (12.5cm) high.
£200–230 / € 300–340
$380–430 ⊞ BET

A Royal Winton Mecca foot warmer, Pattern No. 1094, marked, early 20thC, 10¼in (26cm) high.
£140–165 / € 210–250
$260–310 ⇗ SWO

A James Kent milk jug and sugar bowl, decorated with Florita pattern, c1930, sugar bowl 2in (5cm) high.
£65–75 / € 100–115
$120–140 ⊞ BEV

A Royal Winton breakfast set, comprising teapot, creamer, sugar bowl, tea cup and tray, 1930s, tray 10in (25.5cm) wide.
£250–280 / € 380–420
$470–520 ⊞ JFME

A Royal Winton breakfast set, comprising teapot, creamer, sugar bowl, tea cup and tray, 1934, tray 10in (25.5cm) wide.
£360–400 / € 540–600
$670–750 ⊞ JFME
With sets, check marks and patterns to ensure that all pieces match and that they are all of the same period. Occasionally a broken piece is replaced with a later addition.

A Royal Winton breakfast set, comprising teapot, creamer, sugar bowl, tea cup and tray, decorated with Welbeck pattern, with associated toast rack, 1940s.
£110–130 / € 165–190
$200–240 ⇗ CHTR

A Royal Winton trio, decorated with Somerset pattern, c1940, plate 6in (12.5cm) diam.
£75–85 / € 115–130
$140–160 ⊞ RH

◀ **A Royal Winton toast rack,** decorated with Kew pattern, c1940, 7in (18cm) wide.
£150–170 / € 230–260
$280–320 ⊞ RH

Clarice Cliff

Clarice Cliff (1899–1972) is arguably the most famous name in Art Deco ceramics. In 1916 she joined the firm of A. J. Wilkinson where she caught the eye of her boss (later husband) Colley Shorter. He set Clarice up in her own studio, and 1928 saw the launch of the Bizarre range – affordable, brightly coloured, hand-decorated earthenware – that was to prove a huge success. In the 1920s and 1930s Cliff designed over 500 shapes and 2,000 patterns. Rarity, shape, pattern and of course condition determine desirability. One of her best-known designs was Crocus, which was manufactured in quantity from the late 1920s until 1939. Crocus remains one of Cliff's more affordable designs, though rarer shapes and more unusual colour schemes such as Blue Crocus will command a premium. Some patterns are particularly desirable (for example May Avenue, Appliqué and Inspiration). Collectors also focus on more unusual shapes. Conical sugar casters are very sought after, as are sabots or clogs, which were designed to hold cacti.

Ceramics should always be checked for damage and beware of fakes. Tell-tale signs include washed out colours, an uneven slightly murky 'honey glaze', and a deliberately aged, crackled glaze around the mark on the base.

A Clarice Cliff egg cup, decorated with Crocus pattern, c1928, 2½in (5.5cm) high.
£175–195 / €260–290 $330–370 ⊞ JFME

A Clarice Cliff toilet set, comprising jug, bowl, chamber pot and covered soap dish, decorated with Broth pattern, printed marks, 1929.
£1,800–2,150 / €2,700–3,250 $3,350–4,000 ➢ GAK

A Clarice Cliff Odilion preserve pot and cover, decorated with Delecia Pansies pattern, c1930, 4in (10cm) diam.
£220–260 / €330–390 $410–480 ➢ Bri

A Clarice Cliff Bizarre candlestick, decorated with Gayday pattern, c1930, 3in (7.5cm) high.
£130–155 / €195–230 $240–290 ➢ Bri

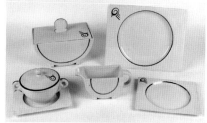

A Clarice Cliff Biarritz dinner service, comprising 45 pieces, some damage, c1930.
£360–400 / €540–600 $670–750 ➢ FHF

A Clarice Cliff Bizarre teapot, slight damage, printed mark, c1930, 5¾in (14cm) high.
£170–200 / €260–300 $320–370 ➢ CDC

▶ **A Clarice Cliff tea-for-two set,** decorated with Crocus pattern, marked, c1930.
£280–330 / €420–500 $520–620 ➢ SWO

Insurance values

Always insure your valuables for the cost of replacing them with similar items, regardless of the original price paid. Both dealers and auctioneers can provide a valuation service for a fee.

A Clarice Cliff Bizarre ashtray,
painted with a geometric design,
c1930, 4¾in (12cm) diam.
£150–180 / €230–270
$280–330 ✗ G(L)

A Clarice Cliff Bizarre plate,
marked, c1930, 10in (25.5cm) diam.
£440–520 / €660–780
$820–970 ✗ G(B)

A Clarice Cliff Bizarre bowl,
decorated with Inspiration Caprice
pattern, marked, c1930,
7in (18cm) diam.
£200–240 / €300–360
$370–440 ✗ E
**The Inspiration range was
produced using metallic oxide
glazes over the design.**

A Clarice Cliff plate, decorated
with Solomon's Seal pattern, 1930,
9in (23cm) diam.
£95–110 / €145–165
$180–200 ⊞ TAC
**In an attempt to find cheaper
production methods, Solomon's
Seal had a printed outline that
was coloured in by hand.
Appearing far more regular than
Cliff's more typical free-hand
designs, the pattern was not a
success and was withdrawn.**

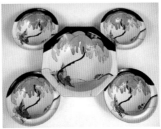

A Clarice Cliff fruit bowl set,
comprising five pieces, decorated
with Woodland pattern, printed and
impressed marks, c1931.
£400–480 / €600–720
$750–900 ✗ SWO

A Clarice Cliff jug, decorated with
Blue-Eyed Marigold pattern, 1931,
6½in (16.5cm) high.
£760–850 / €1,150–1,300
$1,400–1,600 ⊞ JFME

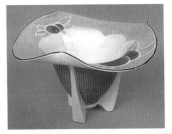

A Clarice Cliff Bizarre vase,
decorated with Nuage pattern,
printed and impressed marks,
c1931, 10¾in (27.5cm) diam.
£140–165 / €210–250
$260–310 ✗ M

A Clarice Cliff vase, decorated
with My Garden pattern, on three
moulded feet, printed and painted
marks, 1930s, 8¼in (21cm) high.
£120–140 / €180–210
$220–260 ✗ CDC

A Clarice Cliff preserve pot,
decorated with Blue Japan pattern,
c1934, 3in (7.5cm) wide.
£450–500 / €680–750
$840–930 ⊞ JFME

A Clarice Cliff sabot, decorated
with Capri pattern, 1935,
4½in (11.5cm) long.
£300–330 / €450–500
$560–620 ⊞ JFME

A Clarice Cliff Bizarre plate, decorated with Appliqué Idyll pattern, 1930s, 9in (23cm) diam.
£320–380 / €480–570
$600–710 ➶ Bri

A pair of Clarice Cliff vases, moulded with a parrot on a branch, 1930s, 6in (15cm) high.
£140–165 / €210–250
$260–310 ➶ L&E

A Clarice Cliff Lotus jug, decorated with Nasturtium pattern, 1930s, 11½in (29cm) high.
£320–380 / €480–570
$600–710 ➶ G(L)

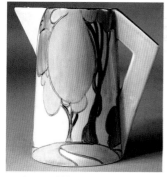

A Clarice Cliff Bizarre jug, decorated with Pastel Autumn pattern, 1930s, 6½in (16.5cm) high.
£340–400 / €510–500
$640–750 ➶ DA

A Clarice Cliff Royal Staffordshire Water-lily bowl, printed mark, 1930s, 8¾in (22cm) diam.
£60–70 / €90–105
$110–130 ➶ WW

A Clarice Cliff Bizarre Stamford jug, decorated with Crocus pattern, 1930s, 5in (12.5cm) high.
£300–360 / €450–540
$560–670 ➶ Bri

A Clarice Cliff jug, decorated with Celtic Harvest pattern, 1930s, 10in (25.5cm) high.
£150–170 / €230–260
$290–320 ⊞ JFME

A Clarice Cliff Lotus jug, decorated with Blue Crocus pattern, 1930s, 11½in (29cm) high.
£900–1,050 / €1,350–1,600
$1,700–1,950 ➶ CHTR

A Clarice Cliff Bizarre mug, decorated with Windbells pattern, 1930s, 4½in (11.5cm) high.
£340–400 / €510–600
$640–750 ➶ WiLP

Susie Cooper

Susie Cooper (1902–95) joined Gray's pottery as a paintress in 1922, producing hand-decorated wares in enamel and lustre that reflected the contemporary craze for abstract patterns. Early wares are very desirable today. In 1929 she left Gray's to set up her own company, and by the early 1930s she was designing her own shapes and experimenting with a range of techniques, from crayoning to banding to transfer printing, in order to create stylish but affordable everyday tableware. 'I wanted to do nice things for people who had taste,

but didn't have the money to satisfy it,' she explained. After the war, Susie Cooper moved into bone china, her pottery merged with R. H. & S. L. Plant in 1958 and became part of the Wedgwood group in 1966. New designs such as the can shape, and a range of sophisticated patterns inspired by everything from Scandinavian ceramics to Carnaby-style Op Art, ensured that her china remained fashionable in the 1950s and 1960s. In 1972 Cooper retired as a director, and in 1980 Wedgwood closed the Susie Cooper Pottery.

A Susie Cooper coffee pot, decorated with Persian Bird pattern, c1928, 7in (18cm) high.
£770–850
€ 1,150–1,300
$1,450–1,600 ⊞ MMc

A Susie Cooper vase, with hand-painted decoration, 1920s, 5½in (14cm) high.
£300–330 / € 450–500
$560–620 ⊞ JFME

A Susie Cooper teapot, with hand-painted decoration, c1928, 8in (20.5cm) high.
£410–460 / € 620–690
$770–860 ⊞ MMc

◀ **A Susie Cooper Crown Works part tea and dinner service,** comprising 26 pieces decorated with Dresden Spray pattern, some damage, c1935.
£100–120 / € 150–180
$185–220 ➢ Bri

A Susie Cooper trio, decorated with Tigerlily pattern, c1950, plate 7in (18cm) diam.
£55–65 / € 85–100
$100–120 ⊞ RH

◀ **A Susie Cooper coffee pot,** decorated with Talisman pattern, c1958, 8½in (21.5cm) high.
£90–100 / € 135–150
$170–190 ⊞ CHI

A Susie Cooper Crown Works Kestrel coffee service, comprising 16 pieces, decorated with Patricia Rose pattern, c1940.
£220–260 / € 330–390
$410–490 ➢ Bri

Three Susie Cooper coffee cups and saucers, decorated with Black Fruit pattern, c1958, 3in (7.5cm) high.
£30–35 / € 45–50
$55–65 each ⊞ CHI

A Susie Cooper teapot, decorated with Corinthian pattern, 1950s, 4½in (11.5cm) high.
£60–70 / € 90–105
$110–130 ⊞ CHI

◀ **A Susie Cooper tea cup and saucer,** decorated with Polka Dot pattern, 1950s, 2½in (6.5cm) high.
£35–40 / € 50–60
$65–75 ⊞ CHI

A Susie Cooper jug, decorated with Keystone pattern, c1969, 6in (15cm) high.
£45–50 / € 70–80
$75–85 ⊞ CHI

A Susie Cooper vegetable dish, decorated with Diablo pattern, c1969, 9in (23cm) diam.
£90–100 / € 135–150
$170–190 ⊞ CHI

A Susie Cooper soup bowl and saucer, decorated with Venetian pattern, 1960s, 5½in (14cm) diam.
£35–40 / € 50–60
$65–75 ⊞ CHI

▶ **A Susie Cooper Wedgwood coffee pot,** decorated with Neptune pattern, 1960s, 6½in (16.5cm) high.
£70–80 / € 105–120
$130–150 ⊞ CHI

Crown Devon

◀ **A Crown Devon ashtray,** modelled with a golfer, c1930, 3in (7.5cm) high.
£135–150 / € 200–230
$250–280 ⊞ BEV

A Crown Devon jug, decorated with a geometric pattern, c1930, 4in (10cm) high.
£90–100 / € 135–150
$170–190 ⊞ RH

A Crown Devon flower vase, with insert and hand-painted decoration, c1930, 5in (12.5cm) high.
£150–165 / € 230–260
$280–310 ⊞ BET

A Crown Devon ginger jar, 1930s, 9in (23cm) high.
£230–260 / € 350–390
$430–490 ⊞ JFME

Condition
Condition is vital when assessing the value of ceramics. Perfect examples appreciate more than damaged pieces, although rare ceramics may command higher prices even when damaged.

A Crown Devon jug, 1930s,
4in (10cm) high.
£80–90 / € 120–135
$150–170 ⊞ JFME

A Crown Devon lustre vase,
with Oriental decoration, 1930s,
9¾in (25cm) high.
£120–140 / € 180–210
$220–260 ✗ Pott

◄ **A Crown Devon honey pot,**
restored, 1940, 5in (12.5cm) wide.
£140–165 / € 210–250
$260–310 ⊞ CCs

A Crown Devon jug, 1930s,
9in (23cm) high.
£330–370 / € 500–560
$620–690 ⊞ JFME

▶ **A Crown
Devon cup
and saucer,**
decorated with
Stockholm
pattern, c1950,
saucer 7in
(18cm) wide.
£45–50
€ 70–80
$85–95 ⊞ BEV

A Crown Devon vase, 1950s,
8in (20.5cm) wide.
£35–40 / € 50–60
$65–75 ⊞ HO

A Crown Devon mug, decorated
with Stockholm pattern, c1950,
4in (10cm) high.
£30–35 / € 45–50
$55–65 ⊞ BET

A Crown Devon jar, with cover,
1950s, 4¼in (11cm) high.
£15–20 / € 22–30
$28–38 ⊞ HEI

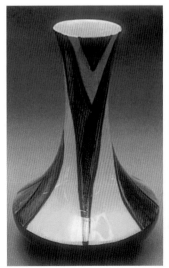

A Crown Devon vase, hand-painted
by Dorothy Ann, entitled 'Flames',
c1960, 10½in (26.5cm) high.
£45–50 / € 70–80
$85–95 ✗ AMB

Crown Ducal

A Crown Ducal vase, transfer-printed with a floral pattern, 1920s, 10in (25.5cm) high.
£30–35 / €45–50
$55–65 ⊞ HO

A Crown Ducal vase, by Charlotte Rhead, decorated with a floral pattern, blue printed marks, 1930s, 8¾in (22cm) high.
£170–200 / €260–300
$320–370 ⋌ L&E

◄ **A Crown Ducal vase,** by Charlotte Rhead, slight damage, 1930s, 5¾in (14.5cm) high.
£30–35 / €45–50
$55–65 ⋌ BBR

A Crown Ducal bowl, by Charlotte Rhead, decorated with Rhodian pattern, printed mark and tube-lined signature, 1930s, 7¾in (19.5cm) diam.
£110–130 / €165–195
$210–240 ⋌ PFK

A Crown Ducal coffee pot, by Charlotte Rhead, decorated with Padua pattern, 1930s, 8in (20.5cm) high.
£550–650 / €830–980
$1,050–1,200 ⊞ MMc

A Crown Ducal wall plaque, by Charlotte Rhead, No. 4491, decorated with Tudor Rose pattern, printed and painted marks, 1930s, 17¼in (44cm) diam.
£270–320 / €410–480
$500–600 ⋌ CDC

A Crown Ducal wall plaque, by Charlotte Rhead, No. 5983, decorated with Ankara pattern, slight damage, printed marks, signed, 1930s,
£85–100 / €130–150
$160–185 ⋌ RTO
Charlotte Rhead (1885–1947) was born into a family of potters and learnt many techniques from her father Frederic Alfred Rhead, including tube-lining, a distinctive feature of her work. Charlotte worked for many different potteries, including Wardle & Co, Bursley Ltd, the Elgreave Pottery and Burgess & Leigh, sometimes with her father and her brother Frederick Hurten Rhead. In 1931 she moved to A. G. Richardson, makers of Crown Ducal Ware. Sought-after pieces include nursery ware, chargers and vases. Early examples by Charlotte Rhead have a tube-lined C. Rhead signature. Later wares have a transfer mark of her full signature.

◄ **A Crown Ducal bowl,** No. 6778, 1930s, 10in (25.5cm) diam.
£110–130 / €165–195
$210–240 ⋌ DA

Cruet Sets

A Clarice Cliff cruet set, decorated with Crocus pattern, c1930, 3¼in (8.5cm) high.
**£420–470 / €630–710
$790–880** ⊞ JFME

An Art Deco cruet set, in the form of elephants, c1930, 5in (12.5cm) wide.
**£120–135 / €180–200
$220–250** ⊞ BEV

An Art Deco cruet set, in the form of Native Americans, c1930, 5in (12.5cm) high.
**£100–115 / €150–175
$190–220** ⊞ BEV

▶ **A cruet set,** in the form of Humpty Dumpty, c1930, 2in (5cm) high.
**£50–55
€75–85
$95–105**
⊞ BEV

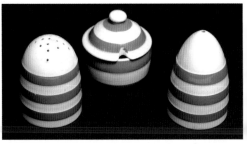

A T. G. Green Cornish Ware cruet set, 1930s–50s, pepper 2½in (6.5cm) high.
**£45–50 / €70–80
$85–95** ⊞ CAL
With a matching tray, this cruet set could be worth double this amount.

A Carlton Ware cruet set, in the form of fruit, c1950, 7in (18cm) wide.
**£40–45 / €60–70
$75–85** ⊞ CoCo

A Carlton Ware cruet set, in the form of vegetables, 1950s, 9in (23cm) wide.
**£45–50 / €70–80
$85–95** ⊞ RTT

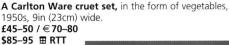

A cruet set, in the form of Noddy and Big Ears, 1950s, 3½in (9cm) high.
**£155–175 / €230–260
$290–330** ⊞ HYP

An Adams cruet set, decorated with Blue Daisy pattern, 1960s, 4½in (11.5cm) high.
**£20–25 / €30–35
$35–45** ⊞ CHI

▶ **A Carlton Ware cruet set,** 1960, 5½in (14cm) high.
**£20–25
€30–35
$35–45** ⊞ HEI

Cups, Saucers & Mugs

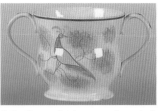

A Prattware loving cup, decorated with a bird, c1800, 4in (10cm) high.
£150–170 / €230–260
$280–320 ✗ Mit

A Vienna cup and saucer, painted with a classical and an Oriental landscape, late 18thC.
£180–210 / €270–320
$340–390 ✗ SWO

A Prattware mug, c1790, 5in (12.5cm) high.
£150–170 / €230–260
$280–320 ✗ Mit

◄ **A Sunderland lustre coffee can,** c1830, 2in (5cm) high.
£45–50 / €70–80
$85–95 ⊞ SER

► **A Davenport cup and saucer,** 1870–88, cup 2in (5cm) diam.
£45–50 / €70–80
$85–95 ⊞ DEB

A George Jones cup and saucer, slight damage, 1870–80, saucer 3in (7.5cm) diam.
£60–70 / €90–105
$110–130 ⊞ DEB

A McIntyre cup and saucer, the handle in the form of a crane, c1875, cup 3in (7.5cm) high.
£135–150 / €200–220
$250–280 ⊞ BEV

A Bodley cup and saucer, c1880, 2in (5cm) diam.
£25–30 / €40–45
$50–55 ⊞ DEB

A Coalport coffee can, late 19thC, 1½in (4cm) diam.
£130–145 / €195–220
$230–270 ⊞ HER

► **A trio,** with transfer-printed decoration, c1890, 4in (10cm) diam.
£10–15
€15–22
$19–28 ⊞ DEB

► **A cup and saucer,** c1890, 2½in (6.5cm) diam.
£20–25 / €30–35
$35–45 ⊞ DEB

An Aynsley cup and saucer, c1905, 2in (5cm) diam.
£35–40 / €50–60
$65–75 ⊞ DEB

A mug, c1900, 6½in (16.5cm) high.
£35–40 / €50–60
$65–75 ⊞ AL

◄ **A Susie Cooper trio,** decorated with Dresden Spray pattern, c1930, 7in (18cm) diam.
£75–85 / €115–130
$140–160 ⊞ RH

A Coalport coffee cup and saucer, c1937, 2½in (6.5cm) diam.
£30–35 / €45–50
$55–65 ⊞ DEB

A Copeland coffee can and saucer, c1940, 2in (5cm) diam.
£30–35 / €45–50
$55–65 ⊞ DEB

▶ **A Royal Cauldon cup and saucer,** c1940s, saucer 3½in (9cm) diam.
£1–5 / €2–7
$3–9 ⊞ HO

An Aynsley Butterfly tea set, comprising 18 pieces, 1940s, cup 3¼in (8.5cm) diam.
£1,050–1,200 / €1,600–1,800
$2,000–2,250 ⊞ SCH
In 1775 John Aynsley founded a pottery at Lane End in Stoke on Trent. In the mid-19th century the family invested in the new process of making bone china and built a factory in 1861, which remains in operation today. This tea set is an extremely fragile and attractive design and it is in perfect condition, which is rare, hence the price range.

◀ **A tea cup and saucer,** c1950, saucer 3in (7.5cm) diam.
£25–30
€40–45
$50–55
⊞ MRW

A Royal Albert cup and saucer, decorated with Masquerade pattern, 1950s, 3in (7.5cm) high.
£15–20 / €22–30
$28–38 ⊞ CHI

An Adams cup and saucer, decorated with Blue Butterfly pattern, c1966, 3in (7.5cm) diam.
£30–35 / €45–50
$55–65 ⊞ CHI

A pair of Royal Albert Gossamer cups and saucers, 1960s, cup 3in (7.5cm) high.
£20–25 / €30–35
$35–45 each ⊞ CHI

A Franciscan Honeycomb trio, 1960s, cup 3in (7.5cm) high.
£15–20 / €22–30
$28–38 ⊞ CHI

A Royal Albert TV cup and saucer, decorated with Braemar pattern, 1955–65, saucer 9in (23cm) wide.
£35–40 / €50–60
$65–75 ⊞ CHI

Denby

A Denby whisky flask, applied with a town crier, marked, c1930, 7in (18cm) high.
£220–250 / €330–380
$410–470 ⊞ KES

▶ A Denby model of a lamb, mid-20thC, 12in (30.5cm) high.
£125–145 / €190–220
$230–270 ⊞ HeA

A Denby plate, designed by Glyn Colledge, c1960, 10in (25.5cm) diam.
£10–15 / €15–22
$19–28 ⊞ HeA

A Denby Danesby Ware vase, c1930, 9in (23cm) high.
£110–130 / €165–195
$210–240 ⊞ HeA

A Denby cloisonné ramekin, designed by Glyn Colledge, c1960, 4in (10cm) diam.

▶ A Denby coffee pot, cup and saucer, 1961, coffee pot 7in (18cm) high.
£45–50 / €70–80
$85–95 ⊞ CHI

A Denby Falstaff coffee pot, c1971, 12in (30.5cm) high.
£60–70 / €90–105
$110–130 ⊞ CHI

◀ A pair of Denby Arabesque ice buckets, 1960s, larger 10in (25.5cm) high.
£130–145 / €195–220
$240–270 ⊞ CHI

A Denby tankard, designed by Glyn Colledge, 1950s, 5in (12.5cm) high.
£45–50 / €70–80
$85–95 ⊞ HeA

A Denby cloisonné ramekin, designed by Glyn Colledge, c1960, 4in (10cm) diam.
£15–20 / €22–30
$28–38 ⊞ HeA

A Denby Potters Wheel plate, bowl, cup, saucer, wine goblet and cutlery, designed by David Yorath, c1973, plate 10in (25.5cm) diam.
£80–90 / €120–135
$150–170 ⊞ CHI

Doulton

A Doulton jug, c1880, 7in (18cm) high.
£85–95 / € 130–145
$160–180 ⊞ SAT

◀ **A pair of late Victorian Doulton Burslem ewers,** decorated with irises, 13in (33cm) high.
£80–95 / € 120–145
$150–180 ↗ NSal

◀ **A Royal Doulton plate,** 1895–1900, 15in (38cm) wide.
£85–95
€ 130–145
$160–180
⊞ BEV

A Royal Doulton Slater patent tyg, decorated with flowers, silver rim, c1885, 6in (15cm) high.
£200–240 / € 300–360
$380–450 ↗ G(B)
Slater patent was a decorative process in which lace and other materials were impressed into the ware.

A Doulton Lambeth stoneware jug, by Emily Welch, 1882, 7¾in (19.5cm) high.
£150–180 / € 230–270
$280–330 ↗ DA

A Doulton stoneware vase, c1900, 3½in (9cm) high.
£50–60 / € 75–90
$95–110 ⊞ HO

◀ **A Royal Doulton flambé bowl,** decorated with a woodland landscape, slight damage, signed 'Noke and Jung', early 20thC, 8in (20.5cm) diam.
£320–380
€480–570
$600–710
⚲ FHF

Further reading

Miller's Twentieth-Century Ceramics, Miller's Publications, 1999

A Royal Doulton Slater patent vase, marked, early 20thC, 14in (35.5cm) high.
£80–95 / €120–140
$150–180 ⚲ G(B)

A Royal Doulton vase, decorated with Periwinkle pattern, c1905, 10in (25.5cm) high.
£85–95 / €130–145
$160–180 ⊞ BET

A Royal Doulton Art Deco vase, 1920s, 5in (12.5cm) high.
£75–85 / €115–130
$140–160 ⊞ BET

A Royal Doulton jug, c1920, 2¼in (5.5cm) high.
£30–35 / €45–50
$55–65 ⊞ HER

▶ **A Royal Doulton Touchstone character jug,** 1930–60, 5½in (14cm) high.
£100–120
€150–180
$185–220
⚲ L&E

A Royal Doulton figure, entitled 'Pickwick', model No. HN556, 1923–39, 7¼in (18.5cm) high.
£160–190 / €250–290
$300–360 ⚲ SWO

A Royal Doulton figure, entitled 'Mephistopheles and Marguerite', model No. HN755, on a mahogany base, printed, painted and impressed marks, 1925–45, 7¾in (19.5cm) high.
£750–900 / €1,150–1,350
$1,450–1,700 ⚲ CDC

Character Jugs

Inspired by Toby jugs, which were first produced in the 18th century and feature the whole body of a figure, character jugs focus on the head and shoulders. Doulton designer Charles Noke (1851–1941) created the first Doulton character jug, John Barleycorn, in 1934. Other modellers, including Harry Fenton and Leslie Harradine, soon expanded the range, and the company went on to become a leading producer in the field. Subjects are typically inspired by legend, history, literature and contemporary events. Some jugs had a limited production run, others were manufactured over a long period, and values vary accordingly. In 1963, Doulton began issuing themed groups of jugs with the Williamsburg collection, and 1991 saw the introduction of Character Jug of the Year, produced for one year only. Jugs were often produced in different sizes and colour variations. The quality of modelling and the mark add to desirability.

▶ **A Royal Doulton Franciscan jug,** by C. J. Noke and H. Fenton, No. 471 of 500, 1933, 10½in (26.5cm) high.
£620–740
€930–1,100
$1,200–1,400
⚘ DA

A Doulton Lambeth stoneware tyg, moulded with topers and a hunting scene, the handles in the form of hounds, impressed marks, 1930s, 6¼in (16cm) high.
£65–75 / €100–115
$120–140 ⚘ L&E

A Royal Doulton jug, entitled 'The Regency Coach', No. 158 of 500, printed mark, 1930s, 11in (28cm) high.
£320–380 / €480–570
$600–710 ⚘ G(B)

◀ **A Royal Doulton figure,** entitled 'Do You Wonder Where Fairies Are That Folks Declare Have Vanished', model No. HN1544, printed, painted and impressed marks, 1933–49, 5in (12.5cm) high.
£260–310
€400–470
$490–580
⚘ FHF

A Royal Doulton loving cup, designed by C. Noke, commemorating the Silver Jubilee of George V and Queen Mary, No. 845 of 1000, 10½in (26.5cm) high.
£520–620 / €780–930
$970–1,150 ⚘ PF

A Royal Doulton figure, entitled 'Gladys', model No. HN1740, 1935–49, 5in (12.5cm) high.
£280–330 / €420–500
$520–620 ⚘ SWO

A Royal Doulton model of a bulldog, c1942, 6in (15cm) wide.
£450–500 / €680–750
$840–940 ⊞ JFME

A Royal Doulton Drake character jug, designed by Harry Fenton, 1940–41, 6in (15cm) high.
£1,600–1,900
€2,400–2,850
$3,000–3,550 ⚘ DA
This is a rare character jug, hence its high value.

▶ **A Royal Doulton Monty character jug,** designed by Harry Fenton, marked, 1946–54, 6¼in (16cm) high.
£55–65 / €85–100
$100–120 ⚘ BBR

A Royal Doulton figure, entitled 'Sir Walter Raleigh', model No. HN2015, 1948–55, 11¾in (30cm) high.
£210–250 / €320–380
$400–470 ➤ SWO

A Royal Doulton figure, entitled 'Marianne', model No. HN2074, painted and printed marks, 1951–53, 5in (12.5cm) high.
£260–310 / €400–470
$490–580 ➤ FHF

Royal Doulton figures

In 1913 Royal Doulton launched its famous series of figures, pioneered by designer Charles Noke. Figures were given a HN numbering system (after Harry Nixon, chief colourist for Doulton at that period) and began with HN1 for 'Darling', the first figure to be introduced. Numbers are now in the thousands and all figures can be approximately dated by their name and production number. Between 1913 and 1917 fewer than 50 characters were represented. After WW1, Leslie Harradine (1887–1965) produced many popular models, developing the Fair Ladies series of romanticized, often crinolined, female figures which captured the mood of the 1930s and came to epitomize the Doulton style. Other major designers include Peggy Davies, who first joined Doulton in 1939 and became well known for her pretty lady figures, and Mary Nichol, who produced many character models (including seafaring figures) from the mid-1950s until her death in 1974. Some enthusiasts collect by artist, others by subject. Leslie Harradine's work is often a focus for collectors and her Fair Ladies are a favourite subject. Collectors sometimes focus their collections around the colour of dress or even the type of fashion accessories portrayed.

A Royal Doulton figure, entitled 'The Cellist', model No. HN2226, 1960–67, 8in (20.5cm) high.
£180–210 / €270–320
$340–390 ➤ G(L)

A Royal Doulton figure, designed by M. Nicoll, entitled 'Omar Khayyam', model No. HN2247, marked, 1965–83, 6in (15cm) high.
£80–95 / €120–140
$150–180 ➤ BBR

A Royal Doulton coffee pot, decorated with Forest Glen pattern, 1973, 9in (23cm) high.
£40–45 / €60–70
$75–85 ⊞ CHI

A Royal Doulton figure, entitled 'The Milk Maid', model No. HN2057, 1975–81, 7½in (19cm) high.
£80–95 / €120–145
$150–180 ➤ WilP

A Royal Doulton coffee pot, decorated with Indian Summer pattern, 1970s, 10in (25.5cm) high.
£15–20 / €22–30
$28–38 ⊞ CHI

A Royal Doulton Henry V character jug, designed by Robert Tabbenor, marked, 1982–84, 7in (18cm) high.
£55–65 / €85–100
$100–120 ➤ BBR

◀ A Royal Doulton figural group, entitled 'The Bisto Kids', 2002.
£210–230 / €310–350
$390–430 ⊞ MCL
This figural group was manufactured in a limited edition of 1,000 exclusively for Millennium Collectables Ltd.

Egg Cups

A Minton egg cup, c1845,
2¼in (5.5cm) high.
£60–70 / €90–105
$110–130 ⊞ AMH

A Pillivuyt Limoges egg cup,
c1875, 2in (5cm) high.
£40–45 / €60–70
$75–85 ⊞ HER

◄ **A Staffordshire egg cup,**
c1870, 2in (5cm) high.
£50–55 / €75–85
$95–105 ⊞ AMH

A Bonzo egg cup,
1920s–30s, 3in (7.5cm) high.
£65–75 / €100–115
$120–140 ⊞ HYP

**A Royal Worcester
egg cup,** c1904,
2½in (6.5cm) high.
£10–15 / €15–22
$19–28 ⊞ POS

**A Royal Worcester egg
cup,** 1912, 2¾in (7cm) high.
£45–50 / €70–80
$85–95 ⊞ HER

A Copeland egg cup,
1920s, 2½in (6.5cm) high.
£45–50 / €70–80
$85–95 ⊞ HER

◄ **A Shelley double egg cup,** c1930,
3½in (9cm) high.
£75–85 / €115–130
$140–160 ⊞ BET
Double egg cups could be turned over,
one end for hens' eggs and the other end
for goose eggs.

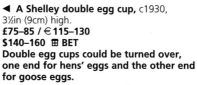

A Royal Winton egg cup,
1930s, 2½in (6.5cm) high.
£25–30 / €40–45
$50–55 ⊞ HER

◄ **An egg cup,** in the
form of a rhinoceros,
1995, 4in (10cm) wide.
£1–5 / €2–7
$3–9 ⊞ POS

Fairings

Fairings derive their name from the English fairs where they were sold or given as prizes from 1850 to 1914. The small figural groups were made from porcelain, and often brightly coloured. Cheap, cheerful and aimed at the popular end of the market, fairings anticipated the saucy humour of the seaside postcard, complete with punning captions. Favourite subjects included marital scenes, canoodling lovers, cats, dogs and children. Events from everyday life, such as a visit to the dentist, are featured and the Crimea and the Franco-Prussian Wars also inspired models. Though English in theme and caption, fairings were in fact made in Germany for export. The principal manufacturer was Conta & Boehme of Possnek. Though the firm's early fairings were unmarked, from the late 1870s models were stamped on the base with a crooked arm holding a dagger, and the pieces were also given an impressed serial number. After 1891 the words 'Made in Germany' were added. Early fairings are often better modelled than later examples. Quality had declined by the end of the century and new products such as Goss and crested china provided increasing competition in the souvenir market. Demand for these German-made items came to an end with the outbreak of WWI.

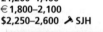

A fairing, entitled 'Don't You Like the Change', impressed marks, German, 19thC, 5½in (14cm) wide.
£1,200–1,400
€1,800–2,100
$2,250–2,600 ✗ SJH

A fairing, entitled 'The Last in Bed to Put Out the Light', 1850–1914, 4in (10cm) wide.
£45–50 / €70–80
$85–95 ⊞ DHJ

A fairing, entitled 'Little Boy Blue', 1850–1914, 4in (10cm) wide.
£90–100 / €135–150
$170–190 ⊞ DHJ

A fairing, entitled 'A Doubtful Case', c1870, 4in (10cm) wide.
£430–480 / €650–720
$800–900 ⊞ Cas

A fairing, entitled 'Don't Awake the Baby', 1850–1914, 4in (10cm) high.
£220–250 / €330–380
$420–470 ⊞ DHJ

A fairing, entitled 'After Marriage', c1870, 2½in (6.5cm) high.
£310–350 / €470–530
$580–650 ⊞ Cas

A fairing, entitled 'Kiss Me Quick', 1850–1914, 4in (10cm) wide.
£135–150 / €200–230
$250–280 ⊞ DHJ

A fairing, entitled 'Alone at Last', c1870, 3½in (9cm) high.
£100–110 / €150–165
$185–210 ⊞ Cas

A fairing, entitled 'A Long Pull and a Strong Pull', 1850–1914, 4in (10cm) high.
£350–400 / €530–600
$650–750 ⊞ DHJ

A fairing, entitled 'Baby's First Steps' by Conta & Boehme, c1870, 4in (10cm) wide.
£220–250 / €330–380
$420–470 ⊞ Cas

A fairing, entitled 'Pluck', c1870, 5½in (14cm) wide.
£165–185 / €250–280
$310–350 ⊞ Cas

A fairing, entitled 'Between Two Stools you Fall to the Ground', c1870, 3½in (9cm) high.
£360–400 / €540–620
$670–750 ⊞ Cas

A fairing, entitled 'Oyster Day', c1870, 3½in (9cm) high.
£110–125 / €165–185
$210–230 ⊞ Cas

A fairing, entitled 'Can You Do This Grandma?', c1870, 4in (10cm) wide.
£310–350 / €470–530
$580–650 ⊞ Cas

▶ **A spill holder fairing,** entitled 'The Welsh Tea Party', c1870, 3½in (9cm) wide.
£30–35 / €45–55
$55–65 ⊞ Cas
Though most fairings were simply decorative, some examples had other purposes, such as match strikers or spill holders.

A fairing, entitled 'Please Sir What Would You Charge to Christen my Doll?', c1870, 4in (10cm) wide.
£310–350 / €470–530
$580–650 ⊞ Cas

A fairing, entitled 'Spoils of War', c1870, 5in (12.5cm) wide.
£125–140 / €190–210
$230–260 ⊞ Cas

A fairing, entitled 'Very Much Frightened', c1870, 3in (7.5cm) high.
£100–110 / €150–165
$185–210 ⊞ Cas

A fairing, entitled 'English Neutrality is Attending the Sick and the Wounded', c1870, 4in (10cm) wide.
£500–600 / €750–900
$940–1,100 ↗ G(L)

A fairing, entitled 'Who Said Rats?', c1870, 3¾in (9.5cm) wide.
£150–170 / €230–260
$280–320 ⊞ Cas

A fairing, entitled 'Who is Coming?', c1870, 3½in (9cm) wide.
£155–175 / €230–260
$290–330 ⊞ Cas

A fairing, entitled 'Checkmate', c1870, 4in (10cm) wide.
£330–370 / €500–560
$620–690 ⊞ Cas

◄ **A fairing,** entitled 'Free and Independent Elections', c1870, 4in (10cm) wide.
£450–500 / €680–750
$840–940 ⊞ Cas

► **A fairing,** by Conta & Boehme of Possnek, entitled 'The Orphans', c1870, 4in (10cm) wide.
£175–195 / €260–290
$330–370 ⊞ Cas

A fairing, entitled 'Hark Tom, Somebody's Coming', c1870, 3in (7.5cm) wide.
£145–160 / €210–240
$270–300 ⊞ Cas

► **A fairing,** entitled 'If Old Age Could!', c1870, 4in (10cm) wide.
£400–450 / €600–680
$750–840 ⊞ Cas

A fairing, entitled 'Ladies of Llangollen', c1870, 6in (15cm) high.
£45–50 / €70–80
$85–95 ⊞ Cas

Figures

A **figural group**, of a milkmaid and a cow, minor restoration, mid-19thC, 7½in (19cm) wide.
£75–85 / €115–130
$140–160 ✗ **G(L)**

A **Minton Parian figure of a classical maiden**, seated beside a heron, entitled 'Solitude', impressed 'Art Union of London 1852' and 'J. Lawlor Sculpt', impressed factory marks, c1853, 19¾in (50cm) high.
£270–320 / €400–480
$500–600 ✗ **RTo**

▶ A **Meissen figure**, entitled 'Envie', German, c1880, 7½in (19cm) high.
£260–290 / €390–440
$490–540 ⊞ **SER**

A **Victorian bisque figural group**, of a young boy and a girl in beach clothing, 11½in (29cm) high.
£30–35 / €45–50
$55–65 ✗ **JAA**

◀ A **Victorian bisque piano baby**, 10in (25.5cm) long.
£200–240
€300–360
$370–440
✗ **DuM**

◀ A **Goldscheider figure of a lady**, monogrammed 'G. J.', Austrian, late 19thC, 13½in (34.5cm) high.
£1,000–1,200 / €1,500–1,800
$1,900–2,250 ✗ **G(L)**

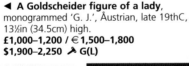

A **pair of bisque piano babies**, model Nos 7480 and 7394, c1900, 7½in (19cm) long.
£190–220 / €290–330
$360–410 ✗ **G(L)**

A **pair of Gerbrüder Heubach bisque figures**, of a Dutch boy and girl, c1920, 8in (20.5cm) high.
£720–800 / €1,100–1,250
$1,350–1,500 ⊞ **YC**

◀ A **bisque wedding cake figure**, symbolizing good luck, 1910–20, 2½in (6.5cm) high.
£65–75 / €100–115
$120–140 ⊞ **CCs**

An Ashtead Pottery figure of a girl with a cane, by Phoebe Stabler, 1920s, 6in (15cm) high.
£800–880
€1,200–1,350
$1,500–1,650 ⊞ MMc

◀ **A Lenci figure of a woman,** entitled 'Il Vento', Italian, 1920s, 16in (40.5cm) high.
£4,250–4,750
€6,400–7,100
$7,900–8,900 ⊞ BD

A Brentleigh Ware figure of a pixie, c1930, 6in (15cm) high.
£75–85 / €115–130
$140–160 ⊞ BEV

A Goebel figure of a girl with flowers, German, 1930s, 3½in (9cm) high.
£110–125 / €170–190
$210–230 ⊞ SCH

A Crown Staffordshire figure of a nymph, 1930s, 5in (12.5cm) high.
£280–330 / €420–500
$520–620 ⊞ SCH

A Goldscheider figure of a girl with a suitcase, Austrian, 1950s, 6in (15cm) high.
£250–280 / €380–420
$470–520 ⊞ SCH

A Bovey Pottery figure, entitled 'Pilot', c1940, 7in (18cm) high.
£170–190 / €260–290
$320–360 ⊞ BRT
The Bovey Pottery Company was founded in Bovey Tracey Devon in 1894. Among the most collectable wares produced by the factory are a series of wartime, military and political figures, designed in the 1940s by Gwyneth Holt and Fenton Wyness. The models were known as 'Our Gang on Parade' and included both the Pilot and the Scotty. The rarest figures in the series however are depictions of Mussolini and Hitler.

A Bovey Pottery figure, entitled 'Scotty', c1940, 7in (18cm) high.
£170–190 / €260–290
$320–360 ⊞ BRT

A Margit Kovacs figure of a woman, impressed marks, Hungarian, c1960, 13½in (34.5cm) high.
£340–400 / €510–600
$630–750 ➶ JAA

A Hummel figure of a boy, entitled 'Retreat to Safety', 1960–72, 4¼in (11cm) high.
£125–145 / €210–220
$240–270 ⊞ TAC

Goss & Crested China

With the development of the Victorian railways and the introduction of bank holidays in 1871, British tourism flourished. Everyone wanted to bring back a memento of their day out, and in the 1880s, W. H. Goss developed a new kind of porcelain for the visitors' market. These were ivory-coloured miniatures, hand-painted with crests of British towns and inspired by artefacts of local interest. Portable and affordable, Goss was a huge success and a host of other companies leapt on the heraldic bandwagon, producing a stream of crested china in the form of everything from animals to new inventions such as aeroplanes. Collecting crested china became a national hobby, peaking in the Edwardian period, when an estimated 90 per cent of British homes contained at least one miniature, and ending with the Depression in the 1930s, when many factories either switched production or shut down.

A selection of teapots, 1905–29, largest 2½in (6.5cm) high.
£8–12 / €12–18
$15–22 ⊞ G&CC

A model of a pig, with London crest, 1920–25, 2½in (6.5cm) high.
£20–25 / €30–35
$35–45 ⊞ JMC

A model of a top hat, with Wembley Exhibition crest, 1920s, 1¾in (4.5cm) high.
£20–25 / €30–35
$35–45 ⊞ JMC

A model of a bulldog, with Progress Blackpool crest, 1920s, 4in (10cm) wide.
£30–35 / €45–50
$55–65 ⊞ HeA

A model of a dog kennel, with Bournemouth crest, 1920s, 3in (7.5cm) high.
£20–25 / €30–35
$35–45 ⊞ HeA

An Arcadian model of a bathing hut, entitled 'Morning Dip', c1910, 4in (10cm) wide.
£30–35 / €45–50
$55–65 ⊞ JUN

An Arcadian model of a black cat on a bicycle, with Lands End crest, 1924–39, 3in (7.5cm) high.
£190–220 / €290–330
$360–410 ⊞ G&CC

A Belleek model of a wine pourer,
with Tramore crest, Second Period,
1891–1926, 2½in (6.5cm) high.
£270–300 / €410–460
$500–560 ⊞ WAA

**A Caledonia model of a curling
stone,** with arms of Ayr, 1910–33,
2¾in (7cm) wide.
£20–25 / €30–35
$35–45 ⊞ G&CC

A Carlton model of a range,
inscribed 'We Kept the Home Fires
Burning till the Boys Came Home',
1914–18, 2¾in (7cm) wide.
£20–25 / €30–35
$35–45 ⊞ G&CC

A Carlton model of a WWI E9 submarine,
with Dublin crest, 1916, 6in (15cm) wide.
£80–90 / €120–135
$150–170 ⊞ BtoB

**A Corona model of a WWI Red
Cross van,** with Margate crest,
c1916, 4in (10cm) wide.
£50–60 / €75–90
$95–110 ⊞ BtoB

A Goss loving cup,
moulded in relief with Mary
Queen of Scots, 1896–28,
4¼in (11cm) high.
£90–100 / €135–150
$170–190 ⊞ G&CC

A Goss Bagware jug,
with arms of Ilfracombe,
1900–28, 2½in (6.5cm) high.
£30–35 / €45–50
$55–65 ⊞ G&CC

**A Goss model of the
Portland lighthouse,**
with Loughborough crest,
1908–28, 4¾in (12cm) high.
£70–80 / €105–120
$130–150 ⊞ G&CC

◄ **A Goss ewer,** with
Blockley crest, 1907–28,
2¼in (5.5cm) high.
£4–8 / €6–12
$8–15 ⊞ G&CC

◀ **A Goss urn,** decorated with four flags of the Allies, 1914–18, 3¾in (9.5cm) high.
£20–25 / €30–35
$35–45 ⊞ G&CC

A Goss model of a WWI tank, with Knaresborough crest, c1915, 4¼in (11cm) wide.
£75–85 / €115–130
$140–160 ⊞ BtoB

A Goss model of a shell, with Blackgang crest, 1920s, 3in (7.5cm) wide.
£30–35 / €45–50
$55–65 ⊞ HeA

A Goss model of a Longships lighthouse, with Walton-on-the-Naze crest, 1920s, 5in (12.5cm) high.
£30–35 / €45–50
$55–65 ⊞ HeA

A Savoy model of a HMS Donner Blitzen tank, 1914–18, 6in (15cm) wide.
£60–70 / €90–105
$110–130 ⊞ G&CC

A Shelley model of a camel, with arms of Blackpool, 1903–23, 4in (10cm) wide.
£20–25 / €30–35
$35–45 ⊞ G&CC

◀ **A Shelley model of a WWI armoured car,** 1915, 5in (12.5cm) wide.
£110–130 / €165–195
$210–240 ⊞ BtoB

A Shelley model of a WWI Red Cross van, model No. 330, with Woolwich crest, c1916, 4in (10cm) wide.
£50–60 / €75–90
$95–110 ⊞ BtoB

◀ **A Willow Art model of an owl,** with Hastings crest, 1920s, 4in (10cm) high.
£50–55 / €75–85
$95–105 ⊞ HeA

T. G. Green

A T. G. Green jug,
decorated with flowers,
1920s, 7½in (19cm) high.
**£80–90 / €120–135
$150–170 ⊞ CAL**

A T. G. Green Polka Dot butter dish,
c1930s, 6in (15cm) diam.
**£30–35 / €45–50
$55–65 ⊞ CAL**

**A T. G. Green Polka Dot coffee
set,** comprising 23 pieces, c1930s,
coffee pot 6in (15cm) wide.
**£135–150 / €200–230
$250–280 ⊞ CAL**

**A T. G. Green coffee cup and
saucer,** decorated with
Physalis pattern, c1930s,
cup 2½in (6.5cm) diam.
**£20–25 / €30–35
$35–45 ⊞ CAL**

**A T. G. Green Cornish Ware milk
jug,** 1930s–50s, 4½in (11.5cm) high.
**£45–50 / €70–80
$85–95 ⊞ CoCo**

◀ **A T. G. Green Blue Domino milk
jug,** 1930s–50s, 4in (10cm) high.
**£75–85 / €115–130
$140–160 ⊞ CHI**

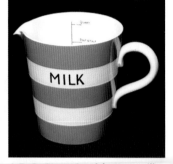

**A T. G. Green Cornish Ware milk
jug,** 1930s–50s, 6in (15cm) high.
**£70–80 / €105–120
$130–150 ⊞ CAL**

Cross Reference
Kitchenware
see pages 269–279

A T. G .Green Cornish Ware jug,
designed by Judith Onions, 1966,
5in (12.5cm) high.
**£35–40 / €50–60
$65–75 ⊞ CAL**

◀ **A T. G. Green Hunt Club pot
stand,** mid-1950s,
6½in (16.5cm) diam.
**£50–60 / €75–90
$95–110 ⊞ CAL**

**A T. G. Green Cornish Ware sugar
shaker,** 1960s, 5½in (14cm) high.
**£25–30 / €40–45
$50–55 ⊞ CAL**

A T. G .Green Cornish Ware marmalade jar, designed by Judith Onions, 1966, 3½in (9cm) high.
£50–55 / € 75–85
$95–105 ⊞ CAL

A T. G. Green Channel Islands storage jar, designed by Judith Onions, 1968, 5½in (14cm) high.
£15–20 / € 22–30
$28–38 ⊞ CAL

A T. G. Green Cornish Ware storage jar, inscribed 'Sugar', 1996–2000, 5in (12.5cm) high.
£25–30 / € 40–45
$50–55 ⊞ CAL

Hornsea

◄ **A Hornsea vase,** c1950, 11in (28cm) high.
£55–65 / € 85–100
$100–120 ⊞ BEV

A Hornsea jardinière, c1950, 7in (18cm) high.
£35–40 / € 50–60
$65–75 ⊞ BEV

◄ **A Hornsea spill vase,** 1950s, 5in (12.5cm) high.
£5–10 / € 9–15
$12–19 ⊞ PrB

A Hornsea Swan Lake jug, 1983–92, 3½in (9cm) high.
£15–20 / € 22–30
$28–38 ⊞ CHI

◄ **A Hornsea Image pepper pot,** 1980, 3in (7.5cm) high.
£15–20 / € 22–30
$28–38 ⊞ CHI

A Hornsea vase, c1970s, 9in (23cm) high.
£30–35 / € 45–50
$55–65 ⊞ LUNA

Japanese Pottery & Porcelain

An Imari porcelain charger, decorated with a *ho-o* bird in a garden, surrounded by a tendril border, 19thC, 13½in (34.5cm) diam.
£170–200 / € 260–300
$320–370 ↗ RTo
Japanese Imari porcelain was first made at Arita in the early 18th century and was shipped from the port of Imari. It was painted in several colours including underglaze blue and dark red, the patterns being influenced by textiles. Imari proved so popular that it was copied throughout China and Europe.

A Kutani tea caddy, signed, late 19thC, 4in (10cm) diameter.
£35–40 / € 50–60
$65–75 ⊞ BAC
Kutani porcelain from Kaga Province is noted for its strong colours in reserved panels on a red patterned ground.

A Satsuma vase, c1880, 13in (33cm) high.
£400–450 / € 600–680
$750–840 ⊞ SAT
Satsuma pottery was made from the early 17th century by Korean potters who had settled in Satsuma on Kyushu Island. Early wares were unpainted; enamels and gilding were then introduced, developing into the most elaborate decorations that covered the whole body of the object. Satsuma-style ware was made in other areas of Japan for the export market.

An Imari charger, printed with flowering branches, damaged, c1900, 12½in (32cm) diam.
£160–190 / € 240–290
$290–360 ↗ SWO

A Satsuma bowl, with an applied figure, painted with Immortals, c1890, 4½in (11.5cm) high.
£100–120 / € 150–180
$185–220 ↗ SWO

A Satsuma koro, with metal-mounted rim and enamelled and gilded decoration, restored, signed, Meiji period 1868–1911, 4¾in (12cm) high.
£400–480 / € 600–720
$750–900 ↗ RTo

A Noritake bottle, decorated with gold and enamel and hand-painted flowers, c1912, 4in (10cm) high.
£110–125 / € 170–190
$210–230 ⊞ BAC

◀ **A Satsuma vase and two plates,** with floral decoration, signed, early 20thC, vase 7in (18cm) high.
£90–100 / € 135–150
$170–190 ⊞ BAC

A Noritake vase, decorated with a mountain scene, marked, c1920, 4in (10cm) high.
£105–120 / €160–180
$195–220 ⊞ DgC

A Noritake trio, marked, c1920.
£30–35 / €45–50
$55–65 ⊞ DgC

A Noritake trio, marked, c1920.
£40–45 / €60–70
$75–85 ⊞ DgC

A Noritake trio, marked, c1920, cup 3in (7.5cm) high.
£40–45 / €60–70
$75–85 ⊞ DgC

A pair of Imari vases, signed, c1920, 6in (15cm) high.
£50–55 / €75–85
$95–105 ⊞ BAC

A Satsuma vase, decorated with wisteria and a landscape, signed, c1920, 6in (15cm) high.
£110–125 / €170–190
$210–230 ⊞ BAC

A Noritake jar and cover, marked, 1920s, 7½in (19cm) high.
£135–150 / €200–230
$250–280 ⊞ DgC

A Kutani model of a dancer, impressed mark, Taisho period, 1912–26, 7in (18cm) high.
£150–165 / €225–250
$280–310 ⊞ BAC

A geisha lithophane cup and saucer, 1930s, cup 2½in (6.5cm) diam.
£30–35 / €45–50
$65–75 ⊞ BAC

Jugs

A Baggerley & Ball pearlware jug, with transfer-printed and painted chinoiserie panels, blue printed mark, painted number '31', 1822–36, 5½in (14cm) high.
£90–100 / €135–150
$170–190 ⚒ PFK

A stoneware jug, possibly Mortlake, applied with hunting scenes, early 19thC, 8¾in (22cm) high.
£460–550 / €690–830
$860–1,000 ⚒ Bea

A Davenport china jug, with gilt and floral decoration, red mark, 1825–50, 1½in (4cm) high.
£80–90 / €120–135
$150–170 ⚒ PFK

A Samuel Alcock Parian jug, probably by Owen Jones, decorated with a geometric Gothic leaf band, pattern No. 3/7427, mid-19thC, 7½in (19cm) high.
£100–120 / €150–180
$185–220 ⚒ WW

An Elsmore & Forster puzzle jug, decorated with Grimaldi the Clown and three cock-fighting scenes, inscribed 'Thomas Jones, 1860', 1853–71, 8¼in (21cm) high.
£160–190 / €240–290
$300–360 ⚒ DN

▶ **A Swansea Pottery Cymro stone jug,** decorated with a Japanese pattern, 19thC, 7½in (19cm) high.
£150–180
€230–270
$290–340 ⚒ PF

A set of three majolica fish jugs, possibly Holdcroft, 1875–1925, largest 11½in (29cm) high.
£120–140 / €180–210
$220–260 ⚒ SWO

A Bishop & Stonier jug, with transfer-printed and hand-coloured decoration, c1890, 6in (15cm) high.
£30–35 / €45–50
$55–65 ⊞ HO

A Copeland Spode harvest jug, with applied decoration, c1894, 6in (15cm) high.
£50–60 / €75–90
$95–110 ⊞ SAT

A Derby jug and sugar bowl, with gilt and floral decoration, 1905, jug 2½in (6.5cm) high.
£50–55 / €75–85
$95–105 ⊞ HER

◀ **A jug,** with hand-painted decoration, the handle in the form of a dragon, c1930, 16in (40.5cm) high.
£200–230 / €300–340
$370–430 ⊞ BEV

A Bishops Art Deco jug, with hand-painted tulips, c1930, 13in (33cm) high.
£105–115 / €160–175
$195–220 ⊞ BEV

A Radford jug, with hand-painted decoration, c1930, 4½in (11.5cm) high.
£80–90 / €120–135
$150–170 ⊞ BEV

An Arthur Wood & Son Smokey the Cat jug, c1930, 8in (20.5cm) high.
£65–75 / €100–115
$120–140 ⊞ BEV

An Arthur Wood & Son Ritz jug, c1934, 8in (20.5cm) high.
£30–35 / €45–50
$55–65 ⊞ SAT

A jug and basin, with hand-painted floral decoration, 1930s, basin 16in (40.5cm) diam.
£75–85 / €115–130
$140–160 ⊞ SAT

A water jug, decorated with a Cecil Aldin dog, some crazing, 1930s, 5¼in (13.5cm) high.
£280–330 / €420–500
$520–620 ⋌ Pott

A jug, with hand-painted decoration, 1940s, 8in (20.5cm) high.
£110–125 / €170–190
$210–230 ⊞ SCH

A Wood's Radford Harvest jug, c1950, 10in (25.5cm) high.
£60–70 / €90–105
$110–130 ⊞ HO

A Golden Shred Golly water jug, 1970s, 6in (15cm) high.
£20–25 / €30–35
$35–45 ⊞ TASV

Limoges

Kaolin, the white china clay used in the manufacture of Limoges porcelain, was discovered in the Limoges region of France in the 18th century. The first porcelain factory (later a subsidiary of Sèvres) opened in the 1770s. By the early 19th century there were over 30 potteries operating in the area, rising to some 48 by the 1920s. Well-known names include Haviland, Guerin, Pouyat and others. Much Limoges porcelain was made for export to the USA, where it was a fashionable wedding present. Although the Great Depression of the 1930s, followed by WWII, severely damaged the prosperity of the industry, Limoges still remains a major centre for the manufacture of porcelain.

A Limoges cup and saucer,
French, signed, c1880,
saucer 5½in (14cm) diam.
£65–75 / € 100–115
$120–140 ⊞ SER

A Rendon Limoges cup and saucer,
French, c1880, cup 3in (7.5cm) diam.
£30–35 / € 45–50
$55–65 ⊞ DEB

◀ **A J. Pouyat Limoges cup and saucer,** French, 1894–1930,
4in (10cm) diam.
£60–70 / € 90–105
$110–130 ⊞ DEB

A Limoges plate, depicting an 18thC lady, French, c1890, 9in (23cm) diam.
£45–50 / € 70–80
$85–95 ⊞ SER

Pâte-sur-pâte

Pâte-sur-pâte is a technique where semi-fluid white slip is applied to porcelain, built up into layers, and a relief design carved on a tinted ground before firing.

A Limoges *pâte-sur-pâte* plaque,
by Marcel Chauffiresse, signed,
c1900, 6 x 4¼in (15 x 11cm).
£190–210 / € 290–320
$360–390 ⊞ SER

A Limoges *pâte-sur-pâte* plaque,
by A. Barriere, depicting the Virgin and Child, signed, c1920,
7¼in (18.5cm) diam.
£110–125 / € 170–190
$210–230 ⊞ SER

A Legrand Limoges coffee cup and saucer, c1920,
cup 2in (5cm) diam.
£35–40 / € 50–60
$65–75 ⊞ DEB

▶ **A Limoges part dinner service,**
comprising 80 pieces, with swag decoration, damaged, c1930.
£300–360 / € 450–540
$560–670 ➹ SWO

Lustreware

A copper lustre jug, the body applied with a pheasant among flowers, damaged and restored, c1830, 10¼in (26cm) high.
£100–120 / €150–180
$185–220 ⚒ TEN

A Sunderland lustre cup and saucer, c1840, cup 4in (10cm) diam.
£20–25 / €30–35
$35–45 ⊞ SER

A Sunderland lustre plaque, inscribed 'Thou God Sees't Me', c1840, 6¾in (17cm) diam.
£200–230 / €300–340
$370–430 ⊞ SER

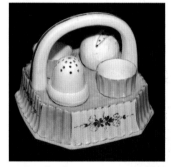

A Moore & Co lustre bowl, decorated with 'The *Agamemnon* in a Storm', a Masonic armorial, the bridge of the River Wear and two panels of verse, 19thC, 11½in (29cm) diam.
£100–120 / €150–180
$185–220 ⚒ WW

A lustre plaque, printed with a frigate, entitled 'Northumberland 74', impressed Dixon mark, 19thC, 8in (20.5cm) wide.
£170–200 / €260–300
$320–370 ⚒ SJH

A Victorian lustre egg cup and cruet set, 5in (12.5cm) square.
£20–25 / €30–35
$35–45 ⊞ POS

◄ **An Arthur Wood & Son lustre Astoria vase,** c1930, 9in (23cm) high.
£35–40 / €50–60
$65–75 ⊞ HO

A lustre vase, by Sicard Weller, decorated with an iridescent glaze, c1910, 6in (15cm) high.
£380–450 / €570–680
$700–840 ⚒ DuM

A Pilkington's Lancastrian lustre vase, c1910, 9½in (24cm) high.
£210–240 / €320–360
$390–450 ⊞ C&W

▶ **A lustre napkin ring,** in the form of a bird with an open beak, c1930, 3in (7.5cm) diam.
£40–45 / €60–70
$75–85 ⊞ BEV

A lustre egg timer, in the form of a duck, German, c1930, 5in (12.5cm) high.
£55–65 / €85–100
$100–120 ⊞ BEV

Majolica

A set of three Victorian majolica jugs, moulded with water lilies and lily pads, largest 9in (23cm) high.
£130–155 / €195–230
$240–290 ♪ PF

A majolica Stilton dish, in the form of a beehive moulded with vine leaves and grapes, 19thC, 13in (33cm) high.
£180–210 / €270–320
$340–390 ♪ HYD

A majolica bust of a young boy, by Brothers Urbach, minor damage, impressed mark, 19thC, 19in (48.5cm) high.
£400–480 / €600–720
$750–900 ♪ JAA

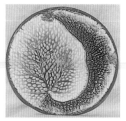

A majolica plate, decorated with a leaf, 19thC, 6½in (16.5cm) diam.
£65–75 / €100–115
$125–150 ♪ DuM

A Palissy-style majolica plate, decorated with a fish, snake, butterfly, shells and ferns, minor damage, Portuguese, 19thC, 4in (10cm) diam.
£110–130 / €165–195
$210–240 ♪ PFK

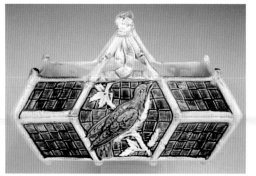

A majolica basket, possibly by Thomas Forrester, decorated in relief with a bird on a branch, 19thC, 9¾in (25cm) wide.
£180–210 / €270–320
$340–390 ♪ SWO

A majolica jug and cover, the handle in the form of a dog, the cover with a barrel finial, slight damage, Portuguese, c1890, 12½in (32cm) high.
£430–510 / €650–770
$800–950 ♪ TEN

Further reading
Miller's Ceramics Buyers Guide,
Miller's Publications, 2000

Five Dunmore Pottery majolica dessert dishes, in the form of vine leaves, impressed mark, Scottish, late 19thC, largest 11in (28cm) wide.
£100–120 / €150–180
$185–220 ♪ PFK

A Victorian majolica flowerpot, decorated with a salmon, 7in (18cm) wide.
£90–105 / €135–160
$170–195 ♪ LAY

▶ **A majolica umbrella stand,** in the form of a stork, Continental, early 20thC, 22¾in (58cm) high.
£190–220 / €290–330
$360–410 ♪ SWO

Maling

Maling (1762–1963) built its success in the 19th century when the company pioneered a mechanized process for the production of commercial ceramics for the food and drink industry, eventually manufacturing most of the jam and marmalade jars used in the UK. In the early 20th century Maling produced a range of hand-crafted decorative ceramics including lustreware and brightly enamelled tube-lined pieces.

A Maling lustre dish, 1930s, 11in (28cm) wide.
£90–100 / € 135–150
$170–190 ⊞ TAC

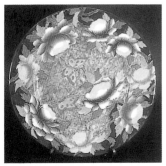

A Maling plate, decorated with Peona pattern, No. 6503, printed mark, impressed '447', 1940s, 11in (28cm) diam.
£110–130 / € 165–195
$210–240 ➤ PFK

A Maling trinket box, 1940s, 5in (12.5cm) wide.
£70–80 / € 105–120
$130–150 ⊞ JFME

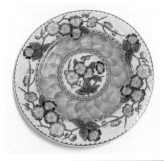

◄ **A Maling plate,** 1948–50, 11in (28cm) diam.
£100–110 / € 150–165
$185–210 ⊞ HeA

A Maling bowl, decorated with Dahlia pattern, c1950, 10in (25.5cm) wide.
£45–50 / € 70–80
$85–95 ⊞ HO

Mason's Ironstone

A Mason's Ironstone vase, decorated with Old School House pattern, impressed mark, c1820, 8¼in (21cm) high.
£380–450 / € 570–680
$710–840 ➤ WW

A Mason's Ironstone sauce tureen and stand, decorated with Japan pattern, the cover with a knop in the form of a dog, slight damage, printed marks, 1825–40, tureen 7¾in (19.5cm) wide.
£260–310 / € 400–470
$490–580 ➤ DN

A Mason's Ironstone water pail, with Oriental decoration, with a wicker handle, 19thC.
£150–180 / € 230–270
$280–340 ➤ JAd

A Mason's Ironstone vase, decorated with exotic birds among foliage, printed marks, 19thC, 12in (30.5cm) high.
£75–90 / € 115–135
$140–170 ➤ GAK

Midwinter

Established in 1910, Midwinter pottery became very successful after WWII, when, inspired by American ceramics, Roy Midwinter introduced a new range of organic shapes and contemporary patterns to British tableware. In recent years 1950s designs by Terence Conran, Hugh Casson and the firm's resident designer, Jessie Tait, have escalated in price, and interest has also grown in Midwinter pottery from the 1960s and 1970s.

A Midwinter coffee pot, designed by Jessie Tait, decorated with Red Domino pattern, 1953, 7in (18cm) high.
£50–60 / €75–90
$95–110 ⊞ RET

A Midwinter cream jug, designed by Hugh Casson, decorated with Riviera pattern, 1954, 2in (5cm) high.
£15–20 / €22–30
$28–38 ⊞ RET

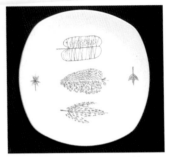

A Midwinter plate, designed by Terence Conran, decorated with Nature Study pattern, 1955, 10in (25.5cm) wide.
£50–55 / €75–85
$95–105 ⊞ CHI

A Midwinter hors d'oeuvre dish, designed by Eve Midwinter, adapted by Jessie Tait, decorated with Bella Vista pattern, c1960, 9in (23cm) diam.
£50–55 / €75–85
$95–105 ⊞ CHI

A Midwinter Fine coffee pot, designed by Eve Midwinter, decorated with Tango pattern, c1969, 8in (20.5cm) high.
£30–35 / €45–50
$55–65 ⊞ CHI

A Midwinter Stonehenge plate, designed by Eve Midwinter, decorated with Summer pattern, 1970s, 10in (25.5cm) diam.
£12–16 / €18–24
$22–30 ⊞ CHI

A Midwinter bowl, designed by Eve Midwinter, decorated with Earth pattern, 1970s, 6½in (16.5cm) diam.
£10–15 / €15–22
$19–28 ⊞ CHI

A Midwinter sugar bowl and cover, designed by Angela Atkinson, decorated with Crocus pattern, 1970s, 4in (10cm) high.
£20–25 / €30–35
$35–45 ⊞ CHI

A Midwinter Stonehenge jug, designed by Jessie Tait, decorated with Nasturtium pattern, 1974–82, 5in (12.5cm) high.
£20–25 / €30–35
$35–45 ⊞ CHI

Minton

A Minton majolica jug, with a mask spout, decorated with stylized flowerheads, 1872, 11in (28cm) high.
£200–240 / €320–360
$370–450 ✗ MAR

A pair of Minton majolica figural candlesticks, each with three cherubs and a gun dog beside them, model No. 657, impressed mark, 1873, 8½in (21.5cm) high.
£950–1,100 / €1,450–1,750
$1,800–2,050 ✗ PFK

A Minton jardinière, decorated with incised foliage and scroll borders, 1878, 12in (30.5cm) high.
£85–95 / €130–145
$160–180 ⊞ G(L)

A Minton majolica vase, modelled as Cupid beside a vase, restored, impressed mark, 1878, 10½in (26.5cm) high.
£500–600 / €750–900
$940–1,100 ✗ PFK

A Minton Seccessionist candlestick, 1890, 6in (15cm) high.
£170–185 / €250–280
$310–350 ⊞ MMc

▶ **A Minton nut dish,** moulded as leaves and nuts, c1910, 9in (23cm) wide.
£30–35 / €45–50
$55–65 ⊞ HO

◀ **A late Victorian Minton model of a dog,** moulded mark, 5½in (14cm) high.
£210–250 / €320–380
$400–470 ✗ G(L)

A Minton two-handled mug, decorated with enamelled flowers and gilding, 1912, 1in (2.5cm) high.
£90–100 / €135–150
$170–190 ⊞ HER

A Minton hors d'oeuvre dish, c1920, 12in (30.5cm) wide.
£70–80 / €105–120
$130–150 ⊞ HO

A Minton vase, No. 42, 1890, 5in (12.5cm) high.
£170–185 / €250–280
$310–350 ⊞ MMc

A Minton Byzantine ware dish, 1930s–40s, 14¼in (36cm) diam.
£70–85 / €110–130
$135–160 ✗ AMB

Moorcroft

William Moorcroft joined the pottery of James Macintyre & Co in Burslem, Staffordshire in 1897. He soon gained a reputation as a talented designer, experimenting with slip trailing and rich jewel-like colours and pioneering the English Art Nouveau style with his famous Florian ware range.

Moorcroft won several major international awards and built up strong links with Liberty & Co, who financed him to leave Macintyre in 1912, enabling him to establish his own pottery. The firm was hugely successful in the 1920s, and William Moorcroft continued to develop the floral and landscape patterns conceived in the Edwardian period, using rich flambé glazes and introducing new lines such as the Powder Blue porcelain range of speckled blue tableware, which continued in production until the 1960s.

After William's death in 1945, his son, Walter Moorcroft, took over the factory and continued the tradition for decorative hand-made pieces, introducing new floral patterns such as Hibiscus, which was based on pressed flowers sent to him from Jamaica. In 1962 Walter's half-brother John Moorcroft joined the company. From the 1980s onwards the family shares were sold and different owners became involved in the business.

Sally Tuffin was chief designer in the 1980s, and in 1992 Rachel Bishop joined the company. The methods pioneered by William Moorcroft 100 years previously continue to be employed today. Modern Moorcroft by various designers attracts many collectors. Highest prices, however, are reserved for the early William Moorcroft pieces, and auction records include £32,900 / €49,400 / $61,500 achieved by Sotheby's for a rare Macintyre Hesperian Carp jardinière and stand.

▶ **A Moorcroft Macintyre Florian ware bowl,** decorated with stylized flowers, slight damage, signed, stamped, painted No. M1685, c1900, 9in (23cm) diam.
£340–400 / €510–600
$640–750 ♣ TRM

A Moorcroft bowl, decorated with Big Poppy pattern, c1920, 6¾in (17cm) high.
£450–500 / €680–750
$840–940 ⊞ PGO

A Moorcroft Powder Blue vase, decorated with Cornflower pattern, c1925, 3½in (9cm) high.
£450–500 / €680–750
$840–940 ⊞ GOv

A Moorcroft salt-glazed dish, decorated with a fish, c1930, 4¼in (11cm) diam.
£300–330 / €450–500
$560–620 ⊞ JFME

▶ **A Moorcroft bowl,** decorated with Pomegranate pattern, with Liberty Tudric pewter cover, impressed marks, signed, c1930, 6in (15cm) wide.
£400–480 / €600–720
$750–900 ♣ SWO

A Moorcroft flambé bowl, decorated with Orchid pattern, impressed marks, c1935, 8¾in (22cm) wide.
£250–300 / €380–450
$470–560 ⚒ **SWO**

A Moorcroft powder bowl, decorated with Pansy pattern, c1935, 5½in (14cm) diam.
£260–310 / €400–470
$490–580 ⚒ **G(L)**

A Moorcroft bowl, decorated with Orchid pattern, impressed marks, signed, c1940, 11in (28cm) diam.
£180–210 / €270–320
$330–390 ⚒ **SWO**

Two Moorcroft Yacht vases, c1997, 9in (23cm) high.
£310–350 / €470–530
$580–650 each ⊞ **MPC**

◄ **A Moorcroft lamp,** decorated with Hibiscus pattern, impressed mark, c1950, 11½in (29cm) high.
£130–150 / €195–220
$240–280 ⚒ **G(L)**

A Moorcroft Year plate, designed by Rachel Bishop, decorated with blackberries, 1998, 8½in (21.5cm) diam.
£70–80 / €105–120
$130–150 ⚒ **G(B)**

Myott

In the 1920s the Staffordshire firm of Myott built up a thriving tableware business. Alongside more traditional designs, the firm became known for a range of adventurous Art Deco shapes that were hand-painted in brilliant colours. Jugs, vases and centrepieces are the most popular wares and the more inventive the shape, the higher the value.

A Myott jug, with hand-painted decoration, c1930, 8in (20.5cm) high.
£100–115 / €150–170
$200–220 ⊞ **BEV**

A Myott vase, with hand-painted decoration, c1930, 8in (20.5cm) high.
£165–185 / €250–280
$310–350 ⊞ **BEV**

A Myott vase, 1930s, 9in (23cm) high.
£270–300 / €400–450
$500–560 ⊞ **JFME**

A Myott vase, with hand-painted decoration, c1930, 8in (20.5cm) high.
£360–400 / €540–600
$670–750 ⊞ **BEV**

Nursery Ware

A Staffordshire creamware plate,
with transfer-printed decoration,
inscribed 'For a Good Girl', c1820,
6in (15cm) diam.
£360–400 / €540–600
$670–750 ⊞ ReN

Three plates, transfer-printed with
Alice in Wonderland illustrations
by John Tenniel, c1900,
largest 5in (12.5cm) wide.
£40–45 / €60–70
$75–85 each ⊞ BtoB

A plate, decorated with a steam train,
inscribed 'All Change' and 'Baby's
Plate', c1910, 7¼in (18.5cm) diam.
£120–135 / €180–200
$220–250 ⊞ BtoB
This plate is decorated with
characters from the children's
books created from the 1890s by
American sisters Florence and
Bertha Upton.

A creamware christening mug,
transfer-printed with initial 'R',
early 19thC, 1½in (4cm) high.
£35–40 / €50–60
$65–75 ➶ PFK

▶ **A Staffordshire plate,** with
transfer-printed decoration within
a moulded alphabet border, c1860,
5in (12.5cm) diam.
£270–300 / €400–450
$500–560 ⊞ ReN

A Swan beaker,
illustrated with the nursery
rhyme 'The Maid was in
the Garden...', 1900–04,
4½in (11.5cm) high.
£60–70 / €90–105
$110–130 ⊞ BtoB

A Staffordshire pearlware plate,
with transfer-printed decoration,
c1840, 7in (18cm) diam.
£250–280 / €380–420
$470–520 ⊞ ReN

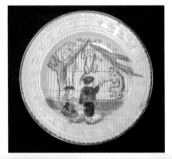

◀ **A bowl,**
with a decorated
border, inscribed
'Porridge',
c1910, 9in
(23cm) diam.
£90–100
€135–150
$170–190
⊞ SMI

A hot water bowl, decorated with Little Bo
Peep illustrations, 1930s–40s, 8in (20.5cm) diam.
£35–40 / €50–60
$65–75 ⊞ LAS

◀ **A Royal Doulton beaker,** decorated with
Cock a Doodle Do pattern, 1920s,
3in (7.5cm) high.
£80–90 / €120–135
$150–170 ➶ Pott

A bowl, decorated with Pinky and Perky, late 1950s, 6½in (16.5cm) diam.
£10–15 / €15–22
$19–28 ⊞ LAS

A Keele Street Pottery mug, decorated with Winnie the Pooh and Christopher Robin, 1960, 4in (10cm) high.
£25–30 / €40–45
$50–55 ⊞ IQ

A Staffordshire mug, decorated with a Thelwell cartoon, 1967, 3in (7.5cm) high.
£15–20 / €22–30
$28–38 ⊞ LAS

▶ **A Washington Pottery mug,** decorated with Joe 90, 1968, 3in (7.5cm) high.
£15–20
€22–30
$28–38 ⊞ RTT

A pair of mugs, one decorated with Sooty, the other with Sweep, 1970s, 3in (7.5cm) high.
£15–20 / €22–30
$28–38 ⊞ LAS

A set of six Midwinter Fashion plates, decorated with nursery rhymes, 1970s, 5in (12.5cm) wide.
£60–70 / €90–105
$110–130 ⊞ LAS

A mug, decorated with Gollies playing cricket, silver crane mark, 1980s, 3½in (9cm) high.
£90–100 / €135–150
$170–190 ⊞ HYP

A teapot, decorated with Tom and Jerry, 1989, 6in (15cm) high.
£10–15 / €15–22
$19–28 ⊞ LAS

Paragon

Paragon China Co was established c1899 as the Star China Co, and was renamed Paragon in 1919. During the interwar years the company produced high-quality tea, coffee, breakfast and dessert china, as well as nursery ware. In 1926, Paragon was commissioned to create china for the nursery of Princess Elizabeth, which initiated a host of royal commissions, including a tea service to celebrate the birth of Princess Margaret Rose. After WWII, Paragon remained well known for its commemorative ware and particularly its royal pieces.

A Paragon mug, decorated with the nursery rhyme 'Hey Diddle Diddle', 1920s, 3½in (9cm) high.
£130–145 / €200–220
$240–270 ⊞ SCH

A Paragon trio, c1930, plate 7in (18cm) diam.
£65–75 / €100–115
$120–140 ⊞ BEV

A Paragon trio, decorated with Crocus pattern, c1930, plate 7in (18cm) diam.
£70–80 / €105–120
$130–150 ⊞ BEV

◀ **A Paragon cup and saucer,** decorated with a floral pattern, c1930, cup 3in (7.5cm) high.
£150–165 / €220–250
$280–310 ⊞ BEV

A Paragon plate, signed 'A. J. Plant', c1939, 8½in (21.5cm) diam.
£80–90 / €120–135
$150–170 ⊞ DEB

A Paragon Patriotic series cup and saucer, entitled 'There will always be an England', 1940, cup 4in (10cm) high.
£125–145 / €200–220
$240–270 ⊞ BtoB

A Paragon Patriotic series cup and saucer, entitled 'Britain shall triumph', 1940, cup 4in (10cm) high.
£65–75 / €100–115
$120–140 ⊞ BtoB

A Paragon Country Lane tea service, comprising six pieces, 1960s, teapot 5in (12.5cm) high.
£125–140 / €190–210
$230–260 ⊞ CHI

A Paragon Michelle jug, 1970s, 5in (12.5cm) high.
£15–20 / €22–30
$28–38 ⊞ CHI

A Paragon Coniston coffee pot, 1970s, 10in (25.5cm) high.
£50–55 / €75–85
$95–105 ⊞ CHI

Poole

◄ A Carter, Stabler & Adams tin-glazed teapot, by Ruth Pavely, c1920, 8in (20.5cm) wide.
£220–250
€340–380
$420–470
⊞ MMc

A Carter, Stabler & Adams plate, with hand-painted decoration, c1921, 7in (18cm) diam.
£80–90 / €120–135
$150–170 ⊞ BAC

A Poole Pottery slipware dish, 1922, 15in (38cm) wide.
£420–470 / €630–710
$790–880 ⊞ MMc

A Carter, Stabler & Adams plate, decorated with Little Miss Muffet, 1920s, 8in (20.5cm) diam.
£165–185 / €250–280
$310–350 ⊞ MMc

A Poole candlestick, by Harold Brownsword, in the form of a cherub, 1928–30, 5in (12.5cm) high.
£270–300 / €410–450
$500–560 ⊞ MMc

▶ A Carter, Stabler & Adams book end, by Harold Brownsword, in the form of an elephant, 1930, 5½in (14cm) wide.
£310–350 / €470–530
$580–650 ⊞ MMc

A Poole Pottery vase, decorated with Blue Bird pattern, No. 335, initialled 'HE', impressed marks, 1930s, 7½in (19cm) high.
£140–160 / €210–240
$260–300 ➹ PFK

A Poole Pottery jug, 1930s, 6in (15cm) high.
£620–690 / €950–1,050
$1,150–1,300 ⊞ MMc

A Poole Pottery vase, 1930s, 8in (20.5cm) high.
£670–750 / €1,000–1,100
$1,250–1,400 ⊞ MMc

A Poole Pottery jug, decorated with stylized flowers, incised '120', painted '170', impressed seal mark, 8¼in (21cm) high.
£130–155 / €195–230
$240–280 ⚒ PFK

◀ **A Poole Pottery vase,** 1940s, 10½in (26.5cm) high.
£270–300
€400–450
$500–560
⊞ **JFME**

▶ **A Poole Pottery bottle vase,** designed by Alfred Read, c1953, 15¼in (39cm) high.
£210–250
€320–380
$400–480
⚒ **Bri**

A Poole Pottery plate, decorated with Trudiana pattern, 1950s, 9in (23cm) diam.
£30–35 / €45–50
$55–65 ⊞ BAC

◀ **A Poole Pottery Charcoal breakfast cup and saucer,** designed by Robert Jefferson, c1965, cup 3in (7.5cm) high.
£10–15 / €15–22
$19–28 ⊞ CHI

A Poole Pottery Delphis charger, probably decorated by Betty Bantten, factory and painter's marks, 1960s, 14½in (37cm) diam.
£340–400 / €510–600
$640–750 ⚒ SJH

A Poole Pottery charger, decorated by Tony Morris, printed and painted marks, 1960s–70s, 10½in (26.5cm) diam.
£240–280 / €360–420
$450–520 ⚒ SWO

A Poole Pottery vase, 1970s, 13in (33cm) high.
£70–80 / €105–120
$130–150 ⚒ AMB

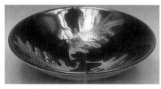

A Poole Pottery charger, decorated with autumn leaves, early 1970s, 13¼in (33.5cm) diam.
£20–25 / €30–35
$35–45 ⚒ AMB

◀ **A Poole Pottery Aegean vase,** decorated with a jousting knight, 1970s, 12¾in (32.5cm) diam.
£50–60 / €75–90
$95–110 ⚒ WilP

Portmeirion

In the 1950s Susan Williams-Ellis started to design ceramics for the gift shop in Portmeirion, the famous holiday village in Wales created by her father. Manufactured in Stoke-on-Trent, her designs were so popular that Susan and her husband took over the Gray's and Kirkham's factories and from 1962 traded as Portmeirion Potteries. Portmeirion became extremely fashionable. The tall cylinder shape of cups and coffee pots captured the streamlined look of the swinging sixties, and patterns were varied and imaginative. Totem (1963), a raised decoration inspired by Victorian tiles, was an immediate best seller, spawning other embossed lines and establishing the success of the company.

In the 19th century, Kirkham's had produced pot lids and other printed wares. Susan discovered their original copper plates and used them to create black and white china that epitomized pop art style and the trend for Victorian revivalism. The Greek Key pattern was another major success story, based on a Kirkham's border for Victorian pub barrels and grocers' jars, it was translated onto coffee sets and tableware and produced in gold from 1968. Designs were drawn from a range of different sources, from Islamic pottery to astrological drawings.

In 1971, Susan and her husband began collecting antiquarian, botanical and natural history books. The following year they introduced the design Botanic Garden, still in production today and now considered a design classic.

A Portmeirion tea caddy, decorated with Tiger Lily pattern, c1962, 4in (10cm) diam.
£125–140 / €190–210
$230–260 ⊞ CHI

A Portmeirion cheese dish, decorated with Totem pattern, c1963, 4in (10cm) high.
£150–165 / €220–250
$280–310 ⊞ CHI

A Portmeirion coffee pot, decorated with Totem pattern, c1963, 12in (30.5cm) high.
£45–50 / €70–80
$85–95 ⊞ CHI

A Portmeirion storage jar, designed by Susan Williams-Ellis, c1963, 5in (12.5cm) high.
£12–16 / €18–24
$22–30 ⊞ TAC

A Portmeirion jam pot, decorated with Totem pattern, c1963, 4in (10cm) high.
£50–55 / €75–85
$95–105 ⊞ CHI

◄ **Two Portmeirion storage jars,** decorated with Tivoli pattern, c1964, 6in (15cm) high.
£65–75 / €100–115
$120–140 ⊞ CHI

► **A set of three Portmeirion storage jars,** designed by Susan Williams-Ellis, decorated with Greek Key pattern, 1960s, tallest 5½in (14cm) high.
£20–25 / €30–35
$35–45 ⊞ TAC

A Portmeirion apothecary jar, decorated with Dolphin pattern, c1965, 8in (20.5cm) high.
£125–140 / € 190–210
$230–260 ⊞ CHI

A Portmeirion rolling pin, decorated with Magic City pattern, c1966, 13in (33cm) long.
£100–110 / € 150–165
$185–210 ⊞ CHI

A Portmeirion coffee pot, decorated with Greek Key pattern, c1968, 13in (33cm) high.
£65–75 / € 100–115
$120–140 ⊞ CHI

A Portmeirion mug, inscribed 'Back in 10 Minutes', 1960s, 4in (10cm) high.
£20–25 / € 30–35
$35–45 ⊞ CHI

Three Portmeirion plates, decorated with Velocipedes pattern, c1968, largest 10in (25.5cm) diam.
£25–30 / € 40–45
$50–55 each ⊞ CHI

A Portmeirion mug, decorated with Phoenix pattern, 1960s, 5in (12.5cm) high.
£15–20 / € 22–30
$28–38 ⊞ CHI

A Portmeirion mug, inscribed 'Britain Into Europe', 1973, 4in (10cm) high.
£25–30 / € 40–45
$50–55 ⊞ CHI

A Portmeirion duck tureen, by Susan Williams-Ellis, 1975–83, 10in (25.5cm) wide.
£90–100 / € 135–150
$170–190 ⊞ CHI

A Portmeirion mug, decorated with Magic Garden pattern, 1970, 5in (12.5cm) high.
£15–20 / € 22–30
$28–38 ⊞ CHI

◀ **Two Portmeirion plates,** decorated with Botanic Garden pattern, 1970s, 10in (25.5cm) diam.
£20–25
€ 30–35
$35–45 each
⊞ CHI

A Portmeirion Parmesan pot, designed by Susan Williams-Ellis, decorated with Botanic Garden pattern, 1975–82, 5½in (14cm) wide.
£6–10 / € 9–15
$12–19 ⊞ TAC

A Portmeirion bottle, decorated with Botanic Garden pattern, 1970s, 11in (28cm) high.
£50–60 / € 75–90
$95–110 ⊞ CHI

Pot Lids

'High Life', by F. & R. Pratt, c1850, 3¼in (8.5cm) diam.
£50–60 / €75–90
$95–110 ♪ SJH

A pot lid, by F. &. R. Pratt, printed with a French street scene, c1850, 4¾in (12cm) diam.
£45–50 / €70–80
$85–95 ♪ SJH

'Christmas Eve', No. 238, c1851, 3in (7.5cm) diam.
£190–220 / €290–330
$360–410 ♪ SAS

'Allied Generals', No. 168, c1854, 4in (10cm) diam.
£140–165 / €210–250
$260–310 ♪ SAS

▶ **'Wimbledon, July 1860'**, No. 223, c1860, 4in (10cm) diam.
£100–120 / €150–180
$185–220 ♪ SAS

'Children Sailing Boats in a Tub', No. 263, c1855, 3in (7.5m) diam.
£75–85 / €115–130
$140–160 ♪ SAS

'Bear, Lion and Cock', No. 19, c1855, 3in (7.5m) diam.
£190–220 / €290–330
$360–410 ♪ SAS

'HRH The Prince of Wales Visiting Tomb of Washington', No. 263, c1861, 4in (10cm) diam.
£110–130 / €165–195
$200–240 ♪ SAS

'Rifle Contest Wimbledon 1864', by F. & R. Pratt, in a mahogany frame, 4in (10cm) diam.
£125–150 / €200–230
$240–280 ♪ GAK

Condition

The condition is absolutely vital when assessing the value of a collectable. Damaged pieces on the whole appreciate much less than perfect examples. However, a rare desirable piece may command a high price even when damaged.

'Rimmels Cherry Tooth Paste',
No. 126, 1865, 3in (7.5cm) diam.
£180–210 / €270–320
$330–390 ⚲ SAS

'Shells', 1865, 5in (12.5cm) diam.
£20–25 / €30–35
$35–45 ⚲ SAS

**'L' Exposition Universelle de
1867'**, c1867, 4in (10cm) diam.
£80–95 / €120–140
$150–180 ⚲ SAS

◄ **'James Atkinson's Bears Grease'**,
1880–1920, 2½in (6.5cm) diam.
£65–75 / €100–115
$120–140 ⚲ BBR

'Trouchet's Corn Cure',
1880–1920, 2in (5cm) diam.
£50–60 / €75–90
$95–110 ⚲ BBR

'Genuine Bears Grease',
1890–1900, 3¾in (9cm) diam.
£850–1,000 / €1,300–1,550
$1,600–1,900 ⚲ BBR

Bear's grease

Bear's grease, a cosmetic preparation for the hair, was popular with gentlemen from the 17th century onwards, resulting in the slaughter of thousands of Russian bears. The leading British manufacturer from 1799 to 1934 was James Atkinson of Old Bond Street, London, but there were many other companies, all of whom produced their own packaging, which was often decorated with bear pictures. These are the most consistently collected pot lids, hence the spiralling prices of rare examples.

'Bale's Mushroom Savoury',
1880–1920, 3½in (9cm) diam.
£110–130 / €165–195
$200–240 ⚲ BBR

Further reading

*Miller's Bottles & Pot Lids:
A Collector's Guide,*
Miller's Publications, 2002

▶ **'Rowland's Otto of Rose Cold
Cream'**, c1900, 3in (7.5cm) diam.
£30–35 / €45–50
$55–65 ⊞ YT

**'Burgess's Genuine Anchovy
Paste'**, c1910, 4in (10cm) diam.
£35–40 / €50–60
$65–75 ⊞ YT

Quimper

A Quimper bagpipe dish, 20thC, 8¾in (22cm) wide.
£55–65 / €85–100
$100–120 ⊞ SER

▶ **A Quimper cup and saucer,** by Paul Fouillen, 1930s, 6in (15cm) high.
£20–25 / €30–35
$35–45 ⊞ SER
Paul Fouillen trained at the HB factory in the early 1920s before establishing his own pottery business.

A HB Quimper jug, c1940, 6¼in (16cm) high.
£45–50 / €70–80
$85–95 ⊞ SER
In 1690 Jean-Baptiste Bousquet started a pottery in Quimper, France, producing simple utilitarian pottery and clay pipes. The firm was successful and expanded into more decorative ware, including faïence. Eventually it was taken over by family descendants called de la Hubaudière and became known as the HB factory.

A pair of Quimper clogs, c1920, 3½in (9cm) long.
£45–50 / €70–80
$85–95 ⊞ SER

A Quimper butter cooler, c1940, 5in (12.5cm) high.
£45–50 / €70–80
$85–95 ⊞ SER

▶ **A Quimper bowl,** 1943–68, 7in (18cm) wide.
£25–30 / €40–45
$50–55 ⊞ SER

A Quimper-style wall pocket, decorated with a lady carrying a basket, 1920s, 9¾in (25cm) high.
£40–45 / €60–70
$75–85 ⚒ LF

A Quimper udder vase, c1940, 5in (12.5cm) high.
£45–50 / €70–80
$85–95 ⊞ SER

A Quimper plate, c1940, 10in (25.5cm) diam.
£45–50 / €70–80
$85–95 ⊞ SER

Royal Copenhagen

A Royal Copenhagen Flora Danica wine cooler, decorated with flowers, c1920, 4½in (11.5cm) high.
£210–250 / €320–380
$400–480 ➤ Bea

A Royal Copenhagen model of a pair of geese, c1961, 8in (20.5cm) wide.
£320–360 / €480–540
$600–670 ⊞ PSA

A pair of Royal Copenhagen models of bears, by Knud Kyhn, 1960s, 3in (7.5cm) high.
£65–75 / €100–115
$120–140 each ⊞ MARK

▶ **A Royal Copenhagen faïence dish,** 1960s, 6½in (16.5cm) square.
£35–40 / €50–60
$65–75 ⊞ MARK

A Royal Copenhagen figure of a herder with a dog, c1945, 8in (20.5cm) high.
£190–210 / €290–320
$350–390 ⊞ PSA

A Royal Copenhagen figure of a faun on a turtle, c1962, 4in (10cm) high.
£145–160 / €220–250
$270–300 ⊞ PSA

A Royal Copenhagen Marselis vase, by Nils Thorsson, printed marks, 1950s, 10½in (26.5cm) high.
£140–165 / €210–250
$260–310 ➤ SWO

A Royal Copenhagen figure of a girl with a doll, c1961, 5in (12.5cm) high.
£145–160 / €220–240
$270–300 ⊞ PSA

A Royal Copenhagen plate, entitled 'Hare in Winter', 1971, 7¼in (18.5cm) diam.
£10–15 / €15–22
$19–28 ⊞ HEI

Royal Winton

A Royal Winton
Byzantaware lustre vase,
1920s, 7in (18cm) high.
**£85–95 / €130–145
$160–180 ⊞ SCH**

**A Royal Winton jam
pot,** in the form of a
wishing well, with hand-
painted decoration,
c1930, 4in (10cm) diam.
**£165–185 / €250–280
$310–350 ⊞ BEV**

A Royal Winton jug,
decorated with Tartan
pattern, c1930,
5in (12.5cm) high.
**£100–115 / €150–170
$190–210 ⊞ BEV**

**A Royal Winton lustre
vase,** with hand-painted
decoration, 1930s,
9in (23cm) high.
**£210–240 / €320–360
$400–450 ⊞ SCH**

**A Royal Winton lustre
vase,** decorated with
flowers, a fairy and a
spider's web, 1930s,
8½in (21.5cm) high.
**£300–330 / €450–500
$560–620 ⊞ SCH**

A Royal Winton lustre charger,
with hand-painted floral decoration,
1936, 12in (30.5cm) diam.
**£310–350 / €470–530
$580–650 ⊞ SCH**

▶ **A Royal Winton trio,** 1930s,
saucer 5¾in (14.5cm) diam.
**£15–20 / €22–30
$28–38 ⊞ HEI**

A Royal Winton jam pot, in the form of a
Pekingese dog, 1930s, 5in (12.5cm) wide.
**£160–180 / €240–270
$300–340 ⊞ SCH**

Cross Reference
Chintzware
see page 94

Chintzware
see page 94

**A Royal Winton cheese/butter
dish,** in the form of a castle on a
hill, 1930s, 7in (18cm) high.
**£300–330 / €450–500
$560–620 ⊞ SCH**

◀ **A Royal
Winton preserve
pot,** in the form
of a cottage,
1930s, 5in
(12.5cm) high.
**£145–160
€220–240
$270–300
⊞ SCH**

**A Royal Winton musical
Toby jug,** plays 'Just A
Wee Deoch-an-Doris',
1940s, 7in (18cm) high.
**£360–400 / €540–600
$670–750 ⊞ SCH**

Shelley

Shelley, founded as Wileman & Co in 1853 and later using the trade name Foley, became known as Shelley in 1925, although the Shelley stamp had been in use from around 1910. The firm produced a range of inventive, high-quality ceramics in the 1920s and 1930s.

Shelley Art Deco tea ware is much sought after by collectors. Famous cup shapes include Vogue and Mode (both with solid triangular handles), Eve (with an open triangular handle), Regent (with an open circular handle), and the best-selling Queen Anne shape, with scalloped, octagonal panels and an upward curving open handle. Solid handles were hard to hold, resulting in short production runs, which makes these more uncomfortable cups particularly collectable.

Other popular interwar lines include chintz ware, lustreware and Harmony ware – a colourful streaky pattern, said to have been inspired by accident when a pottery decorator dropped some paint. Shelley was also known for nursery ware commissioned from such designers as Mabel Lucie Attwell and Hilda Cowham.

A Shelley Intasario vase, c1900, 9in (23cm) high.
£260–290 / €390–440
$490–540 ⊞ JFME

▶ **A Shelley Cecil jelly mould,** 1920–30, 8in (20.5cm) diam.
£35–40 / €50–60
$65–75 ⊞ HO

A Shelley jug, decorated with Mason pattern, c1910, 6in (15cm) high.
£165–185 / €250–280
$310–350 ⊞ BET

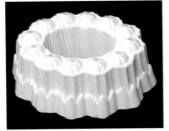

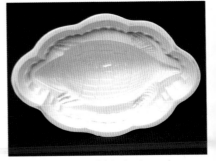

A Shelley jelly mould, in the form of an armadillo, 1912–25, 7in (18cm) wide.
£210–230 / €310–350
$390–430 ⊞ BS

Shelley was well known for its ceramic jelly and blancmange moulds. By the 1920s the company was producing some 50 different moulds, many inspired by Victorian copper examples. These ranged from traditional castellated designs (some of which were named after famous London hotels, such as the Ritz, Carlton and Cecil) to animals, including rabbits, hens, swans, crayfish and even an armadillo. These came in different sizes and are sought after by both kitchenware and Shelley collectors.

A Shelley dish, decorated with birds among sprigs and foliage, printed mark, c1920, 9½in (24cm) diam.
£100–120 / €150–180
$185–220 ➢ GAK

A Shelley teapot and cream jug, by Mabel Lucie Attwell, in the form of animals, c1926, teapot 7in (18cm) high.
£360–430 / €540–650
$670–800 ➢ BBR

A Shelley Harmony vase, c1930, 6in (15cm) wide.
£75–85 / €115–130
$140–160 ⊞ BET

A Shelley toast rack, decorated with Wild Flowers pattern, c1930, 5in (12.5cm) wide.
£125–140 / €190–210
$230–260 ⊞ BEV

A Shelley Eve tea service, comprising 37 pieces, some damage, pattern No. U11952, 1930s, teapot 4¾in (12cm) high.
£320–380 / €480–570
$600–710 ↗ SWO

A Shelley Harmony toast rack, 1930s, 5in (12.5cm) wide.
£35–40 / €50–60
$65–75 ⊞ TAC

A Shelley Volcano Harmony vase, 1930s, 7in (18cm) wide.
£50–55 / €75–85
$95–105 ⊞ HO

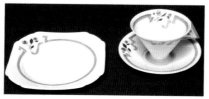

A Shelley Vogue trio, decorated with green J pattern, No. 11740, 1930s, cup 4in (10cm) high.
£270–300 / €400–450
$500–560 ⊞ SCH

A Shelley Queen Anne tea service, for six places, printed and painted with floral decoration, printed mark, No. 723 404, 1930s.
£200–240 / €300–360
$370–450 ↗ L&E

▶ **A Shelley Harmony vase,** No. 946, 1930s, 5in (12.5cm) high.
£25–30 / €40–45
$50–55 ⊞ HeA

A Shelley Regent tea service, comprising 21 pieces, pattern No. W12207/B, 1930s.
£170–200 / €260–300
$320–370 ↗ G(L)

Shelley wares have a printed back stamp and a painted number which can be used to identify the date when the pattern was first produced. Some pieces also carry a design registration number that indicated the year in which the shape or pattern was officially recorded in order to prevent copying.

▶ **A Shelley Harmony vase,** 1930s, 5in (12.5cm) high.
£80–90 / €120–135
$150–170 ⊞ HeA

A Shelley lamp, decorated with Daffodil pattern, 1930s, 9in (23cm) high.
£180–200 / €270–300
$340–370 ⊞ BEV

A Shelley Harmony vase, 1930s, 7in (18cm) high.
£25–30 / €40–45
$50–55 ⊞ HEI

Staffordshire

A Staffordshire figure of a female gardener, repaired, late 18thC, 8¾in (22cm) high.
£80–95 / €120–145 $150–180 ⚒ G(L)

A Staffordshire figure of a boy with a squirrel, early 19thC, 6¼in (16cm) high.
£280–330 / €420–500 $520–620 ⚒ G(L)

A pair of Staffordshire models of spaniels, 19thC, 8in (20.5cm) high.
£50–60 / €75–90 $95–110 ⚒ G(L)

◀ **A Staffordshire dish and cover,** modelled as a hen, 19thC, 6½in (16.5cm) high.
£350–420 €530–630 $650–780 ⚒ DA

A Staffordshire spill vase, modelled as a Biblical figural group, 19thC, 12in (30.5cm) high.
£50–60 / €75–90 $95–110 ⚒ GAK

▶ **A Staffordshire figural group of a woman and child,** inscribed 'Widow', some damage, early 19thC, 8½in (21.5cm) high.
£60–70 / €90–105 $110–130 ⚒ G(L)

A Staffordshire model of a castle, 19thC, 9in (23cm) high.
£50–60 / €75–90 $95–110 ⚒ G(L)

A Staffordshire model of a deer, attributed to Walton, some damage, early 19thC, 7½in (19cm) high.
£150–180 / €230–270 $280–330 ⚒ G(L)

▶ **A Staffordshire money box,** modelled as a cottage flanked by standing figures, early 19thC, 5in (12.5cm) high.
£180–210 / €270–320 $340–390 ⚒ PFK

A Staffordshire figural group, probably of Christ and Mary Magdalene, early 19thC, 5½in (14cm) high.
£135–160 / €200–240 $250–300 ⚒ GAK

A Staffordshire group of musicians, surrounded by farmyard animals, c1810, 8¼in (21cm) high.
£310–350 / €470–530
$580–650 ⊞ SER

A Staffordshire pearlware figure of a girl leaning against an urn, by F. & J. Pratt, c1815, 6¾in (17cm) high.
£410–450 / €620–680
$770–850 ⊞ SER

A Staffordshire spill vase, modelled as a sheep and a lamb, c1815, 5¼in (13.5cm) high.
£260–290 / €390–440
$490–540 ⊞ SER

A Victorian Staffordshire model of Mother Goose, 7¼in (18.5cm) high.
£90–105 / €135–160
$170–195 ↗ HOLL

▶ **A pair of Victorian Staffordshire models of sheep,** 1½in (4cm) high.
£220–260 / €330–390
$410–490 ↗ CHTR

A Victorian Staffordshire model of a bird, and a nest, 8½in (21.5cm) high.
£320–380 / €480–570
$600–710 ↗ G(L)

A Victorian Staffordshire group of a milkmaid and a cow, 8¼in (21cm) high.
£170–200 / €250–300
$320–380 ↗ HOLL

◀ **A Victorian Staffordshire figure of St Luke,** beside a calf, some damage, 7½in (19cm) high.
£90–105 / €135–160
$170–200 ↗ G(L)

A Victorian model of a greyhound, carrying a dead hare, repaired, 9½in (24cm) high.
£60–70 / €90–105
$110–130 ↗ G(L)

▶ **A Victorian Staffordshire model of a zebra,** 5in (12.5cm) high.
£40–45 / €60–70
$75–85 ↗ HOLL
With the rise of zoological gardens in the 19th century, exotic animals became a favourite subject with Staffordshire potters. Zebras could easily be produced by giving a horse model a stripey coat.

A Staffordshire vase, modelled as a cow beside a fence, c1840, 4in (10cm) high.
£300–330 / €450–500
$560–620 ⊞ SER

A Staffordshire figure of Columbine, attributed to Thomas Parr, c1845, 5½in (14cm) high.
£135–150 / €200–230
$250–280 ⊞ SER

▶ **A Staffordshire figural group,** of children bird-nesting, c1850, 8in (20.5cm) high.
£300–350 / €450–530
$560–650 ⊞ SER

A Staffordshire figure of Elizabeth Barrett Browning, holding her dog Flush, c1850, 9in (23cm) high.
£210–240 / €320–360
$400–450 ⊞ SER

A Staffordshire figure of George Gordon-Cumming, standing on a lion, c1850, 15¼in (38.5cm) high.
£290–320 / €430–480
$540–600 ⊞ SER
Staffordshire figures often represented celebrities of the day. George Gordon-Cumming (1820–66) was a Scottish traveller and sportsman, famously known as the 'Lion Hunter'. His collection of hunting trophies from South Africa was shown at the Great Exhibition of 1851.

A Staffordshire figural group of Fenella and Masaniello, c1850, 14in (35.5cm) high.
£250–280 / €380–420
$470–520 ⊞ SER
Fenella and Masaniello are the heroes of Daniel François Espirit Auber's opera *The Mute Girl of Patici* (1828).

◀ **A Staffordshire group of Darby and Joan,** c1860, 11in (28cm) high.
£260–290 / €390–440
$490–540 ⊞ SER
Darby and Joan first appeared in a ballad written by Henry Woodfall in 1735 celebrating the loving relationship of John Darby and his wife. The names subsequently became a generic expresson for a settled and content couple.

A Staffordshire bust of William Shakespeare, 1860–70, 8¾in (22cm) high.
£200–220 / €300–330
$370–410 ⊞ SER

A pair of Staffordshire inkwells, modelled as greyhounds on cushions, 1850–1900, 6in (15cm) high.
£180–210 / €270–320
$340–390 ⚲ WW

A pair of Staffordshire models of cats, c1900, 8in (20.5cm) high.
£110–130 / €165–195
$200–240 ⚲ WW

SylvaC

SylvaC was produced by the Staffordshire firm of Shaw & Copestake (1894–1982). The firm began making small animal figures in the late 1920s. The trade name SylvaC was used from 1936 and was taken from the firm's Sylvan works factory, with the final 'C ' added for Copestake. SylvaC animals were very popular. Famous lines included rabbits (produced for over 40 years in different colours and sizes),

dogs (over 200 different designs) and a wide range of other creatures from squirrels to bears. The pottery also produced household goods: vases, jugs, wall pockets and covered jars, often decorated with moulded forms. As well as animals, popular subjects included pixies and natural and floral themes. Most SylvaC is impressed on the base with a model number, the company name and 'England'.

A SylvaC model of a squirrel, No. 1144, 1930s, 8in (20.5cm) high.
£80–90 / €120–135
$150–170 ⊞ JFME

A SylvaC jug, moulded with an Egyptian pattern, No. 829, 1930s, 8in (20.5cm) high.
£70–80 / €105–120
$130–150 ⊞ JFME

A SylvaC jug, moulded with a floral pattern, 1930s, 8in (20.5cm) high.
£130–145 / €195–220
$240–270 ⊞ JFME

◄ **A SylvaC model of a poodle,** 1940s, 3½in (9cm) high.
£45–50 / €70–80
$85–95 ⊞ JFME

A SylvaC model of a polar bear, 1940s, 6in (15cm) wide.
£50–55 / €75–85
$95–105 ⊞ JFME

A SylvaC model of a lamb, 1940s, 4in (10cm) high.
£50–60 / €75–90
$95–110 ⊞ JFME

◄ **A SylvaC model of a dog,** 1940s, 6½in (16.5cm) high.
£80–90 / €120–135
$150–170 ⊞ JFME

◄ **A SylvaC jug,** modelled as an acorn, the handle in the form of a squirrel, No. 1958, some damage, 1950s, 7½in (19cm) high.
£15–20 / €22–30
$28–38 ⊞ HEI
If this jug were in perfect condition it could be worth £30–35 / €45–50 / $55–65.

Teapots

Teapots are a favourite collecting area. When tea was first imported from China in the second half of the 17th century it was expensive and heavily taxed. A pound of tea cost the equivalent of a week's wages for a craftsman. The new drink was the preserve of the wealthy, and the precious leaves were kept in the drawing room, locked up in finely crafted caddies.

The first British teapot, made from silver, is said to have been produced c1670. In Asia tea was brewed in bowls and the early ceramic teapots used in the West were inspired by Chinese wine pots. In the 18th century taxes were lifted and tea became increasingly popular, stimulating demand for ceramic teapots, with potteries such as Whielden and Wedgwood supplying designs in the latest fashionable shapes. The growing need for affordable tea ware also helped stimulate the development of transfer-printed pottery. By the 19th century, the teapot was a standard item in every home. Tea was being imported from India and Ceylon (Sri Lanka) and had become Britain's national drink. Annual consumption grew from around 1½lbs (70g) per head in the 1800s to 6lbs (2.75kg) in 1900. By 1930 it had reached a record high of 10lbs (4.5kg) per capita – the equivalent of five cups a day for every man, woman and child in Britain.

The interwar years were the golden age of tea drinking with the development of Lyons Corner Houses and tea dances. Pots were produced in every imaginable style, from Art Deco 'tea-for-two' sets for grown-up breakfast in bed to novelty designs for the nursery tea table. The growing popularity of coffee after WWII affected tea consumption, which never again reached such leafy heights, and the introduction of the tea bag, enabling tea to be made in a mug, reduced the need for a range of teapots in the home.

A Whieldon teapot, 18thC, 7in (18cm) wide.
£290–340 / €440–530
$540–650 ➤ SJH

▶ **A Sèvres teapot,** 19thC, 5¼in (13.5cm) high.
£95–110 / €145–165
$180–210 ➤ Gam

A New Hall teapot, pattern No. 195, early 19thC.
£120–140 / €180–210
$220–260 ➤ DA

A Whieldon creamware teapot, slight damage, c1770, 4in (10cm) high.
£160–190 / €240–290
$300–360 ➤ SWO

A black basalt teapot, 1790–1800, slight damage, 10in (25.5cm) wide.
£60–70 / €90–105
$110–130 ➤ PFK

A Chinese export teapot, 19thC, 5½in (14cm) high.
£80–90 / €120–135
$150–170 ➤ COBB

◀ **A Yorkshire pottery Bachelor teapot,** c1820, 2½in (6.5cm) high.
£175–195 / €260–290
$330–370 ⊞ ReN

A teapot, possibly Hackwood, c1830, 6in (15cm) wide.
£175–195 / €260–290
$330–370 ⊞ ReN

A Foley teapot, by Charles Wileman, 1895–1900, 9in (23cm) wide.
£120–135 / €180–200
$220–250 ⊞ BEV

A Copeland Spode teapot, commemorating Queen Victoria's Diamond Jubilee, 1897, 8in (20.5cm) high.
£470–530 / €700–800
$880–990 ⊞ H&G

A nursery teapot, illustrating the nursery rhyme 'Where Are You Going To My Pretty Maid?', c1920, 8in (20.5cm) wide.
£140–155 / €210–240
$260–290 ⊞ BEV

A teapot, decorated with 'Halt Near Ruins' and 'Cows in Stream Near Ruins', restored, c1870, 4¾in (12cm) high.
£40–45 / €60–70
$75–85 ✈ SAS

A Foley teapot, by Charles Wileman, 1895–1900, 9in (23cm) wide.
£165–185 / €250–280
$310–350 ⊞ BEV

A Staffordshire bargeware teapot, inscribed 'To Hetty from Joshua 1887', the cover with a teapot finial, late 19thC, 12in (30.5cm) high.
£210–250 / €310–370
$390–460 ✈ CAG

A Belleek teapot, decorated with Hawthorn pattern, printed and impressed marks, First Period, 1863–96, 4¼in (11cm) high.
£160–190 / €240–290
$300–360 ✈ SWO

An earthenware teapot, commemorating Queen Victoria's Diamond Jubilee and advertising Tower Tea, 1897, 6in (15cm) high.
£155–175 / €260–290
$330–370 ⊞ H&G

A Clews teapot, modelled as an artillery gun, printed mark, early 20thC, 6in (15cm) wide.
£20–25 / €30–35
$35–45 ✈ G(L)

Buying teapots

Always check condition of teapots. Look for staining and crazing and remember that lids are particularly vulnerable to damage.

◄ **A Johnson teapot and stand,** decorated with enamels and gilding, c1920, 7in (18cm) high.
£60–70 / €90–105
$110–130 ⊞ SAT

A **Sadler teapot**, modelled as a racing car, with OKT42 number plate, c1930, 9in (23cm) wide.
£200–230 / €300–340
$380–430 ⊞ BEV
First produced in 1937, Sadler's Racing Car was one of the most popular novelty teapot designs of the day. According to London Art Deco ceramics dealer Beverley, this teapot has been found in over 42 different colourways, and value depends largely on rarity of the colour. Up until 1939 teapots were finished with platinum lustre, were given an OKT42 number plate, and were marked underneath 'Made in England registered number 820236'. The most common colours are cream, yellow and green, and rarer variations include shades of blue, black, grey, pink and maroon. Post-war chrome plating was replaced by a sponged, mottled glaze, the number plate was left off and pots were backstamped with the Sadler name and mark. These later models tend to command lower prices. Manufacture ceased in 1952, although modern reproductions have also been made. 'Spouts tend to be more elongated on the newer versions,' advises Beverley, 'and if you can't read the registration mark properly, it could well be a reproduction.'

A **General Household Utilities teapot**, commemorating the Coronation of King George VI and Queen Elizabeth, 1937, 6in (15cm) high.
£220–250 / €330–380
$410–470 ⊞ H&G

A **Sudlow's teapot**, modelled as an aeroplane, c1930, 9in (23cm) wide.
£1,050–1,200 / €1,600–1,800
$2,000–2,250 ⊞ BEV
Aeroplane teapots are rare, largely because of the fragility of the design. The winged lid is easily damaged, which not only makes surviving examples rare but deterred retailers from stocking these novelty pots in the first place, thus limiting the number produced. Though the initial date of manufacture is not known, these pots were popular in the 1930s and 1940s with those involved in the air force, and can sometimes be found personalized with a pilot's name or, very rarely, a squadron crest.

A **Wood & Sons teapot**, modelled as a pug dog, c1930, 10in (25.5cm) high.
£150–165 / €220–250
$280–310 ⊞ BEV

A **Susie Cooper Rex teapot**, decorated with Acorn pattern, 1930s, 5in (12.5cm) high.
£110–125 / €165–190
$210–230 ⊞ BD

A **Beswick teapot**, modelled as Sam Weller, c1930, 6in (15cm) high.
£90–100 / €135–150
$170–190 ⊞ BEV
Sam Weller is a character in Charles Dickens' novel *The Pickwick Papers*.

A **Lingard Pottery teapot**, modelled as Humpty Dumpty on a wall, c1930, 8in (20.5cm) wide.
£150–165 / €220–250
$280–310 ⊞ BEV
This teapot was also produced in green. Lingard manufactured a matching sugar basin and milk jug.

A **New Chelsea China Co nursery teapot**, c1936, 4in (10cm) high.
£60–70 / €90–105
$110–130 ⊞ BtoB

A **Crown Ducal teapot**, inscribed 'War Against Hitlerism', 1939, 6in (15cm) high.
£135–150 / €200–230
$250–280 ⊞ H&G

A Royal Venton Ware Circus teapot, by John Steventon & Sons, modelled as an elephant being ridden by a monkey, 1930s, 5in (12.5cm) high.
£670–750 / €1,000–1,150 $1,250–1,400 ⊞ SCH
A number of teapots modelled as elephants were produced in the interwar years, including one being ridden by Sabu. Sabu was the Indian boy actor who achieved great popularity in the 1930s in a series of films by Sir Alexander Korda, including *The Jungle Book.*

▶ **An Arthur Wood & Son teapot,** modelled as a cat, inscribed 'Good Health', 1930s, 6in (15cm) high.
£175–195 / €260–290 $320–360 ⊞ BEV

A Wade Heath teapot, modelled as Donald Duck, 1930s, 7in (18cm) high.
£600–680 / €920–1,050 $1,100–1,250 ⊞ SCH

A Noritake teapot and stand, marked, 1930s, 5½in (14cm) high.
£50–60 / €75–90 $95–110 ⊞ DgC

A Burleigh Ware teapot, 1930s–40s, 7in (18cm) high.
£80–90 / €120–135 $150–170 ⊞ JFME

A Sadler Kleen Ware teapot and stand, 1940s, 6in (15cm) high.
£50–60 / €75–90 $95–110 ⊞ SCH

A teapot, sugar basin and jug, modelled as a wagon train, 1950s, teapot 9in (23cm) wide.
£125–140 / €190–210 $230–260 ⊞ LAS

A Kensington teapot, decorated with flowers and bees, 1940s–50s, 6in (15cm) high.
£160–180 / €240–270 $300–340 ⊞ SCH

An Arthur Wood & Son teapot, modelled as a football, the finial in the form of a whistle, 1950s, 7in (18cm) wide.
£55–65 / €85–100 $100–120 ⊞ BEV

A T. G. Green Blue Domino teapot, early 1950s, 7in (18cm) high.
£70–80 / €105–120 $130–150 ⊞ JWK

A Sadler lustre teapot,
commemorating the Coronation
of Queen Elizabeth II, 1953,
6½in (16.5cm) wide.
**£70–80 / €105–120
$130–150 ⊞ H&G**

A Portmeirion teapot, decorated
with Magic City pattern, 1966,
7in (18cm) high.
**£85–95 / €130–145
$160–180 ⊞ CHI**

◀ **An Adams teapot,** decorated
with Old Colonial pattern, 1970s,
7in (18cm) high.
**£60–70 / €90–105
$110–130 ⊞ CHI**

◀ **A Robertson's Golly teapot,**
designed by J. & G. Morton, silver
crane mark, 1980s, 9in (23cm) high.
**£250–280 / €380–420
$470–520 ⊞ HYP**

A Ridgways Metro teapot,
decorated with Homemaker pattern,
c1960, 9in (23cm) wide.
**£270–300 / €410–450
$500–560 ⊞ BEV**
**Though vast amounts of
Homemaker tableware sold
through Woolworths, tea and
coffee pots were only produced
as special order items. Comparatively few were made and they
are very sought after today.**

A Royal Doulton teapot,
decorated with Westwood pattern,
1960s, 6in (15cm) high.
**£35–40 / €50–60
$65–75 ⊞ CHI**

A Royal Collection teapot,
commemorating the Golden Jubilee
of Queen Elizabeth II, limited edition
of 750, 2002, 6in (15cm) high.
**£220–250 / €330–380
$410–470 ⊞ H&G**

An Adams teapot, transfer-printed
with Scenic pattern, c1962,
6in (15cm) high.
**£45–50 / €70–80
$85–95 ⊞ CHI**

A Royal Worcester teapot,
decorated with Hyde Park pattern,
1960s, 5in (12.5cm) high.
**£85–95 / €130–145
$160–180 ⊞ CHI**

**A Carlton Ware Red Baron
teapot,** 1980s, 9in (23cm) wide.
**£75–85 / €115–130
$140–160 ⊞ BET**

A Sadler teapot and cup, inscribed
'The History of Tea', 2002–03.
**£15–20 / €22–30
$28–38 ⊞ KWCC**

Tiles

A set of four majolica tiles, 17thC, 5in (12.5cm) square.
£250–280 / €380–420
$470–520 ⊞ OLA

A set of six Delft tiles, depicting ships, 17thC, 5in (12.5cm) square.
£230–270 / €350–410
$430–500 ⚲ VSP

▶ A set of 10 Delft tiles, depicting figures in rural landscapes, 18thC, 5in (12.5cm) square.
£500–600 / €750–900
$940–1,100 ⚲ HYD

◀ A set of three delft tiles, printed by Sadler, depicting actors in character, in an ebonized frame, c1750, each tile 4¾in (12cm) square.
£480–570 / €720–860
$900–1,050 ⚲ SWO

▶ A Bristol delft tile, depicting a figure in a landscape, c1750, 5¼in (13.5cm) wide.
£95–105 / €140–155
$175–195 ⊞ JHo

A Sadler & Green delftware tile, transfer-printed with a shepherd and a shepherdess, repaired, c1775, 5in (12.5cm) square.
£60–70 / €90–105
$110–130 ⚲ PFK

A Victorian tile, with floral decoration, 6in (15cm) square.
£10–15 / €15–22
$19–28 ⊞ TASV

◀ A Minton & Hollins tile, transfer-printed with a bird among bullrushes, one of 12, c1875, 6in (15cm) square.
£100–110 / €150–165
$185–210 ⊞ ReN

A Minton tile, designed by William Wise, from the Animals of the Farm Series, depicting horses, c1879, 6in (15cm) square.
£100–115 / €150–170
$185–210 ⊞ C&W

A tile, probably Minton, depicting a cricketing scene, 1870s, 6in (15cm) square.
£180–200 / €270–300
$330–370 ⊞ MSh

A pair of William de Morgan tiles, decorated with Tudor roses, slight damage, impressed Chelsea period marks, c1880, 6in (15cm) square.
£320–380 / €480–570
$600–720 ✗ Bea

A pair of William De Morgan tiles, with floral decoration, one cracked, impressed Chelsea period marks, c1880, 6in (15cm) square.
£440–520 / €660–780
$820–970 ✗ Bea

A Malkin Edge tile, depicting a game of bowls, from the Pastimes Series, c1883, 6in (15cm) square.
£135–150 / €200–230
$250–280 ⊞ ReN

A Wedgwood tile, transfer-printed with a hunting dog and a game bird, c1885, 8in (20.5cm) square.
£155–175 / €230–260
$290–330 ⊞ ReN

A set of four tiles, depicting months of the year, from a series of 12, c1890, 6in (15cm) square.
£135–150 / €200–230
$250–280 each ⊞ ReN

An H. & R. Johnson Art Nouveau tile, with tube-lined decoration, depicting a lady, marked 'Cristal', early 20thC, 6in (15cm) square.
£75–85 / €115–130
$140–160 ✗ PFK

A Minton butcher's tile, depicting a pig, late 19thC, 12in (30.5cm) square.
£270–300 / €410–450
$500–560 ⊞ SMI

A tile, depicting an 18thC couple, set into a pewter tray, Continental, c1910, 10in (25.5cm) wide.
£50–55 / €75–85
$95–105 ⊞ BET

▶ **A tile,** designed by Salvador Dali, initialled, printed marks, 1954, 17in (43cm) high.
£220–250 / €330–380
$410–470 ⊞ EMH

Troika

Troika was founded in St Ives in 1963 by sculptor Lesley Illsley, potter Benny Sirota and architect Jan Thompson, hence the name which means triumvirate. For 20 years the firm sold innovative, hand-crafted pottery to leading stores across the world. Each pot was conceived as an individual work of art. Troika was known for its distinctive,

moulded forms and a sculptural abstracted style, inspired by contemporary art and the Cornish landscape. Troika, which ceased trading in 1983, has become increasingly collectable since the 1990s and rare pieces can command high prices. As well as the Troika mark, look out for the initials of the individual designer.

A Troika vase, marked 'HC', possibly for decorator Honor Curtis, 1960s, 12¼in (31cm) high.
£350–420 / €530–630
$660–790 ⚲ HOLL

A Troika lamp base, decorated with incised geometric pattern, marked 'Troika AB Cornwall', 1960s–70s, 10¾in (27.5cm) high.
£220–250 / €330–380
$410–470 ⚲ SWO

◄ **A Troika vase,** with incised geometric pattern, painted mark, 1960s, 8¾in (22cm) high.
£190–220
€290–310
$350–410
⚲ SWO

A Troika vase, painted marks, 1960s, 6½in (16.5cm) high.
£220–250 / €330–380
$410–470 ⚲ SJH

A Troika vase, decorated with incised geometric pattern, painted mark, 1970s, 8½in (21.5cm) high.
£350–420 / €530–630
$650–790 ⚲ G(L)

A Troika lamp base, by Julian Greenwood–Penny, one side depicting The Godolphin Arms, Marazion, the other St Michael's Mount, c1980, 11½in (29cm) wide.
£850–1,000
€1,300–1,500
$1,600–1,850 ⚲ LAY

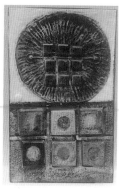

A Troika wall plaque, decorated with geometric motifs, marked, c1970, 12 x 8in (30.5 x 20.5cm).
£1,300–1,550
€1,950–2,300
$2,450–2,900 ⚲ HOLL

Two Troika vases, decorated with incised geometric patterns, painted marks, 1970s, 3½in (9cm) high.
£130–150 / €195–230
$240–280 ⚲ G(L)

► **A Troika model of an Aztec mask,** marked, c1980, 10in (25.5cm) high.
£2,200–2,600
€3,300–3,900
$4,100–4,850
⚲ G(B)

Wade

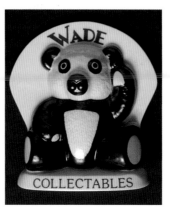

A Wade Family Favourites model of Priscilla the pig, 2000, 2½in (6.5cm) high.
£10–15 / €15–22
$19–28 ⊞ JMC

A Wade Disney Blow Up model of Lady, 1961, 4¼in (11cm) high.
£50–60 / €75–90
$95–110 ↗ BBR

◄ **A Wade Collectables model of a panda,** 1998, 8in (20.5cm) high.
£35–40 / €50–60
$65–75 ⊞ LAS

Wall Pockets

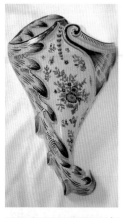

◄ **A Desvres faïence wall pocket,** French, c1900, 13in (33cm) high.
£135–150 / €200–230
$250–280 ⊞ SER

An Auvergne pottery wall pocket, French, early 20thC, 7in (18cm) high.
£130–145 / €195–220
$240–270 ⊞ SER

A Kensington lustre wall pocket, 1930, 7in (18cm) high.
£40–45 / €60–70
$75–85 ⊞ BET

◄ **A Crown Devon wall pocket,** modelled as a female hiker, No. 219, c1932, 10in (25.5cm) high.
£220–250
€330–380
$410–470
⊞ JFME

A Simpson Potters Solian ware wall pocket, modelled as a straw bonnet, decorated with flowers, marked, 1930s, 7in (18cm) high.
£10–15 / €15–22
$19–28 ↗ SJH

A Crown Ducal wall pocket, by Charlotte Rhead, decorated with Oak Leaves pattern, No. 5391, printed mark, signed, 1930s, 8in (20.5cm) wide.
£240–280 / €360–420
$450–520 ↗ PFK

Wedgwood

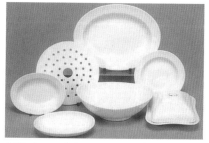

A Wedgwood Queen's ware child's part dinner service, comprising 57 pieces, some damage, impressed marks, c1800.
£380–450 / €570–680
$710–840 ➤ DN

A pair of Wedgwood creamware soup plates, enamelled with a coat-of-arms within a leaf and scroll border, repaired, impressed marks, 1780–90, 9¾in (25cm) diam.
£260–310 / €400–480
$490–580 ➤ LFA

A Wedgwood pearlware pickle dish, in the form of a leaf, with a stalk handle, impressed mark, 1800–10, 4¼in (11cm) wide.
£140–165 / €210–250
$260–310 ➤ LFA

◀ **A Wedgwood Queen's ware basket and stand,** with pierced rims, painted No. N899, impressed marks, c1810, stand 10¼in (26cm) wide.
£200–240 / €300–360
$380–450 ➤ DN

A Wedgwood majolica tray, decorated in Whieldon-type colours, impressed mark, 1869, 16½in (42cm) wide.
£200–240 / €300–360
$370–450 ➤ PFK

A pair of Wedgwood majolica wall pockets, each in the form of a bird's nest with a bird, marked, c1872, 12in (30.5cm) wide.
£400–480 / €600–720
$750–900 ➤ G(B)

A Wedgwood plate, by E. Jones, decorated with hand-painted roses, signed, c1880, 10in (25.5cm) wide.
£30–35 / €45–50
$55–65 ⊞ HO

A Wedgwood cream jug, 1891–1900, 3in (7.5cm) high.
£60–70 / €90–105
$110–130 ⊞ HER

A Wedgwood maiolica cheese dish and cover, relief-moulded with primroses, base repaired, pattern No. M1744, impressed mark, late 19thC, 10in (25.5cm) diam.
£200–240 / €300–360
$380–450 ⚶ CAG

A Wedgwood jasper ware jug, with a white metal hinged cover, impressed marks, 19thC, 6½in (16.5cm) high.
£40–45 / €60–70
$75–85 ⚶ SJH

A Wedgwood Queen's ware teapot, inscribed 'The Elder Brewster Teapot, The Original Was Brought to America in Ye Mayflower, AD 1620...', impressed mark, 1890–1900, 4½in (11.5cm) high.
£340–400 / €510–600
$640–750 ⚶ LFA

A Wedgwood lustre dish, decorated with birds of paradise, a gilt kingfisher and geese, marked, early 20thC, 4¼in (11cm) diam.
£1,100–1,300 / €1,650–1,950
$2,050–2,450 ⚶ PFK

A Wedgwood Moonstone vase, designed by Keith Murray, blue printed mark and 'K. M.' initials, 1930s, 9½in (24cm) high.
£420–500 / €630–750
$790–940 ⚶ DMC

▶ **A Wedgwood teapot,** decorated with Peony pattern, 1960s, 4in (10cm) high.
£45–50 / €70–80
$85–95 ⊞ CHI

A Wedgwood model of a bull, attributed to Arnold Machin, 1950s, 13in (33cm) wide.
£250–280 / €380–420
$470–520 ⊞ JFME

A Wedgwood Basalt coffee can and saucer, 1950s, can 2in (5cm) high.
£7–11 / €11–17
$13–20 ⊞ HEI

LOCATE THE SOURCE
The source of each illustration in Miller's can be found by checking the code letters below each caption with the Key to Illustrations, pages 443–451.

A Wedgwood coffee pot, sugar bowl and milk jug, decorated in Gold Florentine pattern, c1961, coffee pot 10in (25.5cm) high.
£300–330 / €450–500
$560–620 ⊞ CHI

A Wedgwood Peter Rabbit paperweight, early 1980s, 2in (5cm) high.
£70–80 / €105–120
$130–150 ⊞ CCH

Worcester

A Chamberlain's Worcester part dessert service, comprising nine pieces, decorated with Blind Earl pattern, impressed mark, comport 2½in (6.5cm) high.
£260–310 / €390–470
$490–580 ➚ HYD

Fifteen Chamberlain's Worcester plates, painted with Imari flowers, largest 9½in (24cm) wide.
£380–450 / €570–680
$710–840 ➚ SWO

A Royal Worcester two-handled vase, painted with flowers, No. 1024, 1891, 14½in (37cm) high.
£300–360 / €450–540
$560–670 ➚ G(L)

A Royal Worcester comport, by J. Rushton, painted with vignettes of satyrs and nymphs, late 19thC, 12in (30.5cm) diam.
£210–250 / €320–380
$390–470 ➚ SWO

A Royal Worcester vase, with moulded foliate decoration, printed mark, c1912, 3¼in (8.5cm) high.
£25–30 / €40–45
$50–55 ➚ SAS

A Royal Worcester model of a monkey, 1916, 3in (7.5cm) high.
£250–280 / €380–420
$470–520 ⊞ WAC

A Royal Worcester mug, painted with a robin, signed 'W.J.B.', c1922, 2¼in (5.5cm) high.
£80–90 / €120–135
$150–170 ➚ SAS

A Royal Worcester posy vase, by Kitty Blake, painted with blackberries and flowers, signed, 1931.
£210–250 / €320–380
$390–470 ➚ G(L)

A Royal Worcester coffee service, comprising 12 pieces, decorated with flowers and scrolls within Greek Key borders, printed mark, 1933, with box.
£130–155 / €195–230
$240–290 ➚ G(L)

A Royal Worcester figure of a Dutch boy, 1935, 5in (12.5cm) high.
£175–195 / €260–290
$330–370 ⊞ WAC

A Royal Worcester cream jug, 1939, 2in (5cm) high.
£40–45 / €60–70
$75–85 ⊞ HER

A Royal Worcester model of a corgi, 1955, 4in (10cm) wide.
£135–150 / €200–230
$250–280 ⊞ WAC

A Royal Worcester pre-production figure of a boy holding a toy galleon, by Freda Doughty, entitled 'Mayflower', No. RW3656, repaired, painted 'Please Return', signed, c1958, 7¾in (19.5cm) high.
£150–180 / €230–270
$280–340 ⋩ Bea

A Royal Worcester figure, entitled 'Sunday's Boy', c1962, 5in (12.5cm) high.
£180–200 / €270–300
$340–370 ⊞ WAC

► **A Royal Worcester model of a robin,** by Dorothy Doughty, entitled 'Robin in the Autumn Woods', c1964, 7in (18cm) high, with case, stand and certificate.
£160–190
€240–290
$300–360 ⋩ DN

A Royal Worcester model of a Hereford bull, by Doris Lindner, entitled 'Hereford Bull', limited edition, printed mark, c1975, 7in (18cm) high.
£600–720 / €930–1,100
$1,100–1,300 ⋩ SAS

Further reading

Miller's Collecting Porcelain, Miller's Publications, 2002

A Royal Worcester equestrian group, by Doris Lindner, entitled 'Stroller and Marion Coakes', printed marks, c1970, 10¼in (26cm) high, with stand and certificate.
£280–330 / €420–500
$520–620 ⋩ DN

◄ **A Royal Worcester equestrian group,** by Doris Lindner, entitled 'Huntsman and Hounds', printed mark, c1975, 7¾in (19.5cm) high.
£550–660
€830–990
$1,050–1,250
⋩ SAS

Christmas

Many Yuletide traditions started in the 19th century. On Christmas day 1800, Queen Charlotte held a party for the children of Windsor, of which the centrepiece was Britain's first recorded Christmas tree, a yew decorated with sweetmeats, toys and candles. Prince Albert and Queen Victoria popularized the tradition when they allowed the *Illustrated London News* to produce an engraving of their Christmas tree in 1848. Initially decorations were home made, including gilded walnuts, shaped biscuits and paper chains. Commercial ornaments were produced from the late 19th century. Early glass baubles (often imported from Germany), 'Dresden' tree decorations (animals and figures made from pressed cardboard) and other vintage ornaments are collectable today, although their fragility makes them very rare. Christmas cake decorations made from bisque or tin also became popular from the Victorian

period, although as with all other Christmas decorations most extant examples date from the 1930s to the 1950s. Electric Christmas tree lights were invented in New York by an associate of Thomas Edison in 1882. Look out for lights from the 1930s to the 1960s, particularly those decorated with Disney figures and other novelty characters. Early Christmas cards are another popular collecting area. The first ever printed Christmas card was sent in 1843 by Sir Harry Cole (1808–82), the public servant and instigator of the Great Exhibition of 1851. Being too busy to write to his friends individually, Cole commissioned an illustrated card from artist John Calcott Horsley. One thousand copies were printed and, to the delight of the Post Office, a new tradition was born. One of Cole's original Christmas cards recently sold for a world record auction price of £22,350 / €33,500 / $41,800.

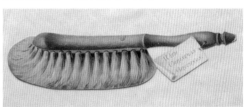

A Christmas card, 1890s, 7in (18cm) wide.
£15–20 / €22–30
$28–38 ⊞ Qua

◀ **A Christmas card,**
1890s, 6½ x 3in
(16.5 x 7.5cm) high.
£40–45 / €60–70
$75–85 ⊞ Qua

A Hall & Holtz Christmas Exposition publicity card, with woodblock decoration, some damage, signed, Japanese, 1882, 13 x 9in (33 x 23cm) high.
£100–120 / €150–180
$185–220 ⋌ SWO

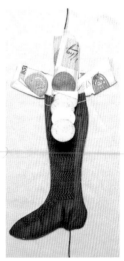

A Dresden tree decoration, modelled as a fish, slight rubbing, German, c1900, 3in (7.5cm) wide.
£80–90 / €120–135
$150–165 ⊞ LEI

A Christmas postcard, by Raphel Tuck & Sons, 1890s, 5 x 3in (12.5 x 7.5cm).
£15–20 / €22–30
$28–38 ⊞ Qua

A pop-up Christmas card, 1890s, 8in (20.5cm) high.
£75–85 / €115–130
$140–160 ⊞ Qua

A Christmas postcard, by Raphael Tuck & Sons, c1900, 4 x 6in (10 x 15cm).
£1–5 / €2–7
$3–9 ⊞ POS

Three bisque and plaster Father Christmas cake decorations, c1935, 2in (5cm) high.
£15–20 / €22–30
$28–38 each ⊞ YC

An enamel Christmas tree brooch, 1950s, 2½in (6.5cm) high.
£25–30 / €40–45
$50–55 ⊞ DRE

A bisque Christmas cake decoration, 1920s, 3in (7.5cm) wide.
£45–50 / €70–80
$85–95 ⊞ MURR

A Henry Clive sweet tin, American, 1925, 7½in (19cm) diam.
£90–100 / €135–150
$170–190 ⊞ HUX

▶ **A Rowntree's coffee tin,** in the form of Santa's House, 1930s, 5¼in (13.5cm) wide.
£220–250
€330–380
$410–470
⊞ HUX

A set of Mazda Disney Christmas lights, 1960, box 13¼in (33.5cm) wide.
£100–110 / €150–165
$185–210 ⊞ GTM

◀ **Picture Post magazine,** Christmas issue, 1952, 13 x 10 (33 x 25.5cm).
£3–7 / €4–10
$6–13 ⊞ RTT

A cast-iron Christmas tree door porter, French, 1930s, 8½in (21.5cm) high.
£50–55 / €75–85
$95–105 ⊞ BET

A plastic brooch, in the form of Father Christmas, with a bell bobble, American, 1950s, 2½in (6.5cm) high.
£20–25 / €30–35
$35–45 ⊞ DRE

A Caithness paperweight, by William Manson, designed by Colin Terris, entitled 'Christmas Weight', No. CT-80, limited edition No. 113/500, together with certificate of authenticity, 1977, 2½in (6.5cm) high.
£75–85 / €115–130
$140–160 ➹ FHF

Cigarette, Trade & Trading cards

Collecting cigarette and trade cards is known as cartophily. Cigarette cards were first introduced in the USA in the second half of the 19th century as packet stiffeners. Initially they were blank, but manufacturers later included advertising information on the cardboard slip and the late 19th century saw the introduction of the pictorial card, which was designed to be collected. In order to encourage the purchase of more cigarettes, cards were produced in sets, typically of 50. Many of the most desirable cards date from before 1918, when Edwardian tobacco manufacturers were competing for a share in the market. Production slowed during WWI, with some cards being withdrawn for political reasons, which can make surviving examples very sought after today. The 1920s to the 1930s was a golden age for cigarette cards. A huge number of sets were produced and they became a popular collecting craze, with albums to keep them in, clubs and specialist shops. Production was again suspended during WWII, after which very few cigarette cards were manufactured.

Cigarette Cards

► **W. D. & H. O. Wills,** Cricketers, set of 50, 1908.
£310–350
€470–530
$580–650 ⊞ JBa

R. M. Mason & Co, Naval and Military Phrases, set of 40, 1904, 2½in (6.5cm) high.
£40–45 / €60–70
$75–85 each ⊞ LCC

John Player & Sons, Football Charactatures, set of 50, 1927, 2¾in (7cm) high.
£50–60 / €75–90
$95–110 ⊞ LCC

British American Tobacco, Indian Chiefs, set of 50, 1930.
£340–380 / €510–570
$640–710 ⊞ SAT

Kensitas, silk embroidered Flowers, set of 60, 1933.
£240–270 / € 360–410
$450–500 ⊞ JBa

John Player & Sons, Boy Scout and Girl Guide Badges, set of 50, 1933.
£15–20 / € 22–30
$28–38 ⊞ SOR

Carreras, Famous Airmen and Air Women, set of 50, 1936, framed.
£100–110 / € 150–165
$185–210 ⊞ JBa

John Player & Sons, Coronation Series, Ceremonial Dress, set of 50, 1937.
£6–10 / € 9–15
$12–19 ⊞ MUR

◀ **John Player & Sons,** Speedway Riders, set of 50, 1937.
£100–110 / € 150–165
$185–210 ⊞ SAT

JOAN CRAWFORD

John Player & Sons, Film Stars, third series, set of 50, 1938, 2¾in (7cm) high.
£35–40 / € 50–60
$65–75 ⊞ LCC

John Bartholomew

CIGARETTE CARDS TRADE CARDS

**Heirloom Antiques
68 High Street
Tenterden
Kent**

▶ OPEN 7 DAYS A WEEK ◀

SHOP:
+44 (0)1580 765535

HOME:
+44 (0)1580 241556

W. D. & H. O. Wills, Dogs, set of 50, 1937, 2¾in (7cm) high.
£25–30 / € 40–45
$50–55 ⊞ LCC

John Player & Sons, Bicycling, set of 50, 1939.
£40–45 / € 60–70
$75–85 ⊞ JBa

Carreras, Film and Stage Beauties, set of 54, 1939.
£65–75 / € 100–115
$120–140 ⊞ SAT

Trade Cards

Trade cards are cards produced by manufacturers of products other than cigarettes. Famous makers include the Liebig Extract of Meat Co (est. 1856), creators of the Oxo cube in c1910, who over a period of years issued approximately 2,000 sets of handsomely decorated cards. Tea companies such as Brooke Bond and sweet manufacturers also issued cards.

In the USA, in the late 19th and early 20th centuries, trade cards were handed out by store keepers with the purchase of a product and often included the shop address. These cards were produced in small numbers. They would be beautifully illustrated and, depending on the appeal of the subject matter, fine examples can fetch high sums. Gum factories were major manufacturers of trade cards which were supplied with confectionery. They produced cards inspired by baseball, football, film and TV to attract children. Famous 1930s firms include Goudey Gum and Gum Inc. After WWII, Bowman Gum and Topps Inc (creators of Bazooka gum) became leading producers of trade cards.

American Eagle Bank, Toy Savings Bank, lithographed trade card, damaged, American, 1883.
£120–140 / €180–210
$220–260 ✎ Bert

Liebig Extract of Meat Co, Raw Materials for our Clothes, set of six, 1907.
£10–15 / €15–22
$19–28 ▦ LENA

Typhoo Tea, Aesop's Fables, 1924.
£60–70 / 90–105
$110–130 ▦ JBa

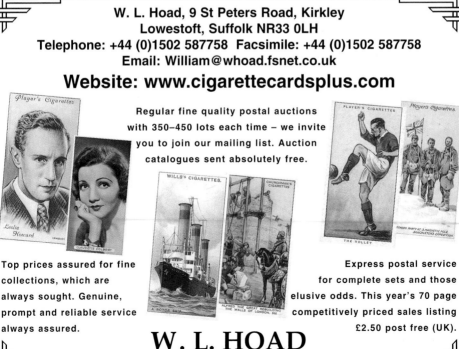

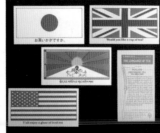

Liebig Extract of Meat Co,
American Skyscrapers, set of six, 1935.
£35–40 / € 50–60
$65–75 ⊞ JBa

Brooke Bond, The Language of
Tea, set of 12, 1958.
£1–5 / € 2–7
$3–9 ⊞ MUR

Brooke Bond, African Birds, set of
50, Rhodesian issue, 1965.
£100–120 / € 150–180
$185–220 ⊞ MRW

▶ **Topps,** *Star Wars* gum cards, Series three and five,
sets of 60, 1978.
£60–70 / € 90–105
$110–130 ⊞ STa
During the production of the Series three set of
cards, a joke card of C3PO was made and was
printed in error. Once this was discovered the card
was quickly withdrawn. This card, in perfect
condition, is now worth up to £100 / € 150 / $190.

Trading Cards

Trading cards are cards that are sold as
collectables, unlike trade or cigarette cards
which come free with the purchase of a
product. Cards are sold in packs often filled
with a random assortment, so that the collector
will have to either buy more cards or swap
them in order to acquire a complete set.
Some cards are produced in smaller numbers to
make them rarer than others. Some trading
cards are also designed to be played with in
what are known as 'customizable card games' –
Pokémon is a famous example. Collectors begin
with a starter pack that is then added to with
smaller booster sets. Typically, for most young
enthusiasts, acquiring the cards is much more
important than playing the game.

Independence Day, Topps widevision trade
cards, set of 72, 1996.
£6–10 / € 9–15
$12–19 ⊞ SSF

Star Trek Voyager,
autograph series, Robert
Beltran as First Officer
Chakotay, 1998.
£50–60 / € 75–90
$95–110 ⊞ SSF

Star Wars, Episode 1, Chase Cards,
set of 8, 1999.
£45–50 / € 70–80
$85–95 ⊞ STa

◀ *Lord of the Rings,* Chase Cards, set of 10 prismatic foil cards, 200?
£25–30 / € 40–45
$50–55 ⊞ SSF

Coca Cola & Pepsi Cola

In 1886 Atlanta pharmacist Dr John S. Pemberton invented a medicinal syrup that included cocoa extract and cola nuts and which he named Coca Cola. The following year he added carbonated water to the recipe, and with the rise of the soda fountain and the temperance movement, Coca Cola became not just a patent medicine but a favourite soft drink. By 1910 sales had reached 11,500 gallons (52,279 litres) a day and the company was spending £454,500 / €681,700 / $850,000 per annum on advertising.

This heavy promotion, which continues to the present day, has resulted in a wealth of Coca Cola collectables. Favourite areas include tin trays, which were first produced in 1897. Prior to 1903 these trays were round, but after that other shapes appeared, including oval and rectangular examples. Vintage trays can fetch

high prices but beware of modern reproductions. The Edwardian-style beauties that featured on early trays also appeared on calendars and enamel signs which, with cardboard cut-outs and paper advertisments, are another popular collecting area. Here again, early material tends to command the highest prices, and condition is crucial to value.

The famous Coca Cola bottle, patented in 1915, was inspired by the shape of the cocoa pod and is known as the hobble-skirt bottle because it resembles the fashions of the day. Cans first appeared in 1955 and were initially created for US army personnel overseas. Commemorative bottles and cans and examples bearing more unusual labelling are sought after by enthusiasts. Shop memorabilia is another major collecting area, and vintage coolers and vending machines can command strong prices.

◀ **A Coca Cola clock,** inscribed 'Relieves Exhaustion Delicious Refreshing', restored, 1893–96, 30½in (77.5cm) high.
£1,150–1,350
€1,700–2,000
$2,150–2,550 ⚒ JDJ

A Coca Cola tin sign, depicting a six pack, inscribed 'Take Home a Carton', 1939, 27½ x 19½in (70 x 49.5cm).
£490–590 / €740–880
$920–1,100 ⚒ JDJ

A Coca Cola Bakelite radio prototype, with painted decoration, 1951.
£1,050–1,250
€1,550–1,850
$1,950–2,350 ⚒ S(P)

A Coca Cola vending machine, 1950s, 67in (170cm) high.
£3,700–4,100
€5,600–6,200
$6,900–7,700 ⊞ DRU

◀ **A Coca Cola tin tip tray,** slight damage, 1914, 6in (15cm) wide.
£90–105 / €135–160
$170–200 ⚒ JDJ

A Coca Cola tin tip tray, slight damage, 1916, 6in (15cm) wide.
£105–125 / €155–185
$200–240 ⚒ JDJ

A Coca Cola tin tray, 1955, 13in (33cm) wide.
£45–50 / €70–80
$85–95 ⊞ HUX

◀ **A Coca Cola enamel drinks cooler,** 1950s, 25in (63.5cm) wide.
£1,500–1,700
€2,250–2,550
$2,800–3,150   ⊞ DRU

A Coca Cola metal sign, with screen-printed decoration, c1960, in a later wood frame, 35 x 72in (89 x 183cm).
£180–210 / €270–310
$340–400   ⚲ JAA

A set of four Coca Cola bottles, commemorating the World Cup, 2002, 9in (23cm) high.
£6–10 / €9–15
$12–19   ⊞ HeA

◀ **A Pepsi Cola enamel vending machine,** 1950s, 61in (155cm) high.
£5,200–5,800 / €7,800–8,700
$9,700–10,800   ⊞ DRU

▶ **A Pepsi Cola Bakelite radio prototype,** by Radio Display Co, with painted decoration, 1951, 23¼in (59cm) high.
£350–420 / €530–630
$650–780   ⚲ S(P)

Pepsi Cola

Pepsi Cola was devised by a North Carolina pharmacist c1898. Initially the beverage was known as Brad's Drink, but was renamed Pepsi Cola after the cola nut and the Pepsin (a digestive aid) said to be included in the original mixture. Pepsi Cola was trademarked in 1903.

Comics & Annuals

Action Comics, No. 33, published by DC Comics, slight damage, 1940, **£380–450 / €570–680 $710–840** ✗ CBP

Amazing Fantasy comic, No. 15, introducing Spider Man, 1962. **£1,050–1,250 €1,550–1,850 $1,950–2,300** ✗ CBP

Authentic Police Cases comic, No. 33, 1954. **£20–25 / €30–35 $35–45** ✗ CBP

A Basinful of Fun comic, No. 97, 1954. **£2–6 / €3–9 $4–11** ⊞ RTT

◀ **The Beano comic,** Nos 546–597, complete year in bound volume, 1953. **£480–570 €720–860 $900–1,050** ✗ CBP

Batman comic, No. 14, Penguin Returns, slight damage, 1942. **£120–140 / €180–210 $220–260** ✗ CBP

The Beano comic, No. 103, Big Eggo gets an Elephant Shower, slight damage, 1940. **£135–160 / €200–240 $250–300** ✗ CBP

Black Cat Mystery comic, No. 50, 1954. **£170–200 / €260–300 $320–370** ✗ CBP

Blackie's Children's Annual, with illustrations by Mabel Lucie Attwell and Alice Woodward, c1923. **£15–20 / €22–30 $28–38** ⊞ HTE

Bonzo's Annual, published by
Dean, Golly Jack in the Box, 1947.
£45–50 / €70–80
$85–95 ⊞ HYP

Bonzo's Annual, published by
Dean, 1948.
£45–50 / €70–80
$85–95 ⊞ HYP

Bonzo's Annual, published by
Dean, 1949.
£45–50 / €70–80
$85–95 ⊞ HYP

The Boy's Own Paper, 1919.
£1–5 / €2–7
$3–9 ⊞ RTT

The Champion comic,
Nos 1092–1143, complete year in
bound volume, 1943.
£175–210 / €260–310
$330–390 ↗ CBP

The Dandy comic, No. 70,
2nd April Fool edition, The Elephant
Stands on its Trunk, 1939.
£120–140 / €180–210
$220–260 ↗ CBP

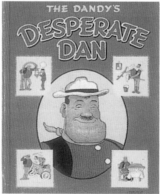

Dennis the Menace annual,
No. 1, 1956.
£120–140 / €180–210
$220–260 ↗ CBP

**The Dandy's Desperate Dan
annual,** No. 1, 1954.
£120–140 / €180–210
$220–260 ↗ CBP

Detective Comics, No. 120, published
by DC Comics, American, 1950.
£290–340 / €440–510
$540–640 ↗ CBP

Detective Comics, published by DC
Comics, Batman and Robin,
American, 1961.
**£25–30 / €40–45
$50–55 ⊞ SSF**

Detective Comics, published by DC
Comics, Batman and Robin,
American, 1978.
**£5–9 / €8–13
$10–16 ⊞ CoC**

Fantastic Four comic, No. 61,
published by Marvel Comics
Group, 1967.
**£6–10 / €9–15
$12–19 ⊞ NOS**

Giant Size X-Men comic,
No. 1, published by Marvel
Comics Group, 1975.
**£200–240 / €300–360
$370–440 ⚲ CBP**

The Hotspur comic, Nos
305–331, half year in
bound volume, 1939.
**£270–320 / €410–480
$500–600 ⚲ CBP**

Mad comic, No.2,
slight damage, 1952–3.
**£300–360 / €450–540
$560–670 ⚲ CBP**

The Magic Comic,
No.1, Koko by E. H.
Banger, Peter Piper by
Dudley Watkins,
slight damage, 1939.
**£1,300–1,550
€1,950–2,300
$2,450–2,900 ⚲ CBP
Only eight copies of the
first issue of this comic
are known to exist.**

Masters of the Universe
Annual, 1986.
**£6–10 / €9–15
$12–19 ⊞ STa**

Mickey Mouse Annual,
Disney Studios, published
by Dean & Son, 1930.
**£370–440 / €560–660
$690–820 ⚲ BBA**

Mysterious Adventures
comic, No.1, published by
Story Comics, 1951.
**£65–75 / €100–115
$120–140 ⚲ CBP**

**LOCATE THE
SOURCE**

The source of each
illustration in
Miller's can be found
by checking the code
letters below each
caption with the Key
to Illustrations,
pages 443–451.

Radio Fun Annual, 1955.
£6–10 / €9–15
$12–19 ⊞ STa

School Friend Annual, published by Fleetwood House, 1955.
£1–5 / €2–7
$3–9 ⊞ HeA

Showcase Adam Strange comic, No. 19, 1959.
£50–60 / €75–90
$95–110 ⚹ CBP

Strange Tales comic, No. 97, 1962.
£220–260 / €330–390
$410–490 ⚹ CBP

Strange Worlds comic, No. 1, 1958.
£170–200 / €260–300
$320–370 ⚹ CBP

Superboy Annual, No. 2, 1954–5.
£20–25 / €30–35
$35–45 ⚹ CBP

Superman comic, No. 4, The Origin of Superman, 1948.
£40–45 / €60–70
$75–85 ⚹ CBP

Items in the Comics & Annuals section have been arranged in alphabetical order.

Superman comic, No. 147, 1961.
£80–90 / €120–135
$150–170 ⊞ PICC

Teddy Tail's Annual, 1937.
£1–5 / €2–7
$3–9 ⊞ HeA

Louis Wain's Summer Book, published by Hutchinson & Co, 1903.
£135–150 / €200–220
$250–280 ⊞ J&J

Commemorative Ware

A ceramic plate, commemorating John Wesley, with transfer-printed decoration, 1850, 11in (28cm) diam.
£260–290 / € 390–440
$490–540 ⊞ BRT

A bronze seal, commemorating the Great Exhibition, engraved with an all-seeing eye, inscribed 'Exhibition Of All Nations 1851',
20in (51cm) wide.
£90–100 / € 135–150
$170–190 ⊞ TML

A ceramic tile trivet, commemorating Charles Dickens, transfer-printed with a portrait, 1870, 6in (15cm) square.
£115–130 / € 175–195
$210–240 ⊞ H&G

◀ **A ceramic plate,** commemorating the Denby Dale Pie, 1928, 9½in (24cm) diam.
£105–120 / € 160–180
$195–220 ⊞ WeA
The Denby Dale Pie was 216in (550cm) long, and 60in (152.5cm) wide. It was baked to raise money for the Huddersfield Royal Infirmary.

◀ **A Doulton stoneware jug,** commemorating Cardinal Manning, printed with a portrait, c1892, 9¼in (23.5cm) high.
£220–260
€ 330–390
$410–490
⋩ SAS

A plastic plate, commemorating the landing on the moon, c1969, 10in (25.5cm) wide.
£45–50 / € 70–80
$85–95 ⊞ BRT

A Farewell to Concorde crystal, by Swarovski Crystal, 2003,
1½in (4cm) wide.
£30–35 / € 45–50
$55–65 ⊞ PeJ

Exploration

A pottery plate, commemorating the Emir Pacha Relief Expedition, with printed decoration and a gilt rim, slight damage, c1887, 10in (25.5cm) wide.
£120–140 / € 180–210
$220–260 ⚲ SAS

A silver-plated tray, from the wardroom of *Discovery*, engraved '*Discovery* Antarctic Expedition, 1901', worn, 11¾in (30cm) diam.
£3,150–3,750 / € 4,700–5,600
$5,900–7,000 ⚲ BBA

The Daily Mirror, Captain Scott Memorial Service Number, 15 February 1913, slight damage.
£40–45 / € 60–70
$75–85 ⚲ VS

Captain Scott

At the turn of the 20th century, explorers were competing to be the first to reach the North and South Poles. Captain Robert Falcon Scott (1868–1912) became the first person to explore Antarctica extensively by land on his expedition aboard the ship *Discovery* (1901–04). In 1910 he embarked on a second voyage to Antarctica on the Terra Nova. After huge trials and an 800-mile sledge journey, Scott and his four companions (including Captain Oates) reached the South Pole in January 1912, only to discover that the Norwegian explorer Roald Amundsen had beaten them to it by a month. On the return journey, pulling the sledges themselves, they were assailed by appalling weather conditions, illness, starvation and frostbite. Recognizing that he was too sick to continue, Captain Oates left the tent on 11 March with the famous line 'I am just going outside and I may be some time'. Scott and his team died a few days later, only 11 miles from their next fuel and food depot. Their bodies and diaries were not found until November 1912, and news of the tragedy only reached Britain in February 1913. Scott was posthumously knighted and a huge memorial service was held in St Paul's Cathedral. Original material associated with Scott and his expeditions is very sought after.

The Daily Mirror, depicting Captain Scott's tomb in Antarctica, 21 May 1913, slight damage.
£40–45 / € 60–70
$75–85 ⚲ VS

◄ **A memorial postcard,** commemorating Captain Scott, 1913.
£50–60 / € 75–90
$95–110 ⚲ VS

► **A copper commemorative plaque,** depicting Captain Scott's Antarctic expedition, early 20thC, in an ebonized frame,10 x 14in (25.5 x 35.5cm).
£230–270 / € 350–410
$430–500 ⚲ SWO

Military & Naval

A Royal Patent Ironstone plate, commemorating the Crimean War, 1855, 7¼in (18.5cm) diam.
£60–70 / €90–105
$110–130 ⋋ DA

A ceramic sugar bowl, commemorating the Boer War, decorated with a portrait of Sir Redvers Buller and flags, 1899–1900, 3in (7.5cm) diam.
£75–85 / €115–130
$140–160 ⊞ BtoB

A ceramic mug, commemorating the Boer War and the relief of Mafeking, decorated with a portrait of Robert Baden-Powell, 1900, 3in (7.5cm) diam.
£210–240 / €320–360
$390–450 ⊞ BRT
Lord Robert Baden-Powell was a soldier, a writer and founder of the world scouting movement. He joined the 13th Hussars in India in 1876 and served in South Africa, where he was mentioned in dispatches and recruited by the Secret Service. He disguised himself as a butterfly collector and transported military plans concealed in drawings of butterfly wings. By the time of the Boer War he had been promoted to Colonel and was Commander during the famous siege of Mafeking. Though the British Garrison was surrounded by a Boer army of over 8,000 men, they managed to withstand the siege for 217 days. After Mafeking was relieved on 16 May 1900, Baden-Powell was promoted to Major General and became a national hero. His book *Aids to Scouting*, which was originally intended for military use, was published during the siege and achieved a far wider audience. On his return to England, Baden-Powell rewrote it as *Scouting for Boys* and initiated the scouting movement that was to spread across the globe.

▶ **An Aller Vale ceramic mug,** commemorating the Boer War, depicting Tommy Atkins, 1899–1900, 4½in (11.5cm) high.
£160–180 / €240–270
$300–340 ⊞ BtoB
'Tommy Atkins' or 'Tommy' is a generic term used for English soldiers. The name (the military equivalent of Mr Smith or John Doe) first appears on War Office forms in 1815. According to military legend, it was chosen by the Duke of Wellington in memory of Tommy Atkins, a soldier who died from horrible wounds at the Battle of Boxtel in 1795 with the final words 'It's alright Sir, it's all in a day's work'. The term became well known during the 19th century (particularly after Rudyard Kipling published his poem 'The Ballad of Tommy Atkins' in 1892). By WWI 'Tommy' had become the universal nickname for an English soldier.

◀ **A Chlorodyne Lozenges tin,** commemorating the Boer War, 1900, 9½in (24cm) wide.
£90–100
€135–150
$170–190
⊞ HUX

▶ **A porcelain plate,** commemorating WWI, Continental, c1914, 8¼in (21cm) diam.
£100–120
€150–180
$185–220
⋋ SAS

A character jug, in the form of Admiral Jellicoe, 1914–18, 7in (18cm) high.
£75–85 / €115–130
$140–160 ⊞ Tus

An Adderley's porcelain mug, decorated with the Union flag, a bulldog and HMS *Birmingham*, 1914–18, 3in (7.5cm) high.
£80–95 / €120–140
$150–180 ✗ SAS

A pottery jug, inscribed 'Verdun 1916', French, c1916, 9½in (24cm) high.
£40–45 / €60–70
$75–85 ✗ SAS

An embroidered panel, commemorating WWI, inset with a photograph, 1914–18, 19 x 20in (48.5 x 51cm).
£140–165 / €220–260
$270–320 ✗ G(L)

A pottery mug, commemorating WWI, with portraits of David Lloyd George, Field Marshall Haig and Admiral Beatty, 1918, 3in (7.5cm) high.
£25–30 / €40–45
$50–55 ⊞ BtoB

A Collingswood bone china mug, commemorating WWI, with hand-painted and transfer-printed decoration, 1919, 3in (7.5cm) high.
£55–65 / €85–100
$100–120 ⊞ H&G

A T. G. Green mug, commemorating WWI, with transfer-printed decoration, 1919, 3in (7.5cm) diam.
£50–55 / €75–85
$95–105 ⊞ H&G

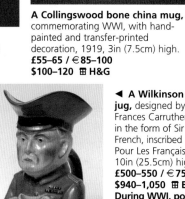

◄ **A Wilkinson Toby jug,** designed by Sir Frances Carruthers Gould, in the form of Sir John French, inscribed 'French Pour Les Français', 1920, 10in (25.5cm) high.
£500–550 / €750–830
$940–1,050 ⊞ BRT
During WWI, political cartoonist Sir Frances Carruthers Gould (1844–1925) produced designs for a series of 11 Toby jugs depicting military and political leaders of the day. These are now very sought after, the rarest figure being the South African Louis Botha.

A badge, inscribed 'Welcome Home Our Heroes', 1940s, 1¼in (3cm) diam.
£15–20 / €22–30
$28–38 ⊞ HUX

A tin, commemorating the end of WWII, decorated with portraits of the Allied leaders, Dutch, 1939–45, 9½in (24cm) high.
£40–45 / €60–70
$75–85 ⊞ HUX

▶ **A Wedgwood mug,** decorated with a relief-moulded bust of President Roosevelt, inscribed 'This can be done...', c1941, 4¼in (11cm) high.
£160–180 / €240–270
$300–340 ⊞ BtoB

Political

A ceramic jug, commemorating Sir Robert Peel, 1885, 8in (20.5cm) high.
£250–280 / €380–420
$470–520 BRT

A brass watch fob, depicting Theodore Roosevelt and Charles Fairbanks, inscribed 'Trade follows the flag and protection, prosperity and Panama', c1904, 5½in (14cm) long.
£35–40 / €50–60
$70–80 JAA

A silver stamp moistener, by Messrs Hutton, in the form of a scroll, embossed with the mask of David Lloyd George, Sheffield 1912, 3in (7.5cm) high.
£640–760 / €960–1,150
$1,200–1,400 WW

An RAF Benevolent Fund cast-metal bell, cast with a portrait of Sir Winston Churchill, 1939–45, 6in (15cm) high.
£25–30 / €40–45
$50–55 HUX
This bell was made from the remains of a German aircraft that was shot down over Britain.

Sir Winston Churchill

Sir Winston Leonard Spencer Churchill (1874–1965) was one of the most famous figures of the 20th century. He is also perhaps the most collectable British politician both in the UK and America (Churchill was half American and mantained a close relationship with the United States). Churchill's distinctive physical image, set off with his trademark cigar, was used to great propaganda effect during WWII and inspired a wealth of commemoratives from mugs to ashtrays. Manufacture of Churchilliana (such as Toby jugs) continues to this day. Along with his political commitments, Churchill was also a prolific writer and received the Nobel Prize for Literature in 1953. First editions of Churchill's works also attract dedicated collectors.

A Wilton Pottery character jug, in the form of Winston Churchill as Prime Minister, 1940, 7½in (19cm) high.
£220–250 / €330–380
$410–470 BtoB

A ceramic mug, celebrating the 1979 conservative victory, with photographic portraits of Margaret Thatcher and James Callaghan, 1979, 3in (7.5cm) diam.
£40–45 / €60–70
$75–85 BRT

◀ **A glass,** decorated with a Cummings cartoon of James Callaghan, 1960s, 4in (10cm) high.
£10–15 / €15–22
$19–28 RTT

A Royal Crown Derby loving cup, with a portrait of John Major, edition of 651, c1992, 3in (7.5cm) high.
£20–25 / €30–35
$35–45 SAS

▶ **A Bairstow Manor Pottery and Carlton Ware character jug,** by Ray Noble, in the form of John Prescott, entitled 'Johnny Two Jags', edition of 500, 2002, 8in (20.5cm) high.
£75–85 / €115–130
$140–160 IQ

Royal

A pearlware jug, commemorating Queen Caroline, printed with portraits, inscribed 'Long Live Queen Caroline', slight damage, c1820, 6in (15cm) high.
£60–70 / €90–105
$110–130 ✗ **WW**

▶ **An earthenware jug,** commemorating the marriage of Princess Victoria and Prince Frederick of Prussia, 1858, 7¾in (19.5cm) high.
£100–120 / €150–180
$185–220 ✗ **SAS**

A Wileman ceramic mug, commemorating the Royal wedding of King George V and Queen Mary, enamelled with a heraldic shield, 1893.
£60–70 / €90–105
$110–130 ✗ **SAS**

▶ **A child's mug,** commemorating King William IV, transfer-printed with a portrait, 1831, 2½in (6.5cm) high.
£360–400
€540–600
$670–750
⊞ **WAA**

A pottery plate, commemorating Queen Victoria's Diamond Jubilee, printed with castles, 1897, 9½in (24cm) diam.
£65–75 / €100–115
$120–140 ✗ **SAS**

A Worcester porcelain scent bottle, commemorating Queen Victoria's Golden Jubilee, inscribed 'Australia', 'India' and 'Canada', the cover in the form of a crown, c1887, 3½in (9cm) high.
£420–500 / €630–750
$790–940 ✗ **WW**

> Items in the Commemorative Ware section have been arranged in date order.

A mother-of-pearl card case, engraved with a portrait of Queen Victoria and a vignette of Brighton Pavilion, c1850, 4in (10cm) high.
£500–600 / €750–900
$940–1,100 ✗ **HYD**

A pottery mug, commemorating the Prince of Wales's visit to Royal Victoria Hospital, Bournemouth, with printed portraits, 1890.
£140–165 / €210–250
$260–310 ✗ **SAS**

A printed ticket, for the Service of Thanksgiving for Queen Victoria's Diamond Jubilee, 1897.
£70–80 / €105–120
$130–150 ✗ **MUL**

A Copeland Spode mug, commemorating Queen Victoria's Diamond Jubilee, 1897, 3in (7.5cm) high.
£145–160 / €210–240
$270–300 ⊞ **H&G**

A Hammersley plaque, commemorating the coronation of King Edward VII, moulded with a portrait, 1902, 9¾in (25cm) diam.
£75–85 / €115–130
$140–160 ✗ **SAS**

A Rowntree's chocolate tin, commemorating the coronation of King Edward VII, 1902, 5in (12.5cm) wide.
£25–30 / €40–45
$50–55 ⊞ HUX

A Royal Doulton porcelain dish, commemorating the coronation of King George V and Queen Mary, decorated with a portrait of the Queen, 1911, 13¼in (33.5cm) wide.
£30–35 / €45–50
$55–65 ⋋ SAS

A Ridgways wall plaque, printed with a photograph of King George V, 1911, 8 x 6in (20.5 x 15cm).
£80–90 / €120–135
$150–170 ⊞ H&G

A porcelain mug, commemorating the Silver Jubilee of King George V and Queen Mary, 1935, 3in (7.5cm) diam.
£50–60 / €75–90
$95–110 ⊞ H&G

A Cadbury's chocolate tin, commemorating the Silver Jubilee of King George V, with contents, 1935, 5½in (14cm) wide.
£55–65 / €85–100
$100–120 ⊞ HUX

An Aynsley bone china beaker, commemorating the Silver Jubilee of King George V and Queen Mary, 1935, 4in (10cm) high.
£55–65 / €85–100
$100–120 ⊞ H&G

▶ **A ceramic loving cup,** commemorating the coronation of King George VI and Queen Elizabeth, 1937, 3in (7.5cm) diam.
£120–140 / €180–210
$220–260 ⊞ BRT

A metal badge, commemorating the coronation of King George VI, 1937, 1½in (4cm) high.
£4–8 / €6–12
$8–15 ⊞ HUX

A Melba ceramic globe, commemorating King Edward VIII, with inscription, 1937, 3½in (9cm) high.
£70–80 / €105–120
$130–150 ⋋ SAS

A Royal Doulton ceramic beaker, commemorating the coronation of King George VI, 1937, 4in (10cm) high.
£360–400 / €540–600
$670–750 ⊞ H&G

▶ **A Bryant & May matchbox holder,** commemorating the coronation of King George VI, 1937, 2¼ x 1½in (5.5 x 4cm).
£15–20
€22–30
$28–38 ⊞ ATK

A ceramic vase, commemorating the coronation of King George VI, 1937, 6in (15cm) high.
£50–60 / €75–90
$95–110 ⊞ WAA

A plastic cameo brooch, commemorating the coronation of Queen Elizabeth II, 1953, 1¼in (3cm) high.
£4–8 / €6–12
$8–15 ⊞ HUX

A Royal Worcester equestrian model, by Doris Lindner, 'HRH Duke of Edinburgh on his polo pony', printed marks, c1968, with certificate and stand.
£200–240 / €300–360
$380–450 ⚒ DN

A Royal Doulton figure, model No. HN2502, entitled 'HM Queen Elizabeth II', 1973–76, 7¾in (19.5cm) high.
£150–180 / €230–270
$280–330 ⚒ WilP

◄ **A silver paper knife,** by Stuart Devlin, commemorating the Silver Jubilee of Queen Elizabeth II, London 1977, 7in (18cm) long, 2oz, cased.
£120–140 / €180–210
$220–260 ⚒ WW

A miniature tea service, commemorating the Silver Jubilee of Queen Elizabeth II, 1977 teapot 1in (2.5cm) high.
£30–35 / €45–50
$55–65 ⊞ Ans

► **A pottery tankard,** commemorating the Silver Jubilee of Queen Elizabeth II, 1977, 6in (15cm) high.
£35–40 / €50–60
$65–75 ⊞ H&G

A bone china mug, by Panorama Studio, commemorating the 50th birthday of Princess Margaret, 1980, 4in (10cm) high.
£65–75 / €100–115
$120–140 ⊞ H&G

An Aynsley bone china mug, commemorating the 30th birthday of the Princess of Wales, 1991, 4in (10cm) high.
£60–70 / €90–105
$110–130 ⊞ H&G

A Royal Doulton bone china loving cup, commemorating the 40th anniversary of the ascension of Queen Elizabeth II, edition of 2,500, 1992, 3½in (9cm) high.
£65–75 / €100–115
$120–140 ⊞ H&G

A bone china mug, commemorating the divorce of the Prince and Princess of Wales, edition of 150, 1996, 4in (10cm) high.
£80–90 / €120–135
$150–170 ⊞ H&G

Royal Photographs

A colour tint photograph of Queen Alexandra, c1880, 10 x 6½in (25.5 x 16.5cm).
£310–350 / €470–530
$580–650 ⊞ AEL

A photograph of Queen Victoria, Princess Patricia of Connaught and various princesses, in the grounds of Osborne House, titled by the Queen, 1887, 7 x 10in (18 x 25.5cm).
£2,500–2,750 / €3,750–4,150
$4,650–5,200 ⊞ CFSD

▶ A photograph of the Duke and Duchess of York with Princesses Elizabeth and Margaret, by Marcus Adams, signed 'Bertie and Elizabeth', 1931, 9½in x 10in (24 x 25.5cm).
£1,550–1,750
€2,350–2,650
$2,900–3,250 ⊞ AEL

▶ A photograph of HRH Prince John, signed, 1905–19, 5 x 3½in (12.5 x 9cm).
£1,650–1,850
€2,500–2,800
$3,100–3,450
⊞ AEL

A pair of presentation portraits of Emperor Hirohito and Empress Nagako, signed in Japanese, 1938, 9 x 6in (23 x 15cm), in sterling silver frames, with original wooden boxes.
£15,700–17,500 / €23,600–26,300
$29,400–33,000 ⊞ CFSD
Hirohito was the 124th Emperor of Japan, and the first Japanese Prince to visit the West in 1921. He acceded to the throne in 1926 and his reign was marked by rapid militarization and the aggressive wars against China and the USA, ending with the atomic bombs being dropped on Hiroshima and Nagasaki. Under American occupation, in 1946 the Emperor renounced his legendary divinity and most of his powers to become a democratic constitutional monarch.

A pair of presentation photographs of Queen Elizabeth II and Prince Philip, 1972, framed, 12½ x 9in (32 x 23cm).
£1,550–1,750 / €2,350–2,650
$2,900–3,250 ⊞ AEL

A photograph of Prince Rainier III, Princess Grace and family, by Howell Conant, signed, c1980, 5 x 4in (12.5 x 10cm).
£220–250 / €330–380
$410–470 ⊞ CFSD

Cross Reference
Autographs see
pages 41–43

With all Good Wishes for Christmas and the New Year

A Christmas card, to Miss Glasier from Charles and Diana, signed, 1980s, 7¼ x 5in (18.5 x 12.5cm).
£1,450–1,650 / €2,200–2,500
$2,700–3,100 ➶ TYA

Corkscrews

A steel corkscrew, the 'Challenge', c1800, 6in (15cm) long.
£50–60 / €75–90
$95–110 ⊞ SAT

A steel 'peg and worm' pocket corkscrew, c1820, 3½in (9cm) long.
£40–45 / €60–70
$75–85 ⊞ CS

A Thomason steel, bone and brass corkscrew, with Royal coat-of-arms, 19thC, 9in (23cm) extended.
£150–180 / €230–270
$280–330 ⚒ G(L)

A steel corkscrew, with a bone handle, dusting brush and Henshall button, c1850, 6in (15cm) long.
£50–55 / €75–85
$95–105 ⊞ CS

A Wolverson's steel corkscrew, with a leather-covered handle, 1876, 5in (12.5cm) long.
£55–65 / €85–100
$100–120 ⊞ SAT

▶ **A Victorian champagne tap,** with two detachable spikes, cased, 4½in (11.5cm) long.
£45–50 / €70–80
$85–95 ⊞ CS

▶ **A brass corkscrew,** in the form of a Scotsman, marked 'R. T. England', c1920, 3in (7.5cm) long.
£40–45
€60–70
$75–85 ⊞ Dall

◀ **A metal corkscrew,** in the form of a pig's hindquarters, marked 'Colonial Crafts Pat Pending', American, 2½in (6.5cm) wide.
£10–15
€15–22
$19–28 ⊞ CS

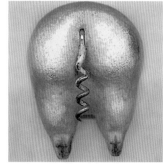

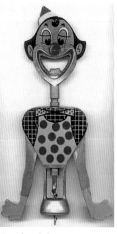

An aluminium corkscrew, in the form of a clown, with painted decoration, Italian, c1950, 10½in (26.5cm) long.
£40–45 / €60–70
$75–85 ⊞ CS

A cast-aluminium corkscrew, in the form of a barman, with painted decoration, 1950s, 10¾in (27.5cm) long.
£30–35 / €45–50
$55–65 ⊞ CS

Cosmetics & Hairdressing

A mantilla-style horn comb, with carved decoration, Agentinian/Spanish, mid-19thC, 10in (25.5cm) wide.
£180–200 / €270–300
$340–380 ⊞ **ACCC**

A silver dressing set, by H. Matthews, comprising a hand mirror, a pair of hairbrushes and a comb, engraved with initials, Birmingham 1900, with original fitted box.
£95–110 / €140–165
$175–210 ⚘ **NSal**

A rosewood toilet box, with mother-of-pearl medallions, containing boxes and jars with silver-plated covers, glass scent bottles and manicure tools, 19thC, 12in (30.5cm) wide.
£220–260 / €330–390
$410–490 ⚘ **G(L)**

An Asprey silver powder compact, with a gold and ruby clasp, 1935, 2½in (6.5cm) wide.
£360–400 / €540–600
$670–750 ⊞ **SUW**

An Art Deco silver and enamel compact, Birmingham 1935, 3in (7.5cm) square.
£50–60 / €75–90
$95–110 ⚘ **G(L)**

A celluloid powder compact, c1930, 3in (7.5cm) diam.
£115–130 / €175–195
$210–240 ⊞ **HUX**

A celluloid shoe horn, 1930s, 7in (18cm) wide.
£50–60 / €75–90
$95–110 ⊞ **SUW**

A tin of Wright's Coal Tar Shaving Soap, 1925–35, 3½in (9cm) high.
£8–12 / €12–18
$15–22 ⊞ **HUX**

A Laurel Ladies Boudoir safety razor, 1930s, 1¾in (4.5cm) wide.
£20–25 / €30–35
$35–45 ⊞ **RTT**

A Potter & Moore's cosmetic set, comprising powder cream, blush and lavender cologne, 1930s, 4¾in (12cm) wide
£15–20 / €22–30
$28–38 ⊞ **RTT**

An enamel and chrome powder compact,
American, 1930s, 4in (10cm) wide.
£75–85 / €115–130
$140–160 ⊞ SUW

A Houbigant enamelled powder compact,
with enamelled decoration, 1930s,
3¼in (8.5cm) long.
£90–100 / €135–150
$170–190 ⊞ SUW

▶ **A card of Record hair clips,** 1940s,
5in (12.5cm) wide.
£5–9 / €8–13
$10–16 ⊞ NFR

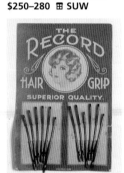

**A Richard Hudnut
powder compact,**
1930s, 2½in (6.5cm) diam.
£135–150 / €200–230
$250–280 ⊞ SUW

◀ **An embroidered tapestry
powder compact,** with a zip
fastening, c1950, 3½in (9cm) diam.
£30–35 /€45–50
$55–65 ⊞ LBr

**A Vogue Vanities powder
compact,** decorated with fairies,
1950s, 4in (10cm) diam.
£50–60 / €75–90
$95–110 ⊞ SUW

◀ **A metal compact,** with
enamelled floral decoration,
1950s, 2¾in (7cm) diam.
£5–9 /€8–13
$10–16 ⊞ CCO

**A Bakelite perfume flask and
compact,** with hand-painted
decoration, French, 1930s,
compact 2½in (6cm) diam.
£150–170 / €230–260
$280–320 ⊞ SUW

A Ziegfield Lucite compact,
American, 1940s, 4¾in (12cm) wide.
£65–75 / €100–115
$120–140 ⊞ SUW

**A Volupté brushed metal and
enamel powder compact,**
with a raised design, 1950s,
3½in (9cm) wide.
£340–380 / €510–570
$640–710 ⊞ SUW
Novelty compacts are very popular
with collectors. The New York
firm Volupté specialized in unusual
designs. Another famous Volupté
piece, dating from the 1940s, is a
compact in the form of praying
hands, which was produced both
with and without nail varnish
and jewellery and even came in
a version with lacy mittens.

Costume & Textiles

Interest in collecting and wearing vintage costume continues to grow, thanks in part to celebrities and the fashion press who regularly promote vintage styles. A further influence has been the *Sex and the City* TV series, which as well as making Manolo Blahnik a household name, also showed the main character Carrie patrolling her favourite thrift stores and successfully teaming old with new. Certain high street shops now sell original period clothes as well as so-called 'new vintage' lines – modern fashions directly inspired by antique dress.

This opening section features clothes from the 19th century to the 1970s. Victorian and Edwardian fashions can be challenging to wear because of the fragility of the fabrics and the small size of the clothes, though coats and cloaks (currently undergoing a modern revival) and looser styles (Edwardian croquet and day dresses) can be wearable. The loose shift shape of the 1920s dresses suit a wide variety of figures. Lamé evening coats and vintage beaded dresses in good condition are very sought after and have a sparkly glamour that never goes out of fashion. Bias-cut dresses from the 1930s can look lovely, but tend to require a slender frame. (It is never a good idea to squeeze into vintage clothes that are too small – old material and seams cannot take the strain.) Clothes from the 1940s often appeal to a specific audience such as swing dancers and WWII re-enactment groups. Fashion from the 1950s and '60s is popular and fun to wear. Big name designers will command high sums, and even more ordinary clothes from the period have risen in value. Certain high-street stores, such as Biba, have also attained an iconic status. Style from the 1970s attracts young enthusiasts, typically the under 30s, who do not remember wearing it the first time around. With all clothes, condition and size are crucial to value.

Victorian & Edwardian

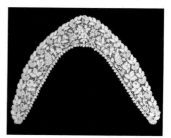

▶ **A Honiton lace collar,** 1850–60, 20in (51cm) long.
£200–220
€300–330
$370–410 ⊞ HL

A Victorian velvet cape, with tape and bead decoration.
£110–130 / €165–195
$210–250 ⚴ G(L)

A silk day dress, with a floral print, c1830.
£115–130 / €170–195
$220–250 ⊞ DE

A shot-silk day dress, c1860.
£160–180 / €240–270
$300–340 ⊞ DE

▶ **A shot-silk bustle dress,** trimmed with lace, 1870s.
£200–220 / €300–330
$370–410 ⊞ L&L

◄ An Edwardian machine-made lace blouse,
£45–50
€70–80
$85–95   ⊞ Ech

An Edwardian cotton lawn and lace croquet dress.
£200–220 / €300–330
$370–410   ⊞ VICT

A silk evening dress, decorated with sequins and jet beads, c1900.
£135–150 / €200–230
$250–280   ⊞ DE

A shot-silk day dress, with a woven polka dot pattern and a lace collar, c1918.
£70–80 / €105–120
$130–150   ⊞ DE

◄ A velvet dress, with embroidered detail, c1918.
£115–130 / €170–195
$220–250   ⊞ DE

Twenties

A Marshalll & Snelgrove silk brocade opera coat, with a velvet lining, 1929.
£750–850 / €1,150–1,300
$1,400–1,600   ⊞ LaF

Three silk velvet dress trims, 1920, 12in (30.5cm) long.
£6–10 / €9–15
$12–19 each   ⊞ DE

◄ A chiffon flapper dress, hand-decorated with sequins carnival glass and mother-of-pearl bugle beads, 1920.
£1,000–1,200
€1,500–1,800
$1,900–2,250   ⊞ LaF

Items in the Costume & Textiles section have been arranged in date order within each sub-section.

A silk and lace dress,
slight damage, 1920s.
£60–70 / €90–105
$110–130 ⊞ DE

**A beaded silk evening
dress,** 1920s.
£310–350 / €460–520
$580–650 ⊞ HSR

A lamé jacket, with self-
covered buttons, 1920s.
£135–150 / €200–220
$250–280 ⊞ Ci

A bridal blouse, with hand-
embroidered decoration,
Hungarian, 1920s.
£20–25 / €30–35
$35–45 ⊞ CCO

A silk kimono, 1920s.
£50–55 / €75–85
$95–105 ⊞ Ech

A net and bead costume trim, 1920s, 11in (28cm) wide.
£25–30 / €40–45
$50–55 ⊞ EV

A net sequinned cape/bolero, 1920s.
£75–85 / €115–130
$140–160 ⊞ Ci

Thirties

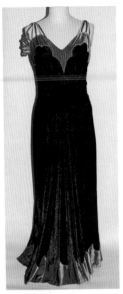

A lurex and velvet
evening dress, c1930.
£340–380 / €510–570
$640–710 ⊞ TIN

◀ A silk backless
evening dress, 1930.
£65–75 / €100–115
$120–140 ⊞ DE

A silk kimono, 1930s.
£200–220 / €300–330
$370–410 ⊞ MARG

A lace dress, 1930s.
£65–75 / €100–115
$120–140 ⊞ Ech

TinTin Collectables
Period Costumes & Accessories, Alfies Antiques Hall,
Unit G38-42, 13-25 Church St. Marylebone, London NW8 8DT
t/f:+44 (0) 20 7258 1305 e:leslie@tintincollectables.com
www.tintincollectables.com (Design - e:hussy.73@virgin.net)

A silk satin wedding
dress, with train, 1930s.
£60–70 / €90–105
$110–130 ⊞ DE

A crepe dress, decorated
with sequins, 1930s.
£155–175 / €230–260
$290–330 ⊞ HSR

Forties

A satin bathing suit,
with hand-embroidered
flowers, c1940.
£20–25 / €30–35
$35–45 ⊞ DE

A linen dress, 1940.
£40–45 / €60–70
$75–85 ⊞ HIP

A taffeta dress, 1940s.
£40–45 / €60–70
$75–85 ⊞ DE

**A Sumrie Original two-
piece suit,** 1940s.
£45–50 / €70–80
$85–95 ⊞ DE

▶ **A net dress,** 1940s.
£75–85 / €115–130
$140–160 ⊞ Ci

▶ **A crepe dress,** 1940s.
£55–65 / €85–100
$100–120 ⊞ HSR

**A Weatherall wool
coat,** 1940s.
£55–65 / €85–100
$100–120 ⊞ NFR

▶ **A Corsonia tweed
jacket,** 1940s.
£35–40 / €50–60
$65–75 ⊞ NFR

**A Jeannie Brand taffeta
dress,** decorated with
sequins, 1940s.
£35–40 / €50–60
$65–75 ⊞ NFR

▶ **A net ball
gown,** 1940s.
£145–165 / €220–250
$270–310 ⊞ HSR

Fifties

A cotton skirt, printed with a bull-fighting scene, 1950.
£35–40 / € 50–60
$65–75 ⊞ DE

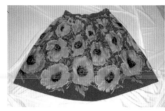

A cotton skirt, 1950s.
£35–40 / € 50–60
$65–75 ⊞ HSR

A cotton bikini, French, 1950s.
£40–45 / € 60–70
$75–85 ⊞ HSR

A brocade cocktail dress, 1950s.
£45–50 / € 70–80
$85–95 ⊞ DE

A lace evening dress, 1950s.
£75–85 / € 115–130
$140–160 ⊞ DE

A Martha Crawford cashmere two-piece, 1950s.
£210–240 / € 320–360
$400–450 ⊞ SpM

A cotton dress, 1950s.
£75–85 / € 115–130
$140–160 ⊞ HSR

A Margie Webb two-piece, 1950s.
£120–135 / € 180–200
$220–250 ⊞ SpM

LOCATE THE SOURCE

The source of each illustration in Miller's can be found by checking the code letters below each caption with the Key to Illustrations, pages 443–451.

▶ **A taffeta dress,** 1950s.
£45–50 / € 70–80
$85–95 ⊞ DE

A Saks jumper, with appliqué poodles, 1950s.
£135–150 / € 200–230
$250–280 ⊞ SpM

Sixties

A Lionel Norman wool coat, 1960.
£40–45 / €60–70
$75–85   ⊞ DE

A Christian Dior silk chiffon and lace dress, 1960.
£210–240 / €320–360
$400–450   ⊞ RER

A cotton dress, American, 1960s.
£35–40 / €50–60
$65–75   ⊞ DRE

▶ **A Frank Usher nylon dress**, 1960s.
£35–40 / €50–60
$65–75   ⊞ DE

A lurex dress, 1960s.
£160–180 / €240–270
$300–340   ⊞ Ci

A nylon dress, 1960s.
£60–70 / €90–105
$110–130   ⊞ HIP

▶ **Two suede belts**, 1960s.
£8–12
€12–18
$15–22 each
⊞ DE

Seventies

A Biba acetate dress, 1970.
£125–140 / €185–210
$230–260 ⊞ DE

A Zandra Rhodes cotton dress, with elasticated waistband, 1970s–80s.
£80–90 / €120–135
$150–170 ⊞ DE

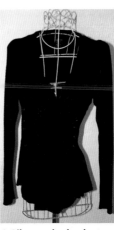

A Biba crushed velvet jacket, 1970s.
£75–85 / €115–130
$140–160 ⊞ HSR

▶ **A Van Allen nylon dress,** 1970s.
£30–35 / €45–50
$55–65 ⊞ DE

Hats

A straw bonnet, relined, 1860.
£75–85 / €115–130
$140–160 ⊞ L&L

▶ **A Walter Bernard & Sons opera hat,** c1870.
£80–90 / €120–135
$150–170 ⊞ TOP

A Victorian baby's lace bonnet, with ribbon ties.
£35–40 / €50–60
$65–75 ⊞ VICT

A wedding headdress, decorated with wax flowers, 1920.
£25–30 / €40–45
$50–55 ⊞ TT

A velvet and kid leather cloche hat, 1920s.
£140–155 / €210–240
$260–290 ⊞ TIN

A straw cloche hat, decorated with flowers, American, 1920s.
£85–95 / €130–145
$160–180 ⊞ RER

Two straw cloche hats, French, 1920.
£50–60 / €75–90
$95–110 each ⊞ DE
The adoption of short hair styles such as the 'Eton Crop' in the 1920s stimulated the fashion for cloche hats, the most famous headgear of the Art Deco period. Felt cloches were worn in winter, and straw in summer. Vintage cloche hats are often very small in size.

A Bradley's straw hat, decorated with silk flowers, 1940s.
£25–30 / €40–45
$50–55 ⊞ CCO

A Maddie Lemieux silk velvet half-hat, decorated with silk and velvet flowers, American, 1950s.
£35–40 / €50–60
$65–75 ⊞ DRE

A net and velvet half-hat, decorated with flowers and a bow, American, 1950s.
£25–30 / €40–45
$50–55 ⊞ DRE

◀ **A straw boater,** with a ribbon band, 1950s.
£25–30
€40–45
$50–55 ⊞ HO

An Evelyn Varon net hat, decorated with fabric flowers, 1950s.
£35–40 / €50–60
$65–75 ⊞ DRE

A cotton sunhat, 1960.
£2–6 / €3–9
$4–11 ⊞ DE

▶ **An Adams tweed riding hat,** Irish, Cork, early 1960s.
£45–50
€70–80
$85–95 ⊞ OH

Linen & Lace

A Honiton lace handkerchief,
c1860, 7in (18cm) square.
**£130–145 / €195–220
$240–270 ⊞ HL**

A hand- and machine-worked
linen mat, c1920, 5½in (14cm) diam.
**£10–15 / €15–22
$19–28 ⊞ HILL**

A crochet-edged linen table mat,
1930, 10in (25.5cm) square.
**£6–10 / €9–15
$12–19 ⊞ L&L**

▶ A pair of linen tray cloths,
hand-embroidered with flying ducks,
1930s, 24 x 16in (61 x 40.5cm).
**£12–16 / €18–24
$22–30 ⊞ HILL**

A Mountmellick linen
tablecloth, Irish, c1880,
with runners, tablecloth
50in (127cm) square.
**£100–110 / €150–160
$185–210 ⊞ JUC**
Mountmellick work is a
form of raised white
embroidery that
originated in
Mountmellick, Ireland in
1830. It was produced
by amateur
needlewomen, both for
their own homes and to
subsidize the family
income. The favoured
material was white 'jean'
(used for upholstery),
which was sturdily
embroidered with white
cotton thread, making
Mountmellick work very
suitable for table linen.
Typical decoration
included flowers and
leaves and, from the
mid-19th century
onwards, this hand-
worked Irish linen was
popular in the USA.

A linen tablecloth, with a hand-worked
decorative border, 1890–1910, 65 x 64in
(165 x 162.5cm).
**£75–85 / €115–130
$140–160 ⊞ HILL**

A set of eight linen needlepoint table
mats, decorated with buttonhole,
drawn thread and satin stitches, 1920s,
11 x 16in (28 x 40.5cm).
**£175–195 / €260–290
$320–360 ⊞ HILL**

◀ A hand-
embroidered
linen tablecloth,
1930s–40s,
50 x 48in
(127 x 122cm).
**£45–50
€70–80
$85–95 ⊞ HILL**

▶ A hand-
embroidered
linen tablecloth,
1930s–40s, 40in
(101.5cm) wide.
**£50–55
€75–85
$95–105
⊞ HILL**

Menswear

A silk-embroidered
satin waistcoat, with a
linen back, some damage,
late 18thC.
**£85–95 / €130–145
$160–180 ♪ WW**

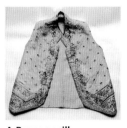

A Regency silk-
embroidered waistcoat.
**£590–650 / €890–980
$1,100–1,250 ⊞ JPr**
This waistcoat is in mint
condition, hence the price.

A Victorian page-boy's
velvet suit, comprising
knee breeches, tail coat,
bicorn hat and two collars.
**£130–155 / €195–230
$250–290 ♪ G(L)**

◀ An evening shirt,
in a Victoria Dry Cleaners
bag, 1940s.
**£10–15 / €15–22
$19–28 ⊞ NFR**

A pair of silk stockings,
1867, with a letter
of provenance.
**£490–590 / €740–890
$920–1,100 ♪ LCM**
The letter of provenance
states that these
stockings belonged to
Maximilian I, Emperor
of Mexico. They were
removed from his
corpse in October 1867
prior to his body being
re-embalmed.

A box of ties, 1920s.
**£6–10 / €9–15
$12–19 each ⊞ OH**

Further reading

*Miller's Collecting
the 1950s,* Miller's
Publications, 2004

A General Post Office
uniform jacket, 1940s.
**£25–30 / €40–45
$50–55 ⊞ NFR**

A Calicraft gabardine
pullover, late 1950s.
**£240–270 / €360–410
$450–500 ⊞ CAD**
This garment is very
rare and 1950s
enthusiasts will pay
high prices for classic
examples and more
unusual pieces of
period fashion.

A wool dressing
gown, 1940s.
**£20–25 / €30–35
$35–45 ⊞ DE**

For further
information on
fashion see Rock &
Pop pages 324–332

A Tootal rayon
scarf, 1950s.
**£8–12 / €12–18
$15–22 ⊞ CCO**

A dinner jacket, with a shawl collar, 1950s.
£50–60 / €75–90
$95–110 ⊞ OH

A pair of leopard print pyjamas, 1950s.
£85–95
€130–145
$160–180 ⊞ CAD

A printed cotton leisure shirt, by Banner, 1950s.
£10–15 / €15–22
$19–28 ⊞ HSt

A Hawaiian shirt, by National Sports Wear, Jamaican, 1960s.
£12–16 / €18–24
$22–30 ⊞ HSt

A Duke Kahanamaku Hawaiian shirt, c1960.
£20–25 / €30–35
$35–45 ⊞ REPS

A barrister's wig, with a tin box, 1960s, box 10in (25.5cm) diam.
£250–280 / €380–420
$470–520 ⊞ OH

A Terylene double-breasted suit, 1960s.
£45–50 / €70–80
$85–95 ⊞ REPS

A Philips & Piper Pychley hacking jacket, 1960s.
£65–75 / €100–115
$120–140 ⊞ OH

A Burberry raincoat, 1970s.
£75–85 / €115–130
$140–160 ⊞ OH

A silver-mounted seal skin sporran, c1970, 9in (23cm) long.
£540–600 / €810–900
$1,000–1,100 ⊞ BWA

Cross Reference
Eighties see
pages 218–221

A Vivienne Westwood cotton Pirate shirt, c1981.
£220–250 / €330–380
$410–470 ⊞ ID

Samplers

A George III needlework text, by Mary Jarman, entitled 'Religion', dated 1798, in a line-inlaid figured satinwood and parquetry frame, 13¾ x 11¾in (35 x 30cm).
£480–570 / €720–860
$900–1,050 ➤ Bri

A sampler, depicting Adam and Eve at the Tree of Knowledge, c1820, 10in (25.5cm) square, framed.
£450–500 / €680–750
$840–940 ⊞ HIS

A sampler, by Margaret Lockie, embroidered with initials, birds, flowers, trees and a house, dated 1835, 17 x 12in (43 x 30.5cm), in a rosewood frame.
£1,900–2,250 / €2,850–3,400
$3,550–4,200 ➤ JNic

◀ **A school sampler,** worked with the alphabet, numbers and a darning patch, 1936, 4 x 5½in (10 x 14cm), framed.
£135–150 / €200–230
$250–280 ⊞ HIS

A linen handkerchief and bag, the bag embroidered with The Lord's Prayer, the handkerchief monogrammed and dated 1843, bag 2½in (6.5cm) wide.
£270–300 / €400–450
$500–560 ⊞ HIS

◀ **A sampler,** depicting a house, 1830s, 7¾ x 6½in (19.5 x 16.5cm), in a maple frame.
£450–500
€680–750
$840–940
⊞ HIS

A sampler, by Sarah Sowersby, worked with flowers, a bird, dogs and a text, some damage, 19thC, 15 x 17in (38 x 43cm), in a maple frame.
£120–140 / €180–210
$220–260 ➤ DA

▶ **A sampler,** by Alice Mary Underdown, commemorating Queen Victoria's Golden Jubilee, worked with a verse, birds and floral motifs within a border of strawberries, 1887, 16 x 19in (40.5 x 48.5cm), in a rosewood frame.
£280–330 / €420–500
$520–620 ➤ G(L)

◀ **A sampler,** by Louisa Hawkins, worked with alphabets and a verse above a house, trees and animals, 19thC, 16½ x 12½in (42 x 32cm).
£580–690 / €880–1,050
$1,100–1,300 ➤ GH

Shawls & Scarves

A tartan shawl, c1840, 144 x 72in (284.5 x 183cm).
£350–390 / €530–590
$650–730 ⊞ GAU

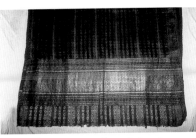

A Victorian cotton and wool shawl, 66in (167.5cm) square.
£45–50 / €70–80
$85–95 ⊞ CCO

An embroidered silk shawl, 1900–20, 55in (139.5cm) square.
£160–180 / €240–270
$300–340 ⊞ DE

Two hand-embroidered silk scarves, 1920, 72in (183cm) long.
£35–40 / €50–60
$65–75 each ⊞ DE

A hand-knitted silk shawl, with appliquéd flowers, 1920s, 54in (137cm) long.
£65–75 / €100–115
$120–140 ⊞ DE

A red silk shawl, with an embroidered net panel and a silk fringe, c1920, 55in (139.5cm) long.
£200–230
€300–350
$380–430 ⊞ DE

A rayon scarf, decorated with poodles, American, 1950s, 26½in (67.5cm) square.
£10–15 / €15–22
$19–28 ⊞ DRE

A Jacqmar silk scarf, c1950, 25in (63.5cm) square.
£15–20 / €22–30
$28–38 ⊞ JUJ

◀ **A Schiaparelli silk scarf,** 1950s, 28in (71cm) square.
£25–30 / €40–45
$50–55 ⊞ JUJ

▶ **A Hermès silk scarf,** c1960, 16in (40.5cm) square.
£50–60 / €75–90
$95–110 ⊞ HIP

Shoes

Finding vintage shoes to actually wear can be a challenge. Over the decades, with improved nutrition, average foot sizes have increased. Vintage shoes are often comparatively small, and the further back in time you go, the smaller they get. Size does affect the value of shoes. More wearable sizes will command a premium and costume dealers will sometimes hang on to a decent-sized pair of vintage shoes because they can make more money hiring them out than selling them. Condition is another factor, and enthusiasts often save their period footwear for special occasions and indoor events. Vintage shoes are also purchased as decorative items or pieces of fashion history. The values depend largely on how much a shoe epitomizes the fashion of the period.

A pair of Edwardian suede and leather button-up boots.
£145–160 / €210–240
$270–300 ⊞ DE

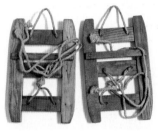

A pair of wooden snow shoes, c1910, 14in (35.5cm) long
£30–35 / €45–50
$55–65 ⊞ HO

A pair of Victorian boots.
£200–220 / €300–330
$370–410 ⊞ DE

A pair of leather shoes, 1920s.
£65–75 / €100–115
$120–140 ⊞ TIN

A pair of Russell & Bromley leather Stella shoes, c1930.
£50–60 / €75–90
$95–110 ⊞ DE

A pair of kid leather and lamé shoes, 1920.
£85–95 / €130–145
$160–180 ⊞ TIN

A pair of wooden mules, with hand-painted decoration, Lucite heels and straw straps, 1940s.
£210–240 / €320–360
$400–450 ⊞ SpM

A pair of Hollywood lamé shoes, c1940.
£60–70 / €90–105
$110–130 ⊞ DE

◀ **A pair of Van-Dal leather Norfolk Broads shoes,** 1940s.
£40–45 / €60–70
$75–85 ⊞ NFR

A pair of **Honnor & Goldberg suede platform shoes,** with metal-trimmed ankle straps, 1940s.
£270–300 / €400–450
$500–560 ⊞ SpM

A pair of **wood and fabric lace-up sandals,** 1950s.
£80–90 / €120–135
$150–170 ⊞ SpM

A pair of **Manfield suede shoes,** c1960.
£15–20 / €22–30
$28–38 ⊞ DE

A pair of **SAKS Springolator Lucite shoes,** with carved heels, 1950s.
£130–150 / €195–230
$240–280 ⊞ Ci

A pair of **Andrew Geller silk and leather La Rose shoes,** late 1950s.
£35–40 / €50–60
$65–75 ⊞ TWI

A pair of **Ricky Dean Collection platform shoes,** 1970.
£60–70 / €90–105
$110–130 ⊞ DE

A pair of **Biba brocade boots,** late 1960s.
£130–150 / €200–230
$240–280 ⊞ Ci

A pair of **Thom McAn leather shoes,** American, early 1970s.
£40–45 / €60–70
$75–85 ⊞ TWI

◄ A pair of **leather shoes,** decorated with Batman logo, 1989.
£15–20 / €22–30
$28–38 ⊞ IQ

A pair of **Dolly Mixture platform sandals,** 1970s.
£35–40 / €50–60
$65–75 ⊞ DE

Tea Cosies

Tea cosies are something of a British speciality, particularly during the interwar years when tea drinking in Britain was at its height. Most are homemade and are typically embroidered on to linen or pieced together from felt. Ladies' magazines and contemporary sewing manuals provided patterns and stencils that the housewife could copy, and cosies were often made to match napkins and tray cloths etc. Favourite themes included flowers, garden scenes, country cottages and the ubiquitous crinoline lady, who remained a favourite decorative subject from the 1920s to the 1950s. Like much embroidered table linen from the period, these hand-produced items can still be picked up very cheaply and provide a charming reminder of a more leisurely age (before the arrival of the television and tea bags) when afternoon tea was a daily ritual, and every lady practised her needlework.

A hand-made lace tea cosy, 1910–20, 14in (35.5cm) wide.
£15–20 / €22–30
$28–38 HILL

A felt tea cosy, in the form of a crinoline lady, with silk lining, 1920s, 13in (33cm) wide.
£10–15 / €15–22
$19–28 DE

A hand-worked double-sided linen tea cosy, with floral decoration, 1920s–30s, 14in (35.5cm) wide.
£25–30 / €40–45
$50–55 HILL

A felt tea cosy, depicting South African Red Cross projects, 1920s–30s, 9in (23cm) high.
£20–25 / €30–35
$35–45 HILL

A hand-worked linen tea cosy, with embroided decoration, 1920s–30s, 15in (38cm) wide.
£10–15 / €15–22
$19–28 HILL

A linen tea cosy, hand-worked with a crinoline lady watering a garden, 1920s–30s, 13in (33cm) wide.
£20–25 / €30–35
$35–45 HILL

A hand-worked double-sided linen tea cosy, 1930s, 15in (38cm) wide.
£10–15 / €15–22
$19–28 HILL

A felt tea cosy, with appliqué and embroidered decoration, c1940, 15in (38cm) wide.
£10–15 / €15–22
$19–28 DE

A felt tea cosy, decorated with appliqué flowers, c1950, 15in (38cm) wide.
£6–10 / €9–15
$12–19 DE

Textiles

A Berlin woolwork panel, c1840, 26in (66cm) wide.
£200–220 / €300–330
$370–410 ⊞ JPr

A beadwork pillow, c1860, 28in (71cm) wide.
£250–300 / €380–450
$470–560 ↗ LHA

A Victorian woolwork picture, depicting a naval ship and national flags, glazed and framed, 9¾ x 13½in (25 x 34.5cm).
£460–550 / €690–830
$860–1,000 ↗ PF

A patchwork quilt, with embroidered decoration, c1880, 100 x 98in (254 x 249cm).
£100–120 / €150–180
$185–220 ↗ MCA

A Log Cabin quilt, American, 19thC, 90 x 85in (228.5 x 216cm).
£110–130 / €165–195
$200–240 ↗ COBB

▶ **A length of upholstery fabric,** 1930s, 52in (132cm) long.
£110–125 / €165–190
$200–230 ⊞ EMH

A wool honeycomb blanket, Welsh, early 1950s, 70 x 84in (178 x 213.5cm).
£30–35 / €45–50
$55–65 ⊞ JWK

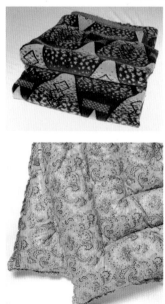

A wool travel rug, 1940s, 55 x 68in (139.5 x 172.5cm).
£10–15 / €15–22
$19–28 ⊞ JWK

◀ **An eiderdown,** 1950s, 50 x 62in (127 x 157.5cm).
£50–60 / €75–90
$95–110 ⊞ JWK

Underwear & Nightwear

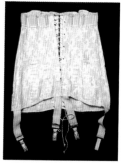

A pair of rayon pyjamas, c1930, with original box.
£25–30 / €40–45
$50–55 ⊞ DE

A corsetted girdle, with suspender snaps, 1910–20.
£175–195 / €260–290
$320–360 ⊞ LU

▶ **A boned satin, elastic and aertex corset,** 1940s.
£35–40 / €50–60
$65–75 ⊞ AFA

A Jeufels Olympia-Suspensor jock strap, in original box depicting the opening ceremony of the Olympics at the Brandenburg Gate, 1936, 5½in (14cm) wide.
£40–45 / €60–70
$75–85 ↗ VS
The value of this vintage jock strap lies in its packaging, which illustrates the 1936 Berlin Olympics.

◀ **A box of Camp seamfree stockings,** late 1950s, with original packaging.
£10–15 / €15–22
$19–28 ⊞ SpM

A rayon, lace and elastic corselet, by Milady, American, c1950.
£40–45 / €60–70
$75–85 ⊞ AFA

A satin and cotton bra, 1950s.
£60–70 / €90–105
$110–130 ⊞ SpM

A nylon suspender belt, 1960.
£10–15 / €15–22
$19–28 ⊞ HIP

◀ **A Kayser Bondor nylon nightdress and bed jacket,** 1950s.
£45–50 / €70–80
$85–105 ⊞ HIP

A pair of polyester pants, decorated with sporting vignettes, 1980s.
£4–8 / €6–12
$8–15 ⊞ TWI

Dolls & Dolls' Houses
Bisque

Dolls are categorized by the medium in which the head is made. From the mid-19th century bisque – unglazed tinted porcelain – was the most popular material used. The major centres of manufacture were Germany and France. Competition was fierce, resulting in the manufacture of some very fine examples. Dolls tend to be marked on the back of the head or shoulders with a name or initials and a mould number. Since as much as 80 per cent of a doll's value can lie in the head, this should always be checked both for

indentification and for any damage such as hairline cracks.

Dolls by famous makers are always desirable, and other factors affecting value include size (large dolls are very sought after), original condition of the body and period clothing. In this, as in every other field, rarity is all important and the mould number can be a good indicator. Only one Kämmer & Reinhardt mould No. 108 is known to exist and when sold at auction in 1994, the doll fetched a record price of £188,500 / €282,800 / $352,500.

A bisque-headed doll, with glass eyes, pierced ears, leather body, bisque lower arms, slight damage, wearing later clothes, marked '193.5', c1870, 17in (43cm) high.
**£380–450 / €570–680
$710–840** ➤ **Bert**

A Kämmer & Reinhardt bisque-headed doll, No. 116A, with sleeping eyes, open/closed mouth, metal tongue and crying voice box, marked, German, 1910, 16in (40.5cm) high.
**£1,900–2,150
€2,850–3,250
$3,600–4,000** ⊞ **SaB**

A bisque-headed doll, dressed as a clown, with glass eyes, mohair wig, five-piece composition body, damaged, German, 1900, 4¾in (12cm) high.
**£310–350 / €470–530
$590–650** ⊞ **SaB**

◀ **A Gebrüder Heubach bisque-headed Stuart doll,** No. 7684, with glass eyes and composition body, German, 1910, 13in (33cm) high.
**£1,100–1,250
€1,650–1,900
$2,100–2,350** ⊞ **SaB**

A Kämmer & Reinhardt bisque-headed Elise doll, No. 109, fully-jointed composition body, German, 1909, 12in (30.5cm) high.
**£1,800–2,000
€2,700–3,100
$3,400–3,800** ⊞ **SaB**
This is a rare mould number, hence the high price.

> Items in the Dolls & Dolls' Houses section have been arranged in date order within each sub-section.

A Kämmer & Reinhardt bisque-headed baby doll, No. 126, with a metal tongue and crying voice box, marked, German, 1910, 12in (30.5cm) high.
**£310–350 / €470–530
$590–650** ⊞ **SaB**

A Simon & Halbig bisque-headed doll, No. 550, with sleeping eyes, mohair wig and fully-jointed composition body, marked 'Gimbels Bros', German, 1910, 23in (58.5cm) high.
**£390–430 / €590–650
$720–800** ⊞ **SaB**
Gimbels was a department store in New York.

An S. F. B. J. bisque-headed googly doll, No. 245, French, 1910, 13in (33cm) high.
£2,200–2,450
€3,300–3,700
$4,150–4,600 ⊞ SaB
In 1899 10 companies amalgamated to form the *Societé Française de Fabrication de Bébés et Jouets (S. F. B. J.)* in order to compete with German doll and toy imports.

An Armand Marseille bisque-headed doll, No. 390, German, 1910–25, 20in (51cm) high.
£250–290 / €380–440
$470–550 ⊞ HeA

A William Goebel bisque-headed doll, with a lace dress and a felt hat, German, c1915, 19in (48.5cm) high.
£180–200 / €270–300
$340–380 ⊞ HeA

An Armand Marseille bisque-headed baby doll, No. 351, German, c1920, 16in (40.5cm) high.
£145–160 / €210–240
$270–300 ⊞ HeA

◀ **An Ernst Heubach character doll,** marked 'Heubach Koppelsdorf', with sleeping eyes and open mouth, German, c1925, 12in (30.5cm) high.
£160–180 / €240–270
$300–340 ⊞ HeA
Ernst Heubach (1887–1930) of Koppelsdorf, Germany made a range of less expensive bisque dolls, including characters, babies and jointed girl dolls. He is often confused with Gebrüder Heubach (active 1820–1945), another German manufacturer, based in Thuringia and very sought after for character-headed dolls.

◀ **An Armand Marseille doll,** No. 995 A3M, German, 1930s, 16in (40.5cm) high.
£180–200 / €270–300
$340–380 ⊞ HeA

◀ **A bisque-headed souvenir doll,** with mohair wig and bisque lower arms and legs, American, 1987, 6in (15cm) high, seated.
£10–15 / €15–22
$20–25 ➢ Bert

◀ **A Maryanne Oldenburg bisque-headed souvenir doll,** with painted eyes, American, 1996, 13½in (34.5cm) high.
£16–20 / €22–30
$30–45 ➢ Bert

China

A porcelain boy doll, with painted features, cloth body, bisque lower arms and wooden legs, slight damage, wearing later clothes, German, c1860, 9in (23cm) high.
£130–155 / €195–230 $250–290 ✗ Bert

A porcelain Dolly Madison doll, with a cloth body and porcelain arms, hairline crack, German, c1880, 18in (45.5cm) high.
£40–45 / €60–70 $75–85 ✗ Bert

A Jayco porcelain-headed doll, with a cloth body, 1940s, 17in (43cm) high.
£70–80 / €105–120 $130–150 ⊞ HeA

▶ **A porcelain articulated Betty Boop doll,** c1980, 11in (28cm) high.
£145–160 / €210–240 $270–300 ⊞ HeA

Cloth

◀ **A Martha Chase oil-painted stockinet doll,** marked, American, early 1900s, 16in (40.5cm) high.
£480–540 / €720–810 $900–1,000 ⊞ SaB

▶ **A Käthe Kruse cloth doll,** with painted features and jointed body, wearing original clothes, 1930s, 17in (43cm) high.
£880–990 €1,300–1,500 $1,650–1,850 ⊞ SaB

A Norah Wellings felt schoolboy doll, 1950s, 11in (28cm) high.
£100–120 / €150–180 $185–220 ⊞ LAS

Composition

◀ **A pair of Armand Marseille composition dolls,** No. 1353, in a basket pram, German, 1930s–40s, 18in (45.5cm) long.
£700–800 / €1,050–1,200 $1,300–1,500 ⊞ UD

▶ **A King Features Syndicate composition Popeye doll,** with wooden joints, hand-painted, damaged, 1935, 13½in (34.5cm) high.
£130–155 / €195–230 $250–290 ✗ Bert

A Reliable Toy Co composition Highland Scottish Lassie doll, Canadian, Toronto, 1930s, 15in (38cm) high.
£80–90 / €120–135 $150–170 ⊞ HeA

Papier-Mâché, Wax & Wood

A papier-mâché shoulder-headed doll, with kid body and wooden arms, wearing original clothes, German, 1830–60, 15in (38cm) high.
£600–670 / €900–1,000
$1,100–1,250 ⊞ SaB

A Schoenhut Baby Face doll, with painted eyes and original mohair wig, wearing later clothes, slight damage, with label, American, 1913, 12in (30.5cm) high.
£250–300 / €380–450
$470–560 ➤ Bert

▶ **Two carved wood fertility dolls,** c1860, 13in (33cm) high.
£100–120 / €150–170
$190–220 each ⊞ NEW

A Schoenhut boy doll, with mohair wig, wearing original clothes, marked, American, 1911, 20in (51cm) high.
£990–1,150
€1,450–1,750
$1,850–2,150 ➤ Bert
Descended from a family of German toy makers, Albert Schoenhut emigrated to Philadelphia in 1866 where he established a business manufacturing wooden toys. By the early 20th century the company produced dolls. With their steam-pressed wooden heads and metal-jointed wooden bodies, these dolls were far sturdier than the bisque-headed, elastic-strung alternatives. Patented in 1911, Schoenhut dolls were popular. Albert died in 1912 and the quality of dolls declined by the 1920s. The firm failed to survive the Depression and went out of business in the mid-1930s.

◀ **A Schoenhut boy doll,** with sleeping eyes and mohair wig, slight damage, with label, stamped, American, 1921, 17in (43cm) high.
£270–320 / €400–480
$500–600 ➤ Bert

A Schoenhut doll, Miss Dolly, wearing original clothes, American, 1911, 17in (43cm) high.
£400–450 / €600–680
$750–840 ⊞ SaB

◀ **A Schoenhut baby doll,** with painted hair and eyes and bent limbs, with label, American, 1913, 13in (33cm) high.
£160–190 / €240–280
$300–360 ➤ Bert

Plastic & Vinyl

A Pedigree hard plastic doll, late 1940s, 12in (30.5cm) high.
£85–95 / €130–145
$160–180 ⊞ UD

A Pedigree hard plastic walking talking doll, c1950, 20in (51cm) high.
£65–75 / €100–115
$120–140 ⊞ UD

A Pedigree hard plastic Elizabeth doll, c1950, 19in (48.5cm) high.
£110–125 / €165–190
$200–230 ⊞ UD

A Pedigree hard plastic walking talking Belles of Brighton doll, 1955, 28in (71cm) high.
£145–160 / €210–240
$270–300 ⊞ UD

An Alexander Doll Co hard plastic Jo doll, American, c1958, 5in (12.5cm) high.
£220–250 / €330–380
$410–470 ⊞ UD
The Alexander Doll Co was founded in New York in 1925. Dolls were inspired by both living figures (such as film stars) and fictional characters. This doll combines the two. The character represented is Jo, from Louisa M. Alcott's famous novel *Little Women*. The face used for this and the other sisters in the Little Women series was known as the 'Margaret face', because the mould was based on Margaret O'Brien, the famous Hollywood child actress, who starred as Beth in the 1949 film version of *Little Women*. Little Women dolls are very sought after.

A Pedigree hard plastic doll, 1950s, 20in (51cm) high.
£220–250 / €330–380
$410–470 ⊞ POLL

A Pedigree plastic walking doll, 1950s, 20in (51cm) high.
£180–200 / €270–300
$330–370 ⊞ POLL

◀ **A Rosebud doll,** with original mohair wig, 1950s, 11in (28cm) high.
£30–35 / €45–50
$55–65 ⊞ POLL

▶ **A Roddy hard plastic doll,** 1950s, 21in (53.5cm) high.
£65–75 / €100–115
$120–140 ⊞ UD

A Rosebud baby doll, wearing hand-knitted clothes, 1950s, 17in (43cm) high.
£200–230 / €300–350
$370–430 ⊞ POLL

◀ **A Roddy walking doll,** slight damage, 1950s, 13in (33cm) high.
£45–50 / € 70–80
$85–95 ⊞ POLL

A Roddy hard plastic doll, wearing Scottish costume, 1950s, 12in (30.5cm) high.
£30–35 / € 45–50
$55–65 ⊞ POLL

A Roddy hard plastic baby doll, 1950s, 21in (53.5cm) high.
£130–145 / € 195–220
$240–270 ⊞ POLL
This large baby doll is difficult to find.

A Pedigree vinyl baby doll, with moulded hair, late 1950s, 11in (28cm) high.
£30–35 / € 45–50
$55–65 ⊞ POLL

◀ **A Roddy vinyl doll,** 1950s–60s, 27in (68.5cm) high.
£175–195 / € 260–290
$320–360 ⊞ POLL

A Kewpie plastic Ned doll, 1950s–60s, 8in (20.5cm) high.
£10–15 / € 15–22
$19–28 ⊞ HeA

A Palitoy vinyl Patsy doll, c1960, 16in (40.5cm) high, in original box.
£65–75 / € 100–115
$120–140 ⊞ UD

A Pedigree vinyl Melanie doll, 1962, 36in (91.5cm) high.
£160–180 / € 240–270
$300–340 ⊞ UD

◀ **A vinyl Tiny Tears doll,** 1966, 15in (38cm) high.
£30–35 / € 45–50
$55–65 ⊞ POLL
Tiny Tears was launched in Britain by Palitoy in 1965. The principal selling points were that when fed with a bottle, the baby doll cried real tears and wet herself. Teeny Tiny Tears, a smaller version at 12in (30.5cm) high, was introduced later, followed in 1980 by Teeny Weeny Tiny Tears, at just 9in (23cm) high. In the USA, drinking and wetting dolls had been popular for several decades. Tiny Tears first appeared in 1950, introduced by American Character Doll Co and later manufactured by Ideal, who also produced another American drinking, wetting, crying favourite, named Betsy Wetsy doll.

A Hummelwerk clockwork plastic dancing doll, German, Limmer, 1965, 4in (10cm) high.
£25–30 / € 40–45
$50–55 ⊞ HeA

A pair of Käthe Kruse hard plastic dolls, with cloth bodies, marked 'US Zone', German, 1960s, 14in (35.5cm) high.
£560–640 / €840–960
$1,050–1,200 ⊞ SaB

A Palitoy vinyl doll, 1960s, 14in (35.5cm) high.
£25–30 / €40–45
$50–55 ⊞ POLL

A Mattel vinyl Francie doll, with bendable legs, American, c1966, 6in (15cm) high.
£330–370 / €500–560
$620–690 ⊞ T&D
Francie was introduced as Barbie's cousin.

A Mattel vinyl Bubblecut Barbie doll, wearing 'Invitation To Tea' outfit, American, c1967, 11½in (29cm) high.
£530–590 / €800–890
$990–1,100 ⊞ T&D
The outfit worn by this doll would cost £400–450 / €600–680 / $750–840 if purchased separately.

A Teeny Tiny Tears doll, 1960s, 12in (30.5cm) high.
£35–40 / €50–60
$65–75 ⊞ POLL

A plastic hedgehog doll, 1960–70s, 4in (10cm) high.
£4–8 / €6–12
$8–15 ⊞ HeA

◄ **A pair of Larry Harmon plastic talking and singing Laurel and Hardy dolls,** for Berman & Anderson, American, 1973, 14in (35.5cm) high.
£140–160 / €210–240
$260–300 ⊞ IQ

► **A Pedigree vinyl First Love doll,** 1974, 15in (38cm) high.
£35–40 / €50–60
$65–75 ⊞ POLL
This doll was similar in concept to Tiny Tears but the water-tight arm and leg sockets made it easier to bathe.

► **A set of seven Remco McDonald's dolls,** including Hamburglar, Professor, Mayor McCheese, Grimace, Big Mac, Captain Crook and Ronald, 1976, 6in (15cm) high.
£120–135 / €180–200
$220–250 ⊞ IQ
These figures are based on McDonald's television commercials from the 1970s. The dolls are fully poseable and have levers in their backs that move their heads. They come with removable clothing and Remco also manufactured a play set.

Two Pedigree vinyl Sindy dolls, 1970s, 12in (30.5cm) high.
£20–25 / €30–35
$35–45 ⊞ LAS

A vinyl Amanda Jane doll, in a carry cot, 1970s, 8in (20.5cm) high.
£35–40 / €50–60
$65–75 ⊞ POLL

▶ **Two vinyl Sasha dolls,** wearing original clothes, 1970s, 16in (40.5cm) high.
£175–195 / €260–290
$330–360 each ⊞ POLL

A Palitoy Action Man, wearing 'Red Devil' outfit, 1970s, 12in (30.5cm) high.
£50–60 / €75–90
$95–110 ⊞ LAS
This Red Devil uniform was used on dolls produced between 1973 and 1976. The dolls had realistic hair, rubber gripping hands and fixed eyes.

◀ **A plastic clockwork crawling doll,** 1970s, 4in (10cm) high.
£2–6 / €3–9
$4–11 ⊞ HeA

A vinyl Amanda Jane doll, wearing a school uniform, 1970s, 7in (18cm) high.
£60–70 / €90–105
$110–130 ⊞ POLL
Amanda Jane dolls became popular in the 1960s. These small dolls came with different hair styles and a wide range of clothes and accessories.

A vinyl Amanda Jane doll, 1970s–80s, 7½in (19cm) high.
£55–65 / €85–100
$100–120 ⊞ POLL

A vinyl Australian Aborigine doll, 1970s, 16in (40.5cm) high.
£25–30 / €40–45
$50–55 ⊞ UD

A Cabbage Patch Kids plastic Cabbage Patch doll, first edition, 1991, 12in (30.5cm) high.
£15–20 / €22–30
$28–38 ⊞ HeA

Two rubber Muppet figures, 1990s, Kermit 9in (23cm) high, Miss Piggy 8in (20.5cm) high.
£20–25 / €30–35
$35–45 each ⊞ LAS

▶ **A Franklin Mint vinyl Elizabeth Taylor portrait doll,** 2000, 18in (45.5cm) high.
£80–90 / €120–135
$150–170 ⊞ IQ

Dolls' Accessories

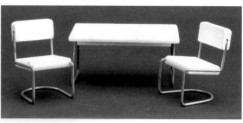

A set of painted wood and metal doll's furniture, 1950s, table 4½in (11.5cm) wide.
£15–20 / €22–30
$28–38 ⊞ MSB

A Crown Staffordshire doll's house chocolate set, comprising eight pieces, 1930s, tray 6in (15cm) long.
£400–440 / €600–660
$740–820 ⊞ SCH

◄ **A set of Model Toys Daisy doll's clothes,** designed by Mary Quant, 1960s–70s, 8in (20.5cm) high.
£8–12 / €12–18
$15–22 each
⊞ LAS

A Lines Brothers Tri-ang doll's pram, 1950s, 28in (71cm) high.
£175–195 / €260–290
$320–360 ⊞ POLL

► **A Mattel Skipper outfit,** 'School Days', c1964, in unopened box, 7in (18cm) square.
£145–160 / €210–240
$270–300 ⊞ T&D

Three sets of Palitoy Action Man accessories, 1970s, in unopened packaging, largest 8in (20.5cm) high.
£10–15 / €15–22
$19–28 each ⊞ HAL

Dolls' Houses

► **A Lines Brothers wooden doll's house,** c1920, 31in (78.5cm) high.
£310–350
€470–530
$580–650 ⊞ HOB

A doll's house, 1907, 36in (91.5cm) wide.
£630–700 / €950–1,050
$1,150–1,300 ⊞ DOL

A wooden doll's house, c1910, 36in (91.5cm) wide.
£400–450 / €600–680
$750–840 ⊞ HOB

► **A Brakspear wooden doll's house,** complete with furniture, signed and dated, 1929, 45in (114.5cm) wide.
£1,800–2,000 / €2,700–3,000
$3,350–3,750 ⊞ HOB

A Tri-ang wooden doll's house,
with tinplate windows, c1930,
48in (122cm) high.
£500–550 / €750–830
$940–1,050 ⊞ HOB

**A hand-made wooden doll's
house,** 1930s, 21in (53.5cm) wide.
£760–850 / €1,150–1,300
$1,400–1,600 ⊞ EMH
Modernist dolls' houses are rare
because, like Modernist houses,
they were not very popular in
the interwar years. Both adults
and children preferred to live in
or play with more traditional,
suburban-style constructions.
However, these Bauhaus-inspired
dolls' houses are very much
sought after by collectors today.

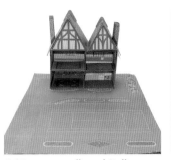

**A Meccano cardboard Dolly
Varden House,** 1934–36,
19in (48.5cm) wide.
£1,050–1,200 / €1,600–1,800
$1,950–2,250 ⊞ HOB
Mock-Tudor half-timbered homes
became all the rage in the leafy
suburbs that sprang up across
Britain in the interwar years and
dolls' houses followed the
prevailing architectural trend.
The Dolly Varden House, made
by Meccano, Liverpool –
manufacturers of Dinky toys –
was named after a coquettish
character in Charles Dickens'
novel *Barnaby Rudge*. The
cardboard house was collapsible
and came in a container that
opened out to form a garden
and a tennis court. It was
especially designed for Dinky
doll's house furniture. Its
fragility makes it rare and very
collectable today.

A wooden doll's house, c1935,
23in (58.5cm) high.
£220–250 / €330–380
$410–470 ⊞ HOB

A wooden doll's house, modelled
as a butcher's shop, 1930s,
30in (76cm) high.
£200–230 / €300–350
$370–430 ⊞ HOB

Doll's House Accessories

A set of doll's house tin washing utensils,
with painted decoration, 1890–1910,
largest 4½in (11.5cm) high.
£120–135 / €180–200
$220–250 ⊞ MSB

A set of doll's house metal furniture,
1930s, settee 4½in (11.5cm) long.
£135–150 / €200–230
$250–280 ⊞ EMH

**A doll's house punched tin and
glass cruet set,** c1900,
1¾in (4.5cm) wide.
£60–70 / €90–105
$110–125 ⊞ MSB

▶ **A set of Ma Cuisine doll's house
metal kitchen utensils,** French,
early 1930s, on original card,
framed, 24½ x 18¼in (62 x 46.5cm).
£145–160 / €220–240
$270–300 ⊞ MSB

**A set of doll's house
punched tin weighing
scales,** early 1900s,
2½in (6.5cm) wide.
£25–30 / €40–45
$50–55 ⊞ MSB

Eighties

The 1980s was a fascinating decade and objects from the period are already becoming collectable. Post-Modernism added a touch of humour to architecture and interior decoration. Leading post-Modern designers included the Memphis group, spearheaded by Ettore Sottsass, whose colourful and eclectic designs captured the playful mood of the moment and are sought after by collectors. Style for style's sake became increasingly important in the decade that gave us *nouvelle cuisine*, and the cachet of a designer label was applied to everything from furniture to trainers to designer mineral water.

The 1980s saw a domestic electronic revolution with the introduction of affordable home computers and portable technology, most famously the mobile phone. Children embraced computer gaming and vintage favourites, such as Nintendo's hand-held Game and Watch sets, are popular with enthusiasts. Electronic instruments such as drum machines and synthesizers also changed the sound and style of popular music. Major 1980s pop stars range from Madonna to Michael Jackson.

In fashion, one of the leading designers of the decade was Vivienne Westwood, who pioneered the Pirate look adopted by the New Romantics and whose clothes, expensive at the time, continue to rise in value. At the other end of the fashion scale, yuppies (both male and female) sported big hair and power suits. Charity and thrift shops are still full of garments made of shiny material with shoulder pads, which tend to appeal to young collectors who don't remember wearing them first time around.

Major events of the decade are recorded in commemoratives which range from traditional-style mugs marking royal events, most notably the wedding of Charles and Diana in 1981, to objects satirizing such major figures and political leaders as Margaret Thatcher and Ronald Reagan. Memorabilia inspired by the *Spitting Image* television series is very desirable. As time progresses the best 1980s material can only become harder to find and more desirable, so collectors are already beginning to stock up.

A fibreglass, metal and rubber Super lamp, by Martine Bedin for Memphis, 1981, 23in (58.5cm) wide.
£700–830 / €1,050–1,250
$1,300–1,550 ⚲ S(NY)

Two MDF prototype drawer units, by Alessandro Mendini for Neuvo Alchimia, with hand-painted decoration, mirror tops and chrome handles, 1981, larger 48½in (123cm) wide.
£6,700–7,500 / €10,100–11,300
$12,500–14,000 ⊞ EMH

A Porcellane San Marco porcelain Ladoga cocktail goblet, by Matteo Thun for Memphis, impressed marks, 1982, 10¼in (26cm) high.
£125–150 / €195–230
$240–280 ⚲ S(NY)

◄ **A Toso Vetri d'Arte glass Cassiopea vase,** by Marco Zanini for Memphis, Italian, 1982, 6¾in (17cm) high.
£260–300 / €390–450
$480–570 ⚲ S(NY)

► **A glass goblet,** attributed to Ettore Sottsass, possibly for Memphis, c1983, 6in (15cm) high.
£125–150 / €195–230
$240–280 ⚲ S(NY)

Further reading

Miller's 20th-Century Design Buyers Guide, Miller's Publications, 2003

Cross Reference
Tiles see pages 157–158

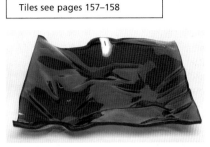

A metal and lacquered-wood First chair, by Michele de Lucchi for Memphis, 1983, 35½in (90cm) high.
£640–750 / €960–1,150
$1,200–1,400 ✗ S(NY)

A glazed ceramic tile, by Ettore Sottsass and Marco Zanini, Italian, marked, c1984, 8½in (21.5cm) square.
£55–65 / €85–100
$100–120 ✗ S(NY)

An acrylic tray, by Verner Panton, 1989, 20in (51cm) wide.
£380–430 / €570–650
$710–800 ⊞ MARK
This tray was also made in yellow, red, grey and black.

Commemorative & Memorabilia

Two J. & J. May porcelain mugs, commemorating the engagement and wedding of Prince Charles and Lady Diana Spencer, 1981, 3½in (9cm) high.
£65–75 / €100–115
$120–140 ⊞ H&G

An Aynsley mug, commemorating the birth of Prince William, damaged, 1982, 2½in (6.5cm) high.
£40–45 / €60–70
$75–85 ⊞ ATK

A ceramic mug, commemorating the Falklands campaign, edition of 500, 1982, 4in (10cm) high.
£10–15 / €15–22
$19–28 ⊞ IQ

Cross Reference
Mining Memorabilia
see pages 301–302

A set of Carlton Ware *Spitting Image* egg cups, depicting Prince Charles, Princess Diana and Prince William, 1982, largest 5in (12.5cm) high.
£65–75 / €100–115
$120–140 each ⊞ H&G

A pair of *Spitting Image* slippers, in the form of Margaret Thatcher in bed, 1984.
£20–25 / €30–35
$35–45 ⊞ IQ

▶ **The *Sun*,** 'Freddie Starr Ate My Hamster', 13 March 1986, 15in (38cm) wide.
£75–85 / €115–130
$140–160 ⊞ IQ
Tabloid papers became ever more extreme in the 1980s and none was more outrageous or successful than the *Sun*, which took over from the *Mirror* to become Britain's most popular paper with a circulation of 4.5 million. This was one of the *Sun*'s most celebrated front covers in the 1980s (the line has entered modern dictionaries of quotations), only matched by another famous/infamous *Sun* headline 'Gotcha' celebrating the sinking of the Argentine warship the *Belgrano* during the Falkland's War.

Fashion & Jewellery

A pair of Caroline Delzoppo
enamelled earrings, c1980.
£80–100 / € 125–150
$155–185 ✦ TEN

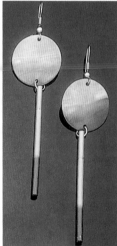

A Malcolm McLaren and Vivienne
Westwood jacket, from the Pirate collection,
with Worlds' End label, 1981.
£540–600 / € 810–900
$1,000–1,100 ⊞ REK

◄ A pair of Gerd Bachmann titanium
earrings, c1980.
£80–100 / € 125–150
$155–185 ✦ TEN

A Malcolm McLaren and Vivienne
Westwood hat, from the Buffalo
collection, with Worlds' End
label, 1982.
£310–350 / € 470–530
$570–650 ⊞ REK

A Malcolm McLaren and
Vivienne Westwood
jersey, from the Savage
collection, with Worlds'
End label, c1983.
£310–350 / € 470–530
$570–650 ⊞ REK

A Malcolm McLaren and Vivienne
Westwood top, with Keith Haring print, from
the Witches collection, c1984.
£450–500 / € 670–750
$840–930 ⊞ REK

A Vivienne Westwood sash, from
the Pirate collection, Worlds' End
label, 1980s, 86in (218.5cm) long.
£200–220 / € 300–330
$370–410 ⊞ REK

A Frank Usher
jacket, 1980s.
£10–15 / € 15–22
$19–28 ⊞ HSt

A pair of L. A. Gear Michael Jackson
trainers, boxed, 1989.
£85–95 / € 130–145
$160–180 ⊞ IQ

Technology & Toys

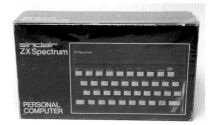

A Sinclair Flat-screen pocket television, boxed, c1982, 8in (20.5cm) wide.
£45–50 / €70–80
$85–95 ⊞ IQ

A Hasbro plastic Mork from Ork gum ball machine, c1980, 9in (23cm) high.
£40–45 / €60–70
$75–85 ⊞ IQ

A Sinclair ZX Spectrum personal computer, 48 RAM, boxed, 1982, 14in (35.5cm) wide.
£140–160 / €210–240
$260–300 ⊞ STa
Launched in 1982 and originally priced at £125 / €190 / $230 the ZX Spectrum was the most famous and successful product created by British inventor Clive Sinclair (b1940). With its rubber membrane keyboard, colour graphics and basic sound, the ZX Spectrum was designed for the home computer market but was principally used for games. Between 1982 and 1988 some seven versions of the ZX Spectrum were produced, the rarest examples include the original Spectrum 16K (1982) and the Spectrum 128 (1985).

◄ A Universal Studios ET costume, American, 1982, boxed, 11in (28cm) wide.
£10–15 / €15–22
$19–28 ⊞ IQ

A Tomy Bjorn Borg electronic tennis game, Japanese, c1982, 10in (25.5cm) wide.
£30–35 / €45–50
$55–65 ⊞ IQ

An LJN plastic *Knight Rider* stunt set, 1980s, boxed, 30in (76cm) wide.
£40–45 / €60–70
$75–85 ⊞ IQ

A Nintendo Mario Brothers electronic Game and Watch game, 1983, 5in (12.5cm) square, with box.
£45–50 / €70–80
$85–95 ⊞ STa

◄ A plastic hairdryer, in the form of Snoopy, c1984, 11in (28cm) high.
£20–25 / €30–35
$35–45 ⊞ IQ

A Sega electronic After Burner game, 1987, 5in (12.5cm) wide.
£4–8 / €6–12
$8–15 ⊞ IQ

Ephemera

A manuscript, detailing the sale of 20,000 acres of land in East Florida, wax and paper seal, slight damage, American, 1767, 2°.
£1,000–1,200
€1,500–1,800
$1,850–2,200 ⚒ BBA

A Valentine card, c1900, 4 x 3in (10 x 7.5cm).
£1–5 / €2–7
$3–9 ⊞ POS

A paper Valentine card, c1900, 6 x 4in (15 x 10cm).
£2–6 / €3–9
$4–11 ⊞ POS

A Minster Fireplaces catalogue, 1920s, 9½ x 7in (24 x 18cm).
£6–10 / €9–15
$12–19 ⊞ J&S

▶ A calendar, 1931, 10 x 15in (25.5 x 38cm).
£45–50 / €70–80
$85–95 ⊞ JUN

A paper chocolate box cover, c1930, 8 x 10in (20.5 x 25.5cm).
£1–5 / €2–7
$3–9 ⊞ POS

A Co-operative Wholesale Society booklet, 1930s, 7½ x 5in (19 x 12.5cm).
£5–9 / €8–13
$10–16 ⊞ RTT

◀ A Brilliant Signs catalogue, c1939, 10in (25.5cm) high.
£55–65 / €85–100
$100–120 ⊞ JUN

A Cunard Line RMS *Queen Elizabeth I* dinner menu, 1953, 11 x 9in (28 x 23cm).
£3–7 / €4–10
$6–13 ⊞ J&S

Erotica

A Munich bronze figure, on a marble plinth, signed and dated, c1898, 12½in (32cm) high.
£260–310 / €400–470
$490–580 ⚒ **G(L)**

A miniature painting of a slave girl, on ivory, signed, late 19thC, in a silver-gilt turquoise-set frame.
£950–1,100
€1,400–1,650
$1,750–2,050 ⚒ **LAY**

An advertising postcard, depicting a girl in a camisole and stockings, c1910.
£30–35 / €45–50
$55–65 ⚒ **VS**

A Bergman bronze figure of a female dancer, Austrian, early 20thC, 7½in (19cm) high.
£260–310 / €400–480
$490–580 ⚒ **G(L)**

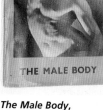

▶ **A silver cigarette case,** decorated with an enamelled panel, Chester 1919, 3in (7.5cm) square.
£490–590
€740–890
$920–1,100
⚒ **DD**

A silver cigarette case, by Reznicek, decorated with an enamel panel, signed, inscribed, Continental, 1912, 3½in (9cm) high.
£900–1,050
€1,350–1,600
$1,700–2,000 ⚒ **TRM**

THE MALE BODY

The Male Body, published by George Routledge & Sons, 1930s, 7½ x 5in (19 x 12.5cm).
£20–25 / €30–35
$35–45 ⊞ **RTT**

◀ **A SylvaC ceramic posy holder,** No. 1326, 1930s, 4in (10cm) wide.
£90–100
€135–150
$170–190
⊞ **JFME**

◀ **A metal bottle opener,** in the form of a nude lady, 1930s–40s, 4¼in (11cm) long.
£6–10 / €9–15
$12–19 ⊞ **RTT**

▶ **An Esquire calendar,** 1951, 12in (30.5cm) high.
£65–75 / €100–115
$120–140 ⊞ **JUN**

***Frou Frou* magazine,** the cover depicting Marilyn
Monroe and Jane Russell, 1953, 9½ x 7in (24 x 18cm).
**£15–20 / €22–30
$28–38 ⊞ RTT**

Serge Jacques, a silver gelatin photograph, entitled
'Brigette Bardot, Pamplone Beach, St Tropez', signed,
numbered 8/10, 1955, 8 x 10¾in (20.5 x 27.5cm).
**£490–590 / €740–890
$920–1,100 ⋏ BBS**
This now famous image of the then unknown
starlet later appeared, colourised, in the December
1959 issue of *Playboy.*

A pin-up postcard,
German, 1950s, 6 x 4in
(15 x 10cm).
**£6–10 / €9–15
$12–19 ⊞ RTT**

**► A pack of
Smiling Brand
playing cards,**
depicting pin-up
girls, 1970s,
2 x 1½in (5 x 4cm).
**£6–10 / €9–15
$12–19 ⊞ RTT**

***Span* magazine,** issue Nos 1, 2 and 4, 1954,
7x 4½in (18 x 11.5cm).
**£10–15 / €15–22
$19–28 each ⊞ RTT**

A pair of silver-gilt cufflinks, with hand-painted
enamel decoration, 1950s.
**£200–230 / €300–350
$370–430 ⊞ JBB**

Phyllis in Censorland,
by Roye, a book of
photographs, 1950s,
5½ x 4½in (14 x 11.5cm).
**£6–10 / €9–15
$12–19 ⊞ RTT**

◄ Irina Ionesco,
solarized gelatin silver
print, entitled 'Fafa with
Top Hat', signed, 1972,
16 x 12in (40.5 x 30.5cm).
**£100–120 / €150–180
$185–220 ⋏ BBA**

**A 3-D peep show
viewer,** 1950s, 27 x 24in
(68.5 x 61cm).
**£400–450 / €600–680
$750–840 ⊞ JUN**

**A glass London Bottle
double-sided calendar,**
1983, 23in (58.5cm) high.
**£25–30 / €40–45
$50–55 ⊞ MRW**

Fans

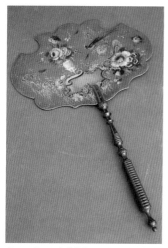

A papier-mâché face screen, the front with painted and gilded decoration, the reverse painted with flowers, with a turned wooden handle, 19thC, 10in (25.5cm) wide.
£60–70 / €90–105
$110–130 ↗ **BWL**

A fan, with carved tortoiseshell sticks, Chinese, 19thC, 7in (18cm) long.
£320–380 / €480–570
$600–710 ↗ **Bea**

A fan, with gilded lacquered sticks and guards, the paper leaf with painted decoration, Chinese, Canton, late 19thC, 11in (28cm) wide.
£100–120 / €150–180
$185–220 ↗ **G(L)**

A silk fan, with mother-of-pearl sticks, the leaf with painted decoration, signed and dated 'H & C Rowley 1883', 23in (58.5cm) wide.
£300–360 / €450–540
$560–670 ↗ **PFK**

A carved ivory fan, with a monogrammed leaf, Chinese, Canton, late 19thC, 8½in (21.5cm) wide.
£110–130 / €165–195
$210–240 ↗ **G(L)**

A silk and lace fan, with bone sticks, c1900, 8in (20.5cm) high.
£45–50 / €70–80
$85–95 ⊞ **CCO**

A paper advertising fan, by Edward Malouze, with wooden sticks, signed, c1920, 9in (23cm) high.
£30–35 / €45–50
$55–65 ⊞ **JPr**

◄ **A paper fan,** with bamboo sticks and hand-painted decoration, 1930s, 10in (25.5cm) wide.
£70–80 / €105–120
$130–150 ⊞ **MARG**

A double-sided paper fan, with bamboo sticks and hand-painted decoration, 1930s, 10in (25.5cm) high.
£1–5 / €2–7
$3–9 ⊞ **POS**

► **A paper foldaway fan,** with an aluminium handle, 1960s, 5in (12.5cm) diam, with box.
£6–10 / €9–15
$12–19 ⊞ **RTT**

A cloth fan, advertising Spanish Air Conditioning, with wooden sticks, c1980, 9in (23cm) high.
£1–5 / €2–7
$3–9 ⊞ **POS**

Fifties

Fifties decorative arts have been performing well in the current market. The clean lines and organic shapes of 'New Look' furnishing sit well in modern interiors, and half a century on many works by leading fifties designers are still in production. Collectors need to distinguish original from more recent editions, and often the materials used provide the evidence. The George Nelson chair shown below, inspired by a broken piece of coconut, is one of the most famous American chairs of the 1950s and was reissued from 1988. Modern versions, however, have a plastic as opposed to steel shell and are lighter in weight than the original.

Fifties lighting is popular. Both works by big designer names and high-quality examples of space-age styling are particularly sought after. Designer textiles have also been making strong prices. They are increasingly being treated as works of modern art and sold as hangings or pictures rather than curtains. The most collectable textiles tend to be good abstract patterns by famous names of the period – preferably still with the selvedge which can include the name of the designer, retailer and the title of the pattern. Condition is a major factor, and material that has never been used or made up and still looks 'factory fresh' will command a premium.

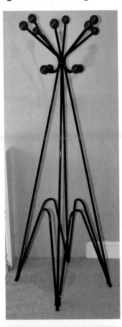

A metal and fabric Coconut chair, by George Nelson for Herman Miller, 1955.
£2,450–2,750
€3,700–4,150
$4,600–5,100 ⊞ MARK
A later version of this chair, with a plastic shell, was produced by Vitra from 1988.

A pair of enamelled table lamps, by Philips, with tripod bases, Dutch, c1955, 14in (35.5cm) high.
£270–300 / €410–450
$500–560 ⊞ BOOM

▶ **An enamelled Atomic hall stand,** with ball hooks, French, c1955, 72in (183cm) high.
£670–750
€1,000–1,150
$1,250–1,400 ⊞ BOOM

A pair of terracotta and metal table lamps, by Philips, with pierced dish shades, Dutch, c1955, 16in (40.5cm) high.
£450–500 / €680–750
$840–940 ⊞ BOOM

▶ **A set of six plastic napkin rings,** by Embee, 1950s, 1¾in (4.5cm) diam.
£10–15
€15–22
$19–28 ⊞ TWI

A Lincoln Beauty Ware metal kitchen canister set, American, 1950s, 16in (40.5cm) wide.
£100–120 / €150–180
$185–220 ⊞ TWI

A chrome and plastic milk jug, sugar bowl and tray, Canadian, 1950s, 11½in (29cm) wide.
£50–60 / €75–90
$95–105 ⊞ GRo

A metal lamp, in the shape of a bomb, on a wooden base, 1950s, 16in (40.5cm) high.
£110–125 / €165–190
$200–230 ⊞ NEW

▶ **A roll of nursery wallpaper,** possibly French, 1950s–60s, 21in (53.5cm) wide.
£45–50 / €70–80
$85–95 per repeat ⊞ TWI

◀ **A brass and metal K10-11 adjustable floor lamp,** by Tapio Wirkkala for Idman Oy, Finnish, 1950s.
£750–900 / €1,100–1,350
$1,400–1,650 ⅄ BUK

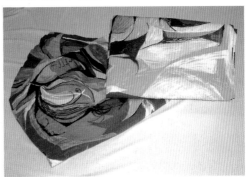

A pair of fabric curtains, designed by Barbara Brown for Heals, decorated with Sweetcorn pattern, 1950s, 45in (114.5cm) wide.
£800–900 / €1,200–1,350
$1,500–1,700 ⊞ EMH

▶ **A set of three plastic nesting tables,** retailed by Maple & Co, 1950s, 9in (23cm) diam.
£140–165 / €210–250
$260–310 ⅄ SWO

Ceramics

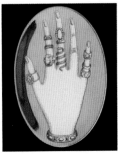

A ceramic ring dish, by Piero Fornasetti, Italian, 1950s, 6½in (16.5cm) wide.
£110–125 / €165–190
$200–230 ⊞ MARK

▶ **A ceramic plate,** by Arthur Meakin, decorated with sailing boats, 1950s–60s, 12in (30.5cm) wide.
£1–5 / €2–7
$3–9 ⊞ FLD

A Napco ceramic vase, modelled as a female head, Japanese, 1950s, 6in (15cm) high.
£55–65 / €85–100
$100–120 ⊞ TWI

Festival of Britain

The Festival of Britain in 1951 was a country-wide celebration designed to showcase modern developments in art and science and to mark the end of forties austerity. The major focus of the Festival was a central exhibition housed in a series of new buildings on London's South Bank. Over five months the exhibition attracted some 10,000,000 visitors, many of whom wanted a souvenir of their visit. The Festival spawned a wealth of memorabilia in every form from mugs and posters (some of the most desirable collectables today) to ashtrays and tea caddies. Look out for the distinctive Festival logo surmounted by the head of Minerva, designed by Abram Games.

A wooden tea caddy, 1951, 5¼in (13.5cm) wide.
£15–20 / €22–30
$28–38 ⊞ HUX

A brass ashtray, with Festival logo, 1951, 4in (10cm) diam.
£15–20 / €22–30
$28–38 ⊞ HUX

A Wedgwood mug, by Norman Makinson, printed and hand-painted with a view of the Great Exhibition, Skylon and the Festival logo, printed and painted marks, 1951, 3in (7.5cm) high.
£500–600 / €750–900
$940–1,100 ⚹ SWO

▶ **A silver teaspoon,** with Festival logo, 1951, 6in (15cm) long.
£35–40 / €50–60
$65–75 ⊞ MURR

Poodles

Good modern design is not the only collectable aspect of the fifties. The period was also famous for kitsch, a style which attracts many collectors. The poodle was a favourite fifties symbol. During WWII the British Bulldog had summoned up the national spirit of resilience, but post-WWII it was time for fun, fantasy and the poodle, which appeared in ceramics, fashion and jewellery. The poodle was associated with France (romantic images of Paris were another favourite fifties decorative theme), but many poodle-decorated items were made in the USA. The poodle skirt was a favourite rock and roll accessory, and poodle items are still popular with rock and roll enthusiasts today.

A cotton handkerchief, decorated with poodles, American, 1950s, 15in (38cm) square.
£20–25 / €30–35
$35–45 ⊞ DRE

A ceramic model of a poodle, American, 1950s, 2¼in (5.5cm) high.
£10–15 / €15–22
$19–28 ⊞ DRE

A metal brooch, in the form of a poodle, 1950s, 1½in (4cm) wide.
£20–25 / €30–35
$35–45 ⊞ LBe

Film & Entertainment

Lotte Jacobi, a silver gelatin print of Ali Ghito, c1932, 9 x 7in (23 x 18cm).
£110–130 / €165–195
$210–240 ➹ BBA

A signed photograph, Fred Astaire and Ginger Rogers, 1930s, 12½ x 10in (32 x 25.5cm).
£450–500 / €680–750
$840–940 ⊞ TYA

A signed photograph, Gary Cooper and Mae West, 1933, 10 x 8in (25.5 x 20.5cm).
£630–700 / €950–1,050
$1,200–1,300 ⊞ TYA
This photograph was taken on 5 December 1933, the day prohibition was repealed in the USA.

◀ **Stan Laurel and Oliver Hardy,** a signed and inscribed postcard, 1940s.
£430–480 / €650–720
$800–900 ⊞ CFSD

Cross Reference
Autographs see pages 41–43

A film poster, *Summer Holiday,* printed by Stafford & Co, c1961, 29¾ x 40in (75.5 x 101.5cm).
£80–90 / €120–145
$150–180 ➹ NSal

Further reading
Miller's Movie Collectibles,
Miller's Publications, 2002

A film poster, *Some Like It Hot,* c1961, 40in (101.5cm) wide.
£360–400 / €540–600
$670–750 ⊞ IQ

A film poster, *Fury of the Kings,* 1961, 28 x 40in (71 x 101.5cm).
£160–175 / €240–260
$260–330 ⊞ MARK

▶ **Jeanloup Sieff,** a gelatin silver print of Alfred Hitchcock and Ina Balke, 1962, 10¾ x 7¼in (27.5 x 18.5cm).
£300–360 / €450–540
$560–670 ➹ BBA

Jeanloup Sieff, a gelatin silver print of Yves Montand, 1961, 10½ x 7¾in (26.5 x 19.5cm).
£165–195 / €250–290
$300–360 ➹ BBA

► **A foyer poster,**
Uncertain Mr Bingo, starring
Stewart Granger, c1965,
15 x 23in (38 x 58.5cm).
**£110–125 / €165–190
$200–230 ⊞ MARK
The English title for this
film was** *Requiem for a
Secret Agent.*

A film poster, *Dr
Strangelove,* directed by
Stanley Kubrick, photographs
by Busta, Italian, 1964,
28 x 12in (71 x 30.5cm).
**£135–150 / €200–230
$250–280 ⊞ SDP**

► **A film poster,** *Alfie,*
starring Michael Caine, c1966,
29 x 13in (73.5 x 33cm).
**£75–85 / €115–130
$140–160 ⊞ IQ**

◄ **Seven foyer
film prints,**
Blow Up, c1966,
each 10 x 8in
(25.5 x 20.5cm).
**£105–120
€160–180
$195–220
⊞ CTO**

A Rank poster, *The Magnificent Two,*
starring Morecambe & Wise, 1967,
30 x 40in (76 x 101.5cm).
**£70–80 / €105–120
$130–150 ⊞ SDP**

► **A film poster,** *Casino
Royale,* Australian, 1968,
30 x 13in (76 x 33cm).
**£75–85 / €115–130
$140–160 ⊞ IQ**

**A 20th Century Fox
poster,** *La Planète des
Singes,* French, 1968,
30 x 22in (76 x 56cm).
**£200–220 / €300–330
$370–410 ⊞ SDP
The English title for this
film was** *The Planet of
the Apes.*

A badge, advertising *Jungle Book,*
1960s, 1½in (4cm) diam.
**£2–6 / €3–9
$4–11 ⊞ RTT**

**A Paramount
poster,** *The
Italian Job,* slight
wear, Australian,
c1969, 30 x 13¼in
(76 x 33.5cm).
**£80–90
€120–135
$150–170
⬈ NSal**

► **A signed photograph,**
of Michael Caine in *Get
Carter,* 1971, 10 x 8in
(25.5 x 20.5cm).
**£150–165 / €220–250
$280–310 ⊞ FRa**

◀ **A film poster,** designed by Maria 'Mucha' Ihnatowicz, *Synowie Szeryfa*, starring John Wayne, 1975, 33½ x 23¼in (85 x 59cm).
£80–90 / €120–140
$150–170 ➹ **VSP**

The Planet of the Apes, authorized edition, 1975, 11in (28cm) high.
£3–7 / €4–10
$6–13 ⊞ **IQ**

◀ **A film poster,** *Le Mariage de Maria Braun*, c1980, 62½ x 46¼in (159 x 117.5cm).
£95–110 / €140–165
$180–210 ➹ **VSP**

A signed photograph, of Al Pacino as Tony Montana in *Scarface*, 1983, 10 x 8in (25.5 x 20.5cm).
£150–165 / €220–250
$280–310 ⊞ **FRa**

A signed photograph, of Harrison Ford as Indiana Jones in *Indiana Jones and the Temple of Doom*, 1984, 10 x 8in (25.5 x 20.5cm).
£200–220 / €300–330
$370–410 ⊞ **FRa**

A Mickey Classic jacket, 1980s.
£180–200 / €270–300
$340–370 ⊞ **COB**

A signed photograph, of Tom Cruise in *Top Gun*, 1998, 10 x 8in (25.5 x 20.5cm), framed and glazed.
£200–220 / €300–330
$370–410 ⊞ **FRa**

A casting crew jacket, used on the set of *The World is not Enough,* 1999.
£135–150 / €200–230
$250–280 ⊞ **CoC**

A signed photograph, of Meg Ryan, 2002, 10 x 8in (25.5 x 20.5cm), framed and glazed.
£150–165 / €230–250
$280–310 ⊞ **FRa**

Games

A mahogany chess and backgammon board, c1790, 15in (38cm) wide.
£450–500 / €680–750
$840–940 ⊞ MSh

◀ **A rosewood games compendium,** with a games board and chess pieces, draughts and dominoes, 1825–75, 12¾in (32.5cm) wide.
£420–500
€630–750
$790–940
⚒ G(L)

A Victorian mahogany solitaire board, with coloured-thread glass marbles, 12in (30.5cm) diam.
£120–140 / €180–210
$220–260 ⚒ Oli

A leather-cased games compendium, with cards, markers and boards for whist, cribbage, piquet and bridge, early 20thC, 12¼in (31cm) wide.
£220–260 / €330–390
$410–490 ⚒ WilP

A set of dominoes, by E. M. Co, with original tin, c1910, 7in (18cm) wide.
£35–40 / €50–60
$65–75 ⊞ TOP

A jigsaw puzzle, depicting SS *Aquitania*, 1920, 14 x 21in (35.5 x 53.5cm), framed.
£75–85 / €115–130
$140–160 ⊞ COB

A set of painted metal chessmen, by W. Britain, 1920s, 9 x 11in (23 x 28cm), with box.
£40–45 / €60–70
$75–85 ⊞ COB

A pack of Great Western Railway playing cards, advertising Lands End, Cornwall and Babbacombe Beach, 1920s, 4 x 2½in (10 x 6.5cm).
£65–75 / €100–115
$120–140 ⊞ MURR

▶ **A Great Western Railway jigsaw puzzle,** entitled 'The Model Railway', c1930, with box, 10in (25.5cm) wide.
£50–60 / €75–90
$95–110 ⊞ JUN

◀ **A Victory jigsaw puzzle,**
depicting a coaching scene, c1930,
11 x 16in (28 x 40.5cm), with box.
£50–60 / €75–90
$95–110 ⊞ RGa

▶ **A Victory wooden jigsaw puzzle,**
depicting RMS *Queen Mary*, 1936,
with box, 8 x 10in (20.5 x 25.5cm).
£40–45 / €60–70
$75–85 ⊞ COB

An Electric Derby game, 1930s, with box,
10½ x 18in (26.5 x 45.5cm).
£55–65 / €85–100
$100–120 ⊞ RTT

An Intalok jigsaw puzzle,
depicting transport, 1930s, with box,
4½ x 7in (11.5 x 18cm).
£20–25 / €30–35
$35–45 ⊞ HUX

**A Can You Solve?
Smoke Screens game,**
1930s, with box,
5 x 3¼in (12.5 x 8.5cm).
£5–9 / €8–13
$10–16 ⊞ RTT

**A boxed set of four John Knight Jig-O-
Lotto jigsaws,** 1940s, 8in (20.5cm) wide.
£35–40 / €50–60
$65–75 ⊞ HUX

**A Chad Valley *Mickey Mouse*
board game,** c1940,
17in (43cm) square.
£25–30 / €40–45
$50–55 ⊞ J&J

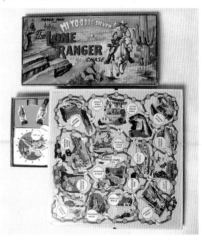

**A Waddingtons Test Match cricket
game,** c1955, 15in (38cm) wide.
£35–40 / €50–60
$65–75 ⊞ HUX

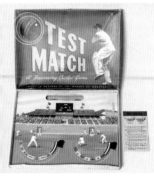

A pack of playing cards,
depicting the Queen
Trooping the Colour,
1952, 3¾in (9.5cm) high,
with box.
£20–25 / €30–35
$35–45 ⊞ HUX

A Lone Ranger Chase game, 1957,
19in (48.5cm) wide.
£40–45 / €60–70
$75–85 ⊞ HUX

A pack of So I Told 'Em Oldham playing cards, 1950s, 3½ x 2⅛in (9 x 6.5cm).
£25–30 / €40–45
$50–55 ⊞ BOB

A pack of Riders of the Range playing cards, from *Eagle* comic, late 1950s, 3¼in (8.5cm) high.
£10–15 €15–22
$19–28 ⊞ HUX

A Subbuteo game, 1957, with box, 18in (45.5cm) wide.
£35–40 / €50–60
$65–75 ⊞ HUX

In the 1920s William Keeling from Liverpool launched a game called New Footy. It consisted of flat cardboard figures on bases that were used to flick a ball into a goal. This game was produced for many years, but in 1947, Englishman Peter Adolph launched a famous competitor – Subbuteo Table Soccer. Adolph had wanted to call his game 'The Hobby', but being unable to trademark this title, named it after the Latin for hobby bird: falco subbuteo. The set included two cardboard teams, metal-framed goals and a celluloid ball. Since post-war shortages were still enforced there was no pitch, and the instructions recommended marking out your own pitch with a piece of chalk on an ex-army blanket. Purchasers were not deterred and Subbuteo was a big success. The 3-D plastic figures were introduced in the 1960s, along with a range of accessories from floodlights to TV towers. In 1968 the company was purchased by Waddingtons, and at its height in the 1970s more than 300 different football teams were produced. In the 1980s demand declined as interest in computer games developed, although the quality and accuracy of figures and strips was extremely high. In the 1990s Hasbro took over Subbuteo and production almost halted. In 2002 the licence was purchased by the Italian company Parodi. Subbuteo is still made today and figures now include bald and pony-tailed players.

A Bruce Forsyth 'I'm in Charge!' game, 1957, 14in (35.5cm) wide.
£30–35 / €45–50
$55–65 ⊞ HUX

A Pepys Punch and Judy card game, 1950s, 3½ x 2⅛in (9 x 6.5cm).
£15–20 €22–30
$28–38 ⊞ J&J

A Waddingtons pack of Young Scotland and Young England playing cards, depicting Scottie dogs and Bulldogs, 1950s, 5 x 4in (12.5 x 10cm).
£15–20 / €22–30
$28–38 ⊞ HUX

◀ **A Michael Miles *Take Your Pick* game,** c1960, 14in (35.5cm) wide.
£25–30 / €40–45
$50–55 ⊞ HUX

A David Nixon Super Magic Box, 1960, 13in (33cm) wide.
£35–40 / €50–60
$65–75 ⊞ HUX

A Standard Toy Craft Supercar Road Race game, American, 1960s, 11 x 15in (28 x 38cm).
£180–200 / €270–300
$340–370 ⊞ HAL

A Beetle Drive game, early 1960s, 7in (18cm) square.
£10–15 / €15–22
$19–28 ⊞ RTT

An Ariel Games Odds-On greyhound race game, c1970, 17in (43cm) square.
£35–40 / €50–60
$65–75 ⊞ ARo

A Frederick Warne & Co Beatrix Potter's *Tailor of Gloucester* jigsaw puzzle, c1970, 8in (20.5cm) square.
£10–15 / €15–22
$19–28 ⊞ JUN

◀ **A Parker Mad game,** c1980, 9 x 18in (23 x 45.5cm).
£40–45 / €60–70
$75–85 ⊞ STa

An Ideal Maniac electronic game, 1979, 11in (28cm) wide, with box.
£30–35 €45–50
$55–65 ⊞ IQ

A Denys Fisher's Toys Morecambe & Wise game, 1980s, 19in (48.5cm) wide.
£30–35 / €45–50
$55–65 ⊞ IQ

A Subbuteo International table football game, 1970s, 22 x 42in (56 x 106.5cm) wide.
£45–50 / €70–80
$85–95 ✣ DA

▸ **A Matchbox Uri Geller's Strike game,** 1980s, 28in (71cm) wide.
£35–40 / €50–60
$65–75 ⊞ IQ

A Mickey Mouse Club bagatelle game, c1990, 15 x 10in (38 x 25.5cm).
£10–15 / €15–22
$19–28 ⊞ HarC

Garden & Farm Collectables

A brass dog collar, with a leather strap and brass buckle, 19thC, 6¾in (17cm) diam.
£340–400 / € 500–600
$640–750 ✦ WW

A brass dog collar, c1820, 5½in (14cm) diam.
£270–300 / € 400–450
$500–560 ⊞ GGv

A Victorian metal and string garden line, 12in (30.5cm) high.
£270–300 / € 400–450
$500–560 ⊞ AL

◄ **Three cast-iron garden seat supports,** c1860, 33in (84cm) high.
£220–250 / € 330–370
$410–460 ⊞ HOP

A Victorian wooden garden seat, with cast-iron legs, 78¾in (200cm) wide.
£130–155 / € 195–230
$240–290 ✦ DD

A drenching horn, c1870, 12in (30.5cm) long.
£85–95 / € 130–145
$160–180 ⊞ NEW

A cast-iron bird bath, c1860, 27in (68.5cm) high.
£430–480 / € 640–720
$800–900 ⊞ HOP

◄ **A stoneware bird feeder,** by Bell Bros & Bowes, 1880–90, 4½in (11.5cm) high.
£230–270 / € 340–400
$430–500 ✦ BBR

A cast-iron water pump, c1890, 25in (63.5cm) high.
£110–125
€ 165–185
$200–230 ⊞ HOP

◄ **An elm wheelbarrow,** with original paint, c1890, 64in (162.5cm) long.
£200–230
€ 300–340
$370–420 ⊞ HOP

A metal watering can, 1885.
£50–55 / € 75–85
$95–105 ⊞ AL

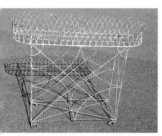

A painted wirework planter,
c1890, 37in (94cm) wide.
€220–250 / €330–370
$410–460 ⊞ HOP

A William Hill steel corn chandler's scoop,
late 19thC, 15in (38cm) long.
£55–65 / €85–100
$100–120 ⊞ BS

A Bingham metal breast plough,
1875–1925, 13in (33cm) wide.
£40–45 / €60–70
$75–85 ⊞ WO

◀ **A pair of Barrows steel pruning shears,**
c1900, 10in (25.5cm) long.
£40–45
€60–70
$75–85
⊞ HOP

▶ **A Cooke's Ploughs catalogue,**
c1910, 5in (12.5cm) wide.
£30–35
€45–50
$55–65 ⊞ JUN

A Haws copper watering can, with a brass rose,
c1910, 26in (66cm) wide.
£135–150 / €200–230
$250–280 ⊞ HOP

A John Riley steel billhook, c1910, 15in (38cm) long.
£30–35 / €45–50
$55–65 ⊞ HOP

A steel daisy grubber, with a wooden handle, c1920,
18in (45.5cm) long.
£35–40 / €50–60
$65–75 ⊞ HOP

A wooden dibber, c1920, 14in (35.5cm) long.
£25–30 / €40–45
$50–55 ⊞ YT

A steel compost and hay thermometer, c1920, 40in (101.5cm) long.
£45–50 / €70–80
$85–95 ⊞ HOP

An iron claw weeder, with a wooden handle, c1920, 10in (25.5cm) long.
£30–35 / €45–50
$55–65 ⊞ HOP

A steel trench spade, with an ash handle, c1920, 22in (56cm) long.
£20–25 / €30–35
$35–45 ⊞ HOP

Three wooden dibbers, c1920, largest 16in (40.5cm) long.
£20–25 / €30–35
$35–45 ⊞ HOP

A painted wood lounger, c1920, 27in (68.5cm) long.
£250–280 / €380–420
$470–520 ⊞ OLA

A pine trug, French, c1920, 18½in (47cm) wide.
£30–35 / €45–50
$55–65 ⊞ AL

An A. & F. Parkes steel fork, with an ash handle, c1920, 38in (96.5cm) long.
£45–50 / €70–80
$85–95 ⊞ HOP

A metal watering can, with a rose, 1920s, 16in (40.5cm) high.
£50–60 / €75–90
$95–110 ⊞ YT

A metal watering can, 1920–30, 16in (40.5cm) high.
£45–50 / €70–80
$85–95 ⊞ FOX

A reed basket, 1920s, 16in (40.5cm) wide.
£45–50 / €70–80
$85–95 ⊞ SMI

▶ **A pair of wooden cloches,** c1930, 24in (61cm) square.
£360–400
€540–600
$670–750
⊞ HOP

▶ **A pair of Astor steel shears,** with wooden handles, c1930, 17in (43cm) wide.
£30–35 / €45–50
$55–65 ⊞ AL

A copper watering can rose,
c1930, 4in (10cm) diam.
£6–10 / €9–15
$12–19 ⊞ HOP

An Eltex copper and brass greenhouse heater, c1930, 7in (18cm) diam.
£25–30 / €40–45
$50–55 ⊞ HOP

A child's beech chair, c1930.
£30–35 / €45–50
$55–65 ⊞ NEW

A Webbs Pedigree Seeds hessian sack, c1938, 17in (43cm) high.
£15–20 / €22–30
$28–38 ⊞ HOP

A painted wood Sussex trug, c1938, 22in (56cm) wide.
£45–50 / €70–80
$85–95 ⊞ HOP

A terracotta garden gnome, 1940s–1950s, 13in (33cm) high.
£10–15
€15–22
$19–28 ⊞ JWK

A pair of steel wavy-edge shears, with wooden handles, c1940, 21in (53.5cm) long.
£30–35 / €45–50
$55–65 ⊞ HOP

A Remex steel hedge trimmer, with wooden handles, c1945, 19in (48.5cm) long.
£55–65 / €85–100
$100–120 ⊞ HOP

▶ **A wire vegetable basket,** with a wooden handle, 1950, 18in (45.5cm) wide.
£60–70
€90–105
$110–130 ⊞ MLL

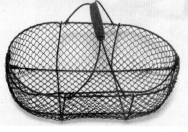

▶ **W. E. Shewell-Cooper,** The Complete Gardener, 1960, 8½ x 6in (21.5 x 15cm).
£1–5 / €2–7
$3–9 ⊞ JWK

Glass

A cut-glass footed vase, c1820, 12in (30.5cm) high.
£850–950 / € 1,250–1,400
$1,600–1,800 ⊞ GLAS

◄ **A glass wine bottle,** with a silver mount marked Birmingham 1844, 13in (33cm) high.
£195–220 / € 300–330
$360–410 ⊞ GLAS

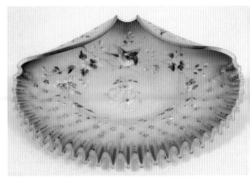

A Victorian Burmese-style glass dish, in the shape of a shell, decorated with a bird and flowers, 11¾in (30cm) wide.
£70–80 / € 105–120
$130–150 ➤ CHTR

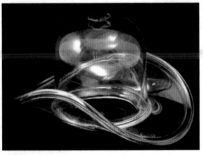

A Nailsea glass frigger, in the form of a bowler hat, mid-19thC, 4in (10cm) high.
£55–65 / € 85–100
$100–120 ➤ G(L)
Friggers were objects made by the glass-maker in his own time, often with left-over glass. They were also known as end-of-day glass and as off-hand glass in the USA.

► **An engraved drinking glass,** Bohemian, 1870, 5½in (14cm) high.
£195–220 / € 300–330
$360–410 ⊞ GLAS

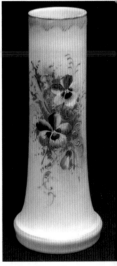

An opaline glass vase, decorated with pansies, c1880, 9in (23cm) high.
£50–55 € 75–85
$95–105 ⊞ DEB

A Stourbridge glass frigger, in the form of a hollow walking cane, c1880, 39in (99cm) long.
£100–120 / € 150–180
$185–220 ⊞ GLAS

◄ **A vaseline glass lemonade jug,** with a reeded handle, c1880, 8in (20.5cm) high.
£250–280 / € 380–420
$470–520 ⊞ GLAS
Vaseline glass contains a small amount of uranium, which creates a milky colour.

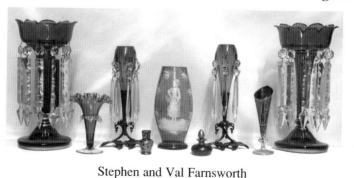

A Moser glass vase, decorated with enamels, Austrian, c1880, 4in (10cm) high.
£70–80 / €105–120 $130–150 ⚹ DuM

A glass centre vase, with clear glass frills, c1880, 11in (28cm) high.
£300–330 / €450–500 $560–620 ⊞ MGA

A glass bowl, with a vaseline glass edge, c1880, 8in (20.5cm) diam.
£50–55 / €75–85 $90–100 ⚹ DuM

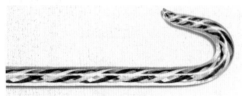

A Stourbridge glass frigger, in the form of a walking cane with red, blue and white twists, c1890, 42in (106.5cm) long.
£135–150 / €200–220 $250–280 ⊞ GLAS
Walking sticks were a popular frigger or novelty. They were produced both in solid glass and as a hollow tube that could be filled with small sweets. In some areas glass canes were hung up in the home to ward off illness, and a broken cane was said to bring bad luck.

◄ **A pair of cranberry glass comports,** on spelter bases, c1890, 8in (20.5cm) diam.
£390–430 €590–650 $730–810 ⊞ GLAS

A Thomas Webb & Sons Queen's Burmese glass vase, 1885, 10½in (26.5cm) high.
£250–280 / €380–420 $470–520 ⊞ GLAS
Burmese glass – opaque art glass that changes from yellow to pink at the top of the object – was developed in the 1880s by the Mount Washington Glass Co, MA, USA. Thomas Webb & Sons patented the technique in England, where it became known as Queen's Burmese Glass in honour of Queen Victoria. The glass was used for tableware and decorative items.

◄ **A cranberry glass pitcher,** c1880, 7in (18cm) high.
£95–105 / €140–155 $180–200 ⚹ DuM

A Peachblow glass pitcher, American, c1880, 3in (7.5cm) high.
£155–175 / €230–260 $290–330 ⚹ DuM
Peachblow glass was produced by several American glassworks during the late 19th century in imitation of the peach-bloom glaze of Chinese porcelain.

An airtrap glass basket, with herringbone decoration, c1885, 7½in (19cm) high.
£130–145 / €195–220 $240–270 ⊞ MGA
Airtrap glass, known as mother-of-pearl glass in the USA, is a layered type of art glass in which the inner layer is blown into a pattern mould then covered with clear or coloured glass to trap air bubbles. Patterns include raindrop, diamond, quilted and herringbone.

◄ **A glass biscuit barrel,** hand-painted with forget-me-nots and trelliswork, c1890, 9in (23cm) high.
£65–75 / €100–115 $120–140 ⊞ GLAS

◄ **A moulded cranberry glass candlestick,** c1890, 9½in (24cm) high.
£100–120 / € 150–180
$185–220 ⊞ GLAS

A pair of crystoleums, illustrating two paintings by Arthur Douglas Vernon,1890–1910, framed, 9¾ x 7½in (25 x 19cm).
£160–190 / € 240–280
$300–360 ♣ G(L)

Crystoleum photographs were popular from the 1880s to c1916. An albumen print was attached to the concave underside of a convex piece of glass. The print was waxed to make it transparent and then coloured with oil paint. Crystoleums were typically mounted in frames, and favourite subjects included popular paintings of the day.

◄ **A Thomas Webb & Sons cameo glass biscuit barrel,** carved with leaves, with a silver-plated collar, cover and swing handle, late 19thC, 7½in (19cm) high.
£600–720 / € 900–1,050
$1,150–1,350 ♣ RTo

A Mary Gregory satin glass vase, depicting a young girl and boy, 1890, 15in (38cm) high.
£220–250 / € 330–380
$410–470 ⊞ GLAS
Mary Gregory glass is the name given to coloured glass that has been decorated, usually in white enamel, with a child or children wearing Victorian dress.

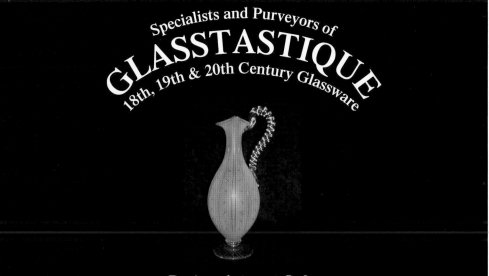

A pair of glass hyacinth vases, c1900, 9¼in (23.5cm) high.
£130–145
€195–220
$240–270
⊞ GAU

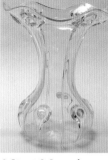

A Stuart & Sons glass Peacock Eye vase, c1900, 10in (25.5cm) high.
£300–330 / €450–500
$560–620 ⊞ MGA

A pair of amethyst glass hyacinth vases, c1900, 7in (18cm) high.
£130–145 / €195–220
$240–270 ⊞ GAU

A glass hyacinth vase, c1900, 5½in (14cm) high.
£50–60 / €75–90
$95–110 ⊞ GAU

A Steuben vaseline cut-glass candlestick, American, c1900, 12in (30.5cm) high.
£110–125
€165–185
$200–230
⚒ DuM

A Stuart & Sons glass vase, c1900, 9in (23cm) high.
£90–100 / €135–150
$170–190 ⊞ MGA

Four glass ice cream licks, 1910–20, largest 3in (7.5cm) high.
£25–30 / €40–45
$50–55 each ⊞ TCG
Penny licks were the precursor of ice cream cones and were used for buying a penny worth of ice cream from the street vendor. After the contents had been licked out, the glass was returned for the next customer. The ice cream seller frequently neglected to wash it and, during the 1920s, in the aftermath of the great flu epidemic, penny licks were banned from many British towns because they spread germs and diseases.

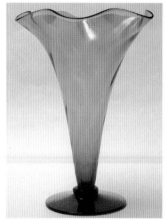

◀ **A John Walsh Walsh glass posy bowl,** with brass flower guide, c1910, 4in (10cm) high.
£40–45 / €60–70
$75–85 ⊞ TCG

A pair of glass candlesticks, c1910, 10in (25.5cm) high.
£110–130 / €165–195
$200–240 ⚒ DuM

A glass vase, decorated with enamels, Czechoslovakian, Haida, c1912, 7½in (19cm) high.
£240–270 / €360–400
$450–500 ⊞ TCG

◀ **A cranberry glass sweetmeat dish,** with applied clear glass handle, c1910, 6in (15cm) wide.
£140–160
€210–240
$260–300
⊞ GLAS

Twenties

A Stourbridge glass frigger, in the form of a walking cane, filled with sweets, c1920, 42in (106.5cm) long.
£125–140 / € 190–210
$230–260 ⊞ GLAS

A Monart glass vase,
1924–61, 4in (10cm) high.
£70–80 / € 105–120
$130–150 ⊞ TCG

A Monart aventurine glass vase, 1924–61, 11in (28cm) high.
£290–320 / € 430–480
$540–600 ⊞ TCG

A Gray-Stan glass vase,
1926–36, 4in (10cm) high.
£45–50 / € 70–80
$85–95 ⊞ TCG

A Lalique frosted glass model of a sparrow,
entitled 'Moineau Hardi', engraved mark 'R. Lalique', French, 1920s–30s, 3¼in (8.5cm) high.
£210–250 / € 310–370
$390–470 ⋋ G(L)

A Webb & Corbett glass goblet, engraved with a hyacinth design, 1920s, 8½in (21.5cm) high.
£220–250 / € 330–380
$410–470 ⊞ TCG
Webb & Corbett was established near Stourbridge in 1897 by Herbert and Thomas Webb (grandsons of Victorian glass-maker Thomas Webb) and George Harry Corbett. They produced high-quality tableware and vases and were particularly known for engraved crystal glass. Also look out for enamel-decorated glass and stone-coloured glass called agate flambé.

A Durand art glass vase,
French, c1922,
8in (20.5cm) high.
£590–700 € 890–1,050
$1,100–1,300 ⋋ DuM

A Gray-Stan glass vase, 1926–36,
8in (20.5cm) high.
£210–240 / € 320–360
$390–450 ⊞ TCG

A Barolac opalescent pressed glass vase,
moulded with poppies, marked, Czechoslovakian, c1928, 10in (25.5cm) high.
£310–350 / € 460–520
$580–650 ⊞ GLAS

A Monart glass vase, 1924–61,
12in (30.5cm) high.
£300–340 / € 450–510
$560–630 ⊞ TCG

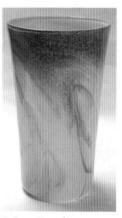

A Gray-Stan glass vase, 1926–36,
11in (28cm) high.
£220–250 / € 330–380
$410–470 ⊞ TCG

A James Powell & Sons Whitefriars ribbed glass decanter, 1920s,
6in (15cm) high.
£90–100 / € 135–150
$170–190 ⊞ TCG

Thirties

A pair of cut-glass ship's decanters, with star-cut bases, 1930s, 9½in (24cm) high.
£300–340 / €450–510
$560–640 ⊞ GLAS

▶ A John Walsh Walsh glass goblet, with enamelled and gilded decoration, 1930s, 9in (23cm) high.
£210–240 / €320–360
$390–450 ⊞ TCG

A Leerdam glass vase, Dutch, 1930s, 11in (28cm) high.
£250–280 / €370–420
$470–520 ⊞ TCG

A Gray-Stan glass vase, engraved mark, c1930, 14in (35.5cm) high.
£220–250 €330–380
$410–470 ⊞ RUSK

A pressed glass water jug, 1930s, 8in (20.5cm) high.
£8–12 / €12–18
$15–22 ⊞ BAC

A Nazeing speckled glass vase, 1930s, 8in (20.5cm) high.
£85–95 / €130–140
$160–180 ⊞ TCG

◀ A Monart aventurine glass vase, 1930s, 7in (18cm) high.
£180–200 / €270–300
$330–370 ⊞ TCG

A Nazeing glass posy bowl, 1930s, 4in (10cm) diam.
£10–15 / €15–22
$19–28 ⊞ TCG

An iridescent glass vase, probably by Loetz, in the form of a pig, 1930s, 5¼in (13.5cm) high.
£150–180 / €230–270
$280–330 ➷ SWO

◀ A Monart glass vase, 1930s, 3in (7.5cm) high.
£175–195
€260–290
$330–370
⊞ SAAC

A Nazeing glass beaker vase, 1930s, 4½in (11.5cm) high.
£25–30 / €40–45
$50–55 ⊞ TCG

A Nazeing glass vase, 1930s, 10in (25.5cm) high.
£110–125 / €165–190
$200–230 ⊞ TCG

A James Powell & Sons Whitefriars Cloudy glass vase, 1930s, 6in (15cm) high.
£85–95 / €130–145
$160–190 ⊞ TCG

A Richardson's Rich Cameo glass vase, 1930s, 10in (25.5cm) high.
£430–480 / €640–720
$800–900 ⊞ MGA
Established in Stourbridge in 1850, the glassworks of H. G. Richardson & Sons developed popular ranges of cameo glass that combined clear glass with a single colour. The firm was taken over by Thomas Webb & Sons but pieces in the Rich Cameo range still featured the Richardson mark. Wares are distinguished by cuttings in the clear glass, which produced a snakeskin-like effect. Favourite colours at the time included green, yellow, blue and amethyst. Red is the rarest and most desirable colour today. Good condition of the cameo decoration is essential to value, since scratches cannot be removed without causing damage. In 1931, Thomas Webb introduced a line of Cameo Fleur vases. Webb's signature appears in the cameo decoration on the base of the vase.

A James Powell & Sons Whitefriars ribbed glass bowl, 1930s, 10in (25.5cm) diam.
£145–160 / €210–240
$270–300 ⊞ TCG

A James Powell & Sons Whitefriars Cloudy glass vase, 1930s, 4in (10cm) diam.
£45–50 / €70–80
$85–95 ⊞ TCG

A Stevens & Williams Caerleon glass bowl, 1930s, 8in (20.5cm) diam.
£165–185 / €250–280
$310–350 ⊞ MGA

A Thomas Webb & Sons Cameo Fleur glass vase, 1930s, 7in (18cm) high.
£430–480 / €640–720
$800–900 ⊞ MGA

◀ **A Vasart glass bowl,** 1946–64, 10in (25.5cm) diam.
£100–120 / €150–180
$185–220 ⊞ TCG

▶ **A Vasart glass vase,** 1947–65, 7in (18cm) high.
£100–120 / €150–180
$185–220 ⊞ TCG

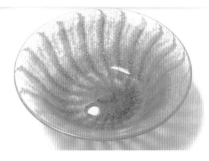

Post-War Glass

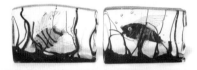

A Whitefriars bubble glass fruit bowl and cover, c1950, 11in (28cm) diam.
£360–400 / €540–600
$670–750 ⊞ SAT

Two Cenedese glass Aquarium Bricks, designed by Ricardo Licata, Italian, Venice, early 1950s, each 6½in (16.5cm) wide.
£155–175 / €230–260
$290–330 ⊞ MARK

A Venini glass pitcher, signed, Italian, Venice, 1950s, 9½in (24cm) high.
£90–100 / €135–150
$170–190 ⊞ MARK

A cased glass ashtray, Italian, 1950s, 4in (10cm) diam.
£20–25 / €30–35
$35–45 ⊞ MARK

A Holmegaard glass cigar ashtray, by Per Lütken, Danish, 1950s–60s, 8in (20.5cm) diam.
£60–70 / €90–105
$110–130 ⊞ ORI

A Bohemia Glassworks lead crystal vase, by Jiri Repásek, Czechoslovakian, c1962, 5½in (14cm) high.
£35–40 / €50–60
$65–75 ⊞ GRo

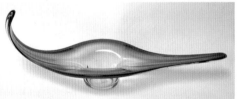

A glass vase, French, 1960, 25in (63.5cm) wide.
£60–70 / €90–105
$110–130 ⊞ ARK

An Ultima Thule Iittala glass tumbler, by Tapio Wirkkala, Finnish, 1960s, 2¾in (7cm) high.
£6–10 / €9–15
$12–19 ⊞ GRo
Textured glass became extremely popular in the 1960s. In 1967 Tapio Wirkkala designed a range of glassware called Ultima Thule for the Finnair airline to commemorate their transatlantic flights. The following year it was put into general commercial production. The moulded pattern was designed to create the effect of drips of water running over ice. Another famous Wirkkala creation from the 1960s was the Finlandia vodka bottle.

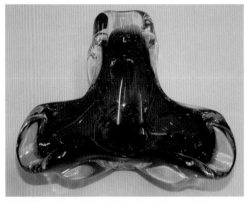

A Murano glass dish, 1960s, 5in (12.5cm) wide.
£25–30 €40–45
$50–55 ⊞ HEI

A glass vase, 1960s, 6¼in (16cm) high.
£4–8 / €6–12
$8–15 ⊞ MARK

A **Murano glass dish,** 1960s, 12in (30.5cm) wide.
£40–45 / €60–70
$75–85 ⊞ HEI

A **glass vase,** Finnish, 1970, 10in (25.5cm) high.
£40–45 / €60–70
$75–85 ⊞ MARK

▶ A **Kosta cased glass bowl,** by Mona Morales-Schildt, Swedish, 1970s, 3½in (9cm) high.
£65–75
€100–115
$120–140
⊞ MARK

A **Bohemia Glassworks moulded lead crystal vase,** by Jiri Repásek, c1970, 10in (25.5cm) high.
£40–45 / €60–70
$75–85 ⊞ GRo

A **glass vase,** with etched decoration, probably Scottish, 1970s, 5in (12.5cm) high.
£10–15 / €15–22
$19–28 ⊞ MARK

An **littala glass vase,** by Alvar Aalto, signed, Finnish, 1988, 14in (35.5cm) high.
£250–280 / €380–420
$470–520 ⊞ PLB

A **moulded glass vase,** 1960s, 9in (23cm) high.
£45–50 / €70–80
$85–95 ⊞ GRo

A **Holmegaard glass bottle vase,** by Otto Brauer, Danish, 1970s, 10in (25.5cm) high.
£35–40 / €50–60
$65–75 ⊞ LUNA

▶ A **Graal glass vase,** by Jonathan Harris, 2001–02, 8½in (21.5cm) high.
£400–440 / €600–660
$750–830 ⊞ RW

A **glass,** printed with musicians, French, 1960s, 4¼in (11cm) high.
£6–10 / €9–15
$12–19 ⊞ RTT

A **glass ewer,** 1970s, 10½in (26.5cm) high.
£10–15 / €15–22
$19–28 ⊞ MARK

Paperweights

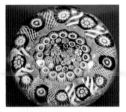

A Paul Ysart glass paperweight, with 13 canes, mid-20thC, 3in (7.5cm) diam.
£250–280 / €380–420
$470–520 ⊞ G(L)

A millefiori paper-weight, 19thC.
£200–240 / €300–360
$380–450 ✗ L&E

A St Louis concentric millefiori glass paperweight, French, mid-19thC, 2½in (6.5cm) diam.
£800–950 / 1,200–1,450
$1,500–1,800 ✗ RTo

A Baccarat scrambled millefiori glass paperweight, with polychrome canes and a ground base, French, 19thC, 7in (18cm) diam.
£220–260 / €330–390
$410–490 ✗ Bri

A Paul Ysart glass paperweight, 1970s, 3in (7.5cm) diam.
£270–300 / €400–450
$500–560 ⊞ RW

◀ **A Baccarat Coeurs de Rose glass paperweight,** No. 9/100, French, 1994, 3½in (9cm) diam.
£500–550 / €750–830
$940–1,050 ⊞ SWB

A St Louis Les Lupins glass paperweight, No. 16/150, French, 1997, 3¼in (8.5cm) diam.
£580–650 / €870–980
$1,050–1,200 ⊞ SWB

Handbags

An enamelled silver purse, by C. Cheshire, decorated with roses, Chester 1912, 4¼in (11cm) wide.
£140–165 / €210–250
$260–310 ⚒ WW

▶ **A silk handbag,** with a Bakelite clasp and beaded fringe, decorated with appliquéd flowers, c1920, 7in (18cm) wide.
£220–250 / €330–380
$410–470 ⊞ HSR

A beaded handbag, with a gilt and enamel frame and hand-painted decoration, French, c1920, 7in (18cm) wide.
£170–190 / €260–290
$320–360 ⊞ HSR

A chain mesh handbag, with a pierced and engraved clasp and metal chain, c1920, 7in (18cm) wide.
£70–80 / €105–120
$130–150 ⊞ DE

A tapestry handbag, with a gilt and enamel frame, 1920s, 7in (18cm) wide.
£15–20 / €22–30
$28–38 ⊞ JPr

A suede clutch bag, with a Bakelite clasp, 1930, 12in (30.5cm) wide.
£180–200 / €270–300
$330–370 ⊞ LBe

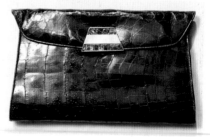

A crocodile skin clutch bag, 1930s, Argentinian, 11in (28cm) wide.
£160–180 / €240–270
$300–340 ⊞ RGA

A velvet handbag, the Bakelite frame decorated with a fruit design, 1930s, 8in (20.5cm) wide.
£130–150 / €200–230
$240–280 ⊞ LBe

◀ **A silver evening purse,** decorated with a crown and the letters CD, with a compartmented interior, 1937, 12in (30.5cm) wide.
£100–120 / €150–180
$185–220 ⚒ G(L)
This purse was reputedly made for the Marchioness of Cambridge.

A leather and Bakelite clutch bag, 1930s, 10in (25.5cm) wide.
£70–80 / €105–120
$130–150 ⊞ JUJ

A silk box bag, with Bakelite top, 1940s, 6½in (16.5cm) wide.
£60–70 / €90–105
$110–130 ⊞ DRE

A moulded Bakelite handbag, 1950s, 9in (23cm) wide.
£130–150 / €200–230
$240–280 ⊞ SUW

A Lucite and gilt-metal handbag, 1950s, 9in (23cm) wide.
£175–195 / €260–290
$320–360 ⊞ SpM

A carry-all handbag, by Evans, containing a cigarette case, lipstick, powder compact and space for coins, American, c1945–50, 5½in (14cm) wide.
£175–195 / €260–290
$320–360 ⊞ SUW

A plastic and fabric handbag, decorated with keys, 1950s, 14in (35.5cm) wide.
£135–150 / €200–230
$250–280 ⊞ LBe

A hand-made tapestry handbag, decorated with flowers, 1950s, 11in (28cm) wide.
£85–95 / €130–145
$160–180 ⊞ HIP

A crocodile skin handbag, 1940s, 10in (25.5cm) wide.
£100–120 / €150–180
$185–220 ⊞ MCa

A wicker handbag, decorated with an owl, 1950s, 10in (25.5cm) wide.
£85–95 / €130–145
$160–180 ⊞ SpM

A tapestry handbag, decorated with a duck, American, 1950s, 17in (43cm) wide.
£60–70 / €90–105
$110–130 ⊞ DRE

A plastic-coated handbag,
decorated with an insert of flowers
and insects, American, 1950s,
11in (28cm) wide.
£60–70 / €90–105
$110–130 ⊞ DRE

A bag, by Cordé, late 1950s,
9in (23cm) wide.
£50–55 / €75–85
$95–105 ⊞ CCO

A beaded shoulder bag, c1960,
12in (30.5cm) high.
£10–15 / €15–22
$19–28 ⊞ DE

A fabric shoulder bag,
by Gucci, with a
leather trim, c1960,
8in (20.5cm) wide.
£85–95 / €130–145
$160–180 ⊞ HIP

A shoe and handbag set, by Miss
Rayne, 1960s, with original box,
15in (38cm) wide.
£65–75 / €100–115
$120–140 ⊞ DE

▶ **A patent leather handbag,** by
Chanel, with authenticity number
card, 1960s, 13in (33cm) wide.
£90–100 / €135–150
$170–190 ⊞ HIP

A beaded handbag, decorated with the King
of Diamonds, American, 1960s,
12in (30.5cm) wide.
£100–120 / €150–180
$185–220 ⊞ LBe

A wicker handbag,
decorated with silk flowers
and plastic fruit, Japanese,
1960s, 12in (30.5cm) wide.
£45–50 / €70–80
$85–95 ⊞ TWI

A wooden box bag, by Collins of
Texas, the cover with inset mirror,
American, c1970, 9in (23cm) wide.
£60–70 / €90–105
$110–130 ⊞ SBL

▶ **A handbag,**
by Karl Lagerfeld,
in the form of a
fan, 1980s,
13in (33cm) wide.
£165–185
€250–280
$310–350
⊞ LBe

Jewellery

This section is devoted to jewellery from the 19th and 20th centuries, focusing on semi-precious and costume jewellery. Pieces from c1850 to the early 1900s can still be very affordable today. In the 19th century jewellery became widely available for the first time, thanks to improved production methods and the employment of cheaper materials. Gems were made using semi-precious stones from garnets to seed pearls. Shell cameos and micro-mosiacs were imported from Italy. Local materials such as Scottish hardstones and Whitby jet (much used in mourning jewellery) were cheap enough to produce the large pieces that set off voluminous crinoline fashions. These heavy designs gave way at the turn of the century to lighter, more delicate styles and naturalistic Art Nouveau patterns. Partly inspired by socialist principles, Arts and Crafts designers also experimented with less costly materials such as silver, pewter and enamel, though today these handcrafted works of art can command high prices.

The 20th century saw the growth of the costume jewellery industry, which took jewellery out of the specialist jewellery shop and on to the high street, catering to every level of the market from five-and-dime store baubles to the smartest designer accessories. The USA was a major centre of manufacture, and from the 1920s onwards jewellery companies flourished in New York and Los Angeles. In Europe, leading couturiers such as Chanel, Schiaparelli and Dior produced lines of jewellery to accessorize their collections.

Many major manufaturers of costume jewellery stamped their work and, when buying, look out for signatures – check necklace clasps, the reverse of earrings and the backs of brooches. Condition is also important to value so examine all jewellery for missing stones and any broken parts. Jewellery was often supplied in sets or 'parures' (necklace, earrings, brooch and bracelet). A complete set will command a premium and original boxes should also be preserved.

Belts

A silver-plated Edwardian belt, 32in (81.5cm) long.
£55–65 / €85–100
$100–120 ⊞ Ech

A hand-made wooden beaded belt, c1940, 32in (81.5cm) long.
£15–20 / €22–30
$28–38 ⊞ DE

Three plastic and metal chain belts, 1960, 30in (76cm) long.
£6–10 / €9–15
$12–19 each ⊞ DE

▶ **A filigree belt,** by Kenneth Jay Lane, with paste decoration, marked 'KJL', 1970s, 32in (81.5cm) long.
£180–200 / €270–300
$330–370 ⊞ HSR

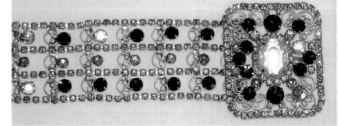

Bracelets

A carved jet snake bangle, 1870–80, 7½in (19cm) long.
£65–75 / €100–115
$120–140 ⊞ AM

A Victorian 15ct gold hinged bangle, set with four sapphires and three diamonds.
£280–330 / €420–500
$500–600 ⚲ G(L)

A Victorian agate and cornelian bracelet, with trefoil and geometric sections.
£100–120 / €150–180
$185–220 ⚲ AMB

◄ **A paste and chrome bracelet,** 1930s, 1in (2.5cm) wide.
£45–50
€70–80
$85–95 ⊞ DRE

A crystal and gilt bracelet, by Emery of Argentina, Austrian, c1940, 1½in (4cm) wide.
£150–170 / €230–260
$290–330 ⊞ LaF
This bracelet was made in Austria for sale in America.

◄ **A copper bracelet,** by Gerry Fells, c1950, 1½in (4cm) wide.
£55–65
€85–100
$100–120 ⊞ JUJ

A Perspex bracelet, inset with flowers, c1950, 1in (2.5cm) wide.
£65–75 / €100–115
$120–140 ⊞ JBB

Brooches

An Edwardian gold and seed pearl flowerhead brooch, centred with a cluster of rose-cut diamonds.
£260–310 / €400–480
$490–580 ⚲ WW

A Victorian gold brooch, set with seed pearls.
£75–90 / €115–135
$140–165 ⚲ HYD

A Victorian yellow metal memorial brooch, with enamel and ivy decoration and a tassel drop, set with a cultured pearl, 2in (5cm) wide.
£100–120 / €150–180
$185–220 ⚲ SWO

◄ **An early Victorian garnet and gold brooch,** in a cannetille frame, with three pendant drops.
£160–190 / €240–280
$300–360 ⚲ HYD
Cannetille (twisted gold wirework) was produced in England and Italy in the first half of the 19th century. It is very fragile, and pieces should be checked for damage and repair work, such as lead soldering, as this reduces the value.

Further reading

Miller's Antiques Checklist: Jewellery, Miller's Publication, 1997

An ivory brooch, in the form of a wheatsheaf with a floral tie, c1880.
£100–120 / €150–180
$190–220 ↗ TEN

A Victorian garnet brooch, with an articulated drop with garnets.
£170–200 / €260–300
$320–370 ↗ G(L)

A carved mother-of-pearl brooch, in the form of a flower, c1900, 3in (7.5cm) long.
£25–30 / €40–45
$50–55 ⊞ FMN

▶ **A silver and paste name brooch,** 1910, 2in (5cm) wide.
£50–60 / €75–90
$95–110 ⊞ FMN

A Victorian gold brooch, set with seven garnets, with a locket back.
£50–60 / €75–90
$95–110 ↗ G(L)

▶ **An Aesthetic Movement brooch,** in the form of a bee, with a pearl body and gold wings, 1870–80, 3in (7.5cm) wide.
£140–165 / €210–250
$260–310 ↗ WW

A 15ct gold brooch, set with opals and diamonds, late 19thC, 2in (5cm) wide.
£310–350 / €470–530
$580–650 ⊞ LaF

A Victorian gold and half-pearl brooch, with entwined ribbon-tied hearts, trefoil bead terminals and bead chain swags.
£90–105 / €135–160
$170–200 ↗ TEN

◀ **A silver and gold bar brooch,** 1894, 2in (5cm) wide.
£30–35 / €45–50
$55–65 ⊞ WAC

A gold and silver brooch, in the form of a spider, set with a blister pearl, cabochon rubies and rose-cut diamonds, c1900, 1½in (4cm) wide.
£400–480 / €600–720
$750–900 ↗ LAY

◀ **A pewter scarf pin,** set with a Ruskin Pottery cabochon, early 20thC, 1½in (4cm) wide.
£45–50 / €70–80
$85–95 ⊞ GLB

Jewellery is affected by fashion and the recent trend for fifties-style tweed jackets accessorized with a brooch on the lapel has stimulated demand for vintage brooches.

A silver and marcasite brooch, in the form of a bird of paradise, French, 1920, 3½in (9cm) wide.
£250–280 / €380–420
$470–520 ⊞ CRIS

A metal novelty brooch, German, c1920, 2½in (6.5cm) wide.
£100–120 / €150–180
$185–220 ⊞ HUX

A carved ivory brooch, in the form of a flower, c1920, 2in (5cm) diam.
£20–25 / €30–35
$35–45 ⊞ FMN

A silver and enamel brooch, with monogram, French, 1920s, 3in (7.5cm) wide.
£115–130 / €175–195
$220–240 ⊞ DRE

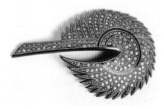

A Bakelite and rhinestone brooch, 1920s–30s, 4in (10cm) long.
£50–55 / €75–85
$95–105 ⊞ SUW

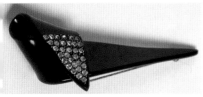

A Bakelite and rhinestone brooch, 1920s–30s, 4in (10cm) long.
£20–25 / €30–35
$35–45 ⊞ SUW

◄ A Bakelite and brass brooch, 1930, 3in (7.5cm) wide.
£85–95 / €130–145
$160–180 ⊞ LBe

A silver brooch, marked `AR' and `ICA', Birmingham 1934, 1in (2.5cm) wide.
£135–150 / €200–230
$250–280 ⊞ AFD

A paste brooch, by Eisenberg, 1940s, 3½in (9cm) wide.
£160–180 / €240–270
$300–340 ⊞ DRE

A metal and enamel brooch, in the form of a Jester, 1930s, 3in (7.5cm) wide.
£100–120 / €150–180
$185–220 ⊞ LBe

► A plastic brooch, decorated with a Scottie dog, 1930s–40s, 3½in (9cm) wide.
£25–30 / €40–45
$50–55 ⊞ DRE

► A Poole Pottery brooch, moulded with a swallow and flowers, 1940s, 2¼in (5.5cm) diam.
£150–180
€230–270
$280–330 ➤ Bri

Three cuttlefish brooches, in the form of dragonflies, 1940s, largest 5in (12.5cm) wide.
£40–45 / € 60–70
$75–85 each ⊞ HSR

A silver and paste articulated brooch, 1940s, 6in (15cm) wide.
£180–200 / € 270–300
$330–370 ⊞ RGA

◀ **A brass, enamel and paste brooch,** by R. Mandle, in the form of a horse's head, c1950, 4in (10cm) wide.
£70–80
€ 105–120
$130–150
⊞ JBB

A paste brooch, by Trifari, in the form of a dancer, 1940s, 3in (7.5cm) long.
£100–120 / € 150–180
$185–220 ⊞ DRE

A 'Russian gold' brooch, by Joseff of Hollywood, in the form of a waterlily, American, 1950s, 2in (5cm) wide.
£80–90 / € 120–135
$150–170 ⊞ LaF
Founded by Eugene Joseff in 1930, Joseff of Hollywood provided costume jewellery for three decades of movies, supplying everything from Shirley Temple's crown in *The Little Princess* (1939) to Elizabeth Taylor's gilded asps in *Cleopatra* (1963). Joseff also launched a retail line c1938 so that 'every American woman could feel like a Hollywood star'. Brass pieces, often modelled on his own dramatic movie designs, were given a matt gold finish (sometimes referred to as Russian gold) devised to minimize the glare from studio lights and create an antique look.

A paste brooch, in the form of a poodle, American, 1950s, 2in (5cm) wide.
£20–25 / € 30–35
$28–38 ⊞ DRE

A gilt-metal brooch, in the form of a woman's head, with bead decoration, 1950s, 3in (7.5cm) long.
£45–50 / € 70–80
$85–95 ⊞ LaF

A paste brooch, 1950s, 3in (7.5cm) wide.
£10–15 / € 15–22
$19–28 ⊞ CCO

▶ **A white metal and paste brooch,** by Pell, in the form of a cat, 1950s, 2in (5cm) high.
£70–80 / € 105–120
$130–150 ⊞ JBB

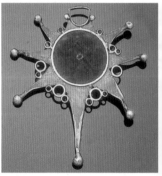

A silver and enamel brooch, inset with a pansy flowerhead, maker's mark 'NG', Edinburgh 1972.
£140–165 / € 210–250
$260–310 ⊞ TEN

Cameos

Cameos became very popular at the turn of the 18th century. 'A fashionable lady wears cameos at her girdle, cameos in her necklace, cameos on each of her bracelets and a cameo on her tiara', noted the *Journal des Dames* in 1805. During the Victorian period, cameos were produced for every level of the market. They ranged from finely carved precious and hard stones (still the most costly cameos today) to more affordable examples made from shell, coral, lava and other materials. Classical subjects were a favourite theme. Values reflect subject matter, crispness of detail in the carving, the presence of an original setting and condition.

A shell cameo brooch, carved with a portrait of Diana the Huntress, in a micro-mosaic easel frame, 19thC, 3½in (9cm) high.
£480–570 / €720–860 $900–1,050 ⚘ G(L)

A hardstone cameo ring, carved with the head of a Roman emperor, in a gold frame, early 19thC.
£360–430 / €540–650 $670–800 ⚘ WW

A necklace mounted with three oyster shell and slate cameos, carved with Aquarius and two putti, in gold mounts, c1800.
£300–360 / €450–540 $560–670 ⚘ WW

A Victorian shell cameo, by Baibati, carved with a portrait of an elderly lady, with a gold frame, signed, in a fitted leather case.
£360–430 / €540–650 $670–800 ⚘ G(L)

A Victorian shell cameo brooch, carved with a portrait of a lady, in a gilt-metal frame, 2in (5cm) high.
£210–250 / €320–380 $380–470 ⚘ G(L)

A Victorian shell cameo brooch, carved with a portrait of a lady, in an engraved gold frame, 1in (2.5cm) high.
£110–130 / €165–195 $210–240 ⚘ G(L)

◀ **A shell cameo brooch,** carved with a portrait of a bacchante, in a gold mount, c1850.
£320–380 / €480–570 $600–710 ⚘ TEN

Further reading
Miller's Antiques Checklists: Jewellery, Miller's Publications, 1997

◀ **A shell cameo brooch,** carved with 'The Triumph of Galatea', in a moulded gold frame, engraved to the reverse 'G. Noto', c1860.
£320–380 / €480–570 $600–710 ⚘ TEN

A shell cameo brooch, carved with a portrait of a lady, c1890, in a silver frame, 1½in (4cm) high.
£135–150 / €200–230 $250–280 ⊞ JBB

Clasps & Buckles

A pair of silver and paste shoe buckles,
19thC, 2in (5cm) square.
£210–240 €320–360
$390–450 ⊞ VK

A pair of stamped-steel shoe buckles, with leather
backing, late 19thC, 2in (5cm) high.
£40–45 / €60–70
$75–85 ⊞ EV

▶ **A paste
buckle,** c1800,
2½in (6.5cm) wide.
£20–25 €30–35
$35–45 ⊞ CCO

An enamel clasp, with Art
Nouveau decoration, c1890,
3in (7.5cm) wide.
£50–60 / €75–90
$95–110 ⊞ JBB

**A silver and niello clasp and four
slides,** c1900.
£75–85 / €115–130
$140–160 ⊞ EV

A brass and glass clasp,
Czechoslovakian, c1920,
3in (7.5cm) wide.
£35–40 / €50–60
$65–75 ⊞ JBB

An enamel clasp, in the form of flowers, c1920,
3in (7.5cm) wide.
£50–60 / €75–90
$95–110 ⊞ JBB

A celluloid and tin clasp, 1920s, 4in (10cm) wide.
£4–8 / €6–12
$8–15 ⊞ JBB

A brass and glass clasp, set with paste
stones, c1920, 3in (7.5cm) wide.
£35–40 / €50–60
$65–75 ⊞ EV

▶ **A brass and
glass buckle,**
in the form of
flowers and
leaves, 1930,
4in (10cm) wide.
£20–25
€30–35
$35–45 ⊞ JBB

Charms

◀ **Three 9ct gold money charms,** containing £1 notes and a 10 shilling note, 1940s–50s, 1in (2.5cm) wide.
£35–40
€50–60
$65–75 ⊞ NEG

A 9ct gold Westminster charm, 1940s–50s, 1in (2.5cm) wide.
£140–160 / €210–240
$260–300 ⊞ NEG

Items in the Jewellery section have been arranged in date order within each sub-section.

A 9ct gold car charm, 1940s–60s, 1in (2.5cm) wide.
£85–95 / €130–145
$160–180 ⊞ NEG

◀ **A 14ct gold charm bracelet,** c1950.
£270–320
€400–480
$500–600
⚲ DuM

▶ **A 9ct gold woodpecker charm,** 1960s, 1in (2.5cm) high.
£15–20 / €22–30
$28–38 ⊞ SPE

Earrings

◀ A pair of Victorian gold earrings, with wirework decoration.
£160–190 / €250–290 $300–360 ⚹ G(L)
Victorian earrings though large in size are often light in weight. They are fragile and are often damaged, therefore perfect and unrestored sets will command a higher premium.

A pair of Victorian gold earrings, set with cat's eyes surrounded with seed pearls.
£130–155 / €195–230 $250–290 ⚹ G(L)

A pair of jet earrings, c1880, 2in (5cm) long.
£220–250 / €330–380 $410–470 ⊞ AM

A pair of gold drop earrings, with later screw-back fittings, 19thC, in a fitted case.
£230–270 / €350–410 $430–500 ⚹ G(L)

A pair of gold earrings, set with rubies and diamonds, 1940s.
£420–500 / €630–750 $790–940 ⚹ G(L)

A pair of Austrian crystal earrings, by Mitchell Mayer for Christian Dior, 1951–54, 1in (2.5cm) high.
£145–165 / €220–250 $270–310 ⊞ LaF

A pair of beaded clip-on earrings, by Trifari, with c1950s, 1in (2.5cm) diam.
£45–50 / €70–80 $85–95 ⊞ LBr

A pair of paste earrings, by Vendome, American, 1960, 1¼in (3cm) wide.
£45–50 / €70–80 $85–95 ⊞ LaF

◀ A pair of brass clip-on earrings, by Givenchy, 1960s, 3in (7.5cm) long.
£50–60 / €75–90 $95–110 ⊞ LBr

▶ A pair of soft-drinks-can earrings, by Val Hunt, 2003, 2in (5cm) high.
£25–30 / €40–45 $50–55 ⊞ LaF

Hatpins

Hatpins came into fashion in the late 19th century along with the vogue for large picture hats. Edwardian hatpins can measure up to 12in (30.5cm) in length and can be viciously sharp. Hatpins with uncovered ends were banned from omnibuses and various patents were taken out for point protectors. Pins came in many different designs and materials, and prominent makers include silversmith Charles Horner. Values depend on maker, medium and style. Check the condition, as many hatpins were shortened when fashions changed after WWI and hats grew smaller, and sometimes the head of the pin can be loosened or damaged by wear. Pairs of hatpins will be worth more than individual examples. Look out for period hatpin holders to display your collection. They were produced both as individual pieces and as part of ladies' dressing table sets.

A ceramic hatpin, decorated with a couple in 18thC dress, c1880, 9in (23cm) long.
£50–60 / €75–90
$95–110 田 JBB

A ceramic hatpin holder, c1900, 5in (12.5cm) high.
£65–75 / €100–115
$120–140 田 JBB

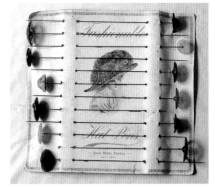

A hatpin sample card, complete with hat pins, 1910, 11in (28cm) square.
£540–600 / €810–900
$1,000–1,100 田 JBB

A glass hatpin, c1910, 6in (15cm) long.
£50–60 / €75–90
$95–110 田 JBB

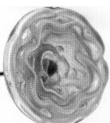

A glass hatpin, c1910, 10in (25.5cm) long.
£30–35 / €45–50
$55–65 田 JBB

A Satsuma hatpin, c1910, 9in (23cm) long.
£110–125 / €165–190
$200–230 田 JBB

An iron hatpin, with gold decoration, c1910, 1in (2.5cm) diam.
£180–200 / €270–300
$330–370 田 VK

A silver and enamel hatpin, Chinese, c1910, 1½in (4cm) diam.
£160–180 / €240–270
$300–340 田 VK

A silver-plated hatpin holder, in the form of a crocodile, Chinese, 1920s, 9in (23cm) long.
£220–250 / €330–380
$410–470 田 JBB

Men's Accessories

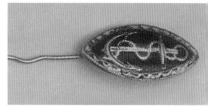

A naval officer's gold and enamel stick pin, decorated with a foul anchor, minor damage, c1880, 2¾in (7cm) long.
£250–280 / €380–420
$470–520 ⊞ TML
A foul anchor is the term used when an anchor is entangled with a rope or a cable. It was first used as a naval insignia by Lord Howard of Effingham during the defeat of the Spanish Armada in 1588.
It subsequently became the seal of the British Admiralty and then a universal naval symbol, used across the world.

A set of six Edwardian mother-of-pearl waistcoat buttons, cased.
£35–40 / €50–60
$65–75 ⊞ OH

A Victorian stick pin, decorated with a lithograph of a horse, 1in (2.5cm) long.
£10–15 / €15–22
$19–28 ⊞ MRW

Three 15ct gold and ruby dress studs, in the form of snakes, c1890, in a case.
£220–250 / €330–380
$410–470 ⊞ CUF

A pair of silver cufflinks, with floral decoration, 1901.
£50–60 / €75–90
$95–110 ⊞ CUF

A metal and diamond stick pin, in the form of a fox mask, in a *faux* morocco case, early 20thC.
£120–140 / €180–210
$220–260 ➤ PFK

A pair of 9ct gold and coral cufflinks, 1920.
£110–125 / €165–190
$200–230 ⊞ JBB

A pair of silver cufflinks, decorated with cricket bats, c1920.
£30–35 / €45–50
$55–65 ⊞ JBB

▶ **A pair of silver and enamel cufflinks,** decorated with silhouettes, 1920.
£175–195 / €260–290
$320–360 ⊞ SPE

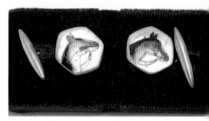

A pair of enamel and silver cufflinks, decorated with horses' heads, 1920s.
£65–75 / €100–115
$120–140 ⊞ CUF

A pair of silver-gilt Monsieur cufflinks, by Christian Dior, French, in a velveteen box, 1920s.
£60–70 / €90–105
$110–130 ⊞ LBr

A set of four mother-of-pearl and diamond dress studs, in a fitted case, c1930.
£220–260 / €330–390
$410–490 ✗ TEN

An 18ct gold and Essex crystal tie clip, decorated with a fox, 1930s, 2in (5cm) wide.
£340–380 / €510–570
$640–710 ⊞ CUF

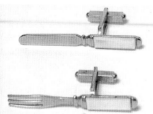

A pair of gilt-metal cufflinks, in the form of a knife and a fork, c1960.
£40–45 / €60–70
$75–85 ⊞ CAD

A pair of silver-gilt and enamel cufflinks, 1960s.
£70–80 / €105–120
$130–150 ⊞ JBB

An 18ct gold, onyx and diamond dress set, 1920s.
£630–700 / €900–1,050
$1,100–1,300 ⊞ CUF

A set of four 14ct white gold cufflinks, set with rubies, 1930s.
£155–175 / €230–260
$290–330 ⊞ CUF

A pair of St George armbands, in a display box, 1930s–40s, 11in (28cm) wide.
£9–13 / €14–19
$17–24 ⊞ RTT

◀ A pair of silver and enamel cufflinks, decorated with terriers, late 1930s.
£110–125
€165–190
$210–230 ⊞ CUF

A pair of 18ct gold cufflinks, French, 1960s.
£310–350 / €470–530
$580–650 ⊞ CUF

Necklaces & Pendants

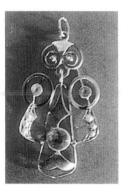

◀ An Edwardian 15ct gold pendant, set with a peridot and seed pearls.
£120–140 / €180–210 $220–260 ≯ PFK

▶ An Edwardian 9ct gold pendant, set with amethysts and seed pearls.
£120–140 / €180–210 $220–260 ≯ G(L)

A gilt-metal pendant, decorated with a micro-mosaic depicting classical ruins, 19thC.
£185–220 / €280–330 $350–410 ≯ G(L)

◀ A jet necklace, with three carved pendants, c1870, 21in (53.5cm) long.
£310–350
€470–530
$580–650
⊞ AM

A 9ct gold pendant frame, set with a $20 coin, American, 1890.
£250–300 / €380–450 $470–560 ≯ G(L)

A white metal and plastic necklace, 1920s–30s, 14in (35.5cm) long.
£50–60 / €75–90 $95–110 ⊞ DRE

A frosted-glass necklace, French, 1920s, 14in (35.5cm) long.
£60–70 / €90–105 $110–130 ⊞ DRE

▶ A Bakelite necklace and bracelet set, in the form of cherries, c1935.
£1,000–1,150
€1,500–1,700
$1,850–2,150 ⊞ SpM
Original 1930s versions of this cherry necklace set are very desirable. It was also reproduced in the post-WWII period. The reproduction necklace is brighter and has broader leaves. It is worth around £130–150 / €195–220 / $240–280.

A sterling silver pendant, designed by Tappio Wirkkala, made by N. Westerback, entitled 'Silvermoon', 1971, Finnish, 4¼in (11cm) diam.
£570–680 / €850–1,000 $1,050–1,250 ≯ BUK

A velvet and paste necklace, 1930s, 24in (61cm) long.
£100–120 / € 150–180
$185–220 ⊞ LBe

A metal necklace, Egyptian, 1930s.
£150–165 / € 220–250
$280–310 ⊞ SUW

A velvet and paste necklace, 1930s, 24in (61cm) long.
£100–120 / € 150–180
$185–220 ⊞ LBe

A gilt cross pendant, by Joseff of Hollywood, set with *faux* pearls, Amerian, late 1940s, 3in (7.5cm) wide.
£310–350 / € 470–530
$580–650 ⊞ JUJ

A *faux* turquoise and gilt necklace, by Philip Hulitar, 1950s, 16in (40.5cm) long.
£115–130 / € 165–190
$210–240 ⊞ LaF

A *faux* pearl necklace, by Miriam Haskell, American, c1950, 17in (43cm) long.
£115–130 / € 165–190
$210–240 ⊞ LaF

◀ **A crystal necklace,** Czechoslovakian, 1950s, 17in (43cm) long.
£55–65 / € 85–100
$100–120 ⊞ DRE

▶ **A gilt and glass necklace,** by Christian Dior, 1960s, 15in (38cm) long, boxed.
£540–600
€ 810–900
$1,000–1,100
⊞ HSR

A silver pendant, by Krug-Baumer, Swedish, 1971, 3in (7.5cm) wide.
£300–340 / € 450–510
$560–640 ⊞ BOOM

A silver and enamel pendant, Italian, Laponnia, c1974, 6in (15cm) long.
£540–600 / € 810–900
$1,000–1,100 ⊞ BOOM

Jewellery Sets

◀ **A metal and glass necklace and earrings set,** Czechoslovakian, 1920s, 14in (35.5cm) long.
£135–150 / €200–230
$250–280 ⊞ DRE

A silver bracelet and earrings set, by Napier, 1940s, earring 1¼in (3cm) diam.
£135–150 / €200–230
$250–280 ⊞ DRE

A copper and enamel bracelet and earrings set, by Gerry Fells for Matisse Renoir, American, 1945–55, bracelet 2in (5cm) wide.
£100–110 / €150–165
$185–210 ⊞ JUJ

◀ **A clear and coloured paste brooch and earrings set,** by Weiss, American, c1950, brooch 2in (5cm) high.
£120–135
€180–200
$220–250
⊞ LaF

A gilt-metal and paste bracelet and earrings set, by Schiaparelli, 1950s.
£720–800 / €1,050–1,200
$1,350–1,500 ⊞ JUJ
Paris couturier Elsa Schiaparelli (1890–1973) was famous for her extravagant and surrealist-inspired dress designs, reflecting the influence of artist friends such as Salvador Dali. Her costume jewellery was similarly inventive. It is currently sought after by collectors and is achieving high prices.

◀ **A gilt and *faux* pearls brooch, earrings and necklace set,** by Kramer, American, 1950, necklace 15in (38cm) long.
£135–150 / €200–230
$250–280 ⊞ LaF

A *faux* turquoise and paste necklace and earrings set, by Mitchell Mayer for Christian Dior, 1950s.
£310–350 / €470–530
$580–650 ⊞ RGA

A gilt metal, enamel and diamante necklace and earrings set, by Nina Ricci, 1970s.
£200–220 / €300–330
$370–410 ⊞ JBB

▶ **A paste necklace and earrings set,** by Butler & Wilson, 1970s, necklace 16¼in (41.5cm) long.
£45–50 / €70–80
$85–95 ⊞ TWI

Kitchenware

Vintage kitchenware is collected both for use and decoration. Victorian and Edwardian objects tend to command the highest prices, but there is also growing interest in more modern material. From jelly moulds to dairy equipment to mechanical apple peelers, 19th-century equipment reflects the Victorian love of ornament, their mechanical ingenuity, and the huge amount of labour required to produce endless courses for the dinner table. Values depend on various factors including material (copper often commands a premium), decoration (typically the more elaborate the design the higher the price) and provenance – such as the Irish soda bread stand illustrated below. Much kitchenware is anonymous,

and though a known manufacturer can add interest and value, in many instances a maker's name is often of less importance than design, rarity and condition.

The 20th century saw the proliferation of mass-production and cheaper man-made materials, the arrival of fitted kitchens, and the replacement of servants with labour-saving appliances. After WWII the introduction of plastics (such as Formica and Fablon) into the kitchen made it a brighter place.

From icing sets to multi-coloured plastic cocktail forks, kitchenware reflected the desire for a bit of fun after war-time austerity. From the modern age, look out for kitsch kitchen material and objects by known designers.

A copper ale muller, 19thC, 7½in (19cm) high.
£120–135 / €180–200
$220–250 ⊞ BS

A copper *bain-marie*, 19thC, 6in (15cm) high.
£165–185 / €250–280
$310–350 ⊞ BS

A copper stockpot, with lid, 19thC, 10in (25.5cm) high.
£270–300 / €400–450
$500–560 ⊞ BS

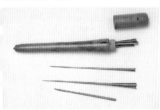

A set of steel larding needles, in a wooden case, 19thC, 10in (25.5cm) long.
£100–115 / €150–175
$185–220 ⊞ BS

◄ **A steel and brass pastry jigger,** c1820, 6in (15cm) long.
£310–350 / €470–530
$580–650 ⊞ NEW

A metal bannoch turner, c1820, 14in (35.5cm) long.
£110–125 / €165–190
$200–230 ⊞ Cot

◄ **A Queen cast-iron firelighting fan,** with tin cover and clockwork bellows, 19thC, 12in (30.5cm) long.
£420–470 / €630–710
$790–880 ⊞ BS

A wrought-iron soda bread stand, Irish, mid-19thC, 16in (40.5cm) high.
£220–250 / €330–380
$410–470 ⊞ WeA
This stand was positioned by the fire and used for baking or freshening-up soda bread.

A glass rolling pin, c1860, 29in (73.5cm) long.
£55–65 / €85–100
$100–120 ⊞ HO

An iron pie peel, Welsh, c1870, 21in (53.5cm) long.
£155–175 / €230–260
$290–330 ⊞ NEW

A metal egg beater, American, 1871, 10in (25.5cm) high.
£35–40 / €50–60
$65–75 ⊞ WeA

A wrought-iron bread peel, with a wooden handle,
c1880, 18in (45.5cm) long.
£30–35 / €45–50
$55–65 ⊞ Cot

A copper fish kettle, c1880, 21in (53.5cm) wide.
£270–300 / €400–450
$500–560 ⊞ NEW

A copper kettle, c1880,
15in (38cm) high.
£200–230 / €300–350
$380–430 ⊞ YT

**A brass and copper
cream can,** c1880,
12in (30.5cm) high.
£125–140 / €190–210
$230–260 ⊞ NEW

**A Hudson & Co cast-iron Little
Star mechanical apple peeler,**
American, 1885, 10in (25.5cm) wide.
£150–165 / €220–250
$280–310 ⊞ BS

A cast-iron double-section waffle iron,
c1890, 22in (56cm) long.
£60–70 / €90–105
$110–130 ⊞ DaM

**A cast-iron raisin
seeder,** American, 1896,
6in (15cm) high.
£120–135 / €180–200
$220–250 ⊞ BS

◄ **A W.
Bullock & Co
cast-iron sugar
snip,** with a
wooden handle,
late 19thC, 14in
(35.5cm) wide.
**£180–200
€270–300
$330–370
⊞ WeA**

Three brass pastry cutters and crimpers, late 19thC, 5in (12.5cm) long.
£30–35 / €45–50
$55–65 ⊞ BS

A set of six Wardrobe & Pierce knives, forks and spoons, late 19thC, knife 10in (25.5cm) long.
£115–130 / €175–195
$210–240 ⊞ WeA

A set of three tin pastry cutters, c1900, largest 3in (7.5cm) diam.
£10–15 / €15–22
$19–28 ⊞ Cot

A metal measuring jug, late 19thC, 5¼in (13.5cm) high.
£55–65 / €85–100
$100–120 ⊞ WeA

A steel biscuit pricker, c1900, 3in (7.5cm) diam.
£40–45 / €60–70
$75–85 ⊞ BS

◀ **A cast-iron potato slicer,** American, c1900, 8in (20.5cm) wide.
£200–230 / €320–350
$390–430 ⊞ BS

Four tin grocery price signs, c1910, largest 8in (20.5cm) high.
£35–40 / €50–60
$65–75 each ⊞ SMI

◀ **Two tin butcher's display signs,** c1910, 10in (25.5cm) high.
£45–50 / €70–80
$85–95 each ⊞ SMI

A cast-iron pestle and mortar, late 19thC, mortar 2¾in (7cm) high.
£65–75 / €100–115
$120–140 ⊞ WeA

A sycamore bread board, carved with fruit and flowers, c1900, 12in (30.5cm) diam.
£60–70 / €90–105
$110–130 ⊞ B&R

A tin pigeon roaster, French, c1900, 10in (25.5cm) wide.
£60–70 / €90–105
$110–130 ⊞ B&R

A wire salad spinner, early 20thC, 9½in (24cm) diam.
£55–65 / €85–100
$100–120 ⊞ WeA

A metal egg lifter,
c1920, 7in (18cm) high.
£6–10 / €9–15
$12–19 ⊞ AL

A steel and brass milk can, c1920, 5in (12.5cm) high.
£100–120 / €150–180
$185–220 ⊞ SMI

A wire egg stand, c1920,
12in (30.5cm) high.
£55–65 / €85–100
$100–120 ⊞ Cot

A brass coffee grinder,
French, 1920s,
11in (28cm) high.
£85–95 / €130–145
$160–180 ⊞ DaM

A wire whisk, with a
wooden handle, French,
1920s, 9in (23cm) high.
£10–15 / €15–22
$19–28 ⊞ Cot

Two enamel storage jars, 1920s, 7in (18cm) high.
£35–40 / €50–60
$65–75 ⊞ B&R

A set of five enamel storage jars, French, c1930,
largest 5in (12.5cm) diam.
£100–120 / €150–180
$185–220 ⊞ B&R

**A Victor's wooden
confectionery delivery
box,** with metal bands,
c1930, 19in (48.5cm) wide.
£135–150 / €200–230
$250–280 ⊞ B&R

**A Green Arrow tin
larder box,** 1930s,
19in (48.5cm) high.
£55–65 / €85–100
$100–120 ⊞ DaM

**A pack of 36 birthday
cake candles,** 1930s–40s,
2½in (6.5cm) square.
£1–5 / €2–7
$3–9 ⊞ RTT

An enamel flour tin,
c1935, 9in (23cm) wide.
£40–45 / €60–70
$75–85 ⊞ B&R

**A Blow glass butter
churn,** 1948,
14in (35.5cm) high.
£55–65 / €85–100
$100–120 ⊞ BS

A Samson chrome and Bakelite electric toaster, No. 198, American, 1940s, 10in (25.5cm) wide.
£25–30 / €40–45
$50–55 ⊞ TRA

◀ **A paper doily,** c1950, 12in (30.5cm) diam.
£1–5 / €2–7
$3–9 ⊞ MSB

A metal food mill, with various attachments, 1950s, 9½in (24cm) diam.
£30–35 / €45–50
$55–65 ⊞ WeA

A Brevetti Robbiati aluminium Atomic espresso machine, c1950, 8¼in (21cm) high.
£180–210 / €270–320
$330–390 ↗ SWO

A tin wall-mounted tea dispenser, 1950s, 8in (20.5cm) high.
£30–35 / €45–50
$55–65 ⊞ DaM

A Tala tin icing set, 1950s–60s, 6in (15cm) high, in original box.
£15–20 / €22–30
$28–38 ⊞ DaM

Ceramics

A redware milk bowl, with lead glaze and sponged decoration, American, mid-19thC, 11in (28cm) diam.
**£150–175 / €220–260
$280–330** ⚲ JAA

A Kent's ceramic egg whisk and beater stand, c1880, 7in (18cm) high.
**£135–150 / €200–230
$250–280** ⊞ SMI

◀ **A salt-glazed bread crock,** Scottish, c1880, 20in (51cm) wide.
**£220–250 / €330–380
$410–470** ⊞ B&R

▶ **A Holborn ceramic egg whisk stand,** c1880, 5in (12.5cm) high.
**£135–150
€200–230
$250–280** ⊞ SMI

A stoneware colander, c1880, 9in (23cm) diam.
**£45–50 / €70–80
$85–95** ⊞ Cot

A Dairy Outfit Co ceramic and metal Speedy egg beater, c1900, 8¾in (22cm) high.
**£145–160 / €210–240
$270–300** ⊞ WeA

A ceramic egg crock, c1900, 12in (30.5cm) wide.
**£50–60 / €75–90
$95–110** ⊞ B&R

An Ovum ceramic measuring cup, c1900, 2½in (6.5cm) high.
**£135–150 / €200–230
$250–280** ⊞ SMI

A ceramic nutmeg storage jar, c1930, 3½in (9cm) high.
**£45–50 / €70–80
$85–95** ⊞ Cot

A painted porcelain cake decoration, 1920–40, 2in (5cm) wide.
**£10–15 / €15–22
$19–28** ⊞ FMN

A Sadler Kleen Ware ceramic milk jug, 1940s, 5½in (14cm) high.
**£25–30 / €40–45
$50–55** ⊞ SCH

Choppers

► **A steel sugar cleaver,** probably Continental, early 19thC, 10½in (26.5cm) long.
£510–570 / €770–860
$950–1,050 ⊞ BS

A steel herb chopper, c1870, 11in (28cm) wide.
£165–185 / €240–270
$310–350 ⊞ NEW

A steel herb chopper, with a wooden handle, 1778, 22in (56cm) long.
£130–145
€195–220
$240–280
⊞ NEW

An iron chopper, with a wooden handle, 19thC, 11in (28cm) high.
£60–70 / €90–105
$110–130 ⊞ NEW

► **A metal chopper,** with a wooden handle, late 19thC, 9¼in (23.5cm) wide.
£75–85 / €115–130
$140–160 ⊞ WeA

Moulds

During the 19th century eating habits became increasingly elaborate. Food was required to be decorative and moulds were a kitchen essential. There were 500 food moulds in the kitchens of Apsley House, residence of the Duke of Wellington. Mrs Beeton included a variety of moulds in her *Book of Household Management* (1861), the bible of the middle-class housewife, while Mrs Marshall – chef, writer and founder of a successful cookery school – illustrated 1,000 different designs in her *Book of Moulds* (1886).

Moulds were produced in every material from copper to earthenware, and came in every size and shape. Small copper moulds were used for aspics while larger examples were for sweet jellies and blancmanges as well as savoury dishes. Though some copper moulds will bear the marks of a retailer or even the monogram of the owner, principal value lies in size and shape. Double-sided tin moulds were for making chocolate, and here again the more elaborate the design, the higher the price.

Pewter was used for ice cream moulds, which were distinguished from jelly moulds by the fact that they close up completely so that the mould could be put into an ice box. Ceramic moulds are popular with collectors today both because designs can be attractive and because they are easier to clean than copper moulds. Ceramic moulds were sometimes marked by the pottery, and here the manufacturer can make a difference to the value. Pressed glass was employed from the 1880s onward, aluminium moulds appeared in the 1920s, and plastics took over in the post-war period, when packet jelly replaced the home-made variety, and jelly was relegated from the adult dinner party to the children's tea table.

Very affordable simple moulds in all these materials can be found, but look out for more interesting novelty designs. Glass rabbits are fairly common but tortoises are rarer, and as such are more expensive.

A cast-iron mould, c1880, 15in (38cm) wide.
£40–45 / €60–70
$75–85 ⊞ DaM

A copper aspic mould, in the form of a crown, 19thC, 3in (7.5cm) high.
£70–80 / €105–120
$130–150 ⊞ BS

A pewter three-piece ice cream mould, c1880, 6in (15cm) high.
£60–70 / €90–105
$110–130 ⊞ DaM

A Copeland ceramic jelly mould, in the form of a chicken, 19thC, 9in (23cm) wide.
£110–125 / €165–190
$200–230 ⊞ BS

◀ **A copper jelly mould,** 19thC, 2¼in (5.5cm) high.
£60–70 / €90–105
$110–130 ⊞ BS

A tin chocolate mould, in the form of a swan, c1900, 4in (10cm) wide.
£35–40 / €50–60
$65–75 ⊞ Cot

A stoneware jelly mould, with a
relief a cow, c1920, 6in (15cm) wide.
£70–80 / €105–120
$130–150 ⊞ SMI

A tin chocolate mould, in the form
of a tiger, Continental, c1920,
6in (15cm) wide.
£35–40 / €50–60
$65–75 ⊞ B&R

A stoneware jelly mould, with a
relief of a greyhound, c1920,
7in (18cm) wide.
£70–80 / €105–120
$130–150 ⊞ SMI

A tin cheese mould, French,
c1920, 6in (15cm) wide.
£25–30 / €40–45
$50–55 ⊞ B&R

A tin chocolate mould, in the form
of a cockerel, Continental, c1920,
5in (12.5cm) wide.
£35–40 / €50–60
$65–75 ⊞ B&R

A Brown & Polson's earthenware
shortbread mould, early 20thC,
9in (23cm) wide.
£110–125 / €165–190
$200–230 ⊞ WeA

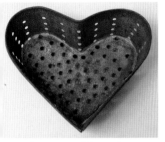

A pressed glass jelly mould, in
the form of a rabbit, c1930,
6in (15cm) wide.
£10–15 / €15–22
$19–28 ⊞ AL

A ceramic jelly mould, with relief of
four rabbits, c1930, 7in (18cm) diam.
£65–75 / €100–115
$120–140 ⊞ SMI

A pressed glass jelly mould, in
the form of a tortoise, 1930–50,
6in (15cm) wide.
£35–40 / €50–60
$65–75 ⊞ DaM

A set of five aluminium moulds,
each in the form of a dog, c1950,
5in (12.5cm) wide.
£1–5 / €2–7
$3–9 each ⊞ AL

▶ A set of six plastic jelly
moulds, 1960s, 3¾in (9.5cm) diam.
£2–6 / €3–9
$4–11 ⊞ TWI

A plastic jelly mould, in the form
of a cat, 1980s, 8in (20.5cm) wide.
£4–8 / €6–12
$8–15 ⊞ TWI

Plastics

A Bakelite squeezer, 1930s–40s, 5½in (14cm) wide.
£50–55 / €75–85
$95–105 ⊞ BS

An Embee plastic cruet set, 1950s, 3½in (9cm) high.
£20–25 / €30–35
$35–45 ⊞ TWI

A plastic cruet set, in the form of a cat and a dog, American, 1940s, 3in (7.5cm) high.
£15–20 / €22–30
$28–38 ⊞ TWI

▶ **A Bel plastic cream maker,** 1950s–60s, 12in (30.5cm) high, with original box.
£45–50 / €70–80
$85–95 ⊞ DaM

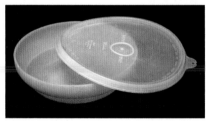

A set of six Tupperware breakfast bowls, with lids, 1960, 6½in (16.5cm) diam.
£40–45 / €60–70
$75–85 ⊞ Mo

◀ **Two plastic ice buckets,** 1960s, 7½in (19cm) high.
£15–20 / €22–30
$28–38 each ⊞ TWI

A Bakemaster 5 in 1 plastic pastry set, comprising rolling pin, flour scoop, flour shaker, scone cutter and filling funnel, 1960s, boxed, 13½in (34.5cm) long.
£15–20 / €22–30
$28–38 ⊞ TWI

◀ **A set of 12 plastic and stainless steel cocktail forks,** 1970s, boxed, 5in (12.5cm) wide.
£4–8 / €6–12
$8–15 ⊞ TWI

A McDougall's plastic weighing spoon, 1950s, 12in (30.5cm) long, with original box.
£45–50 / €60–70
$75–85 ⊞ DaM

A set of Salter plastic kitchen scales, 1960s, 8½in (21.5cm) high.
£20–25 / €30–35
$35–45 ⊞ TWI

Items in the Kitchenware section have been arranged in date order within each sub-section.

A Jonas plastic jug, by Bjarne Bo, 1970s, 7in (18cm) high.
£20–25 / €30–35
$35–45 ⊞ TWI

Wood

A lignum vitae pestle, 19thC,
11in (28cm) long.
£80–90 / €120–135
$150–170 ⊞ BS

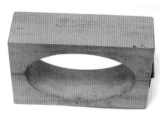

▶ **A sycamore butter mould and stamp,**
19thC, 10½in (26.5cm) wide.
£330–370 / €500–560
$620–690 ⊞ BS

**An R. A. Lister & Co oak
butter churn,** with cast-
iron fittings, 19thC,
48in (122cm) high.
£120–140 / €180–210
$220–260 ⚲ SJH

A wooden pin, 1860,
11in (28cm) long.
£100–120 / €150–165
$185–210 ⊞ WeA

▶ **A set of sycamore
spice drawers,** c1880,
8in (20.5cm) high.
£145–165 / €220–250
$270–310 ⊞ NEW

**A fruitwood and
birchwood salt box,**
c1840, 13in (33cm) high.
£95–110 / €145–165
$180–210 ⊞ F&F

◀ **A birch
butter pot,**
with pokerwork
decoration, with
lid, Norwegian,
1891, 11¼in
(28.5cm) wide.
£80–90
€120–135
$150–170
⚲ PFK

An oak butter churn,
with steel bands, 19thC,
19½in (49.5cm) high.
£155–175 / €230–270
$290–330 ⚲ JAA

▶ **An oak flour barrel,**
c1880, 10in (25.5cm) high.
£120–135 / €180–200
$220–250 ⊞ Cot

A beech rolling pin, c1900, 18in (45.5cm) long.
£30–35 / €45–50
$55–65 ⊞ Cot

▶ **Two sycamore butter stamps,** one carved with a
thistle, the other with a swan, 1920s,
larger 5in (12.5cm) diam.
£70–80 / €105–120
$130–150 ⊞ SMI

Lighting

A Victorian glass ceiling light,
decorated with fruit,
21in (53.5cm) diam.
£230–270 / €350–410
$430–510 ↗ JAA

**A wrought-iron
floating wick
pendant lamp,**
French, c1770,
19in (48.5cm)
high.
£340–380
€510–570
$640–710 ⊞ SEA

A Victorian oil lamp, the
frosted glass shade etched
with butterflies, on an ebony
base, 29in (73.5cm) high.
£90–105 / €135–160
$170–200 ↗ GH

A pair of brass candlesticks, the
galleries with pierced decoration,
c1850, 6in (15cm) high.
£175–195 / €260–290
$320–360 ⊞ SAT

A Victorian oil lamp,
with a vaseline glass
shade, the brass column
applied with sphinx,
30in (76cm) high.
£600–720 / €900–1,050
$1,100–1,300 ↗ GH

A steel candlestick, with
a wooden base, French,
c1850, 7in (18cm) high.
£130–145 / €195–220
$240–270 ⊞ NEW

**A Fratelli Tosso glass
lamp,** Italian, 1890,
18in (45.5cm) high.
£500–550 / €750–830
$940–1,050 ⊞ GLAS

A gilt-brass ceiling light,
with a cut-glass shade,
19thC, 9¾in (25cm) high.
£50–60 / €75–90
$95–110 ↗ L&E

▶ **A brass gas ceiling
lamp,** with an etched
glass shade, converted for
electricity, 1890–1900,
21in (53.5cm) high.
£145–165 / €220–250
$270–310 ⊞ JeH

A set of four brass wall lights, decorated with eagles, c1900, 29in (73.5cm) high.
£420–500 / €630–750
$790–940 ⚒ **E**

◀ **An oak table lamp,** late 19thC, 19in (48.5cm) high.
£220–250 / €330–380
$410–470 ⊞ **JeH**

A vaseline glass pendant lamp, 1890–1900, 9in (23cm) diam.
£340–380 / €510–570
$640–710 ⊞ **JeH**

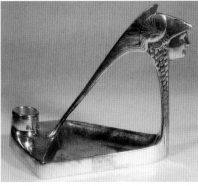

A satin glass shade, c1910, 4in (10cm) high.
£50–60 / €75–90
$95–110 ⊞ **JeH**

A WMF silver-plated candlestick, stamped mark, numbered '104', German, early 20thC, 6in (15cm) high.
£100–120 / €150–180
$185–220 ⚒ **CDC**

A cut-glass ceiling lamp, c1910, 11in (28cm) high.
£165–185 / €250–280
$310–350 ⊞ **JeH**

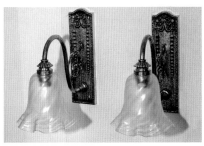

A pair of cast brass wall lights, with glass shades, c1910, 9in (23cm) high.
£200–230 / €300–340
$370–430 ⊞ **JeH**

Sets/pairs

Unless otherwise stated, any description which refers to 'a set' or 'a pair' includes a guide price for the entire set or the pair, even though the illustration may show only a single item.

A copper desk lamp, 1910–20, 24in (61cm) high.
£175–195 / €260–290
$330–370 ⊞ **JeH**

A Jefferson Glass Co opaque glass pendant lamp, with a brass rose, American, 1910s–20s, 17in (43cm) diam.
£270–300 / €410–450
$500–560 ⊞ **EAL**

An Edward Miller & Co caramel glass and bronze desk lamp, American, c1920, 13in (33cm) high.
£220–260 / €330–390
$400–480 ✧ **DuM**

▶ **A Bohemian-style overlay glass bag chandelier,** with hand-painted decoration, French, c1950, 17in (43cm) high.
£310–350 / €470–530
$580–650 ⊞ **JPr**

◀ **A chrome Sputnik ceiling lamp,** 1960s, 30in (76cm) diam.
£700–800
€1,050–1,200
$1,300–1,500 ⊞ **HSR**

◀ **A Hertel, Schwab & Co boudoir lamp,** numbered '13', impressed mark, 1920s, 12in (30.5cm) high.
£400–450 / €600–680
$750–840 ⊞ **SUW**

A brass and enamelled-steel desk lamp, with adjustable light box, American, c1935, 15in (38cm) high.
£300–340 / €450–510
$560–640 ⊞ **BOOM**

A chromed steel Fase desk lamp, with a revolving base, Spanish, Madrid, c1960, 16in (40.5cm) high.
£300–340 / €450–510
$560–640 ⊞ **BOOM**

▶ **A Vistosi chrome and glass chandelier,** Italian, 1960s, 18in (45.5cm) wide.
£310–350 / €470–530
$580–650 ⊞ **HSR**

A Japanese-style Ghost lamp, German, 1965, 40in (101.5cm) high.
£250–280 / €380–420
$470–520 ⊞ **BOOM**

A Flower Pot lamp, by Verner Panton for Louis Poulsen, 1969, 8in (20.5cm) diam.
£180–200 / €270–300
$330–370 ⊞ **HSR**
Blue versions of this lamp are rare.

A Murano cased glass table lamp, Italian, c1970, 18in (45.5cm) high.
£400–450 / €600–680
$750–840 ⊞ **BOOM**

◀ **A chrome and frosted glass lamp,** 1970s, 12in (30.5cm) high.
£65–75 / €100–115
$120–140 ⊞ **MARK**

Lions

This section is devoted to lions. The 'King of Beasts' is traditionally associated with royalty and leadership and has a long history of representation in the decorative arts. Lions were said to have decorated the throne of King Solomon and they appear in the heraldic devices of various monarchies. The arms of England are three Lions Passant Gardant (i.e. walking and showing full face), and a Lion Rampant is the device of Scotland.

In religion the lion was an emblem of the resurrection, because, according to tradition, lion whelps were born dead, only coming to life when their father breathed onto their faces. Jesus was referred to as 'The Lion of Judah', a winged lion was the symbol of St Mark the Evangelist (patron saint of Venice), and like Androcles, St Jerome gained the friendship of a lion through pulling a thorn from its paw.

Leo is the fifth sign of the zodiac (23 July–22 August). For the ancient Egyptians, this period coincided with the inundation of the Nile, hence the tradition of the lion's head fountain (in which water issued from the lion's mouth), a device adopted in Greece and Rome and still used today. Lion-head mounts on furniture and decorative arts also derive from classical prototypes. The lion is a symbol of strength, masculinity and vigilance, and lion sculptures are placed before doorways in both Eastern and Western cultures. In the Middle Ages lions appeared on tombs and by church entrancies and from this evolved the tradition of stone lions and lion door knockers guarding the entrance to the home.

A tile, decorated with a lion, restored, Continental, 17thC, 5in (12.5cm) square.
£100–120 / €150–180
$185–210 ⚒ VSP

A Victorian Staffordshire figural group, entitled 'Death of the Lion Queen', damaged and restored, 14½in (37cm) high.
£750–900
€1,150–1,350
$1,450–1,700 ⚒ G(L)

A pair of Victorian terracotta garden ornaments, 27in (68.5cm) long.
£500–600 / €750–900
$940–1,100 ⚒ HYD

A Staffordshire figural group, entitled 'Samson and the Lion', 19thC, 9in (23cm) high.
£150–180 / €230–270
$280–330 ⚒ SWO

A copper mould, in the form of a lion, 19thC, 16in (40.5cm) wide.
£520–580 / €780–870
$970–1,100 ⊞ KEY
This is a very rare jelly mould.

▶ **A painted terracotta model of a lion,** probably 19thC, 32½in (82.5cm) high.
£1,000–1,200
€1,500–1,800
$1,850–2,200 ⚒ COBB

A ceramic box, the cover surmounted with a lion, with three compartments, possibly Italian, c1820, 7in (18cm) wide.
£1,050–1,200
€1,600–1,800
$1,950–2,200 ⊞ ReN

An earthenware mug, entitled with a 'A visit to Van Amburgh's Lions', printed with a scene of a lion tamer with lions, 1839, 4in (10cm) high.
£70–80 / €105–120
$130–150 ⚒ SAS

◀ **A pair of cast-iron door porters,** in the form of lions, 1860, 12in (30.5cm) high.
£155–175
€230–260
$290–330
⊞ **GBr**

A metal penknife, the handle in the form of a recumbent lion, 1900, 3in (7.5cm) long.
£40–45 / €60–70
$75–85 ⊞ **NLS**

A London Scottish Rifle Volunteers silver-plated brooch, decorated with a lion in a thistle wreath, stamped 'Merton', c1908.
£180–200 / €270–300
$340–370 ↗ **WAL**

A brass coal bucket, with lion-mask handles and lion-paw feet, c1910, 15in (38cm) high.
£130–150 / €200–230
$250–280 ⊞ **JeH**

A two-handled mug, commemorating the Empire Exhibition, Glasgow, Scotland, the handles in the form of lions, 1938, 4in (10cm) high.
£70–80 / €105–120
$130–150 ⊞ **WAA**

◀ **An Abingdon Bowling Club gilded-silver and enamel badge,** c1938, 1½in (4cm) high.
£10–15 / €15–22
$19–28 ⊞ **MRW**

A Portmeirion mug, decorated with Gold Lion pattern, 1963, 3in (7.5cm) high.
£15–20 / €22–30
$28–38 ⊞ **CHI**

A W. H. Goss thistle vase, commemorating the Empire Exhibition, Glasgow, Scotland, with transfer lion mark, 1938, 3¼in (8.5cm) high.
£55–65 / €85–100
$100–120 ⊞ **G&CC**

Cross Reference
Commemorative Ware
see pages 177–185

Commemorative Ware
see pages 177–185

A Steiff mohair lion, German, 1960s, 13in (33cm) long.
£70–80 / €105–120
$130–150 ⊞ **POLL**

▶ **A Coalport mug,** commemorating the Silver Jubilee of Queen Elizabeth II, decorated with the English coat-of-arms, 1977, 4in (10cm) high.
£45–50 / €70–80
$85–95 ⊞ **H&G**

Luggage

A leather hat box, c1870, 13in (33cm) wide.
£200–230 / €300–350
$370–430 ⊞ **TOP**

A silver-plate, steel and ivory cutlery set, in a leather case, comprising a fork, spoon, knife with corkscrew and condiment tower, with a leather pad with four pockets, in a leather case, late 19thC, 5in (12.5cm) long.
£130–145 / €195–220
$240–270 ⊞ **ChC**

► **A leather case,**
by Erskine & Son, monogrammed 'J.F.', 1910, 24in (61cm) wide.
£110–130 / €165–195
$220–240 ⊞ **SPT**

A late Victorian painted wood hat box,
14in (35.5cm) high.
£175–195 / €260–290
$320–360 ⊞ **SDA**

A leather attaché case,
c1910, 14in (35.5cm) wide.
£85–95 / €130–145
$160–180 ⊞ **MCa**

LOCATE THE SOURCE

The source of each illustration in Miller's can be found by checking the code letters below each caption with the Key to Illustrations, pages 443–451.

An Edwardian leather Gladstone bag, with brass fittings, 31in (78.5cm) wide.
£340–380 / €510–570
$640–710 ⊞ **MINN**

A leather collar box,
decorated with a horseshoe, 1930s, 7in (18cm) high.
£25–30 / €40–45
$50–55 ⊞ **MCa**

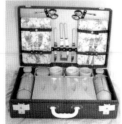

A Brexton picnic set and matching drinks set,
1950s, 20in (51cm) wide.
£220–250 / €330–380
$410–470 ⊞ **PPH**

Medals & Tokens

Commemorative & Tokens

A silver Royalist badge, possibly by T. Rawlins, decorated with a crowned bust of Charles II, c1660, 1½in (4cm) high.
£340–380 / €510–570 $640–710 ⊞ TML

► **An Indian Peace medal,** commemorating James Monroe, President of America, 1817, 3in (7.5cm) diam.
£430–510 / €650–770 $800–950 ↗ WAL

A silver medal, commemorating the coronation of King William III, signed, 1689, 2¼in (5.5cm) diam.
£280–330 / €420–500 $520–620 ↗ G(L)

A bronze ticket, for Anglesey Druids Society, c1780, 1⅜in (3.5cm) high.
£165–185 / €250–280 $310–350 ⊞ TML

A bronze ticket, for Richardson's Coffee House, Covent Garden, 1793, 1¼in (3cm) diam.
£75–85 / €115–130 $140–160 ⊞ TML

◄ **A literary prize medal,** inscribed 'Merited by Rapid Improvement in Penmanship', c1829, 1in (2.5cm) wide.
£200–240 / €300–360 $380–450 ↗ WW

A white metal medal, by T. Halliday, commemorating the opening of the Grand Junction Railway, depicting Liverpool Railway Station, 1837, 2in (5cm) diam.
£155–175 / €230–260 $290–330 ⊞ TML

A bronze medal, by B. Pistrucci, commemorating Field Marshal Arthur Duke of Wellington, 1841, 2¼in (5.5cm) high.
£250–280 / €380–420 $470–520 ⊞ TML

A bronze medal, by W. J. Taylor, commemorating the completion of the Thames Tunnel, depicting the tunnel and the head of Sir Marc Isambard Brunel, 1842, 1½in (4cm) diam.
£110–125 / €165–190 $210–230 ⊞ TML

◄ **A white metal medal,** by J. Davis, commemorating the Jubilee of the London Missionary Society, depicting a preacher and a kneeling congregation, 1844, 1½in (4cm) diam.
£65–75 / €100–115 $120–140 ⊞ TML

A white metal medal, by T. Ottley, commemorating Queen Victoria's visit to the Château d'Eu, 1843, 2in (5cm) diam.
£110–125 / €165–190 $210–230 ⊞ TML
The Château d'Eu was the private residence of the French royal family, and the Queen and Prince Albert were entertained there in September 1843.

A white metal medal, for Amateur Gardening, 1855, 2in (5cm) diam.
£10–15 / €15–22 $19–28 ⊞ HOP

Cross Reference
Shipping see pages 340–344

A white metal medal, by J. Moore, commemorating the death of Isambard Kingdom Brunel, depicting SS *Great Eastern*, 1859, 1½in (4cm) diam.
£45–50 / €70–80
$85–95 ⊞ TML

A bronze gilt medal, after W. Wyon, for the Telford Prize, Institution of Civil Engineers, depicting Thomas Telford and the Menai Bridge, 1864, 2¼in (5.5cm) diam.
£155–175 / €230–260
$290–330 ⊞ TML

◀ **A medal,** for the Royal Humane Society, 1865.
£110–125 / €165–190
$210–230 ⤢ AMB
This medal, dated 22 April 1865, was awarded to John Perry for rescuing a drowning boy at Maldon in Essex.

A silver medal, by O. Yencesse, commemorating Gustave Servois, French, 1908, 2½in (6.5cm) diam, with original box.
£75–85 / €115–130
$140–150 ⤢ DNW
Gustave Servois was the director of France's Archive Nationales between 1888 and 1902.

A silver prize medal, by H. Maryon, for the National Pig Breeders' Association, 1923, 2in (5cm) diam.
£65–75 / €100–115
$120–150 ⊞ TML

A gardening medal, in original box, 1924, 2in (5cm) diam.
£15–20 / €22–30
$28–38 ⊞ HOP

A silver prize medal, by J. Moore, for the Great Thurlow Poultry Society Suffolk, depicting birds at a pond, 1896, 1½in (4cm) diam, with original case.
£75–85 / €115–130
$140–160 ⊞ TML

▶ **Three copper bread tokens,** for the Northampton Cooperative Society, 1920s, 1¼in (3cm) wide.
£20–25
€30–35
$35–45 ⊞ BS

A bronze medal, by M. Delannoy, celebrating the Paris *Exposition Coloniale Internationale*, French, 1931, 2in (5cm) diam.
£35–40 / €50–60
$65–75 ⤢ DNW

A silver pass, for the Henriot Champagne cellars in Reims, French, c1950, 1¾in (4.5cm) diam.
£20–25 / €30–35
$35–45 ⤢ DNW

Military

A group of miniature medals, awarded to Sergeant A. Thomson: Victoria Cross; Crimea 1854–56 with three bars; Indian Mutiny 1857–58 with one bar; and Turkish Crimea 1855.
£750–900 / €1,150–1,350
$1,400–1,650 ≯ DNW

▶ A pair of medals, awarded to Private J. Williams, Cheshire Regiment: India General Service medal; Victoria Long Service medal, 1887–89.
£220–250 / €330–380
$410–470 ⊞ JBM

▶ A Crimea medal, awarded to G. King Gr & Dr 6th Battalion Royal Artillery, with Sebastopol bar, slight damage, c1855.
£140–165 / €210–250
$260–310 ≯ G(L)
Because Queen Victoria wanted her troops to receive Crimea medals quickly, they were awarded unnamed and could be returned for inscription. Some recipients never bothered, others had their names engraved privately. Comparatively few medals were sent back for official naming, and today these can command a high premium.

An East and West Africa medal, awarded to W. H. Tamlyn, with a Witu bar, 1887–1900.
£250–300
€380–450
$470–560
≯ HOLL

▶ A Volunteers Officer's decoration, with a miniature, 1892–1908, in a fitted leather case, 5in (12.5cm) wide.
£130–145
€195–230
$240–270 ⊞ Tus

A pair of medals, awarded to Sergeant E. Wells, Transport Corps: India General Service medal with Chin Hills 1892–93 bar; India medal with Relief of Chitral 1895 bar, 1892–95.
£550–660 / €830–990
$1,050–1,250 ≯ G(L)
Clasps and bars add significantly to the history and value of medals. This Indian General Service Medal includes a rare 1892–93 Chin Hills bar. The more desirable bars have been faked and something like a Queen's South Africa medal with a Relief of Mafeking clasp should be checked against the medal rolls.

A pair of medals, awarded to Private N. Watts, 21st Lancers: Queen's Sudan medal; Khedive's Sudan medal, with a Khartoum bar.
£1,500–1,800 / €2,250–2,700 $2,800–3,350 ⚒ WAL

A group of miniature Boer War dress medals, comprising Victoria Cross; Queen's South Africa medal with four bars; King's South Africa medal with two bars; and an Army Long Service and Good Conduct medal, 1899–1902.
£220–260 / €330–390 $410–490 ⚒ BR

A Queen's South Africa medal, awarded to Private A. Fort, with three bars, 1899–1902.
£210–250 / €320–380 $390–470 ⚒ HOLL

▶ **A silver Melton Mowbray tribute medal,** for soldiers returning from the Boer War, presented to Patrick Nolan, 1900–01, 1½in (4cm) diam.
£400–480 / €600–720 $750–890 ⚒ DNW

A Toronto tribute medal, for soldiers returning from the Boer War, presented to Sergeant W. Lang, inscribed 'Canada's Brave Boys, South Africa, Welcome Home', 1900, with original brooch bar.
£450–540 / €670–800 $840–1,000 ⚒ DNW

A 15ct gold and enamel Londonderry tribute medal, by Vaughton & Son, for soldiers returning from the Boer War, presented to J. Thompson, Birmingham 1900, 1in (2.5cm) diam.
£600–720 / €900–1,050 $1,150–1,350 ⚒ DNW

A silver and enamel Portsmouth tribute medal, by W. J. D., inscribed 'Naval Brigade, South Africa 1899–1900, North China 1900', Birmingham 1902, 1in (25cm) diam.
£230–270 / €350–410 $430–500 ⚒ DNW

Two medals, awarded to Private J. Wassall, Worcestershire Regiment: Queen's South Africa medal with two bars; King's South Africa medal with five bars, c1901.
£250–300 / €380–450 $470–560 ⚒ CDC

A group of Serbian medals, comprising: Order of the White Eagle; Order of the Crown; Order of St Saviour; Oblitch medal with palms; Oblitch medal; King Peter's medal; 1915 Albania medal; 1912 Serbo-Turkish War medal; 1913 Serbo-Bulgarian War; 1914–18 Communist War medal, 8in (20.5cm) wide.
£520–580 / €780–870
$970–1,100 ⊞ ABCM

A group of seven medals, awarded to Sergeant W. H. Simmonds: including 1914 Star with clasp; Defence and War medals, c1914.
£900–1,050 / €1,350–1,600
$1,700–1,950 ⚬ WAL

A group of three medals, awarded to Private A. J. Burton, Cheshire Regiment: 1914–15 Star; British War medal; Victory medal.
£50–60 / €75–90
$95–110 ⊞ JBM
The British War Medal is sometimes missing from WWI trios. Being silver, it could be pawned if the recipient fell on hard times. Bronze medals had comparatively little 'hocking' value.

A group of 10 medals, awarded to S. J. Hassett: South African Medal for Korea; South African Defence Force Good Service Medal; South Africa Permanent Force Good Service Medal; 1939–45 Star; Italy Star; War Medal 1939–45; Africa Service Medal; American Bronze Star; UN Korea Medal; South Korean War Service Medal, together with related fitment for USA Presidential unit commendation.
£880–1,050 / €1,300–1,550
$1,650–1,950 ⚬ DNW

A Third Reich Spanish Cross, for the Condor Legion, in gilt with swords, the reverse inscribed 'L15', 1933–45, 3in (7.5cm) diam, in original case.
£300–360 / €450–540
$560–670 ⚬ WAL

A group of five medals, awarded to Sergeant R. Angus, RAF: including Royal Air Force General Service medal with Bomber Mine Clearance bar; 1939–45 Star Defence War medal; Canada Decoration with extra bar 1939–45.
£540–600 / €810–900
$1,000–1,100 ⊞ GBM

A group of seven WWII medals, awarded to Lieutenant Commander George D. P. Townsend, RNR: comprising DSC; 3945 Atlantic; Burma and Italy Stars; Victory Medal with oak leaf; Long Service Royal Naval Reserve medal, 1939–45.
£2,100–2,500 / €3,150–3,750
$3,950–4,700 ⚬ WilP
Groups of medals chart the personal military career of the recipient. It is often worth researching the individual concerned, since the recipient's history can add considerable interest and value to a medal. Groups of medals should not be broken up as this spoils their story and lessens their worth.

◀ **A Campaign Services medal,** with Cyprus bar, 1958–59, 4in (10cm) high.
£35–40 / €50–60
$65–75 ⊞ ABCM

An Iron Cross, first class, German, 1939, 2in (5cm) wide, in original case.
£155–175 / €230–260
$290–330 ⊞ ChM

Medical

◄ **A tin stomach warmer,** with brass carrying handle and maker's label, 19thC, 10in (25.5cm) wide.
£330–370 / € 500–560
$620–690 ⊞ BS

► **A silver nipple shield,** by T. Phipps & E. Robinson, London 1807, 2½in (6.5cm) diam, ½oz.
£220–260 / € 330–390
$410–490 ⚒ WW

A pair of white metal dental elevators, with ebony handles, c1820, 5¾in (14.5cm) long.
£180–200 / € 270–300
$340–410 ⊞ FOF
These implements were used to dig out the roots of teeth.

A metal Chassaignac's pattern *écraseur*, 1850–1900, 12¼in (31cm) long.
£200–230 / € 300–350
$370–430 ⊞ FOF
This rather bizarre device was originally used for the removal of haemorrhoids, but also served for the excision of uterine tumours and polyps. When the handle is turned, the chain drops down, the offending swelling is placed in the loop and, using the reverse procedure, clamps the part tightly. The restricted blood loss causes the swelling to wither and fall off.

A *faux* tortoiseshell ear trumpet, French, 1870, 5in (12.5cm) wide.
£250–280 / € 380–420
$470–520 ⊞ CuS

A metal abscess knife, with a mother-of-pearl handle, c1880, 4½in (11.5cm) long, with a leather case.
£40–45 / € 60–70
$75–85 ⊞ WAC

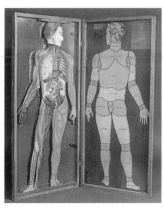

► **A wood and tin 'Smith's New Outline Map of the Human System',** by the American Manikin Co, American, 1888, with an oak carrying case, 44in (112cm) wide.
£400–480
€ 600–720
$740–890
⚒ JAA

A late Victorian mahogany apothecary's cabinet, comprising two drawers, a two-piece Baird & Tatlock Bunsen burner, three graduated heating crucibles, test tube rack and a ceramic heat-proof tablet, 38in (96.5cm) wide.
£250–280 / € 380–420
$470–520 ⊞ FOF

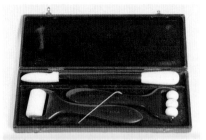

A set of ivorine and composition reflexology instruments, by Henri Simons, signed, cased, German, c1900, 8¾in (22cm) wide.
£180–200 / €270–300
$340–370 ⊞ FOF

A Vapo Resolene vaporizer, c1900, 7in (18cm) high, in original box.
£25–30 / €40–45
$50–55 ⊞ OIA

◀ **A Prosthetic Appliances, Tools and Materials catalogue,** by S. S. White Dental Manufacturing Co, American, 1918, 10 x 7in (25.5 x 18cm).
£15–20 / €22–30
$28–38 ⊞ J&S

A metal auriscope, by Brunton's, cased, c1905, 4in (10cm) wide.
£100–110 / €150–165
$185–210 ⊞ WAC

◀ **A tin of Zotos Sea Sickness Preventatives,** with original packaging, 1920s, 3½in (9cm) wide.
£8–12 / €12–18
$15–22 ⊞ HUX

▶ **A Capac Bin–Aural stethoscope,** in original wooden case, 1920, 13in (33cm) wide.
£220–250
€330–380
$410–470
⊞ SAT

A set of metal minor surgical instruments, c1925, in a leather roll case, 6in (15cm) wide.
£150–170 / €230–260
$280–320 ⊞ WAC

◀ **A ceramic Dr Nelson's Improved Inhaler,** 1930s, 11in (28cm) high.
£15–20 / €22–30
$28–38 ⊞ JWK

▶ **A rubber model of a head,** on a stand, 1950, 23in (58.5cm) high.
£175–195
€260–290
$330–360
⊞ CuS

A tin of Junior Elastoplast, 1960s, 3¼in (8.5cm) wide.
£4–8 / €6–12
$8–15 ⊞ RTT

yebaths

yebaths, also known as eye or eyewash cups, ave been produced in a surprising variety of hapes, colours and media. Typical shapes include ucket, stemmed and reservoir (a waisted design). ilass is perhaps the most common medium. arly examples were hand-blown. Later, mass- roduction techniques took over and eyebaths vere moulded. Some are unmarked, others are mbossed with a product logo or a maker's mark.

The most easily found colours include blue and clear glass. While more commonplace eyebaths can be found very cheaply, early hand-blown examples and more unusual colours such as amber and lime green, are more costly. Eyebaths have also been made from other materials, including ceramic, metal and plastic. Rarities such as 19th-century silver, rubber and blue and white ceramic examples can fetch high prices.

A silver-plated eyebath, with engraved decoration, 1900–10, 1½in (4cm) high.
£140–165 / €210–250 $260–310 ⚲ BBR

A glass eyebath, embossed 'Sterling Eyebath', 1910–20, 2in (5cm) high.
£10–15 / €15–22 $19–28 ⚲ BBR

A glass eyebath, the ase with a ground ontil, 1890–1900, ¾in (7cm) high.
60–70 / €90–105 110–130 ⚲ BBR

A glass eyebath, with hand-painted decoration, signed, 1900–10, 2¾in (7cm) high.
£55–65 / €85–100 $100–120 ⚲ BBR

► **A glass pedestal** yebath, 1910–20, ½in (6.5cm) high.
20–25 / €30–35 35–45 ⚲ BBR

► **A pair of glass eyebaths,** the Flint eyebath and the Salva eyebath, 1910–20, larger 2½in (6.5cm) high, with original boxes.
£6–10 / €9–15 $12–19 ⚲ BBR

glass eyebath, 1920s, ½in (6.5cm) high.
10–15 / €15–22 19–28 ⊞ TASV

A glass eyebath, with reservoir, 1930s, 2½in (6.5cm) high.
£4–8 / €6–12 $8–15 ⊞ TAC

A glass eyebath, 1930s, 2½in (6.5cm) high.
£10–15 / €15–22 $19–28 ⊞ TASV

An Optrex glass eyebath, 1970s, 2in 5cm) wide.
£1–5 / €2–7 $3–9 ⊞ TAC

Militaria

◄ A cast-iron and brass model gun carriage, 19thC, 19in (48.5cm) wide.
£100–120
€150–180
$185–220
🏹 WilP

A Short Account of the Battle of Waterloo fought on the 18th of June 1815, a manuscript booklet, with watercolour frontispiece, 200 painted paper cutouts of soldiers, a naive sketch of six types of troops and 26pp text, cardboard covers, 1830s, 5½ x 3½in (14 x 9cm).
£290–340 / €430–510
$540–640 🏹 WAL

► A copper powder flask, with graduated charger, spring missing, signed 'James Dixon & Sons, Sheffield', c1830, 7½in (19cm) long.
£60–70 / €90–105
$110–130 🏹 WD

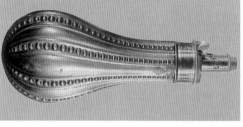

A decommissioned metal grenade, 1914–20, 4in (10cm) high.
£25–30 / €40–45
$50–55 ⊞ Tus

A 'Soldiers Own' diary, 1918, 4in (10cm) high.
£6–10 / €9–15
$12–19 ⊞ COB

◄ A wood and canvas shell carrier, with a leather handle, 1914–18, 34in (86.5cm) high.
£175–195 / €260–290
$330–360 ⊞ MCa

A bronze death plaque, inscribed 'Arthur Cecil Abbott', 1920, 4¾in (12cm) diam.
£60–70 / €90–105
$110–130 ⊞ Tus
During WWI all next-of-kin of service personnel who lost their lives during the conflict were presented with a memorial scroll and a bronze memorial plaque. Names, but not ranks, were included on the plaque in order to show equality in death. Troops nicknamed the plaque 'the Dead Man's Penny'. A tragic 1,350,000 plaques were made for men but only 600 were produced for women, and a Dead Woman's Penny could be worth in the region of £2,000 / €3,000 / $3,750.

A plastic ration and identity card wallet, 1939–44, 6½in (16.5cm) wide.
£10–15 / €15–22
$19–28 ⊞ RTT

◄ A silver-plated military coffee pot, by Mappin & Webb, inscribed 'Officer's Mess, Stanley Camp, Hong Kong', c1961, 6in (15cm) high.
£30–35 / €45–50
$55–65 ⊞ OLD

Armour & Uniform

A metal cabasset, with 'pear stalk' finial to crown, decorated with brass rosettes, slight damage and repair, c1600.
£340–400 / €510–600
$640–750 ✗ WAL

A copper-gilt gorget, with applied silver arms and supporters, c1800, 4in (10cm) wide.
£200–240 / €300–360
$370–450 ✗ WAL

A Victorian 1st (Brighton) Sussex Artillery Volunteers white metal helmet plate.
£150–180 / €230–270
$290–340 ✗ WAL

◄ A military uniform, issued to James Bourne of Demarara on his appointment as Lieutenant at Georgetown, with a tin trunk and a copy of the original documentation, 1868.
£240–280 / €360–420
$450–520 ✗ G(L)

A Victorian Carmarthenshire Rifle Volunteers white metal helmet plate, with a separate bugle centre.
£150–180 / €230–270
$290–340 ✗ WAL

A 53rd Shropshire Light Infantry metal shako plate, 1869.
£170–200 / €260–300
$320–370 ✗ WAL

An American Civil War officer's woollen frock coat, by Horstmann Co, American, Philadelphia, 1860s.
£300–360 / €450–540
$570–680 ✗ JDJ

A Montgomery Yeomanry Cavalry other rank's full dress tunic, with W. M. Dragoon collar badges, T. Y. Montgomery shoulder titles and regimental buttons, c1900.
£160–190 / € 240–290
$300–360 ⚔ WAL

◀ A Cameronians officer's cloth shako, with patent leather peak and chin, lace headbands, plaited cords, bugle badge, side hooks, silk lining, and plume holder with ostrich and vulture feather plume, 1900.
£600–720 / € 900–1,050
$1,150–1,350 ⚔ WAL

A Royal Marines Artillery field officer's cap, with gilt-embroidered peak, the gilt-embroidered badge with silver-plated globe, patent leather chinstrap, gilt crest buttons, and separate crossed gilt cannons, some damage, 1901–23.
£160–190 / € 240–290
$300–360 ⚔ WAL

A Royal Artillery helmet, with a brass and gilt badge, 1902–10.
£400–450 / € 620–680
$770–850 ⊞ Tus

◀ An Imperial Officer's leathe and brass *Pikelhaube*, German, 1914–18, 9in (23cm) high.
£500–550
€ 750–830
$940–1,050
⊞ ChM

An officer's cotton peaked cap and neck protector, the cord chinstrap with leather buttons, some wear, 1914–18.
£160–190 / € 240–290
$300–360 ⚔ WAL

A metal Hampshire Battalion cyclist badge, 1914–18, 2in (5cm) high.
£35–40 / € 50–60
$65–75 ⊞ ABCM

A Boy's Brigade cotton cap, 1930s.
£6–10 / € 9–15
$12–19 ⊞ Tus

▶ A leather and mesh Luftwaffe fighter pilot helmet, c1941.
£160–180 / € 240–270
$300–340 ⊞ OLD

◀ A pair of leather Royal Air Force flying gauntlets, c1941, 16in (40.5cm) long.
£145–165 / € 220–250
$270–310 ⊞ OLD
Like most wartime gloves, the left and the right were made by different contractors to reduce the likelihood of theft.

A Royal Air Force Warrant Officer's peaked cap, 1939–45.
£65–75 / €100–115
$120–140 ⊞ ChM

An Army Air Force parachute pack, by Eagle Parachute Corp, canopy missing, American, c1945.
£175–195 / €260–290
$330–370 ⊞ OLD

A Tanganyika administration officer's jacket, belonging to Sir E. C. Richards, 1948.
£100–120 / €150–180
$185–220 ⊞ ABCM

A Scout shirt, with badges, 1950–60.
£25–30 / €40–45
$50–55 ⊞ MRW

▶ **A British Intelligence Corps dress uniform,** c1955.
£135–150 / €200–230
$250–280 ⊞ ABCM

▶ **A Welsh Guards non-commissioned officer's bearskin,** c1950, 16in (40.5cm) high.
£500–550
€750–830
$940–1,050
⊞ ChM

Edged Weapons

◀ **A late Georgian smallsword,** with steel hilt, blade 30in (76.5cm) long, with vellum-covered steel-mounted scabbard.
£200–240 / €300–360
$380–450 ➶ **WAL**

A Malayan *parang*, with a wooden hilt and an embossed silver ferrule, 19thC, blade 14½in (37cm) long, with a silver-mounted ebony sheath.
£220–260 / €330–390
$410–490 ➶ **WAL**

A Victorian court sword, with a gilt hilt, blade 32in (82cm) long, with gilt-mounted leather scabbard and cloth shoulder strap.
£300–360 / €450–540
$560–670 ➶ **WAL**

◀ **A naval officer's sword,** with a leather and brass scabbard, 19thC, 34½in (87.5cm) long.
£230–270 / €350–410
$450–500 ➶ **SWO**

▶ **A double-edged SA dagger,** with a wooden grip, the blade engraved 'Alles Für Deutschland', German, c1933, blade 8½in (21.5cm) long.
£110–130
€165–195
$210–240 ➶ **WD**

An officer's sword and scabbard, French, early 20thC, 38¼in (97cm) long.
£150–180 / €230–270
$290–340 ➶ **SWO**

A Medieval Revival sword, with a steel hilt, the blade etched with 12 bust portraits on a ground of Arabic Naskh inscriptions, Persian, Qajar period, 19thC, blade 29½in (75cm) long.
£175–210 / €270–320
$330–390 ➶ **WAL**

A dagger, by F. W. Holler, with a Bakelite grip, German, c1938, 14½in (37cm) long.
£200–230 / €310–350
$370–430 ⊞ **Tus**

▶ **A British Light Infantry officer's sword,** by Wilkinson, 1939–45, 39in (99cm) long, with a leather-covered cabbard.
£250–280
€380–420
$470–520
⊞ **ChM**

A KAR.98 bayonet, with a cavalry frog mount, German, 1939–45, 16½in (42cm) long.
£100–120 / €150–180
$185–220 ⊞ **TLA**

Firearms

A .45 calibre percussion Kentucky rifle, by J. Forker, with brass fittings, 19thC, 37in (94cm) long.
£720–860 / €1,100–1,300
$1,350–1,600 ✗ JDJ

A 32-bore percussion travelling pistol, by T. North, with walnut full stock, c1830, 8½in (21.5cm) long.
£350–420 / €530–630
$650–780 ✗ WAL

A cavalry pistol, with colony armoury mark, 1830s, 15½in (39.5cm) long.
£580–650 / €870–980
$1,000–1,200 ⊞ Tus

A double-action five-shot pistol revolver, by Adams & Deane, engraved marks, 1851, 32¾in (83cm) long.
£680–810 / €1,000–1,200
$1,250–1,500 ✗ SWO

A 12-bore double-barrelled hammer gun, by H. Holland, with a figured walnut stock, c1860, barrel 30in (76cm) long.
£340–400 / €510–600
$640–750 ✗ G(B)

A pin fire revolver, plated barrel and cylinder, Belgian, barrel 4in (10cm) long.
£50–60 / €75–90
$95–110 ✗ WD

An 11mm M1874 Gras SS military rifle, cleaning rod missing, marked, French, 1876, 51½in (131cm) long, with a steel scabbard.
£300–360 / €450–540
$560–670 ✗ WAL

An iron Panzerfaust rocket grenade launcher, German, 1939–45, 42in (106.5cm) long.
£250–280 / €380–420
$470–520 ⊞ TLA

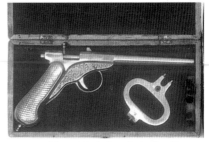

A .177 calibre nickel-plated air pistol, by Eisenwerke, German, early 20thC, 9½in (24cm) long, with wooden box, stripping tool, trigger spring and six darts.
£410–490 / €620–740
$770–920 ✗ WAL

Police & Rescue

A Victorian painted beech truncheon, decorated with royal arms and a crest, 18in (45.5cm) long.
£20–25 / €30–35
$35–45 🔨 G(L)

▶ **A brass fire service lamp,** 1900, 10in (25.5cm) high.
£50–60 / €75–90
$95–110 ⊞ COB

A fire officer's brass helmet, embossed with dragons, slight damage, early 20thC, 11¾in (30cm) wide.
£400–480 / €600–720
$750–900 🔨 BR

A pair of steel handcuffs, by Hiatt, 1900–20s, 9in (23cm) long.
£100–115 / €150–170
$190–220 ⊞ BS

A brass Metropolitan Police whistle, 1900–20s, 3in (7.5cm) long.
£30–35 / €45–50
$55–65 ⊞ BS

◀ **A set of eight white metal St John Ambulance Brigade buttons,** 1930s, 1in (2.5cm) diam.
£15–20 / €22–30
$28–38 ⊞ Tus

▶ **A Metropolitan Mounted Police helmet,** 1930–50.
£180–200 / €270–300
$340–380 ⊞ Q&C

◀ **A hardwood police truncheon,** 1920s–60s, 17in (43cm) long.
£20–25 / €30–35
$35–45 ⊞ Tus

A Civil Defence Corps Rescue armband, embroidered with a crown, 1950s, 18in (45.5cm) long.
£1–5 / €2–7
$3–9 ⊞ Tus

A Police Inspector's hat, French, c1975.
£20–25 / €30–35
$35–45 ⊞ Tus

A Metropolitan Mounted Police helmet, 1970s, 7in (18cm) high.
£55–65 / €85–100
$100–120 ⊞ UCO

Mining Memorabilia

Mining memorabilia is a subject new to this guide. This material is often collected by those who have had a personal or related family involvement in the mining industry. Popular areas include 'paranumismatics' – the term used to describe the various tokens and checks that were issued to miners in the 19th and 20th century. These served various purposes, from payment to work tallies. Pit or colliery checks (metal discs inscribed with a personal number) would be handed in by the miner at the start of the day and retrieved at the end. In some mines a personal check or token was exchanged for a lamp, which not only ensured that the miner received his designated equipment, but also provided a record of who was down the pit, particularly important in case of an accident. Values of tokens and checks depend on rarity and the desirability of a specific colliery.

Miner's lamps are also sought after. The Flame safety lamp (shown below) was developed in the early 19th century by various inventors including, most famously, Sir Humphrey Davy, who introduced the metal mesh funnel that prevented the flame from explosion when it came into contact with methane gas. 'Davy' lamps were used by miners until c1910, when they were replaced by electric hand lamps, superseded in the 1940s by lamps on helmets. However, 'Davy' lamps were still employed to check the safety of mines, since changes to the flame visibility reflected the levels of gas in the atmosphere.

Another important collecting area is memorabilia connected with the British Miners' Strike of 1984–85, ranging from badges issued by the National Union of Miners to commemorative ceramics. As one of the most significant events of Margaret Thatcher's premiership, which marked the closing of pits and the changing of a whole way of life, this material is sought after by enthusiasts of political and social history, as well as mining memorabilia collectors.

A miner's wage tin, c1900, 2in (5cm) wide.
£25–30 / €40–45
$50–55 ⊞ HO

A badge, commemorating the South & West Yorkshire Miners' Association founded 1858 and the Yorkshire Miners' Association founded 1881, c20thC, 1¼in (3cm) wide.
£8–12 / €12–18
$15–22 ⊞ DOM

◄ **A 2BA Flame safety lamp,** by John Davis, Derby, c1900, 10¾in (27.5cm) high.
£210–240 / €320–360
$390–450 ⊞ FOF

A steel and brass A3 miner's lamp, c1914, 10¼in (26cm) high.
£155–175 / €230–260
$290–330 ⊞ FOF

A Guy's Dropper carbide caver's and miner's lamp, by Universal Lamp Co, American, 1930s, 3½in (9cm) high.
£25–30 / €40–45
$50–55 ⊞ OIA

▶ **A miner's pit helmet,** for Kiveton Park Colliery, 1930s–40s, 5in (12.5cm) high.
£30–35 / €45–50
$55–65 ⊞ DOM
Due to the relatively small size of this helmet, it is probable that it was made to fit a boy. It was common in mining communities at the time for a boy to leave school at 14 and follow in his father's footsteps by going to work down the pit.

A Bakelite TELE 77 telephone, by Automatic Telephone & Electric Co, with inscribed plaque, c1948, 9½in (24cm) high.
£135–150 / €200–230
$250–280 ⊞ DOM
This telephone would have been for surface use at a colliery.

A ceramic plate, commemorating the Miners' Strike, c1985, 10in (25.5cm) diam.
£50–55 / €75–85
$95–105 ⊞ H&G

A ceramic plate, by Edwardian China, for the National Union of Mineworkers, commemorating Michael McGahey, 1987, 10in (25.5cm) diam.
£50–55 / €75–85
$95–105 ⊞ H&G

A brass pit check, for Manton Colliery, No. 3606, 1970s–80s, 1½in (4cm) diam.
£10–15 / €15–22
$19–28 ⊞ DOM
Sadly, as with many coal mines throughout Yorkshire, Nottinghamshire and the UK, Manton Colliery was closed in the early 1990s.

▶ **A badge,** for the National Union of Mineworkers, issued by the Cortonwood Colliery, commemorating the death of two miners, c1985, 1in (2.5cm) diam.
£10–15 / €15–22
$19–28 ⊞ DOM
The 1984–85 miners' strike began at Cortonwood Colliery.

A ceramic plate, commemorating the miners' strike, inscribed 'Justice for Mineworkers', c1985, 10in (25.5cm) diam.
£50–55 / €75–85
$95–105 ⊞ H&G

▶ **A packet of three colliery emergency tallies,** 1980s–90s, 6 x 4in (15 x 10cm).
£4–8 / €6–12
$8–15 ⊞ DOM
Tallies were discs given to the emergency services and other persons authorized to enter the mine after an accident. Each packet contained three plastic discs, one of which was to be worn at all times, one to be handed to the Lampman and the other to the Banksman. These discs were collected before returning to the surface and handed back to the issuer.

A ceramic mug, for SOGAT, commemorating the Women in Action Mining Strike, 1985, 4in (10cm) high.
£35–40 / €50–60
$65–75 ⊞ H&G
SOGAT is the acronym for the Society of Graphical and Allied Trades.

Three enamel badges, for the National Union of Mineworkers, supporting the 1984–85 strike, c1985, largest 1in (2.5cm) diam.
£15–20 / €22–30
$28–38 each ⊞ DOM

Money Boxes

A J. Stiff stoneware money box, in the form of a house, impressed mark, 1870s, 4¼in (11cm) high.
£110–130 / € 165–195
$200–240 ⚡ SWO

A 'single peanut' money box, by Kyser & Rex Co, in the form of a lion and two monkeys, one monkey replaced, American, 1883, 8½in (21.5cm) high.
£450–500 / € 680–750
$850–940 ⚡ Bert
This bank comes in two sizes, one having a taller tree than the other. On the taller version there is a double peanut shape on the trunk as opposed to the single peanut shape shown here.

◀ **A wooden money box,** with a sliding cover, c1900, 4in (10cm) wide.
£70–80 / € 105–120
$130–150 ⊞ CoHA

A cast-iron money box, by John Harper, 1892, 9in (23cm) high.
£1,600–1,800
€ 2,400–2,700
$3,000–3,350 ⊞ HAL

▶ **A tin money box,** in the form of a church, German, c1905, 3in (7.5cm) high.
£80–90 / € 120–135
$150–170 ⊞ HAL

A tin money box, by John Wright, entitled 'The Aero', in the form of a fireplace, 1910–20, 4in (10cm) high.
£90–100 / € 135–150
$170–190 ⊞ MRW

▶ **A tin money box,** in the form of a wizard, with inscribed verse, c1912, 6in (15cm) high.
£100–110 / € 160–180
$185–210 ⊞ HAL

A ceramic money box, in the form of Old Bill peering out of a tank, inscribed 'Where's that blinking Kaiser?', c1918, 4in (10cm) wide.
£50–55 / €75–85 $95–105 ⊞ JUN
Old Bill was a WWI cartoon character created by Bruce Bairnsfather (1888–1959), inspired by the British Tommy.

A tin mechanical money box, in the form of a clown, German, c1920, 5in (12.5cm) high.
£700–800 / €1,050–1,200 $1,350–1,500 ⊞ HAL

A painted cast-iron mechanical money box, by Tammany, in the form of a seated gentleman, marked, American, c1920, 5in (12.5cm) high.
£310–350 / €470–530 $580–650 ⊞ JUN
Produced between 1875 and 1920 this was one of the most popular mechanical money boxes of the period.

A painted cast-iron money bank, by Hubley, in the form of Porky Pig, American, c1930, 5in (12.5cm) high.
£120–140 / €180–210 $220–260 ♪ Bert

◄ A tin money box, in the form of a post box, 1930s, 4½in (11.5cm) high.
£10–15 / €15–22 $19–28 ⊞ COB

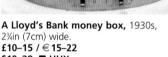

A Lloyd's Bank money box, 1930s, 2¾in (7cm) wide.
£10–15 / €15–22 $19–28 ⊞ HUX

A Nottingham Savings Bank, in the form of a leather book, 1940s, in original box, 5½ x 4in (14 x 10cm).
£10–15 / €15–22 $19–28 ⊞ HUX

A Muffin the Mule money box, by Chad Valley, c1951, 3in (7.5cm) high.
£220–250 / €330–380 $410–470 ⊞ MTMC

► A plastic money box, by Trex, 1950s–60s, 4in (10cm) high.
£20–25 / €30–35 $35–45 ⊞ RTT

A money box, commemorating the coronation of Queen Elizabeth II, 1950s, 5in (12.5cm) high.
£15–20 / €22–30 $28–38 ⊞ OIA

A Trustee Savings Bank tin money box, 1960s, 2¾in (7cm) high.
£10–15 / €15–22 $19–28 ⊞ RTT

Newspapers & Magazines

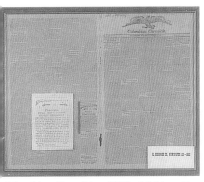

Colombian Chronicle of Philadelphia, with an advertisement for Henry Deringer's firearms shop, slight damage, American, 1812, 20 x 25¼in (51 x 64cm), framed and glazed.
£150–175 / €220–260
$280–330 ⚒ JDJ

Sphere, reporting the sinking of the *Titanic,* slight damage, 1912.
£100–120 / €150–180
$185–220 ⚒ VS

Ship Builder, No.98, 1918, 10 x 8in (25.5 x 20cm).
£6–10 / €9–15
$12–19 ⊞ COB

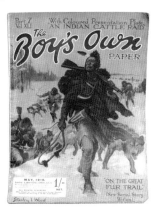

Boy's Own Paper, 1919, 11½ x 8¼in (29 x 21cm).
£1–5 / €2–7
$3–9 ⊞ RTT

Baltimore News, Al Capone Starts for Federal Penitentiary, 1932, 21 x 16in (53.5 x 40.5cm), framed.
£165–185 / €250–280
$310–350 ⊞ IQ

Detective Weekly, No. 1, February 1933, 13 x 10in (33 x 25.5cm).
£30–35 / €45–50
$55–65 ⊞ ADD

The Humorist magazine, Easter number, 1936, 12 x 9½in (30.5 x 24cm).
£6–10 / €9–15
$12–19 ⊞ RTT

Melody Maker, December 1950, 17 x 11in (43 x 28cm).
£6–10 / €9–15
$12–19 ⊞ IQ

Picture Post, with Bill Haley and his Comets cover, 1957, 13 x 10in (33 x 25.5cm).
£10–15 / €15–22
$19–28 ⊞ RTT

Maiden Voyage, SS *Canberra* souvenir number, 1961, 13in (33cm) high.
£30–35 / €45–50
$55–65 ⊞ COB

Paper Money

Collecting paper money or bank notes (notaphily) is a worldwide hobby. Many factors can make a note desirable. Some enthusiasts are attracted by a pictorial image, others by a particular historical period, or a specific denomination (for examples white £5 notes).

Notes with errors or misprints are very sought after; signatures and unusual serial numbers (for example the first and last number in any series) can also make a difference to value.

Condition is vital and notes are graded, with the highest condition being 'unc' for uncirculated. Early notes often command the highest sums. In 1998 a record £423,500 / €635,000 / $792,000 was paid at auction for a US series 1863 $1,000 Treasury note, known as the watermelon on account of its colouring and the shape of the figures on the back. In the UK, a record £45,000 / €67,500 / $84,200 was paid for a £100 note issued by the Bank of England in 1790.

A State of North Carolina $2 note, American, 1778.
£90–100 / €135–150
$170–190 ⊞ NAR

An Essex & Suffolk Bank £10 note, No. 14680, for Sparrow, Brown, Hanbury Saville and Simpson, signature cut, cancelled, c1814.
£780–930 / €1,200–1,400
$1,500–1,750 ⚲ SWO

A Craven Bank £10 note, for Self and Other Partners, depicting a Burnley Heifer, unissued, 19thC.
£130–155 / €195–230
$250–290 ⚲ SWO

▶ **A Stanford & Rutland Bank £5 note,** No. A376, for Stephen Eaton and Edward Cayley, hand-written marks, February 1834.
£50–60 / €75–90
$95–110 ⚲ LAY

A Boer War £5 note, No. 6098, signed, fold marks and stains, South African, Pretoria, 1900.
£50–60 / €75–90
$95–110 ⚲ WW

A Siege of Mafeking 1 shilling note, 1900.
£90–100 / €135–150
$170–190 ⊞ NAR

Bank notes

During the early 19th century banks were set up in towns throughout Britain. The notes they issued were generally well printed, often carrying a design identifying the place of issue. Unfortunately the majority of these banks went into liquidation and many investors lost their money. Some lasted until the end of the century before being absorbed into the large clearing banks of today. It is common to see the marks of the bankruptcy court stamped on the note. These notes are highly collectable both for their decorative qualities and the opportunity to own a piece of local history.

◀ **A United States of America $20 and $10 note,** 1913.
£60–70 / €90–105
$110–130 ⚲ JAA

▶ **A Clydesdale Bank £1 note,** No. 2660389, 1917.
£180–200 / €270–300
$330–370 ⊞ NAR

A Bank of England £20 note, 1918.
£990–1,100 / €1,500–1,650
$1,850–2,050 ⊞ WP

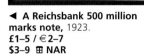

◀ A Reichsbank 500 million marks note, 1923.
£1–5 / €2–7
$3–9 ⊞ NAR

A Bank of Scotland £1 note, 1926.
£135–150 / €200–230
$250–280 ⊞ WP

◀ A Currency Commission Irish Free State £5 note, 1937.
£180–200
€270–300
$330–370 ⊞ WP

A Bank of Ireland £1 note, depicting a ploughman, 1938.
£90–100 / €135–150
$170–190 ⊞ NAR

A Bank of Canada 'Devil's Head' $1 note, 1954.
£20–25 / €30–35
$35–45 ⊞ NAR
'Devil's Head' is the nickname for the Canadian bank notes issued to mark Queen Elizabeth II's accession to the throne in 1952. Various design changes were made to this new series of notes, including moving the monarch from the centre to the right-hand side in order to minimize damage from folding. Unfortunately, however, highlights added to the Queen's hair created an image of a grinning imp behind her ear. In 1956 the Bank of Canada had the offending curls darkened on all denominations, but so-called Devil's Head notes are now sought after.

▶ A Bank of England £5 note, signed by Hollom, 1960s.
£15–20
€22–30
$28–38 ⊞ NAR

A Bank of England £10 note, No. A01 000099, signed by Page, 1975.
£360–400 / €540–600
$670–750 ⊞ NAR
The serial number makes this note very desirable. A note with an ordinary number would have a price range of £20–25 / €30–35 / $35–45.

Photography

Charles Milton Bell, an imperial cabinet card photograph of a Pawnee chief, slight damage, 19thC, 12 x 9in (30.5 x 23cm).
£250–290 / €380–440
$460–550 ⋟ JDJ

► **Carlo Ponti,** a set of 14 albumen prints of buildings and views of Venice, stamped, Italian, 1860–70, 9 x 12in (23 x 30.5cm).
£380–450 / €570–680
$710–840 ⋟ HOLL
Albums such as this were usually prepared by Ponti to a tourist's specific order. The use of French rather than Italian on the title page suggests that this album was originally produced for a French visitor.

◄ **A photograph of four military drummers,** the reverse with inscription, 1862–63, 13 x 16in (33 x 40.5cm).
£400–480
€600–720
$740–890
⋟ JDJ

Robert Demachy, an albumen print of a young woman, c1890, 7¾ x 6in (19.5 x 15cm) .
£165–195 / €250–290
$300–360 ⋟ BBA
Better known for his gum prints, Demachy's earlier albumen prints are rare.

A photograph of the launching of the yacht *Bertha*, 1900, 9 x 11in (23 x 28cm).
£35–40 / €50–60
$65–75 ⊞ HO

A book of photographs, entitled 'Fine Art Views of Straits Settlements and Federated Malay States', 1920, 9 x 11in (23 x 28cm).
£8–12 / €12–18
$15–22 ⊞ J&S

A photograph of Josephine Baker at the Paris Casino, gelatin silver print 1931, 6¼ x 8¼in (16 x 21.5cm).
£185–220 / €280–330
$350–410 ⋟ BBA

Robert Doisneau, a gelatin silver print of Gabaroche, Saint-Germain-des-Prés, stamped and numbered, 1947, 8¼ x 8in (21 x 20.5cm).
£420–500 / €630–750
$790–940 ⋟ BBA

Sharok Hatami, a gelatin silver print of Coco Chanel, signed, titled, numbered 1/10, dated 1965, 13½ x 9¼in (34.5 x 23.5cm).
£85–100 / €130–150
$160–190 ⋟ BBA

Frames & Albums

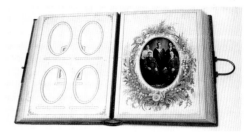

◀ A ceramic photograph frame, French, 19thC, 22in (56cm) wide.
£650–750
€980–1,150
$1,200–1,400
⚒ G(L)

A Victorian tooled leather photograph album, with some original photographs, 12 x 9in (30.5 x 23cm).
£90–100 / €135–150
$170–190 ⊞ TAC

◀ A Victorian carved oak double photograph frame, 7 x 9in (18 x 23cm).
£65–75 / €100–115
$120–140 ⊞ AMR

A Victorian leather photograph case, with gilt-bronze mounts, the expandable interior lined with silk, 5¾ x 6¾in (14.5 x 17cm).
£55–65 / €85–100
$100–120 ⚒ JAA

▶ A gutta-percha photograph frame, French, 1860–70, 11in (28cm) high.
£300–340 / €450–510
$560–640 ⊞ HaH

A boullework photograph frame, late 19thC, 8 x 6in (20.5 x 15cm).
£360–430 / €540–650
$670–800 ⚒ G(L)

An amboyna and fruitwood photograph frame, Italian, c1900, 7in (18cm) high.
£165–185 / €250–280
$310–350 ⊞ HaH

A copper photograph frame, 1920s, 6½in (16.5cm) high.
£75–85 / €115–130
$140–160 ⊞ HaH

A silver-plated photograph frame, c1930, 10in (25.5cm) high.
£145–165 / €220–250
$270–310 ⊞ SAT

Postcards

A Souvenir of Bethlehem postcard,
c1900, 4 x 6in (10 x 15cm).
£15–20 / €22–30
$28–38 ⊞ S&D

A Stockholm postcard, c1900,
4 x 6in (10 x 15cm).
£15–20 / €22–30
$28–38 ⊞ S&D

An Atlantic City postcard,
published by Raphael Tuck & Sons,
from the Views of US Cities series,
No. 5073, 1900–05.
£4–8 / €6–12
$8–15 ⊞ JMC

◄ **An embossed
postcard,** depicting
a military romance,
c1900, 4 x 6in
(10 x 15cm).
£35–40 / €50–60
$65–75 ⊞ POS

► **A glamour
postcard,** by
Angelo Asti, with
a portrait of a
lady, c1900,
4½ x 3½in
(11.5 x 9cm).
£2–6 / €3–9
$4–11 ⊞ POS

A postcard, depicting Spanish
royalty, 1903, 4 x 6in (10 x 15cm).
£6–10 / €9–15
$12–19 ⊞ S&D

◄ **A Cupid's Alphabet 'B'
postcard,** from the Tuck Art series,
No. 6114, c1906.
£6–10 / €9–15
$12–19 ⊞ JMC

An American Line postcard, depicting SS
New York, advertising the Southampton-
Cherbourg-New York service, American, 1904.
£20–25 / €30–35
$35–45 ➹ DAL

A 'Fab' patchwork postcard,
c1906, 4 x 6in (10 x 15cm).
£4–8 / €6–12
$8–15 ⊞ POS

◄ **A photographic name
postcard,** 'Marie', published by
Rotary Photo, depicting actresses,
1906, 4 x 6in (10 x 15cm).
£1–5 / €2–7
$3–9 ⊞ POS

► **A photographic postcard,**
published by Kingsway, depicting the
interior of Portsmouth station, 1909.
£25–30 / €40–45
$50–55 ➹ VS

A Maidstone Horse Repository postcard, depicting a hunter, the reverse advertising an auction of '56 Valuable Horses' on 6 December 1910.
£8–12 / €12–18
$15–22 ⊞ JMC

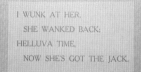

A postcard, American, c1910, 4 x 6in (10 x 15cm).
£1–5 / €2–7
$3–9 ⊞ POS
Sometimes humorous postcards can become unwittingly more humorous as words change their meaning with the passage of time.

A Selfridges advertising postcard, c1910, 4 x 6in (10 x 15cm).
£1–5 / €2–7
$3–9 ⊞ POS

▶ **A pack of BDS Line advertising postcards,** 1910–18, 2½ x 4½in (6.5 x 11.5cm), with original leather case.
£45–50 / €70–80
$85–95 ⊞ MURR
BDS stands for Bergenske Dampskibsselskab (Bergen Steamship Company), founded in 1851.

◀ **A postcard,** celebrating New Year, 1913, 4 x 6in (10 x 15cm).
£1–5 / €2–7
$3–9 ⊞ POS

A Yeoward Line postcard, depicting five shipping views, c1910.
£10–15 / €15–22
$19–28 ⋌ DAL

An advertising postcard, for the first International Hunting Exhibition, German, 1910, 6 x 4in (15 x 10cm).
£20–25 / €30–35
$35–45 ⊞ S&D

Two postcards, depicting children and teddy bears, c1910.
£45–50 / €70–80
$85–95 each ⊞ BeB
These cards are rare and would appeal to both collectors of postcards and teddy bears.

A Fry's Milk Chocolate advertising postcard, c1910.
£10–15 / €15–22
$19–28 ⋌ DAL

◀ **A photographic postcard,** published by Rotary Photo, entitled 'London Life, Early Morning in Rotten Row, Hyde Park', 1914.
£35–40 / €50–60
$65–75 ✗ VS

▶ **A photographic postcard,** depicting Electric Avenue in Brixton, c1920, 5 x 6in (12.5 x 15cm).
£1–5 / €2–7
$3–9 ⊞ POS

A velvet and celluloid postcard, with hand-painted decoration, French, c1914, 4 x 6in (10 x 15cm).
£1–5 / €2–7
$3–9 ⊞ POS

A glamour postcard, published by Alpha, with a portrait by René Méras, French, c1920, 4 x 6in (10 x 15cm).
£1–5 / €2–7
$3–9 ⊞ POS

A photographic postcard, depicting suffragettes, 1926.
£75–85 / €115–130
$140–160 ✗ VS

A Fairies of the Countryside postcard, published by M. W. Tarrant, depicting the Scots-Pine Fairies, c1933.
£1–5 / €2–7
$3–9 ⊞ JMC

A Nora Davidson postcard, 'Never run away from trouble. lest it turn and overtake thee', c1936.
£1–5 / €2–7
$3–9 ⊞ JMC

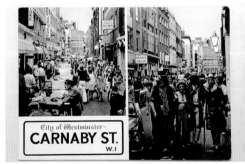

A photographic postcard, depicting Carnaby Street, London, c1960, 4 x 6in (10 x 15cm).
£1–5 / €2–7
$3–9 ⊞ POS

Posters

A Chocolat Mexicain/ Masson Paris poster, by Eugene Grasset, printed by G. de Malherbe, French, 1892, 46½ x 31in (118 x 78.5cm).
£510–610 / € 770–920 $960–1,150 ➤ S(NY)

A Music Hall Tous les Soirs poster, 'Eldorado', by Jules Chéret, 1894, 22½ x 15½in (57 x 39.5cm).
£460–550 / € 690–830 $860–1,000 ➤ VSP

A Quinquina Dubonnet poster, by Jules Chéret, 1896, 22½ x 15½in (57 x 39.5cm).
£360–430 / € 540–640 $670–800 ➤ VSP

A Harper's October poster, by Edward Penfield, 1896, 46 x 35in (117 x 89cm).
£360–430 / € 540–640 $670–800 ➤ VSP

A travel poster, 'The Colne River at Uxbridge by Tram', by Edward McKnight Kauffer, printed by Sanders Phillips & Co, The Baynard Press, signed, 1924, 30 x 20in (76 x 51cm).
£860–1,000 / € 1,300–1,500 $1,600–1,850 ➤ ONS

A London Midland and Scottish poster, 'Edinburgh, Scotland's Historic Capital', by Healy Hislop, printed by McCorquodale & Co, mounted on linen, 1928, 40¼ x 50in (102 x 127cm).
£2,000–2,400 / € 3,000–3,600 $3,750–4,500 ➤ ONS

A theatre poster, by John Hassall, for *The Gondoliers*, repaired, 60 x 40in (152.5 x 101.5cm).
£15–20 / € 22–30 $28–38 ➤ NSal

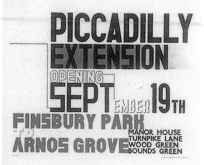

◄ **A travel poster,** 'Piccadilly Extension', by Edward McKnight Kauffer, printed by S. C. Allen & Co, c1930, 10 x 13¼in (25.5 x 33.5cm).
£250–300 / € 380–450 $470–560 ➤ VSP

► **A travel poster,** 'Dubrovnik', by Hans Wagula, printed by Lit. Z. T. Narodhih Novina, on japan paper, 1935, 37½ x 24½in (95.5 x 62cm).
£250–300 / € 380–450 $470–560 ➤ VSP

An Inter-Tribal Indian Ceremony poster, illustrated by Ed Rawlins, 1936, 22 x 14in (56 x 35.5cm).
£180–210 / €270–320 $340–400 ↗ JDJ

A travel poster, 'Chamonix Mont Blanc', by Max Ponty, on linen, 1936, 39¼ x 24½in (99.5 x 62cm).
£490–590 / €740–890 $920–1,100 ↗ VSP

An Exposition Internationale Paris poster, by Jean Carlu, printed by Jules Simon, 1937, 23½ x 15½in (59.5 x 39.5cm).
£80–95 / €120–140 $150–175 ↗ VSP

A British Railways poster, 'Bristol, Travel by Train', by Claude Buckle, c1938, 40¼ x 25¼in (102 x 64cm), framed and glazed.
£490–590 / €740–890 $920–1,100 ↗ DW

A London and North Eastern Railway poster, by G. Stanislus Brien, printed by McCorquodale & Co, mounted on linen, restored, 1938, 40¼ x 50in (102 x 127cm).
£4,400–5,300 / €6,600–7,900 $8,200–9,800 ↗ ONS
This London and North Eastern Railway poster is very rare, hence the high value .

A poster, 'Plaisir et Santé au Bain de Saint–Josse', by Noël Tolmar, printed by Affiches Marci, on linen, c1940, 28 x 20in (71 x 51cm).
£320–380 / €480–570 $600–710 ↗ VSP

A poster, by John Gilroy, 1940s, 29 x 20in (73.5 x 51cm).
£200–230 / €300–340 $370–430 ⊞ IQ

A British Railways poster, 'Unceasing Service on the Lines Behind the Lines', No. 526, by Frank H. Mason, printed by The Haycock Press, slight damage, 1945, 40¼ x 50in (102 x 127cm).
£1,700–2,000 / €2,550–3,000 $3,200–3,750 ↗ ONS

A poster, 'Østrig', 1947, 35 x 23¾in (89 x 60.5cm).
£410–490 / €620–740 $770–920 ↗ VSP

A travel poster, 'Harwich Hook of Holland', by P. H. Huveneers, printed by The Haycock Press, c1955, 39¼ x 25in (99.5 x 63.5cm).
£220–260 / €330–390 $410–480 ↗ VSP

A travel poster, 'Indonesia Hindu temples in Central Java', by Victor J. Trip, c1955, 39¼ x 26¾in (99.5 x 68cm).
£160–190 / € 240–280 $300–360 ⚒ **VSP**

A poster, 'Pathe Marconi', by Bernard Villemot, printed by Aussel, Paris, on linen, c1955, 63 x 45¾in (160 x 116cm).
£430–510 / € 640–770 $800–950 ⚒ **VSP**

A poster, 'What's on a man's mind, Sigmund Freud', c1960, 39 x 29in (99 x 73.5cm).
£70–80 / € 105–120 $130–150 ⚒ **VSP**

A Netherlands Railways poster, 'See Holland', printed by Senefelder, Dutch, c1960, 39 x 24½in (99 x 62cm).
£80–95 / € 120–140 $150–175 ⚒ **VSP**

A British Railways poster, 'Glasgow Electric', by Terence Cuneo, printed by Waterlow & Sons, signed on reverse, 1960, 40¼ x 50in (102 x 127cm).
£420–500 / € 630–750 $790–940 ⚒ **ONS**

A poster, 'Galerie Adrien Maeght', by Joan Miró, printed by Imprimerie Arte, French, c1965, 25¼ x 19¼in (64 x 49cm).
£70–80 / € 105–120 $130–150 ⚒ **VSP**

A Levi's poster, printed by Vita Nova, c1965, 38 x 26in (96.5 x 66cm).
£125–150 / € 190–220 $240–280 ⚒ **VSP**

A Levi's poster, printed by Vita Nova, c1965, 26 x 38in (66 x 96.5cm).
£125–150 / € 190–220 $240–280 ⚒ **VSP**

▶ **A poster,** 'Chiquita, Snoecks', c1970, 27¼ x 20¾in (69 x 52.5cm).
£110–130 / € 165–195 $200–240 ⚒ **VS**

A poster, 'Peaceful Country', 1979, 38½ x 26in (98 x 66cm).
£70–80 / € 100–120 $130–150 ⚒ **VSP**

Puppets

A Minnie Mouse hand puppet, with a rubber head, 1950s, 9in (23cm) high.
**£10–15 / € 15–22
$19–28 ⊞ LAS**

A Pelham Professor Popkiss string puppet, from Gerry Anderson's *Supercar* series, 1960s, 10in (25.5cm) high.
**£135–150 / € 200–230
$250–280 ⊞ ARo**

A papier-mâché Dutch girl string puppet, probably German, early 1900s, 23in (58.5cm) high.
**£210–240 / € 320–360
$390–450 ⊞ SaB**

A Picot schoolboy string puppet, c1960, 8in (20.5cm) high, with box.
**£70–80 / € 105–120
$130–150 ⊞ ARo**

▶ **A Pelham poodle string puppet,** 1950s–80s, 9in (23cm) high.
**£35–40 / € 50–60
$65–75 ⊞ LAS**

A Pelham Mickey Mouse string puppet, c1980, 12in (30.5cm) high, with box.
**£65–75 / € 100–115
$120–140 ⊞ UD**

A Pelham Parker string puppet, from Gerry Anderson's *Thunderbirds* series, 1990s, 11in (28cm) high.
**£75–85 / € 115–130
$140–160 ⊞ LAS**

A Pelham Pinky string puppet, 1980s, 9in (23cm) high, with box.
**£80–90 / € 120–135
$150–170 ⊞ LAS**

Radios, Televisions & Gramophones

Radios

A twin crystal receiver, in a walnut case, 1924, 11in (28cm) wide.
£270–300 / €400–450
$500–560 ⊞ OTA

A Celestion moving iron speaker, in a mahogany case, 1929, 12in (30.5cm) square.
£35–40 / €50–60
$65–75 ⊞ GM

An Ekco AD76 radio, in a Bakelite case, repaired, 1930s, 15½in (39.5cm) diam.
£180–200 / €270–300
$340–370 ⚒ G(L)

An Ekco AC97 radio, in a black and ivory Bakelite case, 1937, 20in (51cm) wide.
£700–800 / 1,050–1,200
$1,300–1,500 ⊞ OTA
This colour is rare. In the more typical brown Bakelite this radio would have a price range of £300–400 €450–600 / $560–750

A Philco A535 radio, in a walnut-veneered case, 1937, 19in (48.5cm) wide.
£90–100 €135–150
$170–190 ⊞ OTA

A Strad radio, in a Bakelite case, 1940s, 11¾in (30cm) wide.
£25–30 / €40–45
$50–55 ⚒ L&E

A Sparkling Champagne Music radio, in a Bakelite case, with painted decoration, c1950, 23½in (59.5cm) high.
£220–240 €300–360 $380–450 ⚒ S(P)
The cork of this radio is the tuner, the speaker is located in the base.

► A Bush DAC 90A radio, in a Bakelite case, 1950, 12in (30.5cm) wide, with original box.
£100–110 / €150–165
$185–210 ⊞ LFi

An Ultra Twin Deluxe Valve portable mains/battery radio, with a simulated crocodile skin case and sliding doors, c1953, 14in (35.5cm) wide.
£130–150 / €200–230
$240–280 ⊞ OTA

A Crosley table clock radio, in a plastic case, c1955, 13in (33cm) wide.
£135–160 / €200–240
$250–300 ⋌ JAA

A single-valve amplifier, disguised as a framed picture, French, 1950s, 12in (30.5cm) high.
£70–80 / €105–120
$130–150 ⊞ LFi

A Decca TPW 70 radio, in a plastic case, 1961, 10in (25.5cm) diam.
£40–45 / €60–70
$75–85 ⊞ RTT
This radio was intended to be wall-mounted for use in bathrooms and kitchens.

A Roberts R300 radio, 1963, 9in (23cm) wide.
£45–50 / €70–80
$85–95 ⊞ GM
This radio was familiarly known as the 'handbag' radio.

A Murphy's radio, in a Perspex-fronted wood case, 1960s, 22¾in (58cm) wide.
£320–350 / €480–530
$600–650 ⊞ MARK

Televisions

◄ **A Pye B18t television,** in a walnut-veneered case, 1950, 18in (45.5cm) wide.
£70–80
€105–120
$130–150 ⊞ OTA

A Bush TV 62 television, in a Bakelite case, 1956, 16in (40.5cm) wide.
£180–200 / €270–300
$340–370 ⊞ OTA

A Philips Discoverer colour television, in plastic case, with remote control, 1980s, 17½in (44.5cm) high.
£270–300 / €410–450
$500–560 ⊞ MARK

Gramophones

▶ **An HMV Model 60 hornless gramophone,** with a mahogany case, 1919, 15in (38cm) wide.
£130–150 / €200–230
$240–280 ⊞ OTA

A gramophone, with a painted horn and a mahogany case, c1910, 15½in (39.5cm) wide.
£120–140 / €180–210
$220–260 ⋟ L&E

▶ **An Edison Amberola Model 80 phonograph,** in an oak case, c1920, 16in (40.5cm) wide.
£310–350 / €460–530
$580–650 ⊞ OTA

A Columbia Model 109A portable gramophone, c1930, 16in (40.5cm) wide.
£100–110 / €150–165
$185–210 ⊞ OIA

Needle Tins

As the popularity of the wind-up gramophone took off in the early 1900s, so did demand for needles. Gramophones had no volume knobs and the loudness of the music was controlled by the thickness of the needle: thin, medium and thick needles supplied soft, medium and loud music. Since it was necessary to replace the needle every time a 78rpm record was played, needles were typically sold in tins containing either 100 or 200.

Predominantly produced in Great Britain and Germany, these tins were extremely decorative as different manufacturers competed for a share of the market. Tins came in a wide variety of designs, sometimes in a matching series (such as Herold dance tins, illustrated below), and the same image would also be produced in different colourways. Values depend on rarity, the appeal of the image and condition.

An Edison Bell chromic needles tin, 1900–30, 1½in (4cm) wide.
£10–15 / €15–22
$19–28 ⊞ AAA

Three Herold gramophone needles tins, depicting the Shimmy, Tango and Scottish-Espagnole dances, 1920, 1¾in (4.5cm) wide.
£75–85 / €115–130
$140–160 each ⊞ HUX
These tins are from a set of five. The complete set includes the Boston and the Foxtrot.

An Edison Bell Radio gramophone needles tin, 1920–30, 1½in (4cm) wide.
£10–15 / €15–22
$19–28 ⊞ AAA

A Diamond gramophone needles tin, 1930s, 2in (5cm) wide.
£50–55 / €75–85
$95–105 ⊞ HUX

A Homokord gramophone needles tin, 1930s, 2in (5cm) wide.
£55–65 / €85–100
$100–120 ⊞ HUX

A Pegasus gramophone needles tin, 1930s, 2¼in (5.5cm) wide.
£45–50 / €70–80
$85–95 ⊞ HUX

Three Homocord gramophone needles tins, 1930s, 2in (5cm) wide.
£55–65 / €85–100
$100–120 each ⊞ HUX

Railwayana

◄ **A brass worksplate,** 'Hawthorns & Co, Leith', No. 240, c1861, 11½in (29cm) wide.
£6,300–7,500 / €9,500–11,300
$11,800–14,000 ⚒ SRA
This is one of the earliest known surviving worksplates.

A cast-brass industrial nameplate, 'Beaudesert', carried by a Class B 0–6–OST, repainted, c1875, 29½in (72.5cm) wide.
£2,000–2,400
€3,000–3,600
$3,750–4,500 ⚒ SRA

► **A Great Northern Railway copper station lamp,** with two glass panels inscribed 'Navenby', late 19thC, 35in (89cm) high.
£750–900 / €1,150–1,350
$1,400–1,650 ⚒ SRA

A Bristol & Exeter Railway wooden office chair, the top rail carved 'B. & E.', 19thC.
£500–600 €750–900
$940–1,100 ⚒ SRA

An iron and copper railway lantern, late 19thC, 12in (30.5cm) high.
£30–35 / €45–50
$55–65 ⚒ SJH

A Great Western Railway three-piece brass lavatory door catch, 1880–1900, 3in (7.5cm) wide.
£210–240 / €320–360
$390–450 ⊞ BS

A Dearne Valley Railway cast-iron sign, c1920, 32½in (82.5cm) wide.
£1,150–1,350 / €1,750–2,050
$2,150–2,500 ⚒ SRA

A mahogany station clock, with single fusee movement, 1910–20, with an associated stand, 30in (76cm) diam.
£600–700 / €900–1,050
$1,150–1,300 ⚹ AMB

◄ **An industrial brass nameplate,** 'Patience', cast with workplate 'No. 5 H. W. Johnson & Co Engineers, St Helens', repainted c1921, 24¼in (61.5cm) wide.
£2,600–3,100
€3,900–4,650
$4,850–5,800
⚹ SRA

► **A London Transport bronze and enamel ticket office sign,** 'Swiss Cottage', c1939, 14in (35.5cm) wide.
£1,350–1,550 / €2,000–2,350
$2,500–2,900 ⊞ SRA

◄ **A Great Western Railway Social and Education Union cricket cap,** decorated with silver thread and a tassel, 1929.
£620–720 / €930–1,100
$1,200–1,400 ⚹ SRA

◄ **A British Railways enamel sign,** 'No Smoking', c1940, 20in (51cm) wide.
£140–160
€210–240
$260–300 ⊞ JUN

► **A London & North Eastern Railway cast-iron wagon plate,** 1941, 11in (28cm) wide.
£25–30 / €40–45
$50–55 ⊞ HeA

◄ **A Great Western Railway dinner menu,** with autographs of famous ex-GWR employees, 1947.
£180–200 / €270–300
$340–380 ⊞ MURR

A cast-brass workplate, 'Andrew Barclay Sons & Co, Caledonia Works No. 2119, 1941 Kilmarnock', repainted, 1941, 16⅜in (42.5cm) wide.
£450–540 / €680–810
$840–1,000 ⚹ SRA

A London & North Eastern Railway brass nameplate, 'Irish Elegance', restored, 1948, 71in (180.5cm) wide.
£20,000–24,000 / €30,000–36,000
$37,000–44,000 ⚹ SRA
Nameplates are the most desirable pieces of railwayana and rare examples can make record prices (see Record Breakers on page 427).

A British Rail Western Region headboard, 'Capitals United Express', depicting the crests of London and Cardiff, c1959.
£13,200–15,800 / €19,800–23,700
$24,700–29,500 ⚹ SRA
The Capitals United Express was launched on 9 February 1956 to celebrate Cardiff's new status as the capital of Wales. It ran between Paddington, Cardiff and Swansea until 12 June 1965.

◄ A British Rail Southern Region station totem, 'Sandling for Hythe', 1950s, 36in (91.5cm) long.
£1,550–1,850 / €2,350–2,800
$2,900–3,450 ⚹ SRA

A Pullman Car Co brass table lamp, with a celluloid shade, the base stamped 'Phoenix', early 1950s.
£500–600 / €750–900
$940–1,100 ⚹ SRA
'Phoenix' was a parlour car built at Preston Park, Brighton, in 1952. The interior decoration was specially commissioned from Mary Adshead and depicted the seasons and transport themes in collage work of stamps, used bank notes and bonds. Apparently, it was a favourite car of the royal family, used for state arrivals in conjunction with the 'Golden Arrow'. It was withdrawn from service in September 1972 and is now in the VSOE (Venice Simplon Orient Express) train. This style of lamp, the rarest of all the Pullman lamp designs, was unique to 'Phoenix' and is most redolent of the early 1950s.

► A cast-aluminium headboard, 'Atlantic Coast Express', carried by Bulleid Pacifics, cast 'MOD' to the reverse, 1964, 50in (127cm) wide.
£3,600–4,300 / €5,400–6,500
$6,700–8,000 ⚹ SRA

A London Transport guide, 1966, 6 x 4in (15 x 10cm).
£1–5 / €2–7
$3–9 ⊞ RTT

A British Railways cast-aluminium nameplate, 'County of Cleveland', c1985, 45½in (115.5cm) wide.
£2,000–2,400 / €3,000–3,600
$3,750–4,500 ⚹ SRA

Rock & Pop

Bay City Rollers, a canvas bag, 1975, 13in (33cm) wide.
£60–70 / €90–105
$110–130 ⊞ IQ

Count Basie, concert programme and tickets for the Empire, Liverpool, 1960s, programme 10 x 8in (25.5 x 20.5cm).
£35–40 / €50–60
$65–75 ⊞ CTO

Crazy World of Arthur Brown, and The Pretty Things, a concert poster, 1968, 30 x 20in (76 x 51cm).
£85–95 / €130–145
$160–185 ⊞ BRIG

◀ **Billy Fury,** a hand bill from the Odeon, Leeds, c1964, 7 x 10in (18 x 25.5cm).
£45–50 / €70–80
$85–95 ⊞ CTO

Cross Reference
Eighties see pages 218–221

▶ **Guns & Roses,** a leather jacket from the German tour, 1985.
£145–160
€220–240
$270–300 ⊞ IQ

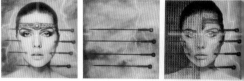

Debbie Harry, museum edition lithograph of cover artwork for 'Koo Koo', by H. R. Giger, signed by the artist and Debbie Harry, 1990, 33in (84cm) wide.
£240–270 / €360–410
$450–500 ⊞ IQ

Buddy Holly, personality photo card by Star Pics, 1959, 10 x 8in (25.5 x 20.5cm).
£4–8 / €6–12
$8–15 ⊞ CTO

Jimi Hendrix, landing card, mounted with a photograph, signed, 1970, 6in (15cm) wide.
£1,800–2,000
€2,700–3,000
$3,350–3,750 ⊞ IQ
This landing card was for Hendrix's last trip to the UK to play at the Isle of Wight Festival. He died one month later.

Leadbelly, a photograph by Bernice Abbott, 'Portrait of Leadbelly', gelatin silver print, stamped 1930s, 9¼ x 7½in (23.5 x 19cm).
£240–280 / €360–420
$450–520 ⚲ BBA

Grace Jones, a gelatin silver print by Greg Gorman, 1991, 9¾ x 7½in (25 x 19cm).
£280–330 / €420–500
$520–620 ⚲ BBA

Madonna, a signed colour photograph, 1996, 10 x 8in (25.5 x 20.5cm).
£450–500 / €680–750
$840–940 ⊞ FRa

◄ **Elvis Presley,** a *Jailhouse Rock* postcard, 1957, 5 x 3in (12.5 x 7.5cm).
£2–6 / €3–9
$4–11 ⊞ CTO

Elvis Presley, a Regal Films *Jailhouse Rock* re-release poster, 1960s, 30 x 40in (76 x 101.5cm).
£130–150 / €200–230
$240–280 ⊞ CTO

Queen, a fan club set of four signed photographs, 1980s, 9 x 6in (23 x 15cm).
£700–800 / €1,050–1,200
$1,300–1,500 ⊞ IQ

Cliff Richard, a postcard, 1960, 6 x 4in (15 x 10cm).
£1–5 / €2–7
$3–9 ⊞ RTT

◄ **Rolling Stones,** a concert poster for the Carlton Ballroom, Slough, 1964, 24½ x 18in (62 x 45.5cm).
£810–900 / €1,200–1,350
$1,500–1,700 ⊞ BRIG

Cross Reference
Posters see pages 313–315

► **Rolling Stones,** a souvenir booklet for the American tour, 1969, 12in (30.5cm) square.
£35–40 / €50–60
$65–75 ⊞ CTO

◄ **Spencer Davis Group,** promotional photo card, c1966, 3 x 6in (7.5 x 15cm).
£35–40
€50–60
$65–75 ⊞ CTO

The Who, Track Records poster for 'Quadrophenia', 1973, 29in (74cm) high.
£160–180 / €240–270
$300–340 ⊞ IQ

The Who, a copy of *The Who* by Gary Herman, signed by all four members of the band, published by Studio Vista, 1971, 8°.
£260–300 / €390–450
$480–560 ➢ DW

The Beatles

◀ **A Beatles tour programme,** 1963, 11¾ x 8¼in (29.5 x 21cm).
£45–50
€70–80
$85–95 ⊞ **BTC**

The Beatles, a postcard, by Valex of Liverpool, c1963, 3 x 5in (7.5 x 12.5cm).
£2–6 / €3–9
$4–11 ⊞ **CTO**

A Beatles poster, published by the *Evening Standard*, advertising journalist Maureen Cleave's interview with the Beatles, early 1960s, 30 x 18¾in (76 x 47.5cm).
£170–200 / €260–300
$320–370 ⚒ **SWO**

▶ *Record Mirror,* Christmas issue, with Beatles front cover, 1966, 17 x 12in (43 x 30.5cm).
£15–20 / €22–30
$28–38 ⊞ **IQ**

A linen tea towel, depicting the Beatles, 1964, 21in (7.5 x 53.5cm) wide.
£110–125 / €165–190
$200–230 ⊞ **IQ**

An Arnhems Museum poster, by Pieter Brattinga, advertising a Peter Blake exhibition, depicting the Beatles, printed by Steendrukkerij de Jong & Co, Danish, 1974, 36¾ x 27½in (70 x 93.5cm) wide.
£95–110 / €140–165
$175–200 ⚒ **VSP**

A 24ct gold-plated 'Imagine' LP record, laser-etched with a picture of John Lennon and lyrics, No. 2,675 of 9,500, 1996, mounted, framed and glazed, 20¼ x 16¼in (51.5 x 41.5cm), with a certificate of authenticity.
£100–120 / €150–180
$185–220 ⚒ **PF**

Jukeboxes

The idea of the jukebox took off in the 1900s with the development of a coin-operated phonograph. Records were played sequentially (in the order they were placed in the machine) until the 1930s, when a mechanism was perfected that allowed listeners to choose what they wanted to hear. The market was dominated by four major American manufacturers: the Rudolph Wurlitzer Co, the Rock-Ola Manufacturing Co, AMI, and the Seeburg Co.

A Wurlitzer 61 jukebox, with 78 selections, 1938, 21¾in (55cm) high.
£2,250–2,700 / €3,350–4,000
$4,200–5,000 ⚡ S(P)

◀ **A Seeburg 147M Ashcan jukebox,** with moulded Plexiglass panels, c1947, 57in (145cm) high.
£800–900
€1,200–1,350
$1,500–1,700
⚡ JAA

A Wurlitzer 1833 jukebox, 1955, 54in (137cm) high.
£6,000–7,000
€9,000–10,500
$11,000–12,500 ⊞ AME

◀ **A Seeburg wall-mounted jukebox,** 1959, 12in (30.5cm) high.
£220–250 / €330–380
$410–470 ⊞ MARK

◀ **A Shyvers table-top Multiphone,** American, 1939–59, 14in (35.5cm) high.
£220–250 / €330–380
$410–470 ⊞ MARK
The Multiphone was developed in the late 1930s by the Shyvers Manufacturing Co in America. At its height of popularity around 8,000 Multiphones were installed in restaurants, drive-ins and bars, placed in booths and on counter tops. The customer would choose a song title from the printed list on the machine, insert coins, and talk through a speaker at the top which provided a direct phone link to a female disc jockey in Seattle who would then play the selected records. Music came out through the speaker at the bottom.

A Seeburg KD 200 Select-o-matic jukebox, the front grill decorated with automotive fins and tail lights, American, 1957, 58in (147.5cm) high.
£3,850–4,250 / €5,800–6,400
$7,200–8,000 ⊞ WAm
Seeburg was established in Chicago in 1907 and by the mid-20th century had become a leading name in the jukebox field. In the late 1940s the company pioneered a machine that could play both sides of 50 records (the first 100-select jukebox), and in 1950 Seeburg introduced the first jukebox that could play 45rpm singles, thus establishing its dominance in the market place.

Punk

Today original Punk fashion and memorabilia is highly collectable. Punk emerged in London in the mid-1970s and the clothing was as important and anarchic as the music. From head to toe punks set out to shock the Establishment and challenge traditional notions of beauty and fashion.

Hair was dyed bright artificial colours (pink, green and bleached-blonde) and gelled into huge spikes and giant mohicans. Make-up was inspired by the vampire look: white faces, black eyes and black lips. Punks also pioneered piercings (most commonly with safety pins), introducing a fashion that some 25 years later was to become mainstream. Favourite jewellery included chains, padlocks and razor blades (another fashion that, translated into gold, was later to become mass-market.) Ripped up T-shirts and long-sleeved muslin tops were emblazoned with aggressive and obscene slogans, and other staples included a baggy loose-knit mohair sweater and a biker-style leather jacket. Bondage trousers with a bum flap and a strap linking the legs were one of the most famous punk garments, and watching a fettered punk trying to run for a bus was an amusing sight in 1970s London. For girls, tight leather skirts and mini tartan kilts were teamed with deliberately ripped fishnets, and the archetypal unisex punk footwear was the boot, either heavy Doc Marten or bondage boots.

The Punk look was most famously pioneered by fashion designers Vivienne Westwood and Malcolm McLaren, whose Kings Road shop became the focus of the movement. The shop went through various permutations. In 1971, as Let it Rock, the shop sold teddy-boy style clothes and, in 1972, fashions were inspired by rockers and bikers. In 1974 the name was changed to Sex. Westwood produced leather, rubber and bondage gear as well as T-shirts printed with anarchic and erotic slogans and McLaren founded the Sex Pistols. In 1977 the shop was named Seditionaries.

Punk was becoming a fully fledged movement, and McLaren and Westwood's fashions were being copied by young people across the world, and by other Kings Road stores, most notably Boy. Early Westwood and McLaren material is highly sought after. 'These pieces are very rare,' says dealer and collector Stephen Phillips. 'Comparatively few garments were made. Many were destroyed by the Punk lifestyle, and today many people buy these items as works of art and will literally put T-shirts in frames.' Since the Vivienne Westwood 2004 exhibition at the Victoria & Albert Museum in London, prices have spiralled. High values, warns Phillips, have also inspired a huge number of fakes, some of which can be hard to spot. 'Be very careful, particularly when buying over the internet, and if you are spending serious amounts of money, go to a reputable dealer,' he advises. Shortage of original Westwood material has also stimulated interest in other punk shops of the period such as Boy, and here again, values have risen.

A pair of Malcolm McLaren and Vivienne Westwood vinyl shoes, from Sex, c1975.
£600–700 / €900–1,050
$1,150–1,300 ⊞ REK

▶ **A Malcolm McLaren and Vivienne Westwood Cambridge Rapist T-shirt,** c1975.
£450–500 / €680–750
$840–940 ⊞ REK
These controversial T-shirts resulted in the prosecution of Westwood and McLaren.

Anarchy in the UK, No.1, the Sex Pistols fanzine, compiled by Vivienne Westwood, Jamie Reid and others, 1976, 18 x 13in (45.5 x 33cm), framed.
£180–200 / €270–300
$330–370 ⊞ IQ

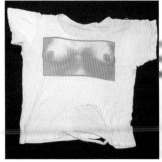

A Malcolm McLaren and Vivienne Westwood Tits T-shirt, with Seditionaries label, torn, c1977.
£360–400 / € 540–600
$670–750 ⊞ REK
The tear does not devalue this T-shirt, which has a classic image that Westwood returned to later in her career.

A Malcolm McLaren and Vivienne Westwood leather skirt, with Seditionaries label, 1976–77.
£900–1,000 / € 1,350–1,500
$1,650–1,850 ⊞ REK

A pair of Malcolm McLaren and Vivienne Westwood leather bondage boots, with Seditionaries label, c1977.
£670–750 / € 1,000–1,150
$1,250–1,400 ⊞ REK

A Malcolm McLaren and Vivienne Westwood muslin God Save the Queen top, with Seditionaries label, c1977.
£550–650 / € 830–980
$1,050–1,200 ⊞ REK
Labels on the muslin tops were inserted between the double-layered muslin on the front left-hand side of shirts.

A Virgin Records promotional poster, for the Sex Pistols' single record 'Holiday in the Sun', 1977, 28in (71cm) square.
£180–200 / € 270–300
$330–370 ⊞ IQ

A Malcolm McLaren and Vivienne Westwood parachute shirt, with Seditionaries label, c1977.
£900–1,000 / € 1,350–1,500
$1,650–1,850 ⊞ REK

◀ **A pair of bondage-style trousers,** with Boy label, 1981.
£90–100
€ 135–150
$170–190
⊞ REK

A parachute shirt, unlabelled, c1980.
£100–120 / € 150–180
$185–220 ⊞ REK

▶ **A plastic Sid Vicious doll,** by S. I. D. Limited, 1998, 12in (30.5cm) high.
£50–55
€ 75–85
$95–100 ⊞ IQ

Records

'Classic Compilations', LP record, by Sire, the cover designed by Kelley Mouse Studios, American, 1976.
£45–50 / €70–80
$85–95 ⊞ CTO

Roy Budd and the London Philharmonic Orchestra, concerto for the *Harry* soundtrack, LP record, by PYE Records, 1972.
£40–45 / €60–70
$75–85 ⊞ PR

Further reading
Miller's Collecting Vinyl, Miller's Publications, 2003

Bill Haley and His Comets, 'Dim Dim the Lights', EP record, by Brunswick, 1956.
£35–40 / €50–60
$65–75 ⊞ BNO

Wolfgang Dauners, 'Et Cetera Live', LP record, by MPS Records, 1973.
£45–50 / €70–80
$85–95 ⊞ TOT

Richard Hell and the Voidoids, 'The Neon Boys', EP record, 1980.
£8–12 / €12–18
$15–22 ⊞ CTO

'The Hitmakers', EP record, by PYE Records, 1965.
£8–12 / €12–18
$15–22 ⊞ BNO

The Hour Glass, LP record, by Liberty, 1968.
£15–20 / €22–30
$28–38 ⊞ TOT

John Mayer and Joe Harriott, 'Indo Jazz-Suite', LP record, by EMI Records, 1966.
£20–25 / €30–35
$35–45 ⊞ PR

Paul McCartney boxed set,
'Flowers in the Dirt', comprising LP
record, 7in single, family tree,
bumper sticker, six postcards and
tour itinerary, 1989.
£25–30 / €40–45
$50–55 ⊞ CTO

Elvis Presley, 'Blue Suede
Shoes'/'Tutti Frutti', 7in single
record, by HMV, 1956.
£125–140 / €190–210
$230–260 ⊞ BNO

The Sapphires, 'Who Do You
Love'/'Oh So Soon', 7in single
record, by Stateside, 1964.
£45–50 / €70–80
$85–95 ⊞ CTO

Yoko Ono, 'Mindtrain', demo EP,
by Apple, 1972.
£35–40 / €50–60
$65–75 ⊞ CTO

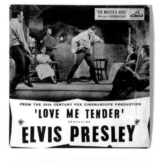

Elvis Presley, 'Love Me Tender', EP
record, by HMV, 1956.
£100–120 / €150–180
$185–220 ⊞ CTO

The Rolling Stones, 'Around
And Around', LP record, by Decca,
German, c1964.
£135–150 / €200–230
$250–280 ⊞ BNO

The Yardbirds, 'Five Yardbirds',
EP record, by Colombia, 1965.
£55–65 / €85–100
$100–120 ⊞ BNO

Perrey & Kingsley, 'Kaleidoscopic
Vibrations', LP record, by Vanguard
Records, 1967.
£20–25 / €30–35
$35–45 ⊞ TOT

Elvis Presley, 'King Creole', EP
record, by RCA, 1958.
£10–15 / €15–22
$19–28 ⊞ BNO

◄ **The Rolling Stones,** 'Around
And Around', LP record, by Decca,
German, c1964.
£135–150 / €200–230
$250–280 ⊞ BNO

'The Sound of the R&B Hits', LP
record, by Stateside, 1963.
£30–35 / €45–50
$55–65 ⊞ CTO

◄ **The Yardbirds,** 'Five Yardbirds',
EP record, by Colombia, 1965.
£55–65 / €85–100
$100–120 ⊞ BNO

Scent Bottles

A cut-glass scent bottle, by Apsley Pellatt, decorated with a sulphide portrait of a gentleman, possibly George III, with step-cut sides and a hobnail back, minor damage, signed, early 19thC, 4in (10cm) high.
£600–700 / € 900–1,050
$1,100–1,300 ♣ RTo

A Coalbrookedale-style ceramic scent bottle, with floral-encrusted decoration, some damage, 19thC, 3¾in (9.5cm) high.
£60–70 / € 90–105
$110–130 ♣ CHTR

A silver-gilt and cut-glass scent bottle, French, 19thC, 5¼in (13.5cm) high.
£105–125 / € 160–190
$195–230 ♣ JAA

A silver-gilt and glass double-ended scent bottle, by Thomas Johnston, one cover with a coral and half-pearl monogram, the other with a turquoise and half-pearl monogram, London 1864, 4¾in (12cm) wide.
£250–300 / € 380–450
$470–560 ♣ WW

A silver-mounted scent bottle, by Sampson Mordan & Co, in the form of a champagne bottle, the hinged cover opens to reveal a vinaigrette, marked, c1870, 5in (12.5cm) high.
£2,300–2,750
€ 3,450–4,150
$4,300–5,100 ♣ WW

A silver-mounted ceramic scent bottle, hand-painted with lovers in a landscape, Birmingham 1903, 2½in (6.5cm) high.
£85–100 / € 130–150
$160–190 ♣ GAK

> **Cross Reference**
> Silver & Metalware
> see pages 345–353

A pair of silver-mounted and cut-glass scent bottles, Birmingham 1903, 6in (15cm) high.
£90–100 / € 135–150
$170–190 ♣ G(L)

▶ **A pair of silver-mounted glass scent bottles,** with hand-painted decoration, London 1920, 4½in (11.5cm) high.
£120–140 / € 180–210
$220–260 ♣ FHF

A gilt-metal-mounted glass scent bottle, by R. Lalique, moulded and etched marks, French, 1920s, 4½in (11cm) high.
£400–480 / €600–720
$750–900 ✏ BR

A Gabilla Rose Perfume glass scent bottle, by Baccarat, French, 1920s–30s, 3in (7.5cm) high, with original box.
£450–500 / €680–750
$840–940 ⊞ LBe

A glass spray perfume bottle, with hand-painted decoration, 1920-30, 5½in (14cm) high.
£85–95 / €130–145
$160–180 ⊞ LBe

A Prince Douka glass scent bottle, modelled as a lady in a cloak, 1930s, 3in (7.5cm) high.
£170–190 / €260–290
$320–360 ⊞ LaF

A Bourjois Evening in Paris scent bottle, in a Bakelite box modelled as an owl, 1930s, 3in (7.5cm) high.
£130–150 / €200–230
$240–280 ⊞ LBr
The box contains a small blue glass vial.

A Schiaparelli Shocking glass scent bottle, in the form of a female torso decorated with flowers, 1930s–1940s, 7in (18cm) high, in a satin-lined box.
£155–175 / €230–260
$290–330 ⊞ LBr
Elsa Schiaparelli (1890–1973) was one of the most famous couturiers of the 1930s. A friend of Salvador Dali and the surrealist circle, both her clothes and her perfume bottles were influenced by surrealist art. Designed by Eleanore Fini, the Shocking bottle was based on a dressmaker's dummy and inspired by the ample proportions of Mae West, a Schiaparelli client. The glass flowers on the head provided a surreal touch and, for the box, Schiaparelli created Shocking Pink, the colour that was to become her trademark. The complete packaging also included a Victorian-style transparent dome that protected the bottle. Most of Schiaparelli's perfumes began with the letter 'S' (see Sleeping below), and they are popular with collectors.

A pair of House for Men glass cologne and aftershave bottles, modelled as Art Deco-style gentlemen, with Bakelite stoppers, American, c1947, 6in (15cm) high.
£250–280 / €380–420
$470–520 ⊞ SUW

◄ **A Schiaparelli Sleeping glass scent bottle,** modelled as a candlestick, 1940s–50s, 5½in (14cm) high.
£200–220
€300–330
$370–410
⊞ LBr

A Calvin Klein Obsession glass counter display bottle, 1980, 11in (28cm) wide.
£220–250 / €330–380
$410–470 ⊞ LaF

Science & Technology

A brass pantograph, by Stanley, in a fitted mahogany case with accessories, 19thC, 27½in (70cm) wide.
£60–70 / € 90–105
$110–130 ↗ LAY

A set of steel and copper hand-held tea scales, by Richard Bastick, stamped and marked, 1828-50, beam 10¼in (26cm) long.
£100–110 / € 150–165
$185–210 ⊞ FOF

A Victorian ivory spy glass, by A. Abraham, with carved decoration and a brass-mounted lens, damaged, signed, 5½in (14cm) extended, with a leather case.
£110–130 / € 165–195
$210–240 ↗ G(L)

A surveyor's brass level, attributed to Miller & Adie, with an ivory scale, jewelled compass, end cap and eyepiece, in a mahogany case, Scottish, c1810, 21½in (54.5cm) wide.
£400–450 / € 600–680
$750–840 ⊞ FOF

▶ **A lacquered-brass gyroscope,** by Newton & Co, c1860, 11in (28cm) high, with original pine case.
£360–400 / € 540–600
$670–750 ⊞ TOM

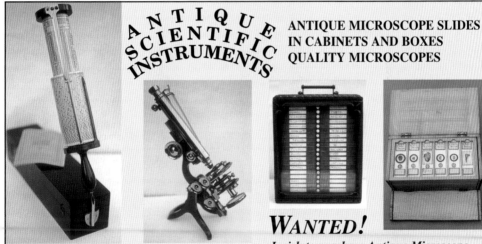

A surveyor's oxidized brass compass and clinometer, by Keufel & Esser Co, American, c1890, 4in (10cm) square.
£220–250 / €330–380
$410–470 ⊞ WAC

◀ **An ebonized stereo graphoscope,** French, 1895, 12in (30.5cm) high.
£180–200 / €270–300
$340–370 ⊞ APC

A folding monocular, with a finger-ring handle, late 19thC, 2¾in (7cm) long, extended.
£200–240 / €300–360
$370–440 ⚒ WW

A late Victorian brass ship's compass, by Dobbie McInnes, with a jewel bearing and brass gimbals, in a mahogany case, 8in (20.5cm) square.
£250–280 / €380–420
$470–520 ⊞ FOF

A wooden cash register, with inlaid decoration, some damage, late 19thC, 18in (45.5cm) wide.
£75–85 / €115–130
$140–160 ⚒ SWO

A brass table telescope, by Dolland, on a turned column, with lens attachments, c1900, 30in (76cm) wide, with a walnut case.
£480–570 / €720–860
$900–1,050 ⚒ CHTR

A Paget angle sextant, by E. R. Watts & Son, with a signed ivorine dial inscribed 'No. 839', in a mahogany case, c1900, 7 x 6in (18 x 15cm).
£500–550 / €750–830
$940–1,050 ⊞ FOF

A late Victorian metal and brass compound microscope, by Phillip Harris, 11in (28cm) high, with a mahogany case.
£240–270 / €360–410
$450–500 ⊞ WAC

A set of brass and steel proportional dividers, by W & D, c1901, in a leather case, 9¾in (25cm) wide.
£160–180 / €240–270
$300–340 ⊞ FOF

◀ **A set of chromed-metal architect's drawing instruments,** by W. H. Harling, three instruments with ivory handles, early 20thC, in a brass-mounted walnut case with an engraved plaque, 9½in (24cm) wide.
£170–200 / €260–300
$320–370 ⚒ DD

A wood and brass Wilmshurst machine, early 20thC, 17¾in (45cm) wide.
£500–600 / €750–900
$940–1,100 ⚒ CHTR

A set of silver postal scales, with a monogrammed platform, Birmingham 1902, 3¼in (8.5cm) high.
£220–260 / €330–390
$410–490 ⚒ SWO

A pair of gilt opera glasses, with engine-turned decoration and mother-of-pearl eyepieces, 4in (10cm) wide, c1910, with a chenille bag.
£70–80 / €100–120
$130–150 ⚒ AMB

An oak aneroid barometer, by C. J. Gowland, with carved decoration and silvered dials, c1910, 32¾in (83cm) high.
£210–250 / €320–380
$390–470 ⚒ DD

A brass gun-laying compass, by F. Barker & Son, 1917, in a mahogany case, 7in (18cm) long.
£55–65 / €85–100
$100–120 ⊞ WAC

A brass weather forecasting dial, by Negretti & Zambra, 1915, 5in (12.5cm) diam, with original cloth case.
£250–280 / €380–420
$470–520 ⊞ ETO

► A ceramic bathroom thermometer, by Dr Forbes, c1920, 11in (28cm) high.
£180–200 / €270–300
$340–370 ⊞ SMI

A brass sextant, by W. Ludolph, No. 736, with sighting tubes and filters, German, 1922, 13in (33cm) wide, with a mahogany box and calibration certificate.
£330–390 / €500–590
$620–730 ⚒ Bri

A Husun sextant, by W. Hughes & Son, c1928, in a fitted mahogany case, 39in (99cm) wide.
£340–410 / €510–610
$640–770 ⚒ WilP

A brass compass, 1942, 3in (7.5cm) diam.
£60–70 / €90–105
$110–130 ⊞ ABCM

A barograph, by C. W. Dixey & Son, in a glazed mahogany case with a drawer, mid-20thC, 14¼in (36cm) wide.
£450–500 / €680–750
$840–930 ⚒ CDC

A reproduction compass, late 20thC, 2in (5cm) diam.
£10–15 / €15–22
$19–28 ⊞ WO
This compass has been artificially aged with the use of chemicals.

Scripophily

An Eastern Counties Railway Co certificate for two shares of £20, York Extensions shares, 1836–62.
£85–95 / €130–145
$160–180 ⊞ GKR

A Royal Terrace Pier £100 share certificate, printed with a vignette of the pier by C. Adlard, signed by the directors, 1845.
£540–600 / €810–900
$1,000–1,100 ⊞ GKR

◀ **An Alliance Marine Assurance Co £100 share certificate,** signed by Samuel Gurney of Overend Gurney & Co, 1850s–70s.
£155–175 / €230–260
$290–330 ⊞ GKR

An American Express Co certificate for four shares of $200, signed by Wm Fargo, Henry Wells and Alex Holland, 1860–61.
£600–670 / €900–1,000
$1,100–1,200 ⊞ GKR
This is one of the rarer types of early American Express certificates. The company was formed in 1850, and the first public shares were issued in 1853. Henry Wells started in the express business in 1841, personally carrying cash and parcels from Albany to Buffalo in a carpet bag by stage coach and train. The company is still going strong today.

▶ **An Oregon Gold Mining Co $100 ten year bond,** American, Louisville, 1888.
£180–200
€270–300
$330–370
⊞ GKR

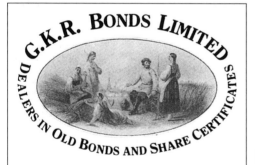

◀ **A John Morgan & Son (Aberdare) £50 share certificate,** No. 21/60, 1920.
£10–15
€15–22
$19–28 ⊞ J&S

▶ **An Evans & Reid Coal Co share certificate,** 1939.
£6–10 / €9–15
$12–19 ⊞ J&S

Sewing

A bone lace bobbin, with glass beads, mid-19thC, 4½in (11.5cm) long.
£15–20 / €22–30
$28–38 ⊞ HL

A Tunbridge ware thread waxer, c1850, 1in (2.5cm) diam.
£100–110 / €150–165
$185–210 ⊞ AMH

◀ A Tunbridge ware needle book, c1870, 2¾in (7cm) wide.
£200–220 / €300–330
$370–410 ⊞ AMH

A Tartan ware egg, enclosing an ivory thimble, c1870, 3in (7.5cm) wide.
£85–95 / €130–145
$160–180 ⊞ RdeR

A Tunbridge ware glove darner, c1880, 5½in (14cm) long.
£140–155 / €200–230
$260–290 ⊞ AMH

▶ A silver pincushion, by Sampson Mordan, modelled as a chick in an eggshell, Chester 1905, 1¾in (4.5cm) high.
£120–140 / €180–210
$220–260 ↗ HOLL

A silver pincushion, by William Comyns, modelled as a salon chair with a stuffed seat, London 1901, 3½in (9cm) high.
£260–310 / €390–460
$490–580 ↗ WW

A silver thimble, Chester 1917, 1in (2.5cm) high.
£25–30 / €40–45
$50–55 ⊞ CoHA

A silver pincushion, by A. & J. Zimmerman, modelled as a crown on a cushion, Birmingham 1910, 2½in (6.5cm) square.
£90–105 / €135–160
$165–195 ↗ WW

◀ A plastic wool holder, 1950s, 8in (20.5cm) high.
£15–20 / €22–30
$28–38 ⊞ HUX

Shipping

The year 2005 sees the bicentennial of the Battle of Trafalgar and the death of Admiral Lord Nelson, and this shipping section opens with Nelson memorabilia. The Battle of Trafalgar (21 October 1805) was the decisive naval action of the Napoleonic Wars and established Britain's supremacy at sea for over 100 years. The battle was fought at Cape Trafalgar on the southwest coast of Spain between a British fleet of 27 ships commanded by Nelson and a combined Franco-Spanish fleet of 33 ships led by Admiral Villeneuve. At 11.50am Nelson hoisted the famous signal 'England expects that every man will do his duty' and, having divided his fleet into two squadrons, attacked Villeneuve's line at right angles. It was a hugely successful strategy. By 5pm the battle was over and won. Some 20 enemy vessels had been captured or sunk without the loss of a single British ship, but in his hour of triumph, Nelson had been shot and died on HMS *Victory* that same afternoon.

The combination of a great triumph combined with the tragic death of a national hero stimulated a demand for commemoratives that has never been matched by any other naval leader. Nelson's funeral procession and interment at St Paul's Cathedral on 9 January 1806 was the greatest spectacle seen in London during the period and brought the souvenir sellers out in force. Commemoratives included medals, china, table cloths and even Trafalgar door handles. A large amount of material was produced in the early years of the 19th century, and demand for mementoes persisted into the Victorian period, particularly in the 1840s with the development in London of Trafalgar Square and the erection of Nelson's column. The centenary of the battle in 1905 spawned another burst of Nelson souvenirs, and modern commemoratives have been produced for the current bicentennial, which has inspired a host of events, including a major Nelson and Napoleon exhibition at the National Maritime Museum in Greenwich.

The most desirable commemoratives are objects that once belonged to or are personally associated with Nelson. These are extremely rare and command very high prices. In 2004 a tiny fragment of Nelson's flag from the *Victory* sold at Bonham's for £25,600 / € 38,400 / $47,800. The flag had been carried by sailors during Nelson's funeral but instead of laying it finally on the coffin, they tore it up for mementoes. Provenance is crucial when dealing with items relating to celebrities whose fame can inspire the manufacture of fakes. Major collections of Nelson material can be seen at the Royal Naval Museum in Portsmouth (home of the *Victory*) and the National Maritime Museum, where one of the most celebrated and moving items on display is the uniform worn by Nelson at the time of his death, complete with bullet hole.

A manuscript, addressed to the 'Masters of his Majesty's Ships *Royal Sovereign*', signed 'Nelson and Bronte', 1805, 9in (23cm) high.
£4,000–4,500 / € 6,000–6,800 $7,500–8,400 ⊞ IQ

An HMS *Defiance* wound certificate, Battle of Trafalgar, 1805, 12in (30.5cm) high.
£2,250–2,500 / € 3,400–3,750 $4,200–4,700 ⊞ IQ

A white metal medal, by C. H. Kuchler, after C. Andras, commemorating the Battle of Trafalgar, depicting Admiral Lord Nelson, 1805, 2in (5cm) diam.
£750–850 / € 1,150–1,300 $1,450–1,600 ⊞ TML

Items in the Shipping section have been arranged in date order.

A lead medal, by T. Wyon Snr, commemorating the Battle of Trafalgar, depicting Admiral Lord Nelson, 1805, 1¾in (4.5cm) diam.
£300–330 / €450–500
$560–620 ⊞ TML
The physician William Turton (1735–1806) sponsored this medal as a tribute to Admiral Lord Nelson. Examples were presented to the authors of 10 memorial poems that were published in *Luctus Nelsoniani – Poems on the Death of Lord Nelson, in Latin and English and Dedicated by Command to His Royal Highness George Prince of Wales, 1807.*

A white metal medal, depicting Victory holding a portrait of Lord Nelson, 1805, 1½in (4cm) diam.
£110–125 / €165–190
$200–230 ⊞ TML

A white metal medal, commemorating the Battle of Trafalgar, depicting Admiral Lord Collingwood, 1805, 1½in (4cm) diam.
£250–280 / €380–420
$470–520 ⊞ TML
Admiral Lord Collingwood's promotion followed closely that of his good friend Nelson. At Trafalgar he was second in command, and his ship, the *Royal Sovereign*, was the first to break through enemy lines. He died in 1810 and was buried alongside Nelson in St Paul's Cathedral.

◄ **A Staffordshire figural group,** entitled 'Death of Nelson', c1840, 8in (20.5cm) high.
£440–490 / €660–740
$820–920 ⊞ SER

An Ironstone plate, printed with a paddle steamer within an Imari-style border, inscribed 'Transatlantic Steam Ship Company', c1840, 8½in (21.5cm) diam.
£130–155 / €195–230
$240–290 ⚲ SAS

A Coleman's California Line for San Francisco trade card, for the *Mary Robinson* clipper ship, 1858, 3¾ x 6½in (9.5 x 16.5cm), in a walnut frame.
£60–70 / €90–105
$110–130 ⚲ JDJ

A *carte de visite*, 'Steamer Leaving Douglas', 1890s, 3 x 4in (7.5 x 10cm).
£20–25 / €30–35
$35–45 ⊞ COB

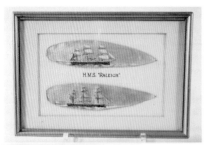

A pair of painted leaves, each depicting HMS *Raleigh*, late 19thC, framed, 6¼ x 8¾in (16 x 22cm).
£80–95 / €120–145
$150–180 ↗ SAS
HMS *Raleigh* was an iron frigate built at Chatham, Kent, in 1873. In 1899, after a long overseas commission, it led the last squadron of naval ships under sail to be put to sea.

A brass Walker's patent Rocket ship-log, with three dials, a measuring gauge and a plumb, stamped, late 19thC, 14½in (37cm) extended.
£240–280 / €360–420
$450–520 ↗ G(L)

▶ **An Irvine brass carbide ship's lamp,** c1900, 20in (51cm) high.
£110–125 / €165–190
$200–230 ⊞ JUN

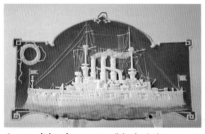

A porcelain plaque, possibly depicting *Kaiserin Augusta*, Continental, c1900, 7¾in (19.5cm) wide.
£35–40 / €50–60
$65–75 ↗ SAS
Kaiserin Augusta was a luxurious German North Atlantic liner made in 1906. After WWI she was surrendered to the British and subsequently became the Canadian Pacific's *Empress of Scotland*. She was scrapped in 1930.

> **Cross Reference**
> Commemorative Ware see pages p177–185

A Cunard Line poster, by N. Wilkinson, depicting RMS *Lusitania* and RMS *Mauretania*, c1910, 12 x 18in (30.5 x 45.5cm).
£450–500 / €680–750
$840–940 ⊞ JUN

A Royal Doulton jug, commemorating the centenary of the death of Admiral Lord Nelson, moulded with a portrait and two views of the Battle of Trafalgar, inscribed 'England Expects Every Man To Do His Duty', c1905, 7¾in (19.5cm) high.
£320–380 / €480–570
$600–710 ↗ SWO

A Carlton porcelain jug, enamelled with a view of RMS *Titanic*, 1912, 2¼in (5.5cm) high.
£120–140 / €180–210
$220–260 ↗ SAS

A Red Star Line ticket wallet, 1920s, 7in (18cm) high.
£20–25 / €30–35
$35–45 ⊞ COB

◀ **A treen spill holder,** c1930, 3½in (9cm) high.
£15–20 / €22–30
$28–38 ⊞ OLD
This spill holder was made from the teak timbers of HMS *Iron Duke*, Admiral Jellicoe's flagship at Jutland in 1916.

An oak ship's wheel, from a London tug boat, with brass fittings, 1930, 30in (76cm) diam.
£340–380 / €510–570
$640–710 ⊞ OLD

A silver cigarette case, engraved 'H. J. D., from Torpedo Man HMS *Neptune*', c1931, 3in (7.5cm) wide.
£110–125 / €165–185
$200–230 ⊞ OLD

A model of a tall ship, by S. C. S. Taws, marked 'Barque Gareloch', 1932, in a glazed case, 33½in (85cm) wide.
£300–350 / €450–540
$560–670 ⚒ L&T

A float salinometer, 1935, in a mahogany box, 8in (20.5cm) wide.
£35–40 / €50–60
$65–75 ⊞ OLD

A Royal Mail Line silver and enamel badge, 1930s, 1in (2.5cm) wide.
£15–20 / €22–30
$28–38 ⊞ COB

A Cunard White Star Line poster, advertising RMS *Mauretania*, 1939, 41 x 26in (104 x 66.5cm), framed.
£40–45 / €60–70
$76–85 ⚒ WL

▶ **A Britannic poster,** advertising 'The Liverpool route to USA and Canada', 1930s, framed, 24 x 23in (61 x 58.5cm).
£450–500 / €680–750
$840–940 ⊞ JUN

An Intalok Zig Zag wooden puzzle, depicting White Star Line *Britannic*, 1930s, with box, 8 x 11in (20.5 x 28cm).
£310–350 / €470–530
$580–650 ⊞ MURR

A brass plaque, 'Dunkirk 1940', 8¾in (22cm) wide.
£165–195 / €250–290
$310–370 ⚒ BR
These plaques were issued to the Dunkirk 'Little Ships' that took part in Operation Dynamo – the rescue of British and Commonwealth troops in 1940.

An Ocean Shipping Co Bakelite ashtray, 1930s, 5in (12.5cm) diam.
£25–30 / €40–45
$50–55 ⊞ HEI

An oak caulking hammer, c1940, 19in (48.5cm) wide.
£40–45 / €60–70
$75–85 ⊞ OLD

A pair of German Navy artillery binoculars, by Carl Zeiss, with lens cover, c1941, 7in (18cm) long.
£380–430 / €570–650
$710–800 ⊞ OLD

A Royal Navy brass and copper navigation lamp, c1945, 9in (23cm) high.
£130–145 / €195–220
$240–270 ⊞ OLD

A Thames Conservancy enamel boat registration plaque, 1948, 4in (10cm) wide.
£40–45 / €70–80
$85–95 ⊞ BS

◀ **A brass lifeboat wheel,** Welsh, c1950, 16in (40.5cm) diam.
£110–125 / €165–185
$200–230 ⊞ OLD

A pair of wood and cotton naval semaphore flags, c1950, 31in (78.5cm) long.
£35–40 / €50–60
$65–75 ⊞ OLD

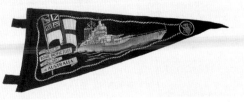

A Royal Navy souvenir pennant, Royal Pacific Fleet in Australia, c1950, 26in (66cm) wide.
£15–20 / €22–30
$28–38 ⊞ OLD

▶ **A brass loud-hailer,** c1950, 13in (33cm) high.
£40–45 / €60–70
$75–85 ⊞ OLD

A P&O hold label, 1950s, 4½ x 7½in (11.5 x 19cm).
£1–5 / €2–7
$3–9 ⊞ RTT

An Airfix model of *Queen Elizabeth 2,* 1990, 21in (53.5cm) wide.
£15–20 / €22–30
$28–38 ⊞ COB

A bronze ship's bell, inscribed 'Lauwers 1953', clapper replaced, 12in (30.5cm) diam.
£75–85 / €115–130
$140–160 ⚒ BRi

◀ **A Louis Vuitton Americas Cup silk scarf,** 2000, 20in (51cm) square.
£60–70 / €90–105
$110–130 ⊞ HIP

Silver & Metalware
Silver

Silver is one of the oldest and most remarkable metals known to man. Polished silver reflects light better than any other metal and in a world without electricity it illuminated as well as decorated the table. Extremely malleable, it could be beaten into sheets, drawn into wire and formed into almost any shape. Silver is the best conductor of heat and electricity, making it a perfect choice for items associated with food and drink. Silver is also self-sterilizing; bacteria cannot survive on silver's surface, which led to it being used for medical instruments as well as eating implements.

Another advantage, particularly for enthusiasts of antique silver, is that the metal is durable. From the 18th until well into the 20th century, the tables of the wealthy were laden with silver from flatware to hollow ware. Much has survived and many pieces can still be used today. Rarities by the finest silversmiths will cost high sums, but smaller and more standard examples of antique tableware can still be very affordable, particularly in this climate where demand and prices for more traditional antiques have dropped.

Antique silver is a joy to use and, with a little bit of care, can prove a good investment for the future and a lasting shiny pleasure. For cleaning, use a good non-abrasive cleaner or wadding polish – silver polishing mitts (cotton gloves ready impregnated with cleaner) are a quick and easy option – then wash the item with warm, soapy water to remove deposits, rinse and dry. Silver should not be over-polished as this can damage the patina and wear away hall marks. Salt should always be removed from salt cellars, and with flatware and serving implements, ivory and other handles should not be immersed in water since this can damage the applied handle and cause it to separate from the blade or eating implement. It is also important to remember that silver should never be put in the dishwasher.

A pair of silver table spoons, by Thomas Wallis, London 1772, 8in (20.5cm) long.
£90–100 / € 135–150
$170–190 ⊞ WAC

A silver and gilt berry spoon, by Thomas Richards, London 1816, 8in (20.5cm) long.
£45–50 / € 70–80
$85–95 ⊞ WAC

▶ **A silver cream jug,** by Solomon Royes, London 1820, 3½in (9cm) high.
£340–380
€ 520–580
$640–710
⊞ GRe

A silver skewer, by George Burrows, London 1796, 12in (30.5cm) long.
£180–200 / € 270–300
$330–370 ⊞ CoHA

A silver fish slice, by John and Henry Lias, with pierced decoration and an ivory handle, initialled 'M. H', London 1817, 11in (28cm) long.
£130–155 / € 195–230
$240–290 ⊅ WW
Serving implements were on display to all the assembled diners and were therefore often extremely decorative. Slices – with a broad flat blade – were used for serving dessert and fish, and in the 19th century often came in a fitted velvet-lined leather case together with a large, matching serving fork. Handles were made from silver, bone, ivory or mother-of-pearl. The head of the fork and the blade of the slice could be enhanced with engraving and piercing. Fish slices, for example, were often decorated with marine scenes, and the ornamental pierced holes allowed fish juices to drain. An original case will enhance the value of a set, and condition should always be checked.

A pierced silver sugar vase and cover, by Messrs Barnard, with a glass liner, London 1845, 5in (12.5cm) high, 8½oz.
£240–280 / € 360–420
$450–520 ⚒ WW

A silver whistle and case, by Joseph Jennens & Co, decorated with a Tudor rose and acanthus leaves, 1849, 4in (10cm) long.
£95–110 / € 140–165
$175–210 ⚒ G(L)
Without its matching case, this whistle would have a price range of £70–80
€ 105–120 / $130–150.

A silver napkin ring, by A. S., Sheffield 1857, 2in (5cm) diam.
£35–40 / € 50–60
$65–75 ⊞ WAC

A silver goblet, repoussé decorated with flowers and fruit, London 1861, 6¾in (17cm) high, 8oz.
£160–190 / € 240–290
$300–360 ⚒ L&E

A set of six silver salt cellars, by Martin Hall & Co, Sheffield 1863, 2in (5cm) diam.
£290–320 / € 430–480
$540–600 ⊞ CoHA
Since salt corrodes metal, cellars were either gilded on the inside or fitted with glass liners (often blue). When not in use, cellars (even those with liners) should be emptied of salt.

A silver christening mug, by R. Martin & E. Hall, with a gilt interior, pierced and engraved with ivy leaves, London 1874, 4in (10cm) high, 5½oz.
£260–310 / € 390–470
$490–580 ⚒ WW

A pair of silver-plated fish servers, c1880, knife 12in (30.5cm) long, in a fitted case.
£65–75 / € 100–115
$120–140 ⊞ FOX

A Victorian silver-plated ham bone holder, by Elkington & Co, 5½in (14cm) long.
£120–140 / € 180–210
$220–260 ⚒ WW

A silver-plated cruet set, in the form of a dairy cart, c1880, 2in (5cm) high.
£310–350 / € 470–530
$580–650 ⊞ SMI

A silver-plated butter knife, with a mother-of-pearl handle, c1880, 7in (18cm) long.
£20–25 / € 30–35
$35–45 ⊞ TASV

Items in the Silver & Metalware section have been arranged in date order within each sub-section.

A silver travelling corkscrew, by W. W. & F. D., with engine-turned decoration and monogram, London 1880, 3¼in (8.5cm) long.
£250–300 / € 380–450
$470–560 ⚒ GAK

A silver trinket box, by William Comyns & Sons, with embossed and crimped decoration, London 1891, 2¼in (5.5cm) wide.
£90–105 / €135–160 $170–200 ⚒ GAK

A silver spoon, by Salters Co, commemorating Queen Victoria's Diamond Jubilee, London 1887, 7in (18cm) long.
£135–150 / €200–230 $250–280 ⊞ CoHA

A silver double-sided menu holder, by Pembroke & Dingley, Birmingham 1896, 2in (5cm) high.
£170–190 / €260–290 $320–360 ⊞ CoHA

A silver miniature chair, Birmingham 1897, 2in (5cm) high.
£90–100 / €135–150 $170–190 ⊞ CoHA

A silver pen wipe, by Sampson Mordan & Co, in the form of a boot scraper, on a wooden base, London 1898, 2¼in (5.5cm) square.
£110–130 / €165–195 $210–240 ⚒ GAK

▶ **A silver sovereign case,** containing a gold sovereign and a half sovereign, Birmingham 1898.
£130–155 €195–230 $250–290 ⚒ G(L)

Hallmarks

Hallmarks on silver have been used in Britain since c1300. British sterling silver usually bears four main marks: the maker's mark, the standard mark (signifying the legal standard of pure silver), the town mark (the location of assay or testing), and the date letter. With the help of a book of hallmarks and a magnifying glass or jeweller's loupe, this information can be decoded.

A silver folding button hook, by Albert Skinner & Co, with a mother-of-pearl handle, Sheffield 1892, 3in (7.5cm) long.
£60–70 / €90–105 $110–130 ⊞ CoHA

▶ **A silver toast rack,** by Heath & Middleton, London 1897, 4¾in (12cm) long.
£55–65 / €85–100 $100–120 ⚒ RTo

A silver napkin ring, by Spurrier & Co, Birmingham 1900, 2in (5cm) diam.
£50–55 / €75–85
$95–105 ⊞ WAC

◀ **A silver-mounted glass decanter,** Sheffield 1900, 10in (25.5cm) high.
£50–60 / €75–90
$95–110 ♪ HYD

Napkin rings

In the Victorian period it became fashionable to decorate tables at dinner parties with damask napkins folded into fanciful shapes, but for less formal occasions the family used napkin rings. Silver napkin rings emerged in the mid-19th century, and were often sold in sets of four or six. In order to identify the user, rings might be engraved with numbers, initials or a monogram. Napkin rings were also popular christening presents, inscribed with the name and occasionally the birth date of the child. Rings can be circular, octagonal or elliptical and can be found in a wide range of styles. While boxed sets can be costly, an affordable and decorative option is to buy individual napkin rings so that everyone has their own design.

A silver-plated tea urn, with engraved decoration, early 20thC, 15¾in (40cm) high.
£60–70 / €90–105
$110–130 ♪ L&E

◀ **A silver toast rack,** Birmingham 1900, 3in (7.5cm) wide.
£80–90 / €120–135
$150–170 ⊞ FOX

▶ **A silver pepperette,** by Louis Willmott, in the form of an articulated doll, with an enamelled head, London 1907, 4½in (11.5cm) high, 2¼oz.
£820–980 / €1,250–1,450
$1,550–1,850 ♪ WW

Casters for shaking condiments and sugar originated in the 17th century. As well as salt and pepper, mustard was originally served in dry powder form in a caster, until c1760, when food fashions changed and it was offered wet and ready-mixed in a mustard pot with a dedicated mustard spoon. The 19th century saw a growing fashion for matching condiments, and miniature sets might be placed before each diner (a small pepper pot is known as a pepperette). Novelty designs became popular in the late 19th and early 20th centuries, and rare designs such as this silver articulated doll can fetch high prices and are very collectable today. Pepper mills emerged in the late 19th century, typically capstan-shaped and often made of wood or ivory with silver banding.

A silver button hook and shoe horn, by C. & N., each in the form of a court jester, with steel shafts, Birmingham 1907, 6in (15cm) high.
£85–100 / €125–150
$160–190 ♪ G(L)

A set of 12 silver coffee spoons, by Elkington & Co, with a pair of matching sugar tongs, Birmingham 1911, in a fitted case.
£115–135 / €170–200
$210–250 ♪ GAK

A silver christening set, Sheffield 1912, in a fitted case.
£35–40 / €50–60
$65–75 ♪ AMB

A silver-mounted glass lemonade jug, by Tiffany & Co, stamped '925', 1910, 12in (30.5cm) high.
£300–360 / € 450–540
$560–670 ✗ HYD

A silver-plated knife stand, with 12 tea knives, 1920s, 9¾in (25cm) high.
£175–195 / € 260–290
$330–370 ⊞ TASV

A silver and glass dressing table stand, comprising a mirror, a nail buffer, four manicure implements and a box, 1926, 7½in (19cm) high.
£140–165 / € 210–250
$260–310 ✗ GAK

A silver toilet box, by Levi & Salaman, Birmingham 1913, 3½in (9cm) high.
£200–220 / € 300–330
$370–410 ⊞ GRe

A silver three-piece cruet set, with matching spoons, c1920, pepper 3½in (9cm) high.
£100–110 / € 150–165
$185–210 ⊞ FOX

A silver dish, with pierced decoration, Birmingham 1927, 11in (28cm) long, 10oz.
£170–200 / € 260–300
$320–370 ✗ FHF

A set of 12 silver-handled knives and forks, by J. B. Wear, Sheffield 1918, in a fitted case, 8 x 6in (20.5 x 15cm).
£80–90 / € 120–135
$150–170 ⊞ WAC

A silver jam spoon, with a mother-of-pearl handle, 1920, 5½in (14cm) long.
£65–75 / € 100–115
$120–140 ⊞ BLm

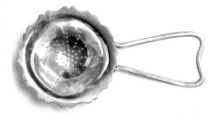

A silver tea strainer, Birmingham 1920, 5½in (14cm) long.
£55–65 / € 85–100
$100–120 ⊞ FOX

A silver five-piece cruet set, by D. F., London 1928, in a fitted case, 5 x 9in (12.5 x 23cm).
£170–190 / € 260–290
$320–360 ⊞ WAC

◄ **A sterling silver bottle label,** for Gin, 1930, 3in (7.5cm) wide.
£75–85 / € 115–130
$140–160 ⊞ JAS

A silver travelling cup, c1930,
3in (7.5cm) high.
£25–30 / €40–45
$50–55 ⊞ **SA**

A silver caddy spoon, by Georg Jensen,
London 1934, 10½in (26.5cm) long.
£130–155 / €195–230
$250–290 ↗ **CHTR**

◄ **A pair of silver servers,**
by Georg Jensen, decorated
with Lily of the Valley
pattern, marked, 1938.
£140–165 / €210–250
$260–310 ↗ **SWO**

▶ **A silver bonbon dish,**
by Roberts & Belk, Sheffield
1965, 12¾in (32.5cm) diam.
£145–165 / €220–250
$270–310 ⊞ **BEX**

◄ **A silver trophy,** on an ebonized
plinth, Birmingham 1930,
11¾in (30cm) high.
£100–120 / €150–180
$185–220 ↗ **WilP**

A silver cruet set, London 1931,
in a fitted case, 8in (20.5cm) wide.
£100–115 / €150–175
$185–210 ⊞ **LaF**

◄ **A silver caddy spoon,** the handle
in the form of a hare, Birmingham
1936, 3in (7.5cm) long, cased.
£100–110 / €150–165
$185–210 ⊞ **BLm**

Folding Knives & Forks

A silver folding fruit fork, with a mother-of-pearl
handle, c1800, 6in (15cm) long, with original box.
£60–70 / €90–105
$110–130 ⊞ **CoHA**

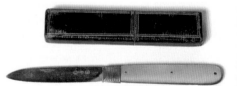

A silver folding fruit knife, by Samuel Kirby & Co,
with a mother-of-pearl handle, Sheffield 1822,
5in (12.5cm) long, with original box.
£80–90 / €120–135
$150–170 ⊞ **CoHA**

◄ **A silver dip pen, pencil and knife,** by Sampson
Mordan & Co, London 1878, 5in (12.5cm) long.
£155–175 / €230–260
$290–330 ⊞ **CoHA**

A silver folding fruit knife, by George Unite, with a seed pick and a mother-of-pearl handle, Birmingham 1885, 6in (15cm) long.
£110–125 / €165–190
$210–230 ⊞ CoHA

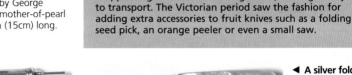

Folding cutlery

Folding knives and forks were used for fruit from the 18th century onwards. Silver was the preferred metal since it would not be damaged by fruit acids, and handles were typically mother-of-pearl, carved or left plain. Knives and forks were housed in a leather carrying case, and another option was a fruit knife and fork that snapped together to form a single unit, making it easy to transport. The Victorian period saw the fashion for adding extra accessories to fruit knives such as a folding seed pick, an orange peeler or even a small saw.

A sterling silver pen, pencil and knife, 1900, 4in (10cm) long.
£100–110 / €150–165
$185–210 ⊞ CoHA

◄ **A silver folding fruit knife and orange peeler,** with a mother-of-pearl handle, Sheffield 1902, 6in (15cm) long.
£60–70
€90–105
$110–130
⊞ CoHA

A silver folding knife and fork set, with a mother-of-pearl handle, Sheffield 1913, 6in (15cm) long.
£110–125 / €165–190
$210–230 ⊞ CoHA
This knife and fork clip together in order to form a single unit.

A brass penknife, c1920, 1in (2.5cm) diam.
£25–30 / €40–45
$50–55 ⊞ MRW

► **A brass penknife,** decorated with pigs, 1930, 3in (7.5cm) long.
£110–125
€165–190
$200–230
⊞ NLS

Locks & Keys

A steel door key, late 19thC, 5in (12.5cm) long.
£8–12 / €12–18
$15–22 ⊞ BS

A brass padlock and key, by Hobbs & Co, c1900, 5in (12.5cm) high.
£120–135 / €180–200
$220–250 ⊞ BS

A steel night latch key, 19thC, 2in (5cm) long.
£60–70 / €90–105
$110–130 ⊞ BS

◄ **Two brass combination padlocks,** c1900, 1in (2.5cm) wide.
£25–30 / €40–45
$50–55 each ⊞ HO

Metalware

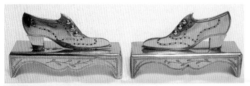

A pair of copper mantel ornaments, in the form of shoes, with engraved decoration, 19thC, 4in (10cm) wide.
£140–160 / €210–240
$260–300 ⊞ BS

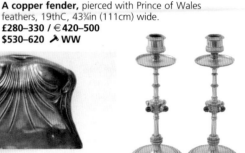

A copper fender, pierced with Prince of Wales feathers, 19thC, 43¾in (111cm) wide.
£280–330 / €420–500
$530–620 ➹ WW

A brass inkwell, with a ceramic liner, c1820, 4in (10cm) square.
£130–145 / €195–220
$240–270 ⊞ SAT

A copper pan and brush, c1890, 11in (28cm) wide.
£75–85 / €115–130
$140–160 ⊞ SAT

A pair of Victorian copper candlesticks, decorated with glass stones, 10in (25.5cm) high.
£160–190 / €240–290
$300–360 ➹ G(L)

A brass and steel bell, c1870, 16in (40.5cm) high.
£40–45 / €60–70
$75–85 ⊞ TOP

▶ **A copper and glass hall lantern,** c1900, 19¾in (50cm) high.
£130–155 / €195–230
$240–290 ➹ SWO

A pair of late Victorian brass candlesticks, with ceramic columns, 9in (23cm) high.
£60–70 / €90–105
$110–130 ➹ CHTR

A copper coal bucket, late 19thC, 16in (40.5cm) high.
£145–165 / €220–250
$260–310 ⊞ WAC

A copper dish, c1902, 6in (15cm) diam.
£10–15 / €15–22
$19–28 ⊞ DEB

A copper and brass ice bucket, with floral decoration, c1900, 11in (28cm) high.
£175–195 / €260–290
$330–370 ⊞ WAC

A copper coal bucket, with an iron frame, early 20thC, 21in (53.5cm) high.
£100–120 / €150–180
$185–220 ➹ G(L)

A brass tipstaff, c1910, 8in (20.5cm) high.
£110–125 / € 165–190
$200–230 ⊞ SA

◀ A brass shop bell, c1910,
3½in (9cm) high.
£25–30 / € 40–45
$50–55 ⊞ AL

A brass jardinière, with embossed
decoration, c1920, 9in (23cm) high.
£65–75 / € 100–115
$120–140 ⊞ JeH

◀ A brass spare bulb box,
the Atlantic Bulb Box, c1920,
6in (15cm) diam.
£25–30 / € 40–45
$50–55 ⊞ JUN

A WMF copper and brass
jardinière, c1915, 10in (25.5cm) high.
£320–360 / € 480–540
$600–670 ⊞ WAC

Skirt Lifters

The combination of long skirts and dirty streets and the growing popularity of bicycling for women created a real need for skirt lifters or port-jupes, which were a popular accessory in the late 19th century. The metal tongs gripped the hem of the skirt and were lifted by a cord or chain. Clips were made from base metal, usually brass or plated, and decorated with engraving. Various different patented designs were produced. The cord could be attached to a chatelaine or wrist bangle, and precautions were taken so that the grippers would not damage the dress fabric. Values depend on design and level of decoration.

A metal skirt lifter, 1890s, 4½in (11.5cm) long.
£65–75 / € 100–115
$120–140 ⊞ SUW

A metal Eureka skirt
lifter, with a diamond
registration mark, 1880s,
3in (7.5cm) long.
£70–80 / € 105–120
$130–150 ⊞ SUW

An Edwardian metal skirt lifter, 3½in (9cm) long.
£30–35 / € 45–50
$55–65 ⊞ HUX

An Edwardian metal skirt
lifter, 2½in (6.5cm) long.
£30–35 / € 45–50
$55–65 ⊞ HUX

Sixties & Seventies

An aluminium Sparklets soda syphon, 1960, 11in (28cm) high.
£35–40 / €50–60 $65–75 ⊞ SAT

◀ **A rosewood ice bucket,** by Jens Quistgaard, Danish, 1961, 18in (46cm) high.
£360–400 €540–600 $670–750 ⊞ BOOM
This design is rarer than the Quistgaard teak ice bucket shown right, a popular design that was produced in large numbers.

A teak ice bucket, by Jens Quistgaard, Danish, 1962, 16in (40.5cm) high.
£180–200 / €270–300 $330–370 ⊞ BOOM

▶ **An 8mm film,** *London Landmarks No.1*, 1964, 5½in (14cm) square.
£10–15 / €15–22 $28–38 ⊞ RTT

A cardboard chair, by Emme Edizioni, Italian, c1964, 17in (43cm) high.
£220–250 / €330–380 $410–470 ⊞ EMH

◀ **John D. Green,** *Birds of Britain*, published by Macmillan Co, New York, American, 1967, 14 x 10¾in (35.5 x 27.5cm) wide.
£110–120 €165–180 $210–220 ⊞ EMH

A teak clock, with a bras face, Danish, c1965, 56in (142cm) high.
£450–500 / €680–750 $840–940 ⊞ BOOM

A stainless steel Cylinda-line teapot set and tray, by Arne Jacobsen for Stelton, Danish, c1967, 4¼in (11cm) high.
£280–330 / €420–500 $520–620 ⋔ SWO

Peter Whitehead, 'Tonite Lets All Make Love In London', by Instant, 1968.
£90–100 / €135–150 $170–190 ⊞ BNO

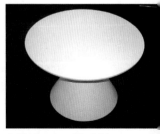

A Mushroom side table, manufactured by Arkana, 1960s, 24in (61cm) diam.
£140–160 / €210–240 $260–300 ⊞ HSR

Two enamel Krenit ware plates, Danish, 1960s, larger 14in (35.5cm) diam.
£65–75 / €100–115
$120–140 ⊞ PLB

A set of Emilio Pucci products, some with contents, 1960s, 6½in (16.5cm) high.
£340–380 / €510–570
$640–710 ⊞ EMH

A nest of three teak tables, with metal bases, Danish, c1970, largest 18in (46cm) high.
£270–300 / €400–450
$500–560 ⊞ BOOM

A plastic stacking chair, by Verner Panton, 1972.
£220–250 / €330–380
$410–470 ⊞ MARK
This was the first one-piece plastic chair.

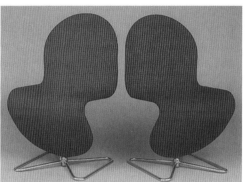

A pair of chrome and wool chairs, by Verner Panton for Fritz Hansen, with later covers, 1973.
£340–400 / €500–600
$640–750 ➴ BUK

A pair of hanging ball speakers, by Grundig, 1970s, 11in (28cm) diam.
£540–600 / €810–900
$1,000–1,100 ⊞ HSR

Ceramics & Glass

A Midwinter Stonehenge sugar bowl, designed by Eve Midwinter, decorated with Moon pattern, 1963–72, 4in (10cm) high.
£20–25 / €30–35
$35–45 ⊞ CHI

Three glass decanters, by Salvador Dali, printed with surrealist views, c1960, 13in (33cm) high.
£150–180 / €230–270
$280–330 ➶ SWO

A Rye Art Pottery pot, c1960, 4in (10cm) high.
£6–10 / €9–15
$12–19 ⊞ HO

A Hornsea vase, 1960–62, 8in (20.5cm) high
£55–65 / €85–100
$100–120 ⊞ EMH

A Whitefriars glass Banjo vase, by Geoffrey Baxter, c1967, 5in (13cm) high.
£55–65 / €85–100
$100–120 ➶ RTo

A pair of Whitefriars glass Drunken Bricklayer vases, by Geoffrey Baxter, c1967, 8in (20.5cm) high.
£190–220 / €290–330
$360–410 ➶ G(L)

Whitefriars

Geoffrey Baxter joined Whitefriars from the Royal College of Art in 1954. Influenced by developments in Italian and Scandinavian glass, he brought a new look to the factory's ranges. Perhaps his most famous designs are the asymmetric and textured soda glass vases that were produced in the late 1960s and '70s in a wide range of fashionable colours, ranging from ruby to kingfisher blue to tangerine. The Banjo and the Drunken Bricklayer vases, shown here, are two of his most successful designs. Like other vases in the textured range, these were produced in various sizes and colours and values vary accordingly. Large pieces in rare colours (i.e. colours that were not popular at the time and so were produced in smaller numbers) are the most sought after and, as the tall pewter vase shown here demonstrates, can fetch high prices.

A Whitefriars pewter glass Drunken Bricklayer vase, by Geoffrey Baxter, 1967–77, 13in (33cm) high.
£820–970 / €1,250–1,450
$1,550–1,800 ➶ RTo

A Meakin ceramic coffee service, comprising a coffee pot, cup and saucer, milk pot and sugar bowl, 1960, largest 10in (25.5cm) high.
£95–105 / €145–160
$175–195 ⊞ CHI

A Gambone Art Pottery bowl, Italian, late 1960s, 6½in (16.5cm) wide.
£220–250 / €330–380
$410–470 ⊞ EMH

Textiles & Wallpaper

Demand is currently strong for good-quality 1960s and '70s textiles. As the following examples demonstrate, this was a time of invention as designers experimented with patterns inspired by pyschedelia and space-age style. Large and colourful abstract designs are typical of the period. Works by leading names carry a premium, and over the past five years prices have risen dramatically. The selvedge of the material, which should not be cut off, should always be checked for the name of the designer,

pattern, manufacturer or retailer.

Condition is important and fading or other damage will reduce value. As prices have risen it has become increasingly common to sell fabric in wall panels that can be hung like a work of art. Textiles by celebrated designers can fetch three- and four-figure sums but equally, unattributed fabrics or works by less-famous designers are comparatively inexpensive and provide an affordable way of achieving the period look.

A length of fabric, by Gabrielle Fountain for Heal's, decorated with Equilibrium pattern, c1964, 26½in (67.5cm) wide.
£120–140 / €180–210
$220–260 ⊞ EMH

A pair of curtains, by John Piper for David Whitehead, decorated with Brittany pattern, 1968, 77¼ x 45¼in (196 x 115cm).
£720–800 / €1,100–1,200
$1,350–1,500 ⊞ EMH

A pair of curtains, by Evelyn Redgrave for Heal's, decorated with Montaine pattern, 1960s, 84½ x 47¼in (214 x 120cm).
£340–380 / €510–570
$640–710 ⊞ EMH

A roll of Crown wallpaper, decorated with Action Man, 1975, 20½in (52cm) wide.
£20–25 / €30–35
$35–45 ⊞ GTM

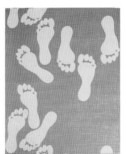

A roll of wallpaper, decorated with footprints, 1970s, 21in (53.5cm) wide.
£20–25 / €30–35
$35–45 ⊞ MARK

A length of fabric, by Giltex, 1970s, 48in (122cm) wide.
£30–35 / €45–50
$55–65 ⊞ HSR

► A length of fabric, 1970s, 55¼in (140.5cm) wide.
£6–10 / €9–15
$12–19 per metre ⊞ MARK

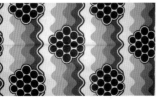

Lighting

◀ **A pair of iron and glass candle holders,** Polish, c1965, 14½in (37cm) high.
£130–145 / €195–220
$240–270 ⊞ BOOM

▶ **A pair of ceramic Skyscraper table lamps,** with hessian shades, American, c1965, 29in (73.5cm) high.
£580–650 / €870–980
$1,100–1,200 ⊞ BOOM

A Fun 1 DM capiz shell lamp, by Verner Panton, 1964, 24in (61cm) high.
£580–650 / €870–980
$1,100–1,200 ⊞ MARK
'A less successful experiment is preferable to beautiful platitude,' claimed Verner Panton (1926–98). Born in a small village in Denmark, Panton became one of the most inventive designers of his generation and a grand master of Pop Art style. He worked in a wide range of media from furniture to textiles and was famous for his lighting designs, which were hugely varied in style. Panton's 'Fun' series shell lights were a Modernist reinterpretation of the chandelier. Inspired by wind chimes traditionally produced by fishermen in the Andaman Islands, these hanging lamps were made from shell discs suspended from metal rings. The mother-of-pearl surfaces reflected the light and with a current of air, the shells made a soft tinkling noise. Typically Panton worked with manmade rather than natural materials and this light was also produced with aluminium discs.

A tin lamp, by Archizoom Associati, Italian, 1966–74, 18in (45.5cm) high.
£630–700 / €950–1,050
$1,200–1,300 ⊞ EMH

◀ **A pair of Murano glass table lamps,** Italian, 1970, 9in (23cm) high.
£200–230
€300–350
$370–430
⊞ BOOM

▶ **An enamelled metal Big Flowerpot lamp,** by Verner Panton for Luber, 1971, 20in (52cm) diam.
£580–650
€870–980
$1,100–1,200
⊞ MARK

◀ **A chrome table lamp,** with a wicker shade, 1970s, 37¼in (94.5cm) high.
£80–90
€120–135
$150–170
⋏ SWO

▶ **pair of chrome table lamps,** American, 1970s, 30in (76cm) high.
£450–500
€680–750
$840–940 ⊞ HSR

Smoking

A boxwood and leather cigar box, in the
form of a photograph album, 19thC,
7in (18cm) wide.
£45–50 / €70–80
$85–95 ⊞ MB

A silver match holder, by J. Grinsell & Sons,
in the form of a wheelbarrow, with a gilt
interior and a glass striker, London 1896,
4½in (11.5cm) long.
£200–240 / €300–360
$370–450 ➹ WW

A white metal vesta case,
advertising Molassine Meal, 1905,
2¼in (5.5cm) wide.
£40–45 / €60–70
$75–85 ⊞ HUX

A wooden pipe rack, c1870,
7in (18cm) high.
£175–195 / €260–290
$330–360 ⊞ SDA

◀ A porcelain humidor, transfer-
printed with a classical scene, with a
white metal cover, the handle in the
form of a pipe, signed 'Kaufmann',
marked 'Victoria Carlsbad Austria',
Austrian, early 20thC,
7½in (19cm) high.
£135–160 / €200–240
$250–300 ➹ JAA

A silver vesta case, with enamelled
decoration, marked 'R.C.',
Birmingham 1906,
2in (5cm) high, 1oz.
£380–450 / €570–680
$710–840 ➹ WW

A poster, by Jules Chéret,
advertising Job cigarettes,
on card, 1895, 18 x 12in
(45.5 x 30.5cm).
£270–300 / €400–450
$500–560 ⊞ Do

◀ A silver-mounted glass match
holder, with engraved floral
decoration, Birmingham 1898,
3in (7.5cm) high.
£240–280 / €360–420
$450–520 ➹ GAK

A Meerschaum pipe, in the form
of a lion's head, with an amber
mouthpiece, late 19thC,
7¼in (18.5cm) long
£200–240 / €300–360
$370–450 ➹ DN(BR)

A silver-mounted oak humidor,
with presentation plaque, 1908,
12in (30.5cm) wide.
£480–570 / €720–680
$900–1,050 ➹ HOLL

A Saphir Cigarettes poster, by Stephano, printed by Moullot, French, Marseille, 1910, 32 x 47in (81.5 x 119.5cm).
£450–500 / €680–750
$840–940 ⊞ Do

▶ A W. D. & H. O. Wills Old Friend cardboard shop sign, 1920s, 10in (25.5cm) high.
£130–145
€195–220
$240–270
⊞ Do

◀ A clay pipe, in the form of King George V's head, 1910–36, 5in (12.5cm) long.
£25–30
€40–45
$50–55 ➤ BBR

A Westward Ho Smoking Mixture showcard, 1920–30, framed and glazed, 20 x 16in (51 x 40.5cm).
£630–700 / €950–1,050
$1,200–1,300 ⊞ AAA

A Black Beauty Shag printed tin sign, 1920s, 9 x 13in (23 x 33cm).
£180–200 / €270–300
$330–370 ⊞ AAA

A box of eight Imperial Tobacco pipes, c1930, 15in (38cm) wide.
£130–145 / €195–220
$240–270 ⊞ JUN

▶ A cigar, 1940, in original box, 15in (38cm) long.
£10–15 / €15–22
$19–28 ⊞ JUN

A spelter match striker, in the form of carpet traders and a camel, 1930s, 7½in (19cm) high.
£100–120 / €150–180
$185–220 ➤ G(L)

◀ A sterling silver cigarette holder, German, 1930s, 1¼in (3cm) long.
£130–145
€195–220
$240–270
⊞ SUW

▶ A Dunhill walnut humidor, with a cedarwood interior, c1950, 13in (22cm) wide.
£360–400
€540–600
$670–750 ⊞ MB

A du Maurier Filter Cigarettes poster, by Greenberg, 1960, framed and glazed, 27½ x 19¾in (70 x 50cm).
£85–100 / €130–150
$160–185 ➤ DW

A Camel Filters poster, by Nick Price, 1975, 35 x 25½in (88.5 x 64.5cm).
£370–440 / €550–660
$690–820 ➤ VSP

Ashtrays

A Player's brass ashtray, 1920s, 4½in (11.5cm) square.
£30–35 / €45–50
$55–65 ⊞ BS

▶ **A brass ashtray,** from a cinema seat, 1920s–30s, 5in (12.5cm) wide.
£35–40 / €50–60
$65–75 ⊞ BS

A Fontana Arte glass ashtray, Italian, 1920s, 6in (15cm) wide.
£100–120 / €150–165
$185–210 ⊞ EMH

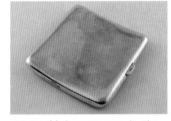

A ceramic Bonzo ashtray, 1920s–30s, 5in (12.5cm) wide.
£50–55 / €75–85
$95–105 ⊞ HYP

A silver smoking set, by The Goldsmith & Silversmiths Co, comprising four ashtrays and four vesta cases, 1936, in a presentation case.
£140–165 / €210–250
$260–310 ↗ SWO

Cigarette Cases

◀ **A silver cigarette case,** by Hermann Jurgens, Braunschweig, German, early 20thC, 5 x 3¼in (12.5 x 8.5cm).
£370–440
€550–660
$690–820
↗ SWO

A 9ct gold cigarette case, by The Goldsmiths & Goldsmiths Co, London 1918, 3½in (9cm) wide.
£220–260 / €330–390
$410–490 ↗ WW

A silver cigarette case, enamelled with a Persian cat, London 1926.
£360–430 / €540–650
$670–800 ↗ LAY

A silver cigarette case, by 'A. B', repoussé-decorated with three horses, marked, Moscow 1930, 4¾in (12cm) wide.
£480–570 / €720–860
$900–1,050 ↗ S(O)

A metal cigarette case, hand-painted with a fairy, 1930, 3½in (9cm) wide.
£125–140 / €190–210
$230–260 ⊞ LBe

A plastic cigarette case, 1930s–40s, 5 x 3in (12.5 x 7.5cm).
£10–15 / €15–22
$19–28 ⊞ RTT

Cigarette Packets & Tins

◀ **A Dandy Fifth Cigarettes packet,** by Salmon & Gluckstein, 1902, 9½in (24cm) wide.
£40–45 / €60–70
$75–85 ⊞ CPCC

A KK Tabak-Regie Cigarettes tin, 1910, 3¾in (9.5cm) high.
£70–80 / €105–120
$130–150 ⊞ HUX

A Pioneer Cigarettes packet, by Hignett Bros & Co, 1919, 1½in (4cm) wide.
£35–40 / €50–60
$65–75 ⊞ CPCC

A Three Nuns Tobacco sample tin, with match holder and striker, 1920s, 2in (5cm) wide.
£20–25 / €30–35
$35–45 ⊞ HUX

▶ **A packet of five W. D. & H. O. Wills Wild Woodbine Cigarettes,** 1920s, 3in (7.5cm) high.
£30–35 / €45–50
$55–65 ⊞ HUX

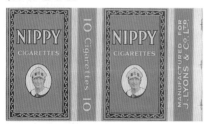

An Associated Tobacco Manufacturers Master Mariner Cigarettes packet, 1930, 1¾in (4.5cm) wide.
£25–30 / €40–45
$50–55 ⊞ CPCC

A Cope's Checkmate Cigarettes packet, c1930, 1¾in (4.5cm) wide.
£25–30 / €40–45
$50–55 ⊞ CPCC

▶ **A W. D. & H. O. Wills Capstan Navy Cut Cigarettes shop display packet,** 1930s, 12in (30.5cm) high.
£90–100 / €135–150
$170–190 ⊞ AAA

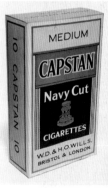

A Nippy Cigarettes packet, for J. Lyons & Co, c1940, 1¾in (4.5cm) wide.
£20–25 / €30–35
$35–45 ⊞ CPCC

▶ **An A. & M. Wix Max Virginia Cigarettes packet,** 1952, 3¼in (8.5cm) wide.
£8–12 / €12–18
$15–22 ⊞ CPCC

Lighters

A *faux* crocodile skin table cigarette lighter, c1930, 4in (10cm) high.
£70–80 / €105–120
$130–150 ⊞ JUN

◀ A cigarette lighter, in the form of a bust of Winston Churchill, signed 'Tallent', 1939–45, 8½in (21.5cm) high.
£200–230 / €300–350
$370–430 ⊞ Tus
The head of the bust would have been filled with cotton wadding, which was soaked in lighter fuel through a metal screw-cap in the back. The cigar is removed and struck against the flint set in the front of the base.

A silver-plated and leather Dunhill Unique petrol table lighter, marked, 1940s, 4in (10cm) high.
£100–120 / €150–180
$185–220 ➶ G(L)

▶ A metal lighter, in the form of a bulldozer, c1950, 6in (15cm) wide.
£30–35
€45–50
$55–65 ⊞ JUN

▶ A chrome lighter, in the form of a pistol, c1960, 2in (5cm) wide.
£25–30
€40–45
$50–55 ⊞ JUN

Sport

A cast-iron dumbell, 19thC, 14in (35.5cm) wide.
£75–85 / €115–130
$140–160 ⊞ BS

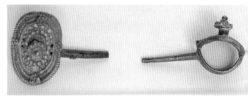

A pair of metal toe spurs, for camel racing, c1900,
3in (7.5cm) wide.
£30–35 / €45–50
$55–65 ⊞ SA

A pair of wooden ping-pong bats, c1910,
13in (33cm) long.
£25–30 / €40–45
$50–55 ⊞ SA

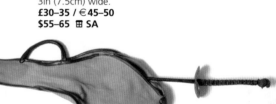

A metal fencing sword, with a case, c1910, 41in (104cm) long.
£45–50 / €70–80
$85–95 ⊞ SA

A white metal cruet set, in the
form of curling stones, c1910,
3in (7.5cm) diam.
£40–45 / €60–70
$75–85 ⊞ SA

▶ **A Slazenger shuttlecock
container,** c1920, 16in (40.5cm) high.
£30–35 / €45–50
$55–65 ⊞ SA

A photograph of a lacrosse team,
1910–20, 12in (30.5cm) wide.
£35–40 / €50–60
$65–75 ⊞ SA

A curling stone, c1920,
11in (30cm) diam.
£85–95 / €130–145
$160–180 ⊞ SA

◀ **A wood and brass croquet
mallet,** c1920, 34in (86.5cm) long.
£45–50 / €70–80
$85–95 ⊞ SA

A velvet sports cap, decorated with
a rose and the initials Y. H. A., boxed,
1928–29, together with a cloth badge.
£35–40 / €50–60
$65–75 ⋗ G(L)

A leather rugby ball, 1920s.
£30–35 / €45–50
$55–65 ⊞ MINN

A pair of leather roller skates, c1930.
£25–30 / €40–45
$50–55 ⊞ SA

A Terry wrist grip,
1950s, boxed, 8 x 5½in
(20.5 x 14cm).
£15–20 / €22–30
$28–38 ⊞ RTT

A souvenir booklet, for
the third Winter Olympic
Games at Lake Placid, New
York, damaged, 1932,
11¾ x 8½in (30 x 21cm).
£110–130 / €165–195
$210–240 ➤ VS

◀ A lacrosse racket,
c1950, 43in (109cm) long.
£15–20 / €22–30
$28–38 ⊞ SA

▶ A fencing mask,
1950s, 12in (30.5cm) long.
£10–15 / €15–22
$19–28 ⊞ AL

An opening ceremony
programme, for the 1948
Olympics, London, signed
by Doug Harris, 1948,
11 x 8½in (28 x 21.5cm).
£35–40 / €50–60
$65–75 ➤ VS

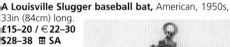

A Louisville Slugger baseball bat, American, 1950s,
33in (84cm) long.
£15–20 / €22–30
$28–38 ⊞ SA

▶ A set of
presentation
darts medals,
1960s, largest
1½in (3cm) wide.
£5–9 / €8–13
$10–16 each
⊞ MRW

◀ An Adidas
plastic sports
bag, 1970s,
22in (60 cm) wide.
£25–30
€40–45
$50–55 ⊞ TWI

Billiards & Snooker

◀ **A Victorian mahogany snooker and billiard scoreboard,** with brass fittings, 34in (86.5cm) wide.
£270–300 / €400–450
$500–560 ⊞ SAT

A metal billiards trophy tankard, 1868, 8in (20.5cm) high.
£90–100 / €135–150
$170–190 ⊞ SA

A Salter billiard table iron and cover, c1900, 12in (30.5cm) wide.
£110–125 / €165–190
$210–230 ⊞ BS

A pair of prints, by L. Thackeray, 'Kissing' and 'Snookered', 1902, image 4¾ x 6¼in (12 x 16cm).
£70–80 / €105–120
$130–150 ⋟ DW

A wood and metal cue holder, c1910, 8in (20.5cm) wide.
£30–35 / €45–50
$55–65 ⊞ SA

▶ **A Billiards and Snooker brochure,** issued by William Sykes Ltd, 1938–39, 8 x 10in (20.5 x 25.5cm).
£25–30 / €40–45
$50–55 ⋟ VS

Boxing

A mezzotint of Richard Humphreys, by Young, published by H. W. Billington, 1788, 21¾ x 16½in (55 x 42cm).
£360–420 / €540–630
$670–790 ⋟ BUDD

▶ **A cameo,** commemorating the 19thC boxer Tom Sayers, carved with a portrait and an inscription, 1856, 3¾in (9.5cm) long.
£700–840 / €1,050–1,250
$1,300–1,500 ⋟ BUDD
Tom Sayers was born at Pimlico, London, on 25 May 1826. He was one of England's most renowned champions and was particularly famed for his first international white heavyweight title bout with John C. Heenan in 1860.

LOCATE THE SOURCE
The source of each illustration in Miller's can be found by checking the code letters below each caption with the Key to Illustrations, pages 443–451.

◀ **A Gray's Pottery tobacco jar and cover,** printed with a vignette of Tom Spring and Jack Langan, early 20thC, 6in (15cm) high.
£210–250
€320–380
$390–470 ⋟ VS

A signed postcard, depicting Jack Johnson, c1914.
£820–980 / €1,250–1,300
$1,550–1,650 ⚹ DW
This is a very rare signature. Jack Johnson defeated Tommy Burns in 1908 to become the world's first African-American heavyweight champion. After an inter-racial marriage and his defeat of several white hopefuls, Johnson was convicted in 1913 under contrived circumstances for violation of a federal law. He fled to Europe and remained a champion in exile until he lost in 1915 to Jess Willard in Cuba.

A set of boxing medals, badges, army service medals and cup, 1937.
£1,750–1,950 / €2,650–2,950
$3,250–3,650 ⊞ ABCM
These boxing medals were won by Winston Churchill's bodyguard, Lance Bombardier G. Preston.

Cross Reference
Medals & Tokens
see pages 286–290

A pair of leather boxing shoes, 1950s.
£25–30 / €40–45
$50–55 ⊞ SA

A pair of leather sparring gloves, c1950.
£25–30 / €40–45
$50–55 ⊞ SA

A cheque, signed by Rocky Marciano, mounted with a photograph, 1966, 16 x 11¾in (40.5 x 30cm).
£200–240 / €300–360
$370–450 ⚹ BUDD

A Muhammad Ali Rope-A-Dope jump rope, American, 1980s, boxed, 9in (23cm) wide.
£70–80 / €105–120
$130–150 ⊞ IQ

Cricket

A Staffordshire figure of a cricketer, mid-19thC, 10¼in (26cm) high.
£550–660 / €830–990
$1,050–1,250 ⚹ BUDD

John Lawrence, *Handbook Of Cricket,* repaired, Irish, 1869–70, 8¼ x 5½in (210 x 148cm).
£100–120 / €150–180
$185–220 ⚹ VS

▶ **A *Vanity Fair* cartoon,** by 'Spy', depicting William Gilbert Grace, entitled 'Cricket', 1877.
£280–330 / €420–500
$520–620 ⚹ DW
'Spy' was the pseudonym of the artist Sir Leslie Ward.

◀ **A Doulton Lambeth tyg,** with raised decoration of cricketers, slight damage, marked, 1880, 5¾in (14.5cm) high.
£880–1,050
€1,300–1,600
$1,650–1,950 ⚹ VS

William Gilbert Grace, a signed letter, declining an invitation to play a cricket match, 1889, 8°.
£280–330 / €420–500
$520–620 ✗ DW

A water jug, with raised decoration of William Clark, Fuller Pilch and Thomas Box, 1880s, 7in (18cm) high.
£1,850–2,200
€2,800–3,300
$3,450–4,100 ✗ VS

◄ **A Coalport plate,** commemorating William Gilbert Grace, 1895, 9in (23cm) diam.
£900–1,050
€1,350–1,600
$1,700–1,950
✗ SAS

A Baines card, depicting a cricketing scene and Lord Hawke, 1890s, 3in (7.5cm) high.
£30–35 / €45–50
$55–65 ✗ VS

A pair of cricket pads, 1900, 26in (66cm) high.
£90–100 / €135–150
$170–190 ⊞ SA

Athletic News Cricket Annual, I, 1901, 6 x 4in (15 x 10cm).
£40–45 / €60–70
$75–85 ✗ VS

A pottery mug, commemorating Herbert Sutcliffe, with printed decoration, slight damage, 1925, 4in (10cm) high.
£380–450 / €570–680
$710–840 ✗ SAS

► **A Parry's Cigarettes tin,** depicting a cricket game, 1930s, 3 x 4in (7.5 x 10cm).
£85–100
€130–150
$160–185
✗ VS

Cross Reference
Commemorative Ware see pages 177–185

A Minton pottery mug, commemorating 150 years of the MCC, with printed decoration, 1937, 4in (10cm) high.
£20–25 / €30–35
$35–45 ✗ SAS

An Ashes souvenir booklet, by W. A. Cricket Association, England v. Australia, 1946, 8 x 5in (20.5 x 12.5cm).
£35–40 / €50–60
$65–75 ✗ VS

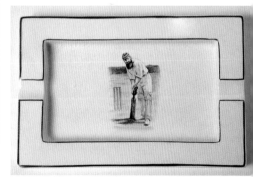

A Sandland ashtray, depicting William Gilbert Grace, 1950s, 9in (23cm) wide.
£55–65 / €85–100
$100–120 ✗ VS

Fishing

A porcelain tea cup and saucer, decorated with a girl fishing by a lake, early 19thC.
£90–105 / € 135–155 $170–195 ⋟ MUL

T. F. Salter, *The Angler's Guide*, third edition, wood-engraved frontispiece, 1 plate, illustrations, 1823, 4pp.
£70–80 / € 105–120 $130–150 ⋟ BBA

A Victorian glass goblet, engraved with a fisherman on a river bank, 3¾in (9.5cm) high.
£180–210 / € 270–320 $330–390 ⋟ AH

A mug, transfer-printed with a fishing scene, inscribed 'Fishing Party', 1860–80, 3in (7.5cm) high.
£50–60 / € 75–90 $95–110 ⊞ SA

▶ **Joseph Crawhall,** *Izaak Walton: His Wallet Booke,* hand-coloured illustrations by Crawhall, printed by the Leadenhall Press, 1885, 8°.
£75–85 / € 115–130 $140–160 ⋟ BBA

Dr Robert Knox, *Fish & Fishing in the Lone Glens of Scotland,* first edition, engraved title vignette, illustrations, later cloth, 1854.
£90–105 / € 135–155 $170–195 ⋟ BBA

▶ **A brass fishing reel,** c1890, 3in (7.5cm) wide.
£45–50 / € 70–80 $85–95 ⊞ SA

◀ **A Hardy wood and brass line winder,** c1900, 12in (30.5cm) wide.
£450–500 € 680–750 $840–940 ⊞ MSh

A Star & Planet salmon fly reel, with a horn handle, brass face and nickel rim, c1900, 5in (12.5cm) diam, with original leather case.
£310–350 / €470–530
$580–650 ⊞ MSh

A late Victorian stuffed and mounted trout, by J. Cooper, in a bowfronted glazed case, trout 23in (58.5cm) long.
£300–360 / €450–540
$560–670 ✗ NSal

An iron spear, c1900, 5½in (14cm) wide.
£25–30 / €40–45
$50–55 ⊞ OTB
This spear would have been used by river keepers to remove pike from trout waters.

A stuffed and mounted sea trout, by Williams & Son, in an ebonized case, inscribed 'This fish weighing 7lbs was caught on 20 August 1903 by J. N. Hartsmith-Pearce, County Mayo, Ireland', case 31¾in (80.5cm) wide.
£350–420 / €530–630
$650–790 ✗ G(L)

John James Hardy, *Salmon Fishing,* first edition, with black and white illustrations, slight damage, 1907.
£70–80 / €105–120
$130–150 ✗ MUL

◀ **Three Norwich spoon lures,** with glass eyes and engraved decoration, c1910, largest 3in (7.5cm) long.
£10–15 / €15–22
$19–28 ⊞ OTB

Three tins, J. Bernard & Son, Hardy Brothers and Kennedy, 1910–30, largest 1½in (4cm) wide.
£10–15 / €15–22
$19–28 each ⊞ OTB

A wood and brass gaff, c1920, 21in (53.5cm) long.
£55–65 / €85–100
$100–120 ⊞ SA

An Archer revolving fly box,
c1920, 4½in (11.5cm) diam.
£40–45 / €60–70
$75–85 ⊞ SA

A bottle of Army & Navy rod varnish,
c1920, 3in (7.5cm) high.
£35–40 / €50–60
$65–75 ⊞ OTB

A Hardy fishing reminder list, c1920,
4½in (11.5cm) high.
£25–30 / €40–45
$50–55 ⊞ OTB

▶ **Walter Shaw Sparrow,** *Angling in British
Art Through Five Centuries: Prints, Pictures,
Books,* first edition, foreword by H. T.
Sheringham, with 200 illustrations, 1923.
£100–120 / €150–180
$185–220 ⋩ MUL

Zane Grey, *Tales of the
Angler's Eldorado New
Zealand,* first edition,
photographic plates,
illustrations, original cloth,
1926, 4°.
£170–200 / €260–300
$320–370 ⋩ BBA

**A Hardy brass and steel
line winder,** 1920s,
10in (25.5cm) wide.
£340–380 / €510–570
$640–710 ⊞ MSh

A fishing creel, c1930,
13in (33cm) wide.
£70–80 / €105–120
$130–150 ⊞ SA

◀ **A wood and brass
fishing reel,** c1930,
6in (15cm) diam.
£45–50 / €70–80
$85–95 ⊞ SA

A Hardy Hotspur steel collapsible line drier, with table clamp, c1930, in original cardboard box, 7½in (19cm) wide.
£35–40 / €50–60
$65–75 ⊞ OTB

A Hardy NAAF fishing rod, in canvas case, c1930, 30in (76cm) long.
£180–200 / €270–300
$330–370 ⊞ SA

Two tin fly boxes, 1930–50, larger 5in (12.5cm) wide.
£25–30 / €40–45
$50–55 ⊞ SA

A Hardy St George trout fly reel, with a brass foot and nickel line guide, with later latch, 1930–55, 3¾in (9.5cm) wide.
£100–120 / €150–180
$185–220 ⊞ OTB

A Hardy steel pipe reamer, 1930s, 2½in (6.5cm) long.
£55–65 / €85–100
$100–120 ⊞ OTB
This pipe reamer would have been sold as an accompaniment to Hardy's Angler's & Sportsman's Pipe.

▶ **A horn fishing priest,** c1950, 6in (15cm) high.
£15–20 / €22–30
$28–38 ⊞ SA

Robert Bruce Lockhart, *My Rod My Comfort,* limited edition, illustrated, 1949.
£80–95 / €120–145
$150–180 ↗ MUL

A Hardy St John trout salmon fly reel, with a two-screw drum release latch, c1955, 3¾in (9.5cm) diam.
£45–50 / €70–80
$85–95 ⊞ OTB

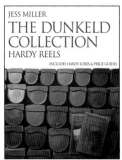

Richard Walker, *Still Water Angling,* second edition, damaged, 1955.
£25–30 / €40–45
$50–55 ↗ MUL

A metal bread bait press, 1950s, 2in (5cm) high.
£15–20 / €22–30
$28–38 ⊞ SA

Football

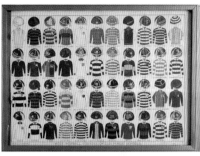

A Britannia FA Cup Winners mug, decorated with a Nottingham County footballer, 1894, 4in (10cm) high.
£300–360 / €450–540
$560–670 ⚲ VS

A *Boy's Own Paper* poster, depicting public school football strip colours, 1900–10, 11 x 15in (28 x 38cm), framed.
£35–40 / €50–60
$65–75 ⊞ SA

Athletic News Football Annual, 1903–04, 6 x 4in (15 x 10cm).
£180–210 / €270–320
$330–390 ⚲ VS

A postcard of Newcastle Football Club, showing players, directors and officials, 1908.
£65–75 / €100–115
$120–140 ⚲ DAL

Alfred Gibson and William Pickford, *Association Football*, published by Caxton Publishing Co, cover by John Hassall, c1905, 10 x 7in (25.5 x 18cm).
£140–165 / €210–250
$260–310 ⚲ VS

A Bristol Porcelain & Glass Co pottery plate, by G. J. Kepple, with records and final league table of the 1st Division of the Football Association English League, and a vignette of the FA cup, 1906–7, 10in (25.5cm) wide.
£900–1,050 / €1,350–1,600
$1,700–1,950 ⚲ VS

◄ **A football programme,** Charlton Athletic v. Northampton, staples missing, 1923, 11 x 8in (28 x 20.5 cm).
£260–310
€390–470
$490–580
⚲ VS

A football programme, Nottingham Forest v. Reading, slight damage, 1927, 10 x 8in (25.5 x 20.5 cm).
£280–330 / €420–500
$520–620 ⚲ VS

A Birmingham City cotton handkerchief, printed with a photograph of the FA Cup Final team, players' names and match results, 1931, 15in (38cm) square.
£30–35 / €45–50
$55–65 ⚲ VS

► **An FA Cup Final programme,** Portsmouth v. Manchester City, with printed wrappers, cover detached, 1934, 8°.
£240–280
€360–420
$450–520
⚲ DW

A football programme, Watford v. Brighton & Hove, 1937, 10 x 7in (25.5 x 18cm).
£140–165 / €210–250
$260–310 ✗ VS

A Tipp-Kick game, by Mieg, German, 1930s, 19in (48.5cm) long.
£80–95 / €120–145
$135–180 ✗ VS

A photograph of Arsenal FC, by Lambert Jackson, with printed titles and players' names, 1947–48, 10 x 12in (25.5 x 30.5cm).
£80–95 / €120–145
$150–180 ✗ VS

A metal medal, inscribed 'British Army XI v. Canadian Army Xi, Central Ground, Aldershot, VE-Day 1945', 1½in (4cm) diam.
£110–130 / €165–195
$200–240 ✗ VS

▶ **A pair of leather football boots,** c1950.
£65–75 / €100–115
$120–140 ⊞ SA

An FA Cup Final programme, Charlton Athletic v. Derby County, 1946, 8 x 5in (20.5 x 12.5cm).
£150–180 / €230–270
$280–330 ✗ VS

Two FA Cup Final programmes, Burnley v. Charlton Athletic 1947 and Arsenal v. Liverpool 1950, damaged and repaired, 8 x 5in (20.5 x 12.5cm).
£100–120 / €150–180
$185–220 ✗ VS

◀ **An FA Cup Final programme,** Blackpool v. Newcastle, 1951, 10 x 7in (25.5 x 18cm).
£25–30 / €40–45
$50–55 ✗ VS

A European Cup Semi-Final programme, Tottenham v. Benfica (Portugal), 1962, 9in (23cm) high.
£1–5 / €2–7
$3–9 ⊞ MRW

▶ **A European Cup Semi-Final pennant,** Manchester United v. A.C. Milan, 1969, 10 x 7in (25.5 x 18cm).
£10–15 / €15–22
$19–28 ⊞ EE

A pair of plastic Bull Boys shin guards, signed by Alan Hansen, 1980s, 11in (28cm) high.
£1–5 / €2–7
$3–9 ⊞ IQ

Golf

A Pater Paxton long-nosed Musselburgh putter, with a beech head, stamped mark, c1880, 36in (91.5cm) long.
**£350–420 / €530–630
$660–790 ⚹ BUDD**

▶ **A Staffordshire plate,** transfer-printed with a golfing scene, inscribed 'Full Swing', c1910, 9in (23cm) diam.
**£110–130 / €165–195
$200–240 ⚹ SWO**

A silver-mounted leather card wallet, by L. & S., decorated with a golfer, Birmingham 1905, 4¼in (11cm) high.
**£300–360 / €450–540
$560–670 ⚹ G(L)**

▶ **A set of six postcards,** depicting golfing scenes, series No. 710, published by Langsdorf & Co, c1908.
**£100–120
€150–180
$185–220
⚹ SWO**

An Auchterlonie putter, c1920.
**£75–85 / €115–130
$140–160 ⊞ MSh**

A jardinière, decorated with a golfing scene, restored, 1920s, 8¾in (22cm) high.
**£390–460 / €590–690
$730–860 ⚹ Pott**

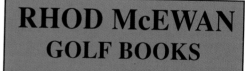

A canvas golf bag, with automatic stand, 1920s, 34in (86.5cm) long.
**£100–120 / €150–180
$185–220 ⊞ MSh**

A Gibson Kinghorn Dominie putter, 1920s, 35in (89cm) long.
**£60–70 / €90–105
$110–130 ⊞ MINN**

A pair of cufflinks and a tie bar, hand-painted with golfers, late 1950s.
**£55–65 / €85–100
$100–120 ⊞ CAD**

Horses & Riding

A Georgian mahogany boot rack,
34in (86.5cm) wide.
£270–320 / € 400–480
$500–600 ≯ BWL

A cotton handkerchief, printed
with Tom Loates riding Donovan,
Derby winner 1889, framed and
glazed, 13½in (34.5cm) square.
£70–80 / € 105–120
$130–150 ≯ VS

An oak crop rack, in the form of a
horseshoe, late 19thC,
16in (40.5cm) high.
£320–360 / € 480–540
$600–670 ⊞ RGA

◀ **A bull's pizzle
riding crop,** with
an antler handle,
c1900, 30in
(76cm) long.
£60–70
€ 990–105
$110–130
⊞ GBr

A stud record book, for Baron
Alfons Rothschild's stud at Oroszvar,
Budapest, 1906–22, 4°, together
with related ephemera.
£700–840 / € 1,050–1,250
$1,300–1,550 ≯ DW
**Baron Rothschild's stud was one
of the major thoroughbred
racehorse studs in Eastern
Europe in the early part of the
20th century.**

A polo hat, 1920–30.
£65–75 / € 100–115
$120–140 ⊞ SA

A silver Chester Vase trophy,
on an onyx plinth, Sheffield 1923,
10in (25.5cm) high.
£200–240 / € 300–360
$380–450 ≯ SWO

◀ **A pair of leather riding
boots,** 1930s.
£135–150 / € 200–230
$250–280 ⊞ JUN

A Seton Pottery water jug,
depicting Grand National winner
Miinnehoma, 1994, 6in (15cm) high.
£40–45 / € 60–70
$75–85 ≯ VS

Tennis

A pair of glass negative plates, depicting lawn tennis matches, c1880, 4¾ x 6½in (12 x 16.5cm).
£400–480 / €600–720
$750–900 ➢ BUDD

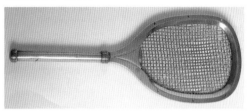

A Victorian terracotta figure of a female tennis player, model No. 186, signed 'W. C. Lawton', impressed marks, 8½in (21.5cm) high.
£45–50 / €70–80
$85–95 ➢ G(L)

A Staffordshire figure of a tennis player, c1880, 8in (20.5cm) high.
£55–65 / €85–100
$100–120 ⊞ SA

A brass tennis racket, c1890, 12in (30.5cm) long.
£155–175 / €230–260
$290–330 ⊞ SA

A Davis Cup souvenir booklet, 1913, 8°.
£180–210 / €270–320
$330–390 ➢ DW

A mahogany tennis racket press, with brass mounts, c1900, 14in (35.5cm) long.
£95–110 / €140–165
$175–210 ➢ COBB

◄ **A print,** depicting women playing tennis, entitled 'London Life', c1930, 12in (30.5cm) high.
£10–15 / €15–22
$19–28 ⊞ SA

A wooden tennis racket, c1930, 27in (68.5cm) long.
£75–85 / €115–130
$140–160 ⊞ SA
The groove in the handle of this racket was designed to enable sweat to run off the hand.

A ceramic plate, with printed decoration, inscribed 'Le Tennis', c1920, 7in (18cm) diam.
£65–75 / €100–115
$120–140 ⊞ SA

Teddy Bears & Soft Toys

A Merrythought Panda, 1938, 24in (61cm) high.
£360–400 / €540–600
$670–750 ⊞ POLL

A Chiltern walker, 1940s, 24in (61cm) high.
£145–165 / €220–250
$270–310 ⊞ POLL

A golly, 1940s–50s, 11in (28cm) high.
£35–40 / €50–60
$65–75 ⊞ LAS

A Chad Valley teddy bear, with glass eyes, jointed body and velvet pads, c1950, 23in (58.5cm) high.
£220–260 / €330–390
$410–490 ⋏ G(L)

A Merrythought Cheshire cat, c1950, 8in (20.5cm) high.
£25–30 / €40–45
$50–55 ⊞ UD

A Chiltern mohair teddy bear, with glass eyes, 1950s, 14in (35.5cm) high.
£270–300 / €400–450
$500–560 ⊞ BBe

A Chad Valley mohair teddy bear, with plastic eyes and velvet pads, 1950s, 22in (56cm) high.
£360–400 / €540–600
$670–750 ⊞ BBe

A Merrythought velvet bendy Noddy, 1950s, 14in (35.5cm) high.
£270–300 / €400–450
$500–560 ⊞ BBe

A Steiff tiger, 1950s, German, 33in (84cm) long, together with a miniature version.
£60–70 / €90–105
$110–130 ⋏ LAY

▶ **A Gebrüder Hermann mohair teddy bear,** with glass eyes, felt pads repaired, German, 1950s, 13in (33cm) high.
£85–95 / €130–145
$160–180 ⊞ BBe

A plush Bugs Bunny, 1950s, 20in (51cm) high.
£25–30 / €40–45
$50–55 ⊞ LAS

◀ **A Fechter Zotty-style mohair teddy bear,** with plastic eyes and original label, Austrian, 1950s, 12in (30.5cm) high.
£100–115
€150–175
$185–210 ⊞ BBe

▶ **A Wendy Boston Sweep,** late 1950s, 12in (30.5cm) high.
£75–85
€115–130
$140–160 ⊞ LAS

▶ **A Merrythought nylon Cheeky bear,** with plastic eyes, late 1950s, 8in (20.5cm) high.
£360–400 / €540–600
$670–750 ⊞ BBe
Introduced in 1957, Cheeky was a successful design for Merrythought and was produced in a number of different sizes and materials. Distinguishing features included large ears containing bells, an embroidered nose, a cheeky grin on the velvet muzzle and the Merrythought label on the footpad. The pads were made of felt and often had to be replaced over the years, resulting in the loss of the label.

A Steiff Zotty mohair teddy bear, with glass eyes and ear tag, German, 1950s–60s, 10in (25.5cm) high.
£140–155 / €200–230
$260–290 ⊞ BBe
Zotty bears were developed by Steiff from c1951. Bears were made in brown and caramel-coloured mohair with white tips and had a peach-coloured mohair chest. Many other factories produced Zotty-style bears.

A Gabrielle Designs Paddington Bear, by Shirley Clarkson, with felt hat and coat and Dunlop Wellington boots, 1970s, 19in (48.5cm) high.
£85–95 / €130–145
$160–180 BBe

Paddington Bear

Paddington Bear, born in darkest Peru and named after the famous London station, came to fame in 1958 when Michael Bond wrote *A Bear called Paddington*. The character was based on a teddy bear that Bond had bought for his wife from Selfridges department store, London, in 1956. The bear was given a hat and a duffel coat, although the famous wellingtons did not appear in the stories until after Shirley Clarkson (mother of television presenter Jeremy Clarkson) had given her soft toy Paddington a pair of wellingtons. As well as books (including 11 novels and two collections of short stories), Paddington appeared on stage, radio and television, and the animated puppet television series launched in 1975 was sold across the world, bringing Paddington an international following. A host of merchandising celebrated the marmalade-loving bear and Gabrielle Designs produced the first soft toy Paddington in 1972. From 1975, Eden Toys Inc, New York, held the licence for manufacturing soft toy Paddingtons outside the UK, but unlike the British bears, their Paddington did not have a safety pin in the hat due to health and safety regulations.

◄ **A James Blackmore Guinness toucan,** with original labels, 1980, 20in (51cm) high.
£55–65 / €85–100
$100–120 POLL

A House of Nisbet mohair Aloysius bear, edition of 5,000, 1980s, 13in (33cm) high.
£175–195 / €260–290
$330–370 BBe
Aloysius was the teddy bear that belonged to Sebastian Flyte in Evelyn Waugh's famous novel *Brideshead Revisited.* When Granada Television produced their TV adaptation in 1981 they needed a suitably ancient bear to play Sebastian's (actor Anthony Andrews) companion. Fellow actor and bear collector Peter Bull provided them with Delicatessen, an American teddy produced c1907 by the Ideal Toy Co, which had languished for some 50 years on the shelf of a dry goods store and delicatessen in Maine before being given to Bull by its owner. Renamed Aloysius, the teddy bear was seen around the world. In the 1980s, the House of Nisbet produced a copy of Aloysius complete with replica of the Daks of Simpson scarf given to the bear by Anthony Andrew's wife. The Nisbet bear is made from mohair plush, and the unusual chamois leather patches on the pads are modelled on those of the original 1907 bear. Look out for the label on the pad.

A nylon Automobile Association advertising bear, 1990s, 14in (35.5cm) high.
£25–30 / €40–45
$50–55 COB

◄ **A Marvel plush Spiderman,** 2002, 15in (38cm) high.
£6–10 / €9–15
$12–19 CoC

Telephones

A Bakelite and brass candlestick telephone, 1920s, 12in (30.5cm) high.
£155–175 / €230–260
$290–330 ⊞ JUN

▶ **A Meccano telephone,** with white Bakelite extension buttons, late 1930s.
£420–500 / €630–750
$780–930 ✗ VEC
This telephone is from the Meccano office. Its value lies in the fact that it is a piece of memorabilia for Meccano enthusiasts.

A Weidman wall telephone, Swiss, 1930, 8in (20.5cm) wide.
£135–150 / €200–230
$250–280 ⊞ SAT

An Automatic Telephone System booklet, with inserts, 1938, 7½ x 5in (19 x 12.5cm).
£6–10 / €9–15
$12–19 ⊞ RTT

An Ericsson mahogany and brass wall telephone, with twin bells and a Bakelite handset, 1930s, 30in (76cm) high.
£180–210 / €270–320
$330–390 ✗ G(L)

◀ **An automatic electric monophone,** 1940.
£240–280 / €360–420
$450–520 ✗ S(P)

A metal Gurda telephone, with a Bakelite handset, decorated with gold leaf, Belgian, 1940s, 9in (23cm) wide.
£110–125 / € 165–185
$200–230 ⊞ DHAR

A Bakelite 300 series telephone, with chrome dial and cheese drawer, fully converted, 1940s, 6in (15cm) wide.
£120–135 / € 180–200
$220–250 ⊞ TASV

A cast-iron Teapot telephone, with a Bakelite handset, brass dial and lifting handle, decorated with gold leaf, Belgian, 1940s, 9in (23cm) wide.
£145–165 / € 220–250
$270–310 ⊞ DHAR

A Bakelite 300 series telephone, 1940s–50s, 9in (23cm) wide.
£180–200 / € 270–300
$330–370 ⊞ JAZZ
The 300 phone was designed by Norwegian artist Jean Heiberg (1884–1976) for the Swedish company L. M. Ericsson.

◀ **An Ericsson acrylic Ericofon telephone,** Swedish, 1970s, 8in (20.5cm) high.
£85–95 / € 130–145
$160–180 ⊞ HSR
Familiarly known as the Cobra, this famous one-piece telephone was produced by L. M. Ericsson in Sweden and became a success when it was launched in a wide range of colours in 1954.

◀ **An Allied Telecommunications Equipment Co plastic Superman telephone,** French, 1981, 18½in (47cm) high.
£800–960 / € 1,200–1,400
$1,500–1,800 ⚲ S(P)
This is a very rare telephone, hence its high value.

▶ **A plastic two-piece Alien telephone,** with last number recall, early 1990s, 15¾in (40cm) diam.
£35–40
€ 50–60
$65–75 ⊞ TL

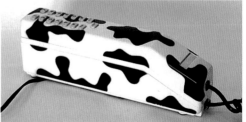

A plastic cow telephone, with 10-number memory, tone/pulse and redial, flashes when rings, early 1990s, 11¾in (30cm) wide.
£10–15 / € 15–22
$19–28 ⊞ TL

Theatre

This new feature is devoted to theatrical memorabilia. Material includes programmes, brochures, posters and flyers. While much of this ephemera can be picked up very affordably, prices are affected by rarity. Memorabilia relating to a famous long-running West End or Broadway show is likely to be less valuable than that deriving from a short provincial run or an infamous flop. Some actors and performers are more collected than others (particularly if they have also found fame in Hollywood movies), and artwork by a well-known artist can also add interest. Certain plays or productions are particularly sought after and this year we include a special section devoted to Peter Pan.

An ivory theatre pass, for the Theatre Royal, Haymarket, London, 1797, 1½in (4cm) diam.
£400–450 / €600–680
$750–840 ⊞ TML
Ivory and metal passes were issued to frequent theatre patrons for admission to their regular box or seat. They could be engraved both with the name of the theatre and the audience member. Famous individuals command a premium and these rare tokens are very collectable.

◄ **A silver theatre pit pass,** for the Royal Liver Theatre, Liverpool, c1800, 1¾in (4.5cm) diam.
£580–650
€870–970
$1,050–1,200
⊞ TML

A coloured illustration, Miss Ellis Jeffreys in *The Sacrament of Judas*, c1900, 10 x 8in (25.5 x 20.5cm).
£1–5 / €2–7
$3–9 ⊞ POS

A menu front, for the Playgoers Club 22nd Annual Dinner, designed by S. H. Sime, signed by Sime and other club members, 1906, mounted, framed and glazed, 8 x 7½in (20.5 x 19cm).
£50–55 / €75–85
$95–105 ➶ NSal

◄ **A theatre programme,** for *The Girl Friend*, Theatre Royal, Chatham, Kent, 1923, 9¾ x 5¼in (25 x 13.5cm).
£3–7 / €4–10
$6–13 ⊞ c20th
Theatrical memorabilia can also appeal to local history enthusiasts, and the photograph on the cover gives this programme added interest.

A theatre programme, for the Empire Theatre, 1922, 8¼ x 5½in (21 x 14cm).
£6–10 / €9–15
$12–19 ⊞ c20th

A theatre programme, for *Lady be Good*, featuring Fred and Adele Astaire, Empire Theatre, 1926, 8½in x 5½in (21.5 x 14cm).
£15–20 / €22–30
$28–38 ⊞ c20th

◄ **A theatre programme,** for *Conversation Piece*, His Majesty's Theatre, London, 1934, 8½ x 5½in (21.5 x 14cm).
£10–15 / €15–22
$19–28 ⊞ CAST

A theatre programme, for *A Kingdom for a Cow*, Savoy Theatre, London, 1935, 8¼ x 5½in (21 x 14cm).
£15–20 / €22–30
$28–38 ⊞ c20th
This Kurt Weill musical was not a success.

A theatre poster, advertising *Call Me Madam* by Irving Berlin, Coliseum Theatre, London, 1952, 19¾ x 12½in (50 x 32cm).
£50–60 / €85–90
$100–110 ⊞ c20th

◄ A theatre flyer, advertising *My Fair Lady*, starring Julie Andrews and Rex Harrison, Theatre Royal, London, 1958, 8 x 5in (20.5 x 12.5cm).
£25–30 / €40–45
$50–55 ⊞ c20th

► A promotional poster, by Barnett Freedman, 'Theatre – go by Underground', printed by Curwen Press, 1936, 40¼ x 50in (102 x 127cm).
£380–450 / €570–670
$710–840 ⋏ ONS

Two theatre programmes, both for Laurel & Hardy at the Bristol Hippodrome, 1947 and 1952, 10 x 8in (25.5 x 20.5cm).
£20–25 / €30–35
$35–45 each ⊞ J&S

A theatre poster, advertising *Dick Whittington*, starring George Formby, Palace Theatre, London, 1956, 19¾ x 12½in (50 x 32cm).
£70–80 / €105–120
$130–150 ⊞ c20th

Cross Reference
Posters see pages 313–315

A theatre poster, advertising *Twenty Minutes South*, St Martin's Theatre, London, 1955, 19¾ x 12½in (50 x 32cm).
£50–60 / €85–90
$100–110 ⊞ c20th

A theatre programme, for *Alice in Wonderland*, Winter Garden Theatre, London, 1959, 7¼ x 5in (18.5 x 12.5cm).
£10–15 / €15–22
$19–28 ⊞ CAST

A theatre flyer, advertising *Wild Thyme*, Duke of York's Theatre, London, artwork by Ronald Searle, 1955, 7¼ x 5in (18.5 x 12.5cm).
£20–25 / €30–35
$35–45 ⊞ c20th

A theatre flyer, advertising *One Over the Eight*, starring Kenneth Williams and Sheila Hancock, Duke of York's Theatre, London, 1961, 7¼ x 4¾in (18.5 x 12cm).
£25–30 / €40–45
$50–55 ⊞ c20th

Billy Bunter's
CHRISTMAS CIRCUS

A theatre programme, for *Billy Bunter's Christmas Circus*, Queen's Theatre, London, 1962, 9 x 6¾in (23 x 17cm).
£25–30 / €40–45
$50–55 ⊞ c20th

A theatre programme, for the musical *Twang* by Lionel Bart, 1965, 9¼ x 6½in (23.5 x 16.5cm).
£3–7 / €4–10
$6–13 ⊞ c20th
This musical was not a success.

A theatre poster, advertising *Cabaret*, starring Judi Dench, Palace Theatre, London, 1968, 19¾ x 12½in (50 x 32cm).
£50–60 / €85–90
$100–110 ⊞ c20th

A theatre flyer, advertising *The Threepenny Opera*, Piccadilly Theatre, London, artwork by David Hockney, 1972, 8 x 5in (20.5 x 12.5cm).
£35–40 / €50–60
$65–75 ⊞ c20th

A theatre brochure, for *Carry on London*, Victoria Palace, London, 1973, 11 x 9in (28 x 23cm).
£20–25 / €30–35
$35–45 ⊞ c20th

A theatre brochure, for *Jeeves*, by Alan Ayckbourn and Andrew Lloyd Webber, 1975, 11 x 8in (28 x 20.5cm).
£100–120 / €150–180
$185–220 ⊞ c20th

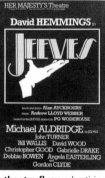

A theatre flyer, advertising *Jeeves*, starring David Hemmings, Her Majesty's Theatre, London, 1975, 8½ x 5½in (21.5 x 14cm).
£6–10 / €9–15
$12–19 ⊞ CAST

A theatre brochure, for the revue *Side by Side by Sondheim*, 1976, 11 x 8in (28 x 20.5cm).
£10–15 / €15–22
$19–28 ⊞ c20th

A theatre flyer, for the musical *Sweeney Todd*, Theatre Royal, London, 1980, 8½ x 5½in (21.5 x 14cm).
£6–10 / €9–15
$12–19 ⊞ CAST

A theatre poster, advertising *American Buffalo*, starring Al Pacino, Duke of York's Theatre, London, 1984, 19¾ x 12½in (50 x 32.5cm).
£10–15 / €15–22
$19–28 ⊞ c20th

A theatre programme, for *Mr & Mrs Nobody* by Keith Waterhouse, starring Judi Dench and Michael Williams, the Garrick Theatre, London, 1986, 8½ x 6in (21.5 x 15cm).
£10–15 / €15–22
$19–28 ⊞ CAST

A theatre programme, for *Medea*, Wyndham's Theatre, London, 1992, 9½ x 6¾in (24 x 17cm).
£10–15 / €15–22
$19–28 ⊞ CAST

Peter Pan

December 2004 saw the 100th anniversary of the first stage performance of *Peter Pan* at the Duke of York's Theatre in London. Written by J. M. Barrie (1860–1937), the story of the boy who never grew up was fuelled by Barrie's own experiences. His elder brother suffered a fatal accident on the eve of his fourteenth birthday, and his devasted mother's only consolation was that her dead son would always remain a boy.

Though childless himself, Barrie was involved with children throughout his life. In 1897 he met the Llewelyn Davis family in Kensington Gardens, London, with whom he was to form a close relationship. When both parents tragically died of cancer he became guardian and adoptive father to their five sons. The play of *Peter Pan* was inspired by the boys, emerging from the stories that he told them, and the central character was named after one of the brothers, Peter Llewelyn Davis. Wendy (a name that Barrie arguably invented) was a tribute to another child friend, Mary Henley, who died at the age of six. Mary was unable to pronounce

the letter 'r' and called Barrie her 'fwendy-wendy', hence the name of the character Wendy. The play can also lay claim to the introduction of the Wendy house, a little wooden house built for Wendy by the Lost Boys.

Peter Pan was an instant success. Even the first-night critics clapped to keep Tinker Bell the fairy alive. Since its inception the play has been regularly performed across the world and translated into various films, including Walt Disney's 1953 animation and J. P. Hogan's 2003 live version.

Over the years *Peter Pan* has stimulated a wide range of memorabilia, ranging from theatrical ephemera to decorative objects that were particularly popular in the 1920s and '30s. Designs were often stylistically inspired by George Frampton's famous Peter Pan monument (1910) in Kensington Gardens. In 1929 Barrie gifted the copyright of *Peter Pan* to Great Ormond Street Children's Hospital in London, and in 2004 the hospital announced a competition to write a sequel.

▶ A *Peter Pan* music score, 1905, 10¾ x 8¾in (27.5 x 22cm).
£135–150 / €200–220 $250–280 ⊞ c20th

A signed postcard, depicting Nina Boucicault as the first Peter Pan, 1904–05, 7½ x 5½in (18.5 x 13.5cm).
£100–120 / €150–180 $185–220 ⊞ c20th

Two *Peter Pan* theatre programmes, from the first run at Duke of York's Theatre, London, 1904–05, 8 x 3½in (20.5 x 9cm).
£135–150 / €200–220 $250–280 each ⊞ c20th
There were two types of programme for this play. The audience in the better seats were given a more colourful one.

A *Peter Pan* Keepsake, souvenir brochure, 1907, 11 x 8¼in (28 x 21cm).
£70–80 / €105–120 $130–150 ⊞ c20th

◀ A set of six Peter Pan prints, by John Hassall, c1909, 10¾in x 29½in (27.5 x 75cm).
£270–300 / €400–450 $500–560 ⊞ c20th

A Royal Worcester figure of Peter Pan, 1951, 8in (20.5cm) high.
£250–280 / €370–420 $470–520 ⊞ WAC

Tools

A cobbler's pine bench, the cupboard top with drawers, the seat with canted gallery work space, c1840, 65in (165cm) wide.
£660–750 / €990–1,100
$1,200–1,400 ⊞ CHES

▶ **A steel and brass miniature saw,** 19thC, 6in (15cm) long.
£200–230
€300–340
$370–430 ⊞ BS

◀ **A brass musical reed gauge,** 19thC, 2¼in (5.5cm) long.
£55–65
€85–100
$100–120 ⊞ WO

A Victorian brass and mahogany plane, Scottish, 9in (23cm) wide.
£155–175 / €230–260
$290–330 ⊞ WiB

A steel pocket auger, in a brass tube, 19thC, 5in (12.5cm) long.
£65–75 / €100–115
$120–140 ⊞ BS

A Spears ⅜in shoulder plane, with an ebony wedge, c1900, 10in (25.5cm) wide.
£140–160 / €210–240
$260–300 ⊞ WO

A pocket tool kit, in a leather case, 19thC, 5in (12.5cm) wide.
£165–185 / €250–280
$310–350 ⊞ BS

A boxwood case of plumber's turnpins, 1900, 5in (12.5cm) high.
£50–60 / €75–90
$95–110 ⊞ BS

A watchmaker's bradawl, with an ebony handle, early 20thC, 3½in (9cm) long.
£20–25 / €30–35
$35–45 ⊞ WO

▶ **A set of five William Mitchell lino cutters,** 1950s–60s, with box, 5in (12.5cm) long.
£25–30 / €40–45
$50–55 ⊞ DaM

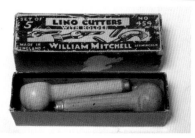

Toys

A wooden pond yacht, c1930,
22in (56cm) wide.
£50–60 / €75–90
$95–110 ⊞ JUN

A metal golly, c1930, 1in (2.5cm) high.
£90–100 / €135–150
$170–190 ⊞ MRW

A Tri-ang wooden milk cart,
with milk churn and bottles, c1938,
13in (33cm) wide.
£250–280 / €380–420
$470–520 ⊞ JUN

**A Chien & Co Pianolodeon plastic
piano,** with four rolls, c1949,
20in (51cm) high.
£35–40 / €50–60
$65–75 ⏊ JAA

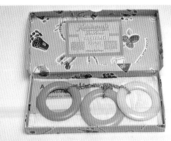

**A set of Kiddicraft De-Luxe plastic
teething rings,** designed by Hilary Page,
1940s–50s, with box, 3½ x 7in (9 x 18cm).
£15–20 / €22–30
$28–38 ⊞ RTT

**A plastic clockwork
Little Bo Peep,** 1950s,
5in (12.5cm) high.
£45–50 / €70–80
$85–95 ⊞ CBB

A wooden toy soldier,
Danish, 1960s,
20in (51cm) high.
£50–55 / €75–85
$95–105 ⊞ LAS

A Crescent Kansas Kid 100 shot toy pistol,
1960s, boxed, 12in (30.5cm) wide.
£60–70 / €90–105
$110–130 ⊞ HAL

**A Bugs Bunny plastic electric
phonograph,** c1975, boxed,
8in (20.5cm) wide.
£30–35 / €45–50
$55–65 ⊞ IQ

◄ **An Airfix plastic Ancient
Britons model kit,** comprising 43
pieces, 1975, boxed,
5in (12.5cm) wide.
£15–20 / €22–30
$28–38 ⊞ HeA

Aircraft

A Steelcraft pressed-steel aeroplane, with painted decoration, 1928, 22½in (57cm) wide.
**£280–330 / €420–500
$520–620** ✗ **Bert**

A tinplate clockwork aeroplane, c1935, 12in (30.5cm) long.
**£200–220 / €300–330
$370–410** ⊞ **JUN**

A tinplate aeroplane toy, c1950, 12in (30.5cm) high.
**£80–90 / €120–135
$150–170** ⊞ **JUN**

An Arnold tinplate Comet 4 airliner, German, 1950s, 12in (30.5cm) long.
**£60–70 / €90–105
$110–130** ✗ **WAL**

A tinplate battery-operated Super Flying Police Helicopter, Japanese, 1960s, 14¼in (36cm) long.
**£80–90 / €120–135
$150–170** ⊞ **RTT**

A tinplate battery-operated Pan Am helicopter, Japanese, 1960s, 13in (33cm) long.
**£75–85 / €115–130
$140–160** ⊞ **LAS**

Britains

The William Britain Company (est. 1845) was known for the manufacture of mechanical lead toys. In 1893 William Britain Junior, son of the original founder, perfected the hollow casting method for model soldiers. Molten lead was poured into a mould and shaken around the sides. The excess was poured back into the melting pot, leaving behind the shell of the figure which was then removed, tidied up and sent off for hand painting. Four hollow-cast figures could be produced from the same quota of lead used to make a single solid figure and thus toys became more affordable.

Figures were standardized in size to match the most popular gauge of toy trains, and Britains began by producing British regiments. Their soldiers were so popular that they inspired copies and

c1900 Britains retooled their moulds to incorporate the company name and date and, in the interim stage, marked figures with paper labels.

During WWI the company began to produce foreign troops and also improved the quality of their packaging. The interwar period saw the introduction of less war-like subjects, such as the popular Home Farm series, and in the 1930s production ranged from Disney figures to Cadbury's Cococubs (animals given away free in tins of cocoa). Model soldiers, however, remained the most famous line. In 1941 the factory halted toy production to make munitions. Manufacture resumed in the post-war period, but by then plastic figures were proving to be a serious competitor and by the 1960s demand for the hollow-cast figures had ceased.

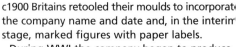

◀ **A Britains RAMC Wagon,** No. 145, 1920s, 11in (28cm) long, with two associated figures.
£95–110 / €145–170
$180–210 ⚒ WAL

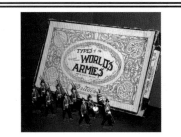

WANTED. Lifelong collector and international expert pays excellent prices for old military toys of all types. Especially wanted are hollow-cast lead soldiers by *"William Britain"*, solids by *"Heyde"*, *"Mignot"*, *"Lucotte"* and composition soldiers and tinplate vehicles by *"Elastolin" and "Lineol"*. Plastic soldiers of all make are required, in particular by *"Britains" and "Timpo"*. Wooden Forts and entrenchments of all types purchased. I am also interested in civilian models by the aforementioned makers. A premium is paid for items in good condition especially in original boxes. Complete collections or singles bought. Distance no object.
Contact G. M. Haley. Hippins Farm, Blackshawhead, Hebden Bridge, W. Yorks.
Telephone: +44 (0)1422 842484

A Britains heavy duty lorry, No. 1641, 1920s, 10in (25.5cm) long, together with an anti-aircraft gun and an army dispatch rider.
£270–320 / €410–480
$500–600 ⚒ WAL

A Britains Royal Engineers Pontoon Section set, No. 203, 1950s, 12in (30.5cm) long, with original box.
£200–240 / €300–360
$370–440 ⚒ WAL

◄ **A Britains Papal State Swiss Guards set,** No. 9371, 1960s, in original box, 15in (38cm) wide.
£130–155 / €195–230
$240–280 ➤ WAL

A Britains Army Staff Car, No. 1448, damaged and repaired, 1950s, 4½in (11.5cm) long, with original box.
£80–95 / €120–145
$150–180 ➤ WAL

► **A Britains Swoppet plastic figure of a War of the Roses Knight,** 1960s, 3in (7.5cm) high.
£10–15 / €15–22
$19–28 ⊞ HAL
Britains Swoppet range revolutionized plastic figures. Soldiers came with heads, legs, bodies and weapons that could be swapped between figures.

Cars & Vehicles

Cast-iron toys, produced from molten iron poured into a mould, became popular in the USA from the second half of the 19th century, and with the development of the automotive age in the 20th century, vehicles became a favourite plaything. Cast-iron cars were typically made in two halves and fastened together with a peened (hammered) rod. Modern reproductions tend to be attached with nuts and bolts and so can be distinguished from period originals. Leading manufacturers illustrated below include Hubley and Arcade. The Hubley Manufacturing Co established in Lancaster, Pennsylvania, in 1894, made electric train-related equipment before moving into toys in 1909. Fire engines, farm wagons, circus wagons and trains were initial successes but model cars became the top sellers in the interwar years. Arcade, founded in Freeport, Illinois, in 1868 was a leading competitor from the 1920s when the company launched a

model of the distinctive yellow cab that plied the streets of New York. The success of this vehicle stimulated a range of other products.

Cast-iron models were finely detailed and durable but they were also heavy and expensive to transport. In the first decade of the 1900s Dowst pioneered die-cast Tootsietoys made from moulded zinc alloy or zamak (known as mazak in the UK). Lighter, less expensive to mass produce and transport, and free from poisonous lead, by the 1940s die-cast vehicles had driven molten-iron cars virtually out of the marketplace. Today, as the following examples show, cast-iron cars can make strong prices. The most collectable cast-iron toys, however, are horse-drawn vehicles that preceded the age of the automobile. Fine 19th-century examples can sell for three- and four-figure sums and auction records include £35,700 / €54,000 / $67,000 for a Carpenter Tally Ho Coach dating from 1885.

◄ **A cast-iron ice truck,** c1920, 3½in (9cm) long.
£55–65 / €85–100
$100–120 ➤ DuM

► **An Arcade cast-iron Ford touring car,** with nickel driver, repainted, American, mid-1920s, 6½in (16.5cm) long, together with a road traffic sign.
£145–170 / €220–260
$270–320 ➤ Bert

An Arcade cast-iron stake truck, with painted decoration and nickel wheels, later rubber tyres and driver, American, 1929, 7in (18cm) long.
£120–140 / €180–210
$220–260 ➤ Bert

◀ **A Hubley cast-iron car carrier,** with two roadsters, American, 1932, 11¾in (30cm) long.
£400–480 / €600–720
$770–920 ⋟ **Bert**
It is unusual to find this carrier complete with cars.

A Hubley cast-iron racing car, with rubber tyres, American, c1932, 6½in (16.5cm) long.
£990–1,150 / €1,500–1,750
$1,850–2,200 ⋟ **Bert**

A Kilgore cast-iron Graham Stake truck, with a nickel grille and bumper, c1933, 6½in (16.5cm) long.
£600–700 / €890–1,050
$1,100–1,300 ⋟ **Bert**

A National Products die-cast Studebaker Land Cruiser, with rubber tyres, rear panel embossed 'Replica of Giant World's Fair Studebaker', 1934, 5¾in (14.5cm) long, with box.
£160–190 / €240–280
$300–360 ⋟ **Bert**

A salesman's sample Arcade cast-iron Ford 9N tractor, with rubber tyres, c1939, 8¾in (22cm) long.
£1,200–1,400 / €1,800–2,100
$2,200–2,600 ⋟ **Bert**

An Arcade cast-iron double decker bus, with a nickel grille, rubber tyres, and three figures, c1940, 7¾in (19.5cm) long.
£350–420 / €520–620
$660–790 ⋟ **Bert**

A Hubley Oliver Orchard tractor, with driver and rubber tyres, American, c1940, 5¼in (13.5cm) long.
£440–520 / €660–780
$820–980 ⋟ **Bert**

A National Products die-cast Buick, with rubber tyres and wooden hubs, embossed '1940 – Best Bet's Buick', 'National Products Corp', 1940, 5¾in (14.5cm) long.
£320–380 / €480–570
$600–720 ⋟ **Bert**

A Tucker promotional model car, axle repaired, 1948, 8in (20.5cm) long.
£240–280 / €360–420
$440–520 ⋟ **Bert**
Promotional vehicles were given to potential Tucker dealers, along with an ashtray, as an added incentive. They are now very desirable.

A Foden die-cast clockwork Shackleton truck, 12in (30.5cm) long, with original box.
£400–450 / €600–680
$750–840 ⊞ **MRW**

A Master Caster die-cast Ford Super Deluxe police car, with rubber tyres and tin hubs, marked, 1948, 7in (18cm) long.
£90–100 / €135–150
$165–185 ⋟ **Bert**

◀ **A Banthrico die-cast Dodge,** marked 'Adrian Federal Savings & Loan Association', American, 1954, 7¾in (19.5cm) long.
£100–120 / €150–180
$190–220 ⋟ **Bert**

► **A Banthrico die-cast Pontiac Star Chief,** marked 'Farmers and Merchants Savings Bank – Framingham, Mass.', American, 1955, 7¾in (19.5cm) long.
£280–330 / €420–500
$520–620 ⚹ **Bert**

Three Benbros die-cast Dunlop Lorries, c1955, largest 1½in (4cm) long.
£6–10 / €9–15
$12–19 each ⊞ **HUX**

A Schuco die-cast Varianto Elecktro 3112U, German, late 1950s, 5in (12.5cm) long.
£60–70 / €90–105
$110–130 ⊞ **CBB**

A Banthrico die-cast Willy's Jeep army truck, marked 'U. S. Army 3F 8062', American, c1967, 6¾in (17cm) long, with box.
£30–35 / €45–50
$65–75 ⚹ **Bert**

A Tri-ang Minic die-cast racing car, 1950s, 6in (15cm) long, with original box.
£70–80 / €105–120
$130–150 ⊞ **CBB**

► **A Solido die-cast Porsche GT Le Mans,** French, 1960s, 4in (10cm) long, with original box.
£50–60 / €75–85
$95–105 ⊞ **HAL**

A Spot-On die-cast Bull Nose Morris, 1960s, with original box, 5in (12.5cm) long.
£30–35 / €45–50
$55–65 ⊞ **HAL**

A Topper Toys plastic battery-operated Johnny 7 car and speed boat, American, 1960s, 14in (35.5cm) long.
£100–120 / €150–180
$185–220 ⊞ **HAL**

A die-cast Carabinieri Fiat Campagnola, 1970s, 6in (15cm) long.
£15–20 / €22–30
$28–38 ⊞ **CBB**

A Lledo die-cast White Star Van, edition of 100, 1983, with original box, 5in (12.5cm) long.
£6–10 / €9–15
$12–19 ⊞ **COB**

◄ **A Presidential Series 1961 Lincoln Continental,** No. 1, The Kennedy Car, 2000, with original box, 10in (25.5cm) long.
£45–50 / €70–80
$85–95 ⊞ **IQ**

► **An Oxford die-cast Volkswagen van,** painted with Tommy Cooper and 'Just Like That', 2002, 4in (10cm) long, with box.
£15–20 / €22–30
$28–38 ⊞ **IQ**

Corgi

A Corgi Toys Man From U.N.C.L.E
Thrush-Buster, No. 497, Waverley
ring missing, 1966, 6in (15cm) long,
with original box.
£160–180 / €240–270
$300–330 ⊞ HAL
With its Waverley ring this car
would have a price range of
£200–230 / €300–350 / $370–430.

A Corgi Toys Batmobile, first
series, 1960s, 6in (15cm) long,
with original box.
£400–450 / €600–680
$750–840 ⊞ CBB

A Corgi Toys Mercedes-Benz
220SE Coupé, No. 230, 1960s,
4in (10cm) long, with box.
£45–50 / €70–80
$85–95 ⊞ HAL

◀ A Corgi Toys Bristol
Bloodhound gift set, comprising
guided missile, launch pad, loading
trolley and Land Rover, 1959–62,
with original box, 11in (28cm) long.
£175–195 / €260–290
$320–360 ⊞ GTM

A Corgi Toys Oldsmobile
Tornado, No. 264, c1960,
5in (12.5cm) long, with original box.
£40–45 / €60–70
$75–85 ⊞ HAL

A Corgi Toys Competition Model
E-Type Jaguar, No. 312, with wire
wheels, 1960s, 4in (10cm) long,
with original box.
£70–80 / €105–120
$130–150 ➢ VEC

A Corgi Toys Major Corporal
Guided Missile and Erector
Vehicle, No. 1113, 1960s,
12in (30.5cm) long, with box.
£200–240 / €300–360
$370–450 ➢ WAL

A Corgi Toys James Bond
Goldfinger Aston Martin DB5,
No. 261, 1965, 6in (15cm) long,
with original box.
£220–250 / €330–380
$410–470 ⊞ HAL
Launched in 1965, the James
Bond Aston Martin was named
toy of the year by the National
Association of Toy Retailers.
During its original three-year
production run it became one of
the most successful toys of all
time with sales of over
3,000,000. Corgi Toys used their
exiting Aston Martin DB4 (1964)
as the basis for the Bond car and
packed it with a range of
exciting new features including
front machine gun, rear bullet-
proof shield and ejector seat.
Although the car is illustrated in
silver on the packaging, it was
painted gold in order to
emphasize its premium quality.
Originally this toy sold for 9s 11
– just under 50p in today's
coinage – but back then it was
equivalent to a month's average
pocket money. In 1968, Corgi
launched a revised version of
James Bond's Aston Martin DB5,
the C270. It was slightly larger,
painted silver and had extra
features including rotating
number plates and tyre slashers.
Today this can be worth three
times as much as the original
gold version, but more
collectable still is a rare bright
gold version of the DB5, only
given to VIPs visiting the Corgi
factory, an example of which
recently sold at auction for
£13,000 / €19,500 / $24,300.

◀ A Corgi Toys Volkswagen
1200 rally car, No. 384, 1960s,
4in (10cm) long, with box.
£70–80 / €105–120
$130–150 ➢ VEC

A Corgi Toys Plymouth US Mail Station Wagon, No. 443, 1960s, 4in (10cm) long, with box.
£130–155 / €195–230
$240–290 ✗ VEC

A Corgi Toys Driving School Austin A60, No. 255, 1960s, 4in (10cm) long, with box.
£80–90 / €120–135
$150–170 ✗ VEC

A Corgi Toys Ford Cortina GXL, No. 313, with Graham Hill figure, 1970, 5in (12.5cm) long, with box.
£50–60 / €75–85
$95–105 ⊞ HAL

A Corgi Toys Batmobile and Batboat gift set, 1979, with box, 11½in (29cm) long.
£300–330 / €450–500
$560–620 ⊞ GTM

A Corgi Toys Heinkel Economy car, No. 233, 1960s, 2in (5cm) long, with box.
£60–70 / €90–105
$110–130 ✗ SAS

A Corgi Toys Avengers gift set, No. 40. comprising John Steed's Bentley, Emma Peel's Lotus Elan, one figure and one umbrella, 1960s, boxed, 6in (15cm) long.
£520–620 / €780–930
$970–1,150 ✗ VEC

A Corgi Toys James Bond Aston Martin DB5, with tyre slashers and revolving number plates, 1973, 6in (15cm) long, with box.
£180–200 / €270–300
$330–370 ⊞ HAL

▶ A Corgi Toys Whizzwheels Chevrolet Astro Experimental, No. 347, 1970s, 4in (10cm) long, with box.
£30–35 / €45–50
$55–65 ⊞ HAL

◀ A Corgi Toys Batboat on Trailer, No. 107, 1970s, 6in (15cm) long, with box.
£70–80 / €105–120
$130–150 ✗ VEC

A Corgi Toys Citroen Safari 1D19, No. 436, 1960s, 4in (10cm) long, with box.
£65–75 / €100–115
$120–140 ✗ SAS

A Corgi Toys Chipperfields Circus gift set, No. 23, first issue, 1960s, with box, 16in (40.5cm) wide.
£580–650 / €870–980
$1,050–1,200 ⊞ HAL

A Corgi Toys James Bond Lotus Esprit, No. 269, from the film The Spy Who Loved Me, 1977, with box, 7in (18cm) long.
£110–125 / €165–190
$210–230 ⊞ GTM

Dinky

Inspired by the success of die-cast Tootsietoys in America, in 1933 Frank Hornby, one of Britain's leading toy manufacturers, produced a range of vehicles known as Modelled Miniatures to accompany the famous Hornby railway system. The pocket-sized toys became a huge success in their own right and in 1934 were renamed Dinky (meaning small). A wide range of vehicles, including cars, buses, commercial and military vehicles were produced in the 1930s, and this early period provides some of the most sought-after Dinkies today. Production ceased during the war and started up again in 1946. Many of the same models were reissued but post-war examples have thicker axles than the 1930s first issues, and the hub caps are more realistic with a raised centre.

In 1947 the Dinky Supertoy range (initially given a 500 series number) was introduced. These were large vehicles with specifically designed die-cast hub caps and treaded rubber tyres that were soon to replace the slick tyres on all Dinky vehicles. The company used a numbering system of one, two or three digit

numbers followed by a letter. From 1954 numbers were standardized. One or two digit numbers were used for accessories, 100s for cars, 200–249 for racing cars, 250–299 for public service vehicles (buses and police vehicles), 300s for agricultural vehicles (and later character cars), 400s for light and medium trucks, 700s for aircraft and accessories and eventually 900s for Supertoys. The 500s and 800s were reserved for toys made at Dinky's French factory, who changed their numbering system in 1959.

With growing competition from other manufacturers such as Corgi Toys in the 1950s, Dinky vehicles became increasingly sophisticated: windows were introduced in 1958, suspension in 1959 and fingertip steering in 1960. Packaging also improved in the 1950s. In the pre-war period (with the exception of special items such as gift sets) small numbers of vehicles were supplied in a trade box to retailers, who would extract cars as they were sold. The first half of the 1950s saw the introduction of individual boxes and these contribute hugely to the value of toys today.

A Dinky Toys motor truck, No. 22C, with rubber tyres, 1935.
£190–220 / €290–330 $350–410 ➶ **WAL**

▶ **A Dinky Toys Power petrol tank wagon,** 1935, 4in (10cm) long.
£600–700 / €900–1,050 $1,100–1,300 ➶ **VEC**

◀ **A Dinky Supertoys Guy 4-ton lorry,** No. 511, 1948–52, 5½in (14cm) long, with box.
£100–120 / €150–180 $185–220 ➶ **VEC**

A Dinky Toys Guy flat truck with tailboard, No. 513, with Supertoys hub caps and 2nd-type cab, 1947–48, 6in (15cm) long, with box.
£100–120 / €150–180 $185–220 ➶ **VEC**

A Dinky Supertoys Guy 4-ton lorry, No. 511, 1947–48, 6in (15cm) long, with box.
£300–360 / €450–540 $560–670 ➶ **VEC**

A Dinky Supertoys Guy 4-ton lorry, No. 511, 1948, 5½in (14cm) long, with box.
£130–145 / €195–220 $240–270 ⊞ **CBB**

A Dinky Supertoys Leyland Octopus Esso tanker, No. 943, 1958–64, 7in (18cm) long, with box.
£340–380 / €510–570
$640–710 ⊞ MRW

A Dinky Toys Rolls-Royce, 1950s, 6in (15cm) long, with box.
£55–65 / €85–100
$100–120 ⊞ HAL

A Dinky Toys Maserati racing car, No. 231, 1950s, 4in (10cm) long, with box.
£50–60 / €75–85
$95–105 ⊞ HAL

A Dinky Toys H.W.M. racing car, No. 23J, 1950s, 4in (10cm) long, with box.
£100–120 / €150–180
$185–220 ⋗ VEC

A Dinky Toys Plymouth estate car, No. 344, 1950s, 4in (10cm) long, with box.
£50–60 / €75–85
$95–105 ⊞ HAL

A Dinky Toys Lyons Swiss Rolls Guy van, No. 514, 1950s, 5½in (14cm) long, with box.
£800–950 / €1,200–1,450
$1,500–1,800 ⋗ VEC

◀ **A Dinky Supertoys Recovery Tractor,** No. 661, 1950s, 5in (12.5cm) long, with box.
£80–90
€120–135
$150–170 ⊞ HAL

▶ **A Dinky Supertoys 10-Ton Army truck,** No. 622, 1950s, 6in (15cm) long, with box.
£70–80
€105–120
$130–150
⊞ HAL

◀ **A Dinky Toys Centurion tank,** No. 651, 1950s, 5in (12.5cm) long, with box.
£60–70
€90–105
$110–130
⋗ SAS

A Dinky Supertoys Foden flat truck, No. 902, 1950s, 7½in (19cm) long, with box.
£270–320 / €400–480
$500–600 ⚲ WAL

A Dinky Supertoys Bedford Pallet-Jekta van, No. 930, with two plastic pallets, 1960–64, 5in (12.5cm) long, with box.
£190–220 / €290–330
$350–410 ⚲ VEC

A Dinky Toys E-Type Jaguar, No. 120, 1965, 3in (7.5cm) long, with original box.
£70–80 / €105–120
$130–150 ⚲ SAS

A Dinky Toys Sinpar 4 x 4 military police car, No. 815, French, 1968, (6.5cm) long, with box.
£155–175 / €230–260
$290–330 ⊞ GTM

A Dinky Toys Peugeot 403 Berline, No. 24B, French, 1960s, 4in (10cm) long, with box.
£90–100 / €135–150
$170–190 ⚲ WAL

A Dinky Toys Peugeot D3A Postes van, No. 25BV, French, 1960s, 4in (10cm) long, with box.
£85–95 / €130–145
$160–180 ⚲ WAL

A Dinky Toys ABC TV Mobile Control Room, 1960s, 5in (12.5cm) long, with camera, cameraman and box.
£130–150 / €195–220
$240–280 ⚲ SAS

A Dinky Toys Klingon Battle Cruiser, No. 357, 1970s, with box, 8in (20.5cm) wide.
£35–40 / €50–60
$65–75 ⚲ SAS

A Dinky Toys 155mm Mobile Gun, No. 654, late 1970s, with box, 7in (18cm) long.
£35–40 / €50–60
$65–75 ⊞ CBB

A Dinky Toys Bell Police helicopter, No. 732, 1970s, with original box, 7in (18cm) long.
£20–25 / €30–35
$35–45 ⚲ SAS

A Dinky Toys Bundesmarine Sea King helicopter, No. 736, 1970s, with original box, 7in (18cm) long.
£45–50 / €70–80
$85–95 ⚲ SAS

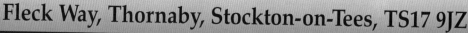

Disney

A Ben Cooper Sleeping Beauty costume, c1930, with box, 11in (28cm) wide.
£220–250 / €330–380
$410–470 ⊞ MRW

A Louis Marx plastic clockwork Pluto, with a wire tail, American, 1950s, 5½in (14cm) high.
£75–85 / €110–125
$135–160 ⋏ Bert

A bendy Donald Duck, Malaysian, 1960s, 8in (20.5cm) high.
£10–15 / €15–22
$19–28 ⊞ LAS

A Louis Marx tinplate clockwork Pinochio the Acrobat, American, 1939, 16½in (42cm) high.
£200–240 / €300–360
$380–450 ⋏ Bert

A Louis Marx tinplate and plastic clockwork Donald Duck Drummer, American, 1950s, 10in (25.5cm) high.
£100–120 / €150–180
$190–220 ⋏ Bert

▶ **A Louis Marx plastic friction-driven Donald Duck on Tractor,** American, 1950s, 3½in (9cm) long.
£35–40 / €50–60
$65–75 ⋏ Bert

A bendy Minnie Mouse, Malaysian, 1970s, 8in (20.5cm) high.
£10–15 / €15–22
$19–28 ⊞ LAS

A Linemar tinplate clockwork Mickey Mouse xylophone player, Japanese, 1950s, 6in (15cm) high.
£350–420 / €520–620
$660–790 ⋏ Bert

A Louis Marx tinplate and plastic clockwork Mickey the Driver, American, 1950s, 6½in (16.5cm) high.
£250–300 / €380–450
$460–550 ⋏ Bert

A Mettoy plastic Movie Viewer, c1984, with box, 14in (35.5cm) wide.
£20–25 / €30–35
$35–45 ⊞ IQ

Kitchenware

A metal strainer, with a wooden handle, 1900–25, 6¾in (17cm) long.
£10–15 / €15–22
$25–30 ⊞ MSB

A rack of tin utensils, early 20thC, 4¼in (11cm) high.
£55–65 / €85–95
$110–125 ⊞ MSB

A steel cooking range, with four tinplate pots and pans, chimney missing, 11½in (29cm) wide.
£95–110 / €140–165
$175–200 ♪ WAL

A set of six painted tin canisters, for coffee, tea, sugar, flour, bread and cake, 1900–25, bread tin 4in (10cm) high.
£165–185 / €250–280
$310–350 ⊞ MSB

A wood and metal coffee grinder, 1900–25, 4in (10cm) high.
£25–30 / €40–45
$50–55 ⊞ MSB

A metal and mesh cutlery basket, with punched metal cutlery, 1930s, 4¼in (11cm) wide.
£25–30 / €40–45
$50–60 ⊞ MSB

A Tri-ang stores, with accessories, 1940s–50s, 15in (38cm) high.
£270–300 / €400–450
$500–560 ⊞ LAS

◀ **A Mettoy sink unit,** 1950s, 16in (40.5cm) high, with original box.
£50–55 / €75–85
$95–105 ⊞ DOL

A Crescent Toys die-cast Garden Party tea set, 1940s, with box, 5in (12.5cm) wide.
£270–300 / €400–450
$500–560 ⊞ MRW

A Casdon battery-operated cooker, 1950–60s, 11in (28cm) high, with box.
£25–30 / €40–45
$50–55 ⊞ LAS

A Greycraft cast-iron Queen range, 1970s, 6in (15cm) wide, with original box.
£50–55 / €75–85
$95–105 ♪ Bert

Matchbox

▶ **A Matchbox E. R. F. Road Tanker,** No. 11a, 1955, 2in (5cm) long.
£190–210 / €290–320
$360–390 ⚲ WAL

A Matchbox Bedford Removals Van, No. 17, c1955, 2½in (6.5cm) long, with box.
£95–110 / €145–165
$180–210 ⚲ WAL

A Matchbox Rolls-Royce Silver Cloud, 1950s, 2½in (6.5cm) long, with box.
£25–30 / €40–45
$50–55 ⊞ HAL

A Matchbox Fire Engine, No. 9, mid–1950s, 2in (5cm) long, with box.
£40–45 / €60–70
$75–85 ⊞ HAL

A Matchbox Snow-Trac, No. 35, 1964, 2½in (6.5cm) long, with box.
£20–25 / €30–35
$35–45 ⊞ GTM

A Matchbox B. R. M. Racing Car, No. 52, 1965, 2½in (6.5cm) long, with box.
£15–20 / €22–30
$28–38 ⊞ GTM

A Matchbox Foden 8-Wheel Sugar Container, No. 10, 1960s, 3in (7.5cm) long, with box.
£25–30 / €40–45
$50–55 ⊞ HAL

Pedal Cars

A tinplate pedal car, damaged, c1930, 24in (61cm) long.
£200–240 / €300–360
$370–450 ⚲ Mit

A painted steel pedal aeroplane, c1937, 44in (112cm) wide.
£220–250 / €330–380
$410–470 ⊞ JUN

A Tri-ang steel Vanwall-style pedal racing car, with wire wheels, front suspension mounts, pneumatic tyres, and plastic steering wheel, 1960s, 48in (122cm) long.
£180–200 / €270–300
$330–370 ⊞ PCCC

Robots & Space Toys

A Merit Dan Dare Planet Gun, 1953, with box, 11in (28cm) wide.
£270–300 / €400–450
$500–560 ⊞ SSF

A Remco plastic battery-operated Jupiter Signal Gun, 1958, 9in (23cm) long, with box.
£90–105 / €135–160
$165–195 ⌿ Bert

▶ **A TM Toys tinplate battery-operated X-7 Flying Saucer,** Japanese, mid-1960s, 8in (20.5cm) diam, with box.
£170–200 / €260–300
$320–370 ⌿ WAL

A Yoshiya plastic battery-operated Spacetrooper, with tin hands and nickel trim, Japanese, 1950s, 6½in (16.5cm) high.
£350–420 / €530–630
$660–790 ⌿ Bert

◀ **A Horikawa tinplate battery-operated Rotate-O-Matic Super Astronaut,** Japanese, 1960s, 12in (30.5cm) high, with box.
£180–200 / €270–300
$330–370 ⊞ GTM

A Naito Shoten tinplate clockwork Inter Planet Space Captain, Japanese, 1950s, 7¾in (19.5cm) high.
£750–880
€1,100–1,300
$1,400–1,650 ⌿ Bert

◀ **A tinplate battery-operated Apollo-7 Moon Traveler,** Japanese, 1968, 12in (30.5cm) long, with box.
£150–170
€230–260
$280–320 ⊞ IQ

A tinplate and plastic battery-operated Space Rocket, Japanese, 1970, 19in (48.5cm) high, with box.
£150–170 / €230–260
$280–320 ⊞ IQ

Rocking Horses

Carved rocking horses are among the earliest known toys. Hobby horse, deriving from the medieval word *hobyn* – a medium-sized horse – was the term applied to the wickerwork horse frame used by Morris dancers and performers in the medieval history plays. From the 16th century, references can be found to children's hobby horses, a stick surmounted by a horse's head.

Rocking horses first appeared in the 17th century and by the Victorian period had become a standard feature of the nursery. Rockers were sharply bowed in the first half of the 19th century, graduating in the second half to a gentle, safer curve. The 1880s and '90s saw the introduction of the trestle-mounted horse, less romantic looking but certainly more space saving and less dangerous. Horses were carved out of blocks of wood (usually pine or beech) that were glued or tennoned together, covered with gesso to smooth over the joints and then painted, traditionally in dapple grey.

Bridles and saddles were made from leather, and real horse hair was used for the mane and tail. Well-known manufacturers of rocking horses include G. & J. Lines, Woodrow & Co, Norton & Baker and Frederick Ayres. Individual makers, however, can be hard to identify since many toys were either not stamped or identification marks were subsequently concealed by repainting or restoration.

Styles of wooden rocking horses changed very little in the 20th century. Vintage rocking horses are very desirable but values are affected by soundness of construction and quality of carving. On a good head, details will be well defined with flared nostrils and pricked ears. In the post-war period, the British firm Mobo Toys (1947–72) introduced a new style of ride-on horse, the Mobo Bronco, made from metal and moved along by pushing the stirrups up and down. Mobo Toys produced a wide range of ride-on, rocking and push-along horses, and many of their products were exported to the USA.

A horse-hide-covered pull-along toy horse, with horsehair mane and tail, on a wooden base with four iron wheels, 19thC, 16in (40.5cm) long.
£320–380 / €480–570
$600–720 ⋔ COBB

A Victorian pine Tumbler horse, with revolving body, 104in (264cm) long.
£850–1,000 / €1,300–1,500
$1,600–1,850 ⋔ TEN

An Edwardian painted rocking horse, on a trestle rocker, 32¼in (82cm) long.
£420–500 / €630–750
$790–940 ⋔ L&T

An Edwardian carved and painted wood rocking horse, restored, 83in (211cm) long.
£1,600–1,800 / €2,400–2,700
$3,000–3,350 ⊞ BaN

▶ **A Frederick Ayres rocking horse,** on a trestle rocker, restored, c1910, 60in (152.5cm) long.
£1,400–1,600 / €2,100–2,400
$2,600–3,000 ⊞ JUN

◀ **A carved and painted rocking horse,** with horsehair mane and tail and a leather and velour saddle, on a pine trestle rocker, 1910, 54in (137cm) long.
£600–720 / €900–1,100
$1,150–1,350 ⚡ **CAG**

A carved and painted wood rocking horse, on a trestle rocker, 1920s, 44in (112cm) long.
£580–650 / €870–980
$1,050–1,200 ⊞ **JUN**

A painted rocking horse, on a trestle rocker, restored, c1920, 54in (137cm) long.
£1,300–1,450 / €1,950–2,200
$2,450–2,700 ⊞ **JUN**

An Orton & Spooner wooden fairground horse, c1930, 39in (99cm) wide.
£270–300 / €400–450
$500–560 ⊞ **JUN**

▶ **A cast-iron tricycle,** in the form of a fairground horse, American, 1930s,
£360–400 / €540–600
$670–750 ⊞ **TNS**

▶ **A Collinson's carved and painted wood rocking horse,** on a trestle rocker, early 1930s, 48in (122cm) long.
£600–700
€930–1,050
$1,150–1,300
⊞ **DEB**

◀ **A Collinwood carved and painted wood rocking horse,** saddle restored, c1950, 50in (127cm) long.
£850–950
€1,250–1,400
$1,600–1,800
⊞ **Cot**

▶ **A Mobo Toys rocking horse,** on a metal stand, 1950s, 39in (99cm) long.
£220–250
€330–380
$410–470 ⊞ **LAS**

Science Fiction & Television

A Waddington's *Thunderbirds* game, 1966, with box, 8¼ x 15¼in (21 x 38.5cm).
£20–25 / €30–35
$35–45 ⊞ TASV

◀ **A set of nine Lone Star plastic *The Man From U.N.C.L.E.* badges,** c1965, on backing board, 8½ x 6in (21.5 x 15cm).
£150–180 / €230–270
$280–330 ↗ WAL

A latex *Dr Who* prop, from The Mutants episode, 1972, 13in (33cm) high.
£400–450 / €600–680
$750–840 ⊞ WHO

A Louis Marx *Lone Ranger* figure, American, 1973, with box, 10in (25.5cm) high.
£45–50 / €70–80
$85–95 ⊞ HeA

The Lone Ranger is perhaps one of the most famous Western characters of all time. The story of the fictional masked law enforcer, his Native American companion Tonto, and his white stallion Silver was created by script writer Fran Striker and producer George W. Trendle for a Detroit radio station and premiered in 1933. By 1937 the famous cry of 'Hi-Yo Silver' could be heard from radios nationwide and the series continued until c1955. The *Lone Ranger* was also translated into comic strips, films and a long-running (and much repeated) television series. From the 1930s onwards the *Lone Ranger* stimulated a vast amount of merchandise from well-known manufacturers including Louis Marx.

A Palitoy plastic battery-operated talking *Dr Who* Dalek, c1975, with box, 7½in (19cm) high.
£120–135 / €180–200
$220–250 ⊞ GTM

A Parker *Star Wars* Adventures of R2D2 board game, 1977, with box, 9 x 17in (23 x 43cm).
£25–30 / €40–45
$50–55 ⊞ SSF

▶ **A *Star Wars* Return of the Jedi storybook,** 1977, 12 x 9¾in (30.5 x 25cm).
£10–15 / €15–22
$19–28 ↗ StDA

A Palitoy *Star Wars* Death Star, 1977, with box, 12 x 17in (30.5 x 43cm).
£360–400 / €540–600
$670–750 ⊞ OW

A Kenner *Star Wars* Land Speeder, American, 1977, with box, 8 x 10in (20.5 x 25.5cm).
£80–90 / €120–135
$150–170 ⊞ OW

A *Star Wars* Boba Fett action figure, 1979, with box, 12in (30.5cm) high.
£500–550 / €750–830
$940–1,050 ⊞ OW

The Art of the Empire Strikes Back, edited by Deborah Call, text by Valerie Hoffman and Vic Bulluck, 1980, 12 x 9¾in (30.5 x 25cm).
£25–30 / €40–45
$50–55 ➢ StDA

A *Dr Who* tin money box, in the form of the Tardis, 1980, 5in (12.5cm) high.
£15–20 / €22–30
$28–38 ⊞ HeA

▶ A Bow Tie *My Little Pony*, 1983, 5in (12.5cm) high.
£1–5 / €2–7
$3–9 ⊞ RAND

A *Star Fleet* Dai-X robot, Japanese, 1982, with box, 6 x 5in (15 x 12.5cm).
£130–150 / €195–230
$240–280 ⊞ OW

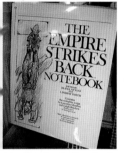

The Empire Strikes Back Notebook, edited by Diana Attias and Lindsay Smith, contains the complete script by Lawrence Kasdan and Leigh Brackett, 1980, 12 x 9¾in (30.5 x 25cm)
£10–15 / €15–22
$19–28 ➢ StDA

A Palitoy *Star Wars Return of the Jedi* X-Wing Fighter Vehicle, 1983, with box, 11in (28cm) high.
£50–60 / €75–85
$95–105 ⊞ OW

A *Star Wars Return of the Jedi* Scout Walker Vehicle, 1983, with box, 11in (28cm) high.
£30–35 / €45–50
$55–65 ⊞ IQ

A Palitoy *Star Wars Return of the Jedi* EV-9D9 action figure, 1983, 4in (10cm) high, on tri-logo card.
£145–160 / €210–240
$270–300 ⊞ SSF

An Arrow *Dr Who* puzzle, 1984, 9 x 11in (23 x 28cm).
£6–10 / €9–15
$12–19 ⊞ HeA

A Tsukuda Hobby *Alien* figure, 1984, 18in (45.5cm) high, with box.
£100–120 / €150–180
$185–220 ⊞ IQ
In 1984, the Tsukuda Hobby Co, Japan, produced a copy of Kenner's 1979 Alien Doll. Kenner objected, which makes this version rare and therefore of high value.

An MB *Transformers* Prowl, French, 1985, with box, 8 x 9in (20.5 x 23cm).
£180–200 / €270–300
$330–370 ⊞ OW

A *Stingray* Troy Tempest action figure, 1992, on card, 7in (18cm) high.
£4–8 / €6–12
$8–15 ⊞ IQ

Two Matchbox *Thunderbirds* action figures, Scott and Virgil, 1992, on card, 8 x 5in (20.5 x 12.5cm).
£10–15 / €15–22
$19–28 each ⊞ LAS

A Hamilton porcelain *Star Trek Generations* plate, American, 1995, 7in (18cm) diam.
£20–25 / €30–35
$35–45 ⊞ CoC

A Hasbro Signature Series *Alien Resurrection* Ripley action figure, 1997, with box, 7in (18cm) high.
£15–20 / €22–30
$28–38 ⊞ SSF

◄ **A Kentucky Fried Chicken *Star Wars* plastic advertising figure of Darth Maul,** from *The Phantom Menace,* 1999, 74in (188cm) high.
£1,300–1,500 / €1,950–2,150
$2,400–2,800 ⊞ WAm

A *Star Trek Insurrection* autograph series trade card, Gregg Henry as Gallatin, 1998, 2½ x 4¾in (6.5 x 12cm).
£35–40 / €50–60
$65–75 ⊞ SSF

Two Mattel Commemorative Series *Masters of the Universe* action figures, He-Man and Battle Cat, edition of 10,000, reissue, 2000, with box, 13 x 17in (33 x 43cm).
£25–30 / €40–45
$50–55 ⊞ SSF

A Sega *The Nightmare Before Christmas* Jack figure, Japanese, 2001, 8in (23cm) high.
£20–25 / €30–35
$35–45 ⊞ NOS

Three Hard Hero Collectors Series *Transformers* cold cast porcelain busts, Megatron, Optimus Prime and Prowl, 2001, 9in (23cm) high, with box.
£55–65 / €85–100
$100–120 each ⊞ OW

A Takara *Transformers* Cybertron Commander Convoy, remould from the 1980s, Japanese, 2002, with box, 8 x 6in (20.5 x 15cm).
£450–500 / €670–750
$840–930 ⊞ NOS

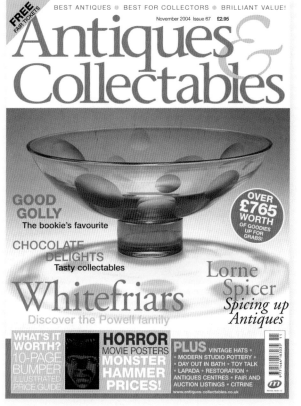

Tinplate

A Johan Hess tinplate saw mill display, the hand-wound motor operates two figures and activates machinery, German, early 20thC, base 22in (56cm) wide.
£170–200 / €250–300
$310–370   ↗ Oli

A tinplate clockwork motor car, German, early 20thC, 12¾in (32.5cm) long.
£340–400 / €500–600
$640–750   ↗ CAG

A Lehmann tinplate clockwork hand-drawn parcel cart and delivery man, No. 770, German, c1910, 7in (18cm) long.
£200–240 / €300–360
$370–440   ↗ WAL

◄ **A Lehmann tinplate clockwork Quack Quack toy,** No. 645, German, c1920, 8in (20.5cm) long.
£160–190 / €240–280
$300–350   ↗ WAL

A tinplate clockwork Maggie and Jiggs toy, 1924, 7in (18cm) long.
£530–630 / €800–940
$990–1,150   ↗ Bert
American illustrator George McManus (1883–1954) started his career drawing hangings and criminals for newspapers before moving on to comic strips. His most famous creation (introduced c1913) was 'Bringing up Father', a cartoon strip featuring the Irish-American Jiggs (a former bricklayer) and his wife, ex-laundress Maggie, who suddenly became rich when they won a lucky ticket in the Irish sweepstake. The comedy centres on Maggie and her daughter trying to raise father Jiggs to his new, elevated social position. The strip was a huge and enduring success and was only withdrawn in 2000. The stories also inspired stage adaptations, numerous films, radio programmes and, as illustrated here, toys.

A Schuco tinplate clockwork Mercedes racing car, No. 1050, with spare parts, German, 1930s, 6in (15cm) long.
£75–85 / €115–130
$140–160   ↗ G(B)

A Meccano tinplate Model Car Constructor, 1930s, 12in (30.5cm) long, with box.
£800–900 / €1,200–1,350
$1,500–1,700   ⊞ HAL

A Unique Art Manufacturing Co tinplate clockwork Li'l Abner and his Dogpatch Band, American, 1945, 9½in (24cm) wide, with box.
£280–330 / €420–500
$520–620   ↗ Bert
L'il Abner was the title character in the long-running (1934–77) syndicated newspaper strip by American cartoonist Al Capp.

◄ **A tinplate clockwork drummer,** Japanese, c1950, 5in (12.5cm) high.
£150–165 / €220–250
$280–310   ⊞ JUN

A Linemar tinplate friction-driven Lincoln Continental Mark II car, with celluloid windshield, Japanese, 1956, 11¼in (28.5cm) long, with box.
£2,800–3,300 / €4,200–5,000 $5,200–6,200 ⚹ Bert

A Linemar tinplate Lincoln Continental Mark II car, with remote control, Japanese, 1956, 11in (28cm) long, with box.
£2,400–2,800 / €3,600–4,200 $4,500–5,200 ⚹ Bert

A Technofix tinplate clockwork motorcycle, German, 1950s, 7in (18cm) long.
£200–230 / €300–350 $370–430 ⊞ CBB

Linemar

In the post-war period Japan became a leading producer of tinplate toys. Since production costs were cheaper in Asia, many American companies commissioned manufacture in Japan. A huge number of toys were made purely for export to the USA and as a result reflected contemporary American culture and taste. Often, however, toys were marked 'foreign' rather than 'made in Japan', so as not to stir up any war-time resentment. Clockwork and friction-powered vehicles were produced from the 1940s, and the mid-1950s saw the introduction of battery-powered vehicles. The Japanese were among the first to use batteries for activating toys. Linemar was founded in the 1950s as an import subsidiary of Louis Marx & Co. This major American toy company was among the first to exploit the advantages of overseas manufacture and to import mechanical and battery-operated toys from Japan. The two handsome examples shown here are rare and in fine condition complete with boxes, hence their high value. One of the disadvantages of battery toys was that batteries could corrode if left in, thus rendering toys unusable.

A tinplate wind-up musical toy, 1950s, 3½in (9cm) high.
£20–25 / €30–35 $35–45 ⊞ RTT

◀ **A tinplate wind-up trolley bus,** with bell and electric lights, French, c1960, 12in (30.5cm) long.
£155–175 €230–260 $290–330 ⊞ GTM

▶ **A tinplate battery-operated Ford 4000 tractor,** Japanese, 1960s, 16in 40.5cm) long.
£320–360 €480–540 $600–670 ⊞ HAL

◀ **A Page tinplate Alice in Wonderland paint box,** 1960s, 20in (51m) wide.
£35–40 €50–60 $65–75 ⊞ LAS

Trains

A Hornby gauge 0 Crawford's Biscuits van, 1924, 6¾in (17cm) long, with box.
£270–300 / €400–450
$500–560 ⊞ MDe

A Hornby No. 3 clockwork gauge 0 locomotive and tender, No. 6100, 'Royal Scot', finished in Great Western livery, 1927–40, 16¾in (42.5cm) long, with box.
£360–450 / €540–670
$710–840 ⊞ MDe
Hornby produced a very popular range of larger locomotives repesenting famous trains from the four railway regions: Great Western, 'Caerphilly Castle'; LNER, 'Flying Scotsman'; Southern, 'Lord Nelson' and LMS, 'Royal Scot'. The fact that the wheel arrangements were not the same as those of the original locomotives did not seem to matter as they sold in large quantities. They were manufactured from 1927 until production ceased in 1940. The electric version of the clockwork locomotive shown here is worth £450–500 / €670–750 / $840–930.

A freight wagon, German, 1930s, 7in (18cm) long.
£40–45 / €60–70
$75–85 ⊞ WOS

Hornby vans
Hornby produced eight different private owner vans, starting in 1923 with the Colman's Mustard van. This is eagerly sought after by collectors today and will fetch upwards of £1,500 / €2,250 / $2,800, and even more if boxed.

A Hornby gauge 0 snow plough, c1930, 6in (15cm) long.
£135–150 / €200–220
$250–280 ⊞ GTM

A Hornby No. E120 electric gauge 0 tank locomotive, No. 826, c1936, 8in (20.5cm) long, with box.
£1,000–1,200 / €1,500–1,800
$1,850–2,400 ⊞ MDe
This locomotive is unusual in that it is finished in black. These were only available to order after 1935. A clockwork version would be worth £150–200 / €220–300 / $280–370.

A Buddy 'L' pressed steel stock van, with opening doors, American, c1926, 22¼in (56.5cm) long.
£640–760 / €960–1,150
$1,200–1,400 ⋟ Bert

A Hornby No. 1 gauge 0 special tank locomotive, No. 8123, finished in LNER livery, c1930, 8½in (21.5cm) long, with box.
£380–450 / €300–670
$710–840 ⊞ MDe
This popular range was introduced in 1929 and is available in both clockwork and electric for all four railway regions. Look out for the electric version in Great Western and Southern, as these will command nearly double the price of clockwork examples.

A Hornby gauge 0 Redline Super petrol tank wagon, 1930s, 7in (18cm) long, with box.
£170–200 / €250–300
$320–370 ⊞ MDe
Hornby first produced their popula series of colourful petrol tank wagons in 1922. They are eagerly sought after by collectors today.

A Bassett Lowke clockwork gauge 0 locomotive and tender, No. 2265, 'Princess Elizabeth', finished in LMS livery, 1930s, 14½in (37cm) long.
£240–280 / €360–420
$450–530 ⋟ WAL

An aluminium electric locomotive, 'American Flyer', with two coaches, c1940, 31½in (80cm) long.
£950–1,100 / € 1,450–1,650
$1,800–2,050 ⚓ S(P)

A Chad Valley tinplate clockwork gauge 0 train, with four coaches, c1950, 6in (15cm) long.
£55–65 / € 85–100
$100–120 ⊞ JUN

▶ **A Trix Twin 4–4–0 locomotive and tender,** with three passenger coaches, two Trix Twin coaches and four goods trucks, c1950.
£140–165 / € 210–250
$260–310 ⚓ AH

A Hornby No. 2 gauge 0 passenger brake end coach, finished in LMS livery, 1940s, 13in (33cm) long, with box.
£200–300 / € 300–450
$370–560 ⊞ MDe
These Hornby passenger coaches were produced immediately after WWII for two years only and are very rare, particularly boxed examples. Great Western and Southern versions will command premium prices.

A Hornby Pool petrol tank wagon, 1940s, 4in (10cm) long, with box.
£90–105 / € 135–155
$165–195 ⚓ VEC

A Hornby gauge 0 NE flat truck with container, 1956–59, 6in (15cm) long, with box.
£35–40 / € 50–60
$65–75 ⊞ GTM

A Hornby Dublo TPO mail van set,
1950s, 11in (28cm) long, with box.
£30–35 / €45–50
$55–65 ⊞ HAL

**A Hornby No. 1 tinplate
gauge 0 crane truck,**
1950s, 6½in (16.5cm)
long, with box.
£25–30 / €40–45
$50–55 ⊞ WOS

**A Bassett Lowke clockwork gauge 0 0–6–0
locomotive and tender,** No. 64193, 1950s,
16in (40.5cm) long, with original box.
£350–420 / €520–620
$650–780 ↗ WAL

**Two Bassett Lowke gauge 0
wagons,** BR 20-ton double-ended
brake van No. 838354 and LMS 13-
ton open wagon No. 36721, 1950s,
5in (12.5cm) long, with original boxes.
£80–90 / €120–135
$150–170 ↗ WAL

**A Hornby Dublo Deltic Diesel electric
locomotive,** No. 9001, 'St Paddy', 1961,
10in (25.5cm) long, with box.
£300–360 / €450–540
$560–670 ↗ VEC

**A Hornby No. 50 gauge
0 gas cylinder wagon,**
early 1960s, 10in (25.5cm)
long, with box.
£35–40 / €50–60
$65–75 ⊞ GTM

**A Hornby Dublo 4–6–2 West
Country class locomotive and
tender,** No. 43005, 'Barnstaple', early
1960s, 11in (28cm) long, with box.
£150–180 / €230–270
$280–330 ↗ WAL

**A Hornby Dublo 2–6–4 4MT tank
locomotive,** No. 80054, three-rail,
early 1960s, 7in (18cm) long, with box.
£90–100 / €135–150
$170–190 ↗ WA

**A Hornby Dublo Electric class AL1
locomotive,** No. E3002, 3,300HP,
with operating pantographs, three-
rail, early 1960s, 9in (23cm) long,
with associated box.
£470–560 / €700–840
$880–1,050 ↗ WAL

**A Hornby Dublo 4–6–2 Duchess
class locomotive and tender,** No.
46245, 'City of London', two-rail,
early 1960s, 12in (30.5cm) long,
with original box.
£150–180 / €230–270
$280–330 ↗ WAL

**A Hornby Dublo Canadian Pacific
Railroad caboose,** No. 437270,
two- or three-rail, early 1960s, 4in
(10cm) long, with original box.
£210–250 / €310–370
$390–460 ↗ WAL

**A Hornby Dublo 4–6–0
locomotive and tender,** No. 4075,
'Cardiff Castle', two-rail, early
1960s, 11in (28cm) long,
with original box.
£100–120 / €150–180
$185–220 ↗ WAL

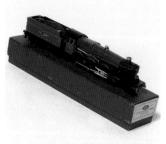

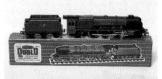

A Hornby Dublo die-cast rail cleaning wagon, with six filter pads and operating instructions, early 1960s, 3in (7.5cm) long, with original box.
£280–330 / €420–500
$520–620 ↗ **WAL**

A Hornby Dublo 4–6–0 Castle class locomotive and tender, No. 7032, 'Denbigh Castle', two-rail, early 1960s, 10½in (26.5cm) long, with original box.
£145–170 / €220–260
$270–320 ↗ **WAL**

▶ **A Hornby Dublo restaurant car,** No. W1910, early 1960s, 9½in (24cm) long, with original box.
£80–90 / €120–135
$150–170 ↗ **WAL**

A Hornby Dublo 4–6–2 locomotive and tender, No. 46245, 'City of London', three-rail, early 1960s, 12in (30.5cm) long, with associated box and instructions.
£120–140 / €180–210
$220–260 ↗ **WAL**

A Hornby Dublo 2–6–4 4MT tank locomotive, No. 80033, three-rail, converted from two-rail, early 1960s, 7in (18cm) long, with original two-rail box.
£80–90 / €120–135
$150–170 ↗ **WAL**

◀ **A Hornby gauge 00 Battle of Britain class locomotive and tender,** No. R374, 'Spitfire', 1980s, 11in (28cm) long, with box.
£65–75 / €100–115
$120–140 ⊞ **GTM**

Treen

A turned beech candle holder, c1670, 6in (15cm) high.
£340–380 / €510–570
$630–710 ⊞ SEA

A burr-birch pot, with locking lid, late 18thC, 5in (12.5cm) diam.
£250–280 / €370–420
$470–520 ⊞ NEW

A Tunbridge ware nutmeg grater, 1845–50, 2in (5cm) diam.
£190–210 / €280–310
$350–390 ⊞ AMH

A Mauchline ware box, decorated with a view of West End Park, Glasgow, inscribed 'Frazer & Green, Chemists, Glasgow', c1860, 3¼in (8.5cm) high.
£85–95 / €130–145
$160–180 ⊞ GAU

A carved bog oak candlestick, Irish, c1860, 6in (15cm) high.
£165–185 / €250–280
$310–350 ⊞ STA

▶ **A wooden bird call,** c1880, 4in (10cm) high.
£45–50 / €70–80
$85–95 ⊞ JUN

A Victorian boxwood gavel, 7in (18cm) long.
£25–30 / €40–45
$50–55 ⊞ WiB

A wooden cruet set, c1890, 3½in (9cm) high.
£20–25 / €300–35
$35–45 ⊞ AL

A carved wood stanhope, in the form of a pig, showing a view of Southend-on-Sea, c1900, ½in (1cm) wide.
£45–50 / €70–80
$85–95 ⊞ MRW

A Black Forest carved softwood model of a bear, holding a thermometer, German, early 20thC.
£40–45 / €60–70
$75–85 ⚒ RTo

A pair of child's pine shoe lasts, c1930, 5in (12.5cm) wide.
£40–45 / €60–70
$75–85 ⊞ Cot

Walking Sticks & Parasols

An ivory and malacca walking stick, with a brass collar, 18thC, 42in (106.5cm) long.
£190–220 / €280–330
$350–410 ⚜ G(L)

A Victorian silver-mounted ivory walking stick handle, in the form of a hare, with glass eyes, 5½in (14cm) long.
£170–200 / €260–300
$320–370 ⚜ G(L)

A malacca walking stick, the handle incorporating a propelling pencil, c1880, 35in (89cm) long.
£270–300 / €400–450
$500–560 ⊞ GBr

A walking stick, with a silver-mounted horn handle, c1890, 35in (89cm) long.
£170–190 / €260–290
$320–360 ⊞ GBr

A wooden walking stick, the handle carved in the form of Cupid's head, Italian, c1890, 35in (89cm) long.
£165–185 / €250–280
$310–350 ⊞ GBr

A silver-mounted ebonized evening cane, c1890, 33in (84cm) long.
£60–70 / €90–105
$110–130 ⊞ GBr

A walnut swordstick, c1890, 35in (89cm) long.
£350–390 / €530–590
$650–730 ⊞ GBr

A brass-mounted carved wood walking stick handle, in the form of a dog's head, with spring-action jaw movement, c1900, 3in (7.5cm) long.
£100–120 / €150–180
$185–220 ⚜ G(L)

A silver-mounted wooden walking stick, the handle carved in the form of an elephant's head, c1900, 40in (101.5cm) long.
£80–95 / €120–145
$150–180 ⚜ G(L)

A cane and brass shooting stick, c1900, 35in (89cm) long.
£90–100 / €135–150
$170–190 ⊞ SA

◀ **A parasol,** with a Black Forest carved wood handle in the form of a bulldog's head, the painted hat containing a powder compact and the mouth holding a lipstick, 1930s, 14in (35.5cm) long.
£360–400 / €540–600
$670–750 ⊞ SUW

Watches & Clocks

A glass mantel clock,
with enamel dial, eight-day
movement and mercury
pendulum, 19thC,
9¼in (23.5cm) high.
**£160–190 / €240–280
$300–360 ✖ Oli**

A slate mantel clock, the enamel dial with
visible escapement, 19thC, 22in (56cm) wide.
**£180–210 / €270–320
$340–400 ✖ G(L)**

**An 18ct gold hunting-cased
watch,** by Robert Monnout, the case
engraved and enamelled, 19thC,
2in (5cm) high, with walnut box.
**£180–210 / €270–320
$340–400 ✖ JAA**

A silver keywind lever pocket watch, by
Joseph Ball, with an enamel dial, the movement
with plain balance, signed, London 1876.
**£55–65 / €85–100
$100–120 ✖ G(L)**

Items in the Watches & Clock section have
been arranged in date order.

**A Black Forest oak
mantel clock,** with a
silvered dial, the Lenzkirch
movement striking on a
bell, German, late 19thC,
12in (30.5cm) high.
**£75–85 / €115–130
$140–160 ✖ G(L)**

An oak wall clock, the glazed door
enclosing a painted dial and a fusee
movement, late 19thC,
15½in (39.5cm) diam.
**£120–140 / €180–210
$220–260 ✖ FHF**

**A brass and glass carriage clock/
barometer,** the top inset with a compass,
c1900, 6½in (16.5cm) wide.
**£200–240 / €300–360
$380–450 ✖ GAK**

**A Movado gold-plated
pocket watch,** inscribed
'Exposition Universelles
Paris', Swiss, c1900.
**£80–90 / €120–135
$150–170 ✖ SWO**

**An Edwardian slate striking
mantel clock,** inlaid with ceramic
panels, 11½in (29cm) high.
**£75–85 / €115–130
$140–160 ✖ WilP**

A silver hunter pocket watch, decorated in relief with portraits of King George V and Edward VII, the silvered dial with royal coat-of-arms, inscribed 'Chronograph Prima', import marks, c1911.
£280–330 / €420–500
$520–620 ↗ CHTR

An 18ct gold wristwatch, with an enamel bezel and a ribbon strap, Glasgow 1912.
£120–140 / €180–210
£220–260 ↗ SWO

A Zenith silver-cased officer's trench watch, 24 hour enamel dial, Swiss, case London 1915.
£240–270 / €360–410
$450–500 ⊞ WAC
Wristwatches were developed in the second half of the 19th century. In 1868 Patek Philippe created a jewelled wristwatch for Countess Kocewicz. In 1886 Girard Perregaux was commissioned to produce wristwatches for the Imperial German Navy, and in 1904 Louis Cartier designed a wristwatch for Alberto Santos Dumont, a Brazilian aviator who needed a convenient timepiece for use on his airship. Generally, however, the pocket watch remained the standard choice for men until WWI, when the rigours of trench life made it far easier to glance at the wrist rather than to extract a pocket watch. Swiss steel watches were mass-produced for military use and in the USA Robert Ingersoll, creator of the $1 watch, supplied inexpensive wristwatches to the armed forces and also devised Radiolite – a luminous paint that would enable troops to see the hands and numerals in the dark. The WWI watch shown here is by the Swiss company Zenith (est. 1865). Military watches are a growing area of the collector's market and examples that are unrestored and in near-mint condition will command more than less well-preserved pieces.

A silver-mounted mahogany mantel clock, by C. L. S, with engine-turned decoration, London 1919, 8½in (21.5cm) high.
£180–210 / €270–320
$330–390 ↗ G(L)

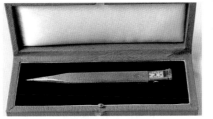

A propelling pencil timepiece, with slide-out mechanism, French, c1920.
£1,750–1,950 / €2,600–2,900
$3,250–3,650 ⊞ AGR

▶ **A metal and glass animated alarm clock,** with moving eyes, German, c1925, 5½in (14cm) high.
£600–700
€900–1,050
$1,100–1,300
↗ S(P)

Further reading
Miller's Wristwatches: How to Compare & Value, Miller's Publications, 2004

An Oswald Clocks carved wood clock, in the form of an owl, with moving eyes, 1920s, 8in (20.5cm) high.
£580–650 / €870–980
$1,050–1,200 ⊞ CCe

▶ **An Oswald Clocks carved wood clock,** in the form of a dog, with moving eyes, 1920s, 8in (20.5cm) high.
£300–350 / €450–530
$560–650 ⊞ CCe
Based in Freiberg, Germany, clockmaker J. Oswald took out an English patent for a clock with revolving eyes in 1926. His novelty clocks, which appear in the form of dogs, Oriental figures and even a skull, are very collectable.

An 18ct white gold wristwatch, with platinum trim, 1920s.
£270–300 / € 400–450
$500–560 ⊞ WAC

An enamelled watch brooch, in the form of cherries hanging from a branch, American, 1930s, 2in (5cm) wide.
£45–50 / € 70–80
$85–95 ⊞ DRE

▶ A Rotary doctor's chrome wristwatch, with seconds dial for measuring pulse, 1930s.
£145–165 / € 220–250
$270–310 ⊞ WAC

A Helvetia chrome-plated waterproof contract watch, stamped 'WWW Q877', 1940s.
£140–155 / € 200–230
$260–290 ⊞ WAC

A Smiths 9ct gold wristwatch, Birmingham 1946.
£220–250 / € 330–380
$410–470 ⊞ WAC

◀ A Rotary stainless steel waterproof sports watch, 1930s.
£230–270 / € 350–410
$430–500 ⊞ WAC

An Ingraham Co metal Buck Rogers pocket watch, initialled, 1935, 2in (5cm) diam.
£300–350 / € 450–530
$500–660 ⚒ Bert

A Driva military-style sterling silver watch, 1940.
£175–195 / € 260–290
$320–360 ⊞ WAC

◀ A Cortebert watch, 1940s.
£165–185 / € 250–280
$310–350 ⊞ WAC

A Charles Nicolet Tramelan 10ct gold-filled chronograph watch, with a coppered dial, 1940s.
£410–470 / € 620–710
$770–880 ⊞ WAC

◀ A Jaeger Le Coultre 18ct gold wristwatch, with a snakelink bracelet, 1940s.
£320–380 / € 480–570
$600–710 ⚒ G(L)

A Bayard Mickey Mouse alarm clock, French, 1940s–50s, 5in (12.5cm) high.
£50–55 / € 75–85
$95–105 ⊞ TASV
The first Mickey Mouse watch was produced by Ingersoll-Waterbury Co in 1933. It originally sold for £2 / € 3 / $3.75 and was then reduced to £1.50 / € 2.25 /$2.75. These cheap watches were apparently notorious for breaking down and gave rise to the pejorative use of the term Mickey Mouse for an inferior or poor-quality product. Mickey Mouse's image has been used on a huge number of watches and clocks since the 1930s.

◀ **A Lorie stainless-steel and 10ct gold wristwatch,** 1940s–50s.
£145–165 / € 220–250
$270–310 ⊞ WAC

An Ingersoll Dan Dare Eagle pocket watch, with a rocket second hand, 1950s.
£380–450 / € 570–680
$710–840 ⋟ CBP

◀ **A watch brooch,** in the form of a train, set with paste stones, American, 1950s, 2in (5cm) high.
£60–70 / € 90–105
$110–130 ⊞ DRE

A Longines 9ct gold wristwatch, signed, Swiss, case Birmingham 1952, with box.
£240–280 / €360–420
$450–520 ↗ TEN

A Bayard travel clock, French, 1950s, 4in (10cm) wide, with case.
£15–20 / €22–30
$28–38 ⊞ OIA

A Rolex Oyster stainless steel wristwatch, with Rolex Superbalance silvered dial, signed, Swiss, c1952.
£480–570 / €720–860
$900–1,050 ↗ S(O)

Rolex

Rolex is one of the most famous names in watches. The company was founded by Hans Wilsdorf in London in 1905. In 1910 Rolex was awarded an Official Chronometer Certification from the Official Bureau in Switzerland, followed in 1914 by a Class A Certificate from the Kew Observatory in Greenwich, the first time that either of these prestigious awards had ever been issued to a wristwatch. After WWI Rolex relocated to Switzerland, where their reputation for technical innovation grew. Wilsdorf's ambition was to produce a truly waterproof watch. In 1926 the Rolex Oyster was launched, and when, in a brilliant piece of advertising, it was worn by Mercedes Gleitz for her Channel swim, Rolex became famous. In 1931 Wilsdorf introduced the Rolex Perpetual system of automatic winding that was eventually copied by almost every maker of self-winding wristwatches, and the Datejust (1945) was the first chronometer with automatic date change. The company continued to lead the way with underwater watches. The Sea Dweller (1971) was guaranteed to a depth of 2,000 feet and was subsequently adapted to make 4,000 feet possible. Rolex watches were worn by everybody from Edmund Hillary when he scaled Mount Everest in 1953, to Sean Connery as James Bond, and in recent years they have confirmed their status as an ultimate accessory. This has resulted in a huge range of fakes, and further identification marks now added by Rolex include a hologram-encoded sticker on the watch case, a tiny laser-etched crown in the glass and watermarked warranty papers. The market for vintage Rolex watches is strong and the most collectable series include Oyster, GMT, Prince, President and bubble-back watches.

A Rolex Oyster steel and gilt wristwatch, No. 6266, the silvered dial with date aperture, signed, Swiss, c1953.
£400–480 / €600–720
$750–900 ↗ S(O)

A Bulova Accutron 14ct gold and stainless steel wristwatch, with railroad dial, 1960s.
£270–300 / €400–450
$500–560 ⊞ WAC

▶ **An Omega De Ville wristwatch,** Swiss, 1970s.
£135–150 / €200–230
$250–280 ⊞ TIC

▶ **An Omega gold-plated wristwatch,** with day and date aperture, Swiss, 1970s.
£220–250 / €330–380
$410–470 ⊞ TIC

An Omega Quartz wristwatch, Swiss, 1978–8
£170–190 / €260–290
$320–360 ⊞ TIC

◀ **A Carlton International Thunderbirds clock,** 1999, 10in (25.5cm) wide.
£15–20 / €22–30
$28–38 ⊞ LAS

Writing

A brass, ebony and ivory rastrum, 19thC, 6½in (16.5cm) long.
£150–170 / € 230–260
$280–320 ⊞ PPL
Rastrum, from the Latin word for rake, is a multi-nibbed pen designed for ruling musical staves. Rastrography, the pattern of stave rulings, is one of the means used to help date historical hand-written musical manuscripts.

A stoneware inkwell, modelled as a grotesque mask, 3in (7.5cm) high.
£120–140 / € 180–210
$220–260 ✒ WilP

▶ **A silver and coral seal,** depicting a whippet, c1830, 2in (5cm) long.
£110–125 / € 165–190
$210–230 ⊞ CoHA

A Sampson Mordan & Co silver slider combination pencil and pen, with machine-engraved decoration, 1860–80, 4in (10cm) long.
£130–150 / € 200–230
$240–280 ⊞ PPL

A treen travelling inkwell, by W. Grahams, 1847, 1½in (4cm) square.
£130–150 / € 200–230
$240–280 ⊞ PPL

▶ **A burr-walnut stationery cabinet,** the two doors enclosing a fitted interior with two gilt-metal-mounted glass inkwells and base drawer, late 19thC, 13in (33cm) wide.
£400–480 / € 600–720
$750–900 ✒ G(L)

Two brass travelling inkwells, with monogrammed initials, c1880, 4in (10cm) high.
£65–75 / € 100–115
$120–140 ⊞ HO

A glass inkwell, in the form of a kettle, c1880, 2½in (6.5cm) high.
£60–70 / € 90–105
$110–130 ⊞ PPL

◀ **A Doulton Lambeth Isobath inkwell,** with stylized decoration, c1885, 7in (18cm) high.
£200–240 / € 300–360
$380–450 ✒ G(B)

A J. Grinsell & Sons silver novelty stamp roller, in the form of a glass grinding wheel, on a marble base, London 1896, 4½in (11.5cm) wide.
£400–480 / € 600–720
$750–900 ✒ WW

An ivory paper knife, the blade carved with a deer, with a deer's foot handle, c1900, 12in (30.5cm) long.
£170–190 / €250–280
$310–350 ⊞ MSh

◀ **A Sampson Mordan & Co silver stamp moistener,** in the form of a Heidseck champagne bottle, with an enamelled label, London 1897, 4½in (11.5cm) high.
£640–760 / €960–1,150
$1,200–1,400 ✗ WW

A Waterman silver filigree Ideal fountain pen, with a rubber barrel, early 20thC, 4½in (11.5cm) long.
£180–200 / €270–300
$330–370 ✗ G(L)

A silver and ivory paper knife, the hilt in the form of a horse's head, marked, Russian, 1908–17, 10¾in (27.5cm) long.
£200–240 / €300–360
$380–450 ✗ WW

A Wemyss inkwell, in the form of a heart, printed with a cockerel, damaged, impressed marks, early 20thC, 7in (18cm) wide.
£220–260 / €330–390
$410–490 ✗ SWO

An Edwardian pressed glass inkwell, with a star-cut cover and a brass collar, 6in (15cm) high.
£55–65 / €85–100
$100–120 ✗ G(L)

A silver stamp roller, in the form of a sleeping pig, surmounted with a calendar, marked, Birmingham 1911, 3¼in (8.5cm) wide.
£560–670 / €840–1,000
$1,050–1,250 ✗ WW

A Milady 'jewelled' metal vanity pen, commemorating the Festival of Britain, 1951, 3½in (9cm) long.
£15–20 / €22–30
$28–38 ⊞ HUX

A Parker 75 sterling silver Cisele fountain pen, c1968, 5in (12.5cm) long.
£45–50 / €70–80
$85–95 ✗ G(L)

A Parker 75 sterling silver Cisele fountain pen, 1975, 5in (12.5cm) long.
£100–120 / €150–180
$200–220 ⊞ RUS

Pocket Money Collectables

A music score, 'Impudence Schottische', by Alan Macey, published by Paxton & Co, c1895, 14 x 10in (35.5 x 25.5cm).
£1–5 / €2–7
$3–9 ⊞ POS

An embroidered tray cloth, 1920s–30s, 15 x 21in (38 x 53.5cm).
£5–9 / €8–13
$10–16 ⊞ HILL

Anne Anson, How to Decorate a Cake, booklet, 1950s, 8in (20.5cm) high.
£1–5 / €2–7
$3–9 ⊞ DaM

A card of Marquita hair clips, 1940s, 7in (18cm high).
£5–9 / €8–13
$10–16 ⊞ NFR

A selection of silk dress trims, c1920, 10in (25.5cm) long.
£6–10 / €9–15
$12–19 each ⊞ DE

◀ A Snowdrop Manchester glass codd bottle, 1910, 9in (23cm) high.
£1–5 / €2–7
$3–9 ⊞ OIA

A pair of plastic sunglasses, with glass lenses, 1940s–50s.
£1–5 / €2–7
$3–9 ⊞ RTT

A pottery egg cup, in the form of a duck, with hand-painted decoration, Italian, c1950, 4in (10cm) wide.
£1–5 / €2–7
$3–9 ⊞ POS

◀ A theatre programme, for Captain Brassbound's Conversion, starring Ingrid Bergman, Cambridge Theatre, 1971, 9 x 5¼in (23 x 13.5cm).
£1–5 / €2–7
$3–9 ⊞ c20th

Collectables of the Future

The *Sun*, front page 'Robbie Williams leaves Take That', 1995, 15 x 12in (38 x 30.5cm).
£1–5 / €2–7
$3–9 ⊞ IQ
Newspapers covering major news events or, as here, key celebrity moments, can be desirable, but in order for them to have any future value they must be in perfect condition.

A Diet Pepsi bottle, illustrated with a photograph of David Beckham, 2002, 8in (20.5cm) high.
£8–12 / €12–18
$15–22 ⊞ HeA

A Royal Collection porcelain mug, commemorating the 21st birthday of Prince William, 2003, 6in (15cm) high.
£20–25 / €30–35
$35–45 ⊞ H&G

◄ **A David Blaine *Vertigo* poster,** from Bryant Park, New York, 2002, 30 x 12in (76 x 30.5cm).
£150–165 / €225–250
$280–310 ⊞ IQ

An aluminium necklace, by Val Hunt, in the form of a fish, made from Fosters and Carlsberg beer cans, 2003, 12in (30.5cm) long.
£80–90 / €120–135
$150–170 ⊞ LaF
Jewellery by contemporary crafts people can be highly inventive, and this example also reflects the current interest in creative recycling.

A Dennis Chinaworks Kingfisher vase, by Sally Tuffin, 2004, 12½in (32cm) high.
£540–600 / €810–900
$1,000–1,100 ⊞ CBi
Sally Tuffin is one of the most collectable names in modern decorative pottery.

An enamel *Queen Mary 2* souvenir badge, in three sections, commemorating the maiden voyage, edition of 100, 2004, 6in (15cm) wide.
£65–75 / €100–115
$120–140 ⊞ COB

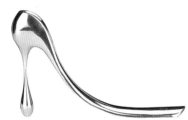

◄ **A Helen MacDonald glass paperweight,** 'Moonlit Meadow', No. L04115, limited edition of 100, 2004, 4in (10cm) high.
£200–230 / €300–340
$380–430 ⊞ Cai

A polished cast-aluminium shoehorn, by Manolo Blahnik for Habitat, 2004, 11¾in (30cm) wide.
£20–25 / €30–35
$35–45 ⊞ MMa
To celebrate its 40th anniversary in 2004, Habitat commissioned a range of objects designed by celebrities, including the famous shoe designer Manolo Blahnik.

Record Breakers

A pottery meat paste jar, 'The Fleet at Anchor', c1855, 4in (10cm) high.
£2,400 / €3,700
$4,500 ↗ **SAS**

Cross Reference
Breweriana
see pages 71–75

A cast-brass nameplate, 'Royal Sovereign', carried by the LNER 'Sandringham' Class B17/4–6–0 LNER 2871, 1937, 59in (150cm) wide.
£25,600 / €38,000
$48,000 ↗ **SRA**
Originally purchased in 1959 when the train was dismantled, this nameplate achieved a record-breaking price due to the fact that it is in completely original condition, has its original BR delivery note, and was from the locomotive frequently used to pull the Royal Train.

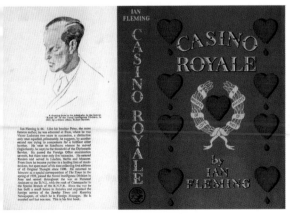

Ian Fleming, *Casino Royale*, dust jacket, first edition, 1953, 8 x19in (20.5 x 48.5cm).
£11,500 / €17,300
$21,500 ↗ **DW**
This dust jacket was on the first edition of Ian Fleming's first and rarest James Bond book.

◄ A Beveridge Bros stoneware whisky jug, with transfer-printed decoration of a stag and thistles, inscribed 'Old Highland Whisky, Beveridge Bros, 446 Duke St, Glasgow', 1900–20, 8¼in (21cm) high.
£1,900 / €2,850
$3,550 ↗ **BBR**
This is a record-breaking auction price for a previously unrecorded transfer-printed whisky jug.

The Dandy comic, No. 1, with free gift Express Whistler, small tear, 1937.
£20,300 / €30,000
$38,000 ↗ **CBP**
The tear to this comic may have been caused by the free gift inclusion. There are fewer than ten first issues known to exist and this copy is the highest grade ever offered at auction. This is also the only known example of an Express Whistler. When sold by Comic Book Postal Auctions in 2004 this *Dandy* No. 1 made a record-breaking auction price for a British comic.

A Matchbox Superfast MB 22 Pontiac sports car, 1969, with original box.
£4,000 / €6,000
$7,500 ↗ **VEC**
This model was unusual since instead of having black plastic wheels it was fitted with chrome and black superwheels, and very few of these toys are known to exist in this form. Made in England in 1969, it would have originally sold for 2/6d, just under 25p at today's values. Sold at auction by Vectis in the USA in 2004 it made a record-breaking price for a Matchbox car of £250 / €5,000 / $6,050.

2004 BACA *Winners...*

CATEGORY 1
General Antiques Dealer

UK: NORTH OF M62
Heathcote Antiques
Cross Hills, Nr Keighley, West Yorkshire BD20 7DS

M62 SOUTH, TO M4 / M25
Christopher Clarke Antiques
Stow-on-the-Wold, Gloucestershire GL54 1JS

LONDON (INSIDE M25)
sponsored by
David Brower
113 Kensington Church Street,
London W8 7LN

SOUTH AND SOUTH-WEST OF ENGLAND
Spencer Swaffer
30 High Street, Arundel, West Sussex BN18 9AB

CATEGORY 2
Specialist Antiques Dealers

FURNITURE
Butchoff Interiors
154 Kensington Church Street, London W8 4BN

COLLECTABLES
H. Blairman & Sons Ltd
119 Mount Street, London W1K 3NL

SILVER & PLATE
Koopman Rare Art
London SIlver Vaults, Chancery House,
Chancery Lane, London WC2A 1QX

ART NOUVEAU & ART DECO
Editions Graphique
3 Clifford Street, London W1S 2LF

OIL PAINTINGS
Messum's Fine Art
8 Cork Street, London W1S 3LJ

CLOCKS, WATCHES & SCIENTIFIC INSTRUMENTS
Trevor Phillips & Son Ltd
75a Jermyn Street, London SW1Y 6NP

JEWELLERY
Tadema Gallery
10 Charlton Place, London N1 8AJ

CERAMICS
Brian Haughton Antiques
3b Burlington Gardens, London W1S 3EP

CATEGORY 3
Auction Houses

UK: NORTH OF M62
Lyon & Turnbull Auctioneers
33 Broughton Place, Edinburgh, Scotland EH1 3RR

M62 SOUTH, TO M4 / M25
Bosley's Military Auctioneers
Marlow, Buckinghamshire SL7 1AH

INSIDE M25
Bonhams
101 New Bond Street, London W1S 1SR

SOUTH AND SOUTH-WEST OF ENGLAND
Dreweatt Neate
Donnington Priory, Newbury,
Berkshire RG14 2JE

CATEGORY 4
Associated Awards

AUCTIONEER OF THE YEAR
Richard Allen
Halls Fine Art Auctions, Welsh Bridge,
Shrewsbury SY3 8LA

MILLER'S CLUB BEST TOWN/VILLAGE
sponsored by
Petworth, West Sussex

BEST ANTIQUES CENTRE VOTED FOR BY THE READERS OF BBC HOMES & ANTIQUES
sponsored by
The Swan Antiques Centre, Tetsworth OX9 7AB

IN-HOUSE EXHIBITION
Art Deco Postmodernism
A Legacy of British Art Deco Glass,
10-20th September 2003, Richard Dennis
Gallery, London W8 (40pp illustrated catalogue
by Jeanette Hayhurst & Nigel Benson)

MILLER'S LIFE-TIME ACHIEVEMENT
sponsored by
Roger Warner
Burford, Oxfordshire

Directory of Specialists

If you require a valuation for an item it is advisable to check whether the dealer or specialist will carry out this service, and whether there is a charge. Please mention Miller's when making an enquiry. Having found a specialist who will carry out your valuation, it is best to send a description and photograph of the item to them, together with a stamped addressed envelope for the reply. A valuation by telephone is not possible. Most dealers are only too happy to help you with your enquiry, however, they are very busy people and consideration of the above points would be welcomed.

BERKSHIRE
Briggs, 54 Lupin Ride, Kings Copse,
Crowthorne, RG45 6UR
Tel: 01344 466022
enquiries@usebriggs.com
www.usebriggs.com
Rock & pop memorabilia

Special Auction Services,
Kennetholme, Midgham, Reading,
RG7 5UX Tel: 0118 971 2949
www.invaluable.com/sas/
*Commemoratives, pot lids &
Prattware, Fairings, Goss & Crested,
Baxter & Le Blond prints. Also toys
for the collector*

BUCKINGHAMSHIRE
Yesterday Child Tel: 01908 583403
djbarrington@btinternet.com
*Antique dolls and dolls house
miniatures. Exhibitors at London doll
fairs*

CAMBRIDGESHIRE
Antique Amusement Co, Mill Lane,
Swaffham Bulbeck, CB5 0NF
Tel: 01223 813041
mail@aamag.co.uk
www.aamag.co.uk
*Vintage amusement machines also
auctions of amusement machines,
fairground art and other related
collectables. Monthly collectors
magazine*

CHESHIRE
The Antique Garden, Grosvenor
Garden Centre, Wrexham Road,
Belgrave, Chester, CH4 9EB
Tel: 01244 629191/07976 539 990
antigard@btopenworld.com
*Original antique garden tools
and accessories*

Collector's Corner, PO Box 8,
Congleton, CW12 4GD
Tel: 01260 270429
dave.popcorner@ukonline.co.uk
Beatles and pop memorabilia

Dollectable, 53 Lower Bridge,
Chester, CH1 1RS
Tel: 01244 344888 or 679195
Antique dolls

M C Pottery Tel: 01244 301800
Sales@Moorcroftchester.co.uk
www.Moorcroftchester.co.uk
Moorcroft pottery

On The Air, The Vintage Technology
Centre, The Highway, Hawarden,
(Nr Chester), Deeside, CH5 3DN
Tel: 01244 530300
www.vintageradio.co.uk
Vintage radios

Specialist Glass Fairs Ltd
Tel: 01260 271975/01260 298042
info@glassfairs.co.uk
www.glassfairs.co.uk
*'National Glass Collectors Fair' (Est.
1991). Bi-annual event held in May &
November. For more details visit
www.glassfairs.co.uk or telephone
01260 271975*

Sweetbriar Gallery Paperweights Ltd.,
3 Collinson Court, off Church Street,
Frodsham, WA6 6PN
Tel: 01928 730064
sales@sweetbriar.co.uk
www.sweetbriar.co.uk
Quality paperweights

Charles Tomlinson Tel: 01244 318395
charles.tomlinson@lineone.net
charlestomlinson@tiscali.co.uk
Scientific instruments

CLEVELAND
Vectis Auctions Ltd, Fleck Way,
Thornaby, Stockton-on-Tees,
TS17 9JZ Tel: 01642 750616
admin@vectis.co.uk www.vectis.co.uk
Toy auctions

DEVON
The Pen and Pencil Lady
Tel: 01647 231619
penpencilady@aol.com
www.penpencilady.com
*Repair service for fountain pens
available, please ring for details.
Specialist dealer for pens, pencils,
dip pens and writing equipment from
the 19th and 20th century*

Sue Wilde at Wildewear
Tel: 01395 577966
compacts@wildewear.co.uk

www.wildewear.co.uk
*Specialists in fashion accessories
1900-1950 including beaded and
leather bags, purses, hats, powder
compacts, buttons and jewellery.
Examples from USA, France, Austria,
East Germany and UK*

DORSET
Books Afloat, 66 Park Street,
Weymouth, DT4 7DE Tel: 01305 779774
*Books on all subjects, liner and naval
memorabilia, shipping company
china, ships bells, old postcards,
models, paintings.*

Murrays' Antiques & Collectables
01202 823870
*Shipping, motoring, railway, cycling
items always required. Also
advertising related items, eg
showcards, enamel signs, tins &
packaging and general quality
collectables. Anything old and
interesting. No valuations given*

Old Button Shop Antiques,
Lytchett Minster, Poole, BH16 6JF
Tel: 01202 622169
info@oldbuttonshop.fsnet.co.uk
Buttons & collectables

ESSEX
20th Century Marks, Whitegates,
Rectory Road, Little Burstead,
Near Billericay, CM12 9TR
Tel: 01268 411 000
info@20thcenturymarks.co.uk
www.20thcenturymarks.co.uk
Original 20th century design

GKR Bonds Ltd, PO Box 1, Kelvedon,
CO5 9EH Tel: 01376 571711
Old bonds and share certificates

Haddon Rocking Horses Ltd,
5 Telford Road, Clacton on Sea,
CO15 4LP Tel: 01255 424745
millers@haddonrockinghorses.co.uk
www.haddonrockinghorses.co.uk
Rocking horse makers and restorers

The Old Telephone Company,
The Old Granary, Battlesbridge
Antiques Centre, Nr Wickford,
SS11 7RF Tel: 01245 400601

gp@theoldtelephone.co.uk
www.theoldtelephone.co.uk
Vintage telephones

FLINTSHIRE
Old Bears 4 U, 45 Chester Close,
Shotton, Deeside, CH5 1AX
Tel: 01244 830066
debbie&paul@oldbears4u.co.uk
www.oldbears4u.co.uk
*Buying, selling, repairing & cleaning
old bears*

GLOUCESTERSHIRE
Cottage Collectibles, Long Street
Antiques, 14 Long Street, Tetbury,
G18 8AQ Tel: 01666 500850
sheila@cottagecollectibles.co.uk
*Open Mon–Sat 10.00am–5.00pm,
Sun 12.00pm-4.00pm & by
appointment. English & Continental
country antiques & kitchenalia.
Showroom at Eccleshall,
Staffordshire. Open by appointment
only - 01785 850210*

Grimes House Antiques, High Street,
Moreton-in-Marsh, GL56 0AT
Tel: 01608 651029
grimes_house@cix.co.uk
www.grimeshouse.co.uk
www.cranberryglass.co.uk
www.collectglass.com
Cranberry glass

Jennie Horrocks Tel: 07836 264896
info@artnouveaulighting.plus.net
www.artnouveaulighting.co.uk
*Also at Top Banana Antiques Mall,
1 New Church St., Tetbury, Glos.
GL8 8DS*

Specialised Postcard Auctions,
25 Gloucester Street, Cirencester,
GL7 2DJ Tel: 01285 659057
Sales of early postcards and ephemera

Telephone Lines Ltd, 304 High
Street, Cheltenham, GL50 3JF
Tel: 01242 583699
info@telephonelines.net
www.telephonelines.net
Antique telephones

HAMPSHIRE
Jim Bullock Militaria, PO Box 217,
Romsey, SO51 5XL Tel: 01794
516455 jim@jimbullockmilitaria.com
www.jimbullockmilitaria.com
War medals, decorations and militaria

Classic Amusements
Tel: 01425 472164
pennyslot@aol.com
www.classicamusements.net
Vintage slot machines

Cobwebs, 78 Northam Road,
Southampton, SO14 0PB
Tel: 023 8022 7458
www.cobwebs.uk.com
*Ocean liner memorabilia. Also naval
and aviation items*

Goss & Crested China Centre &
Museum, incorporating Milestone
Publications, 62 Murray Road,
Horndean, PO8 9JL
Tel: 023 9259 7440
info@gosschinaclub.co.uk
www.gosschinaclub.co.uk

Solent Railwayana Auctions,
9 Wildern Close, Locks Heath,
Southampton, SO31 7EZ
Tel: 01489 574029
nigel@solentrailwayana.com
www.solentrailwayana.com
*Railwayana and transport related
auctions*

KENT
Chris Baker Gramophones,
All Our Yesterdays, 3 Cattle Market,
Sandwich, CT13 9AE
Tel: 01304 614756
cbgramophones@aol.com
www.chrisbakergramophones.co.uk
*Specialist dealer in gramophones
and phonographs*

John Bartholomew, Heirloom
Antiques, 68 High Street, Tenterden,
TN30 6AU Tel: 01580 765535 or
01580 241556
Postcards and cigarette cards

Beatcity, P O Box 229, Chatham,
ME5 8WA Tel: 01634 200444 or
07770 650890
Darrenhanks@beatcity.co.uk
www.beatcity.co.uk
Beatles and rock & roll memorabilia

Candlestick & Bakelite, PO Box 308,
Orpington, BR5 1TB
Tel: 020 8467 3743
candlestick.bakelite@mac.com
www.candlestickandbakelite.co.uk
Telephones from 1920s to 1970s

Dragonlee Collectables
Tel: 01622 729502
Noritake

Stuart Heggie, 14 The Borough,
Northgate, Canterbury, CT1 2DR
Tel: 01227 470422
*Vintage cameras, optical toys and
photographic images*

Lambert & Foster, 102 High Street,
Tenterden, TN30 6HT
Tel: 01580 762083

tenterden@lambertandfoster.co.uk
www.lambertandfoster.co.uk
*Regular monthly sales held
Tenterden Antique Auction Rooms*

The Old Tackle Box, PO Box 55,
Cranbrook, TN17 3ZU
Tel: 01580 713979
tackle.box@virgin.net
Old fishing tackle

The Neville Pundole Gallery,
8A & 9 The Friars, Canterbury,
CT1 2AS Tel: 01227 453471
neville@pundole.co.uk
www.pundole.co.uk
*Moorcroft and contemporary pottery
and glass*

Wenderton Antiques
Tel: 01227 720295 (by appt only)
*Country antiques including kitchen,
laundry and dairy*

Woodville Antiques, The Street,
Hamstreet, Ashford, TN26 2HG
Tel: 01233 732981
woodvilleantiques@yahoo.co.uk
Tools

Wot a Racket, 250 Shepherds Lane,
Dartford, DA1 2PN
Tel: 01322 220619
wot-a-racket@talk21.com
Sporting memorabilia

LANCASHIRE
Decades, 20 Lord St West, Blackburn,
BB2 1JX Tel: 01254 693320
*Original Victorian to 1970s clothing,
accessories, jewellery, decorative
textiles, and more*

Tracks, PO Box 117, Chorley,
PR6 0UU Tel: 01257 269726
sales@tracks.co.uk www.tracks.co.uk
Beatles and pop memorabilia

LEICESTERSHIRE
Pooks Books, Fowke Street, Rothley,
LE7 7PJ Tel: 0116 237 6222
pooks.motorbooks@virgin.net
Motoring books and automobilia

LINCOLNSHIRE
Junktion, The Old Railway Station,
New Bolingbroke,
Boston, PE22 7LB
Tel: 01205 480068/480087
junktionantiques@hotmail.com
*Advertising and packaging,
automobilia, slot machines, pedal cars*

Skip & Janie Smithson Antiques
Tel: 01754 810265
smithsonantiques@hotmail.com
Kitchenware

LONDON

Bloomsbury Auctions Ltd,
Bloomsbury House,
24 Maddox Street, W1S 1PP
Tel: 020 7495 9494
info@bloomsburyauctions.com
www.bloomsburyauctions.com
*Books, manuscripts, art, prints,
collectables auctions*

Chelsea Military Antiques,
F4 Antiquarius, 131/141 Kings Road,
Chelsea, SW3 4PW
Tel: 020 7352 0308
richard@chelseamilitaria.com
*British campaign medals, 19th &
20thc allied & axis militaria*

Christie's South Kensington,
85 Old Brompton Road, SW7 3LD
Tel: 020 7930 6074
info@christies.com
www.christies.com
Collectibles auctions

The Collector, Tom Power,
20 Granville Road, Barnet, EN5 4DS
Tel: 020 8441 2015
collector@globalnet.co.uk
By appointment only. *Contemporary
collectables including Royal Doulton,
Beswick, Pendelfin, Worcester,
Lladro, Border Fine Art, Wade,
Wedgwood, Coalport, Bossons,
Lilliput Lane, David Winter, etc*

Comic Book Postal Auctions Ltd,
40-42 Osnaburgh Street, NW1 3ND
Tel: 020 7424 0007
comicbook@compalcomics.com
www.compalcomics.com
Comic book auctions

Dix-Noonan-Webb, 16 Bolton Street,
Piccadilly, W1J 8BQ Tel: 020 7016
1700 auctions@dnw.co.uk
www.dnw.co.uk
*Auctioneers and valuers of orders,
decorations and medals, coins,
tokens and banknotes*

Eat My Handbag Bitch,
37 Drury Lane, WC2B 5RR
Tel: 020 7836 0830
contact@eatmyhandbagbitch.co.uk
www.eatmyhandbagbitch.co.uk
*Post-war design, furniture, glass,
small decorative items, ceramics,
lighting, etc*

GB Military Antiques,
17-18 The Mall, 359 Upper Street,
Islington, N1 0PD Tel: 020 7354 7334
info@gbmilitaria.com
www.gbmilitaria.com

Michael German Antiques Ltd,
38B Kensington Church Street,
W8 4BX Tel: 020 7937 2771/
020 7937 1776
info@antiquecanes.com
info@antiqueweapons.com
www.antiquecanes.com
Walking canes, arms and armour

IPM Promotions/Memories,
130/132 Brent Street, Hendon,
NW4 2DR Tel: 020 8203 1500
www.memoriespostcards.co.uk
Postcards and photographs

Charles Jeffreys Posters & Graphics,
4 Vardens Road, SW11 1RH
Tel: 020 7978 7976
cjeffreys@cjposters.ision.co.uk
charlie@cjposters.com
www.cjposters.com
*Specialising in selling original, rare
and collectable posters from the
birth of modernism through bauhaus
to the 60s and 70s pop art and
psychedelic culture*

Timothy Millett Ltd. Historic Medals
and Works of Art, PO Box 20851,
SE22 0YN Tel: 020 8693 1111
tim@timothymillett.demon.co.uk
Medals and works of art

Colin Narbeth & Son Ltd,
20 Cecil Court, Leicester Square,
WC2N 4HE Tel: 020 7379 6975
Colin.Narbeth@btinternet.com
www.colin-narbeth.com
Banknotes, bonds and shares

Sotheby's Olympia,
Hammersmith Road, W14 8UX
Tel: 020 7293 5555
www.sothebys.com
Auctions of art, antiques, and collectibles

Tablewhere Ltd, 4 Queens Parade
Close, N11 3FY Tel: UK local rate
0845 130 6111 or 020 8361 6111
kitson@tablewhere.co.uk
www.tablewhere.co.uk
New or discontinued tableware

Tin Tin Collectables, G38-42 Alfies's
Antique Market, 13-25 Church
Street, Marylebone, NW8 8DT
Tel: 020 7258 1305
leslie@tintincollectables.com
www.tintincollectables.com
Period costumes and accessories

Vintage Modes, Grays Antique
Market, Mayfair, W1K 5AB
Tel: 020 7409 0400
www.vintagemodes.co.uk
Vintage fashion emporium

Vintage & Rare Guitars (London) Ltd,
6 Denmark Street, WC2H 8LX
Tel: 020 7240 7500
enquiries@vintageandrareguitars.co
m www.vintageandrareguitars.com
Vintage guitars and accessories

Nigel Williams Rare Books,
25 Cecil Court, WC2N 4EZ
Tel: 020 7836 7757
nigel@nigelwilliams.com
www.nigelwilliams.com
*Books -first editions, illustrated,
childrens and detective*

NORFOLK

Cat Pottery, 1 Grammar School
Road, North Walsham, NR28 9JH
Tel: 01692 402962
Winstanley cats

NORTHAMPTONSHIRE

Jess Miller Tel: 01933 623323
jessmiller@hardyreelbook.com
www.hardyreelbook.com
*Fishing associated items brokerage,
valuation and cataloguing service*

The Old Brigade, 10A Harborough
Road, Kingsthorpe, Northampton,
NN2 7AZ Tel: 01604 719389
theoldbrigade@btconnect.com
stewart@theoldbrigade.co.uk
www.theoldbrigade.co.uk
Military antiques

NOTTINGHAMSHIRE

The Carlton Lady, Helen Martin
Tel: 01636 611171
carltonhelen@aol.com
www.carltonware.biz
*Carlton ware specialist. See me at
Newark and Detling or check my
website*

Millennium Collectables Ltd,
P.O. Box 146,
Newark, NG24 2WR
Tel: 01636 703075
mail@millenniumcollectables.co.uk
www.millenniumcollectables.co.uk
Limited edition Guinness collectables

T. Vennett-Smith, 11 Nottingham
Road, Gotham, NG11 0HE
Tel: 0115 983 0541 info@vennett-
smith.com www.vennett-smith.com
*Ephemera and sporting memorabilia
auctions*

OXFORDSHIRE

Alvin's Vintage Games & Toys
Tel: 01865 772409
alvin@vintage-games.co.uk
www.vintage-games.co.uk
Pelham puppets

Mike Delaney
Tel: 01993 840064
mike@vintagehornby.co.uk
www.vintagehornby.co.uk
Vintage Hornby "0" gauge trains

Julian Eade Tel: 01865 300349
Doulton Lambeth stoneware and signed Burslem wares

Stone Gallery, 93 The High Street, Burford, OX18 4QA
Tel: 01993 823302
mail@stonegallery.co.uk
www.stonegallery.co.uk
Specialist dealers in antique and modern paperweights, gold and silver designer jewellery and enamel boxes

Teddy Bears of Witney,
99 High Street, Witney, OX28 6HY
Tel: 01993 706616
www.teddybears.co.uk
New and old Teddy bears

REPUBLIC OF IRELAND
George Stacpoole, Main Street, Adare, Co. Limerick
Tel: (0)6139 6409
stacpoole@iol.ie
www.georgestacpooleantiques.com
Furniture, pottery, ceramics, silver and prints

SCOTLAND
Rhod McEwan - Golf Books, Glengarden, Ballater, Aberdeenshire, AB35 5UB
Tel: 013397 55429
www.rhodmcewan.com
Rare and out-of-print golfing books

SHROPSHIRE
Mullock & Madeley,
The Old Shippon, Wall-under-Heywood, Nr Church Stretton, SY6 7DS Tel: 01694 771771
auctions@mullockmadeley.co.uk
www.mullockmadeley.co.uk
Sporting auctions

SOMERSET
Antiques & Collectables Magazine, Units 3-4 Riverside Court, Lower Bristol Road, Bath, BA2 3DZ
Tel Subscriptions: 01225 786814
Advertising: 01225 786810
antiques.collectables@btinternet.com
www.antiques-collectables.co.uk
Monthly magazine

Antiques Trade Online, Unit 3, 14 Fountain Buildings, Lansdown Mews, Bath, BA1 5DX

Tel: 01225 311061
info@antiquestradeonline.com
www.AntiquesTradeOnline.com
Antiques and collectables online

Philip Knighton, 1c South Street, Wellington, TA21 8NR
Tel: 01823 661618
philip.knighton@btopenworld.com
Wireless, gramophones and all valve equipment

London Cigarette Card Co Ltd, Sutton Road, Somerton, TA11 6QP
Tel: 01458 273452
cards@londoncigcard.co.uk
www.londoncigcard.co.uk
Cigarette and trade cards

Vintage & Rare Guitars (Bath) Ltd, 7-8 Saville Row, Bath, BA1 2QP
Tel: 01225 330 888
enquiries@vintageandrareguitars.co
m www.vintageandrareguitars.com
Vintage guitars and accessories

STAFFORDSHIRE
Peggy Davies Ceramics, Formerly St Luke's School Lower, Wellington Road, Hanley, Stoke-on-Trent, ST1 3QH Tel: 01782 262002
rhys@peggydavies.com
www.peggydavies.com
Ceramics - Limited edition Toby jugs and figures

Gordon Litherland, 25 Stapenhill Road, Burton on Trent, DE15 9AE
Tel: 01283 567213
Bottles, breweriana and pub jugs, advertising ephemera and commemoratives

The Potteries Antique Centre, 271 Waterloo Road, Cobridge, Stoke on Trent, ST6 3HR
Tel: 01782 201455
sales@potteriesantiquecentre.com
www.potteriesantiquecentre.com
Collectable ceramics

SUFFOLK
Jamie Cross, PO Box 73, Newmarket, CB8 8RY jamiecross@aol.com
www.thirdreichmedals.com
We buy and sell, value for probate and insurance British, German and foreign war medals, badges and decorations

W. L. Hoad, 9 St. Peter's Road, Kirkley, Lowestoft, NR33 0LH
Tel: 01502 587758
William@whoad.fsnet.co.uk
www.cigarettecardsplus.com
Cigarette cards

Suffolk Sci-Fi and Fantasy,
17 Norwich Road, Ipswich, IP1 2ET
Tel: 01473 400655
mick@suffolksci-fi.com
www.suffolksci-fi.com
Science fiction

SURREY
British Notes, PO Box 257, Sutton, SM3 9WW Tel: 020 8641 3224
pamwestbritnotes@aol.com
www.britishnotes.co.uk
Banking collectables

Collectors Choice, PO Box 99, Guildford, GU1 1GA
Tel: 01483 531104
louise@collectors-choice.net
www.collectors-choice.net
Collectable ceramics

The Gooday Gallery, 14 Richmond Hill, Richmond, TW10 6QX
Tel: 020 8940 8652
goodaygallery@aol.com
Arts & Crafts, Art Deco, Art Nouveau, Tribal, 1950s and 60s

Howard Hope, 19 Weston Park, Thames Ditton, KT7 0HW
Tel: 020 8398 7130
howard_hope@yahoo.co.uk
www.gramophones.uk.com
Specialising for 30 years in gramophones, phonographs, anything related to the history of recorded sound and other mechanical/musical items. Dealing by correspondence only, please no visits - call first. Colour pictures of any item in stock can be sent on request by email. Exporting worldwide. Shipping quotations given for any machine

EAST SUSSEX
High Street Retro, 39 High Street, Old Town, Hastings, TN34 3ER
Tel: 01424 460068

Tony Horsley, PO Box 3127, Brighton, BN1 5SS
Tel: 01273 550770
Candle extinguishers, Royal Worcester and other porcelain

Soldiers of Rye, Mint Arcade, 71 The Mint, Rye, TN31 7EW
Tel: 01797 225952
rameses@supanet.com
chris@johnbartholomewcards.co.uk
www.rameses.supanet.com
Military badges, cigarette cards, prints, medals, collectors figurines, dolls' house miniatures

Wallis & Wallis, West Street Auction Galleries, Lewes, BN7 2NJ
Tel: 01273 480208
auctions@wallisandwallis.co.uk
grb@wallisandwallis.co.uk
www.wallisandwallis.co.uk
Specialist auctioneers of militaria, arms, armour, coins and medals. Also die-cast and tinplate toys, Teddy bears, dolls, model railways, toy soldiers and models

WEST SUSSEX
Rupert Toovey & Co Ltd,
Spring Gardens, Washington,
RH20 3BS Tel: 01903 891955
auctions@rupert-toovey.com
www.rupert-toovey.com
Monthly specialist auctions of antiques, fine art and collectors' items. Regular specialist auctions of collectors' toys and dolls and antiquarian and collectors' books

WALES
Jen Jones, Pontbrendu, Llanybydder, Ceredigion, SA40 9UJ
Tel: 01570 480610
quilts@jen-jones.com
www.jen-jones.com
Quilt expert dealing mainly in Welsh quilts and blankets. Between 200 and 300 quilts in stock with a comparable number of blankets. Looking to buy as well as sell

Roberts Emporium (Fleamarket),
58-60 Salisbury Road, Cardiff,
South Glamorgan, CF24 4AD
Tel: 029 20235630
info@cheapaschips.cc
www.cheapaschips.cc
Antiques and collectables

WARWICKSHIRE
Bread & Roses Tel: 01926 817342
Kitchen antiques 1800–1950s.
Also at The Ark Angel, Long St,
Tetbury, Glos. Tel: 01666 505820 &
Zani Lady, Corfe St, Ludlow,
Shropshire. Tel: 01584 877200

Chinasearch, PO Box 1202,
Kenilworth, CV8 2WW
Tel: 01926 512402
info@chinasearch.uk.com
www.chinasearch.uk.com
Discontinued dinner, tea and collectable ware bought and sold

Chris James medalsandmilitaria.co.uk,
Warwick Antiques Centre,
22-24 High Street, Warwick,
CV34 4AP Tel: 01926 495704/
07710 274452

user@chrisjames.slv.co.uk
www.medalsandmilitaria.co.uk
British, German, Japanese and USSR medals, swords, militaria and aviation items. For sale and purchased. 'The International', The National Motorcycle Museum, Birmingham. The U.K's largest militaria fair. A.M.&.S.E., PO Box 194, Warwick. Tel: 01926 497340

WEST MIDLANDS
Fragile Design, 8 The Custard Factory, Digbeth,
Birmingham, B9 4AA
Tel: 0121 693 1001
info@fragiledesign.com
www.fragiledesign.com
Dealers of original 20th century design

WILTSHIRE
Books Illustrated
Tel: 0777 1635 777
booksillustrated@aol.co
www.booksillustrated.com
Illustrated books and original artwork

Dominic Winter Book Auctions,
The Old School, Maxwell Street,
Swindon, SN1 5DR Tel: 01793
611340 info@dominicwinter.co.uk
www.dominicwinter.co.uk
Auctions of antiquarian and general printed books & maps, sports books and memorabilia, art reference & pictures, photography & ephemera (including toys, games and other collectables)

YORKSHIRE
BBR, Elsecar Heritage Centre,
Elsecar, Nr Barnsley, S74 8HJ
Tel: 01226 745156
sales@onlinebbr.com
www.onlinebbr.com
Advertising, breweriana, pot lids, bottles, Cornishware, Doulton and Beswick, etc

Briar's C20th Decorative Arts,
Skipton Antiques & Collectors Centre,
The Old Foundry, Cavendish Street,
Skipton, BD23 2AB
Tel: 01756 798641
bsdecoart@aol.com
Art Deco ceramics and furniture, specialising in Charlotte Rhead pottery

The Camera House, Oakworth Hall,
Colne Road, Oakworth, Keighley,
BD22 7HZ Tel: 01535 642333
Mobile 07984 018951
colin@the-camera-house.co.uk
www.the-camera-house.co.uk

Cameras & photographic equipment from 1850. Cash purchases, part exchanges, sales and repairs. National and International mail order a speciality. Valuations for probate & insurance. Online catalogue. Please ring or email before visiting. Prop. C Cox

Country Collector, 11-12 Birdgate,
Pickering, YO18 7AL
Tel: 01751 477481
www.country-collector.co.uk
Art Deco ceramics, blue and white, pottery and porcelain

The Crested China Co, Highfield,
Windmill Hill, Driffield, YO25 5YP
Tel: 0870 300 1 300
dt@thecrestedchinacompany.com
www.thecrestedchinacompany.com
Goss and crested china

Echoes, 650a Halifax Road,
Eastwood, Todmorden, OL14 6DW
Tel: 01706 817505
Antique costume, textiles including linen, lace and jewellery

James M. Fielding
Tel: 0114 235 0185
m.fielding@btinternet.com
Old fishing tackle

Glasstastique By appointment only
Tel: 0113 287 9308 (office) or
07967 337795/07967 345952
glasstastique@aol.com
www.glasstastique.com
18th, 19th & 20thc glassware

Gerard Haley, Hippins Farm,
Black Shawhead, Nr Hebden Bridge,
HX7 7JG Tel: 01422 842484
Toy soldiers

John & Simon Haley, 89 Northgate,
Halifax, HX1 1XF
Tel: 01422 822148/360434
toysandbanks@aol.com
Old toys and money boxes

Harpers Jewellers Ltd,
2/6 Minster Gates, York, YO1 7HL
Tel: 01904 632634
york@harpersjewellers.co.uk
www.vintage-watches.co.uk
Vintage and modern wrist and pocket watches

Linen & Lace, Shirley Tomlinson,
Halifax Antiques Centre,
Queens Road/Gibbet Street,
Halifax, HX1 4LR
Tel: 01484 540492/01422 366657
Antique linen, textiles, period costume and accessories

Sheffield Railwayana Auctions,
43 Little Norton Lane, Sheffield,
S8 8GA Tel: 0114 274 5085
ian@sheffrail.freeserve.co.uk
www.sheffieldrailwayana.co.uk
Railwayana, posters and models auctions

U.S.A.
20th Century Vintage Telephones,
2780 Northbrook Place,
Boulder, CO 80304
Tel: 303 442 3304

Sara Bernstein Antique Dolls &
Bears, Englishtown, NJ 07726
Tel: 732 536 4101
santiqbebe@aol.com
www.sarabernsteindolls.com
Dolls and Teddy bears

Bertoia Auctions, 2141 DeMarco
Drive, Vineland, NJ 08360
Tel: 856 692 1881
bill@bertoiaauctions.com
www.bertoiaauctions.com
Mechanical bank and toy auctions

Marilynn and Sheila Brass,
PO Box 380503, Cambridge,
MA 02238-0503 Tel: 617 491 6064
shelmardesign1@aol.com
Kitchenware

The Calico Teddy
Tel: 410 366 7011
CalicTeddy@aol.com
www.calicoteddy.com
Antique Teddy bears

Christie's, 20 Rockefeller Plaza,
New York, NY 10020
Tel: 212 636 2000
www.christies.com
Art, antiques and collectibles auctions

Copake Auction, Inc., 266 RT. 7A,
Copake, NY 12516
Tel: 518 329 1142
info@copakeauction.com
www.copakeauction.com
*Americana, antique & classic bicycles
and textiles auctions*

The Dunlop Collection, P.O. Box
6269, Statesville, NC 28687
Tel: 704 871 2626 or
Toll Free Telephone (800) 227 1996
Paperweights

M. Finkel & Daughter, 936 Pine
Street, Philadelphia, PA 19107-6128
Tel: 215 627 7797
mailbox@finkelantiques.com
www.finkelantiques.com
*Antique sampler and needlework
dealer*

Goodfaith Antiques and Fine Art,
By appointment only
Tel: 518 854 7844
ntk@goodfaithantiques.com
www.goodfaithantiques.com
*Broad range of antiques, art, vintage
collectibles*

Karen Michelle Guido, Karen
Michelle Antique Tiles, PMB 243,
1835 US 1 South #119, St Augustine,
FL 32084 Tel: 904 471 3226
karen@antiquetiles.com
www.antiquetiles.com
Antique and collectible tiles

Hunt Auctions, 75 E. Uwchlan Avenue,
Suite 130, Exton, PA 19341
Tel: 610 524 0822
info@huntauctions.com
www.huntauctions.com
*Historical baseball and football
memorabilia auctions*

Hurst Gallery, 53 Mt. Auburn Street,
Cambridge, MA 02138
Tel: 617 491 6888
www.hurstgallery.com
manager@hurstgallery.com
www.hurstgallery.com
*Antiquities, Asian, African, Oceanic,
Pre-Columbian and American Indian
art and artifacts*

Randy Inman Auctions Inc.,
PO Box 726, Waterville,
ME 04903-0726
Tel: 207 872 6900
inman@inmanauctions.com
www.inmanauctions.com
*Advertising, coin-op, gambling
devices, automata, soda pop, Coca
Cola, breweriana, robots and space
toys, C.I. and tin toys, Disneyana,
mechanical music, mechanical and
still banks, quality antiques auctions*

Jackson's International Auctioneers
& Appraisers of Fine Art & Antiques,
2229 Lincoln Street,
Cedar Falls, IA 50613
Tel: 319 277 2256/800 665 6743
www.jacksonsauction.com
Antiques and collectibles auctions

JMW Gallery, 144 Lincoln Street,
Boston, MA 02111 Tel: 617 338
9097 www.jmwgallery.com
*American Arts & Crafts, Decorative
Arts, American Art Pottery, Mission
furniture, lighting, color block prints,
metalwork*

James D Julia, Inc., P O Box 830,
Rte.201 Skowhegan Road,
Fairfield, ME 04937

Tel: 207 453 7125
www.juliaauctions.com
*Americana, firearms, lamps and
glass, advertising, toys and dolls
auctions*

Lamps: By The Book, Inc.,
514 14th West Palm Beach,
FL 33401 Tel: 561 659 1723
booklamps@msn.com
www.lampsbythebook.com
*Gift lamps. Also buy leather bound
books*

Malchione Antiques & Sporting
Collectibles, 110 Bancroft Road,
Kennett Square, PA 19348
Tel: 610 444 3509

Skinner Inc., 357 Main Street,
Bolton, MA 01740
Tel: 978 779 6241
www.skinnerinc.com
*Antiques, fine art and collectibles
auctionsAlso at The Heritage On The
Garden, 63 Park Plaza, Boston, MA
02116 Tel: 617 350 5400*

Sloan's & Kenyon, 4605 Bradley
Boulevard, Bethesda, MD 20815
Tel: 301 634 2330
info@sloansandkenyon.com
www.sloansandkenyon.com
Art, antiques and collectibles auctions

Sotheby's, 1334 York Avenue at
72nd St, New York, NY 10021
Tel: 212 606 7000
www.sothebys.com
*Antiques, fine art and collectibles
auctions*

Toy's N Such Toy's - Antiques &
Collectables, 437 Dawson Street,
Sault Sainte Marie, MI 49783-2119
Tel: 906 635 0356

TreasureQuest Auction Galleries, Inc.
Tel: 772 781 8600
TQAG@TQAG.com www.TQAG.com
*Toys, dolls, bears and collectibles
auctions*

Triple "L" Sports, P O Box 281,
Winthorp, ME 04364
Tel: 207 377 5787 lllsport@att.net
*Winchester collectibles, fishing,
hunting, trapping, knives, primitives,
baseball, football, golf, tennis,
memorabilia and advertising*

VintagePostcards.com, 60-C Skiff
Street, Suite 116, Hamden,
CT 06517 Tel: 203 248 6621
quality@VintagePostcards.com
www.VintagePostcards.com

Directory of Collectors' Clubs

With new Collectors' Clubs emerging every day this directory is by no means complete. If you wish to be included in next year's directory or if you have a change of details, please inform us by 1 June 2005.

Alice in Wonderland Collectors Network, Joel Birenbaum, 765 Shellingham Drive, Lisle, IL 60532-4245, U.S.A.

American Barb Wire Collector's Society, John Mantz, 1023 Baldwin Road, Bakersfield, CA 93304-4203, U.S.A.

American Breweriana Association, Inc., Stan Galloway, PO Box 11157, Pueblo, CO 81001, U.S.A. Tel: 719 544 9267 breweriana1@earthlink.net www.americanbreweriana.org

American Business Card Club UK, Robin Cleeter, 28 Abbotsbury Road, Morden, Surrey SM4 5LQ

American Business Card Club US, Avery N. Pitzak, PO Box 460297, Aurora, CO 80046-0297, U.S.A.

American Credit Card Collectors Society, Bill Wieland, President, PO Box 2465, MI 48640, U.S.A.

American Fan Collectors' Association, Steve Cunningham, PO Box 5473, Sarasota, FL 34277-5473, U.S.A.

American Fish Decoy Collectors Association, PO Box 252, Boulder Junction, WI 54512, U.S.A.

American Hatpin Society, Virginia Woodbury, 20 Montecillo Drive, Rolling Hills Estates, CA 90274, U.S.A. www.americanhatpinsociety.com

American Lock Collectors Association, 36076 Grennada, Livonia, MI 48154, U.S.A.

American Matchcover Collecting Club, PO Box 18481, Asheville, NC 28814, U.S.A.

American Society of Camera Collectors, Sam Rosenfeld, 4570 Kelvin Ave, Canoga Park, CA 91306-4021, U.S.A.

American Toy Emergency Vehicle (ATEV) Club, Jeff Hawkins, President, 11415 Colfax Road, Glen Allen, Virginia 23060, U.S.A.

The Antiquarian Horological Society, Wendy Barr, Secretary, New House, High Street, Ticehurst, East Sussex TN5 7AL Tel: 01580 200 155 secretary@ahsoc.demon.co.uk www.ahsoc.demon.co.uk

Antique Bookmark Collector's Association, Richard W. Kelly, 2224 Cherokee, Saint Louis, MO 63118, U.S.A.

Antique Bottles & Collectibles Club, Willy Young, PO Box 1061, Verdi, NV 89439, U.S.A.

Antique Comb Collectors Club International, Jen Cruse, European Coordinator, 14 Hall Drive, London SE26 6XB jen.cruse@eggconnect.net

Antique Comb Collectors Club International (US), Linda Shapiro, 8712 Pleasant View Road, Bangor, PA 18013, U.S.A.

Antique Wireless Association (AWA), Box E, Breesport, New York 14816, U.S.A.

Association for British Brewery Collectables, 28 Parklands, Kidsgrove, Stoke-on-Trent, Staffordshire ST7 4US Tel: 01782 761048 www.breweriana.org.uk www.abbclist.info

Avon Magpies Club, Mrs W. A. Fowler, 15 Saunders House, Leith Avenue, Paulsgrove, Portsmouth, Hampshire PO6 4NY Tel: 023 92 380975 wendy@avon4magpies.fsnet.co.uk

B.E.A.R. Collector's Club, Linda Hartzfeld, 16901 Covello Street, Van Nuys, California 91406, U.S.A.

Badge Collectors' Circle, c/o Frank Setchfield, 57 Middleton Place, Loughborough, Leicestershire LE11 2BY www.badgecollectorscircle.co.uk

Barbie Collectors Club of Great Britain, Elizabeth Lee, 17 Rosemont Road, Acton, London W3 9LU

Barbie Lover's Club, Amy Reed, 399 Winfield Road, Rochester, New York 14622, U.S.A.

Battery-Operated Toy Collectors of America, Jack Smith, 410 Linden, PO Box 676, Tolono, IL 61880, U.S.A.

The Bead Society of Great Britain, Carole Morris (Dr), 1 Casburn Lane, Burwell, Cambridge CB5 0ED Tel: 01638 742024 www.beadsociety.freeserve.co.uk

Bearly Ours Teddy Club, Linda Harris, 54 Berkinshaw Crescent, Don Mills, Ontario M3B 2T2, Canada

The Beatrix Potter Society, UK Registered Charity No. 281198, c/o Membership Secretary, 9 Broadfields, Harpenden, Hertfordshire AL5 2HJ info@beatrixpottersociety.org.uk www.beatrixpottersociety.org.uk

Beer Can Collectors of America, Don Hicks, 747 Merus Court, Fenton, MO 63026-2092, U.S.A.

Belleek Collectors Group (UK), The Hon Chairman Mr D. Reynolds, 7 Highfield Estate, Wilmslow, Cheshire SK9 2JR www.belleek.org.uk

Black Memorabilia Collectors Association, Sharon Hart, 2482 Devoe Terrace, Bronx, NY 10468, U.S.A.

British Art Medal Society, Philip Attwood, c/o Dept of Coins and Medals, The British Museum, London WC1B 3DG Tel: 020 7323 8260 pattwood@thebritishmuseum.ac.uk www.bams.org.uk/

The British Beermat Collectors' Society, Hon Sec, 69 Dunnington Avenue, Kidderminster, Worcestershire DY10 2YT www.britishbeermats.org.uk

British Button Society, Membership Secretary Mrs June Baron, Jersey Cottage, Parklands Road, Bower Ashton, Bristol, Avon BS3 2JR

The British Compact Collectors' Society, SAE to: PO Box 131, Woking, Surrey GU24 9YR www.thebccs.org.uk

British Doll Collectors Club, Mrs Frances Baird, Publisher & Editor, The Anchorage, Wrotham Road, Culverstone, Meopham, Gravesend, Kent DA13 0QW www.britishdollcollectors.com

British Novelty Salt & Pepper Collectors Club, Ray Dodd (Secretary), Coleshill, Clayton Road, Mold, Flintshire CH7 1SX www.bnspcc.com

British Numismatic Society, c/o Warburg Institute, Woburn Square, London WC1H 0AB Tel: 01329 284661

British Postmark Society, General Secretary John A. Strachan, 12 Dunavon Park, Strathaven ML10 6LP Tel: 01357 522430 johlen@stracml10.freeserve.co.uk

The British Smurf Collectors Club, The Club Secretary, PO Box 5737, Swanage, Dorset BH19 3ZX www.globalserve.net/~astro1/bscc/register.htm

The Brooklands Automobilia & Regalia Collectors' Club (B.A.R.C.C.), Hon. sec. G. G. Weiner, 4-4a Chapel Terrace Mews, Kemp Town, Brighton, East Sussex BN2 1HU Tel: 01273 622722 www.barcc.co.uk www.brmmbrmm.com/barcc

Bubble Gum Charm Collectors, Maureen McCaffrey, 24 Seafoam Street, Staten Island, NY 10306, U.S.A.

The Burleigh Ware International Collectors Circle
Tel: 01664 454570

Butter Pats International Collectors Club, Alice Black,
38 Acton Street, Maynard, MA 01754, U.S.A.

The Buttonhook Society, c/o Paul Moorehead Chairman,
2 Romney Place, Maidstone, Kent ME15 6LE
Tel: 01622 752949

The Buttonhook Society (US contact), c/o Priscilla Stoffel,
White Marsh, Box 287, MD 21162-0287, U.S.A.
Tel: 410 256 5541 buttonhooksociety@tiscali.co.uk
www.thebuttonhooksociety.com

Caithness Glass Paperweight Collectors' Society,
Mrs Caroline Clark, The Caithness Glass Compay Limited,
Inveralmond, Perth, Scotland PH1 3TZ Tel: 01738 492335
collector@caithnessglass.co.uk www.caithnessglass.co.uk

Campbell Soup Collectors International Association,
Betty Campbell Madden, President, 305 East Main Street,
Ligonier, PA 15658, U.S.A.

Cane Collectors Club of America, 2 Horizon Road,
Suite G18, Fort Lee, NJ 07024, U.S.A.

Carlton Ware Collectors International, Carlton Factory
Shop, Carlton Works, Copeland Street, Stoke on Trent,
Staffordshire ST4 1PU Tel: 01782 410504

Carnival Glass Society (UK), PO Box 14, Hayes,
Middlesex UB3 5NU
www.carnivalglasssociety.co.uk

The Cartophilic Society of Great Britain Ltd, Membership
secretary, Alan Stevens, 63 Ferndale Road, Church
Crookham, Fleet, Hampshire GU52 6LN Tel: 01252 621586
membership@csgb.co.uk www.csgb.co.uk

Cash Register Collectors Club, Mike Hennessey,
PO Box 20534, Dayton, OH 45420-0534, U.S.A.
Tel: 937 433 3529 www.crcci.org

Cat Collectables, 297 Alcester Road, Hollywood,
Birmingham, West Midlands B47 5HJ Tel: 01564 826277
cat.collectables@btinternet.com www.cat-collectables.co.uk

Cigarette Case Collectors' Club, Colin Grey, 19
Woodhurst North, Raymead Road, Maidenhead, Berkshire
SL6 8PH Tel: 01628 781800 colin.grey1@virgin.net

Cigarette Pack Collectors Association, Richard Elliot,
61 Searle St, Georgetown, MA 01833, U.S.A.

Cigarette Packet Collectors Club of GB, Barry Russell,
Talisker, Vines Cross Road, Horam, Heathfield, East Sussex
TN21 0HF Tel: 01435 812453

City of London Phonograph and Gramophone Society
www.clpgs.org.uk

Clarice Cliff Collectors' Club, Fantasque House, Tennis
Drive, The Park, Nottingham NG7 1AE www.claricecliff.com

The Coca-Cola Collectors Club, Membership Director,
4780 Ashford-Dunwoody Road Suite. A, Atlanta,
Georgia 30338, U.S.A.
www.cocacolaclub.org

The Coleco Collectors Club, Ann Wilhite,
610 W 17th Freemont, NE 68025, U.S.A.

Collector's Choice, Admail 981, Stoke on Trent,
Staffordshire ST12 9JW Tel: 0870 830 8028

Commemorative Collectors' Society, c/o Steven Jackson,
Lumless House, 77 Gainsborough Road, Winthorpe, Newark,
Nottinghamshire NG24 2NR Tel: 01636 671377
commemorativecollectorssociety@hotmail.com

Compact Collectors Club International, Roselyn Gerson,
PO Box 40, Lynbrook, NY 11563, U.S.A.

Cookie Cutters Collectors Club, Ruth Capper, 1167 Teal
Road S. W., Dellroy, OH 44620-9704, U.S.A.

Corgi Collector Club, c/o Corgi Classics Ltd, Meridian Eas
Meridian Business Park, Leicester LE19 1RL
Tel: 0870 607 1204 susie@collectorsclubs.org.uk

Cornish Collectors Club, PO Box 58, Buxton, Derbyshire
SK17 0FH

The Costume Society, St Paul's House, Warwick Lane,
London EC4P 4BN www.costumesociety.org.uk

The Crested Circle, 42 Douglas Road, Tolworth, Surbiton
Surrey KT6 7SA

Cricket Memorabilia Society, Steve Cashmore, 4 Stoke
Park Court, Stoke Road, Bishop's Cleeve, Cheltenham,
Gloucestershire GL52 8US cms87@btinternet.com
www.cms.cricket.org

Crunch Club (Breakfast Cereal Collectables), John Cah
9 Weald Rise, Tilehurst, Reading, Berkshire RG30 6XB

The Dean's Collectors Club, Euro Collectibles,
PO Box 370565, 49 NE 39th Street, Miami FL33 137, U.S.,
Tel: US toll free 1 800 309 8336 www.deansbears.com

The Dean's Collectors Club, Pontypool, Gwent NP4 6YY
Tel: 01495 764881 www.deansbears.com

Devon Pottery Collectors' Group, Mrs Joyce Stonelake,
19 St Margarets Avenue, Torquay, Devon TQ1 4LW

Die Cast Car Collectors Club, c/o Jay Olins (Chairman),
PO Box 67226, Los Angeles, California 90067-0266, U.S.A
Tel: 310 629 7113 jay@diecast.org www.diecast.org

Dinky Toy Club of America, c/o Jerry Fralick, 6030 Day
Break Circle, Suite A 150, PBM/132, Clarksville, Maryland
21029, U.S.A. Tel: 301 854 2217 mrdinky@erols.com
www.dinkytoyclub.net

Dinosaur Collectors Club, Mike Howgate, 71 Hoppers Ro
Winchmore Hill, London N21 3LP

Doll House & Miniature Collectors, PO Box 159,
Bethlehem, CT 06751-0159, U.S.A.

Door Knob Collectors, ADCA, PO Box126, Eola,
IL 60519-0126, U.S.A.

Egg Cup Collectors' Club of GB, Sue Wright, Subs
secretary, PO Box 39, Llandysul, Wales SA44 5ZD
suewright@suecol.freeserve.co.uk
www.eggcupworld.co.uk

The English Playing Card Society, John Sings - Secretary
PO Box 29, North Walsham, Norfolk NR28 9NQ
Tel: 01692 650496 Secretary@EPCS.org
www.wopc.co.uk/epcs

Ephemera Society of America, Inc., PO Box 95,
Cazenovia, NY 13035-0095, U.S.A. Tel: 315 655 9139
info@ephemerasociety.org www.ephemerasociety.org

The Ephemera Society, Membership secretary, PO Box 11.
Northwood, Middlesex HA6 2WT

ETB Radford Collectors' Club, 27 Forest Mead, Denmea
Waterlooville, Hampshire PO7 6UN www.radfordcollect.co

The European Honeypot Collectors' Society, John Doyl
The Honeypot, 18 Victoria Road, Chislehurst, Kent BR7 6D
Tel: 020 8289 7725 johnhoneypot@hotmail.com
www.geocities.com/tehcsuk

The Fairing Collectors Society, Stuart Piepenstock
Tel: 01895 824830

The Family Circle of Pen Delfin, Susan Beard, 230 Sprin
Street N.W., Suite 1238, Atlanta, Georgia 30303, U.S.A.

Fan Circle International, Sec: Mrs Joan Milligan, "Cronk-
Voddy", Rectory Road, Coltishall, Norwich, Norfolk NR12 7H

Festival of Britain Society, c/o Martin Packer,
41 Lyall Gardens, Birmingham, West Midlands B45 9YW
Tel: 0121 453 8245 martin@packer34.freeserve.co.uk
www.packer34.freeserve.co.uk

The Followers of Rupert, Mrs S. Reeves, The Membership secretary, 31 Whiteley, Windsor, Berkshire SL4 5PJ www.rupertthebear.org.uk

Friends of Blue Ceramic Society, Terry Sheppard, 45a Church Road, Bexley Heath, Kent DA7 4DD www.fob.org.uk

Friends of Broadfield House Glass Museum, June Wilson, Broadfield House Glass Museum, Compton Drive, Kingswinford, West Midlands DY6 9NS Tel: 01384 812745

The Furniture History Society, c/o Dr. Brian Austen, 1 Mercedes Cottages, St. John's Road, Haywards Heath, West Sussex RH16 4EH Tel: 01444 413845 furniturehistorysociety@hotmail.com

The Glove Collector Club, Joe Phillips, 14057 Rolling Hills Lane, Dallas, TX 75240, U.S.A.

Golly Collectors' Club, Keith Wilkinson, 18 Hinton Street, Fairfield, Liverpool, Merseyside L6 3AR

Goss Collectors' Club (est 1970), Brian Waller, 35 Felstead Way, Luton, Bedfordshire LU2 7LH Tel: 01582 732063 commercialofficer@gosscollectorsclub.org

The Hagen-Renaker Collectors Club, Jenny Palmer, 3651 Polish Line Road, Cheboygan, Mitchigan 49721, U.S.A.

Hagen-Renaker Collectors Club (UK), Chris and Derek Evans, 97 Campbell Road, Burton, Christchurch, Dorset BH23 7LY www.priorycollectables.co.uk

The Happy Pig Collectors Club, Gene Holt PO Box 17, Oneida, IL 61467-0017, U.S.A.

The Hat Pin Society of Great Britain, PO Box 110, Cheadle, Cheshire SK8 1GG www.hatpinsociety.org.uk

Historical Model Railway Society, 59 Woodberry Way, London E4 7DY

Honiton Pottery Collectors' Society, Robin Tinkler (Chairman), 2 Redyear Cottages, Kennington Road, Ashford, Kent TN24 0TF Tel: 01233 647898 hpcs@moshpit.cix.co.uk www.hpcs.info

Hornby Collectors Club, PO Box 18, Melton Mowbray, Leicestershire LE13 1ZF

The Hornby Railway Collectors' Association, John Harwood, PO Box 3443, Yeovil, Somerset BA21 4XR

Hornsea Pottery Collectors' and Research Society, c/o Mr Peter Tennant, 128 Devonshire Street, Keighley, West Yorkshire BD21 2QJ hornsea@pdtennant.fsnet.co.uk www.hornseacollector.co.uk

The Illustrated Comic Journal, C.J. Publications, c/o 6 Rotherham Road, Catcliffe, Rotherham, South Yorkshire S60 5SW

Indian Military Historical Society, The Secretary/Editor A N McClenaghan, 33 High Street, Tilbrook, Huntingdon, Cambridgeshire PE28 0JP

Inn Sign Society, Chairman Mr R. P. Gatrell, Flat 19, Stamford Grange, Dunham Road, Altrincham, Cheshire WA14 4AN Raymond@gatrell65.freeserve.co.uk www.bjcurtis.force9.co.uk

Inner-Seal Collectors Club (National Biscuit Co and Nabisco Memorabilia), Charlie Brown, 6609 Billtown Road, Louisville, KY 40299, U.S.A.

International Association of Calculator Collectors, PO Box 345, Tustin, CA 92781-0345, U.S.A.

International Bank Note Society, c/o Milan Alusic, PO Box 1642, Racine, WI 53401, U.S.A.

International Bond and Share Society, c/o Peter Duppa-Miller, Beechcroft, Combe Hay, Bath, Somerset BA2 7EG

International Bond & Share Society, American Branch, Ted Robinson, Vice President, PO Box 814, Richboro, PA, U.S.A. Tel: 215 357 6820 fandr@voicenet.com

International Map Collectors Society (IMCoS), Secretary Yasha Beresiner, 43 Templars Crescent, London N3 3QR

International Paperweight Society, 761 Chestnut Street, Santa Cruz, CA 95060, U.S.A.

International Perfume Bottle Association, Details from Lynda Brine, Assembly Antique Centre, 6 Saville Row, Bath, Somerset BA1 2QP Tel: 01225 448488 lyndabrine@yahoo.co.uk www.scentbottlesandsmalls.co.uk

International Perfume Bottle Association, c/o Membership Secretary, 295 E. Swedesford Road, PMB 185, Wayne PA 19087, U.S.A.

International Philatelic Golf Society, Ron Spiers (Secretary), 8025 Saddle Run, Powell, OH 43065, U.S.A.

International Philatelic Golf Society, Secretary Dr Eiron B.E. Morgan, 50 Pine Valley, Cwmavon, Port Talbot, Wales SA12 9NF

International Playing Card Society, PR Officer Yasha Beresiner, 43 Templars Crescent, London N3 3QR

International Society for Apple Parer Enthusiasts, G.W. Laverty, 735 Cedarwood Terrace, Apt 735B, Rochester, NY 14609, U.S.A.

The International Society of Meccanomen, Adrian Williams, Bell House, 72a Old High Street, Headington, Oxford OX3 9HW www.dircon.co.uk/meccano/

International Swizzle Stick Collectors Association, Ray P. Hoare, PO Box 1117, Bellingham, WA 98227-1117, U.S.A. veray.issca@shaw.com

The James Bond Collectors Club, P O Box 1570, Christchurch, Dorset BH23 4XS Tel: 0870 4423007 www.bondbooks.biz

James Sadler International Collectors Club, Customer Services, Churchill China PLC, High Street, Tunstall, Stoke on Trent ST6 5NZ Tel: 01782 577566 diningin@churchillchina.plc.uk www.james-sadler.co.uk

Jonathan Harris Studio Glass Ltd, Woodland House, 24 Peregrine Way, Apley Castle, Telford, Shropshire TF1 6TH Tel: 01952 246381/588441 jonathan@jhstudioglass.com www.jhstudioglass.com

Just Golly! Collectors Club, SAE to Mrs A. K. Morris, 9 Wilmar Way, Seal, Sevenoaks, Kent TN15 0DN www.gollycorner.co.uk

King George VI Collectors' Society (Philately), Secretary, 17 Balcaskierd, Eltham, London SE9 1HQ

The Lace Guild, The Hollies, 53 Audnam, Stourbridge, West Midlands DY8 4AE

Legend Products International Collector's Club, Sheila Cochrane (Owner and club founder), 1 Garden Villas, Wrexham Road, Cefn Y Bedd, Flintshire LL12 9UT Tel: 01978 760800 sheila@legend-lane.demon.co.uk

Lilliput Lane Collectors' Club, PO Box 498, Itasca, IL 60143-0498, U.S.A.

Lock Collectors' Club, Mr Richard Phillips, "Merlewood", The Loan, West Linton, Peeblesshire, Scotland EH46 7HE Tel: 01968 661039 rphillips52@btinternet.com

The Maling Collectors' Society, Sec David Holmes, PO Box 1762, North Shields NE30 4YJ www.maling-pottery.org.uk

Marble Collectors' Society of America MCSA, PO Box 222, Trumball, CT 06611, U.S.A.

Matchbox International Collectors Association (MICA) of North America, c/o Stewart Orr and Kevin McGimpsey, PO Box 28072, Waterloo, Ontario N2L 6J8, Canada

The Matchbox Toys International Collectors' Association, Editor Kevin McGimpsey, PO Box 120, Deeside, Flintshire CH5 3HE Tel: 01244 539414
kevin@matchboxclub.com
www.matchboxclub.com

Mauchline Ware Collectors Club, Secretary Mrs Christabelle Davey, PO Box 158, Leeds LS16 5WZ
enquiries@mauchlineclub.org
www.mauchlineclub.org

Medal Society of Ireland, 5 Meadow Vale, Blackrock, Co Dublin, Eire Tel: 289 5085

Memories UK Mabel Lucie Attwell Club, Abbey Antiques, 63 Great Whyte, Ramsey, Nr Huntingdon, Cambridgeshire PE26 1HL Tel: 01487 814753

Menucard Collectors' Society, 23 White Hart Wood, Sevenoaks, Kent TN13 1RS www.menucards.org

Merrythought International Collector's Club, Club Sec Peter Andrews, Ironbridge, Telford, Shropshire TF8 7NJ
Tel: 01952 433116 ext 21 contact@merrythought.co.uk
www.merrythought.co.uk

Merrythought International Collector's Club, PO Box 577, Oakdale, California 95361, U.S.A.

Miracle Jewellery Collectors Group
http://groups.yahoo.com/group/miraclecollectors/

The Model Railway Club, The Hon Sec, Keen House, 4 Calshot Street, London N1 9DA

Moorcroft Collectors' Club, W. Moorcroft PLC, Sandbach Road, Burslem, Stoke-on-Trent, Staffordshire ST6 2DQ
Tel: 01782 820510 cclub@moorcroft.com
www.moorcroft.com

Moorland Pottery Collectors Club, Moorland Road, Burslem, Stoke on Trent, Staffordshire ST6 1DY

Muffin the Mule Collectors' Club, 12 Woodland Close, Woodford Green, Essex IG8 0QH Tel: 020 8504 4943
adrienne@hasler.gotadsl.co.uk
www.Muffin-the-Mule.com

Musical Box Society of Great Britain, PO Box 299, Waterbeach, Cambridgeshire CB4 8DT mail@mbsgb.org.uk
www.mbsgb.org.uk

National Association of Avon Collectors, Connie Clark, President, PO Box 7006, Kansas City, MO 64113, U.S.A.

National Association of Breweriana Advertising, Robert E. Jaeger, 2343 Met-to-wee Lane, Milwaukee, WI 53226-1612, U.S.A.

National Button Society, Lois Pool, Secretary, 2733 Juno Pl., Apt 4, Akron, Ohio 44333-4137, U.S.A.

National Doll & Teddy Bear Collector, Rose Morgan, PO Box 4032, Portland, OR 97208-4032, U.S.A.

National Fishing Lure Collectors Club, Secretary-Treasurer NFLCC, 197 Scottsdale Circle, Reeds Springs, MO 65737, U.S.A.

National Toothpick Holder Collectors' Society, PO Box 852, Archer City, TX 76351, U.S.A. garnetoak@aol.com
www.nthcs.org

New Baxter Society, Membership Secretary, 205 Marshalswick Lane, St Albans, Hertfordshire AL1 4XA
Baxter@rpsfamily.demon.co.uk
www.rpsfamily.demon.co.uk

NFFC - The Club for Disneyana Enthusiasts, PO Box 19212, Irvine, CA 92623-9212, U.S.A.
Tel: 714 731 4705 www.nffc.org

Nutcracker Collectors' Club, Susan Otto, 12204 Fox Run Drive, Chesterland, OH 44026, U.S.A. Tel: 440 729 2686
nutsue@adelphia.net

Observer's Pocket Series Collectors Society (OPSCS), Alan Sledger, Secretary, 10 Villiers Road, Kenilworth, Warwickshire CV8 2JB Tel: 01926 857047

The Official Betty Boop Fan Club, Ms Bobbie West, 10550 Western Avenue #133, Stanton, CA 90680-6909, U.S.A. BBOOPFANS@aol.com

The Official International Wade Ceramics Collectors Club, Royal Victoria Pottery, Westport Road, Burslem, Stoke on Trent, Staffordshire ST6 4AG
www.wade.co.uk

Official Popeye Fan Club, 1001 State St, Chester, IL 62233, U.S.A.

Old Appliance Club, PO Box 65, Ventura, CA 93002, U.S.A.

Old Bottle Club of Great Britain, Alan Blakeman, c/o BBR, Elsecar Heritage Centre, Nr Barnsley, Yorkshire S74 8HJ
Tel: 01226 745156 sales@onlinebbr.com
www.onlinebbr.com

The Old Hall Collectors' Club, Nigel Wiggin, Sandford House, Levedale, Stafford ST18 9AH Tel: 01785 780376
oht@gnwiggin.freeserve.co.uk
www.oldhallclub.co.uk

The Old Lawnmower Club, c/o Milton Keynes Museum, McConnell Drive, Wolverton, Milton Keynes, Buckinghamshire MK12 5EL Tel: 01327 830675
enquiry@oldlawnmowerclub.co.uk
www.oldlawnmowerclub.co.uk

On the Lighter Side (OTLS), PO Box 1733, Quitman, TX 75783-1733, U.S.A. Tel: 903 763 2795
www.otls.com

Orders and Medals Research Society OMRS, PO Box 1904, Southam CV47 2ZX Tel: 01295 690009
petedeehelmore@talk21.com www.omrs.org.uk

The Oriental Ceramic Society, The Secretary, 30b Torrington Square, London WC1E 7JL
Tel: 020 7636 7985 ocs-london@beeb.net

Paperweight Collectors Circle, PO Box 941, Comberton, Cambridgeshire CB3 7GQ Tel: 02476 386172

Peanuts Collector Club, Inc., 539 Sudden Valley, Bellingham, WA 98226-4811, U.S.A.

Pedal Car Collectors' Club (P.C.C.C.), Secretary A. P. Gayler, 4/4a Chapel Terrace Mews, Kemp Town, Brighton, East Sussex BN2 1HU Tel: 01273 601960
www.brmmbrmm.com/pedalcars

Pelham Puppets Collectors Club, Sue Valentine, 46 The Grove, Bedford MK40 3JN Tel: 01234 363336
sue.valentine@ntlworld.com

Pen Delfin Family Circle, Pendelfin Studios Ltd, Townley Street, Briercliffe Business Centre, Burnley, Lancashire BB10 2HG Tel: 01282 432301
boswell@pendelfin.co.uk
www.pendelfin.co.uk

The Pewter Society, Llananant Farm, Penallt, Monmouth, NP25 4AP secretary@pewtersociety.org
www.pewtersociety.org

Photographic Collectors Club of Great Britain, Membership Office P.C.C.G.B., 5 Buntingford Road, Puckeridge, Ware, Hertfordshire SG11 1RT
www.pccgb.org

Pilkington's Lancastrian Pottery Society, Wendy Stock, Sullom Side, Barnacre, Garstang, Preston, Lancashire PR3 1GH
www.pilkpotsoc.freeserve.co.uk

Poole Pottery Collectors Club, Poole Pottery Limited, Sopers Lane, Poole, Dorset BH17 7PP Tel: 01202 666200
www.poolepottery.com

Postcard Club of Great Britain, c/o Mrs D. Brennan, 34 Harper House, St James Crescent, London SW9 7LW Tel: 020 7771 9404

The Pot Lid Circle, c/o Ian Johnson, Collins House, 32/38 Station Road, Gerrards Cross, Buckinghamshire SL9 8EL Tel: 01753 279001 ian.johnson@bpcollins.co.uk

Potteries of Rye Society, Membership Secretary Barry Buckton, 2 Redyear Cottages, Kennington Road, Ashford, Kent TN24 0TF Tel: 01233 647898 www.potteries-of-rye-society.co.uk

Road Map Collectors Association, PO Box 158, Channelview, TX 77530-0158, U.S.A.

Royal Doulton International Collectors' Club, Royal Doulton, Sir Henry Doulton House, Forge Lane, Stoke-on-Trent, Staffordshire ST1 5NN www.icc@royal-doulton.com

The Royal Numismatic Society, Hon Sec Andrew Meadows, c/o Department of Coins and Medals, The British Museum, London WC1B 3DG Tel: 020 7323 8577 rns@dircon.co.uk www.rns.dircon.co.uk

Royal Winton International Collectors' Club, Dancers End, Northall, Bedfordshire LU6 2EU

Rugby Memorabilia Society, PO Box 1093, Thornbury, Bristol BS35 1DA www.rugby-memorabilia.co.uk

Scientific Instrument Society, Registered Charity No 326733, 31 High Street, Stanford in the Vale, Faringdon, Oxon SN7 8LH www.sis.org.uk

The Shelley Group (for collectors of Shelley and Wileman wares), Ruskin, 47 St Andrew's Drive, Perton, Staffordshire WV6 7YL 01902 754245 shelley.group@shelley.co.uk www.shelley.co.uk

Silhouette Collectors' Club, c/o Miss Diana B. Joll, Flat 5, 13 Brunswick Square, Hove, East Sussex BN3 1EH Tel: 01273 735760

The Silver Spoon Club of Great Britain, Daniel Bexfield, 26 Burlington Arcade, Mayfair, London W1J 0PU Tel: 020 7491 1730 antiques@bexfield.co.uk

Smurf Collectors Club International, Dept 115 NR, 24 Cabot Road West, Massapeque, New York 11758, U.S.A.

Snowdome Collectors Club, PO Box 53262, Washington, DC 20009, U.S.A.

Snuff Bottle Society, 14 Rossiters Quay, Christchurch, Dorset BH23 1DZ Tel: 01202 469050 Mobile 07977 596 336 snuffbottles@onetel.com

Society of Tobacco Jar Collectors (USA), 19 Woodhurst North, Raymead Road, Maidenhead, Berkshire SL6 8PH Tel: 01628 781800 colin.grey1@virgin.net

The Soviet Collectors Club, PO Box 56, Saltburn by the Sea, TS12 1YD collect@sovietclub.com www.sovietclub.com

Steiff Club - North America, Rebekah Kaufman, Steiff North America, Inc., 425 Paramount Drive, Raynham MA 02767, U.S.A. Tel: 508 828 2377 rkaufman@steiffusa.com www.steiffusa.com

Susie Cooper Collectors Club, Panorama House, 18 Oakley Mews, Aycliffe Village, Co. Durham DL5 6JP www.susiecooper.co.uk

The SylvaC Collectors Circle, 174 Portsmouth Road, Horndean, Waterlooville, Hampshire PO8 9HP Tel: 023 9259 1725 www.sylvacclub.com

TEAMS Club - The official club for Brooke Bond Card Collectors, PO Box 1, Market Harborough, Leicestershire LE16 9HT Tel: 01858 466 441 sales@teamsclub.co.uk www.teamsclub.co.uk

The Thimble Society, c/o Bridget McConnel, Geoffrey Van Arcade, 107 Portobello Road, London W11 2QB Open Sat only www.thimblesociety.co.uk

Toaster Collector Association, PO Box 485, Redding Ridge CT 06876, U.S.A.

Torquay Pottery Collectors' Society, Membership Secretary, c/o Torre Abbey, The Kings Drive, Torquay, Devon TQ2 5JX www.torquaypottery.com

Totally Teapots The Novelty Teapot Collectors Club, Vince McDonald, Euxton, Chorley, Lancashire PR7 6EY Tel: 01257 450366 vince@totallyteapots.com www.totallyteapots.com

Toy Story Collectors' Club, Paul Cross, 20 Thurstons Barton, Whitehall, Bristol, Gloucestershire BS5 7BQ

Trade Card Collector's Association, PO Box 284, Marlton, NJ 08053, U.S.A.

Train Collectors Society, James Day, Membership Secretary, PO Box 20340, London NW11 6ZE Tel: 020 8209 1589 tcsinformation@btinternet.com www.traincollectors.org.uk

The Transport Ticket Society, Membership secretary, David Randell, Oaktree Lodge, 221A Botley Road, Burridge, Hampshire SO31 1BJ

Treasury of Christmas Ornaments Collectors' Club, PO Box 277, Itasca, IL 60143-0277, U.S.A.

UK 1/6th Collectors Club, Adrian Pitman, 1 St Cadocs Rise, Barry, Vale of Glamorgan, South Wales CF63 2FG Tel: 01446 405373 littledevon@ntlworld.com www.onesixthcollectors.com

UK Football Programme Collectors Club, 46 Milton Road, Kirkaldy, Scotland KY1 1TL Tel: 01592 268718 progm@hotmail.com www.pmfc.co.uk

UK Headscarf Collectors Society, 19 Poulton Old Road, Blackpool, Lancashire FY3 7LD

UK McDonald's & Fast Food Collectors Club, c/o Lawrence Yap, 110 Tithelands, Harlow, Essex CM19 5ND bigkidandtoys@ntlworld.com

UK Sucrologists Club, The Membership Secretary, 14 Marisfield Place, Selsey, West Sussex PO20 0PD

United Kingdom Spoon Collectors Club, David Cross General Secretary, 72 Edinburgh Road, Newmarket, Suffolk CB8 0DQ Tel: 01638 665457 david@ukspoons.fsnet.co.uk

Universal Autograph Collectors Club, Michael Hecht, President UACC, PO Box 6181, Washington, DC 20044-6181, U.S.A. www.uacc.org

US Chintz Collectors Club, PO Box 50888, Pasadena, CA 91115, U.S.A.

Vintage Fashion & Costume Jewelry Club, PO Box 265, Glen Oaks, NY 11004, U.S.A.

Vintage Model Yacht Group, Trevor Smith, 1A Station Avenue, Epsom, Surrey KT19 9UD Tel: 020 8393 1100 www.vmyg.org.uk

The Wade Watch, Carole Murdock & Valerie Moody, 8199 Pierson Ct, Arvada, CO 80005, U.S.A. www.wadewatch.com

Directory of Markets & Centres

Derbyshire

Alfreton Antique Centre, 11 King Street,
Alfreton, DE55 7AF Tel: 01773 520781
*30 dealers on 2 floors. Antiques, collectables, furniture,
books, militaria, postcards, silverware. Open 7 days
Mon–Sat 10am-4.30pm, Sundays 11am–4.30pm.
Customer car park.*

Chappells Antiques Centre, King Street,
Bakewell, DE45 1DZ Tel: 01629 812496
ask@chappellsantiquescentre.com
www.chappellsantiques centre.com
*Over 30 dealers inc LAPADA members. Quality period
furniture, ceramics, silver, plate, metals, treen, clocks,
barometers, books, pictures, maps, prints, textiles,
kitchenalia, lighting, furnishing accessories, scientific,
pharmaceutical and sporting antiques from the
17th–20thC. Open Mon–Sat 10am–5pm. Sun 12
noon–5pm. Closed Christmas Day, Boxing Day, New
Years Day. Please ring for brochure.*

Matlock Antiques, Collectables & Riverside Café,
7 Dale Road, Matlock, DE4 3LT Tel: 01629 760808
bmatlockantiques@aol.com
www.matlock-antiques-collectable.cwc.net
*Proprietor W. Shirley. Over 70 dealers.
Open every day 10am-5pm.*

Come and visit the
ANTIQUES CENTRE GLOUCESTER
with over 100 dealers on 5 floors

There is something for everyone from
collector to interior designer. We have antique
silver, glass, costumes, antique & modern
ceramics, furniture, linen, toys, stamps, cards,
clocks, railwayana and much, much more
including a delightful restaurant.
Open Mon–Sat 10am–5pm & Sun 1–5pm.

ADMISSION CHARGE: 50p WEEKENDS AND BANK
HOLIDAYS. TRADE FREE

ANTIQUES CENTRE GLOUCESTER LTD
1 Severn Road, Gloucester GL1 2LE
Tel: +44 (0)1452 529716
www.antiquescentre.com

Devon

Quay Centre, Topsham, Nr Exeter, EX3 0JA
Tel: 01392 874006
office@quayantiques.com
www.quayantiques.com
*80 dealers on 3 floors. Antiques, collectables and
traditional furnishings. Ample parking. Open 7 days,
10am-5pm. All major cards accepted.*

Gloucestershire

Antiques Centre Gloucester, 1 Severn Road,
The Historic Docks, Gloucester, GL1 2LE
Tel: 01452 529716 www.antiques.center.com
Open Mon–Sat 10am–5pm, Sun 1pm–5pm.

Hampshire

Dolphin Quay Antique Centre, Queen Street,
Emsworth, PO10 7BU Tel: 01243 379994
*Open 7 days a week (including Bank Holidays) Mon–Sat
10am-5pm Sun 10am-4pm. Marine, naval antiques,
paintings, watercolours, prints, antique clocks,
decorative arts, furniture, sporting apparel, luggage,
specialist period lighting, conservatory, garden antiques,
fine antique/country furniture, French/antique beds.*

Lymington Antiques Centre, 76 High Street,
Lymington, SO41 9AL Tel: 01590 670934
*Open Mon–Fri 10am–5pm, Sat 9am–5pm. 30 dealers,
clocks, watches, silver, glass, jewellery, toys & dolls,
books, furniture, textiles.*

Kent

Castle Antiques, 1 London Road (opposite Library),
Westerham, TN16 1BB Tel: 01959 562492
*Open 10am-5pm 7 days. 4 rooms of antiques, small
furniture, collectables, rural bygones, costume, glass,
books, linens, jewellery, chandeliers, cat collectables.
Services: advice, valuations, theatre props, house
clearance, talks on antiques.*

Malthouse Arcade, High Street, Hythe,
CT21 5BW Tel: 01303 260103
*Open Fridays and Saturdays Bank holiday Mondays
9.30am-5.30pm. 37 Stalls and cafe. Furniture, china and
glass, jewellery, plated brass, picture postcards, framing.*

Lancashire

The Antique & Decorative Design Centre,
56 Garstang Road, Preston, PR1 1NA
Tel: 01772 882078
info@paulallisonantiques.co.uk
www.paulallisonantiques.co.uk
*Open 7 days a week 10am–5pm. 25,000sq. ft. of quality
antiques, objects d'art, clocks, pine, silverware, porcelain,
upholstery, French furniture for the home and garden.*

GB Antiques Centre, Lancaster Leisure Park,
(the former Hornsea Pottery), Wyresdale Road,
Lancaster, LA1 3LA Tel: 01524 844734

140 dealers in 40,000 sq. ft. of space. Porcelain, pottery, Art Deco, glass, books, linen, mahogany, oak and pine furniture. Open 7 days 10am-5pm.

Kingsmill Antique Centre, Queen Street, Harle Syke, Burnley, BB10 2HX Tel: 01282 431953
antiques@kingsmill.demon.co.uk
www.kingsmill.demon.co.uk
Dealers, packers and shippers.

Leicestershire
Oxford Street Antique Centre, 16-26 Oxford Street, Leicester, LE1 5XU Tel: 0116 255 3006

Lincolnshire
St Martins Antiques Centre, 23a High St, St Martins, Stamford, PE9 2LF Tel: 01780 481158
peter@st-martins-antiques.co.uk
www.st-martins-antiques.co.uk

London
Alfie's Antique Market, 13 Church Street, Marylebone, NW8 8DT Tel: 020 7723 6066
www.alfiesantiques.com
Open Tues–Sat 10am–6pm.

Covent Garden Antiques Market, Jubilee Market Hall, Covent Garden, WC2 Tel: 020 7240 7405
Visit the famous Covent Garden Antique Market.
150 traders selling jewellery, silver, prints, porcelain, objets d'art and numerous other collectables.

Grays Antique Markets, South Molton Lane, W1K 5AB
Tel: 020 7629 7034 grays@clara.net
www.graysantiques.com
Opposite Bond St tube.

Northcote Road Antique Market, 155a Northcote Road, Battersea, SW11 6QB Tel: 020 7228 6850
gillikins@ntlworld.com
www.spectrumsoft.net/nam
Indoor arcade open 7 days, Mon–Sat 10am–6pm, Sun 12noon–5pm. 30 dealers offering a wide variety of antiques & collectables.

Palmers Green Antiques Centre, 472 Green Lanes, Palmers Green, N13 5PA
Tel: 020 8350 0878
Mobile: 07986 730155
Over 40 dealers. Specialising in furniture, jewellery, clocks, pictures, porcelain, china, glass, silver & plate, metalware, kitchenalia and lighting, etc. Open 6 days a week, Mon–Sat 10am–5.30pm (closed Tues), Sun 11am–5pm, open Bank Holidays. Removals & house clearances, probate valuations undertaken, quality antiques and collectables. All major credit cards accepted.

Norfolk
Tombland Antiques Centre, Augustine Steward House, 14 Tombland, Norwich, NR3 1HF
Tel: 01603 761906 or 619129
www.tomblandantiques.co.uk
Open Mon–Sat 10am–5pm. Huge selection on three floors. Ideally situated opposite Norwich Cathedral.

Oxfordshire
Antiques on High, 85 High Street, Oxford, OX1 4BG
Tel: 01865 251075
Open 7 days a week 10am-5pm. Sundays & Bank Holidays 11am-5pm. 35 friendly dealers with a wide range of quality stock.

Scotland
Scottish Antique and Arts Centre, Carse of Cambus, Doune, Perthshire, FK16 6HD Tel: 01786 841203
sales@scottish-antiques.com www.scottish-antiques.com
Over 100 dealers. Huge gift & collectors sections. Victorian & Edwardian furniture. Open 7 days 10am-5pm. Restaurant.

Scottish Antique and Arts Centre, Abernyte, Perthshire, PH14 9SJ Tel: 01828 686401
sales@scottish-antiques.com www.scottish-antiques.com
Over 100 dealers. Huge gift & collectors sections. Victorian & Edwardian furniture. Open 7 days 10am-5pm. Restaurant.

Shropshire
Stretton Antiques Market, Sandford Avenue, Church Stretton, SY6 6BH Tel: 01694 723718
60 dealers under one roof.

Surrey
Maltings Monthly Market, Bridge Square, Farnham, GU9 7QR Tel: 01252 726234
info@farnhammaltings.com
www.farnhammaltings.com
9.30–4.00pm 1st Sat of the month

East Sussex
The Brighton Lanes Antique Centre, 12 Meeting House Lane, Brighton, BN1 1HB Tel: 01273 823121
peter@brightonlanes-antiquecentre.co.uk
www.brightonlanes-antiquecentre.co.uk
A spacious centre in the heart of the historic lanes with a fine selection of furniture, silver, jewellery, glass, porcelain, clocks, pens, watches, lighting and decorative items. Open daily 10am–5.30pm, Sun 12noon–4pm. Loading bay/parking - Lanes car park.

Tyne & Wear
Antique Centre, The 2nd floor, 142 Northumberland Street, Newcastle-upon-Tyne, NE1 7DQ
Tel: 0191 232 9832 time-antiques@btconnect.com

Wales
Offa's Dyke Antique Centre, 4 High Street, Knighton, Powys, LD7 1AT Tel: 01547 528635/ 520145
Open Mon-Sat 10am-5pm. Wide ranging stock. Specialists in ceramics and glass, fine art of the 19th & 20th Centuries. Country Antiques and Collectables.

The Works Antiques Centre, Station Road, Llandeilo, Carmarthenshire, SA19 6NH Tel: 01558 823964
theworks@storeyj.clara.co.uk www.works-antiques.co.uk
Open Tues-Sat 10am-6pm & Sun 10am-5pm. Open Bank Holiday Mondays. 5,000sq ft. 60 dealers. Ample parking. Free tea and coffee.

Warwickshire

Stratford Antiques Centre, 59-60 Ely Street,
Stratford-upon-Avon, CV37 6LN Tel: 01789 204180
*Come and visit Stratford-upon-Avon. A one stop
collectors experience with 2 floors and courtyard full of
shops. Open 7 days a week from 10am-5pm.*

West Midlands

Birmingham Antique Centre, 1407 Pershore Road,
Stirchley, Birmingham, B30 2JR Tel: 0121 459 4587
bhamantiquecent@aol.com
www.birminghamantiquecentre.co.uk
*Open 7 days 9am-5pm Mon-Sat and 10am-4pm Sun.
Cabinets available to rent.*

Wiltshire

Upstairs Downstairs, 40 Market Place, Devizes, SN10 1JG
Tel: 01380 730266 or 07974 074220
devizesantiques@btconnect.com
*Open Mon-Sat 9.30am-4.30pm, Sun 9.30am-3pm,
closed Wed. Antiques & collectables centre on 4 floors
with 30 traders.*

Worcestershire

Worcester Antiques Centre, Reindeer Court,
Mealcheapen Street, Worcester, WR1 4DF
Tel: 01905 610680
WorcsAntiques@aol.com
*Porcelain & pottery, furniture, silver & dining room
accessories, jewellery, period watches & clocks, scientific
instrumentation, Arts & Crafts, Nouveau, Deco, antique
boxes, Mauchline & Tartan wares, books, ephemera,
militaria & kitchenalia with full restoration & repair
services on all of the above.*

Yorkshire

St Nicholas Antique Shops, 33-35 St Nicholas Cliff,
Scarborough, YO11 2ES Tel: 01723 365221/374175
sales@collectors.demon.co.uk
www.collectors.demon.co.uk
*International dealers in stamps, postcards, silver, gold,
medals, cigarette cards, cap badges, militaria, jewellery,
commemorative ware, furniture, clocks, watches and
many more collectables.*

York Antiques Centre, 1a Lendal, York,
YO1 8AA Tel: 01904 641445

U.S.A.

Alhambra Antiques Center, 3640 Coral Way,
Coral Cables, FL Tel: 305 446 1688
*4 antiques dealers that sell high quality decorative pieces
from Europe*

Antique Center I, II, III at Historic Savage Mill,
Savage, MD Tel: 410 880 0918 or 301 369 4650
antiquec@aol.com
*225 plus select quality dealers representing 15 states.
Open every day plus 3 evenings - Sun thru Wed
9.30am-6pm, Thurs, Fri and Sat 9.30am-9pm. Closed
Christmas, Easter and Thanksgiving days. Open New
Year's Day 12 noon-5pm*

Antique Village, North of Richmond, Virginia, on Historic
US 301, 4 miles North of 1-295 Tel: 804 746 8914
*Mon, Tues, Thurs, Fri 10am-5pm, Sat 10am-6pm, Sun
12 noon-6pm, closed Wed. 50 dealers specialising in Art
Pottery, country & primitives, Civil War artifacts, paper
memorabilia, African art, toys, advertising, occupied
Japan, tobacco tins, glassware, china, holiday
collectibles, jewellery, postcards*

Antiques at Colony Mill Marketplace, 222 West Street,
Keene, NH 03431 Tel: 603 358 6343
*Open Mon-Sat 10am-9pm, Sun 11am-6pm. Over 200
booths. Period to country furniture, paintings and prints,
Art Pottery, glass, china, silver, jewellery, toys, dolls, quilts.*

The Hayloft Antique Center, 1190 First NH Turnpike
(Rte. 4), Northwood, NH 03261
Tel: 603 942 5153
TheHayloftAntiqueCenter@NHantiqueAlley.com
*Over 150 dealers offering Estate jewelry, sterling silver,
rare books, glass, porcelain, pottery, art, primitives,
furniture, toys, ephemera, linens, military, sporting
collectibles and much more. Open 10am-5pm Daily.
Closed major holidays, please call ahead*

Madison Antique Mall, 320 Gallatin Rd, S. Nashville, TN
Tel: 615 865 4677
18th and 19thc English antiques and objets d'art

Michiana Antique Mall, 2423 S. 11th Street, Niles,
MI 49120 www.michianaantiquemall.com
Open 7 days a week 10am-6pm

Morningside Antiques, 6443 Biscayne Blvd., Miami,
FL Tel: 305 751 2828
*The city's newest antiques market specialising in English,
French and American furniture and collectibles in a mall
setting with many different vendors*

Nashville Wedgewood Station Antique Mall,
657 Wedgewood Ave., Nashville, TN
Tel: 615 259 0939

Parker-French Antique Center, 1182 First NH Turnpike
(Rt. 4), Northwood, NH 03261
Tel: 603 942 8852
ParkerFrenchAntiqueCenter@NHantiqueAlley.com
*135 antique dealers all on one level offering a good mix
of sterling silver, jewelry, glassware, pottery, early
primitives. No crafts, reproductions or new items. Open
10am-5pm daily. Closed major holidays, please call ahead*

Quechee Gorge Antiques & Collectibles Center,
Located in Quechee Gorge Village Tel: 1 800 438 5565
*450 dealers. Open all year, 7 days a week. Depression
glass, ephemera, tools, toys, collectibles, Deco,
primitives, prints, silver and fine china*

Showcase Antique Center, PO Box 1122, Sturbridge MA
01566 Tel: 508 347 7190 www.showcaseantiques.com
*Open Mon, Wed, Thurs, 10am-5pm, Fri, Sat
10am-5pm, Sun 12 noon-5pm, closed Tues. 170 dealers*

Tennessee Antique Mall, 654 Wedgewood Ave.,
Nashville, TN Tel: 615 259 4077

Key to Illustrations

Each illustration and descriptive caption is accompanied by a letter code. By referring to the following list of Auctioneers (denoted by 🔨), Dealers (⊞) and Clubs (§), the source of any item may be immediately determined. Inclusion in this edition in no way constitutes or implies a contract or binding offer on the part of any of our contributors to supply or sell the goods illustrated, or similar articles, at the prices stated. Advertisers in this year's directory are denoted by (†).

If you require a valuation for an item, it is advisable to check whether the dealer or specialist will carry out this service and if there is a charge. Please mention Miller's when making an enquiry. Having found a specialist who will carry out your valuation it is best to send a photograph and description of the item to the specialist together with a stamped addressed envelope for the reply. A valuation by telephone is not possible. Most dealers are only too happy to help you with your enquiry; however, they are very busy people and consideration of the above points would be welcomed.

AAA ⊞ Ad-Age Antique Advertising, Maidstone, Kent
Tel: 01622 670595

ABCM ⊞ A B Coins & Medals, 23–25 'Old' Northam Road, Southampton, Hampshire SO14
Tel: 023 8023 3393

ACCC § Antique Comb Collectors Club International, Jen Cruse European Coordinator, 14 Hall Drive, London SE26 6XB
jen.cruse@eggconnect.net

ADD ⊞ Addyman Books, 39 Lion Street, Hay-on-Wye, Herefordshire HR3 5AD Tel: 01497 821136

AEL ⊞ Argyll Etkin Ltd, 1–9 Hills Place, Oxford Circus, London W1F 7SA Tel: 020 7437 7800
philatelists@argyll-etkin.com
www.argyll-etkin.com

AFA ⊞ Alex Fane

AFD ⊞ Afford Decorative Arts Tel: 01827 330042
afforddecarts@fsmail.net

AGR • Anthony Green Antiques, Unit 39, The Bond Street Antique Centre, 124 New Bond Street, London W1S 1DX Tel: 020 7409 2854
vintagewatches@hotmail.com
www.anthonygreen.com

AH 🔨 Andrew Hartley, Victoria Hall Salerooms, Little Lane, Ilkley, Yorkshire LS29 8EA
Tel: 01943 816363
info@andrewhartleyfinearts.co.uk
www.andrewhartleyfinearts.co.uk

AL ⊞ Ann Lingard, Ropewalk Antiques, Rye, East Sussex TN31 7NA Tel: 01797 223486
ann-lingard@ropewalkantiques.freeserve.co.uk

AM ⊞ Alison Massey, MBO 32/33 Grays Antiques, 1–7 Davies Mews, London W1K 5AB
Tel: 020 7629 7034

AMB 🔨 Ambrose, Ambrose House, Old Station Road, Loughton, Essex IG10 4PE Tel: 020 8502 3951

AME ⊞ American Dream, Unit 10 Stephenson Road, St Ives, Huntingdon, Cambridgeshire PE27 3WJ Tel: 01480 495444
chris2americandream.co.uk
www.americandream.co.uk

AMH ⊞ Amherst Antiques, Monomark House, 27 Old Gloucester Street, London WC1N 3XX
Tel: 01892 725552 info@amherstantiques.co.uk
www.amherstantiques.co.uk

AMR ⊞ Amron Antiques, Staffordshire
Tel: 01782 566895

AnS No longer trading

APC ⊞ Antique Photographic Company Ltd
Tel: 01949 842192 alpaco47@aol.com

ARK ⊞ The Ark Angel, 33 Long Street, Tetbury, Gloucestershire GL8 8AA Tel: 01666 505820

ARo ⊞† Alvin's Vintage Games & Toys
Tel: 01865 772409 alvin@vintage-games.co.uk
http://www.vintage-games.co.uk

ARP ⊞ Arundel Photographica, The Arundel Antiques Centre, 51 High Street, Arundel, West Sussex BN18 9AJ 01903 882749

ATK ⊞ J & V R Atkins Tel: 01952 810594

AU ⊞ Auto Suggestion Tel: 01428 751397

AVT ⊞ Alexander von Tutschek Tel: 01225 465532
vontutschek@onetel.net.uk

B&R ⊞† Bread & Roses Tel: 01926 817342

BAC ⊞ The Brackley Antique Cellar, Drayman's Walk, Brackley, Northamptonshire NN13 6BE
Tel: 01280 841841 antiquecellar@tesco.net

BAJ ⊞ Beaulieu Autojumble, Beaulieu, Hampshire

BaN ⊞ Barbara Ann Newman Tel: 07850 016729

BAY ⊞ George Bayntun, Manvers Street, Bath, Somerset BA1 1JW Tel: 01225 466000
EBayntun@aol.com

BBA 🔨† Bloomsbury Auctions Ltd, Bloomsbury House, 24 Maddox Street, London W1S 1PP
Tel: 020 7495 9494
info@bloomsburyauctions.com
www.bloomsburyauctions.com

BBe ⊞ Bourton Bears help@bourtonbears.co.uk
www.bourtonbears.com

BBR 🔨† BBR, Elsecar Heritage Centre,Elsecar, Nr Barnsley, S. Yorkshire S74 8HJ
Tel: 01226 745156 sales@onlinebbr.com
www.onlinebbr.com

BD ⊞ Banana Dance Ltd, 155A Northcote Road, Battersea, London SW11 6QT
Tel: 01634 364539
jonathan@bananadance.com
www.bananadance.com

Bea 🔨 Bearnes, St Edmund's Court, Okehampton Street, Exeter, Devon EX4 1DU
Tel: 01392 207000 enquiries@bearnes.co.uk
www.bearnes.co.uk

Bert 🔨 Bertoia Auctions, 2141 DeMarco Drive, Vineland, New Jersey 08360, U.S.A.
856 692 1881 bill@bertoiaauctions.com
www.bertoiaauctions.com

BET ⊞ Beth, GO 43–44, Alfies Antique Market, 13–25 Church Street, Marylebone, London NW8 8DT
Tel: 020 7723 5613/0777 613 6003

BEV ⊞ Beverley, 30 Church Street, Marylebone, London NW8 8EP Tel: 020 7262 1576

BEX ⊞ Daniel Bexfield Antiques, 26 Burlington Arcade, London W1J 0PU Tel: 020 7491 1720
antiques@bexfield.co.uk www.bexfield.co.uk

BI ⊞† Books Illustrated Tel: 0777 1635 777
booksillustrated@aol.com
www.booksillustrated.com

BIB ⊞ Biblion, 1–7 Davies Mews, London W1K 5AB
Tel: 020 7629 1374 info@biblion.com
www.biblionmayfair.com

BLm ⊞ Lyn Bloom & Jeffrey Neal, Vault 27,
The London Silver Vaults, Chancery Lane,
London WC2A 1QS Tel: 020 7242 6189
bloomvault@aol.com www.bloomvault.com

BNO ⊞ Beanos, Middle Street, Croydon, London
CR0 1RE Tel: 020 8680 1202
enquiries@beanos.co.uk www.beanos.co.uk

BOB ⊞ Bob's Collectables Tel: 01277 650834

BOOM ⊞ Boom Interiors, 115–117 Regents Park Road,
Primrose Hill, London NW1 8UR
Tel: 020 7722 6622 www.boominteriors.com

BR **See DN(BR)**

Bri **See DN(Bri)**

BRIG ⊞† Briggs, 54 Lupin Ride, Kings Copse, Crowthorne,
Berkshire RG45 6UR Tel: 01344 466022
enquiries@usebriggs.com www.usebriggs.com

BrL ⊞ The Brighton Lanes Antique Centre,
12 Meeting House Lane, Brighton, East Sussex
BN1 1HB Tel: 01273 823121
peter@brightonlanes-antiquecentre.co.uk
www.brightonlanes-antiquecentre.co.uk

BRT ⊞ Britannia, Grays Antique Market, Stand 101,
58 Davies Street, London W1Y 1AR
Tel: 020 7629 6772 britannia@grays.clara.net

BS ⊞ Below Stairs, 103 High Street, Hungerford,
Berkshire RG17 0NB Tel: 01488 682317
hofgartner@belowstairs.co.uk
www.belowstairs.co.uk

BTC ⊞† Beatcity, P O Box 229, Chatham,
Kent ME5 8WA
Tel: 01634 200444 or 07770 650890
Darrenhanks@beatcity.co.uk
www.beatcity.co.uk

BtoB ⊞ Bac to Basics Tel: 07787 105609
bcarruthers@waitrose.com

BUDD ⚒ Budd Auctions Ltd, Graham Auctioneers &
Valuers gb@grahambuddauctions.co.uk

BUK ⚒ Bukowskis, Arsenalsgatan 4, Stockholm,
Sweden Tel: +46 (8) 614 08 00
info@bukowskis.se www.bukowskis.se

BWA ⊞ Bow Well Antiques, 103 West Bow, Edinburgh
EH1 2JP, Scotland Tel: 0131 225 3335
murdoch.mcleod@virgin.net

BWL ⚒ Brightwells Fine Art, The Fine Art Saleroom,
Easters Court, Leominster, Herefordshire
HR6 0DE Tel: 01568 611122
fineart@brightwells.com www.brightwells.com

c20th ⊞ www.c20th.com, Simon Moss
Tel: 07775 704052
simon@c20th.com www.c20th.com

C&W ⊞ Carroll & Walker Tel: 01877 385618

CAD ⊞ The Girl Can't Help It!, Sparkle Moore & Cad
Van Swankster, Alfies Antique Market, G100
& G116 Ground Floor, 13–25 Church Street,
Marylebone, London NW8 8DT
Tel: 020 7724 8984 sparkle.moore@virgin.net
www.sparklemoore.com

CAG ⚒ The Canterbury Auction Galleries,
40 Station Road West, Canterbury,
Kent CT2 8AN Tel: 01227 763337
auctions@thecanterburyauctiongalleries.com
www.thecanterburyauctiongalleries.com

CaH ⊞ The Camera House, Oakworth Hall, Colne Road,
Oakworth, Keighley, Yorkshire BD22 7HZ
Tel: 01535 642333
colin@the-camera-house.co.uk
www.the-camera-house.co.uk

CAL ⊞ Cedar Antiques Ltd, High Street,
Hartley Wintney, Hampshire RG27 8NY
Tel: 01252 843222 or 01189 326628

Cas ⊞ Castle Antiques www.castle-antiques.com

CAST ⊞ Castaside, FO13 Alfie's Antique Market,
13–25 Church Street, Marylebone, London
NW8 8DT Tel: 020 7723 7686
post@ealfies.com

CBB ⊞ Colin Baddiel, Gray's Mews, 1–7 Davies Mews,
London W1Y 1AR
Tel: 020 7408 1239/020 8452 7243

CBi ⊞ Collector Bits Tel: 02476 746981
collectorbits@aol.com www.collectorbits.com

CBP ⚒† Comic Book Postal Auctions Ltd,
40–42 Osnaburgh Street, London NW1 3ND
Tel: 020 7424 0007
comicbook@compalcomics.com
www.compalcomics.com

CCe ⊞ Clock Centre, London Tel: 020 7278 9660
clockcentre@aol.com www.clockcentre.com

CCH ⊞† Collectors Choice, PO Box 99, Guildford,
Surrey GU1 1GA Tel: 01483 531104
louise@collectors-choice.net
www.collectors-choice.net

CCO ⊞ Collectable Costume, Showroom South,
Gloucester Antiques Centre, 1 Severn Road,
Gloucester GL1 2LE Tel: 01989 562188

CCs ⊞ Coco's Corner, Unit 4, Cirencester Antique
Centre, Cirencester, Gloucestershire
Tel: 01452 556 308
cocos-corner@blueyonder.co.uk

CDC ⚒ Capes Dunn & Co, The Auction Galleries,
38 Charles Street, Off Princess Street, Greater
Manchester M1 7DB Tel: 0161 273 6060/1911
capesdunn@yahoo.co.uk

CFSD • Clive Farahar & Sophie Dupre, Horsebrook
House, XV The Green, Calne,
Wiltshire SN11 8DQ Tel: 01249 821121
post@farahardupre.co.uk
www.farahardupre.co.uk

ChC ⊞ Christopher Clarke (Antiques) Ltd, The Fosse
Way, Stow-on-the-Wold, Gloucestershire
GL54 1JS Tel: 01451 830476
cclarkeantiques@aol.com
www.campaignfurniture.com

CHES • Chesapeake Antique Center, Inc., Rt. 301,
PO Box 280, Queenstown, MD 21658, U.S.A.
Tel: 410 827 6640
antiques@chesapeakeantiques.com
www.chesapeakantiques.com

CHI ⊞† Chinasearch, PO Box 1202, Kenilworth,
Warwickshire CV8 2WW Tel: 01926 512402
info@chinasearch.co.uk
www.chinasearch.uk.com

ChM ⊞ Chelsea Military Antiques, F4 Antiquarius,
131/141 Kings Road, Chelsea, London
SW3 4PW Tel: 020 7352 0308
richard@chelseamilitaria.com

CHTR ⚒ Charterhouse, The Long Street Salerooms,
Sherborne, Dorset DT9 3BS
Tel: 01935 812277
enquiry@charterhouse-auctions.co.uk
www.charterhouse-auctions.co.uk

Ci ⊞ Circa, 8 Fulham High Road, London SW6
Tel: 020 7736 5038

COB ⊞† Cobwebs, 78 Northam Road, Southampton,
Hampshire SO14 0PB Tel: 023 8022 7458
www.cobwebs.uk.com

COBB ⤴ The Cobbs Auctioneers LLC, Noone Falls Mill,
50 Jaffrey Rd, Peterborough, NH 03458,
U.S.A. Tel: 603 924 6361 info@thecobbs.com
www.thecobbs.com

CoC ⊞ Comic Connections, 4a Parsons Street,
Banbury, Oxfordshire OX16 5LW
Tel: 01295 268989
comicman@freenetname.co.uk

CoCo ⊞ Country Collector, 11–12 Birdgate, Pickering,
Yorkshire YO18 7AL Tel: 01751 477481
www.country-collector.co.uk

CoHA ⊞ Corner House Antiques and Ffoxe Antiques,
Gardners Cottage, Broughton Poggs, Filkins,
Lechlade-on-Thames, Gloucestershire GL7 3JH
Tel: 01367 860078
jdhis007@btopenworld.com
www.corner-house-antiques.co.uk

Cot ⊞ Cottage Collectibles, Long Street Antiques,
14 Long Street, Tetbury,
Gloucestershire G18 8AQ Tel: 01666 500850
sheila@cottagecollectibles.co.uk

CPCC § Cigarette Packet Collectors Club of GB,
Barry Russell, Talisker, Vines Cross Road,
Horam, Heathfield, East Sussex TN21 0HF
Tel: 01435 812453

CRIS ⊞ Cristobal, 26 Church Street, London NW8 8EP
Tel: 020 7724 7230

CS ⊞ Christopher Sykes, The Old Parsonage, Woburn,
Milton Keynes, Bedfordshire MK17
9QM Tel: 01525 290259
www.sykes-corkscrews.co.uk

CTO ⊞† Collector's Corner, PO Box 8, Congleton,
Cheshire CW12 4GD Tel: 01260 270429
dave.popcorner@ukonline.co.uk

CUF ⊞ The Cufflink Shop, Stand G2 Antiquarius,
137 Kings Road, London SW3 4PW
Tel: 020 7352 8201

CuS ⊞ Curious Science, 319 Lillie Road, Fulham,
London SW6 7LL Tel: 020 7610 1175
curiousscience@medical-antiques.com

DA ⤴ Dee, Atkinson & Harrison, The Exchange
Saleroom, Driffield, East Yorkshire YO25 6LD
Tel: 01377 253151 info@dahauctions.com
www.dahauctions.com

DAL ⤴ Dalkeith Auctions Ltd, Dalkeith Hall,
Dalkeith Steps, Rear of 81 Old Christchurch
Road, Bournemouth, Dorset BH1 1YL
Tel: 01202 292905
how@dalkeith-auctions.co.uk
www.dalkeith-auctions.co.uk

Dall ⊞ P&R Dallimore Antique Collectibles,
Cheltenham, Gloucestershire
Tel: 01242 820119 rdalli5760@aol.com

DaM ⊞ Martin's Antiques & Collectibles, The Shed
Antiques Collectibles Centre, West Midlands
Tel: 01386 438387
Jackiem743710633@aol.com
www.martinsantiquescollectibles.co.uk

DD ⤴ David Duggleby, The Vine St Salerooms,
Scarborough, Yorkshire YO11 1XN
Tel: 01723 507111
auctions@davidduggleby.com
www.davidduggleby.com

DE ⊞† Decades, 20 Lord St West, Blackburn,
Lancashire BB2 1JX Tel: 01254 693320

DEB ⊞ Debden Antiques, Elder Street, Debden,
Saffron Walden, Essex CB11 3JY
Tel: 01799 543007 info@debden-antiques.co.uk
www.debden-antiques.co.uk

DgC ⊞ Dragonlee Collectables Tel: 01622 729502

DHAR ⊞ Dave Hardman Antiques, West Street,
Witheridge, Devon EX16 8AA
Tel: 01884 860273
dave@hardmanantiques.freeserve.co.uk

DHJ ⊞ Derek H Jordan chinafairings@aol.com
www.chinafairings.co.uk

DMC ⤴ Diamond Mills & Co, 117 Hamilton Road,
Felixstowe, Suffolk IP11 7BL Tel: 01394 282281

DN ⤴ Dreweatt Neate, Donnington Priory,
Donnington, Newbury, Berkshire RG14 2JE
Tel: 01635 553553 donnington@dnfa.com
www.dnfa.com/donnington

DN(BR) ⤴ Dreweatt Neate, formerly Bracketts Fine Art
Auctioneers, The Auction Hall, The Pantiles,
Tunbridge Wells, Kent TN2 5QL
Tel: 01892 544500 tunbridgewells@dnfa.com
www.dnfa.com/tunbridgewells

DN(Bri) ⤴ Dreweatt Neate, formerly Bristol Auction
Rooms, St John's Place, Apsley Road, Clifton,
Bristol, Gloucestershire BS8 2ST
Tel: 0117 973 7201 bristol@dnfa.com
www.dnfa.com/bristol

DNW ⤴† Dix-Noonan-Webb, 16 Bolton Street,
Piccadilly, London W1J 8BQ Tel: 020 7016 1700
auctions@dnw.co.uk www.dnw.co.uk

Do ⊞ Liz Farrow T/As Dodo, Stand F071/73, Alfie's
Antique Market, 13–25 Church Street, London
NW8 8DT Tel: 020 7706 1545

DOL ⊞† Dollectable, 53 Lower Bridge, Chester CH1 1RS
Tel: 01244 344888 or 679195

DOM ⊞ Peter Dome, Sheffield, Yorkshire
peterdome@onetel.com

DRE ⊞ Dreamtime, Shop 7, Georgian Village,
30–31 Islington Green, London N1 8DU
Tel: 020 8880 6695

DRU ⊞ Drummonds Architectural Antiques Ltd,
The Kirkpatrick Buildings, 25 London Road (A3),
Hindhead, Surrey GU26 6AB
Tel: 01428 609444 info@drummonds-arch.co.uk
www.drummonds-arch.co.uk

DuM ⤴ Du Mouchelles, 409 East Jefferson, Detroit,
Michigan 48226, U.S.A. Tel: 313 963 6255

DW ⤴† Dominic Winter Book Auctions, The Old
School, Maxwell Street, Swindon, Wiltshire
SN1 5DR Tel: 01793 611340
info@dominicwinter.co.uk
www.dominicwinter.co.uk

E ⤴ Ewbank Auctioneers, Burnt Common Auction
Rooms, London Road, Send, Woking, Surrey
GU23 7LN Tel: 01483 223101
antiques@ewbankauctions.co.uk
www.ewbankauctions.co.uk

EAL ⊞ The Exeter Antique Lighting Co., Cellar 15,
The Quay, Exeter, Devon EX2 4AP
Tel: 01392 490848
www.antiquelightingcompany.com

Ech ⊞† Echoes, 650a Halifax Road, Eastwood,
Todmorden, Yorkshire OL14 6DW
Tel: 01706 817505

EE ⊞ Empire Exchange, 1 Newton Street, Piccadilly,
Manchester Tel: 0161 2364445

EMH ⊞† Eat My Handbag Bitch, 37 Drury Lane, London WC2B 5RR Tel: 020 7836 0830 contact@eatmyhandbagbitch.co.uk www.eatmyhandbagbitch.co.uk

ES ⊞ Ernest R Sampson, 33 West End, Redruth, Cornwall TR15 2SA Tel: 01209 212536

ETO ⊞ Eric Tombs, 62a West Street, Dorking, Surrey RH4 1BS Tel: 01306 743661 ertombs@aol.com www.dorkingantiques.com

EV ⊞ Marlene Evans, Headrow Antiques Centre, Headrow Centre, Leeds, Yorkshire Tel: 0113 245 5344

F&F ⊞ Fenwick & Fenwick, 88–90 High Street, Broadway, Worcestershire WR12 7AJ Tel: 01386 853227/841724

FHF ⤳ Fellows & Sons, Augusta House, 19 Augusta Street, Hockley, Birmingham, West Midlands B18 6JA Tel: 0121 212 2131 info@fellows.co.uk www.fellows.co.uk

FLD ⊞ Flying Duck, 320/322 Creek Road, Greenwich, London SE10 9SW Tel: 020 8858 1964

FMN ⊞ Forget Me Knot Antiques, Antiques at Over the Moon, 27 High Street, St Albans, Hertfordshire AL3 4EH Tel: 01923 261172 sharpffocus@hotmail.com

FOF ⊞ Fossack & Furkle, PO Box 733, Abington, Cambridgeshire CB1 6BF Tel: 01223 894296 fossack@btopenworld.com www.fossackandfurkle.freeservers.com

FOX ⊞ Fox Cottage Antiques, Digbeth Street, Stow-on-the-Wold, Gloucestershire GL54 1BN Tel: 01451 870307

FRa ⊞ Fraser's, 399 Strand, London WC2R 0LX Tel: 020 7836 9325/836 8444 sales@frasersautographs.co.uk www.frasersautographs.com

G(B) ⤳ Gorringes Auction Galleries, Terminus Road, Bexhill-on-Sea, East Sussex TN39 3LR Tel: 01424 212994 bexhill@gorringes.co.uk www.gorringes.co.uk

G(L) ⤳ Gorringes, inc Julian Dawson, 15 North Street, Lewes, East Sussex BN7 2PD Tel: 01273 478221 auctions@gorringes.co.uk www.gorringes.co.uk

G&CC ⊞† Goss & Crested China Centre & Museum, incorporating Milestone Publications, 62 Murray Road, Horndean, Hampshire PO8 9JL Tel: 023 9259 7440 info@gosschinaclub.co.uk www.gosschinaclub.co.uk

GAK ⤳ Keys, Off Palmers Lane, Aylsham, Norfolk NR11 6JA Tel: 01263 733195 www.aylshamsalerooms.co.uk

Gam ⤳ Clarke & Gammon, The Guildford Auction Rooms, Bedford Road, Guildford, Surrey GU1 4SJ Tel: 01483 880915

GAU ⊞ Becca Gauldie Antiques, The Old School, Glendoick, Perthshire, Scotland PH2 7NR Tel: 01738 860 870 webuy@scottishantiques.freeserve.co.uk

GBM ⊞† GB Military Antiques, 17–18 The Mall, 359 Upper Street, Islington, London N1 0PD Tel: 020 7354 7334 info@gbmilitaria.com www.gbmilitaria.com

GBr ⊞ Geoffrey Breeze Antiques, Top Banana Antiques Mall, 1 New Street, Tetbury, Gloucestershire GL8 8OS Tel: 01225 466499 antiques @geoffreybreeze.co.uk www.antiquecanes.co.uk

GGD ⊞ Great Grooms of Dorking, 50/52 West Street, Dorking, Surrey RH4 1BU Tel: 01306 887076 www.great-grooms.co.uk

GGv ⊞ G.G. van Schagen, Antiquair Tel: 31 229 275692 g.schagen@wxs.nl

GH ⤳ Gardiner Houlgate, The Bath Auction Rooms, 9 Leafield Way, Corsham, Nr Bath, Somerset SN13 9SW Tel: 01225 812912 gardiner-houlgate.co.uk www.invaluable.com/gardiner-houlgate

GKR ⊞† GKR Bonds Ltd, PO Box 1, Kelvedon, Essex CO5 9EH Tel: 01376 571711

GLAS ⊞† Glasstastique By appointment only Tel: 0113 287 9308 or 07967 337795/ 07967 345952 glasstastique@aol.com www.glasstastique.com

GLB ⊞ Glebe Antiques, Scottish Antique Centre, Doune, Scotland FK16 6HG Tel: 01259 214559 RRGlebe@aol.com

GM ⊞† Philip Knighton, 1c South Street, Wellington, Somerset TA21 8NR Tel: 01823 661618 philip.knighton@btopenworld.com

GOv ⊞ Glazed Over Tel: 0773 2789114

GRe ⊞ Greystoke Antiques, 4 Swan Yard, (off Cheap Street), Sherborne, Dorset DT9 3AX Tel: 01935 812833

GRo ⊞ Geoffrey Robinson, GO77–78, GO91–92 (Ground floor), Alfies Antique Market, 13–25 Church Street, Marylebone, London NW8 8DT Tel: 020 7723 0449 info@alfiesantiques.com www.alfiesantiques.com

GTM ⊞† Gloucester Toy Mart, Ground Floor, Antique Centre, Severn Road, Old Docks, Gloucester GL1 2LE Tel: 07973 768452

H&G ⊞ Hope & Glory, 131A Kensington Church Street, London W8 7LP Tel: 020 7727 8424

HaH ⊞ Hayman & Hayman, Antiquarius Stand K3, 135 Kings Road, London SW3 4PW Tel: 020 7351 6568 georgina@haymanframes.co.uk

HAK ⊞ Paul Haskell Tel: 01634 891796 www.antiqueslotmachines.inuk.com

HAL ⊞† John & Simon Haley, 89 Northgate, Halifax, Yorkshire HX1 1XF Tel: 01422 822148/360434 toysandbanks@aol.com

HarC ⊞ Hardy's Collectables Tel: 07970 613077 www.poolepotteryjohn.com

HeA ⊞ Heanor Antiques Centre, 1–3 Ilkeston Road, Heanor, Derbyshire DE75 7AE Tel: 01773 531181/762783 sales@heanorantiquescentre.co.uk www.heanorantiques.co.uk

HEI ⊞ Heirloom Antiques, 68 High Street, Tenterden, Kent TN30 6AU Tel: 01580 765535

HER ⊞ Hermitage Antiques Tel: 01384 296544

HILL ⊞ Hillhaven Antique Linen & Lace Tel: 0121 358 4320

HIP ⊞ Hilary Proctor, Shop 6 Admiral Vernon Antiques Market, 141–151 Portobello Road, London W11 2DY Tel: 07956 876428 hproctor@antiquehandbags.fsnet.co.uk

HIS ⊞ Erna Hiscock & John Shepherd, Chelsea Galleries, 69 Portobello Road, London W11 Tel: 01233 661407

HL ⊞ Honiton Lace Shop, 44 High Street, Honiton, Devon EX14 1PJ Tel: 01404 42416 shop@honitonlace.com www.honitonlace.com

HO ⊞ Houghton Antiques, Houghton,
Cambridgeshire Tel: 01480 461887

HOB ⊞ Hobday Toys Tel: 01895 636737
wendyhobday@freenet.com

HOLL ⚲ Holloway's, 49 Parsons Street, Banbury,
Oxfordshire OX16 5PF Tel: 01295 817777
enquiries@hollowaysauctioneers.co.uk
www.hollowaysauctioneers.co.uk

HOP ⊞† The Antique Garden, Grosvenor Garden
Centre, Wrexham Road, Belgrave, Chester
CH4 9EB Tel: 01244 629191/07976 539 990
antigard@btopenworld.com

HSR/ ⊞ High Street Retro, 39 High Street, Old Town,
HSt Hastings, East Sussex TN34 3ER
Tel: 01424 460068

HTE ⊞ Heritage, 6 Market Place, Woodstock,
Oxfordshire OX20 1TA Tel: 01993 811332/
0870 4440678 dealers@atheritage.co.uk
www.atheritage.co.uk

HUX ⊞ David Huxtable, Saturdays at: Portobello Road,
Basement Stall 11/12, 288 Westbourne Grove,
London W11 Tel: 07710 132200
david@huxtins.com www.huxtins.com

HYD ⚲ Hy Duke & Son, The Dorchester Fine Art
Salerooms, Weymouth Avenue, Dorchester,
Dorset DT1 1QS Tel: 01305 265080
www.dukes-auctions.com

HYP ⊞ Hyperion Collectables

ID ⊞ Identity, 100 Basement Flat, Finsborough
Road, London SW10 9ED Tel: 020 7244 9509

IQ ⊞ Cloud Cuckooland, 12 Fore Street, Mevagissey,
Cornwall PL26 6UQ Tel: 01726 842364
Paul@cloudcuckooland.biz
www.cloudcuckooland.biz

J&J ⊞ J & J's, Paragon Antiquities Antiques & Collectors
Market, 3 Bladud Buildings, The Paragon,
Bath, Somerset BA1 5LS Tel: 01225 463715

J&S ⊞ J.R & S.J Symes of Bristol Tel: 117 9501074

JAA ⚲ Jackson's International Auctioneers &
Appraisers of Fine Art & Antiques, 2229
Lincoln Street, Cedar Falls, IA 50613, U.S.A.
Tel: 319 277 2256/800 665 6743
www.jacksonsauction.com

JAd ⚲ James Adam & Sons, 26 St Stephen's Green,
Dublin 2, Republic of Ireland
Tel: 3531 676 0261
www.jamesadam.ie/

JAM ⊞ Jam Jar Tel: 078896 17593

JAS ⊞ Jasmin Cameron, Antiquarius, 131–141 King's
Road, London SW3 4PW Tel: 020 7351 4154
jasmin.cameron@mail.com

JAZZ ⊞ Jazz Art Deco Tel: 07721 032277
jazzartdeco@btinternet.com
www.jazzartdeco.com

JBa ⊞† John Bartholomew, Heirloom Antiques,
68 High Street, Tenterden, Kent TN30 6AU
Tel: 01580 765535 or 01580 241556

JBB ⊞ Jessie's Button Box, Bartlett Street Antique
Centre, Bath, Somerset BA1 5DY
Tel: 0117 929 9065

JBM ⊞† Jim Bullock Militaria, PO Box 217, Romsey,
Hampshire SO51 5XL Tel: 01794 516455
jim@jimbullockmilitaria.com
www.jimbullockmilitaria.com

JDJ ⚲ James D Julia, Inc., P O Box 830, Rte.201,
Skowhegan Road, Fairfield, ME 04937, U.S.A.
Tel: 207 453 7125
www.juliaauctions.com

JeH ⊞ Jennie Horrocks Tel: 07836 264896
info@artnouveaulighting.plus.net
www.artnouveaulighting.co.uk

JFME ⊞ James Ferguson & Mark Evans
Tel: 0141 950 2452 or 01388 768108
james@dec-art.freeserve.co.uk
mark@evanscollectables.co.uk
www.evanscollectables.co.uk

JHo ⊞ Jonathan Horne, 66 Kensington Church Street,
London W8 4BY Tel: 020 7221 5658
JH@jonathanhorne.co.uk
www.jonathanhorne.co.uk

JMC ⊞ J & M Collectables Tel: 01580 891657
jandmcollectables@tinyonline.co.uk

JNic ⚲ John Nicholson, The Auction Rooms,
Longfield, Midhurst Road, Fernhurst, Surrey
GU27 3HA Tel: 01428 653727

JPr ⊞ Antique Textiles & Lighting, 34 Belvedere,
Lansdown Hill, Bath, Somerset BA1 5HR
01225 310795 antiquetextiles@aol.co.uk
www.antiquetextiles.co.uk

JuC ⊞ Julia Craig, Bartlett Street Antiques Centre,
5–10 Bartlett Street, Bath, Somerset BA1 2QZ
Tel: 01225 448202/310457

JUJ ⊞ Just Jewellery

JUN ⊞† Junktion, The Old Railway Station, New
Bolingbroke, Boston, Lincolnshire PE22 7LB
Tel: 01205 480068/480087
junktionantiques@hotmail.com

JWK ⊞ Jane Wicks Kitchenalia, Country Ways, Strand
Quay, Rye, East Sussex Tel: 01424 713635
janes_kitchen@hotmail.com

KES ⊞ Keystones, PO Box 387, Stafford ST16 3FG
Tel: 01785 256648
gkey@keystones.demon.co.uk
www.keystones.co.uk

KEY ⊞ Key Antiques of Chipping Norton, 11 Horsefair,
Chipping Norton, Oxfordshire OX7 5AL
Tel: 01608 644992/643777
info@keyantiques.com www.keyantiques.com

KWCC § James Sadler International Collectors Club,
Customer Services, Churchill China PLC,
High Street, Tunstall, Stoke on Trent ST6 5NZ
Tel: 01782 577566
diningin@churchillchina.plc.uk
www.james-sadler.co.uk

L ⚲ Lawrence Fine Art Auctioneers, South Street,
Crewkerne, Somerset TA18 8AB
Tel: 01460 73041 www.lawrences.co.uk

L&E ⚲ Locke & England, 18 Guy Street,
Leamington Spa, Warwickshire CV32 4RT
Tel: 01926 889100
www.auctions-online.com/locke

L&L ⊞† Linen & Lace, Shirley Tomlinson,
Halifax Antiques Centre, Queens Road/Gibbet
Street, Halifax, Yorkshire HX1 4LR
Tel: 01484 540492/01422 366657

L&T ⚲ Lyon & Turnbull, 33 Broughton Place,
Edinburgh, Scotland EH1 3RR
Tel: 0131 557 8844 info@lyonandturnbull.com

LaF ⊞ La Femme Tel: 07971 844279
jewels@joancorder.freeserve.co.uk

LAS ⊞ Reasons to be Cheerful, Georgian Village,
30–31 Islington Green, London N18 DU
Tel: 0207 281 4600

LAY ⚲ David Lay (ASVA), Auction House, Alverton,
Penzance, Cornwall TR18 4RE Tel: 01736 361414
david.lays@btopenworld.com

LBe ⊞ Linda Bee, Art Deco Stand L18–21, Grays Antique Market, 1–7 Davies Mews, London W1Y 1AR Tel: 020 7629 5921

LBr ⊞ Lynda Brine By Appointment only lyndabrine@yahoo.co.uk www.scentbottlesandsmalls.co.uk

LCM ➤ Galeria Louis C. Morton, GLC A7073L IYS, Monte Athos 179, Col. Lomas de Chapultepec, CP11000, Mexico Tel: 52 5520 5005 glmorton@prodigy.net.mx www.lmorton.com

LEI ⊞ Joyce M. Leiby, PO Box 6048, Lancaster, PA 17607, U.S.A. Tel: 717 898 9113 joyclei@aol.com

LENA ⊞ Lena Baldock, Mint Arcade, 71 The Mint, Rye, East Sussex TN31 7EW Tel: 01797 225952

LF ➤ Lambert & Foster, 77 Commercial Road, Paddock Wood, Kent TN12 6DR Tel: 01892 832325

LFA ➤ Law Fine Art Tel: 01635 860033 info@lawfineart.co.uk www.lawfineart.co.uk

LFi ⊞ Laurence Fisher Tel: 07977 368 288

LHA ➤ Leslie Hindman, Inc., 122 North Aberdeen Street, Chicago, Illinois 60607, U.S.A. Tel: 312 280 1212 www.lesliehindman.com

LU ⊞ Lucia Collectables, (open Saturdays) Stalls 57–58, Admiral Vernon Antique Arcade, Portobello Road, London Tel: 01793 790607 sallie_ead@lycos.com

LUNA ⊞ Luna, 23 George Street, Nottingham NG1 3BH Tel: 0115 924 3267 info@luna-online.co.uk www.luna-online.co.uk

M ➤ Morphets of Harrogate, 6 Albert Street, Harrogate, Yorkshire HG1 1JL Tel: 01423 530030

MAR ➤ Frank R Marshall & Co, Marshall House, Church Hill, Knutsford, Cheshire WA16 6DH Tel: 01565 653284

MARG ⊞† Margaret Williamson, Vintage Modes, Grays Antique Market, 1–7 Davies Mews, Mayfair, London W1K 5AB Tel: 0207 40 90 400 chelsealace@aol.com www.vintagemodes.co.uk

MARK ⊞† 20th Century Marks, Whitegates, Rectory Road, Little Burstead, Near Billericay, Essex CM12 9TR Tel: 01268 411 000 info@20thcenturymarks.co.uk www.20thcenturymarks.co.uk

MB ⊞ Mostly Boxes, 93 High Street, Eton, Windsor, Berkshire SL4 6AF Tel: 01753 858470

MCA ➤ Mervyn Carey, Twysden Cottage, Scullsgate, Benenden, Cranbrook, Kent TN17 4LD Tel: 01580 240283

MCa ⊞ Mia Cartwright Tel: 07956 440260 mia.cartwright@virgin.net

MCL ⊞† Millennium Collectables Ltd, P.O. Box 146, Newark, Nottinghamshire NG24 2WR Tel: 01636 703075 mail@millenniumcollectables.co.uk www.millenniumcollectables.co.uk

MDe ⊞† Mike Delaney Tel: 01993 840064 mike@vintagehornby.co.uk www.vintagehornby.co.uk

MF ⊞ Maurice Flinton Tel: 01723 863215

MFB ⊞ Manor Farm Barn Antiques Tel: 01296 658941 mfbn@btinternet.com btwebworld.com/mfbantiques

MGA ⊞ M. G. Antiques Tel: 01489 783724

MINN ⊞ Geoffrey T. Minnis, Hastings Antique Centre, 59–61 Norman Road, St Leonards-on-Sea, East Sussex TN38 0EG Tel: 01424 428561

Mit ➤ Mitchells, Fairfield House, Station Road, Cockermouth, Cumbria CA13 9PY Tel: 01900 827800 info@mitchellsfineart.com

MLa ⊞ Marion Langham Tel: 028 895 41247 marion@ladymarion.co.uk www.ladymarion.co.uk

MLL ⊞ Millers Antiques Ltd, Netherbrook House, 86 Christchurch Road, Ringwood, Hampshire BH24 1DR Tel: 01425 472062 mail@millers-antiques.co.uk www.millers-antiques.co.uk

MMa Madeleine Marsh

MMc ⊞ Marsh-McNamara Tel: 07790 759162

Mo ⊞ Mr Moore

MPC ⊞† M C Pottery, Cheshire Tel: 01244 301800 Sales@Moorcroftchester.co.uk www.Moorcroftchester.co.uk

MRW ⊞ Malcolm Welch Antiques, Wild Jebbett, Pudding Bag Lane, Thurlaston, Nr Rugby, Warwickshire CV23 9JZ Tel: 01788 810 616 www.rb33.co.uk

MSB ⊞ Marilynn and Sheila Brass, PO Box 380503, Cambridge, MA 02238-0503, U.S.A. Tel: 617 491 6064 shelmardesign1@aol.com

MSh ⊞ Manfred Schotten, 109 High Street, Burford, Oxfordshire OX18 4RG Tel: 01993 822302 www.antiques@£schotten.com

MTMC § Muffin the Mule Collectors' Club, 12 Woodland Close, Woodford Green, Essex IG8 0QH Tel: 020 8504 4943 adrienne@hasler.gotadsl.co.uk www.Muffin-the-Mule.com

MUL ➤† Mullock & Madeley, The Old Shippon, Wall-under-Heywood, Nr Church Stretton, Shropshire SY6 7DS Tel: 01694 771771 auctions@mullockmadeley.co.uk www.mullockmadeley.co.uk

MUR ⊞ Murray Cards (International) Ltd, 51 Watford Way, Hendon Central, London NW4 3JH Tel: 020 8202 5688 murraycards@ukbusiness.com www.murraycard.com/

MURR ⊞ Murrays' Antiques & Collectables Tel: 01202 823870

NAR ⊞ Colin Narbeth & Son Ltd, 20 Cecil Court, Leicester Square, London WC2N 4HE Tel: 020 7379 6975 Colin.Narbeth@btinternet.com www.colin-narbeth.com

NEG ⊞ C Negrillo Antiques, Antiquarius P1/P2/P3, 135 Kings Road, London SW3 4PW Tel: 020 7349 0038 negrilloc@aol.com

NEW ⊞ Newsum Antiques, 2 High Street, Winchcombe, Gloucestershire GL54 5HT Tel: 01242 603446/07968 196668 mark@newsumantiques.co.uk www.newsumantiques.co.uk

NFR ⊞ The 40's Room, Unit 40 Rugeley Antiques Centre, Main Road, Brereton, Rugeley, Staffordshire WS15 1DX Tel: 01889 577166 info@cc41homefrontdisplays.co.uk

NLS ⊞ Lenson-Smith, 153 Portobello Road, London W11 2DY Tel: 020 8340 8767

OS ⊞ Nostalgia and Comics, 14–16 Smallbrook Queensway, City Centre, Birmingham, West Midlands B5 4EN Tel: 0121 643 0143

Sal ⚒ Netherhampton Salerooms, Salisbury Auction Centre, Netherhampton, Salisbury, Wiltshire SP2 8RH Tel: 01722 340 041

W ⊞ Nigel Williams Rare Books, 25 Cecil Court, London WC2N 4EZ Tel: 020 7836 7757 nigel@nigelwilliams.com www.nigelwilliams.com

H ⊞ Old Hat, 66 Fulham High Road, London SW6 3LQ Tel: 020 7610 6558

IA ⊞ The Old Ironmongers Antiques Centre, 5 Burford Street, Lechlade, Gloucestershire GL7 3AP Tel: 01367 252397

LA ⊞ Olliff's Architectural Antiques, 19–21 Lower Redland Road, Redland, Bristol, Gloucestershire BS6 6TB Tel: 0117 923 9232 marcus@olliffs.com www.olliffs.com

LD ⊞ Oldnautibits, PO Box 67, Langport, Somerset TA10 9WJ Tel: 01458 241816 geoff.pringle@oldnautibits.com www.oldnautibits.com

li ⚒ Olivers, Olivers Rooms, Burkitts Lane, Sudbury, Suffolk CO10 1HB Tel: 01787 880305 oliversauctions@btconnect.com

NS ⚒ Onslow's Auctions Ltd, The Coach House, Manor Road, Stourpaine, Dorset DT8 8TQ Tel: 01258 488838

RI ⊞ Origin 101, Gateway Arcade, Islington High Street, London N1 Tel: 07769 686146/07747 758852 david@origin101.co.uk www.naturalmodern.com www.origin101.co.uk

TA ⊞† On The Air, The Vintage Technology Centre, The Highway, Hawarden, (Nr Chester), Deeside, Cheshire CH5 3DN Tel: 01244 530300 www.vintageradio.co.uk

TB ⊞† The Old Tackle Box, PO Box 55, Cranbrook, Kent TN17 3ZU Tel: 01580 713979 tackle.box@virgin.net

W **See STa**

CCC § Pedal Car Collectors' Club (P.C.C.C.), Secretary A. P. Gayler, 4/4a Chapel Terrace Mews, Kemp Town, Brighton, East Sussex BN2 1HU Tel: 01273 601960 www.brmmbrmm.com/pedalcars

eJ ⊞ Peter Jones, Dept 1128, 22 Westgate, Wakefield, Yorkshire WF1 1LB Tel: 01924 362510 www.peterjoneschina.com

F ⚒ Peter Francis, Curiosity Sale Room, 19 King Street, Carmarthen, Wales SA31 1BH Tel: 01267 233456 Peterfrancis@valuers.fsnet.co.uk www.peterfrancis.co.uk

FK ⚒ Penrith Farmers' & Kidd's plc, Skirsgill Salerooms, Penrith, Cumbria CA11 0DN Tel: 01768 890781 info@pfkauctions.co.uk www.pfkauctions.co.uk

GO ⊞ Pamela Goodwin, 11 The Pantiles, Royal Tunbridge Wells, Kent TN2 5TD Tel: 01892 618200 mail@goodwinantiques.co.uk www.goodwinantiques.co.uk

CC ⊞ Piccypicky.com Tel: 020 8206 2001 www.piccypicky.com

PLB ⊞ Planet Bazaar, 149 Drummond Street, London NW1 2PB Tel: 020 7387 8326 info@planetbazaar.co.uk www.planetbazaar.co.uk

POL ⊞ Politico Book Shop, 8 Artillery Row, London SW1 Tel: 020 7828 0010

POLL ⊞ Pollyanna, 34 High Street, Arundel, West Sussex BN18 9AB Tel: 01903 885198

POS § Postcard Club of Great Britain, c/o Mrs D. Brennan, 34 Harper House, St James Crescent, London SW9 7LW Tel: 020 7771 9404

Pott ⚒ Potteries Specialist Auctions, 271 Waterloo Road, Cobridge, Stoke on Trent, Staffordshire ST6 3HR Tel: 01782 286622

PPH ⊞ Period Picnic Hampers Tel: 0115 937 2934

PPL ⊞ The Pen and Pencil Lady Tel: 01647 231619 penpencilady@aol.com www.penpencilady.com

PR ⊞ Prime Cuts, 85 Gloucester Road, Bishopston, Bristol BS7 8AS Tel: 0117 9830007

PrB ⊞ Pretty Bizarre, 170 High Street, Deal, Kent CT14 6BQ Tel: 07973 794537

PSA ⊞ Pantiles Spa Antiques, 4, 5, 6 Union House, The Pantiles, Tunbridge Wells, Kent TN4 8HE Tel: 01892 541377 psa.wells@btinternet.com www.antiques-tun-wells-kent.co.uk

Q&C ⊞ Q & C Militaria, 22 Suffolk Road, Cheltenham, Gloucestershire GL50 2AQ Tel: 01242 519815 john@qc-militaria.freeserve.co.uk www.qcmilitaria.com

Qua ⊞ Quadrille, 146 Portobello Road, London W11 2DZ Tel: 01923 829079/020 7727 9860 (sat only)

RaA ⊞ Race Art, 33 Westgate Street, Southery, Norfolk PE38 0PA Tel: 01366 377069 simon@race-art.com www.race-art.com

RAND ⊞ Becky Randall, c/o 36 Highfield Road, Wilmslow, Buckinghamshire MK18 3DU Tel: 07979 848440

RdeR ⊞ Rogers de Rin, 76 Royal Hospital Road, London SW3 4HN Tel: 020 7352 9007

REK ⊞ Rellik, 8 Golborne Road, London W10 5NW Tel: 020 8962 0089

ReN ⊞ Rene Nicholls, 56 High Street, Malmesbury, Wiltshire SN16 9AT Tel: 01666 823089

REPS ⊞ Repsycho, 85 Gloucester Road, Bishopston, Bristol BS7 8AS Tel: 0117 9830007

RER ⊞† Red Roses, Vintage Modes, Shops 57 & 58, Admiral Vernon Antiques Markets, 141–149 Portobello Road, London W11 2DY Tel: 01793 790 607 sallie_ead@lycos.com

RET ⊞ Retro-Spective Tel: 07989 984659 retro_spective1@hotmail.com

RGa ⊞ Richard Gardner Antiques, Swanhouse, Market Square, Petworth, West Sussex GU28 0AN Tel: 01798 343411

RGA ⊞ Richard Gibbon, Shop 4 34/34a Islington Green, London N1 8DU Tel: 020 7354 2852 neljeweluk@aol.com

RH ⊞ Rick Hubbard Art Deco, 3 Tee Court, Bell Street, Romsey, Hampshire SO51 8GY Tel: 07767 267607 rick@rickhubbard-artdeco.co.uk www.rickhubbard-artdeco.co.uk

RTo ⚒ Rupert Toovey & Co Ltd, Spring Gardens, Washington, West Sussex RH20 3BS Tel: 01903 891955 auctions@rupert-toovey.com www.rupert-toovey.com

RTT ⊞ Rin Tin Tin, 34 North Road, Brighton, East Sussex BN1 1YB Tel: 01273 672424 rick@rintintin.freeserve.co.uk

RUS ⊞ Trevor Russell Vintage Fountain Pens, PO Box 1258, Uttoxeter, Staffordshire ST14 8XL tjrussell@onetel.net.uk

RUSK ⊞ Ruskin Decorative Arts, 5 Talbot Court, Stow-on-the-Wold, Cheltenham, Gloucestershire GL54 1DP Tel: 01451 832254 william.anne@ruskindecarts.co.uk

RW ⊞ Robin Wareham, Warminster

S(NY) ⚒ Sotheby's, 1334 York Avenue at 72nd St, New York, NY 10021, U.S.A. Tel: 212 606 7000 www.sothebys.com

S(O) ⚒ Sotheby's Olympia, Hammersmith Road, London W14 8UX Tel: 020 7293 5555 www.sothebys.com

S(P) ⚒ Sotheby's France SA, 76 rue du Faubourg, Saint Honore, Paris 75008, France Tel: 33 1 53 05 53 05

S&D ⊞ S&D Postcards, Bartlett Street Antique Centre, 5–10 Bartlett Street, Bath, Somerset BA1 2QZ Tel: 07979 506415 wndvd@aol.com

SA ⊞ Sporting Antiques, St Ives, Cambridgeshire 01480 463891 john.lambden@virgin.net

SAAC ⊞ Scottish Antique Centre, Abernyte PH14 9SJ, Scotland Tel: 01828 686401 sales@scottish-antiques.com www.scottish-antiques.com

SaB ⊞ Sara Bernstein Antique Dolls & Bears, Englishtown, New Jersey 07726, U.S.A. Tel: 732 536 4101 santiqbebe@aol.com www.sarabernsteindolls.com

SAS ⚒† Special Auction Services, Kennetholme, Midgham, Reading, Berkshire RG7 5UX Tel: 0118 971 2949 www.invaluable.com/sas/

SAT ⊞ The Swan at Tetsworth, High Street, Tetsworth, Nr Thame, Oxfordshire OX9 7AB Tel: 01844 281777 antiques@theswan.co.uk www.theswan.co.uk

SBL ⊞ Twentieth Century Style Tel: 01822 614831

SCH ⊞ Scherazade Tel: 01708 641117 scherz1@yahoo.com

SDA ⊞ Stephanie Davison Antiques, Bakewell Antiques Centre, King Street, Bakewell, Derbyshire DE45 1DZ Tel: 01629 812496 bacc@chappells-antiques.co.uk www.chappells-antiques.co.uk

SDP ⊞ Stage Door Prints, 9 Cecil Court, London WC2N 4EZ Tel: 020 7240 1683

SEA ⊞ Mark Seabrook Antiques, PO Box 396, Huntingdon, Cambridgeshire PE28 0ZA Tel: 01480 861935 enquiries@markseabrook.com www.markseabrook.com

SER ⊞ Serendipity, 125 High Street, Deal, Kent CT14 6BB Tel: 01304 369165/ 01304 366536 dipityantiques@aol.com

SJH ⚒ S.J. Hales, 87 Fore Street, Bovey Tracey, Devon TQ13 9AB Tel: 01626 836684

SMI ⊞† Skip & Janie Smithson Antiques Tel: 01754 810265 smithsonantiques@hotmail.com

SOR ⊞ Soldiers of Rye, Mint Arcade, 71 The Mint, Rye, East Sussex TN31 7EW Tel: 01797 225952 rameses@supanet.com chris@johnbartholomewcards.co.uk www.rameses.supanet.com

SPE ⊞ Sylvie Spectrum, Stand 372, Grays Market, 58 Davies Street, London W1Y 2LB Tel: 020 7629 3501

SpM ⊞ The Girl Can't Help It!, Sparkle Moore & Cad Van Swankster, Alfies Antique Market, G100 & G116 Ground Floor, 13–25 Church Street, Marylebone, London NW8 8DT Tel: 020 7724 8984 sparkle.moore@virgin.net www.sparklemoore.com

SPT ⊞ Sporting Times Gone ByTel: 01903 885656 or 07976 942059 www.sportingtimes.co.uk

SRA ⚒†Sheffield Railwayana Auctions, 43 Little Norton Lane, Sheffield, Yorkshire S8 8GA Tel: 0114 274 5085 ian@sheffrail.freeserve.co.uk www.sheffieldrailwayana.co.uk

SSF ⊞ Suffolk Sci-Fi and Fantasy, 17 Norwich Road, Ipswich, Suffolk IP1 2ET Tel: 01473 400655 mick@suffolksci-fi.com www.suffolksci-fi.com

STa ⊞ Starbase-Alpha, Unit 19–20, Rumford Shopping Halls, Market Place, Rumford, Essex RM1 3AT Tel: 01708 765633 starbasealpha1@aol.com www.starbasealpha.cjb.net

STA ⊞ George Stacpoole, Main Street, Adare, Co. Limerick, Republic of Ireland Tel: 6139 6409 stacpoole@iol.ie www.georgestacpooleantiques.com

StC ⊞ Carlton Factory Shop, Carlton Works, Copeland Street, Stoke on Trent, Staffordshire ST4 1PU Tel: 01782 410504

StDA ⚒ St. David's Auctions, Mill Road Trading Estate, Barnstaple, North Devon EX31 1JH Tel: 01271 343123 info@stdavidsauctions.co.uk www.stdavidsauctions.co.uk

SUW ⊞ Sue Wilde at Wildewear Tel: 01395 577966 compacts@wildewear.co.uk www.wildewear.co.uk

SWB ⊞† Sweetbriar Gallery Paperweights Ltd., 3 Collinson Court, off Church Street, Frodsham, Cheshire WA6 6PN Tel: 01928 730064 sales@sweetbriar.co.uk www.sweetbriar.co.uk

SWO ⚒ Sworders, 14 Cambridge Road, Stansted Mountfitchet, Essex CM24 8BZ Tel: 01279 817778 auctions@sworder.co.uk www.sworder.co.uk

T&D ⊞ Toys & Dolls, 367 Fore Street, Edmonton, London N9 0NR Tel: 020 8807 3301

TAC ⊞ Tenterden Antiques Centre, 66–66A High Street, Tenterden, Kent TN30 6AU Tel: 01580 765655/765885

TASV ⊞ Tenterden Antiques & Silver Vaults, 66 High Street, Tenterden, Kent TN30 6AU Tel: 01580 765885

TB ⊞ Millicent Safro, Tender Buttons, 143 E.62nd Street, New York, NY10021, U.S.A. Tel: 212 758 7004

TCG ⊞ 20th Century Glass, Nigel Benson Tel: 07971 859848 nigelbenson@20thcentury-glass.com

TDG ⊞ The Design Gallery 1850–1950, 5 The Green, Westerham, Kent TN16 1AS Tel: 01959 561234 sales@thedesigngalleryuk.com www.thedesigngalleryuk.com

TEN ⚒ Tennants, The Auction Centre, Harmby Road, Leyburn, Yorkshire DL8 5SG Tel: 01969 623780 enquiry@tennants-ltd.co.uk www.tennants.co.uk

▦† Tony Horsley, PO Box 3127, Brighton,
East Sussex BN1 5SS Tel: 01273 550770

▦ Tickers, 37 Northam Road, Southampton,
Hampshire SO14 0PD Tel: 02380 234431
kmonckton@btopenworld.com

▦† Tin Tin Collectables, G38–42 Alfies's Antique
Market, 13–25 Church Street, Marylebone,
London NW8 8DT Tel: 020 7258 1305
leslie@tintincollectables.com
www.tintincollectables.com

▦† Telephone Lines Ltd, 304 High Street,
Cheltenham, Gloucestershire GL50 3JF
Tel: 01242 583699 info@telephonelines.net
www.telephonelines.net

▦ The Lanes Armoury, 26 Meeting House Lane,
The Lanes, Brighton, East Sussex BN1 1HB
Tel: 01273 321357
enquiries@thelanesarmoury.co.uk
www.thelanesarmoury.co.uk

▦ Timothy Millett Ltd, Historic Medals and Works
of Art, PO Box 20851, London SE22 0YN
Tel: 020 8693 1111
tim@timothymillett.demon.co.uk

▦ Toy's N Such Toy's - Antiques & Collectables,
437 Dawson Street, Sault Sainte Marie,
MI 49783-2119, U.S.A. Tel: 906 635 0356

▦† Charles Tomlinson, Chester Tel: 01244 318395
charles.tomlinson@lineone.net
charlestomlinson@tiscali.co.uk

▦ The Top Banana Antiques Mall, 1 New Church
Street, Tetbury, Gloucestershire GL8 8DS
Tel: 0871 288 1102
info@topbananaantiques.com
www.topbananaantiques.com

▦ Totem, 168 Stoke Newington, Church Street,
London N16 0JL Tel: 020 7275 0234
sales@totemrecords.com
www.totemrecords.com

✦ Thomson, Roddick & Medcalf Ltd
www.thomsonroddick.com

▦ Treasures in Textiles, 53 Russian Drive,
Liverpool, Merseyside L13 7BS
Tel: 0151 281 6025

▦ Tussie Mussies, The Old Stables, 2b East Cross,
Tenterden, Kent TN30 6AD Tel: 01580 766244
tussiemussies@btinternet.com
www.tussiemussies.co.uk

▦ Twinkled, 1st Floor, Old Petrol Station,
11–17 Stockwell Street, Greenwich, London
SE10 9JN Tel: 020 8269 0864
info@twinkled.net www.twinkled.net

▦ Tony Young Autographs, 138 Edward Street,
Brighton, East Sussex BN2 0JL Tel: 01273 732418

▦ Unique Collections, 52 Greenwich Church
Street, London SE10 9BL Tel: 020 8305 0867
glen@uniquecollections.co.uk
www.uniquecollections.co.uk

▦ Upstairs Downstairs, 40 Market Place, Devizes,
Wiltshire SN10 1JG Tel: 01380 730266 or
07974 074220
devizesantiques@btconnect.com

✦† Vectis Auctions Ltd, Fleck Way, Thornaby,
Stockton-on-Tees, Cleveland TS17 9JZ
Tel: 01642 750616 admin@vectis.co.uk
www.vectis.co.uk

▦† June Victor, Vintage Modes, S041–43,
Alfies Antique Market, 13–25 Church Street,
London NW8 8DT Tel: 020 7723 6066

VK ▦ Vivienne King of Panache Tel: 01934 814759
Kingpanache@aol.com

VS ✦† T. Vennett-Smith, 11 Nottingham Road,
Gotham, Nottinghamshire NG11 0HE
Tel: 0115 983 0541 info@vennett-smith.com
www.vennett-smith.com

VSP ✦ Van Sabben Poster Auctions, PO Box 2065,
1620 EB Hoorn, The Netherlands
Tel: 31 229 268203
uboersma@vsabbenposterauctions.nl
www.vsabbenposterauctions.nl

WA ✦ Whyte's Auctioneers, 38 Molesworth Street,
Dublin 2, Republic of Ireland Tel: 676 2888
info@whytes.ie www.whytes.ie

WAA ▦ Woburn Abbey Antiques Centre, Woburn,
Bedfordshire MK17 9WA Tel: 01525 290350
antiques@woburnabbey.co.uk

WAC ▦ Worcester Antiques Centre, Reindeer Court,
Mealcheapen Street, Worcester WR1 4DF
Tel: 01905 610680 WorcsAntiques@aol.com

WAL ✦† Wallis & Wallis, West Street Auction Galleries,
Lewes, East Sussex BN7 2NJ Tel: 01273 480208
auctions@wallisandwallis.co.uk
grb@wallisandwallis.co.uk
www.wallisandwallis.co.uk

WAm ▦ Williams Amusements Ltd, Bluebird House,
Povey Cross Road, Horley, Surrey RH6 0AG
Tel: 01293 782222
adrian@williams-amusements.co.uk
www.williams-amusements.co.uk

WD ✦ Weller & Dufty Ltd, 141 Bromsgrove Street,
Birmingham, West Midlands B5 6RQ
Tel: 0121 692 1414 sales@welleranddufty.co.uk
www.welleranddufty.co.uk

WeA ▦ Wenderton Antiques Tel: 01227 720295
(by appt only)

WHO ▦ The Who Shop International Ltd, 4 Station
Parade, High Street North, East Ham, London
E6 1JD Tel: 020 8471 2356
mwhoshop@hilly.com www.thewhoshop.com

WiB ▦ Wish Barn Antiques, Wish Street, Rye,
East Sussex TN31 7DA Tel: 01797 226797

WilP ✦ W&H Peacock, 26 Newnham Street, Bedford
MK40 3JR Tel: 01234 266366

WL ✦ Wintertons Ltd, Lichfield Auction Centre,
Fradley Park, Lichfield, Staffordshire WS13 8NF
Tel: 01543 263256 enquiries@wintertons.co.uk
www.wintertons.co.uk

WO ▦ Woodville Antiques, The Street, Hamstreet,
Ashford, Kent TN26 2HG Tel: 01233 732981
woodvilleantiques@yahoo.co.uk

WOS ▦ Wheels of Steel, Grays Antique Market,
Stand A12–13, Unit B10 Basement, 1–7 Davies
Mews, London W1Y 2LP Tel: 0207 629 2813

WP ▦† British Notes, PO Box 257, Sutton, Surrey
SM3 9WW Tel: 020 8641 3224
pamwestbritnotes@aol.com
www.britishnotes.co.uk

WW ✦ Woolley & Wallis, Salisbury Salerooms,
51–61 Castle Street, Salisbury, Wiltshire SP1 3SU
Tel: 01722 424500/411854
junebarrett@woolleyandwallis.co.uk
www.woolleyandwallis.co.uk

YC ▦† Yesterday Child Tel: 01908 583403
djbarrington@btinternet.com

YT ▦ Yew Tree Antiques, Woburn Abbey Antiques
Centre, Woburn, Bedfordshire MK17 9WA
Tel: 01525 872514

Index to Advertisers

Index

Bold numbers refer to information and pointer boxes